D1117403

Uncertain Rule-Based Fuzzy Logic Systems:
Introduction and New Directions

Jerry M. Mendel
University of Southern California
Los Angeles, CA

Prentice Hall PTR
Upper Saddle River, NJ
07458
www.phptr.com

ISBN 0-13-040969-3

90000

9 780130 409690

Library of Congress Cataloging-in-Publication Data

Mendel, Jerry M., 1938-
 Uncertain rule-based fuzzy logic systems : introduction and new directions / Jerry M. Mendel.
  p. cm.
 Includes bibliographical references and index.
 ISBN 0-13-040969-3
  1. Fuzzy logic. I. Title

QA9.64 .M46 2000
511.1--dc21

00-053050

Production Editor: Wil Mara
Acquisitions Editor: Bernard Goodwin
Editorial Assistant: Michelle Vincenti
Marketing Manager: Dan DePasquale
Manufacturing Manager: Alexis R. Heydt
Cover Designer: Talar Agasyan
Cover Design Direction: Jerry Votta
Art Director: Gail Cocker-Bogusz
Composition: Jerry Mendel

© 2001 Prentice Hall PTR
Prentice-Hall, Inc.
Upper Saddle River, NJ 07458

All rights reserved. No part of this book may be reproduced, in any form or by any means, without permission in writing from the author and publisher.

The publisher offers discounts on this book when ordered in bulk quantities. For more information contact: Corporate Sales Department, Prentice Hall PTR, One Lake Street, Upper Saddle River, NJ 07458. Phone: 800-382-3419; Fax: 201-236-7141; E-mail: corpsales@prenhall.com

Printed in the United States of America

10 9 8 7 6 5 4 3 2 1

ISBN 0-13-040969-3

Prentice-Hall International (UK) Limited, *London*
Prentice-Hall of Australia Pty. Limited, *Sydney*
Prentice-Hall Canada Inc., *Toronto*
Prentice-Hall Hispanoamericana, S.A., *Mexico*
Prentice-Hall of India Private Limited, *New Delhi*
Prentice-Hall of Japan, Inc., *Tokyo*
Pearson Education Asia Pte. Ltd.
Editora Prentice-Hall do Brasil, Ltda., *Rio de Janeiro*

To Ashlee
who thinks
"fuzzy logic is cool"

About the Web Site

More than 30 MATLAB M-files are available as freeware on the Internet at the following URL: *http://sipi.usc.edu/~mendel/software*. They are being made available so that you will be able to immediately use the results in this book. Brief descriptions of M-files appear at the end of each chapter for which they are most applicable. Appendix C collects the M-files together as they are organized on the Internet, i.e., in the three folders: *type-1 FLSs, general type-2 FLSs*, and *interval type-2 FLSs*.

Contents

PART 1: PRELIMINARIES

◆ 1 INTRODUCTION

SUPPLEMENTARY MATERIAL: SHORT PRIMERS ON FUZZY SETS AND FUZZY LOGIC

◆ 2 SOURCES OF UNCERTAINTY   66

◆ 3 MEMBERSHIP FUNCTIONS AND
UNCERTAINTY   79

◆ 4 CASE STUDIES 110

PART 2: TYPE-1 FUZZY LOGIC SYSTEMS

◆ 5 SINGLETON TYPE-1 FUZZY LOGIC SYSTEMS: NO UNCERTAINTIES 131

◆ 6 NON-SINGLETON TYPE-1 FUZZY LOGIC SYSTEMS   186

Part 3: Type-2 Fuzzy Sets

◆ 7 OPERATIONS ON AND PROPERTIES OF

TYPE-2 FUZZY SETS   213

◆ 8 TYPE-2 RELATIONS AND COMPOSITIONS

235

PART 4: TYPE-2 FUZZY LOGIC

SYSTEMS

◆ 10 SINGLETON TYPE-2 FUZZY LOGIC SYSTEMS   287

◆ 11 TYPE-1 NON-SINGLETON TYPE-2 FUZZY LOGIC SYSTEMS   353

◆ 12 Type-2 Non-Singleton Type-2

Fuzzy Logic Systems   382

◆ 13 TSK Fuzzy Logic Systems   421

◆ **14 EPILOGUE**   **454**

◆ A JOIN, MEET, AND NEGATION OP-ERATIONS FOR NON-INTERVAL TYPE-2 FUZZY SETS 502

◆ B PROPERTIES OF TYPE-1 AND TYPE-2 FUZZY SETS 517

◆ C COMPUTATION   526

REFERENCES   530

INDEX   547

Preface

Uncertainty is the fabric that makes life interesting. For millenia human beings have developed strategies to cope with a plethora of uncertainties, never absolutely sure what the consequences would be, but hopeful that the deleterious effects of those uncertainties could be minimized. This book presents a complete methodology for accomplishing this within the framework of fuzzy logic (FL). This is not the original FL, but is an expanded and richer FL, one that contains the original FL within it.

The original FL, founded by Lotfi Zadeh, has been around for more than 35 years, as of the year 2000, and yet it is unable to handle uncertainties. By *handle*, I mean *to model and minimize the effect of*. That the original FL—type-1 FL—cannot do this sounds paradoxical because the word *fuzzy* has the connotation of uncertainty. The expanded FL—type-2 FL—is able to handle uncertainties because it can model them and minimize their effects. And, if all uncertainties disappear, type-2 FL reduces to type-1 FL, in much the same way that if randomness disappears, probability reduces to determinism.

Although many applications were found for type-1 FL, it is its application to *rule-based systems* that has most significantly demonstrated its importance as a powerful design methodology. Such rule-based fuzzy logic systems (FLSs), both type-1 and type-2, are what this book is about. In it I show how to use FL in new ways and how to effectively solve problems that are awash in uncertainties.

FL has already been applied in numerous fields, in many of which uncertainties are present (e.g., signal processing, digital communications, computer and communication networks, diagnostic medicine, operations research, financial investing, control, etc.). Hence, the results in this book can immediately be used in all of these fields. To demonstrate the performance advantages for type-2 FLSs over their type-1 counterparts, when uncertainties are present, I describe and provide results for the following applications in this book: forecasting of time series, knowledge-mining using surveys, classification of video data working directly with compressed data, equalization of time-varying nonlinear digital communication channels, overcoming co-channel interference and intersymbol interference for time-varying nonlinear digital communication channels, and connection admission control for asynchronous transfer mode networks. No control applications have been included, because to date type-2 FL has not yet been applied to them; hence, this book is not about FL control, although its methodologies may someday be applicable to it.

I have organized this book into four parts. Part 1— *Preliminaries* — contains four chapters that provide background materials about uncertainty, membership functions, and two case studies (forecasting of time-series and knowledge mining using surveys) that are carried throughout the book. Part 2—*Type-1 Fuzzy Logic Systems*—contains two chapters that are included to provide the underlying basis for the new type-2 FLSs, so that we can compare type-2 results for our case studies with type-1 results. Part 3—*Type-2 Fuzzy Sets*—contains three chapters, each of which focuses on a different aspect of such sets. Part 4—*Type-2 Fuzzy Logic Systems*—which is the heart of the book, contains five chapters, four having to do with different architectures for a FLS and how to handle different kinds of uncertainties within them, and one having to do primarily with four specific applications of type-2 FLSs.

This book can be read by anyone who has an undergraduate BS degree and should be of great interest to computer scientists and engineers who already use or want to use rule-based systems and are concerned with how to handle uncertainties about such systems. I have included many worked-out examples in the text, and have also included homework problems at the end of most chapters so that the book can be used in a classroom setting as well as a technical reference.

Here are some specific ways that this book can be used:

- For the person totally unfamiliar with FL who wants a quick introduction to it, read the Supplement to Chapter 1 and Chapter 5 (Sections 5.1–5.8).

- For the person who wants an in-depth treatment of type-1 rule-based FLSs, read the Supplement to Chapter 1 and Chapters 4–6.

- For the person who is only interested in type-2 fuzzy set theory, read Chapters 3, 7–9, and Appendices A and B.

- For a person who wants to give a course on rule-based fuzzy logic systems, use Chapters 1–12 and 13 (if time permits). Chapter 14 should be of interest to people with a background in digital communications, pattern recognition, or communication networks and will suggest projects for a course.

- For a person who is a proponent of Takagi-Sugeno-Kang (TSK) fuzzy systems and wants to see what their type-2 counterparts look like, read Chapters 3, 7–9, and 13.

- For a person who is interested in forecasting of time-series and wants to get a quick overview of the benefits to modeling uncertainties on forecasting performance when using rule-based forecasters, read Chapters 4 (Section 4.2), 5 (Section 5.10), 6 (Section 6.7), 10 (Section 10.11), 11 (Section 11.5), and 12 (Section 12.5).

- For a person who is interested in knowledge mining and wants to get a quick overview of the benefits to modeling uncertainties on judgment making when using rule-based advisors, read Chapters 4 (Section 4.3), 5 (Section 5.11), and 10 (Section 10.12).

So that people will start using type-2 FL as soon as possible, I have made free software available online for implementing and designing type-1 and type-2 FLSs. It is MATLAB®-based (MATLAB is a registered trademark of The MathWorks, Inc.), was developed by my former PhD students Nilesh Karnik and Qilian Liang, and can be reached at: _http://sipi.usc.edu/~mendel/software_. A computation section, which directs the reader to very specific M-files, appears at the end of most chapters of this book. Appendix C summarizes all of the M-files so that the reader can see the forest from the trees.

This book is an amalgamation of the research of some of my past PhD students who have worked with me during the past 14 years on FLSs. Therefore, I want to give each of them the credit here that they so richly deserve. Li-Xin Wang was my first student to study model-free applications of FL. The work we did together on singleton type-1 FLSs is the basis for Chapter 5. George Mouzouris extended Li-Xin's works from singleton fuzzification to non-singleton fuzzification. This represented our first attempt at handling one kind of uncertainty (uncertain measurements that are the inputs to a FLS) totally within the framework of a FLS, and is the basis for Chapter 6. Nilesh Karnik provided the entire foundation and framework for singleton type-2 FLSs.[1] Some of the new concepts that were developed by him to do this are overviewed in Section 1.3, and his work is the basis for some of Chapter 3, all of Chapters 7–9, some of Chapter 10, and Appendices A and B. Qilian Liang made type-2 FLSs practical by focusing on how to design such systems when the uncertainties about type-1 fuzzy sets are modeled as _interval sets_. He did this for singleton and two kinds of non-singleton fuzzification (type-1 and type-2), and also developed type-2 TSK FLSs. Some of the new concepts that were developed by him are overviewed in

---

[1]Although Lotfi Zadeh introduced the concept of a type-2 fuzzy set in 1975, and after that date a very small number of other papers were published about type-2 fuzzy sets (see Section 1.6), no one prior to our work had developed a type-2 FLS.

Section 1.3, and his work is the basis for some of Chapters 3 and 10, all of Chapters 11–13, and the four applications in Chapter 14. Chapter 13 is co-authored by him.

All of the simulations in this book were performed by Qilian Liang. I wish to express my sincere appreciation to him for helping me in this way. I also wish to thank him and Hongwei Wu for reviewing the entire book, and to Katarina Vukadinovic for reviewing parts of the first draft of the book. Special thanks also go to Robert John (DeMontfort University, Leicester, England) and George Klir (State University of New York at Binghamton). Bob John, who also works on type-2 fuzzy sets and their applications, acted as a sounding board for the material that is in Chapters 3, 7, and 8 when I visited and worked jointly with him in June 2000. Those chapters are immeasurably clearer as a result of our collaboration. George Klir reviewed Chapter 2 and shared his great wisdom about uncertainty, and was a big influence on the final version of Section 2.1. All of the inputs from these people helped me in reaching the final version of the book. Any remaining errors in content or publishing are my responsibility.

The author gratefully acknowledges material quoted from books or journals by AIAA, American Association for the Advancement of Science, Elsevier Science, IEEE, McGraw-Hill, Prentice-Hall, and Springer-Verlag. For a complete listing of quoted books or articles, please see the "References." The author also gratefully acknowledges Nilesh Karnik for material quoted from a report that I co-authored with him.

I am also very grateful to my editor Bernard Goodwin, who is always a pleasure to work with; to my production editors Lisa Iarkowski and Wil Mara, who guided me through the final production of the book; and to other staff members at Prentice Hall for their help in the production of this book.

I want to thank my wife Letty for providing me, for more than 40 years, with a wonderful environment that has made the writing of this book possible. Finally, I have dedicated this book to my granddaughter, Ashlee Cabral, who, I hope, will someday be a user of fuzzy logic.

Jerry M. Mendel
Los Angeles, CA
December 2000

Part 1—
Preliminaries

CHAPTER 1

Introduction

For many problems, two distinct forms of problem knowledge exist: (1) *objective knowledge*, which is used all the time in engineering problem formulations (e.g., mathematical models), and (2) *subjective knowledge*, which represents linguistic information (e.g., rules, expert information, design requirements) that is usually impossible to quantify using traditional mathematics. Examples of objective knowledge are: equations of motion for a robot, submarine, spacecraft, automobile, etc.; a convolutional model that describes a communication channel or a reflection seismology experiment; and, a probability density function for random parameters or noise. Some examples of rules are:

> If a target is being tracked at one time point, then it will not be too far away at the next time point,

which might be valid for tracking a submarine or any other slowly moving large object; or,

> If the data do not contain too many significant events, then those events are very close to one another,

which might be valid for processing a specific section of reflection seismology data.

Subjective knowledge is usually ignored at the front end of engineering designs; but, it is frequently used to evaluate such designs. I believe that both types of knowledge should and can be used to solve real problems.

The two forms of knowledge can be coordinated in a logical way using *fuzzy logic* (FL). Two approaches for doing this have appeared in the literature: (1) *model-based approach*, in which objective knowledge is represented by mathematical models and subjective knowledge is represented by linguistic statements that are converted to rules, which are then quantified using FL, [e.g, Popoli and Mendel (1989, 1993)]; and (2) *model-free approach*, in which rules are extracted from numerical data and are then combined with linguistic knowledge (collected from experts), both using FL. In this book I focus on the model-free approach because it is very applicable when real data do not agree with an assumed data-generating model, a situation that is quite common.

Today, the two major approaches to model-free designs are artificial neural networks and FL.[1] In this book, I focus on the latter because, as I will explain and demonstrate throughout the book, uncertainties can be handled within the framework of FL.

The model-free approach that is based on rules and FL leads to a system that we shall refer to as a *fuzzy logic system* (FLS). Such systems are what this book is all about. In general, a FLS is a nonlinear mapping of an input data (feature) vector into a scalar output; the vector output case decomposes into a collection of independent multi-input/single-output systems. The richness of FL is that there are enormous numbers of possibilities that lead to lots of different mappings. This richness does require a careful understanding of FL and the elements that comprise a FLS. One can, of course, challenge the validity of some of these possibilities. To me, this is analogous to the representation problem that we always face in engineering, i.e., do we use a linear model, time-domain or frequency-domain model, lumped-parameter or distributed parameter model, state-space or input-output model, deterministic or random model, etc.? Once we agree on the representation, we can proceed. The same is true about a FLS.

---

[1]The term *model-free* may be a bit of a misnomer, because both neural networks and fuzzy logic provide mathematical descriptions for a problem. Perhaps, the difference between the *model-based* and *model-free* approaches is that, in the former, the assumed mathematical model is believed to represent truth (or a close approximation thereof), whereas in the latter, the associated mathematical model is a representation of an architecture that is only meant to solve a specific problem.

   Some people object, on principle, to using FL instead of a more familiar model-based approach to design. To dispel the notion of crispness (i.e., dual-valued concepts, which are either true or not true), I list a collection of terms (see Table 1-1) that are widely used in control, signal processing, and communications. While we frequently strive for crisp values of these terms, we usually use them in fuzzy contexts, where they actually convey more useful information than would a crisp value.

   Correlation is an interesting example, because it can be defined mathematically so that, for a given set of data, we can compute a crisp number for it. Let's assume that correlation has been normalized so that it can range between zero and unity, and that for a given set of data we compute the correlation value as 0.15. When explaining the amount of data correlation to someone else, it is usually more meaningful to explain it as "these data have low correlation." When we do this, we are actually fuzzifying the crisp value of 0.15 into the fuzzy set "low correlation."

   Stability is another very interesting example. A system is either stable or not stable; there is nothing fuzzy about this. However, if the system is stable, we frequently describe its degree of relative stability, using any of the terms listed in Table 1-1. These terms may be more meaningful than the following description: The system has four complex poles and the effective damping ratio for the system is 0.3. We just describe the response of such a system as "lightly damped." Once again, we are fuzzifying the crisp value of 0.3 into the fuzzy set "lightly damped."

Table 1-1: Engineering terms whose contextual usage is usually quite fuzzy (Mendel, 1995, © 1995a, IEEE).

Term	Contextual Usage
Alias	none, a bit, high
Bandwidth	narrowband, broadband
Blur	somewhat, quite, very
Correlation	low, medium, high, perfect
Errors	large, medium, small, alot of, not so great, very large, very small, almost zero
Frequency	high, low, ultra-high
Resolution	low, high
Sampling	low-rate, medium-rate, high-rate, very high-rate
Stability	stable (lightly damped, highly damped, over damped, critically damped), unstable

For interesting historical perspectives on FL, including its earlier origins (when it was called continuous-valued logic), see McNeill and Freilberger (1992).

1.1 RULE-BASED FLSs

As just mentioned, rule-based FLSs are what this book is all about. They contain four components—rules, fuzzifier, inference engine, and output processor—that are inter-connected, as shown in Figure 1-1. Once the rules have been established, a FLS can be viewed as a mapping from inputs to outputs (the solid path in Figure 1-1, from "Crisp inputs" to "Crisp outputs"), and this mapping can be expressed quantitatively as $y = f(\mathbf{x})$. This kind of FLS is very widely used in many engineering applications of FL, such as in FL controllers and signal processors, and is also known as a fuzzy controller or fuzzy system.

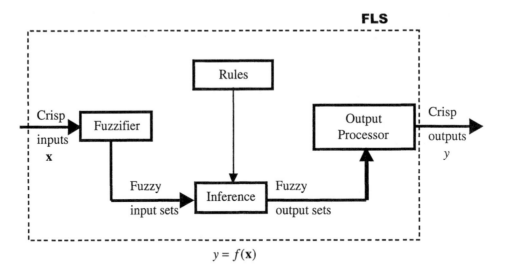

Figure 1-1: Fuzzy logic system.

Rules are the heart of a FLS, and may be provided by experts or can be extracted from numerical data. In either case, the rules that we are interested in can be expressed as a collection of IF–THEN statements, e.g.,

IF the total average input rate of real-time voice and video traffic is *a moderate amount*, and the total average input rate of the non-real-time data traffic is *some*, THEN the confidence of accepting the telephone call is *a large amount*.

The IF-part of a rule is its *antecedent*, and the THEN-part of a rule is its *consequent*.

Fuzzy sets are associated with terms that appear in the antecedents or consequents of rules, and with the inputs to and output of the FLS. Membership functions[2] are used to describe these fuzzy sets. In this book we use two kinds of fuzzy sets, type-1 and type-2. Type-1 fuzzy sets are described by membership functions that are totally certain, whereas type-2 fuzzy sets are described by membership functions that are themselves fuzzy. The latter let us quantify different kinds of uncertainties that can occur in a FLS. For example, quite often the knowledge that is used to construct rules is *uncertain*. Such uncertainty leads to rules whose antecedents or consequents are uncertain, which translates into uncertain antecedent or consequent membership functions.

A FLS that is described completely in terms of type-1 fuzzy sets is called[3] a *type-1 FLS*, whereas a FLS that is described using at least one type-2 fuzzy set is called a *type-2 FLS*. Type-1 FLSs are unable to directly handle rule uncertainties, because they use type-1 fuzzy sets that are certain. Type-2 FLSs, on the other hand, are very useful in circumstances where it is difficult to determine an exact membership function for a fuzzy set; hence, they can be used to handle rule uncertainties, and even measurement uncertainties.

Returning to the Figure 1-1 FLS, the fuzzifier maps crisp numbers into fuzzy sets. It is needed to activate rules that are in terms of linguistic variables, which have fuzzy sets associated with them. The inputs to the FLS prior to fuzzification may be certain (e.g., perfect measurements) or uncertain (e.g., noisy measurements). The membership function for a type-2 fuzzy set lets us handle either kind of measurement.

The inference engine of the Figure 1-1 FLS maps fuzzy sets into fuzzy sets. It handles the way in which rules are activated and combined. Just as we humans use many different types of inferential procedures to help us understand things or to make decisions, there are many different FL inferential procedures. In this book, we only focus on two of them, the *minimum* and *product*. We leave the extensions of our results to all other inference procedures to others.

In many applications of a FLS, crisp numbers must be obtained at its output. This is accomplished by the output processor, and is known as *defuzzification*. In a control-system application, for example, such a number corresponds to a control action. In a signal processing application, such a number could correspond to the prediction of next year's sun-spot activity, a financial forecast,

---

[2]For readers who are unfamiliar with fuzzy sets and FL, some background material has been added to this chapter as Supplementary Material. Even readers who are already familiar with this material may be advised to read the Supplementary Material so that they can become familiar with my perspectives on fuzzy sets and FL, since those perspectives are used throughout this book.

[3]Prior to the work on type-2 FLSs, it was never necessary to refer to a FLS as a type-1 FLS. Now, to distinguish between the two kinds of FLSs, we need to use the prefix *type-1* or *type-2*.

or the location of a target. The output processor for a type-1 FLS is just a defuzzifier; however, the output processor of a type-2 FLS contains two components: the first maps a type-2 set into a type-1 set and the second performs defuzzification on the latter set.

How to handle rule uncertainties as well as measurement uncertainties by a FLS is also what this book is about. We shall show that all of this can be done by a type-2 FLS.

1.2 A NEW DIRECTION FOR FLSS

Type-2 FLSs move the world of FLSs into a fundamentally new and important direction. What is this new direction and why is it important? To make the answers to these questions as clear as possible, let us briefly digress to review some things that are, no doubt, familiar to the reader.

Probability theory is used to model random uncertainty, and within that theory we begin with a probability density function (pdf) that embodies total information about random uncertainties. In most practical real-world applications it is impossible to know or determine the pdf; so, we fall back on using the fact that a pdf is completely characterized by all of its moments (if they exist). If the pdf is Gaussian, then, as is well known, two moments—the mean and variance—suffice to completely specify it. For most pdfs, an infinite number of moments are required. Of course, it is not possible, in practice, to determine an infinite number of moments; so, instead, we compute as many moments as we believe are necessary to extract as much information as possible from the data. At the very least we use two moments, the mean and variance; and, in some cases, we even use higher-than-second-order moments.

To use just the first-order moments would not be very useful, because random uncertainty requires an understanding of dispersion about the mean, and this information is provided by the variance. So, our accepted probabilistic modeling of random uncertainty focuses to a large extent on methods that use *at least* the first two moments of a pdf. This is, for example, why designs based on minimizing a mean-squared error are so popular.

Should we expect any less of a FLS for rule uncertainties or any other types of uncertainties? To-date, we may view the output of a type-1 FLS—the defuzzified output—as analogous[4] to the mean of a pdf. Just as variance provides a measure of dispersion about the mean, and is almost always used to capture more about probabilistic uncertainty in practical statistical-based designs, a FLS also

---

[4]We do not wish to get stuck in the quagmire about the equivalence between subjective probability and type-1 fuzzy sets; our "analogy" between the defuzzified output of a FLS and the mean of a pdf is meant to be just that and nothing more.

needs some measure of dispersion—*the new direction*—to capture more about its uncertainties than just a single number. Type-2 FL provides this measure of dispersion and (I hope to convince you) seems to be as fundamental to the design of systems which include linguistic and/or numerical uncertainties that translate into rule or input uncertainties, as variance is to the mean—*the importance of the new direction.*

1.3 NEW CONCEPTS AND THEIR HISTORICAL BACKGROUND

Although the concept of a type-2 fuzzy set was first introduced by Zadeh (1975), until the works of Karnik and Mendel (e.g., 1998b) no one had extended a type-1 FLS to a type-2 FLS. In retrospect, the major obstacles to doing this were: (1) characterization of type-2 fuzzy sets; (2) performing operations with type-2 fuzzy sets; (3) inferencing with type-2 fuzzy sets; and (4) going from the output of a type-2 inference engine (see Figure 1-1), which is a type-2 fuzzy set, to a defuzzified value, which is a type-0 set. All of these obstacles have been overcome with the introduction of some new concepts, which we briefly describe next[5].

Characterizing a type-2 fuzzy set is not as easy as characterizing a type-1 fuzzy set. Instead of being two-dimensional, as a type-1 fuzzy set is, a type-2 fuzzy set is three-dimensional. It is this additional dimension that lets uncertainty be handled within the framework of FL. The concept of a *footprint of uncertainty*,[6] along with the associated concepts of *lower* and *upper membership functions* [first described in Mendel and Liang (1999)] lets us easily characterize type-2 fuzzy sets. The concept of an *active branch* [first described in Liang and Mendel (2000a)] of a lower or upper membership function lets us design an interval type-2 FLS (i.e., a type-2 FLS whose type-2 fuzzy sets use interval sets to characterize their fuzziness).

We who use type-1 fuzzy set theory are so used to performing the common operations of union, intersection, and complement that we take them for granted, as well we should. How to perform these operations is covered in every book about (type-1) fuzzy sets and logic. Operating with type-2 fuzzy sets—obtaining their union, intersection, and complement—is another matter. Although some work on how to do this existed in the literature before the works of Karnik and Mendel (e.g., 1998b), it had not been developed far enough to be

---

[5]For the newcomer to FL, this section can be skipped on first reading without any loss in continuity.
[6]This term does not appear in the earliest works of Karnik and Mendel (1998a, b, c). It was coined by Mendel as a simple way to verbalize and describe the two-dimensional domain of support for a type-2 fuzzy set's membership function, and appears for the first time in Karnik et al. (1999) and Karnik and Mendel (2000a).

very practical. By focusing on a very special but very useful kind of type-2 fuzzy set—the interval set—and using the concepts of lower and upper membership functions, it is now possible to perform all of these operations very simply.

The *sup-star* composition (described in Section 1.10.11) is the fundamental mapping from the fuzzy input sets that excite the inference mechanism (Figure 1-1) to its output. All type-1 FLSs make use of it, and it can be viewed as a nonlinear mapping of a type-1 input fuzzy set into another type-1 output set. A comparable result for type-2 fuzzy sets needed to be developed. By using Zadeh's Extension Principle, this has now been done, and is called the *extended sup-star composition.*[7] All type-2 FLSs make use of it, and it can be viewed as a nonlinear mapping of a type-2 input fuzzy set into another type-2 output fuzzy set. To perform the calculations associated with the extended sup-star composition one needs to use the operations of union and intersection for type-2 fuzzy sets; so, the developments of practical algorithms for these operations come in quite handy.

Going from the output of a type-2 inference engine (see Figure 1-1), which is a type-2 fuzzy set, to a defuzzified value, which is a type-0 set, was virgin territory. Inspired by what we do in a type-1 FLS, when we defuzzify the (combined) output of the inference engine using a variety of defuzzification methods that all do some sort of centroid calculation, it became clear that the concept of the *centroid of a type-2 fuzzy set* was needed. Using the Extension Principle, Karnik and Mendel (1998b) defined the centroid of a type-2 fuzzy set; it is a type-1 fuzzy set. Associated with this new concept are the related new concepts of *embedded type-2 and type-1 fuzzy sets* [first described in Karnik and Mendel (1998b)]. These sets are easy to visualize on the footprint of uncertainty of a type-2 fuzzy set, and let us interpret a type-2 FLS as a collection of type-1 FLSs.

Computing the centroid of a general type-2 fuzzy set can be very intensive, because the number of its embedded type-1 fuzzy sets can be enormous; however, for an interval type-2 fuzzy set, an exact method for computing its centroid has been developed [Karnik and Mendel (1998b)]. This was possible because the centroid of an interval type-2 fuzzy set is an interval type-1 fuzzy set. Interval sets are completely characterized by their left- and right-end points; hence, computing the centroid of an interval type-2 fuzzy set only requires computing the centroid of *two* embedded type-1 fuzzy sets, one each for the left- and right-end points of this centroid.

Returning to the output of the inference engine in a type-2 FLS, it is a type-2 fuzzy set. In fact, we get one such set for each rule that is fired by the input to the inference engine, and, in general, (just as in a type-1 FLS) more than one rule will be fired. These type-2 fuzzy sets can be combined in different ways, just as they can be in a type-1 FLS. The result is another type-2 fuzzy set.

---

[7]For a short history of who developed this, see footnote 4 in Chapter 8 on p. 242.

The operation that maps this type-2 set into a type-1 fuzzy set is called *type-reduction* [first described in Karnik and Mendel (1998a, b, c)], which is also a new concept. Just as there are many different kinds of centroid-based defuzzifiers, there are many different and comparable type-reducers, but all are based on computing the centroid of the combined type-2 fuzzy set. Type-reduction is easy for interval type-2 fuzzy sets, and leads to an interval type-1 fuzzy set. Going from it to a defuzzified output for the type-2 FLS is simple—just average the end-points of the interval type-reduced set.

Putting all of these new concepts together lets us mathematically describe a type-2 FLS, just as we can mathematically describe a type-1 FLS. Doing this then lets us develop design procedures for type-2 FLSs that are analogous to those that have already been developed for type-1 FLSs. Design procedures for both type-1 and type-2 FLSs are covered in this book so that the reader will be able to immediately apply the book's results to new applications.

1.4 FUNDAMENTAL DESIGN REQUIREMENT

Behind everything that we do in this book is the following *fundamental design requirement* [Karnik and Mendel (1998a, b)]:

> When all sources of uncertainty disappear, a type-2 FLS must reduce to a comparable type-1 FLS.

So, for example, when all uncertainty disappears, the extended sup-star composition reduces to the usual sup-star composition and type-reduction reduces to defuzzification. In this way, a type-2 FLS represents a generalization of a type-1 FLS and not a replacement.

This design requirement is analogous to what happens to a probability density function when random uncertainties disappear. In that case, the variance of the pdf goes to zero, and a probability analysis reduces to a deterministic analysis. So, just as the capability for a deterministic analysis is embedded within a probability analysis, the capability for a type-1 FLS is embedded within a type-2 FLS.

1.5 THE FLOW OF UNCERTAINTIES

Just as random uncertainties flow through a system and their effects can be evaluated using the mean and variance, linguistic and random uncertainties flow through a type-2 FLS and their effects can be evaluated using the defuzzified output and the type-reduced output of that system. Just as the variance provides a measure of dispersion about the mean, and is often used in confidence intervals, the type-reduced output can be interpreted as providing a measure of dispersion about the defuzzified output and can be thought of as (or related to) a linguistic confidence interval. Just as the variance increases as random uncertainty increases, the type-reduced set also increases as linguistic or random uncertainties increase. So, a type-2 FLS is *analogous* (see footnote 4) to a probabilistic system through first and second moments, whereas a type-1 FLS is analogous to a probabilistic system only through the first moment.

A pdf captures complete knowledge about a random quantity, and from it one computes its moments; so, working with higher-than-second-order moments (e.g., cumulants) when a pdf is non-Gaussian can be very useful. The higher order moments can extract more information about the non-Gaussian quantity than can just the mean and variance. To date, there is nothing comparable to a pdf for linguistic uncertainties. Perhaps someone will someday establish a *knowledge density function*, whose first-order moment will be associated with a type-1 fuzzy set, and whose combined first- and second-order moments will be associated with a type-2 fuzzy set. Perhaps there is a knowledge density function that is analogous to a Gaussian pdf, for which a type-2 FLS contains all the useful information about rule-based knowledge. Otherwise, the knowledge density function could be used to develop even higher type FLSs (or fuzzy sets) that would extract even more information about rule-based knowledge than does a type-2 FLS.

1.6 EXISTING LITERATURE ON TYPE-2 FUZZY SETS

In 1999, Zadeh communicated (to members of an Internet Berkeley Institute on Soft Computing Group) the news that more than 27,000 publications had already appeared using the word *fuzzy*. A search of this literature by myself using the Internet revealed that less than 40 of those publications had anything to do with type-2 fuzzy sets or logic. This is very good news for anyone wishing to do research in type-2 FLSs.

Although we provide references to much of this literature in the later chapters of this book, it is useful to provide an historical perspective of them in one place.

As already mentioned, Zadeh (1975) introduced the concept of a type-2 fuzzy set as an extension of an ordinary fuzzy set, i.e., a type-1 set. Mizumoto and Tanaka (1976) studied the set theoretic operations of type-2 fuzzy sets and properties of membership grades of such sets; they also examined type-2 fuzzy sets under the operations of algebraic product and algebraic sum [Mizumoto and Tanaka (1981)]. Nieminen (1977) provided more detail about the algebraic structure of type-2 fuzzy sets. Karnik and Mendel [(1998a, b), (2000a)] extended the works of Mizumoto and Tanaka and obtained practical algorithms for performing union, intersection, and complement for type-2 fuzzy sets. They also developed the concept of the centroid of a type-2 fuzzy set and provided a practical algorithm for computing it for interval type-2 fuzzy sets in Karnik and Mendel [(1998b), (2000b)].

Dubois and Prade [(1978), (1979), (1980)] discussed fuzzy valued logic and gave a formula for the composition of type-2 relations as an extension of the type-1 sup-star composition; but their formula is only for the minimum t-norm. A general formula for the extended sup-star composition of type-2 relations was given by Karnik and Mendel (1998b, c) and Karnik et al. (1999). Based on this formula, Karnik and Mendel (1998a, b, c) and Karnik et al. (1999) established a complete type-2 FLS theory, one that includes type-reduction, although the latter was developed first by Karnik and Mendel (1998b, c).

Hisdal (1981) studied rules and interval sets for higher-than-type-1 FL; however, her work proceeded quite differently from that of Liang and Mendel [(2000a), (2000c)], who developed a complete theory for interval type-2 FLSs. They did this for different kinds of fuzzifiers, and showed how such FLSs can be designed, i.e., how the free parameters within interval type-2 FLSs can be tuned using training data.

The two most popular FLSs used by engineers today are the Mamdani and Takagi-Sugeno-Kang (TSK) systems. Both are characterized by IF–THEN rules and have the same antecedent structures. They differ in the structures of the consequents. The consequent of a Mamdani rule is a fuzzy set, whereas the consequent of a TSK rule is a function. Mamdani FLSs were first developed by Mamdani (1974) and represent one of the first really useful applications of Zadeh's fuzzy sets and logic. TSK FL controllers are very widely used in control system applications of FL [e.g., Takagi and Sugeno (1985), Sugeno and Kang (1988)]. Liang and Mendel [(1999), (2000f)] developed type-2 TSK FLSs.

To date, type-2 fuzzy sets and FLSs have been used for:[8]

- classification of coded video streams [Liang and Mendel (2000h)]
- co-channel interference elimination from nonlinear time-varying communication channels [Liang and Mendel (2000 g)]
- connection admission control [Liang et al. (2000)]
- control of mobile robots [Wu (1996)]
- decision making [Yager (1980), Chaneau et al. (1987)]

---

[8]This list is in alphabetical order by application.

- equalization of non-linear fading channels [Karnik et al. (1999), Mendel (2000), Liang and Mendel (2000b, 2000d)]

- extracting knowledge from questionnairre surveys [Karnik and Mendel (1998b, 1999b), Liang et al. (2000)]

- forecasting of time-series [Karnik and Mendel (1999a), Mendel (2000), Liang and Mendel (2000c)]

- function approximation [Karnik and Mendel (1998b)]

- pre-processing radiographic images [John et al. (1997, 1998)]

- relational databases [Chiang et al. (1997)]

- solving fuzzy relation equations [Wagenknecht and Hartmann (1988)]

- transport scheduling [John (1996)]

There are also some articles about type-2 fuzzy sets that have appeared in the Japanese literature, but are only in Japanese. Two examples are [Izumi et al. (1983)] and [Sugeno (1983)]. No doubt, there are other articles that have eluded this author, and, if there are, I hope that we hear about them.

1.7 COVERAGE

This book has been organized into four parts: Preliminaries, Type-1 Fuzzy Logic Systems, Type-2 Fuzzy Sets, and Type-2 Fuzzy Logic Systems. Part 1—Preliminaries—contains four chapters, including this *Introduction*. Short primers about fuzzy sets and fuzzy logic are included at the end of this chapter.

In Chapter 2, *Sources of Uncertainty*, we describe what we mean by an *uncertain* rule-based FLS. "Uncertain," as we use this word, is not an abstract theoretical notion; instead, it is a concrete notion that is conditioned on the structure of the Figure 1-1 FLS. We demonstrate that, because words can mean different things to different people, there is uncertainty associated with the words that are used in rules. This translates into uncertainty about membership functions and the need to capture it using type-2 fuzzy sets.

In Chapter 3, *Membership Functions and Uncertainty*, we formally introduce membership functions for type-2 fuzzy sets, and carefully define and explain many terms that are associated with them. The new concepts of footprint of uncertainty, lower and upper membership functions, and embedded type-2 and embedded type-1 fuzzy sets are also defined.

In Chapter 4, *Case Studies*, we describe two case studies that are carried through the entire book. They are *forecasting of time-series* and *knowledge mining using surveys*, and should be understandable to all the readers of this book.

Part 2—Type-1 Fuzzy Logic Systems—contains two chapters that are included to provide the underlying basis for our type-2 FLSs so that we can compare type-2 results for our case studies with type-1 results.

In Chapter 5, *Singleton Type-1 Fuzzy Logic Systems: No Uncertainties*, we lay the groundwork and provide the baseline for the rest of the book. We discuss and quantify each of the blocks in the Figure 1-1 FLS for the case when there are no rule uncertainties and the inputs to the FLS are measured perfectly. The tremendous simplification of the computations in the singleton case is due to the easy computation of the supremum operation in the sup-star composition, due to singleton fuzzification. We interpret the FLS as a FL basis function expansion, which lets us put the FLS into the context of other basis function expansions. And we also discuss, without proof, the important universal approximation property of a FLS. Because a FLS has parameters associated with it that must somehow be specified, we describe some design methods to do this. All of the design methods are associated with the following problem:

> We are given a collection of N input–output numerical data training pairs, $(\mathbf{x}^{(1)}:y^{(1)}),(\mathbf{x}^{(2)}:y^{(2)}),...,(\mathbf{x}^{(N)}:y^{(N)})$, where $\mathbf{x}$ is the vector input and y is the scalar output of a FLS. Our goal is to completely specify the FLS using the training data.

We examine the following design methods: two one-pass methods, a least-squares method, a back-propagation (steepest descent) method, and a singular-value decomposition (SVD)–QR method. Some of these methods require tuning of the FLS parameters and others do not. The SVD–QR method is very useful for reducing the number of rules in the FLS.

In Chapter 6, *Non-Singleton Type-1 Fuzzy Logic Systems*, we continue to lay the groundwork and provide a baseline for the rest of the book. We discuss and quantify each of the blocks in the Figure 1-1 FLS for the case when there are no rule uncertainties but the inputs to the FLS are corrupted by additive measurement noise—the first kind of uncertainty treated in this book. Non-singleton fuzzification leads to more complicated calculations than singleton fuzzification, because in the former the supremum operation in the sup-star composition is difficult to perform, whereas in the latter it is easy to perform. When, however, all membership functions are Gaussian, it is easy to perform the sup-star composition in the non-singleton case; so, we emphasize this choice of membership function. As in all of the later chapters that are about FLSs, the developments in this chapter parallel those in Chapter 5; so, for example, we cover design methods for non-singleton type-1 FLSs that parallel those given for singleton type-1 FLSs.

Part 3—Type-2 Fuzzy Sets—contains three chapters, each of which focuses on a different aspect of such sets. Much of the material in these chapters is theoretical and detailed; but for the newcomer to type-2 fuzzy sets it needs to be digested at least one time. This is analogous to studying probability for the first time, where one learns many important facts by proving them (e.g., the expected value of a sum of two independent random variables equals the sum of the expected values of each of the random variables). Once the proofs of these facts are understood, we can then use them in new situations without having to re-prove them each time (e.g., we can treat expectation as a linear operator). We make very heavy use of the results of these three chapters in the rest of the book.

In Chapter 7, *Operations on and Properties of Type-2 Fuzzy Sets*, we examine set theoretic operations on and properties of type-2 fuzzy sets. The Extension Principle plays a very important role in this chapter. First, we give results for union, intersection, and complement of general type-2 fuzzy sets; then, we give results for algebraic operations—addition and multiplication—of general type-2 fuzzy sets. Results are given for the minimum and product t-norms, since they are the most widely used t-norms. In the second part of the chapter we focus on interval type-2 fuzzy sets because, to date, they are the only ones that are practical to use, and we use them extensively in the rest of the book. In Appendixes A and B we provide additional results about operations and properties of general type-2 fuzzy sets.

In Chapter 8, *Type-2 Relations and Compositions*, we provide the extended sup-star composition, which, as we have already mentioned, is the fundamental mapping of the inputs by the Figure 1-1 inference engine into its output. To compute the extended sup-star composition, we make heavy use of the results from Chapter 7. We conclude this chapter by describing the membership function for a type-2 implication.

In Chapter 9, *Centroid of a Type-2 Fuzzy Set: Type-Reduction*, we provide results that are used in the rest of this book. We describe the new concept of a centroid of a type-2 fuzzy set first for general type-2 fuzzy sets, and then for interval type-2 fuzzy sets. We emphasize how to compute the centroid for both kinds of sets, and provide a very practical algorithm for computing the centroid of an interval type-2 fuzzy set. This algorithm is very heavily used in the rest of the book. We also describe *type-reduction* in this chapter, because it is equivalent to calculating the centroid of very specific type-2 fuzzy sets. The starting point for type-reduction is a particular defuzzification method (e.g., centroid, height). Just as there are many different kinds of defuzzification methods, there are many different but comparable type-reduction methods. We describe five of them in this chapter, first for general type-2 fuzzy sets and then for interval type-2 fuzzy sets.

Part 4—Type-2 Fuzzy Logic Systems—contains five chapters, three having to do with Mamdani type-2 FLSs, one having to do with TSK type-2 FLSs, and an epilogue.

In Chapter 10, *Singleton Type-2 Fuzzy Logic Systems*, we describe a type-2 FLS that accounts for uncertainties about either the antecedents or consequents in rules but does not explicitly account for input measurement uncertainties. We return to the blocks of Figure 1-1 and discuss and quantify each of them, first for general type-2 fuzzy sets and then for interval type-2 fuzzy sets. As in Chapter 5, singleton fuzzification simplifies the computations of the extended sup-star composition. Somewhat surprisingly, fuzzy basis functions do not seem to be very useful for general type-2 FLSs; but, they are very useful for interval type-2 FLSs. We show that the concepts of *lower* and *upper membership functions* play an extremely important role in interval type-2 FLSs, and let us obtain analytical results that make the calculations for such FLSs very practical. In fact, we show that an interval singleton type-2 FLS is characterized by just two fuzzy basis function expansions. In the rest of this chapter we focus on how to design singleton type-2 FLSs, using one-pass, back-propagation (steepest descent), and SVD–QR methods. While the former method is a straightforward extension of its type-1 counterparts, the latter two are not. The back-propagation method is where we need the concept of an active branch of a lower or upper membership function. Which branch is activated depends on the numerical values of the inputs that are applied to the FLS.

In Chapter 11, *Type-1 Non-Singleton Type-2 Fuzzy Logic Systems*, we describe a type-2 FLS that not only accounts for uncertainties about either the antecedents or consequents in rules but also accounts for input measurement uncertainties. We model the latter as type-1 fuzzy numbers, just as we did in Chapter 6. This chapter parallels the developments in Chapter 10, especially for interval type-2 fuzzy sets. Except for the calculations of the upper and lower membership functions for the firing intervals, all the calculations described in Chapter 10 apply to the present chapter. As in Chapter 6, the non-singleton fuzzifier complicates the calculation of the extended sup-star composition; but again, using Gaussian membership functions makes these calculations fairly straightforward.

In Chapter 12, *Type-2 Non-Singleton Type-2 Fuzzy Logic Systems*, we describe, as we did in Chapter 11, a type-2 FLS that not only accounts for uncertainties about either the antecedents or consequents in rules but also accounts for uncertainties in the input measurements; however, in this chapter, we model the latter as type-2 fuzzy numbers. Doing this is useful, e.g., in time-series forecasting when the additive measurement noise is non-stationary. As we did in Chapter 11, this chapter also parallels the developments in Chapter 10, especially for interval type-2 fuzzy sets, and, except for the calculations of the upper and lower membership functions for the firing intervals, all the calculations described in Chapter 10 apply to the present chapter. The type-2 non-singleton fuzzifier complicates the calculation of the extended sup-star composition even more than it did in Chapter 11; but again, using Gaussian membership functions makes these calculations fairly straightforward.

In Chapter 13, *TSK Fuzzy Logic Systems*, we cover type-1 and type-2 TSK FLSs. Because we could not find any discussions about non-singleton type-1 TSK FLSs in the literature, we only cover singleton type-1 and type-2 TSK FLSs. We also include some design methods for TSK FLSs—least-squares and back-propagation for type-1 TSK FLSs, and back-propagation for type-2 TSK FLSs.

In Chapter 14, *Epilogue*, we provide a brief summary of the book, including a table that lets the reader easily compare type-1 and type-2 singleton and non-singleton FLSs. We also provide some guidance about the kinds of situations that at present seem to be most appropriate for using type-2 FLSs. We then describe four applications to which type-2 FLSs have already demonstrated much better performance than type-1 FLSs: rule-based classification of video traffic, equalization of time-varying non-linear digital communication channels, overcoming co-channel interference and inter-symbol interference for time-varying nonlinear digital communication channels, and connection admission control for ATM networks. Finally, we conclude with some potential application areas for type-2 FLSs, including the architecture for a *perceptual computer*.

1.8 APPLICABILITY OUTSIDE OF RULE-BASED FLSs

Although the focus of this book is on rule-based FLSs, the material in Chapters 3, 7, 8, and 9 should also be applicable to non-rule-based applications of type-2 fuzzy sets. We leave it to the reader to explore such applications.

1.9 COMPUTATION

MATLAB is a large collection of more than 500 subroutines, which are called *M-files*. They are easily linked together by the end-user. Although no MATLAB M-files are packaged with this book, more than 30 are available as freeware on the Internet at the following URL: *http://sipi.usc.edu/~mendel/software*. They are being made available so that you will be able to immediately use the results in this book.

Brief descriptions of M-files appear at the end of each chapter for which they are most applicable. Appendix C collects the M-files together as they are organized on the Internet, i.e., in the three folders: type-1 FLSs, general type-2 FLSs, and interval type-2 FLSs. Some additional M-files that appear in these folders, but are not listed in Appendix C, are needed by some of the ones that are listed in Appendix C.

Supplementary Material

Short Primers on Fuzzy Sets and Fuzzy Logic

1.10 PRIMER ON FUZZY SETS

Fuzzy sets are a natural outgrowth and generalization of crisp sets; so, to begin we review some important aspects of crisp sets.[9]

1.10.1 Crisp sets

Recall that a *crisp set A* in a universe of discourse X (which provides the set of allowable values for a variable) can be defined by listing all of its members or by identifying the elements $x \subset A$. One way to do the latter is to specify a condition or conditions for which $x \subset A$; thus, A can be defined as $A = \{x \mid x \text{ meets some condition(s)}\}$. Alternatively, we can introduce a zero-one *membership function* (also called a characteristic function, discrimination function, or indicator function) for A, denoted $\mu_A(x)$, such that

$$A \Rightarrow \mu_A(x) = \begin{cases} 1 & \text{if } x \in A \\ 0 & \text{if } x \notin A \end{cases} \tag{1-1}$$

Set A (which can also be treated as a subset of X) is mathematically equivalent to its membership function $\mu_A(x)$ in the sense that knowing $\mu_A(x)$ is the same as knowing A itself.

Example 1-1: Consider the set of all automobiles in New York City; this is X.

---

[9]Most of the material in this supplement is taken from Mendel (1995a), © 1995, IEEE.

The elements of X are individual cars; but, there are many different types of subsets that can be established for X, including the three that are depicted in Figure 1-2. Either a car has or does not have six cylinders. This is a very crisp requirement. Hence, if our car has four cylinders, its membership function value (i.e., membership grade) for the subset of four cylinder cars is unity, whereas its membership grades for the subsets of six cylinder or eight cylinder cars are zero. ■

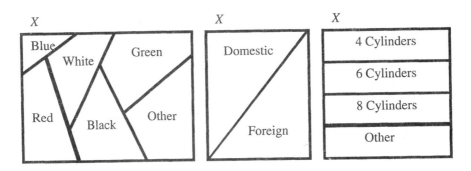

Figure 1-2: Partitioning of the set of all automobiles in New York City into subsets by (a) color, (b) domestic or foreign, and (c) number of cylinders (Mendel, 1995a, © 1995, IEEE).

1.10.2 From crisp sets to fuzzy sets

A *fuzzy set F* is a generalization of a crisp set. It is defined on a universe of discourse X and is characterized by a membership function $\mu_F(x)$ that takes on values in the interval $[0, 1]$. A membership function provides a *measure of the degree of similarity* of an element in X to the fuzzy set. Note that F can also be treated as a subset of X.

Example 1-1 (Continued): A car can be viewed as "domestic" or "foreign" from different perspectives. One perspective is that a car is domestic if it carries the name of a U. S. auto manufacturer; otherwise it is foreign. There is nothing fuzzy about this perspective. Many people today, however, feel that the distinction between a domestic and foreign automobile is not as crisp as it once was, because many of the components for what we consider to be domestic cars (e.g., Fords, GMs, and Chryslers) are produced outside of the United States. Additionally, some "foreign" cars are manufactured in the United States. Consequently, one could think of the membership functions for domestic and foreign cars looking like $\mu_D(x)$ and $\mu_F(x)$ depicted in Figure 1-3. Observe that a specific car (located along the horizontal axis by determining the percentage of its parts made in the United States) exists in both subsets simultaneously—domestic cars and foreign cars—but to different degrees of membership. For example, if a car has 75% of its parts made in the United States, then $\mu_D(75\%) = 0.90$ and $\mu_F(75\%) = 0.25$. Ultimately, we would describe the car as domestic. In fact, when we do this, we decide on the subset by choosing it to be associated with the maximum of $\mu_D(75\%) = 0.90$ and $\mu_F(75\%) = 0.25$.

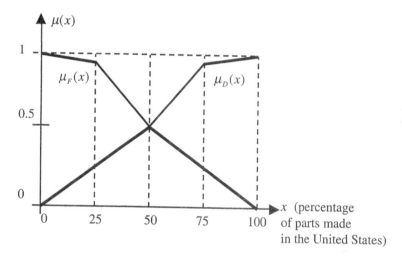

Figure 1-3: Membership functions for domestic and foreign cars, based on the percentage of parts in the car made in the United States (Mendel, 1995a, © 1995, IEEE).

Describing a car by its color is also not a crisp description, because each color has different shades associated with it.

The main point of this example is to demonstrate that in fuzzy logic an element can reside in more than one set to different degrees of similarity. This cannot occur in crisp set theory. ∎

A fuzzy set F in X may be represented as a set of ordered pairs of a generic element x and its grade of membership function, $\mu_F(x)$, i.e.,

$$F = \{(x, \mu_F(x)) \mid x \in X\} \tag{1-2}$$

For type-1 fuzzy sets we frequently use the terms *membership function* and *grade of membership function* interchangeably. Recall that a *function* is an ordered pair of elements no two of which have the same first element. Hence, strictly speaking, $(x, \mu_F(x)) \; \forall x \in X$ denotes the membership function whereas $\mu_F(x)$ denotes the grade of the membership function. It is common practice, however, to refer to $\mu_F(x)$ as the membership function, and doing so does not cause confusion.

When X is continuous (e.g., the real numbers), F is commonly written as

$$F = \int_X \mu_F(x)/x \qquad (1\text{-}3)$$

In this equation, the integral sign does not denote integration; it denotes the collection of all points $x \in X$ with associated membership function $\mu_F(x)$. When X is discrete (e.g., the integers), F is commonly written as

$$F = \sum_X \mu_F(x)/x \qquad (1\text{-}4)$$

In this equation, the summation sign does not denote arithmetic addition; it denotes the collection of all points $x \in X$ with associated membership function $\mu_F(x)$; hence, it denotes the set theoretic operation of union. The slash in (1-3) and (1-4) associates the elements in X with their membership grades, where $\mu_F(x) > 0$.

Example 1-2: [Zimmerman (1991)] Let F = integers close to 10; then, one choice for $\mu_F(x)$ is:

$$F \equiv 0.1/7 + 0.5/8 + 0.8/9 + 1/10 + 0.8/11 + 0.5/12 + 0.1/13 \qquad (1\text{-}5)$$

Three points to note from F are:

1. The integers not explicitly shown all have membership functions equal to zero—by convention, we do not list such elements.
2. The values for the membership functions were chosen by a specific individual; except for the unity membership value when $x = 10$, they can be modified based on our own personal interpretation of the word "close."
3. The membership function is symmetric about $x = 10$, because there is no reason to believe that integers to the left of 10 are close to 10 in a different way than are integers to the right of 10; but again, we are free to make other interpretations.

■

1.10.3 Linguistic variables

Zadeh (1975, p. 201) states:

In retreating from precision in the face of overpowering complexity, it is natural to explore the use of what might be called linguistic variables, that is, variables whose values are not numbers but words or sentences in a natural or artificial language. The motivation for the use of words or sentences rather than numbers is that linguistic characterizations are, in general, less specific than numerical ones.

Let u denote the name of a linguistic variable (e.g., temperature). Numerical (measured) values of a linguistic variable u are denoted x, where $x \in X$. Sometimes x and u are used interchangeably, especially when a linguistic variable is a letter, as is sometimes the case in engineering applications. A linguistic variable is usually decomposed into a set of terms, $T(u)$, which cover its universe of discourse.

Example 1-3: [Cox (1992)] Let *pressure* (u) be interpreted as a linguistic variable. It can be decomposed into the following set of terms: T(pressure) = {*weak, low, okay, strong, high*}, where each term in T(pressure) is characterized by a fuzzy set in the universe of discourse $X = [100 \text{ psi}, 2300 \text{ psi}]$. We might interpret *weak* as a pressure below 200 psi, *low* as a pressure close to 700 psi, *okay* as a pressure close to 1050 psi, *strong* as a pressure close to 1500 psi, and *high* as a pressure above 2200 psi. These terms can be characterized as fuzzy sets whose membership functions are shown in Figure 1-4. Measured values of pressure (x) lie along the pressure axis. In this example, a vertical line from any measured value intersects, at most, two membership functions. So, for example, $x = 300$ resides in the fuzzy sets *weak pressure* and *low pressure*, but to different degrees of similarity. ∎

Recently, Zadeh (1999, p. 107) has used the word *perception* to describe the terms associated with linguistic variables. For example, he states:

A fundamental difference between measurements and perceptions is that, in general, measurements are crisp numbers whereas perceptions are fuzzy numbers or, more generally, fuzzy granules, that is, clumps of objects in which the transition from membership to nonmembership is gradual rather than abrupt.

Indeed, in Example 1-3, the terms *weak, low, okay, strong,* and *high* are perceptions about the level of pressure.

1.10.4 Membership functions

In rule-based applications of FL, *membership functions*, $\mu_F(x)$, are associated with terms that appear in the antecedents or consequents of rules, or in phrases (e.g., *foreign* cars).

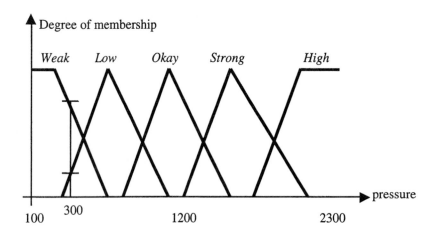

Figure, 1-4: Membership functions for *T*(pressure) = {*weak, low, okay, strong, high*}. The shapes of the membership functions as well as their degree of overlap are quite arbitrary. (©1992 IEEE. This figure has been taken from E. Cox, "Fuzzy Fundamentals," *IEEE Spectrum*, pp. 58-61, Oct. 1992.)

Example 1-4: Some examples of rules and associated membership functions (shown in brackets) are: (1) IF we are tracking a *large* target at one instant of time, THEN the target will not be *too far away* at the next instant of time [$\mu_{LARGE}(t), \mu_{TOO-FAR-AWAY}(x)$]; (2) IF the horizontal position is *medium positive* and the angular position is *small negative*, THEN the control angle is *large positive* [$\mu_{MEDIUM-POSITIVE}(x)$, $\mu_{SMALL-NEGATIVE}(\theta)$, $\mu_{LARGE-POSITIVE}(\phi)$]; and, (3) IF y(t) is *close to 0.5*, THEN *f*(y) is *close to zero* [$\mu_{CLOSE-TO-0.5}(y)$, $\mu_{CLOSE-TO-ZERO}(f(y))$]. ∎

The most commonly used shapes for membership functions are triangular, trapezoidal, piecewise-linear, Gaussian, and bell-shaped. Membership functions can either be chosen by the user arbitrarily, based on the user's experience (hence, the membership functions for two users could be quite different depending upon their experiences, perspectives, cultures, etc.), or, they can be designed using optimization procedures (e.g., [Horikawa et al. (1992)], [Jang (1992)], [Wang and Mendel (1992a, b)].

Example 1-5: Let *X* be the set of all men. The term "height" can mean different things to different people. Figure 1-5 depicts two sets of membership functions for the set of terms {*short men, medium men, tall men*}. Clearly, the terms *short men, medium men,* and *tall men* will have a very different meaning to a professional basketball player than they will to most other people. This illustrates the fact that membership functions can be quite context dependent. ■

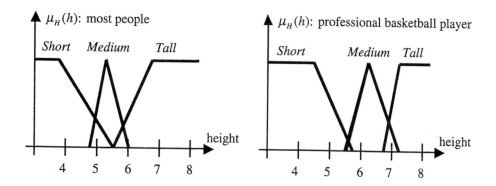

Figure 1-5: Membership functions for T(height) = {*short men, medium men, tall men*}. (a) Most people's membership functions, and (b) professional basketball player's membership functions (Mendel, 1995a, © 1995, IEEE).

The number of membership functions is up to us. Greater resolution is achieved by using more membership functions at the price of greater computational complexity. Membership functions don't have to overlap; but, one of the great strengths of FL is that membership functions can be made to overlap. This expresses the fact that "the glass can be partially full and partially empty at the same time." In this way (as will become clear in later chapters, e.g., Chapter 5) we are able to distribute our decisions over more than one input class, which helps to make FL systems robust. Although membership functions do not have to be scaled between zero and unity, most people do this so that variables are normalized. We can always normalize a fuzzy set by dividing $\mu_F(x)$ by its largest value, $\sup_{x \in X} \mu_F(x)$.

1.10.5 Some terminology

The *support* of a fuzzy set F is the crisp set of all points x in X such that $\mu_F(x) > 0$. For example, the support of the fuzzy set *short* in Figure 1-5 (a) is $x \in [0, 5.5]$. A fuzzy set whose support is a single point in X with $\mu_F(x) = 1$ is called a (type-1) *fuzzy singleton*. A *normal* fuzzy set is one for which $\sup_{x \in X} \mu_F(x) = 1$.

1.10.6 Set theoretic operations for crisp sets

Now that we have defined fuzzy sets, *what can we do with them?* We could ask the same question about crisp sets, and we know that there are lots of things we can do with them; hence, we expect that we can do analogous things with fuzzy sets. To begin, let us briefly review the elementary crisp-set operations of union, intersection, and complement.

Let A and B be two subsets of X. The *union* of A and B, denoted $A \cup B$, contains all of the elements in either A or B, i.e.,

$$\mu_{A \cup B}(x) = \begin{cases} 1 & \text{if } x \in A \text{ or } x \in B \\ 0 & \text{if } x \notin A \text{ and } x \notin B \end{cases} \tag{1-6}$$

The *intersection* of A and B, denoted $A \cap B$, contains all of the elements that are simultaneously in A and B, i.e.,

$$\mu_{A \cap B}(x) = \begin{cases} 1 & \text{if } x \in A \text{ and } x \in B \\ 0 & \text{if } x \notin A \text{ or } x \notin B \end{cases} \tag{1-7}$$

Let $\overline{A}$ denote the *complement* of A; it contains all the elements that are not in A, i.e.,

$$\mu_{\overline{A}}(x) = \begin{cases} 1 & \text{if } x \notin A \\ 0 & \text{if } x \in A \end{cases} \tag{1-8}$$

From these facts, it is easy to show that:

$$A \cup B \Rightarrow \mu_{A \cup B}(x) = \max[\mu_A(x), \mu_B(x)] \tag{1-9}$$

$$A \cap B \Rightarrow \mu_{A \cap B}(x) = \min[\mu_A(x), \mu_B(x)] \tag{1-10}$$

$$\mu_{\overline{A}}(x) = 1 - \mu_A(x) \tag{1-11}$$

Consider $\mu_{A \cup B}(x)$ for example. In this case, $x \in A$ or $x \in B$ means

$$\left(\mu_A(x) = 1, \mu_B(x) = 1 \right) \text{ or } \left(\mu_A(x) = 1, \mu_B(x) = 0 \right) \text{ or } \left(\mu_A(x) = 0, \mu_B(x) = 1 \right);$$

for each of these situations, $\max[\mu_A(x), \mu_B(x)] = 1$. Additionally, $x \notin A$ and $x \notin B$ means $\left(\mu_A(x) = 0, \mu_B(x) = 0\right)$ for which $\max[\mu_A(x), \mu_B(x)] = 0$. Consequently, $\max[\mu_A(x), \mu_B(x)]$ for $\forall x$ does provide the correct membership function, given in (1-6), for union.

The formulas for $\mu_{A \cup B}(x)$, $\mu_{A \cap B}(x)$, and $\mu_{\overline{A}}(x)$ are very useful for proving other theoretical properties about crisp sets. Note, also, that the maximum and minimum are not the only ways to describe $\mu_{A \cup B}(x)$ and $\mu_{A \cap B}(x)$. While these formulas are not usually part of conventional set theory, they are esssential to fuzzy set theory; however, as we have just demonstrated, they really do occur in conventional set theory. See, e.g., [Klir and Folger (1988)] and [Yager and Filev (1994b)] for other ways to characterize these operations.

The crisp union and intersection operations satisfy many properties (see Table B-1 for an extensive list of these properties), including:

1. *Commutative* (e.g., $A \cup B = B \cup A$)
2. *Associative* (e.g., $A \cup B \cup C = (A \cup B) \cup C = A \cup (B \cup C)$)
3. *Distributive* (e.g., $A \cap (B \cup C) = (A \cap B) \cup (A \cap C)$ and
$$A \cup (B \cap C) = (A \cup B) \cap (A \cup C))$$

These properties can be proved either by Venn diagrams or by means of the membership function definition given in (1-1).

De Morgan's laws for crisp sets are:

$$\overline{A \cup B} = \overline{A} \cap \overline{B} \text{ and } \overline{A \cap B} = \overline{A} \cup \overline{B}$$

These laws, which are also very useful in proving things about more complicated operations on sets, can also be proved either by Venn diagrams or by means of the membership function definition given in (1-1).

The two fundamental (Aristotelian) laws of crisp set theory are:

1. *Law of Excluded Middle*: $A \cup \overline{A} = X$ (i.e., a set and its complement must comprise the universe of discourse).
2. *Law of Contradiction* $A \cap \overline{A} = \varnothing$ (i.e., an element can either be in its set or its complement; it cannot simultaneously be in both).

1.10.7 Set theoretic operations for fuzzy sets

In FL, union, intersection, and complement are defined in terms of their membership functions. Let fuzzy sets A and B be described by their membership functions $\mu_A(x)$ and $\mu_B(x)$. One definition of *fuzzy union* leads to the membership function

$$\mu_{A\cup B}(x) = \max[\mu_A(x), \mu_B(x)], \qquad (1\text{-}12)$$

and one definition of *fuzzy intersection* leads to the membership function

$$\mu_{A\cap B}(x) = \min[\mu_A(x), \mu_B(x)] \qquad (1\text{-}13)$$

Additionally, the membership function for *fuzzy complement* is

$$\mu_{\bar{A}}(x) = 1 - \mu_A(x) \qquad (1\text{-}14)$$

Obviously, these three definitions were motivated by their crisp counterparts in equations (1-9)–(1-11).

Although equations (1-12)–(1-14) and (1-9)–(1-11) look exactly alike, we must remember that:

1. Sets A and B in (1-12)–(1-14) are fuzzy, whereas in (1-9)–(1-11) they are crisp; and,
2. Fuzzy sets can *only* be characterized by their membership functions, whereas crisp sets can be characterized either by their membership functions, a description of their elements, or a listing of their elements.

Example 1-6: Consider the fuzzy sets A = damping ratio x *considerably larger* than 0.5, and B = damping ratio x *approximately* equal to 0.707. Note that damping ratio is a positive real number, i.e., its universe of discourse, X, is the positive real numbers $0 \le x \le 1$. Consequently, $A = \{(x, \mu_A(x)) | x \in X\}$ and $B = \{(x, \mu_B(x)) | x \in X\}$, where, for example, $\mu_A(x)$ and $\mu_B(x)$ are specified, as:

$$\mu_A(x) = \begin{cases} 0 & \text{if } 0 \le x \le 0.5 \\ 1/[1 + (x - 0.5)^{-2}] & \text{if } 0.5 < x \le 1 \end{cases} \qquad (1\text{-}15)$$

and

$$\mu_B(x) = \frac{1}{[1 + (x - 0.707)^4]} \quad 0 \le x \le 1 \qquad (1\text{-}16)$$

Figure 1-6 depicts $\mu_A(x)$, $\mu_B(x)$, $\mu_{A\cup B}(x)$, $\mu_{A\cap B}(x)$, and $\mu_{\bar{B}}(x)$. Observe, from Figure 1-6 (d), that the point $x = 5$ exists in both B and $\bar{B}$ simultaneously, but to different degrees, because $\mu_B(0.5) \neq 0$ and $\mu_{\bar{B}}(0.5) \neq 0$. ∎

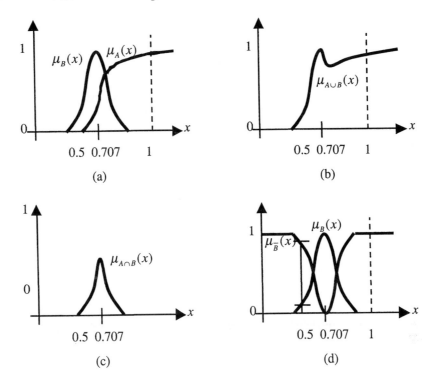

Figure 1-6: Membership functions associated with A = damping ratio x *considerably larger* than 0.5, and B = damping ratio x *approximately* 0.707. (a) $\mu_A(x)$ and $\mu_B(x)$, (b) $\mu_{A \cup B}(x)$, (c) $\mu_{A \cap B}(x)$, and (d) $\mu_{\bar{B}}(x)$.

This example demonstrates that for fuzzy sets the Laws of Excluded Middle and Contradiction are broken, i.e., *for fuzzy sets*: $A \cup \bar{A} \neq X$ and $A \cap \bar{A} \neq \emptyset$. We have also seen this in the automobile Example 1-1. In fact, one of the ways to describe the difference between crisp set theory and fuzzy set theory is to explain that these two laws do not hold in fuzzy set theory.

The maximum and minimum operators are not the only ones that could have been chosen to model fuzzy union and fuzzy intersection. Zadeh (1965), in his pioneering first paper, defined two operators each for fuzzy union and fuzzy intersection, namely:

1. **Fuzzy union:** *maximum* and *algebraic sum*, where for the latter

$$\mu_{A\cup B}(x) = \mu_A(x) + \mu_B(x) - \mu_A(x)\mu_B(x) \qquad (1\text{-}17)$$

2. **Fuzzy intersection**: *minimum* and *algebraic product*, where for the latter

$$\mu_{A\cap B}(x) = \mu_A(x)\mu_B(x) \qquad (1\text{-}18)$$

Later, other operators, that have a strong axiomatic basis (e.g., [Klir and Yuan, 1995]) were introduced (in all cases, $x, y \in [0,1]$):

1. **t-conorm operators** for fuzzy union (also known as *s*-norm and denoted $\oplus$). The maximum and algebraic sums are t-conorms; some other examples of t-conorms are:

    - *Bounded sum*: $x \oplus y = \min(1, x + y)$

    - *Drastic sum*: $x \oplus y = \begin{cases} x & \text{if } y = 0 \\ y & \text{if } x = 0 \\ 1 & \text{otherwise} \end{cases}$

2. **t-norm operators** for fuzzy intersection (denoted $\star$). The minimum and algebraic product are t-norms; some other examples of t-norms are:

    - *Bounded product*: $x \star y = \max(0, x + y - 1)$

    - *Drastic product*: $x \star y = \begin{cases} x & \text{if } y = 1 \\ y & \text{if } x = 1 \\ 0 & \text{otherwise} \end{cases}$

There is even an axiomatic definition for the complement of a fuzzy set (denoted c). In engineering applications, most people use the fuzzy complement whose membership function is given in (1-14).

As pointed out by Zimmerman (1991), pairs of t-norms and t-conorms satisfy the following generalization of DeMorgan's laws [Bonissone and Decker (1986)]:

$$s[\mu_A(x), \mu_B(x)] = c\left\{ t\left[c(\mu_A(x)), c(\mu_B(x)) \right] \right\} \qquad (1\text{-}19)$$

$$t[\mu_A(x), \mu_B(x)] = c\{s[c(\mu_A(x)), c(\mu_B(x))]\} \tag{1-20}$$

where $x \in X$. For example,

$$\max[\mu_A(x), \mu_B(x)] = 1 - \min[1 - \mu_A(x), 1 - \mu_B(x)] \tag{1-21}$$

and

$$\min[\mu_A(x), \mu_B(x)] = 1 - \max[1 - \mu_A(x), 1 - \mu_B(x)] \tag{1-22}$$

Note, also, that there are other ways of combining fuzzy sets, e.g., the *fuzzy and*, *fuzzy or*, *compensatory and*, and *compensatory or*; e.g., see [Zimmerman (1991)] and [Yager and Filev (1994b)].

The different t-norms, t-conorms, and complements that are available to us in fuzzy set theory provide us with a plethora of richness and also with some (tough) choices that will have to be made in our FLS. Zimmerman (1991, pp. 42-43) provides eight criteria that might be helpful in selecting the connective's operator. Unfortunately, I found most of those criteria to be so subjective that I could not use them in my engineering applications of FL.

Most engineering applications of fuzzy sets use: (1) the minimum or algebraic product t-norm for fuzzy intersection, (2) the maximum t-conorm for fuzzy union, and (3) $1 - \mu_A(x)$ for the membership function of the fuzzy complement. We do likewise. Finally, we note that all of the operators that are available for fuzzy union, intersection, and complement reduce to their crisp set counterparts when the membership functions are restricted to the values 0 or 1.

1.10.8 Crisp relations and compositions on the same product space

According to Klir and Folger (1988, p. 65), "A *crisp relation* represents the presence or absence of association, interaction, or interconnectedness between the elements of two or more sets." Here we limit our attention to relations between two sets U and V, i.e., to binary relations denoted $R(U,V)$. We let $U \times V$ denote the *Cartesian product* of the two crisp sets U and V, i.e.,

$$U \times V = \{(x,y) | x \in U \text{ and } y \in V\} \tag{1-23}$$

$R(U,V)$ is a subset of $U \times V$.

Crisp relation $R(U,V)$ can be defined by the following membership function:

$$\mu_R(x,y) = \begin{cases} 1 & \text{if and only if } (x,y) \in R(U,V) \\ 0 & \text{otherwise} \end{cases} \tag{1-24}$$

For binary relations defined over a Cartesian product whose elements come from a discrete universe of discourse, it is convenient to collect the membership functions into a *relational matrix* whose elements are either zero or unity. An equivalent representation for a binary relation is a *sagittal diagram*, in which the sets U and V are each represented by a set of nodes in the diagram that are clearly distinguished from one another. Elements of $U \times V$ with non-zero membership grade in $R(U,V)$ are represented in the diagram by lines connecting the respective nodes. Although not explicitly shown, the lines have membership values equal to unity.

Example 1-7: Let R represent the relation of *stability* between the set of all linear, second-order continuous-time systems and the set of the poles of such systems. Of all the possible pairings of linear second-order continuous-time systems and poles, we know that only those pairs whose members are time-invariant with poles lying either in the left-half of the complex s-plane or on the imaginary axis of that plane are stable.

Let $U = \{x_1, x_2\} = \{$linear second-order time-varying continuous-time system, linear second-order time-invariant continuous-time system$\}$, and $V = \{y_1, y_2, y_3\} = \{$poles lie in the left-half s-plane, poles lie on the $j\omega$ axis, poles lie in the right-half s-plane$\}$. The Cartesian product $U \times V$ can be visualized as a 2×3 array of ordered pairs, e.g., the (1-2) element is (linear second-order time-varying continuous-time system, poles lie on the $j\omega$ axis). Clearly, our stability relation $R(U,V)$ is the following subset of $U \times V$:

$R(U,V) = \{$(linear second-order time-invariant continuous-time system, poles lie in the left-half s-plane), (linear second-order time-invariant continuous-time system, poles lie on the $j\omega$ axis)$\}$.

The relational matrix for our stability relation is:

$$\begin{array}{c c} & \begin{array}{ccc} y_1 & y_2 & y_3 \end{array} \\ \begin{array}{c} x_1 \\ x_2 \end{array} & \begin{pmatrix} 0 & 0 & 0 \\ 1 & 1 & 0 \end{pmatrix} \end{array}$$

The sagittal diagram for our stability relation is depicted in Figure 1-7. ■

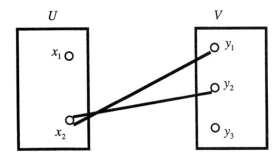

Figure 1-7: Sagittal diagram for relation of stability between the set of all linear, second-order continuous-time systems and the set of poles of such systems (Mendel, 1995a, © 1995, IEEE).

Let $R(u,v)$ and $S(u,v)$—R and S for short—be two crisp relations in the same Cartesian product space $U \times V$. The intersection and union of R and S, which are *compositions* of the two relations, are computed using (1-9) and (1-10), because a relation is a set.

1.10.9 Fuzzy relations and compositions on the same product space

Fuzzy relations represent a *degree* of presence or absence of association, interaction, or interconnectedness between the elements of two or more fuzzy sets. Some examples of binary fuzzy relations are:

- x is much larger than y
- y is very close to x
- z is much greener than y
- system 1 is less damped than system 2
- bandwidth of system A is larger than that of system B
- tone C is of higher local signal-to-noise ratio than tone D

Fuzzy relations play an important role in a FLS.

Let U and V be two universes of discourse. A *fuzzy relation*, $R(U,V)$, is a fuzzy set in the Cartesian product space $U \times V$, i.e., it is a fuzzy subset of $U \times V$

and is characterized by membership function $\mu_R(x,y)$ where $x \in U$ and $y \in V$, i.e.,

$$R(U,V) = \left\{ \left((x,y), \mu_R(x,y) \right) \middle| (x,y) \in U \times V \right\} \qquad (1\text{-}25)$$

The difference between a crisp relation and a fuzzy relation is that for the former $\mu_R(x,y) = 0$ or 1, whereas for the latter $\mu_R(x,y) \in [0,1]$. The generalization of a fuzzy relation to an n-dimensional Cartesian product space is straightforward and is described in Section 8.2.

Example 1-8: Let U and V be the real numbers, and consider the fuzzy relation "target x is *close* to target y." Here is one membership function for this relation:

$$\mu_c \left(|x - y| \right) \equiv \max \left\{ (5 - |x - y|)/5, 0 \right\} \qquad (1\text{-}26)$$

This relational membership function is depicted in Figure 1-8. Note that the distance between the two targets $|x - y|$ is treated as the independent variable. ∎

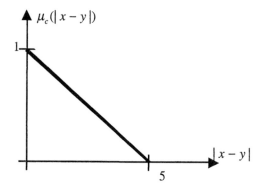

Figure 1-8: Relational membership function $\mu_c(|x-y|)$, (Mendel, 1995a, © 1995, IEEE).

Because fuzzy relations are fuzzy sets in a Cartesian product space, set theoretic and algebraic operations can be defined for them using our earlier operators for fuzzy union, intersection and complement. Let $R(U,V)$ and $S(U,V)$ (shortened in the sequel to R and S) be two fuzzy relations in the *same* Cartesian product space $U \times V$. The intersection and union of R and S, which are *compositions* of the two relations, are then defined as:

$$\mu_{R \cap S}(x, y) = \mu_R(x, y) \star \mu_S(x, y) \tag{1-27}$$

$$\mu_{R \cup S}(x, y) = \mu_R(x, y) \oplus \mu_S(x, y) \tag{1-28}$$

where $\star$ is any t-norm, and $\oplus$ is any t-conorm.

Example 1-9: Consider the two somewhat contradictory fuzzy relations "u is close to v" *and* "u is smaller than v," and also the less-contradictory relations "u is close to v" *or* "u is smaller than v." All relations are on the same Cartesian product space $U \times V$. For simplicity, let us assume that $U = \{u_1, u_2\} = \{2, 12\}$ and $V = \{v_1, v_2, v_3\} = \{1, 7, 13\}$. Here we calculate the membership grades for the union and intersection of the two relations. Let the membership functions for *close* and *smaller* be denoted as $\mu_c(u, v)$ and $\mu_s(u, v)$, respectively, where the numbers in $\mu_c(u, v)$ and $\mu_s(u, v)$ have been chosen to agree with a comparison of the numbers in U and V.

$$\mu_c(u, v) \equiv \begin{array}{c} \\ u_1 \\ u_2 \end{array} \begin{array}{ccc} v_1 & v_2 & v_3 \\ \left(0.9 \right. & 0.4 & \left. 0.1 \right) \\ \left. 0.1 \right. & 0.4 & \left. 0.9 \right) \end{array} \tag{1-29}$$

and

$$\mu_s(u, v) \equiv \begin{array}{c} \\ u_1 \\ u_2 \end{array} \begin{array}{ccc} v_1 & v_2 & v_3 \\ \left(0 \right. & 0.6 & \left. 1 \right) \\ \left. 0 \right. & 0 & \left. 0.3 \right) \end{array} \tag{1-30}$$

The membership grades for the union and intersection of these relations, assuming minimum t-norm ($\wedge$) and maximum t-conorm ($\vee$), can be found as

$$\mu_{c \cup s}(u_i, v_j) = \mu_c(u_i, v_j) \vee \mu_s(u_i, v_j) \tag{1-31}$$

and

$$\mu_{c \cap s}(u_i, v_j) = \mu_c(u_i, v_j) \wedge \mu_s(u_i, v_j) \tag{1-32}$$

where $i = 1, 2$ and $j = 1, 2, 3$. Using (1-31) and (1-32), it is easy to show that

$$\mu_{c\cup s}(u,v) = \begin{array}{c} \\ u_1 \\ u_2 \end{array} \begin{array}{ccc} v_1 & v_2 & v_3 \\ \left(0.9 \quad 0.6 \quad 1 \right. \\ \left. 0.1 \quad 0.4 \quad 0.9 \right) \end{array} \qquad (1\text{-}33)$$

and

$$\mu_{c\cap s}(u,v) = \begin{array}{c} \\ u_1 \\ u_2 \end{array} \begin{array}{ccc} v_1 & v_2 & v_3 \\ \left(0 \quad 0.4 \quad 0.1 \right. \\ \left. 0 \quad 0 \quad 0.3 \right) \end{array} \qquad (1\text{-}34)$$

From (1-33) and (1-34) we see that "u is close to v" *or* "u is smaller than v" is much more sensible than "u is close to v" *and* "u is smaller than v," because membership values in $\mu_{c\cup s}(u,v)$ are fairly large, whereas those in $\mu_{c\cap s}(u,v)$ are mostly small. ∎

1.10.10 Crisp relations and compositions on different product spaces

Next, we consider the composition of crisp relations, $P(U,V)$ and $Q(V,W)$, from different Cartesian product spaces that share a common set. Klir and Folger (1988, p. 75) state "The *composition* of these two relations is denoted by

$$R(U,W) = P(U,V) \circ Q(V,W) \qquad (1\text{-}35)$$

and is defined as a subset $R(U,W)$ of $U \times W$ such that $(x,w) \in R$ if and only if there exists at least one $y \in V$ such that $(x,y) \in P$ and $(y,w) \in Q$."

Example 1-10: Here we begin with the saggital diagrams depicted in Figure 1-9, from which we conclude that the relational matrices $R_1(U,V)$, $R_2(V,W)$, and $R_3(U,W)$ are:

$$R_1(U,V) = \begin{array}{c} \\ x_1 \\ x_2 \\ x_3 \end{array} \begin{array}{cccc} y_1 & y_2 & y_3 & y_4 \\ \left(0 \quad 1 \quad 0 \quad 1 \right. \\ \left. 1 \quad 0 \quad 0 \quad 0 \right. \\ \left. 0 \quad 0 \quad 1 \quad 1 \right) \end{array} \qquad (1\text{-}36)$$

$$R_2(V,W) = \begin{array}{c} \\ y_1 \\ y_2 \\ y_3 \\ y_4 \end{array} \begin{array}{cccc} z_1 & z_2 & z_3 & z_4 \\ \begin{pmatrix} 1 & 0 & 0 & 0 \\ 0 & 0 & 0 & 1 \\ 1 & 1 & 0 & 0 \\ 0 & 0 & 1 & 0 \end{pmatrix} \end{array}$$ (1-37)

and

$$R_3(U,W) = \begin{array}{c} \\ x_1 \\ x_2 \\ x_3 \end{array} \begin{array}{cccc} z_1 & z_2 & z_3 & z_4 \\ \begin{pmatrix} 0 & 0 & 1 & 1 \\ 1 & 0 & 0 & 0 \\ 1 & 1 & 1 & 0 \end{pmatrix} \end{array}$$ (1-38)

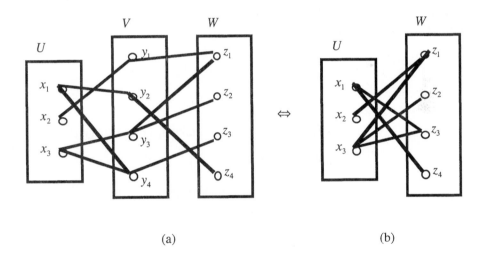

(a)   (b)

Figure 1-9: Saggital diagram for Example 1-10. (a) Original diagram for relations $R_1(U,V)$ and $R_2(V,W)$ and (b) compositional diagram for $R_3(U,W)$, (Mendel, 1995a, © 1995, IEEE).

Because it is not efficient to keep describing our compositions in terms of sagittal diagrams, we need a *formula* that conveys the same information.

Definitions: *The* max–min composition *of relations* $P(U,V)$ *and* $Q(V,W)$ *is defined by the membership function* $\mu_{P \circ Q}(x,z)$, *where*

$$\mu_{P \circ Q}(x,z) = \left\{ (x,z), \ \max_y \left[\min \left(\mu_P(x,y), \mu_Q(y,z) \right) \right] \right\} \qquad (1\text{-}39)$$

The max–product composition *of relations* $P(U,V)$ *and* $Q(V,W)$ *is defined by the membership function* $\mu_{P \times Q}(x,z)$, *where*

$$\mu_{P \times Q}(x,z) = \left\{ (x,z), \ \max_y \left[\mu_P(x,y) \mu_Q(y,z) \right] \right\} \qquad (1\text{-}40)$$

It is a fact that carrying out the operations of either the *max-min* or *max-product* compositions leads to the correct relational matrix $R(U,W)$. A proof of this can be found in [Wang (1997, p. 54)].

Example 1-11: Here we verify (1-39) and (1-40) for the 1-2 element of $R_3(U,W)$ in (1-38). For this element, (1-39) becomes

$$\mu_{R_3}(x_1,z_2) = \left\{ (x_1,z_2), \max_y \left[\min \left(\mu_{R_1}(x_1,y), \mu_{R_2}(y,z_2) \right) \right] \right\}$$

$$= \left\{ (x_1,z_2), \max \left[\min \left(\mu_{R_1}(x_1,y_1), \mu_{R_2}(y_1,z_2) \right), \right. \right.$$

$$\min \left(\mu_{R_1}(x_1,y_2), \mu_{R_2}(y_2,z_2) \right), \min \left(\mu_{R_1}(x_1,y_3), \mu_{R_2}(y_3,z_2) \right),$$

$$\left. \left. \min \left(\mu_{R_1}(x_1,y_4), \mu_{R_2}(y_4,z_2) \right) \right] \right\} \qquad (1\text{-}41)$$

$$= \left\{ (x_1,z_2), \max \left[\min(0,0), \min(1,0), \min(0,1), \min(1,0) \right] \right\}$$

$$= \left\{ (x_1,z_2), \max[0,0,0,0] \right\} = \left\{ (x_1,z_2), 0 \right\}$$

which agrees with (1-38). Similarly, (1-40) becomes

$$\mu_{R_3}(x_1,z_2) = \left\{ (x_1,z_2), \max_y \left[\mu_{R_1}(x_1,y) \mu_{R_2}(y,z_2) \right] \right\}$$

$$= \left\{ (x_1,z_2), \max \left[\mu_{R_1}(x_1,y_1) \mu_{R_2}(y_1,z_2), \mu_{R_1}(x_1,y_2) \mu_{R_2}(y_2,z_2), \right. \right.$$

$$\left. \left. \mu_{R_1}(x_1,y_3) \mu_{R_2}(y_3,z_2), \mu_{R_1}(x_1,y_4) \mu_{R_2}(y_4,z_2) \right] \right\} \qquad (1\text{-}42)$$

$$= \left\{ (x_1,z_2), \max \left[(0 \times 0), (1 \times 0), (0 \times 1), (1 \times 0) \right] \right\}$$

$$= \left\{ (x_1,z_2), \max[0,0,0,0] \right\} = \left\{ (x_1,z_2), 0 \right\}$$

which also agrees with (1-38). ■

While this example is not a proof of the validity of (1-39) and (1-40), it demonstrates that both seem to be correct representations for $R(U,W)$.

The following shortcuts can be used to evaluate the *max-min* or *max-product* compositions.

> **Max-min composition:** (1) Write out each element in the matrix product $Q(U,V)P(V,W)$; but, (2) treat each multiplication as a minimum operation; and, then, (3) treat each addition as a maximum operation.

> **Max-product composition:** (1) Write out each element in the *matrix product* $Q(U,V)P(V,W)$; but, (2) treat each multiplication as an algebraic multiplication operation; and, then, (3) treat each addition as a maximum operation.

Example 1-11 (Continued): Here we use these two shortcuts to again verify (1-39) and (1-40), but this time for the 1-3 element of $R_3(U,W)$ in (1-38). Now applying the shortcut for the max-min composition to the 1-3 element of $R_1(u,v)R_2(v,w)$, we find

$$R_3(x_1,z_3) = 0 \times 0 + 1 \times 0 + 0 \times 0 + 1 \times 1$$
$$= \min(0,0) + \min(1,0) + \min(0,0) + \min(1,1) \qquad (1\text{-}43)$$
$$= \max(0,0,0,1) = 1$$

Similarly, applying the shortcut for the max-product composition to the 1-3 element of $R_1(u,v)R_2(v,w)$, we find

$$R_3(x_1,z_3) = 0 \times 0 + 1 \times 0 + 0 \times 0 + 1 \times 1$$
$$= \max(0,0,0,1) = 1 \qquad (1\text{-}44)$$

Both of these results agree with the 1-3 element of $R_3(U,W)$ in (1-38). ■

The *max-min* and *max-product* compositions are not the only ones that correctly represent $R(U,W)$; however, they seem to be the most widely used ones.

1.10.11 FUZZY RELATIONS AND COMPOSITIONS ON DIFFERENT PRODUCT SPACES

Next, we consider the composition of fuzzy relations from different Cartesian product spaces that share a common set, namely $R(U,V)$ and $S(V,W)$, e.g., x is *smaller* than *y*, and *y* is *close* to *z*. The composition of fuzzy relations from different Cartesian product spaces that share a common set is defined analogously to the crisp composition, except that in the fuzzy case the sets are fuzzy sets. Associated with fuzzy relation *R* is its membership function $\mu_R(x,y)$, where $\mu_R(x,y) \in [0,1]$. Associated with fuzzy relation *S* is its membership function $\mu_S(y,z)$, where $\mu_S(y,z) \in [0,1]$. When *R* and *S* are from discrete universes of discourse, then the fuzzy composition of *R* and *S*, denoted $R \circ S$, can be described either by a sagittal diagram, in which each branch is labeled by its membership function value, or a fuzzy relational matrix, in which each element is a positive real number between and including zero and unity. A mathematical formula for $\mu_{R \circ S}(x,z)$, which is motivated by (1-39) and (1-40), is the following *sup-star composition* of *R* and *S* (e.g., [Wang (1997)]):

$$\mu_{R \circ S}(x,z) = \sup_{y \in V}\left[\mu_R(x,y) \star \mu_S(y,z)\right] \tag{1-45}$$

When *U*, *V*, and *W* are discrete universes of discourse, then the supremum operation is the *maximum*. Motivation for using the "star" operation, which of course is short for a t-norm, comes from the crisp *max-min* and *max-product* compositions, because both the minimum and product are t-norms. Although it is permissible to use other t-norms, the most commonly used sup-star compositions are the *sup-min* and *sup-product*. The shortcuts for computing the sup-min and sup-product, given in Section 1.10.10, apply also to fuzzy compositions over discrete universes of discourse.

Example 1-12: Consider the type-1 relation "*u* is close to *v*" on $U \times V$, where $U = \{u_1, u_2\}$ and $V = \{v_1, v_2, v_3\}$ are given in Example 1-9 as $U = \{2, 12\}$ and $V = \{1, 7, 13\}$, and $\mu_c(u,v)$ is given by (1-29). Now consider another type-1 fuzzy relation "*v* is much bigger than *w*" on $V \times W$, where $W = \{w_1, w_2\} = \{4, 8\}$, with the following membership function, $\mu_{mb}(v,w)$, for *much bigger*:

$$\mu_{mb}(v,w) \equiv \begin{array}{c} \\ v_1 \\ v_2 \\ v_3 \end{array}\begin{array}{cc} w_1 & w_2 \\ \left(0 \right. & \left. 0 \right) \\ 0.6 & 0 \\ 1 & 0.7 \end{array} \tag{1-46}$$

The statement "*u* is close to *v and v* is much bigger than *w*" indicates the composition of these two type-1 relations. This composition can be found by using (1-45) and the minimum t-norm as follows:

$$\mu_{comb}(u_i, w_j) = \left[\mu_c(u_i, v_1) \wedge \mu_{mb}(v_1, w_j)\right] \vee \left[\mu_c(u_i, v_2) \wedge \mu_{mb}(v_2, w_j)\right]$$
$$\vee \left[\mu_c(u_i, v_3) \wedge \mu_{mb}(v_3, w_j)\right] \tag{1-47}$$

where $i = 1, 2, j = 1, 2, 3,$ $\wedge$ denotes minimum, and $\vee$ denotes maximum. For example,

$$\mu_{comb}(u_1, w_1) = \left[\mu_c(u_1, v_1) \wedge \mu_{mb}(v_1, w_1)\right] \vee \left[\mu_c(u_1, v_2) \wedge \mu_{mb}(v_2, w_1)\right]$$
$$\vee \left[\mu_c(u_1, v_3) \wedge \mu_{mb}(v_3, w_1)\right]$$
$$= [0.9 \wedge 0] \vee [0.4 \wedge 0.6] \vee [0.1 \wedge 1] \tag{1-48}$$
$$= 0 \vee 0.4 \vee 0.1 = 0.4 \quad .$$

Doing all the calculations in a similar manner, we get

$$\mu_{comb}(u, w) = \begin{array}{c} \\ u_1 \\ u_2 \end{array}\!\!\begin{array}{c} w_1 \quad w_2 \\ \left(\begin{array}{cc} 0.4 & 0.1 \\ 0.9 & 0.7 \end{array}\right) \end{array} \tag{1-49}$$

Unlike the case of crisp compositions, for which exactly the same results are obtained using either the max-min or max-product compositions, the same results are not obtained in the case of fuzzy compositions. This is a major difference between fuzzy and crisp compositions.

Suppose fuzzy relation R is just a fuzzy set, in which case $V = U$, so that $\mu_R(x, y)$ just becomes $\mu_R(x)$ [or $\mu_R(y)$], e.g., "y is *medium large* and y is *smaller* than z." What happens to the sup-star composition in this case? Because $V = U$,

$$\sup_{y \in V}\left[\mu_R(x, y) \star \mu_S(y, z)\right] = \sup_{x \in U}\left[\mu_R(x) \star \mu_S(x, z)\right], \tag{1-50}$$

which is only a function of output variable z; hence, we can simplify the notation $\mu_{R \circ S}(x, z)$ to $\mu_{R \circ S}(z)$, so that *when R is just a fuzzy set*,

$$\mu_{R \circ S}(z) = \sup_{x \in U}\left[\mu_R(x) \star \mu_S(x, z)\right] \tag{1-51}$$

Example 1-13: Consider again the Example 1-9 relation "u is close to v" on $U \times V$, where $U = \{2, 12\}$ and $V = \{1, 7, 13\}$. The membership function for $\mu_c(u, v)$ is given in (1-29). Let the fuzzy set "small" on U be defined as

$$\begin{matrix} u_1 & u_2 \end{matrix}$$
$$\mu_s(u) = \begin{pmatrix} 0.9 & 0.1 \end{pmatrix} \tag{1-52}$$

The composition of the two statements "u is small *and* u is close to v" can be obtained by using (1-51) as follows:

$$\mu_{s \circ c}(v_j) = \left[\mu_s(u_1) \wedge \mu_c(u_1, v_j)\right] \vee \left[\mu_s(u_2) \wedge \mu_c(u_2, v_j)\right] \tag{1-53}$$

where $j = 1, 2, 3$. Using (1-53) it is straightforward to show that

$$\begin{matrix} v_1 & v_2 & v_3 \end{matrix}$$
$$\mu_{s \circ c}(v) = \begin{pmatrix} 0.9 & 0.4 & 0.1 \end{pmatrix} \tag{1-54}$$

■

For discrete universes of discourse, we can evaluate the max-min or max-product compositions in (1-51) using the shortcuts described earlier; however, we must first create a row matrix for $\mu_R(x)$, i.e., if $x \in U = \{x_1, x_2, ..., x_n\}$, let $R(U) = \left(\mu_R(x_1), \mu_R(x_2), ..., \mu_R(x_n)\right)$. Then, we have, for:

Max-min composition: (1) Write out each element in the matrix product $R(U)S(U,W)$, but (2) treat each multiplication as a minimum operation, and then (3) treat each addition as a maximum operation.

Max-product composition: (1) Write out each element in the *matrix product* $R(U)S(U,W)$, but (2) treat each multiplication as an algebraic multiplication operation, and then (3) treat each addition as a maximum operation.

1.10.12 Hedges

A *linguistic hedge* or modifier is an operation that modifies the meaning of a term, or more generally, of a fuzzy set. For example, if *weak pressure* is a fuzzy set, then *very weak pressure, more-or-less weak pressure, extremely weak pressure*, and *not-so weak pressure* are examples of hedges which are applied to this fuzzy set. *Hedges can be viewed as operators that act on a fuzzy set's membership function to modify it.* Here we give a small sample of these operators; many more can be found in, e.g., Cox (1994).

1. *Concentration*: $\mu_{con(F)}(x) \equiv \left[\mu_F(x)\right]^2$. If, e.g., *weak pressure* has membership function $\mu_{WP}(p)$, then *very weak pressure* is a fuzzy set with membership function $\left[\mu_{WP}(p)\right]^2$, and *very very weak pressure* is a fuzzy set with membership function $\left[\mu_{WP}(p)\right]^4$. Because our membership functions have been assumed to be normalized, it is clear that the operation of concentration leads to a membership function that lies within the membership function of the original fuzzy set (thus, the term *concentration*); both have the same support, and the same membership values where the value of the original membership function equals unity or zero.

2. *Dilation*: $\mu_{dil(F)}(x) \equiv \left[\mu_F(x)\right]^{1/2}$. If, e.g., *weak pressure* has membership function $\mu_{WP}(p)$, then *more or less weak pressure* is a fuzzy set with membership function $\left[\mu_{WP}(p)\right]^{1/2}$. The operation of dilation leads to a membership function that lies outside of the membership function of the original fuzzy set (thus, the term *dilation*); both have the same support, and the same membership values where the value of the original membership function equals unity or zero.

3. *Artificial Hedges*: Two hedges that are quite useful are the *plus* and *minus* hedges, whose membership functions are $\mu_{plus(F)}(x) \equiv \left[\mu_F(x)\right]^{1.25}$ and $\mu_{minus(F)}(x) \equiv \left[\mu_F(x)\right]^{0.75}$. These artificial hedges provide milder degrees of concentration and dilation than those associated with the concentration and dilation hedges.

We have used the $\equiv$ sign in these hedge membership functions to convey the fact that their exponents are quite arbitrary; they can be changed depending upon one's interpretation of the hedges.[10]

Example 1-14: [Zadeh (1973)] In conversations, we frequently use the phrase *highly unlikely*. Here we show how to obtain a membership function for it. Let X denote a universe of discourse associated with an appropriate quantity related to our notion of *likely*. We will clarify X below. Let $\mu_{LIKELY}(x)$ be the membership function for the term *likely*. Then,

$$\mu_{HIGHLY-UNLIKELY}(x) = \left[1 - \mu_{LIKELY}(x)\right]^{4 \times 0.75} \qquad (1\text{-}55)$$

To obtain (1-55), we have interpreted the hedge *highly* as *minus very very* (which, of course, is subjective) and have used the fact that *unlikely* is the complement of *likely*.

---

[10]Because of the uncertainty about the numerical values of the exponents, hedges might be more appropriately modeled within the framework of type-2 fuzzy sets. In fact, it may be appropriate to re-examine the entire concept of a hedge now that type-2 fuzzy sets are more readily available.

From estimation theory (e.g., [Edwards (1972)], [Mendel (1995b)]), it is known that *likelihood is proportional to probability*. This fact helps us to establish the universe of discourse, X, as values of probability (the constant of proportionality between probability and likelihood is irrelevant), i.e., $x \in X$ where $X = [0,1]$. As a concrete example, we assume the following discrete universe of discourse: $X = 0 + 0.1 + 0.2 + 0.3 + \cdots + 0.9 + 1$, where the + sign denotes union rather than arithmetic sum. To evaluate (1-55), we need to specify $\mu_{LIKELY}(x)$. Based on our own perception of the fuzzy set *likely*, we make the following ad hoc choice for $\mu_{LIKELY}(x)$ (your choice may be different):

$$\mu_{LIKELY}(x) \equiv 1/1 + 1/0.9 + 1/0.8 + 0.8/0.7 + 0.6/0.6$$
$$+ 0.5/0.5 + 0.3/0.4 + 0.2/0.3 \tag{1-56}$$

Recall that the terms not shown have zero membership function values. Evaluating (1-55), we find that

$$\mu_{HIGHLY-UNLIKELY}(x) \approx 1/0 + 1/0.1 + 1/0.2$$
$$+ 0.5/0.3 + 0.3/0.4 \tag{1-57}$$

Observe, from (1-56) and (1-57), that the membership function $\mu_{HIGHLY-UNLIKELY}(x)$ seems to make sense, i.e., it agrees with our own notion that something that is highly unlikely has a very very small chance (i.e., probability) of occurring. Consequently, large values for $\mu_{HIGHLY-UNLIKELY}(x)$ should and indeed do occur for small values of probability, x. ∎

1.10.13 Extension principle

The Extension Principle was introduced by Zadeh $(1975)^{11}$ and is an important tool in fuzzy set theory. We make very heavy use of it in later chapters of this book. It lets us extend mathematical relationships between non-fuzzy variables to fuzzy variables. Suppose, for example, that we are given the membership function for the fuzzy set *small* and want to determine the membership function for the fuzzy set $small^2$. The Extension Principle tells us how to determine the membership function for $small^2$ by making use of the non-fuzzy mathematical relationship $y = x^2$ in which the fuzzy set *small* plays the role of x.

Suppose we are given a function of a single variable x, $y = f(x)$, where $x \in U$ and $y \in V$. For illustrative purposes, U is assumed to be a discrete universe of discourse. We are given a fuzzy set A whose universe of discourse also is U, i.e.,

---

[11] According to Klir and Yuan (1995), the Extension Principle was introduced in Zadeh (1975); however, in that paper, Zadeh (1975, p. 236, footnote 18) states that the Extension Principle is implicit in a result given in Zadeh (1965).

$$A = \sum_{x \in U} \mu_A(x)/x \tag{1-58}$$

The Extension Principle states that [Jang et al. (1997)] the image of the fuzzy set A under the mapping $f(\cdot)$ can be expressed as a fuzzy set B, i.e.,

$$B = f(A) = f\left(\sum_{x \in U} \mu_A(x)/x\right)$$
$$= \mu_A(x_1)/y_1 + \mu_A(x_2)/y_2 + \cdots \mu_A(x_N)/y_N \equiv \mu_B(y) \tag{1-59}$$

where $y_i = f(x_i)$, $i = 1, ..., N$. Since $x = f^{-1}(y)$, where $f^{-1}(y)$ is the inverse of f (i.e., $f[f^{-1}(y)] = y$), another way to express B is by $\mu_B(y) = \mu_A[f^{-1}(y)]$, $\forall y \in V$.

Example 1-15: As a concrete illustration of (1-59), suppose that $U = \{1, 2, 3, 4, 5, 6, 7, 8, 9, 10\}$, and $A = small = 1/1 + 0.8/2 + 0.6/3 + 0.3/4$; then,

$$B = small^2 = 1/1 + 0.8/4 + 0.6/9 + 0.3/16$$

■

The version of the Extension Principle given in (1-59) is valid only if the mapping between y and $f(x)$ is one-to-one. It is quite possible that the same value of y can be obtained for different values of x—a many-to-one mapping—in which case (1-59) needs to be modified. For example, we may have $f(x_1) = f(x_2) = y$, but $x_1 \neq x_2$ and $\mu_A(x_1) \neq \mu_A(x_2)$. To resolve this ambiguity, we assign the larger one of the two membership values to $\mu_B(y)$. The general modification to (1-59) is [Wang (1997)]:

$$\mu_B(y) = \max_{x \in f^{-1}(y)} \mu_A(x) \quad y \in V \tag{1-60}$$

where $f^{-1}(y)$ denotes the set of all points $x \in U$ such that $f(x) = y$.

Example 1-16: As an illustration of (1-60), suppose that $U = \{-3, -2, -1, 0, 1, 2\}$ and fuzzy set A is characterized by the membership function values listed in the second column of the following table. Then, $\mu_B(y)$ for $y = f(x) = x^4$ is given in the last column of the table.

Observe that there are two pairs of elements of U that map into the same value of y: -2 and 2 map into 16, and -1 and 1 map into 1. In both cases the membership value of y is obtained by taking the maximum of the membership grades of the respective two elements. From this table, observe that $B = 0.9/0 + 1/1 + 0.6/16 + 0.5/81$. ■

x	$\mu_A(x)$	$y = f(x) = x^4$	$\mu_B(y)$
-3	0.5	81	$\max\{0.5\} = 0.5$
-2	0.6	16	$\max\{0.6, 0.1\} = 0.6$
-1	1.0	1	$\max\{1, 0.4\} = 1$
0	0.9	0	$\max\{0.9\} = 0.9$
1	0.4	1	$\max\{1, 0.4\} = 1$
2	0.1	16	$\max\{0.6, 0.1\} = 0.6$

So far we have stated the Extension Principle just for a mapping of a single variable. Things get a bit more complicated for a function of more than one variable. Suppose, for example, we have a function of two variables x_1 and x_2, i.e., $y = f(x_1, x_2)$, where $x_1 \in X_1$, $x_2 \in X_2$, $y \in V$, and X_1 and X_2 are assumed to be discrete universes of discourse. We are now given two fuzzy sets, A_1 and A_2, where

$$A_1 = \sum_{x_1 \in X_1} \mu_{A_1}(x_1)/x_1 \tag{1-61}$$

and

$$A_2 = \sum_{x_2 \in X_2} \mu_{A_2}(x_2)/x_2 \tag{1-62}$$

Now it is possible for $y = f(x_1, x_2)$ to be many-to-one, just as it was in the single-variable case; so, the Extension Principle for the two-variable case needs to look something like (1-60). The difference between the two- and one-variable cases is that in the latter there is only one membership function that can be evaluated for each value of x, whereas in the former there are two membership functions that can be evaluated, namely $\mu_{A_1}(x_1)$ and $\mu_{A_2}(x_2)$. In this case, the Extension Principle becomes:

$$\mu_{f(A_1, A_2)}(y) \equiv \mu_B(y) = \begin{cases} \sup_{(x_1, x_2) \in f^{-1}(y)} \min\{\mu_{A_1}(x_1), \mu_{A_2}(x_2)\} \\ 0 \text{ if } f^{-1}(y) = \varnothing \end{cases} \tag{1-63}$$

where $f^{-1}(y)$ now denotes the set of all points $x_1 \in X_1$ and $x_2 \in X_2$ such that $f(x_1, x_2) = y$. The condition in (1-63) that $\mu_B(y) = 0$ if $f^{-1}(y) = \varnothing$ means that if there are no values of x_1 and x_2 for which we can reach a specific value of y, then we set the membership function value for that specific value of y equal to zero. Only those values of y that satisfy $y = f(x_1, x_2)$ can be reached. Note that Yager (1986) provides a justification of (1-63) based on the sup-star composition.

Example 1-17: [Lin and Lee (1996, p. 30)] As an illustration of (1-63), suppose that $X_1 = \{-1, 0, 1\}$ and $X_2 = \{-2, 2\}$, and fuzzy sets A_1 and A_2 are characterized by the membership functions listed in the second and fourth columns of the following table. Then the membership function for the fuzzy set B that is associated with $\mu_{f(A_1, A_2)}(y)$, where $y = f(x_1, x_2) = x_1^2 + x_2$, is given in the last column of that table. Observe that the construction of this table first required determining all x_1 and x_2 pairs for which y is defined. These values constitute the Cartesian product of X_1 and X_2, $X_1 \times X_2$. By evaluating $y = f(x_1, x_2) = x_1^2 + x_2$ at all these values, we establish that $V = \{-2, -1, 2, 3\}$.

x_1	$\mu_{A_1}(x_1)$	x_2	$\mu_{A_2}(x_2)$	$y = f(x_1, x_2)$ $= x_1^2 + x_2$	$\mu_{f(A_1, A_2)}(y)$ $\equiv \mu_B(y)$
-1	0.5	-2	0.4	-1	$\max\{0.4, 0.4\} = 0.4$
-1	0.5	2	1.0	3	$\max\{0.5, 0.9\} = 0.9$
0	0.1	-2	0.4	-2	$\max\{0.1\} = 0.1$
0	0.1	2	1.0	2	$\max\{0.1\} = 0.1$
1	0.9	-2	0.4	-1	$\max\{0.4, 0.4\} = 0.4$
1	0.9	2	1.0	3	$\max\{0.5, 0.9\} = 0.9$

There are two ordered pairs $(-1, -2)$ and $(1, -2)$ that map into the same value of y, namely -1, and, there are also two ordered pairs $(-1, 2)$ and $(1, 2)$ that map into the same value of $y = 3$. It is for these two sets of ordered pairs that the respective maximum membership grades must be taken in (1-63).

We illustrate the calculations of $\mu_B(y)$ for $y = -1$:

$$\mu_B(-1) = \max[\min\{\mu_{A_1}(-1), \mu_{A_2}(-2)\}, \min\{\mu_{A_1}(1), \mu_{A_2}(-2)\}$$
$$= \max[\min(0.5, 0.4), \min(0.9, 0.4)] = 0.4 \tag{1-64}$$

From the last two columns of the table, we conclude that $B = 0.1 / -2 + 0.4 / -1 + 0.1 / 2 + 0.9 / 3$. ∎

The generalization of the Extension Principle in (1-63), from 2 to r variables is given in Section 7.2. Some additional comments about its use also appear in that chapter.

1.11 PRIMER ON FL

From Figure 1-1, we see that one of the major components of a FLS is *Rules*. Our rules will be expressed as logical implications, i.e., in the forms of IF–THEN statements, e.g.,

IF x is A, THEN y is B where $x \in X$ and $y \in Y$

A rule represents a special kind of *relation* between A and B; its membership function is denoted $\mu_{A \to B}(x, y)$. What is a proper and appropriate choice for this membership function? Nothing that we have presented so far helps us to answer this question, because an implication resides within a branch of mathematics known as logic, and so far we have been discussing set theory. Fortunately, as stated in Klir and Folger (1988, p. 24):

> It is well established that propositional logic is isomorphic to set theory under the appropriate correspondence between components of these two mathematical systems. Furthermore, both of these systems are isomorphic to a Boolean algebra, which is a mathematical system defined by abstract (interpretation-free) entities and their axiomatic properties. ... The isomorphisms between Boolean algebra, set theory, and propositional logic guarantee that every theorem in any one of these theories has a counterpart in each of the other two theories. ... These isomorphisms allow us, in effect, to cover all these theories by developing only one of them.

Consequently, we will not spend a lot of time reviewing crisp logic; but, we must spend some time on it, especially on the concept of implication, in order to reach the comparable concept in FL.

1.11.1 Crisp logic

Rules are a form of propositions.[12] A *proposition* is an ordinary statement involving terms that have been defined, e.g., "The damping ratio is low." Consequently, we could have the following rule: "IF the damping ratio is low, THEN the system's impulse response oscillates a long time before it dies out." In traditional propositional logic, a proposition must be meaningful to call it "true" or "false," whether or not we know which of these terms properly applies.

Logical reasoning is the process of combining given propositions into other propositions, and then doing this over and over again. Propositions can be

---

[12]Much of this section is paraphrased from [Allendoerfer and Oakley (1955)].

combined in many ways, all of which are derived from three fundamental operations: *conjunction* (denoted $p \wedge q$), where we assert the simultaneous truth of two separate propositions p and q (e.g., damping ratio is low and band-width is large); *disjunction* (denoted $p \vee q$), where we assert the truth of either or both of two separate propositions (e.g., I will design an analog filter or I will design a digital filter); and, *implication* (denoted $p \rightarrow q$), which usually takes the form of an IF–THEN rule, an example of which has been given in the previous paragraph. The IF part of an implication is called the *antecedent*, whereas the THEN part is called the *consequent*.

In addition to generating propositions using conjunction, disjunction, or implication, a new proposition can be obtained from a given one by prefixing the clause "it is false that ...". This is the operation of *negation* (denoted $\sim p$). Additionally, $p \leftrightarrow q$ is the *equivalence* relation; it means that p and q are both true or false.

In traditional propositional logic an implication is said to be *true* if one of the following holds: (1) antecedent is true, consequent is true, (2) antecedent is false, consequent is false, and (3) antecedent is false, consequent is true; and the implication is called *false* when (4) antecedent is true, consequent is false. Situation (1) is the familiar one of common experience. Situation (2) is also reasonable, for if we start from a false assumption we expect to reach a false conclusion, however, intuition is not always reliable. We may reason correctly from a false antecedent to a true consequent (e.g., IF $1 = 2$, THEN $3 = 3$; note that $1 = 2$ is false, but, adding $2 = 1$ to this false statement, lets us correctly conclude that $3 = 3$); hence, a false antecedent can lead to a consequent which is either true or false, and thus both situations (2) and (3) are allowed in traditional propositional logic. Finally, situation (4) is in accord with our intuition, for an implication is clearly false if a true antecedent leads to a false consequent.

A logical structure is constructed by applying the aforementioned five operations to propositions. The objective of a logical structure is to determine the truth or falsehood of all propositions that can be stated in the terminology of this structure.

A *truth table* is very convenient for showing relationships between several propositions. The fundamental truth tables for conjunction, disjunction, implication, equivalence, and negation are collected together in Table 1-2, in which symbol T means that the corresponding proposition is true, and symbol F means that it is false.

The fundamental axioms of traditional propositional logic are: (1) every proposition is either true or false, but not both true or false; (2) the expressions given by defined terms are propositions; and (3) the truth Table 1-2 for conjunction, disjunction, implication, equivalence, and negation. Using truth tables, we can derive many interpretations of the preceding operations and can also prove relationships about them.

Table 1-2: Truth table for five operations that are frequently applied to propositions (Mendel, 1995a, © 1995, IEEE).

p	q	$p \wedge q$	$p \vee q$	$p \rightarrow q$	$p \leftrightarrow q$	$\sim p$
T	T	T	T	T	T	F
T	F	F	T	F	F	F
F	T	F	T	T	F	T
F	F	F	F	T	T	T

A *tautology* is a proposition formed by combining other propositions (p, q, r, ...) which is true regardless of the truth or falsehood of p, q, r, ... The most important tautology for our work is:

$$(p \rightarrow q) \leftrightarrow \sim [p \wedge (\sim q)] \tag{1-65}$$

A proof of this tautology, using truth tables, is given in Table 1-3. Observe that the entries in the two columns $p \rightarrow q$ and $\sim [p \wedge (\sim q)]$ are identical, which proves the tautology. This tautology can also be expressed as

$$(p \rightarrow q) \leftrightarrow (\sim p) \vee q \tag{1-66}$$

the truth of which is also demonstrated in Table 1-3. The importance of these tautologies is that they let us express the membership function for $p \rightarrow q$ in terms of membership functions of either propositions p and $\sim q$ or $\sim p$ and q, which was the main objective for this section.

Table 1-3: Proofs of $(p \rightarrow q) \leftrightarrow \sim [p \wedge (\sim q)]$ and $(p \rightarrow q) \leftrightarrow (\sim p) \vee q$ (Mendel, 1995a, © 1995, IEEE).

p	q	$p \rightarrow q$	$\sim q$	$p \wedge (\sim q)$	$\sim [p \wedge (\sim q)]$	$\sim p$	$(\sim p) \vee q$
T	T	T	F	F	T	F	T
T	F	F	T	T	F	F	F
F	T	T	F	F	T	T	T
F	F	T	T	F	T	T	T

Some of the most important mathematical equivalences between logic and set theory are:

Logic	Set Theory
∧	∩
∨	∪
~	‾()

Additionally, as mentioned earlier, there is a correspondence between elementary logic and Boolean Algebra (0,1). Any statement that is true in one system becomes a true statement in the other, simply by carrying through the following changes in notation:

Logic	Boolean Algebra (0, 1)
T	1
F	0
∧	×
∨	+
~	′
↔	=
$p, q, r,$ ...	$a, b, c,$ ...

In this list, ′ stands for complement, and $a, b, c,$ ... are arbitrary elements of the two-element set $\{0, 1\}$.

Using the facts that $(p \rightarrow q) \leftrightarrow \sim [p \wedge (\sim q)]$ and $(p \rightarrow q) \leftrightarrow (\sim p) \vee q$, and the equivalence between logic and set theory, we can now obtain two membership functions for $p \rightarrow q$. The first of these tautologies lets us show that

$$\mu_{p \rightarrow q}(x, y) = 1 - \mu_{p \cap \bar{q}}(x, y) = 1 - \min\left[\mu_p(x), 1 - \mu_q(y)\right] \qquad (1\text{-}67)$$

and the second of these tautologies lets us show that

$$\mu_{p \rightarrow q}(x, y) = \mu_{\bar{p} \cup q}(x, y) = \max\left[1 - \mu_p(x), \mu_q(y)\right] \qquad (1\text{-}68)$$

To validate the truth of these two membership functions, construct a Boolean truth table, such as the one in Table 1-4. Observe that the entries in the last two columns agree with the entries in Table 1-2 for $p \rightarrow q$, where we are interchanging logical T and F with Boolean 1 and 0, respectively.

Table 1-4: Validations of (1-67) and (1-68) (Mendel, 1995a, © 1995, IEEE).

$\mu_p(x)$	$\mu_q(y)$	$1-\mu_p(x)$	$1-\mu_q(y)$	$1-\min[\mu_p(x),$ $1-\mu_q(y)]$	$\max[1-\mu_p(x),$ $\mu_q(y)]$
1	1	0	0	1	1
1	0	0	1	0	0
0	1	1	0	1	1
0	0	1	1	1	1

The implication membership functions in (1-67) and (1-68) are by no means the only ones that give agreement with $p \rightarrow q$. Two others are shown here (see [Baets and Kerre (1993)] and [Yager (1983)] for many more):

$$\mu_{p \rightarrow q}(x,y) = 1 - \mu_p(x)[1 - \mu_q(y)] \tag{1-69}$$

and

$$\mu_{p \rightarrow q}(x,y) = \min\left[1, 1 - \mu_p(x) + \mu_q(y)\right] \tag{1-70}$$

The membership function in (1-69) is similar to the one in (1-67), except that a *product* operation is used for conjunction instead of the minimum operation.

In traditional propositional logic there are two very important inference rules, *Modus Ponens* and *Modus Tollens*:

Modus Ponens:

> *Premise*: *x* is *A*
> *Implication*: IF *x* is *A* THEN *y* is *B*
> *Consequence:* *y* is *B*

Modus Ponens is associated with the implication "*A* implies *B*" ($A \rightarrow B$). In terms of propositions *p* and *q*, Modus Ponens is expressed as $(p \wedge (p \rightarrow q)) \rightarrow q$.

Modus Tollens:

> *Premise*: *y* is not *B*
> *Implication*: IF *x* is *A* THEN *y* is *B*
> *Consequence*: *x* is not *A*

In terms of propositions *p* and *q*, Modus Tollens is expressed as $(\bar{q} \wedge (p \rightarrow q)) \rightarrow \bar{p}$.

Whereas Modus Ponens plays a central role in engineering applications of logic, due in large part to cause and effect, Modus Tollens does not seem to have yet played much of a role.

1.11.2 From crisp logic to FL

FL begins by borrowing notions from crisp logic, just as fuzzy set theory borrows from crisp set theory. As in our extension of crisp set theory to fuzzy set theory, our extension of crisp logic to FL is made by replacing the bivalent membership functions of crisp logic with fuzzy membership functions. That is all there is to it; hence, the IF–THEN statement "IF x is A, THEN y is B," where $x \in X$ and $y \in Y$, has a membership function $\mu_{A \rightarrow B}(x, y)$ where $\mu_{A \rightarrow B}(x, y) \in [0, 1]$. Note that $\mu_{A \rightarrow B}(x, y)$ measures the degree of truth of the implication relation between x and y, and it resides in the Cartesian product space $X \times Y$. Examples of such membership functions, are:

$$\mu_{A \rightarrow B}(x, y) = 1 - \min\left[\mu_A(x), 1 - \mu_B(y)\right] \tag{1-71}$$

$$\mu_{A \rightarrow B}(x, y) = \max\left[1 - \mu_A(x), \mu_B(y)\right] \tag{1-72}$$

and

$$\mu_{A \rightarrow B}(x, y) = 1 - \mu_A(x)\left(1 - \mu_B(y)\right) \tag{1-73}$$

which, of course, are fuzzy versions of (1-67)–(1-69), respectively.

In FL, Modus Ponens is extended to *Generalized Modus Ponens*:

> *Premise: x* is A^*
> *Implication*: IF x is A THEN y is B
> *Consequence*: y is B^*

Compare Modus Ponens and Generalized Modus Ponens to see their subtle differences, namely, in the latter, fuzzy set A^* is not necessarily the same as rule antecedent fuzzy set A, and fuzzy set B^* is not necessarily the same as rule consequent B.

Example 1-18: Consider the rule "IF a man is short, THEN he will not make a very good professional basketball player." Here fuzzy set A is *short man*, and fuzzy set B is *not a very good professional basketball player*. We are now given Premise 1, as "This man is under five feet tall." Here A^* is the fuzzy set *man under five feet tall*. Clearly $A^* \neq A$; but, A^* is similar to A. We now draw the following consequence: "He will make a poor professional basketball player." Here B^* is the fuzzy set *poor professional basketball player*, and $B^* \neq B$, although B^* is indeed similar to B. ∎

In crisp logic a rule will be fired only if the premise is exactly the same as the antecedent of the rule, and the result of such rule-firing is the rule's actual consequent. In FL, on the other hand, a rule is fired so long as there is a non-zero degree of similarity between the premise and the antecedent of the rule, and the result of such rule-firing is a consequent that has a non-zero degree of similarity to the rule's consequent.

Generalized Modus Ponens is a fuzzy composition where the first fuzzy relation is merely the fuzzy set A^*. Consequently, using (1-51), $\mu_{B^*}(y)$ is obtained from the following sup-star composition:

$$\mu_{B^*}(y) = \sup_{x \in X}\left[\mu_{A^*}(x) \star \mu_{A \to B}(x, y)\right] \tag{1-74}$$

To help us understand the meaning of (1-74), we shall consider some examples. In all these examples we assume that the fuzzy set A^* is a fuzzy singleton, i.e.,

$$\mu_{A^*}(x) = \begin{cases} 1 & x = x' \\ 0 & x \neq x' \text{ and } \forall x \in X \end{cases} \tag{1-75}$$

In Chapter 5 we will call this a *singleton fuzzifier* and will learn why it is so popular. For the singleton fuzzifier, (1-74) becomes:

$$\begin{aligned}\mu_{B^*}(y) &= \sup_{x \in X}\left[\mu_{A^*}(x) \star \mu_{A \to B}(x, y)\right] \\ &= \sup\left[\mu_{A \to B}(x', y), 0\right] = \mu_{A \to B}(x', y)\end{aligned} \tag{1-76}$$

regardless of whether we use minimum or product for $\star$. Observe that for the singleton fuzzifier the supremum operation is very easy to evaluate, because $\mu_{A^*}(x)$ is non-zero at only one point, x'.

Example 1-19: To begin, let us examine the result of using (1-71) for $\mu_{A \to B}(x', y)$ in (1-76), i.e.,

$$\mu_{B^*}(y) = \mu_{A \to B}(x', y) = 1 - \min\left[\mu_A(x'), 1 - \mu_B(y)\right] \tag{1-77}$$

A graphical interpretation of this result is given in Figure 1-10. Starting with $\mu_B(y)$ in (a), we computed $1 - \mu_B(y)$ as shown in (b), and, for the given level of $\mu_A(x')$ shown in (b), we then constructed $\min[\mu_A(x'), 1 - \mu_B(y)]$, also shown in (b). Note that the level shown for $\mu_A(x')$ in (b) was chosen arbitrarily, where $\mu_A(x') \in [0,1]$. Finally, we constructed $1 - \min[\mu_A(x'), 1 - \mu_B(y)]$ as shown in (c).

The result shown in (c) is disturbing for an engineering application. It tells us that, given a specific input $x = x'$, the result of firing a specific rule, whose consequent is associated with a specific fuzzy set of finite support [the base of the triangle in (a)], is a fuzzy set whose support is infinite. Somehow a bias (constant) has gotten into the output so that regardless of x' the output is never zero [unless $\mu_A(x') = 1$]. This does not seem desirable for engineering applications. ∎

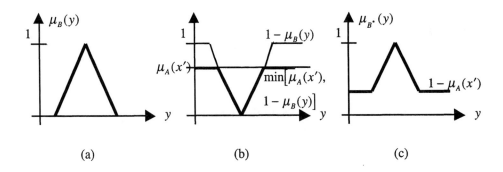

(a)   (b)   (c)

Figure 1-10: Construction of $\mu_{B^*}(y)$ in (1-77). (a) Consequent membership function $\mu_B(y)$, (b) construction of $\min[\mu_A(x'), 1 - \mu_B(y)]$, and (c) $\mu_{B^*}(y)$, (Mendel, 1995a, © 1995, IEEE).

Example 1-20: Perhaps the problem we experienced in Example 1-19 is a result of a poor choice for $\mu_{A \to B}(x', y)$. Therefore, let us examine the result of using $\mu_{A \to B}(x', y)$ obtained from (1-70), i.e.,

$$\mu_{A \to B}(x', y) = \min[1, 1 - \mu_A(x') + \mu_B(y)] \tag{1-78}$$

which, by the way, is the implication membership function given by Zadeh (1973) in his important paper. Substituting this expression for $\mu_{A \to B}(x', y)$ into (1-76), we find that:

$$\mu_{B^*}(y) = \mu_{A \to B}(x', y) = \min[1, 1 - \mu_A(x') + \mu_B(y)] \tag{1-79}$$

A graphical interpretation of this result is given in Figure 1-11. As in Example 1-19, the level shown for $\mu_A(x')$—and subsequently for $1-\mu_A(x')$—was chosen arbitrarily. Once again, we have obtained a result, in Figure 1-11 (b) that includes a bias. It is easy to demonstrate that all of the other choices we have provided for $\mu_{A\rightarrow B}(x,y)$ have the same problem. Even those that we have not listed here have the same problem. ∎

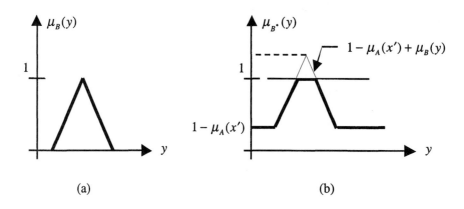

(a)   (b)

Figure 1-11: Construction of $\mu_{B^*}(y)$ in (1-79). (a) Consequent membership function $\mu_B(y)$, (b) construction of $\mu_{B^*}(y)$, (Mendel, 1995a, © 1995, IEEE).

Mamdani (1974) seems to have been the first one to recognize the problem we have just demonstrated. Based on simplifying the computations associated with (1-76), he chose to work with the following *minimum implication* (inference)

$$\mu_{A\rightarrow B}(x,y) \equiv \min\left[\mu_A(x),\mu_B(y)\right] \qquad (1\text{-}80)$$

Later, Larsen (1980) proposed the following *product implication* (inference)

$$\mu_{A\rightarrow B}(x,y) \equiv \mu_A(x)\mu_B(y) \qquad (1\text{-}81)$$

Again, the reason for this choice was simplicity of computation.[13]

---

[13]There is a paragraph in the lower right-hand column on p. 359 of Mendel (1995a) that contains an error. Observe that our derivation of (1-76) has accounted for all values of x, including $x \neq x'$, because it uses (1-75). For some reason that I cannot recall, in the erroneous paragraph, I claim that for all $x \neq x'$, $\mu_{B^*}(y)=1$, which I then interpret as a form of non-causality, i.e., a rule will be fired for all $x \neq x'$. I then argue for the use of a Mamdani or Larsen implication on the basis of their causality. This is incorrect; however, it does not affect anything else in the 1995 tutorial.

Equations (1-80) and (1-81) can be expressed collectively as

$$\mu_{A \to B}(x, y) \equiv \mu_A(x) \bigstar \mu_B(y) \qquad (1-82)$$

where $\bigstar$ is a t-norm, product, or minimum, and is frequently referred to as a *Mamdani implication* regardless of whether the t-norm used is the minimum or product.

Today, minimum and product implications are the most widely used implications in the engineering applications of fuzzy logic; but, what do they have to do with traditional propositional logic? Table 1-5 demonstrates that neither minimum implication nor product implication agrees with the accepted propositional logic definition of implication; hence, minimum and product implications have nothing to do with traditional propositional logic. We suggest, therefore, that minimum and product implications—Mamdani implications—be thought of as *engineering implications*.

Table 1-5: Demonstration that minimum and product implications do not agree with $\mu_{p \to q}(x, y)$ (Mendel, 1995a, © 1995, IEEE).

$\mu_p(x)$	$\mu_q(y)$	$\min\left[\mu_p(x), \mu_q(y)\right]$	$\mu_p(x)\mu_q(y)$	$\mu_{p \to q}(x, y)$
1	1	1	1	1
1	0	0	0	0
0	1	0	0	1
0	0	0	0	1

Example 1-21: The purpose of this example is to demonstrate that both the minimum and product implications lead to output fuzzy sets that seem quite reasonable from an engineering perspective, in that they only alter the shape of $\mu_B(y)$ and do not introduce a bias. As in Examples 1-19 and 1-20, we assume singleton fuzzification, i.e., $\mu_{A'}(x)$ is given by (1-75).

Let us consider minimum implication first; then, (1-76) becomes

$$\mu_{B'}(y) = \min\left[\mu_A(x'), \mu_B(y)\right] \qquad (1-83)$$

A graphical interpretation of this result is given in Figure 1-12. As in those earlier examples, the level shown for $\mu_A(x')$ was chosen arbitrarily. Observe from (b) that given a specific antecedent $x = x'$ the result of firing a specific rule is a fuzzy set whose support is finite and whose shape is a clipped version of $\mu_B(y)$.

Next, we consider the product implication for which (1-76) becomes:

$$\mu_{B'}(y) = \mu_A(x')\mu_B(y) \tag{1-84}$$

A graphical interpretation of this result is given in Figure 1-13. We draw similar conclusions from this figure as we did for minimum implication. In this case, the shape of the fuzzy output set is a scaled (attenuated) version of $\mu_B(y)$.

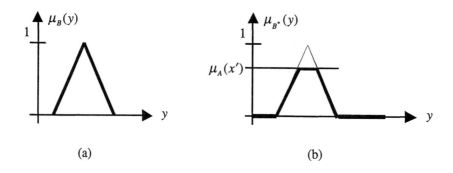

(a)   (b)

Figure 1-12: Construction of $\mu_{B'}(y)$ in (1-83). (a) Consequent membership function $\mu_B(y)$, (b) construction of $\mu_{B'}(y)$, (Mendel, 1995a, © 1995, IEEE).

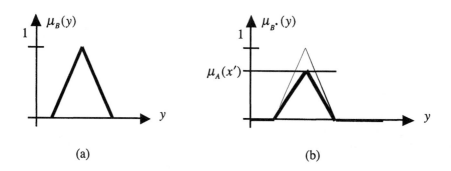

(a)   (b)

Figure 1-13: Construction of $\mu_{B'}(y)$ in (1-84). (a) Consequent membership function $\mu_B(y)$, (b) construction of $\mu_{B'}(y)$, (Mendel, 1995a, © 1995, IEEE).

Our overall conclusions are that minimum and product implications are, indeed, useful engineering implications, and, that $\mu_{B'}(y)$ can be expressed as

$$\mu_{B'}(y) = \mu_A(x')\star\mu_B(y) \tag{1-85}$$

where ★ is either the minimum or product. ∎

So far, all of our discussions about rules have been for rules with single antecedents, e.g., IF x is A, THEN y is B. In Chapter 5 and later chapters we will describe and characterize rules that have more than one antecedent, e.g.,

IF x_1 is F_1 and x_2 is F_2 and ... and x_p is F_p, THEN y is G

In such a multiple-antecedent rule, $x_1 \in X_1,...,x_p \in X_p$, $y \in Y$, and $F_1,...,F_p$ and G are fuzzy sets.

1.12 REMARKS

This completes our primers on fuzzy set theory and FL. Some other topics, which appear frequently in the FL literature and are sometimes used in engineering applications of FL, include: cardinality, quantifiers $\exists x$ and $\forall x$, and α – cut of a fuzzy set. A brief discussion about rules that use quantifiers is given in Section 5.2. Because we do not use cardinality or α – cuts in the rest of this book, we leave discussions about them to the references (e.g., [Dubois and Prade (1980)], [Klir and Folger (1988)], [Klir and Yuan (1995)], [Wang (1997)], [Yager and Filev (1994b)], and [Zimmerman (1991)]).

EXERCISES

1-1: Suppose that a car is described by its *color*. What scale could be used for color? Create five terms for color and sketch membership functions for each term.

1-2: Establish membership functions for:

(a) real numbers close to 10

(b) real numbers approximately equal to 6

(c) integers very far from 10

(d) complex numbers near the origin

(e) light (weight)

(f) heavy (weight)

1-3: List six linguistic variables from the field of acoustics (or any field that is of interest to you).

1-4: Using the rules in Example 1-4 as illustrations, list four more rules and their associated membership functions.

1-5: Let X be the set of all men and Y be the set of all women. Consider the linguistic variable "weight," and the set of terms {*very skinny, skinny, just-right, heavy, very heavy*}. Create membership functions for these terms for both men and women.

1-6: Consider the judgments listed here, and assume that they can be mapped onto an interval scale ranging from 0 to 10. Define five fuzzy sets for each of them and sketch what you feel are appropriate membership functions for them.

(a) touching

(b) eye contact

(c) smiling

(d) acting witty

(e) flirtation

1-7: Prove that, for crisp sets A and B, $\min[\mu_A(x), \mu_B(x)]$ provides the correct membership function for intersection, given in (1-7).

1-8: For crisp sets A and B, prove the:

(a) commutative law

(b) associative laws

(c) distributive laws

(d) De Morgan's laws

1-9: Consider three fuzzy sets, A, B, and C, whose membership functions are (unnormalized) Gaussians, i.e.,

$$\mu_A(x) = \exp\left[-\tfrac{1}{2}(x-3)^2\right], \ \mu_B(x) = \exp\left[-\tfrac{1}{2}(x-4)^2\right], \text{ and } \mu_C(x) = \exp\left[-\tfrac{1}{2}(x-6)^2\right].$$

Sketch each of the following:

(a) $\mu_{A \cap B \cap C}(x)$

(b) $\mu_{A \cup B \cup C}(x)$

(c) $\mu_{(A \cup B) \cap C}(x)$ and $\mu_{A \cup (B \cap C)}(x)$

(d) $\mu_{(A \cap B) \cup C}(x)$ and $\mu_{A \cap (B \cup C)}(x)$

(e) $\mu_{\overline{A \cup B \cup C}}(x)$

1-10: Consider the fuzzy sets A and B, where

$$\mu_A(x) = \exp\left[-\tfrac{1}{2}(x-3)^2\right] \text{ and } \mu_B(x) = \exp\left[-\tfrac{1}{2}(x-4)^2\right].$$

(a) Sketch $\mu_{A \cup B}(x)$ for the following t-conorms: maximum, algebraic sum, bounded sum and drastic sum. Which t-conorm gives the largest and smallest values for $\mu_{A \cup B}(x)$?

(b) Sketch $\mu_{A \cap B}(x)$ for the following t-norms: minimum, algebraic product, bounded product and drastic product. Which t-norm gives the largest and smallest values for $\mu_{A \cap B}(x)$?

1-11: Using (1-31) and (1-32), show that $\mu_{c \cup s}(u,v)$ and $\mu_{c \cap s}(u,v)$ are given by (1-33) and (1-34), respectively.

1-12: Consider the fuzzy relations "u is lighter than v" *or* "u is about the same weight as v." Assume that $u \in U$ and $v \in V$ where U and V are discrete universes of discourse, and U has 4 elements whereas V has 6 elements.

(a) Pick U and V to use in the rest of this exercise.

(b) Establish membership functions for *lighter* and *about the same*, i.e., $\mu_l(u,v)$ and $\mu_{ats}(u,v)$, where the numbers in $\mu_l(u,v)$ and $\mu_{ats}(u,v)$ agree with a comparison of the numbers in U and V.

(c) Compute $\mu_{l \cup ats}(u,v)$.

1-13: Verify the max-min and max-product composition of the crisp relations for the 3-3 element of $R_3(U,W)$ in (1-38).

1-14: Prove the validity of the sup-star composition given in (1-45).

1-15: Perform all of the calculations needed to obtain $\mu_{comb}(u,w)$ given in (1-49).

1-16: Repeat Example 1-12 using the product t-norm. Compare these results with the ones given in (1-49) which were obtained using the minimum t-norm. Are they significantly different?

1-17: Consider the fuzzy relation "u is lighter than v" on $U \times V$, and the fuzzy relation "v is heavier than w" on $V \times W$. Assume that U, V, and W are discrete universes of discourse, and U has four elements, V has six elements, and W has three elements.

(a) Pick U, V, and W to use in the rest of this exercise.

(b) Establish membership functions for *lighter* and *heavier*, i.e., $\mu_l(u,v)$ and $\mu_h(v,w)$, where the numbers in $\mu_l(u,v)$ and $\mu_h(v,w)$ agree with a comparison of the numbers in U, V, and W.

(c) Compute $\mu_{loh}(u,w)$ using minimum t-norm.

(d) Compute $\mu_{loh}(u,w)$ using product t-norm.

(e) Compare the results from (c) and (d).

1-18: Consider the fuzzy relation "u is lighter than v" on $U \times V$. Assume that U and V are discrete universes of discourse, and U has four elements and V has six elements.

(a) Pick U and V to use in the rest of this exercise.

(b) Establish a membership function for *lighter*, i.e., $\mu_l(u,v)$, where the numbers in $\mu_l(u,v)$ agree with a comparison of the numbers in U and V.

(c) Construct a membership function for the fuzzy set *skinny*, $\mu_{skinny}(u)$, on U.

(d) Compute the composition of "u is skinny" *and* "u is lighter than v", $\mu_{skinnyol}(v)$.

1-19: Using the same universe of discourse as in Example 1-14, develop membership functions for:

(a) very likely

(b) not-too-likely

1-20: Suppose that $U = \{-5,-4,-3,-2,-1,0,1,2,3,4,5\}$ and fuzzy set A is characterized by the membership function

$$\mu_A(x) = 0.2 / -5 + 0.4 / -4 + 0.4 / -3 + 0.5 / -2 + 0.5 / -1 + 0.6 / 0 + 0.9 / 1$$
$$+ 1 / 2 + 0.8 / 3 + 0.5 / 4 + 0.1 / 5$$

(a) Given that $y = f(x) = x^3 + 2x^2$, compute $\mu_B(y)$.

(b) Given that $y = |x|$, compute $\mu_B(y)$.

1-21: Suppose that $X_1 = \{1, 2, 3, 4\}$ and $X_2 = \{-1, -2, -3, -4\}$, and fuzzy sets A_1 and A_2 are characterized by the following membership functions:

$$\mu_{A_1}(x_1) = 0.5 / 1 + 0.5 / 2 + 0 / 3 + 1 / 4 \quad \text{and} \quad \mu_{A_2}(x_2) = 1 / -1 + 0 / -2 + 0.25 / -3 + 0.5 / -4$$

Determine the membership function for the fuzzy set B that is associated with $\mu_{f(A_1 A_2)}(y)$, when $y = f(x_1, x_2) = x_1^2 - 2x_2^2$.

1-22: Using truth tables show that the following are tautologies [Allendoerfer and Oakley (1955)]:

(a) $p \wedge (q \vee r) \leftrightarrow (p \wedge q) \vee (p \wedge r)$

(b) $p \vee (q \wedge r) \leftrightarrow (p \vee q) \wedge (p \vee r)$

(c) $p \wedge (q \wedge r) \leftrightarrow (p \wedge q) \wedge r$

(d) $p \vee (q \vee r) \leftrightarrow (p \vee q) \vee r$

1-23: Use truth tables to determine whether or not the following propositions are tautologies:

(a) $(p \wedge q) \rightarrow (p \vee q)$

(b) $[(p \rightarrow q) \wedge (r \rightarrow s) \wedge (p \vee r)] \rightarrow (q \vee s)$

(c) $((p \wedge q) \rightarrow r) \leftrightarrow (p \rightarrow r) \vee (q \rightarrow r)$

1-24: Validate the truth of the crisp implication membership functions given in (1-69) and (1-70).

1-25: Repeat Example 1-19 for the implication membership function given in (1-72).

1-26: Repeat Example 1-19 for the implication membership function given in (1-73).

1-27: When there is some uncertainty about the measurement of input variable x, then that measurement can be modeled as a fuzzy number. Let the measured value of x be denoted x'. In this example, we create a fuzzy number centered about x' by using the following Gaussian membership function for A^*:

$$\mu_{A^*}(x) = \exp\left\{-\tfrac{1}{2}\left[\frac{(x-x')}{\sigma_{A^*}}\right]^2\right\}$$

Here we only consider one single-antecedent rule whose antecedent membership function is also assumed to be a Gaussian, namely

$$\mu_A(x) = \exp\left\{-\tfrac{1}{2}\left[\frac{(x-m_A)}{\sigma_A}\right]^2\right\}$$

We also assume product implication and product t-norm.

(a) Show that the sup-star composition in (1-74) can be expressed as

$$\mu_{B^*}(y) = \sup_{x \in X}\left[\mu_{A^*}(x)\mu_A(x)\right] \times \mu_B(y)$$

(b) Show that $\sup_{x \in X}\left[\mu_{A^*}(x)\mu_A(x)\right]$ occurs at $x = x_{max} = \left(\sigma_{A^*}^2 m_A + \sigma_A^2 x'\right)/\left(\sigma_{A^*}^2 + \sigma_A^2\right)$.

(c) Show that $\sup_{x \in X}\left[\mu_{A^*}(x)\mu_A(x)\right] = \exp\left\{-\tfrac{1}{2}\left(x'-m_A\right)^2/\left(\sigma_{A^*}^2 + \sigma_A^2\right)\right\}$.

(d) Assume a Gaussian consequent membership function, $\mu_B(y)$. Sketch the fired-rule membership function $\mu_{B^*}(y)$. How is this obtained directly from sketches of $\mu_{A^*}(x)$, $\mu_A(x)$ and $\mu_B(y)$?

(e) Repeat part (d) for a triangular consequent membership function.

(f) Compare the result in part (e) with the result in Figure 1-13.

1-28: Everything is the same as in Exercise 1-27, except that in this exercise minimum implication and minimum t-norm are used.

(a) Show that, in this case, the sup-star composition in (1-74) can be expressed as

$$\mu_{B^*}(y) = \min\left[\sup_{x \in X}\left[\min\left[\mu_{A^*}(x), \mu_A(x)\right]\right], \mu_B(y)\right]$$

(b) Show that $\sup_{x \in X}\left[\min\left[\mu_{A^{\bullet}}(x), \mu_A(x)\right]\right]$ occurs at the intersection point of the two Gaussian membership functions, namely at

$$x = x_{max} = \left(\sigma_{A^{\bullet}} m_A + \sigma_A x'\right)\big/\left(\sigma_{A^{\bullet}} + \sigma_A\right).$$

(c) If possible, obtain a formula for $\sup_{x \in X}\left[\min\left[\mu_{A^{\bullet}}(x), \mu_A(x)\right]\right]$.

(d) Assume a Gaussian consequent membership function $\mu_B(y)$. Sketch the fired-rule membership function $\mu_{B^{\bullet}}(y)$. How is this obtained directly from sketches of $\mu_{A^{\bullet}}(x)$, $\mu_A(x)$ and $\mu_B(y)$?

(e) Repeat part (d) for a triangular consequent membership function.

(f) Compare the result in part (e) with the result in Figure 1-12.

CHAPTER 2

Sources of Uncertainty

2.1 UNCERTAINTIES IN A FLS

The title of this book, *Uncertain Rule-Based Fuzzy Logic Systems*, emphasizes the word *uncertain* by using it as its first word. Note, however, that this word applies to the rest of the title, *rule-based fuzzy logic systems*. Hence, this book will not provide a lot of general discussions about the meaning of uncertainty; instead, it will examine its meaning relative to (conditioned on) a rule-based FLS.

2.1.1 Uncertainty: General discussions

Uncertainty comes in many guises and is independent of what kind of FL, or any kind of methodology, one uses to handle it. One of the best sources for general discussions about uncertainty is Klir and Wierman (1998). Professor Klir and his students (e.g., [Klir and Folger (1988)]) have been focusing on uncertainty topics since the 1980s, and this book represents an amalgamation and sharpening of the many ideas from their works. Regarding the *occurrence of uncertainty*, they state (1998, p. 2):

> When dealing with real-world problems, we can rarely avoid uncertainty. At the empirical level, uncertainty is an inseparable companion of almost any measurement, resulting from a combination of inevitable measurement errors and resolution limits of measuring instruments. At the cognitive level, it emerges from the vagueness and ambiguity inherent in natural language. At the social level, uncertainty has even strategic uses and it is often created and maintained by people for different purposes (privacy, secrecy, propriety).

Regarding the *causes of uncertainty*, they state (1998, p. 5):

> Uncertainty involved in any problem-solving situation is a result of some information deficiency. Information (pertaining to the model within which the situation is conceptualized) may be incomplete, fragmentary, not fully reliable, vague, contradictory, or deficient in some other way. In general, these various information deficiencies may result in different types of uncertainty.

Regarding the *nature of uncertainty*, they state (1998, p. 43):

> Three types of uncertainty are now recognized . . . *fuzziness*[1] (or vagueness), which results from the imprecise boundaries of fuzzy sets; *nonspecificity*[2] (or imprecision), which is connected with sizes (cardinalities) of relevant sets of alternatives; and *strife*[3] (or discord), which expresses conflicts among the various sets of alternatives.

They divide these three types of uncertainty into two major classes, *fuzziness* and *ambiguity*, where ambiguity ("one to many relationships") includes *nonspecificity* and *strife*.

Another source for some general discussions about uncertainty is Berenji (1988, p. 233), who states, in agreement with Klir and Wierman (1998), that "uncertainty stems from lack of complete information." He also states that "Uncertainty may also reflect incompleteness, imprecision, missing information, or randomness in data and a process."

Taken out of context, "uncertainty" is relatively abstract because of its many varieties; however, as we demonstrate next, taken in the context of a FLS, uncertainty is easy to understand.

---

[1]Klir and Wierman (1998, p. 103) associate the following synonyms with fuzziness: "vagueness, cloudiness, haziness, unclearness, indistinctness and sharplessness."

[2]Klir and Wierman (1998, p. 103) associate the following synonyms with nonspecificity: "variety, generality, diversity, equivocation and imprecision." The use of *imprecision* both as a synonym for nonspecificity and in the discussion about fuzziness is confusing. In a private correspondence to me, Klir states that "when it comes to the term 'imprecision,' it is meaningful to use it (and it is often used) for both nonspecificity and fuzziness. When it is used for nonspecificity, it refers to information - based imprecision; here, uncertainty results from information deficiency. When it is used for fuzziness, it refers to linguistic imprecision. Clearly, the term 'imprecision' has been used prior to the emergence of fuzzy sets. For example, we talk about limited precision (or imprecision) of measurements (or computations). . . . Nonspecificity and imprecision are thus connected, but . . . we should not consider them as synonyms. The reason is that imprecision is also connected with fuzziness. This ambiguity can be avoided by distinguishing information-based imprecision (equivalent to nonspecificity) with linguistic imprecision (equivalent to fuzziness)."

[3]Klir and Wierman (1998, p. 103) associate the following synonyms with strife: "dissonance, incongruency, discrepancy, conflict, and discord."

2.1.2 Uncertainty: In a FLS

The following sources of uncertainty can occur for the FLS in Figure 1-1:

- Uncertainty about the meanings of the words that are used in the rules
- Uncertainty about the consequent that is used in a rule
- Uncertainty about the measurements that activate the FLS
- Uncertainty about the data that are used to tune the parameters of a FLS

We have already seen that a FLS consists of rules and rules use words. In fact, Zadeh (1996, 1999) has been advocating "computing with words" (CW) and using FL to do this. In his 1996 article, he states (1996, p. 103):

- Computing with words is a necessity when the available information is too imprecise to justify the use of numbers and . . . when there is a tolerance for imprecision which can be exploited to achieve tractability, robustness, low solution cost, and better rapport with reality.
- Fuzzy logic is a methodology for computing with words.
- As used by humans, words have fuzzy denotations.
- A key aspect of CW is that it involves a fusion of natural languages and computation with fuzzy variables.

Our thesis is that *words mean different things to different people* and so there is *uncertainty* associated with words, which means that FL must somehow use this uncertainty when it computes with words [Mendel (1999)].

Type-1 FL handles uncertainties about the meanings of words by using *precise* membership functions that the user believes capture the uncertainty of the words. Once the type-1 membership functions have been chosen, all uncertainty about the words disappears, because type-1 membership functions are totally precise. Type-2 FL, on the other hand, handles uncertainties about the meanings of words by *modeling* the uncertainties. This is accomplished, as we describe in great detail in Chapter 3, by blurring the boundaries of type-1 membership functions into what we call a *footprint of uncertainty*. Although a type-2 membership function will also be totally precise, it includes the footprint of uncertainty that provides new degrees of freedom that let uncertainties be handled by a type-2 FLS in totally new ways.

In rules we distinguish between antecedent words and consequent words; but, there are also connector words (e.g., *and, or*). In this book, we do not assign uncertainty to such connectors, because we believe that their use in language is so well established that there is no uncertainty about them. If there are situations where this is not true then we leave them to others to explore. What we mean by "words mean different things to different people" will be discussed in our next section at great length.

The uncertainty about the meanings[4] of the words that are used in rules seems to me to be in accord with *fuzziness*, which results from imprecise boundaries of fuzzy sets.

Consequents for rules are either obtained from experts, by means of knowledge mining (engineering), or are extracted directly from data. Because experts don't all agree, a survey of experts will usually lead to a histogram of possibilities for the consequent of a rule. This histogram represents the uncertainty about the consequent of a rule, and this kind of uncertainty is different from that associated with the meanings of the words used in the rules. A histogram of consequent possibilities can be handled by a type-2 FLS.

Uncertainty about the consequent used in a rule, as established by a histogram of possibilities, seems to be in accord with *strife*, which expresses conflicts among the various sets of alternatives.

Measurements are usually corrupted by noise; hence, they are uncertain. I do not propose to abandon traditional ideas about noisy measurements (i.e., measurement = signal + noise). What I will abandon (at least in this book) is the frequently made assumption of a priori knowledge of a probability model (i.e., a probability density function) for either the signal or the noise. Doing this gets around the major shortcoming of a probability-based model, namely the assumed probability model, for which results will be good if the data agree with the model, but may not be so good if the data do not. Uncertain measurements can be handled very naturally within the framework of a FLS.[5]

Uncertain measurements (i.e., randomness in the data) can be modeled as fuzzy sets (type-1 or type-2); hence, uncertainty about the measurements that activate the FLS seems to be in accord with *nonspecificity* when nonspecificity is associated with information-based imprecision, as suggested by Klir in footnote 2.

Finally, a FLS contains many design parameters whose values must be set by the designer before the FLS is operational. There are many ways to do this, and all make use of a set of data, usually called the *training set*. This set consists of input–output pairs for the FLS, and, if these pairs are measured signals, then they are as uncertain as the measurements that excite the FLS. In this case—one that is quite common in practice, but has not received much attention in the

---

[4]In a private correspondence to me, Klir pointed out that the term "meaning" has itself many different meanings and is context-dependent. I agree and suggest that all of this contributes to the uncertainty about the meanings of words.

[5]This author has spent most of his career working with probability-based models (e.g., [Mendel (1983, 1990, 1995b,)]) and is in no way recommending that such models be abandoned. When one has a high confidence in the validity of probability-based models, they can provide excellent results. Type-2 FLSs provide a viable alternative to them when one does not have a high confidence in the validity of a probability-based model or cannot determine such a model because of system complexities, such as non-linearity, time-variability, or non-stationarity.

FLS literature—the FLS must be tuned using unreliable data, which is yet another form of uncertainty that can be handled by a type-2 FLS.

The uncertainty about the data that are used to tune the parameters of a FLS also seems to be in accord with *nonspecificity* when nonspecificity is associated with information-based imprecision.

Based on our discussions so far, it would appear that a type-2 FLS is able to directly address all three types of uncertainty—*fuzziness*, *strife*, and *nonspecificity*. Klir and Wierman (1998), however, appear to be dismissive of type-2 fuzzy sets, when they state (1998, p. 20):

> These more general fuzzy sets [*fuzzy sets of type-2*] . . . are not relevant to our discussion of uncertainty measures and principles"

On this point we strongly disagree,[6] and, in fact, in this book, we examine all of these kinds of uncertainty, and show how a type-2 FLS—one that makes use of type-2 fuzzy sets—can be designed to perform well in spite of them. Type-2 fuzzy sets are the means to handling all three types of uncertainty totally within the framework of fuzzy set theory. They are able to do this because they directly model uncertainties.

2.2 WORDS MEAN DIFFERENT THINGS TO DIFFERENT PEOPLE

Today, computing with words must still be done using numbers, and, therefore, numeric intervals must be associated with words. Suppose, for example, that we have established ahead of time that the words or phrases to be used in a collection of rules will all lie on the scale 0–10. An interesting question then is, *How can we cover the scale 0–10 with words (or phrases)?* In typical engineering applications of FL, we don't ask this question, because we choose the number of fuzzy sets that will cover an interval arbitrarily, and then choose the names for these sets just as arbitrarily (e.g., *zero*, *small positive*, *medium positive*, and *large positive*). This works fine for many engineering applications, when rules are extracted from data. However, it is a questionable practice when rules are extracted from people (experts). Put another way, machines don't care about words, but people do.

---

[6]In a private correspondence to me, Klir clarified the intended meaning of this statement, in that his book is restricted only to type-1 fuzzy sets and, hence, the more general fuzzy sets are not relevant to the discussions in the book. The quoted statement was not intended to dismiss the significance of type-2 fuzzy sets.

In the rest of this section, in order to make our discussions concrete, I focus on applying FL to situations where the meanings of words are associated with a scale of 0-10. These discussions can easily be extended to arbitrary scales. Consider the following question, whose meaning will become clear in the following discussions:

What is the *smallest* number of words (or phrases) that cover the interval 0-10?

We will demonstrate that the answer to this question depends on whether or not uncertainty is associated with the words. Note that this question seems to be in accord with another aspect of *nonspecificity*, namely with the sizes of relevant sets of alternatives (cardinalities).

To answer this question, we performed a survey. With the help of a social scientist,[7] who is also an expert in survey methodology, we established 16 words or phrases that we thought would cover the interval 0-10. As is usually done in FL [Zadeh (1975)], we assumed that these terms are generated in a context-free grammar.[8] The 16 phrases (which are referred to as *labels* in the survey) were randomized. Engineering undergraduate students were given the survey, whose wording was as follows:

Below are a number of labels that describe an interval or a "range" that falls somewhere between 0 to 10. For each label, please tell us where this range would start and where it would stop. (In other words, please tell us how much of the distance from 0 to 10 this range would cover.) For example, the range "quite a bit" might start at 6 and end at 8. It is important to note that *not all the ranges are the same size*.

Table 2-1 was provided to the students so that they only had to fill in two numbers for each label. The labels were randomized so that interval information collected about each label would be uncorrelated. A total of 87 surveys were completed; 17 had outliers (e.g., some students filled in 0-10 for the range of all the labels). Of the remaining 70, 40 were from men, 11 from women, and 19 were from students who chose not to identify their sex. In the following results, we did not distinguish between the sex of the respondent, although clearly one

---

[7]Sheila Murphy, University of Southern California Annenberg School of Communications.

[8]Klir and Wierman (1998, p. 13) state: "fuzzy numbers, fuzzy intervals, and other types of fuzzy sets give us enough flexibility to represent, as closely as desirable, states characterized by *expressions in a natural language* that are inherently vague. These expressions are, of course, strongly dependent on the context in which they are used. This implies that membership grade functions by which we attempt to capture the relevant linguistic expressions must be constructed in the context of each application." This raises the important question (to which we provide no answer), "Is there such a thing as a context-free grammar?"

could if that was felt to be important.[9] Survey results are summarized in Table 2-2.

Table 2-1: Survey table with randomized labels.

Range Label	Start	End
None		
Some		
A good amount		
An extreme amount		
A substantial amount		
A maximum amount		
A fair amount		
A moderate amount		
A large amount		
A small amount		
Very little		
A lot		
A sizeable amount		
A bit		
A considerable amount		
A little bit		

Because a range was requested for each label, and a range is defined by two numbers—*start* and *end*—the survey provided sample statistics for these two numbers, namely their mean and standard deviations. The standard deviations represent the uncertainties associated with each label. Observe that standard deviations are not the same for the *start* and *end* values for each label.

The Table 2-2 data are also summarized in Figure 2-1. For each label there are two circles with a solid line between them. The circles are located at the mean *start* and *end* points for each label. The dashed lines to the left of the left-hand circles and to the right of the right-hand circles each terminate in a vertical bar equal to one standard deviation, listed in Table 2-2 for the mean *start* and *end* points, respectively.

---

[9]This would suggest that gender differences may have to be considered when computing with words.

Table 2-2: Processed survey results: ordered labels.

No.	Range Label	Mean		Standard Deviation	
		Start	End	Start	End
1	*None*	0.0143	0.2286	0.1195	0.9036
2	*Very little*	0.8714	2.2571	0.9313	1.3693
3	*A small amount*	1.3000	3.6429	0.8739	1.1800
4	*A little bit*	1.3143	3.0714	0.8434	1.6180
5	*A bit*	1.7000	3.7571	1.4876	1.8371
6	*Some*	1.8286	4.2857	1.2391	1.6694
7	*A moderate amount*	4.1429	6.1714	1.1457	1.1668
8	*A fair amount*	4.2571	6.2286	1.2931	1.3424
9	*A good amount*	4.9429	7.4429	1.4928	1.3688
10	*A considerable amount*	5.3571	7.9857	1.5700	1.5834
11	*A sizeable amount*	5.6571	8.2571	1.9700	1.5575
12	*A large amount*	6.0857	8.9000	1.6572	1.0377
13	*A substantial amount*	6.2571	8.6429	1.8703	1.2399
14	*A lot*	6.7429	9.3857	1.9611	0.7669
15	*An extreme amount*	7.8857	9.6000	2.1027	0.7690
16	*A maximum amount*	8.8857	9.7571	2.4349	1.1221

Observe, from Figure 2-1, that:

1. There is a gap between the mean-value end points of *none* and *very little*, implying that either another word should be inserted between them or they should be combined. For illustrative purposes, in our following discussions, we do the latter.

2. People seem to agree that *none* starts at zero—and there is very little uncertainty about this (see the standard deviation in Table 2-2). To people, the word *none* seems to have a very strong connotation with the number "zero."

3. The same cannot be said for the label *a maximum amount*. The right-hand mean value for its range is 9.7571 and not 10. One explanation for this is that people may be adverse to assigning the largest possible number to any label, because of an expectation that there could be another label that should have the largest number associated with it.[10] Because the labels were randomized, the students may have expected a phrase even stronger than *a maximum*

---

[10]Why, for example, if the top grade on an examination is *excellent* and the range for *excellent* is 8-10, are some people assigned an 8, and probably no one is assigned a 10? Perhaps, it is the expectation that someone else will do better, or that no one is perfect.

amount, and they did not check the complete list of 16 words to see if such a stronger phrase actually occurred.

4. The 16 words do not quite cover the 0-10 interval, but this only occurs at the right-most extreme values.

5. There seems to be a linguistic gap between the labels *some* and *a moderate amount* as evidenced by the small degree of overlap between these labels. Perhaps this gap could be filled by adding the label *somewhat moderate*.

6. The dashed portions of the intervals for each label represent the label's uncertainty.

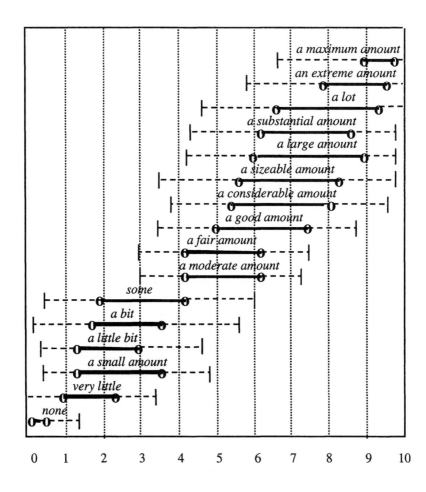

Figure 2-1: All 16 labels and their intervals and uncertainty bands.

What do we do with such uncertainty information, when we compute with words using a type-1 FLS? Usually, in a type-1 fuzzy set we would tend to explicitly *ignore* the uncertainty, either by using just the [mean(*start*), mean(*end*)] range for a label, or perhaps by being conservative, and using the range associated with the interval [mean(*start*) – standard deviation(*start*), mean(*end*) + standard deviation(*end*)]. As Figure 2-1 indicates, it is not correct to do the former, and, as explained next, it is also not correct to do the latter.

The dashed lines in Figure 2-1 represent linguistic uncertainty, in much the same way that standard deviation for a measured random quantity represents its uncertainty. When we work in the province of probability, we find it useful and important to distinguish between the mean and the standard deviation; so, as we have already argued in Chapter 1, why should less be expected of us when we work with linguistic uncertainties? Unfortunately, type-1 fuzzy sets cannot let us distinguish the dashed part of an interval from the solid part. Type-2 fuzzy sets can, and how to do this is explained in Chapter 3.

There is more that can be concluded from the survey results, namely:

1. In Figure 2-2, the sets *none* and *very little* have been combined as explained earlier, and five labels are shown that cover the 0-10 range (except for the right-end anomaly), whose intervals between their mean *start* and *end* points are drawn in very heavy. These are not the only five labels that could have been chosen. For example, instead of using *a moderate amount* we could have used *a fair amount*, or instead of using *a large amount* we could have used *a substantial amount*.

2. The intervals are not of equal size and there is more (or less) overlap between some than between others. Membership functions that are associated with these labels should make use of this information and be designed accordingly. We explain how to do this in Chapter 3.

3. It is possible to cover the 0-10 range with five labels, as indicated in Figure 2-2; however, there is not much overlap between some of the labels. When the standard deviation information is used, then sufficient overlap is achieved.

4. It is also possible to cover the 0-10 interval with four or three labels (see Figure 2-3). The smallest number of labels from the 16 labels used in our survey that cover the interval is three and this is only possible because of linguistic uncertainties; that is, overlap occurs for the three labels only because of uncertainty.[11]

---

[11]In a private correspondence to me, Klir suggests that two labels *none to a small amount* and *large to a maximum amount* could also cover 0-10. Although this could be concluded by combining intervals (as we did for *none* and *very little*), it needs to be verified by means of another survey. It does seem quite plausible that a vocabulary that included these two terms would let the interval 0-10 be covered by as few as two labels. Klir also suggests that a single label such as *any amount* could cover 0-10, but then adds that this would have no pragmatic value (for a FLS).

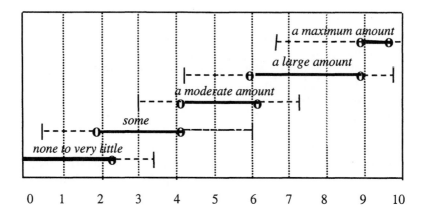

Figure 2-2: Although five labels cover 0–10, there is not much overlap between some of them. It is when the standard deviation information is used that sufficient overlap is achieved.

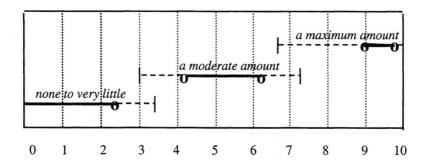

Figure 2-3: The smallest number of labels that cover the interval 0-10 is three, and this is only possible because of uncertainties.

Linguistic uncertainty appears to be useful in that it lets us cover the 0-10 range with a much smaller number of labels than without it. Put another way, in the context of firing rules in a FLS, *uncertainty can fire rules*. This cannot occur in the framework of a type-1 FLS; but, it can occur in the framework of a type-2 FLS. Additionally, *uncertainty can be used to control the rule explosion* that is so common in a FLS. If, for example, we ignored uncertainty, and had rules with two antecedents, each of which has six labels, it would take 36 rules to completely describe the fuzzy rule base. On the other hand, using three labels for each antecedent requires a rule base with only nine rules. This is a 75% reduction in the size of the rule base. For rules with more than two antecedents the rule reduction is even greater.

I conclude this discussion with a conjecture. *Uncertainty is good in that it lets people make decisions (albeit conservative ones) rapidly.* Perhaps this is why some people can make decisions very quickly and others cannot. The latter may have partitioned their variables into so many fine sets that they get hung up among the resulting enormous number of possibilities. They are the eternal procrastinators.

This conjecture seems to be supported by Klir and Wierman (1998), when they state:

> Uncertainty has a pivotal role in any efforts to maximize the usefulness of systems models. . . . Uncertainty becomes very valuable when considered in connection to the other characteristics of systems models: a slight increase in uncertainty may often significantly reduce complexity and, at the same time, increase credibility of the model. Uncertainty is thus an important commodity in the modeling business, a commodity which can be traded for gains in the other essential characteristics of models.

Based on the results in Figure 2-2, we conducted another survey using a different group of engineering students. We randomized the five labels *none to very little, some, a moderate amount, a large amount,* and *a maximum amount.* The same question was asked as in our first survey, and results from 47 students are given in Table 2-3. Note that there is no longer an anomaly about reaching the maximum value of 10. This is probably because only 5 phrases were used and it was easy for the students to check them all to determine that the strongest one was *a maximum amount.*

Table 2-3: Survey results for labels of fuzzy sets.

No.	Range Label	Mean Start	Mean End	Standard Deviation Start	Standard Deviation End
1	*None to very little* (NVL)	0	1.9850	0	0.8104
2	*Some* (S)	2.5433	5.2500	0.9066	1.3693
3	*A moderate amount* (MOA)	3.6433	6.4567	0.8842	0.8557
4	*A large amount* (LA)	6.4833	8.7500	0.7484	0.5981
5	*A maximum amount* (MAA)	8.5500	10	0.7468	0

It seems pretty clear from these surveys that *words do indeed mean different things to different people* and that by utilizing the uncertainties associated with words we can reduce the number of alternatives, which is in accord with the cardinality aspect of *nonspecificity*. In the next chapter, we show how to model the uncertainties of words by using type-2 fuzzy sets.

EXERCISES

2-1: Take the survey in Table 2-1, and then compare your results with those given in Table 2-2. Explain how to modify the results given in Table 2-2 using your survey's results.

2-2: Choose a set of phrases that may include some but not all of the phrases used in Table 2-2 (i.e., include some new phrases) and perform a survey, as we did to obtain the results in Table 2-2. Separate the results by gender and draw conclusions.

2-3: Create, administer, and analyze a survey that tests whether or not the results given in Table 2-2 or Table 2-3 are context-independent.

C H A P T E R   3

Membership Functions and Uncertainty

3.1 INTRODUCTION

Membership functions characterize fuzzy sets, be they type-1 or type-2. In a FLS, membership functions are associated with terms that appear in the antecedents or consequents of rules, and with the input and output to the FLS. In this chapter, we briefly review membership functions for type-1 fuzzy sets, which we now call "type-1 membership functions," and then we formally introduce membership functions for type-2 fuzzy sets, which we call "type-2 membership functions." Important terms that are associated with type-2 membership functions are defined, and how the uncertainties that were described in Chapter 2 can be represented using type-2 membership functions is explained.

3.2 TYPE-1 MEMBERSHIP FUNCTIONS

A type-1 fuzzy set, A, which is in terms of a single variable, $x \in X$, has already been defined and discussed in Section 1.10.2. Recall that such a set may be represented as

$$A = \{(x, \mu_A(x)) \mid \forall x \in X\} \tag{3-1}$$

Type-1 membership function, $\mu_A(x)$, is constrained to be between 0 and 1 for all $x \in X$, and is a two-dimensional (2D) function. The extensions of these no-tions to a type-1 fuzzy set, A_x, which is in terms of two or more variables, $x_1, x_2, ..., x_p$, is given in Section 3.5.1.

As we know, the number of membership functions associated with a linguis-tic variable is free to be chosen. In Figure 3-1 the linguistic variable temperature has been decomposed into five terms {*very negative, medium negative, near zero, medium positive, very positive*}. For illustrative purposes, triangular and piecewise-linear membership functions have been used. Many decisions were made to draw the Figure 3-1 membership functions, including where to center the triangles, where to locate the shoulder points of the piecewise-linear mem-bership functions, where to locate the base-points of the triangles on the x-axis, and how much overlap there should be between the shoulder membership func-tions and the triangles. All of these decisions translate into uncertainties, which as we shall demonstrate here can be handled by type-2 fuzzy sets and their mem-bership functions.

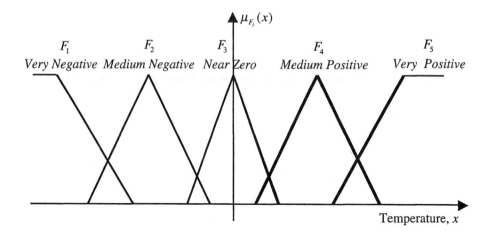

Figure 3-1: Type-1 membership functions.

3.3 TYPE-2 MEMBERSHIP FUNCTIONS

In this section we introduce type-2 fuzzy sets and formally define a large number of associated concepts and terminology.

3.3.1 The concept of a type-2 fuzzy set [Karnik and Mendel (1998b), p. 2]

Consider the transition from ordinary sets to fuzzy sets. When we cannot determine the membership of an element in a set as 0 or 1, we use fuzzy sets of type-1. Similarly, when the circumstances are so fuzzy that we have trouble determining the membership grade even as a crisp number in [0, 1], we use fuzzy sets of type-2, a concept that was first introduced by Zadeh in 1975.

This does not mean that we need to have extraordinary fuzzy circumstances to use type-2 sets. We can look at the situation from a different perspective. When something is uncertain (e.g., a measurement), we have trouble determining its exact value, and in this case using type-1 sets makes more sense of course than using crisp sets. But then, even in the type-1 sets, we specify the membership functions exactly, which seems counter-intuitive. If we cannot determine the exact value of an uncertain quantity, how can we determine its exact membership in a fuzzy set? Of course, this criticism applies to type-2 sets as well, because even though the membership is fuzzy, we specify it exactly, which again seems counter-intuitive. If we continue thinking along these lines, we can say that no finite-type fuzzy set can represent uncertainty "completely." So, ideally, we need to use a type-∞ fuzzy set to completely represent uncertainty. Of course, we cannot do this in practice, so we have to use some finite-type sets. In this book we deal just with type-1 and type-2 fuzzy sets. One may look at higher types too; but, as we go on to higher types, the complexity of the FLS increases rapidly.

3.3.2 Definition of a type-2 fuzzy set and associated concepts

Imagine blurring the type-1 membership function depicted in Figure 3-2 (a) by shifting the points on the triangle either to the left or to the right and not necessarily by the same amounts, as in Figure 3-2(b). Then, at a specific value of x, say x', there no longer is a single value for the membership function; instead, the membership function takes on values wherever the vertical line intersects the blur. Those values need not all be weighted the same; hence, we can assign an amplitude distribution to all of those points. Doing this for all $x \in X$, we create a three-dimensional membership function—a type-2 membership function—that characterizes a type-2 fuzzy set.

We now define a type-2 fuzzy set in a *pointwise* manner.

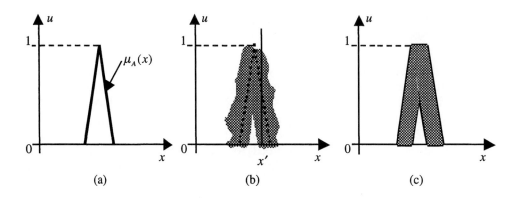

Figure 3-2: (a) Type-1 membership function, (b) blurred type-1 membership function, and (c) FOU.

Definition 3-1: *A type-2 fuzzy set, denoted $\tilde{A}$, is characterized by a type-2 membership function $\mu_{\tilde{A}}(x,u)$, where $x \in X$ and $u \in J_x \subseteq [0,1]$, i.e.,*

$$\tilde{A} = \left\{ \left((x,u), \mu_{\tilde{A}}(x,u) \right) \mid \forall x \in X, \forall u \in J_x \subseteq [0,1] \right\} \tag{3-2}$$

in which $0 \le \mu_{\tilde{A}}(x,u) \le 1$. $\tilde{A}$ can also be expressed as

$$\tilde{A} = \int_{x \in X} \int_{u \in J_x} \mu_{\tilde{A}}(x,u) / (x,u) \quad J_x \subseteq [0,1] \tag{3-3}$$

where $\int\int$ denotes union over all admissible x and u. ■

Example 3-1: Figure 3-3 depicts $\mu_{\tilde{A}}(x,u)$ for x and u discrete. In particular, $X = \{1,2,3,4,5\}$ and $U = \{0,0.2,0.4,0.6,0.8,1\}$. Observe that $J_1 = \{0,0.2,0.4\}$, $J_2 = \{0,0.2, 0.4,0.6,0.8\}$, $J_3 = \{0.6,0.8\}$, $J_4 = J_2$ and $J_5 = J_1$, and, we have only included values in $J_1,...,J_5$ for which $\mu_{\tilde{A}}(x,u) \ne 0$. Each of the spikes in Figure 3-3 represents $\mu_{\tilde{A}}(x,u)$ at a specific (x, u)-pair. ■

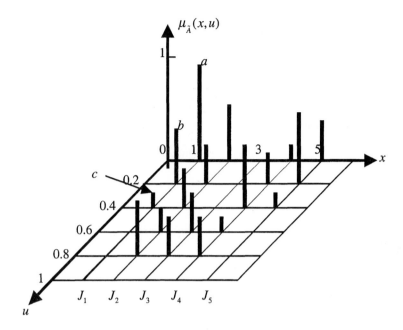

Figure 3-3: Example of a type-2 membership function.

In Definition 3-1, the restriction that $\forall u \in J_x \subseteq [0,1]$ is consistent with the type-1 constraint that $0 \leq \mu_A(x) \leq 1$. That is, if the blur disappears, then a type-2 membership function must reduce to a type-1 membership function, in which case the variable u equals $\mu_A(x)$ and $0 \leq \mu_A(x) \leq 1$. The additional restriction that $0 \leq \mu_{\tilde{A}}(x,u) \leq 1$ is consistent with the fact that the amplitudes of a membership function should lie between or be equal to 0 and 1.

Definition 3-2: *At each value of x, say $x = x'$, the 2D plane whose axes are u and $\mu_{\tilde{A}}(x',u)$ is called a vertical slice of $\mu_{\tilde{A}}(x,u)$. A secondary membership function is a vertical slice of $\mu_{\tilde{A}}(x,u)$. It is $\mu_{\tilde{A}}(x = x',u)$ for $x' \in X$ and $\forall u \in J_{x'} \subseteq [0,1]$, i.e.,*

$$\mu_{\tilde{A}}(x = x',u) \equiv \mu_{\tilde{A}}(x') = \int_{u \in J_{x'}} f_{x'}(u)/u \qquad J_{x'} \subseteq [0,1] \qquad (3\text{-}4)$$

in which $0 \leq f_{x'}(u) \leq 1$. Because $\forall x' \in X$, we drop the prime notation on $\mu_{\tilde{A}}(x')$, *and refer to $\mu_{\tilde{A}}(x)$ as a secondary membership function; it is a type-1 fuzzy set, which we also refer to as a* secondary set. ∎

Based on the concept of secondary sets, we can reinterpret a type-2 fuzzy set as the union of all secondary sets, i.e., using (3-4), *we can re-express $\tilde{A}$ in a vertical-slice manner,* as:

$$\tilde{A} = \{(x, \mu_{\tilde{A}}(x)) \mid \forall x \in X\} \tag{3-5}$$

or,[1] as

$$\tilde{A} = \int_{x \in X} \mu_{\tilde{A}}(x)/x = \int_{x \in X} \left[\int_{u \in J_x} f_x(u)/u \right] \Big/ x \qquad J_x \subseteq [0,1] \tag{3-6}$$

Definition 3-3: *The* domain *of a secondary membership function is called the* primary membership *of x. In (3-6), J_x is the primary membership of x, where $J_x \subseteq [0,1]$ for $\forall x \in X$.* ∎

Definition 3-4: *The* amplitude *of a secondary membership function is called a* secondary grade. *In (3-6), $f_x(u)$ is a secondary grade; in (3-2), $\mu_{\tilde{A}}(x', u')$ ($x' \in X, u' \in J_{x'}$) is a secondary grade.* ∎

If X and J_x are both discrete (either by problem formulation or by discretization of continuous universes of discourse), then the right-most part of (3-6) can be expressed as

$$\tilde{A} = \sum_{x \in X} \left[\sum_{u \in J_x} f_x(u)/u \right] \Big/ x = \sum_{i=1}^{N} \left[\sum_{u \in J_{x_i}} f_{x_i}(u)/u \right] \Big/ x_i$$
$$= \left[\sum_{k=1}^{M_1} f_{x_1}(u_{1k})/u_{1k} \right] \Big/ x_1 + \cdots + \left[\sum_{k=1}^{M_N} f_{x_N}(u_{Nk})/u_{Nk} \right] \Big/ x_N \tag{3-7}$$

Observe that x has been discretized into N values and at each of these values u has been discretized into M_i values (Exercise 3-1). The discretization along each u_{ik} does not have to be the same, which is why we have shown a different upper

---

[1] A type-2 fuzzy set can also be thought of as a fuzzy valued function that assigns to every $x \in X$ a type-1 fuzzy set. In this sense, Karnik and Mendel [e.g., (1998b), (2000a)] call X the *domain* of the type-2 fuzzy set. In this book, I prefer to treat the membership function of a type-2 fuzzy set as having domain $\bigcup_{x \in X} J_x$, in order to emphasize its 3-D nature (see Definition 3-6).

sum for each of the bracketed terms. If, however, the discretization along each u_{ik} is the same, then $M_1 = M_2 = \cdots = M_N \equiv M$.

Expressions similar to (3-7) can be written for the mixed cases when X is continuous but J_x is discrete, or vice-versa. The most important case for us in this book will be (3-7), because when a type-2 membership function is programmed it must be discretized, not only over X but also over J_x.

Example 3-2: Referring to Figure 3-3, observe that the secondary membership function at $x = 1$ is $a / 0 + b / 0.2 + c / 0.4$. Its primary membership values at $x = 1$ are $u = 0, 0.2, 0.4$, and their associated secondary grades are a, b, c, respectively. ∎

Many choices are possible for the secondary membership functions. By convention, the name that we use to describe the entire type-2 membership function is associated with the name of its secondary membership functions; so, for example, if the secondary membership functions are Gaussian, then we refer to $\mu_{\tilde{A}}(x,u)$ as a Gaussian type-2 membership function.

Example 3-3: When $f_x(u) = 1, \forall u \in J_x \subseteq [0,1]$, then the secondary membership functions are interval sets, and, if this is true for $\forall x \in X$, we have the case of an *interval type-2 membership function*. Interval secondary membership functions reflect a uniform uncertainty at the primary memberships of x, and are the ones that we shall emphasize in this book.

Note that an interval set can be represented just by its domain interval, which can be expressed in terms of its left and right end-points as $[l, r]$, or by its center and spread as $[c - s, c + s]$, where

$$c = (l + r) / 2 \text{ and } s = (r - l) / 2 \qquad (3-8)$$

It is customary to express an interval set just by its domain, namely as $[l, r]$ or $[c - s, c + s]$. When we use this notation, it is understood that the membership grade at each point in the domain equals 1. ∎

Example 3-4: *Triangular or Gaussian secondary membership functions* (i.e., triangular or Gaussian type-2 membership functions) are usually centered at the midpoint of the primary memberships of each x, and reflect a diminishing importance for points farther away from the midpoint; hence, the maximum value of $f_x(u)$ for these secondary membership functions occurs at the midpoint of J_x. Their use requires a judgment be made ahead of time that the greatest emphasis should be placed on the midpoint of the primary memberships of each x. This judgment is not necessary when one uses interval type-2 membership functions. A Gaussian type-2 membership function is depicted in Figure 3-4. ∎

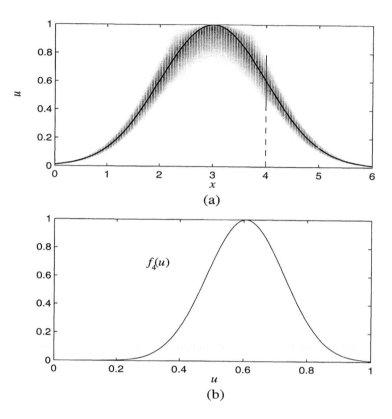

Figure 3-4: (a) Pictorial representation of a Gaussian type-2 fuzzy set. The domain of the membership grade corresponding to $x = 4$ is also shown. The Gaussian secondary membership function at $x = 4$ is shown in (b).

Definition 3-5: *Assume that each of the secondary membership functions of a type-2 fuzzy set has only one secondary grade that equals 1. A principal* membership function *is the union of all such points at which this occurs, i.e.,*

$$\mu_{principal}(x) = \int_{x \in X} u/x \text{ where } f_x(u) = 1 \tag{3-9}$$

and[2] is associated with a type-1 fuzzy set. ∎

Example 3-5: The principal membership function for the Gaussian type-2 fuzzy set whose membership function is depicted in Figure 3-4 is the solid Gaussian curve. ∎

For interval secondary membership functions, we define the principal membership function as occurring at the union of all primary membership *midpoints*. Note that when all membership function uncertainties disappear, a type-2 membership function reduces to its principal membership function.

Definition 3-6: *Uncertainty in the primary memberships of a type-2 fuzzy set, Ã, consists of a bounded region that we call the* footprint *of uncertainty (FOU). It is the union of all primary memberships, i.e.,*

$$FOU(\tilde{A}) = \bigcup_{x \in X} J_x \quad \blacksquare \qquad (3\text{-}10)$$

The term FOU is very useful, because it not only focuses our attention on the uncertainties inherent in a specific type-2 membership function, whose shape is a direct consequence of the nature of these uncertainties, but it also provides a very convenient verbal description of the entire domain of support for all the secondary grades of a type-2 membership function. In all of our applications of type-2 FLSs we have found it very useful to choose appropriate type-2 membership functions by first thinking about their choice in terms of appropriate FOUs.

Example 3-6: An example of a FOU is the shaded regions in Figure 3-5 (a). The FOU is shaded uniformly to indicate that it is for an interval type-2 fuzzy set; hence, a uniformly shaded FOU also represents the entire interval type-2 fuzzy set $\mu_{\tilde{A}}(x,u)$. Shown also on Figure 3-5 are the primary memberships and secondary membership functions at two points. ∎

Example 3-7: Figure 3-6 is an "uncertain" version of Figure 3-1, in which uncertainty has been assumed about the knowledge of where to locate the triangle apex points and where to locate the shoulder points of the two end membership-functions. As in Figure 3-5 (a), the uniformly shaded FOUs denote the fact that the secondary membership functions are interval sets and represent the entire interval type-2 fuzzy set $\mu_{\tilde{A}}(x,u)$. ∎

---

[2]Note that $f_x(u) = 1$ can be solved for u (at $\forall x \in X$), so that u can be expressed as $u = f_x^{-1}(1)$.

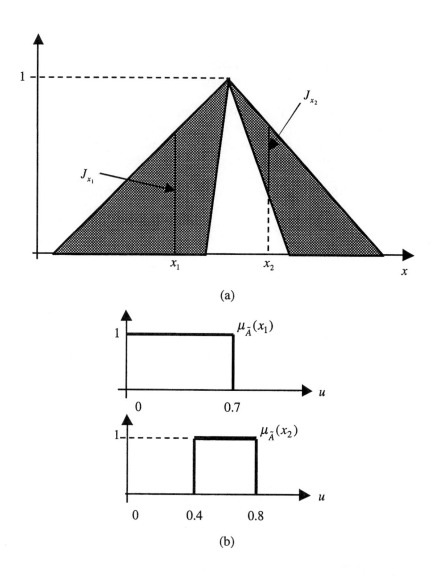

(a)

(b)

Figure 3-5: The shaded region in (a) is the FOU for a type-2 fuzzy set. (a) The primary memberships, J_{x_1} and J_{x_2}, and their associated secondary membership functions $\mu_{\tilde{A}}(x_1)$ and $\mu_{\tilde{A}}(x_2)$ are shown at the two points x_1 and x_2. (b) The secondary membership functions are interval sets.

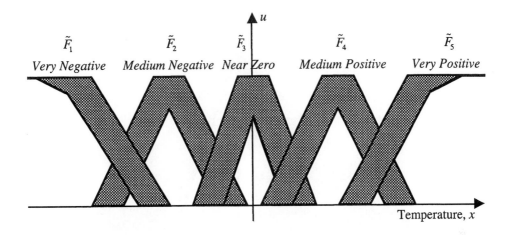

Figure 3-6: FOUs for the Figure 3-1 membership functions.

Example 3-8: As another example of a FOU, let us return to the word-survey described in Chapter 2. Figure 3-7 indicates how the uncertainties associated with the two endpoints of an interval can be translated into a FOU for pre-chosen triangular membership functions. Let a denote the average value for the left-hand point of the interval and b denote the average value for the right-hand point of the interval. The standard deviation for the location of the left-hand point is denoted σ_a, and the standard deviation for the location of the right-hand point is denoted σ_b. Points a and b are shown as solid circles in Figure 3-7. We define the *uncertainty intervals* for the two points as $[a - \sigma_a, a + \sigma_a]$ and $[b - \sigma_b, b + \sigma_b]$, respectively. There are two cases that we must consider: (1) $b - \sigma_b > a + \sigma_a$ and (2) $b - \sigma_b < a + \sigma_a$. In the first case (Figure 3-7), the uncertainty interval for point a does not overlap with the uncertainty interval for point b, but in the second case it does. We provide a construction for the FOU for the first case, and leave the construction of the FOU for the second case as an exercise.

When $b - \sigma_b > a + \sigma_a$, as in Figure 3-7: (1) let $b - a = l$; (2) locate the apex of the triangle at $l/2$, and assign it unity height; (3) the left-hand vertex of the triangle, on the horizontal axis, can range from $a - \sigma_a$ to $a + \sigma_a$; the region of uncertainty for the left-hand leg is the shaded left-hand triangle whose vertices are at: $(a - \sigma_a, 0)$, $(a + \sigma_a, 0)$ and $(l/2, 1)$; (4) the right-hand vertex of the triangle, on the horizontal axis, can range from $b - \sigma_b$ to $b + \sigma_b$; the region of uncertainty for the right-hand leg is the shaded right-hand triangle whose vertices are at: $(b - \sigma_b, 0)$, $(b + \sigma_b, 0)$ and $(l/2, 1)$; and (5) the FOU is the union of all points in the two shaded triangles. This construction also gives some meaning to the FOU shown in Figure 3-5.

This is by no means the only way in which a FOU can be associated with the two end points of a phrase-interval. In Chapter 10 we describe another choice. ■

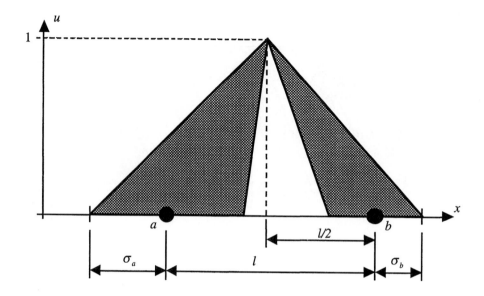

Figure 3-7: FOU when end-point information is requested. Uncertainty interval for *a* does not overlap with the uncertainty interval for *b*.

Another term that is frequently used is *primary membership function*, which is not the same as the term primary membership.

Definition 3-7: *Consider a family of type-1 membership functions* $\mu_A(x \mid p_1, p_2, ..., p_v)$ *where* $p_1, p_2, ..., p_v$ *are parameters, some or all of which vary over some range of values, i.e.,* $p_i \in P_i$ *(i = 1, ..., v). A* primary membership function (MF) *is any one of these type-1 membership functions, e.g.,*

$$\mu_A(x \mid p_1 = p_{1'}, p_2 = p_{2'}, ..., p_v = p_{v'}).$$

For short, we use $\mu_A(x)$ *to denote a primary membership function. It will be subject to some restrictions on its parameters. The family of all primary membership functions creates a FOU.* ∎

Example 3-9: An example of a primary membership function is the triangle, depicted in Figure 3-2 (a) whose vertices have been assumed to vary over some interval of values. The FOU associated with this primary membership function is shown in Figure 3-2 (c). ■

3.3.3 More examples of type-2 fuzzy sets and FOUs

Here we provide some additional examples of useful type-2 fuzzy sets and their FOUs.

Example 3-10: Gaussian primary MF with uncertain mean

Consider the case of a Gaussian primary membership function having a fixed standard deviation, σ, and an uncertain mean that takes on values in $[m_1, m_2]$, i.e.,

$$\mu_A(x) = \exp\left[-\tfrac{1}{2}\left(\frac{x-m}{\sigma}\right)^2\right] \quad m \in [m_1, m_2] \tag{3-11}$$

Corresponding to each value of m we will get a different membership curve (Figure 3-8).

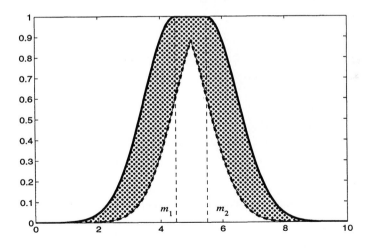

Figure 3-8: FOU for Gaussian primary membership function with uncertain mean.

The uniform shading for the FOU again denotes interval sets for the secondary membership functions and represents the entire interval type-2 fuzzy set $\mu_{\tilde{A}}(x,u)$. We use this primary membership function and its associated interval type-2 membership function a lot, in Chapters 10-14, to characterize the antecedents and consequents of type-2 rules. ∎

Example 3-11: Gaussian primary MF with uncertain
standard deviation

Consider the case of a Gaussian primary membership function having a fixed mean, m, and an uncertain standard deviation that takes on values in $[\sigma_1, \sigma_2]$, i.e.,

$$\mu_A(x) = \exp\left[-\frac{1}{2}\left(\frac{x-m}{\sigma}\right)^2\right] \quad \sigma \in [\sigma_1, \sigma_2] \tag{3-12}$$

Corresponding to each value of σ we will get a different membership curve (Figure 3-9).

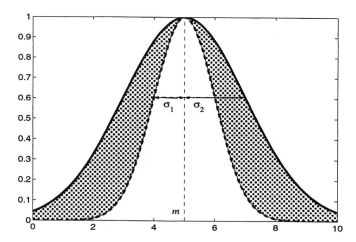

Figure 3-9: FOU for Gaussian primary membership function with uncertain standard deviation.

The uniform shading for the FOU again denotes interval sets for the secondary membership functions and represents the entire interval type-2 fuzzy set $\mu_{\tilde{A}}(x,u)$. We use this primary membership function and its associated interval type-2 membership function in Chapter 12 to model measurements that have been corrupted by non-stationary additive noise. It is also used in Chapter 14. ∎

Example 3-12: Gaussian type-2 fuzzy set

Sometimes it may be appropriate for primary memberships near zero to have less uncertainty associated with them than primary memberships near 1. In other words, it may be appropriate that the uncertainty in a primary membership value be expressible as some percentage of it. Such a type-2 membership function is depicted in Figure 3-4, which shows an example of a Gaussian type-2 fuzzy set, where the secondary membership function for every point is a Gaussian type-1 set contained in [0, 1], and these secondary membership functions are centered about a Gaussian principal membership function (dark curve). Intensity of shading is approximately proportional to secondary grades. Darker areas indicate higher secondary grades. The standard deviations of the secondary Gaussians decrease by design, as x moves away from 3. The flat portion from about 2.5 to 3.5 appears because the primary memberships cannot be greater than 1 and so the Gaussians have to be clipped. ∎

3.3.4 Upper and lower membership functions

The FOU can be described in terms of upper and lower membership functions.

Definition 3-8: *An upper membership function and a lower membership function [Mendel and Liang (1999)] are two type-1 membership functions that are bounds for the FOU of a type-2 fuzzy set $\tilde{A}$. The upper membership function is associated with the upper bound of $FOU(\tilde{A})$, and is denoted $\overline{\mu}_{\tilde{A}}(x)$, $\forall x \in X$. The lower membership function is associated with the lower bound of $FOU(\tilde{A})$, and is denoted $\underline{\mu}_{\tilde{A}}(x)$, $\forall x \in X$, i.e.,*

$$\overline{\mu}_{\tilde{A}}(x) \equiv \overline{FOU(\tilde{A})} \quad \forall x \in X \tag{3-13}$$

and

$$\underline{\mu}_{\tilde{A}}(x) \equiv \underline{FOU(\tilde{A})} \quad \forall x \in X \tag{3-14}$$

Because the domain of a secondary membership function has been constrained in (3-2) to be contained in [0, 1], lower and upper membership functions always exist. ∎

From (3-10), we see that $\overline{FOU(\tilde{A})} = \bigcup_{x \in X} \overline{J_x}$ and $\underline{FOU(\tilde{A})} = \bigcup_{x \in X} \underline{J_x}$, where $\overline{J_x}$ and $\underline{J_x}$ denote the upper and lower bounds on J_x, respectively; hence,

$\overline{\mu}_{\tilde{A}}(x) = \overline{J}_x$ and $\underline{\mu}_{\tilde{A}}(x) = \underline{J}_x$, $\forall x \in X$. We have chosen to use $\overline{\mu}_{\tilde{A}}(x)$ and $\underline{\mu}_{\tilde{A}}(x)$ instead of $\overline{J}_x$ and $\underline{J}_x$ because this notation is already well-entrenched in the type-2 FLS literature (e.g., [Karnik and Mendel (1998b)], [Karnik, et al (1999)], and [Liang and Mendel (2000c)]).

We can re-express (3-6) in terms of upper and lower membership functions, as:

$$\tilde{A} = \mu_{\tilde{A}}(x,u) = \int_{x \in X} \mu_{\tilde{A}}(x)/x = \int_{x \in X} \left[\int_{u \in J_x} f_x(u)/u \right]/x$$

$$= \int_{x \in X} \left[\int_{u \in [\underline{\mu}_{\tilde{A}}(x), \overline{\mu}_{\tilde{A}}(x)]} f_x(u)/u \right]/x \tag{3-15}$$

We see from this equation that the secondary membership function $\mu_{\tilde{A}}(x)$ can be expressed in terms of upper and lower membership functions as:

$$\mu_{\tilde{A}}(x) = \int_{u \in [\underline{\mu}_{\tilde{A}}(x), \overline{\mu}_{\tilde{A}}(x)]} f_x(u)/u \tag{3-16}$$

In the special but important case when the secondary membership functions are interval sets, then (3-15) simplifies to

$$\tilde{A} = \int_{x \in X} \left[\int_{u \in J_x} 1/u \right]/x = \int_{x \in X} \left[\int_{u \in [\underline{\mu}_{\tilde{A}}(x), \overline{\mu}_{\tilde{A}}(x)]} 1/u \right]/x \tag{3-17}$$

We will make great use of upper and lower membership functions in Chapters 10–14.

Example 3-13: Gaussian primary MF with uncertain mean

For the Gaussian primary membership function with uncertain mean (Figure 3-8), the upper membership function, $\overline{\mu}_{\tilde{A}}(x)$, is

$$\overline{\mu}_{\tilde{A}}(x) = \begin{cases} N(m_1, \sigma; x) & x < m_1 \\ 1 & m_1 \leq x \leq m_2 \\ N(m_2, \sigma; x) & x > m_2 \end{cases} \tag{3-18}$$

where, for example, $N(m_1, \sigma; x) \equiv \exp\left[-\frac{1}{2}(x - m_1/\sigma)^2\right]$. The thick solid curve in Figure 3-8 denotes the upper membership function. The lower membership function, $\underline{\mu}_{\tilde{A}}(x)$, is

$$\mu_{\underline{A}}(x) = \begin{cases} N(m_2,\sigma;x) & x \leq \dfrac{m_1+m_2}{2} \\ N(m_1,\sigma;x) & x > \dfrac{m_1+m_2}{2} \end{cases} \qquad (3\text{-}19)$$

The thick dashed curve in Figure 3-8 denotes the lower membership function. We use the results of this example later in Chapters 10–14. ∎

From this example we see that sometimes an upper (or a lower) membership function cannot be represented by just one mathematical function over its entire x-domain. It may consist of several branches each defined over a different segment of the entire x-domain. When the input, x, is located in a specific x-domain segment, we call its corresponding membership function branch an *active branch* [Liang and Mendel (2000a)]; e.g., in (3-19), when $x > (m_1+m_2)/2$, the active branch for $\mu_{\underline{A}}(x)$ is $N(m_1,\sigma;x)$. Some upper and lower membership functions can be represented by one function, as illustrated by the next:

Example 3-14: Gaussian primary MF with uncertain standard deviation

For the Gaussian primary membership function with uncertain standard deviation (Figure 3-9), the upper membership function, $\overline{\mu}_{\tilde{A}}(x)$, is

$$\overline{\mu}_{\tilde{A}}(x) = N(m,\sigma_2;x) \qquad (3\text{-}20)$$

and the lower membership function, $\underline{\mu}_{\tilde{A}}(x)$, is

$$\underline{\mu}_{\tilde{A}}(x) = N(m,\sigma_1;x) \qquad (3\text{-}21)$$

The thick solid curve in Figure 3-9 denotes the upper membership function, and the thick dashed curve in Figure 3-9 denotes the lower membership function. Note that the upper and lower membership functions are simpler for this example than for the preceding one. ∎

These two examples illustrate how to define the upper and lower membership functions so that it is clear how to define them for other situations.

When an upper (or lower) membership function is represented in different segments by different branches, its left-hand and right-hand derivatives at the segment end-point [e.g., $x = (m_1+m_2)/2$ for $\underline{\mu}_{\tilde{A}}(x)$ in (3-19)] may not be equal, so the upper (or lower) membership function may not be differentiable at all points. However, it is piece-wise differentiable, i.e., each branch is differentiable over its segment domain. This fact will be used by us in Chapters 10–14 when we tune the parameters of different type-2 FLSs using a steepest descent algorithm.

Example 3-15: Derivatives of Gaussian primary MF with uncertain mean

Because we will make heavy use of the derivatives of upper and lower membership functions with respect to their parameters in later chapters, we collect these results here. From (3-18) and (3-19), it follows that (Exercise 3-8):

$$
\frac{\partial \bar{\mu}_{\tilde{A}}(x)}{\partial m_1} = \begin{cases} \partial N(m_1, \sigma; x)/\partial m_1 \\ 0 \\ 0 \end{cases} = \begin{cases} (x - m_1)N(m_1, \sigma; x)/\sigma^2 & x < m_1 \\ 0 & m_1 \le x \le m_2 \\ 0 & x > m_2 \end{cases} \tag{3-22}
$$

$$
\frac{\partial \bar{\mu}_{\tilde{A}}(x)}{\partial m_2} = \begin{cases} 0 \\ 0 \\ \partial N(m_2, \sigma; x)/\partial m_2 \end{cases} = \begin{cases} 0 & x < m_1 \\ 0 & m_1 \le x \le m_2 \\ (x - m_2)N(m_2, \sigma; x)/\sigma^2 & x > m_2 \end{cases} \tag{3-23}
$$

$$
\frac{\partial \bar{\mu}_{\tilde{A}}(x)}{\partial \sigma} = \begin{cases} \partial N(m_1, \sigma; x)/\partial \sigma \\ 0 \\ \partial N(m_2, \sigma; x)/\partial \sigma \end{cases} = \begin{cases} (x - m_1)^2 N(m_1, \sigma; x)/\sigma^3 & x < m_1 \\ 0 & m_1 \le x \le m_2 \\ (x - m_2)^2 N(m_2, \sigma; x)/\sigma^3 & x > m_2 \end{cases} \tag{3-24}
$$

$$
\frac{\partial \underline{\mu}_{\tilde{A}}(x)}{\partial m_1} = \begin{cases} 0 \\ \partial N(m_1, \sigma; x)/\partial m_1 \end{cases} = \begin{cases} 0 & x \le \dfrac{m_1 + m_2}{2} \\ (x - m_1)N(m_1, \sigma; x)/\sigma^2 & x > \dfrac{m_1 + m_2}{2} \end{cases} \tag{3-25}
$$

$$
\frac{\partial \underline{\mu}_{\tilde{A}}(x)}{\partial m_2} = \begin{cases} \partial N(m_2, \sigma; x)/\partial m_2 \\ 0 \end{cases} = \begin{cases} (x - m_2)N(m_2, \sigma; x)/\sigma^2 & x \le \dfrac{m_1 + m_2}{2} \\ 0 & x > \dfrac{m_1 + m_2}{2} \end{cases} \tag{3-26}
$$

$$\frac{\partial \mu_{\underline{\tilde{A}}}(x)}{\partial \sigma} = \begin{cases} \partial N(m_2, \sigma; x)/\partial \sigma \\ \partial N(m_1, \sigma; x)/\partial \sigma \end{cases} = \begin{cases} (x - m_2)^2 N(m_2, \sigma; x)/\sigma^3 & x \le \dfrac{m_1 + m_2}{2} \\ (x - m_1)^2 N(m_1, \sigma; x)/\sigma^3 & x > \dfrac{m_1 + m_2}{2} \end{cases} \qquad (3\text{-}27)$$

The important points to remember from these calculations are that, for a Gaussian primary membership function with uncertain mean, we must be very careful to use the correct values for the derivatives of the upper and lower membership functions with respect to their parameters, and these derivatives depend on where the independent variable x is in relation to the means of the left- and right-hand Gaussians, i.e., which branch is active. ∎

Example 3-16: Derivatives of Gaussian primary MF with uncertain standard deviation

Because the upper and lower membership functions in this case can each be represented by one function, they are differentiable over their entire domain, i.e.,

$$\frac{\partial \overline{\mu}_{\tilde{A}}(x)}{\partial m} = \partial N(m, \sigma_2; x)/\partial m = (x - m)N(m, \sigma_2; x)/\sigma_2^2 \qquad (3\text{-}28)$$

$$\frac{\partial \overline{\mu}_{\tilde{A}}(x)}{\partial \sigma_2} = \partial N(m, \sigma_2; x)/\partial \sigma_2 = (x - m)^2 N(m, \sigma_2; x)/\sigma_2^3 \qquad (3\text{-}29)$$

$$\frac{\partial \mu_{\underline{\tilde{A}}}(x)}{\partial m} = \partial N(m, \sigma_1; x)/\partial m = (x - m)N(m, \sigma_1; x)/\sigma_1^2 \qquad (3\text{-}30)$$

$$\frac{\partial \mu_{\underline{\tilde{A}}}(x)}{\partial \sigma_1} = \partial N(m, \sigma_1; x)/\partial \sigma_1 = (x - m)^2 N(m, \sigma_1; x)/\sigma_1^3 \qquad (3\text{-}31)$$

These derivatives are much simpler to compute than those for a Gaussian primary membership function with uncertain mean; however, this fact should not be the deciding point as to which kind of type-2 membership function should be used in a specific application. An understanding about the nature of the application's uncertainties should always be the driving force behind this decision. ∎

Finally, note that when $\mu_{\underline{\tilde{A}}}(x) = \overline{\mu}_{\tilde{A}}(x)$ all sources of uncertainty disappear, and in this case a type-2 membership function reduces to a type-1 membership function, i.e.,

$$\mu_{\tilde{A}}(x)\Big|_{\underline{\mu}_{\tilde{A}}(x)=\bar{\mu}_{\tilde{A}}(x)} \to \mu_A(x) \qquad (3\text{-}32)$$

3.3.5 Embedded type-2 and type-1 sets

A type-2 fuzzy set $\tilde{A}$ can be thought of as a collection of type-2 fuzzy sets $\tilde{A}_e$, that we call *embedded type-2 sets* in $\tilde{A}$.

Definition 3-9: *For continuous universes of discourse X and U, an* embedded type-2 set $\tilde{A}_e$ *is*

$$\tilde{A}_e = \int_{x \in X} \left[f_x(\theta)/\theta \right] \big/ x \qquad \theta \in J_x \subseteq U = [0,1] \qquad (3\text{-}33)$$

Set $\tilde{A}_e$ is embedded in set $\tilde{A}$, and there are an uncountable number of embedded type-2 sets. ■

At each value of x the membership function of $\tilde{A}_e$ has only one primary membership, namely θ, where $\theta \in J_x$, and an associated secondary grade $f_x(\theta)$. A plot of the membership function of $\tilde{A}_e$ would look like a three-dimensional (3D) wavy sheet (a foil). The uncountable number of $\tilde{A}_e$ is due to the continuous natures of X and U. Figure 3-10 shows an example of an embedded type-2 set for an interval type-2 set. Another example of an embedded type-2 set is the principal membership function along with its secondary grades of unity, e.g., Figure 3-4(a).

When we compute using type-2 fuzzy sets, we always discretize X and U, as in (3-7), in which case there are a finite number of embedded type-2 sets.

Definition 3-10: *For discrete universes of discourse X and U, an* embedded type-2 set $\tilde{A}_e$ *has N elements, where $\tilde{A}_e$ contains exactly one element from $J_{x_1}, J_{x_2}, ..., J_{x_N}$, namely $\theta_1, \theta_2, ..., \theta_N$, each with its associated secondary grade, namely $f_{x_1}(\theta_1), f_{x_2}(\theta_2), ..., f_{x_N}(\theta_N)$, i.e.,*

$$\tilde{A}_e = \sum_{i=1}^{N} \left[f_{x_i}(\theta_i)/\theta_i \right] \big/ x_i \qquad \theta_i \in J_{x_i} \subseteq U = [0,1] \qquad (3\text{-}34)$$

Set $\tilde{A}_e$ is embedded in $\tilde{A}$, and, there are a total of $\prod_{i=1}^{N} M_i$ $\tilde{A}_e$. ∎

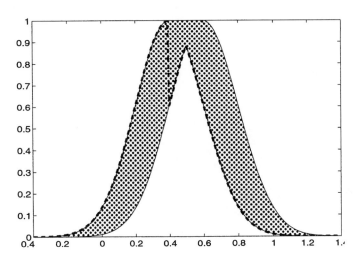

Figure 3-10: Example of an embedded type-1 set (thick dashed line) in a type-2 fuzzy set.

Example 3-17: Figure 3-11 shows two of the possible 450 embedded type-2 sets for the type-2 membership function that is depicted in Figure 3-3. ∎

Associated with each $\tilde{A}_e$ is an embedded type-1 set A_e.

Definition 3-11: *For continuous universes of discourse X and U, an embedded type-1 set A_e is*

$$A_e = \int_{x \in X} \theta/x \qquad \theta \in J_x \subseteq U = [0,1] \tag{3-35}$$

Set A_e is the union of all the primary memberships of set $\tilde{A}_e$ in (3-33), and there are an uncountable number of A_e. ∎

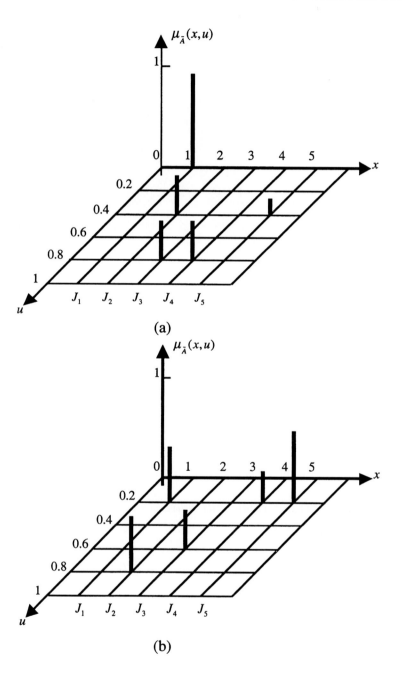

Figure 3-11: Examples of embedded type-2 sets, each associated with the type-2 membership function depicted in Figure 3-3.

Definition 3-12: *For discrete universes of discourse X and U, an embed-ded type-1 set A_e has N elements, one each from $J_{x_1}, J_{x_2}, ..., J_{x_N}$, namely $\theta_1, \theta_2, ..., \theta_N$, i.e.,*

$$A_e = \sum_{i=1}^{N} \theta_i / x_i \quad \theta_i \in J_{x_i} \subseteq U = [0,1] \tag{3-36}$$

Set A_e is the union of all the primary memberships of set $\tilde{A}_e$ in (3-34), and there are a total of $\prod_{i=1}^{N} M_i$ A_e. ∎

Example 3-18: For the two embedded type-2 sets that are depicted in Figure 3-11, their associated embedded type-1 sets are $0/1 + 0.4/2 + 0.8/3 + 0.8/4 + 0.4/5$ and $0.2/1 + 0.8/2 + 0.6/3 + 0.2/4 + 0.2/5$. ∎

Note that a primary membership function, as defined in Definition 3-7, is also an embedded type-1 membership function.

We will use the concepts of embedded type-2 and type-1 sets in Chapters 9 and 10.

So that we can see the forest from the trees, Table 3-1 summarizes the new type-2 fuzzy set terminology and where each term is defined. This new termi-nology is the basis for effective communication about type-2 fuzzy sets and is used throughout the rest of this book.

Table 3-1: Terminology for type-2 fuzzy sets.

Term	Defined in Definition #
Embedded type-1 set	3-11 and 3-12
Embedded type-2 set	3-9 and 3-10
Footprint of uncertainty	3-6
Primary membership	3-3
Primary membership function	3-7
Principal membership function	3-5
Secondary grade	3-4
Secondary membership function	3-2
Secondary set	3-2
Type-2 fuzzy set	3-1
Type-2 membership function	3-1
Upper/lower membership function	3-8

3.3.6 Type-1 fuzzy sets represented as type-2 fuzzy sets

A type-1 fuzzy set can also be expressed as a type-2 fuzzy set. Its type-2 representation is $(1/\mu_F(x))/x$ or $1/\mu_F(x)$, $\forall x \in X$, for short. The notation $1/\mu_F(x)$ means that the secondary membership function has only one value in its domain, namely the primary membership $\mu_F(x)$, at which the secondary grade equals 1.

3.3.7 Zero and one memberships in a type-2 fuzzy set

An element $x = x'$ is said [Mizumoto and Tanaka (1976)] to have a zero membership in a type-2 set if it has a secondary grade equal to 1 corresponding to the primary membership of 0, and if it has all other secondary grades equal to 0. Such a 0 membership is denoted 1/0. Similarly, an element $x = x'$ is said to have a membership of one in a type-2 set if it has a secondary grade equal to 1 corresponding to the primary membership of 1, and, if it has all other secondary grades equal to 0. Such a membership is denoted 1/1.

3.4 RETURNING TO LINGUISTIC LABELS

Sometimes it is necessary to go from membership function numerical values for a variable to a linguistic description of that variable. How to do this for type-1 fuzzy sets is well known; however, how to do this for type-2 fuzzy sets is not so well known. In this section we examine how to do this for both type-1 and type-2 fuzzy sets.

Consider, for example, the type-1 situation depicted in Figure 3-12 (which is a portion of Figure 3-1) at $x = x'$. This value of x only generates a non-zero membership value in the fuzzy set $F_4 =$ *Medium Positive*; hence, $x = x'$ can be described linguistically, without any ambiguity, as "Medium Positive." The situation at $x = x''$ is different, because this value of x generates a non-zero membership value in two fuzzy sets $F_4 =$ *Medium Positive* and $F_5 =$ *Very Positive*. It would be very awkward to speak of x'' as "being Medium Positive to degree $\mu_{F_4}(x'')$ and Very Positive to degree $\mu_{F_5}(x'')$." People just don't communicate this way. Instead, we usually compare $\mu_{F_4}(x'')$ and $\mu_{F_5}(x'')$ to see which is larger, and then assign x'' to the set associated with the larger value; hence, in this example, we would speak of x'' as "being Medium Positive."

We can formally describe what we have just explained, as follows. Given P fuzzy sets F_i with membership functions $\mu_{F_i}(x)$, $i = 1, ..., P$. When $x = x'$, evaluate all P membership functions at this point, and then compute $\max[\mu_{F_1}(x'), \mu_{F_2}(x'), ..., \mu_{F_P}(x')] \equiv \mu_{F_m}(x')$. Let $L(x')$ denote the linguistic label associated with x'. Then, $L(x') \equiv F_m$, i.e.,

$$L(x') = \arg \max_{\forall F_i}\left[\mu_{F_1}(x'), \mu_{F_2}(x'), ..., \mu_{F_P}(x')\right] \qquad (3\text{-}37)$$

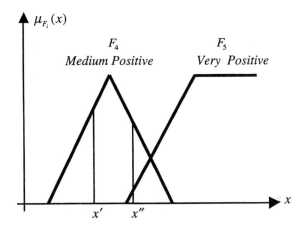

Figure 3-12: Returning to a linguistic label for type-1 fuzzy sets.

Next, consider the type-2 situation depicted in Figure 3-13 (which is a portion of Figure 3-6) at $x = x'$. This value of x again only generates a non-zero membership in the now type-2 fuzzy set $\tilde{F}_4 = $ *Medium Positive*; hence, $x = x'$ can again be described linguistically, without any ambiguity, as "Medium Positive." The situation at $x = x''$ is quite different, because this value of x generates a range of non-zero secondary membership function values in the two type-2 fuzzy sets $\tilde{F}_4 = $ *Medium Positive* and $\tilde{F}_5 = $ *Very Positive*. It would be extraordinarily difficult to communicate this linguistically. One approach, which we describe next, is to first convert the intersection of the vertical line at $x = x''$ with the FOUs into a collection of numbers, after which we can choose the linguistic label at $x = x''$ using an algorithm similar to that in (3-37).

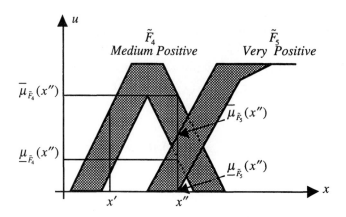

Figure 3-13: Returning to a linguistic label
for type-2 fuzzy sets.

Type-2 membership functions $\mu_{\tilde{F}_4}(x,u)$ and $\mu_{\tilde{F}_5}(x,u)$ are characterized by their FOUs, $FOU(\tilde{F}_4)$ and $FOU(\tilde{F}_5)$, respectively. The upper and lower membership functions for $\tilde{F}_4$ are $\overline{\mu}_{\tilde{F}_4}(x)$ and $\underline{\mu}_{\tilde{F}_4}(x)$, whereas the comparable quantities for $\tilde{F}_5$ are $\overline{\mu}_{\tilde{F}_5}(x)$ and $\underline{\mu}_{\tilde{F}_5}(x)$. Consider, for example, the vertical line at $x = x''$, and its intersections with the FOU for $\tilde{F}_4$ (see Figure 3-13). Associated with the interval $\left[\underline{\mu}_{\tilde{F}_4}(x''), \overline{\mu}_{\tilde{F}_4}(x'')\right]$ is the secondary membership function, $f_{x''}(u)$, $u \in \left[\underline{\mu}_{\tilde{F}_4}(x''), \overline{\mu}_{\tilde{F}_4}(x'')\right]$. Let the center of gravity of $f_{x''}(u)$, $\forall u \in \left[\underline{\mu}_{\tilde{F}_4}(x''), \overline{\mu}_{\tilde{F}_4}(x'')\right]$ be denoted $f_{x''}^{cg}(\tilde{F}_4)$. In a similar manner, we can compute $f_{x''}^{cg}(\tilde{F}_5)$. We can then compare[3] $f_{x''}^{cg}(\tilde{F}_4)$ and $f_{x''}^{cg}(\tilde{F}_5)$. If $f_{x''}^{cg}(\tilde{F}_4) > f_{x''}^{cg}(\tilde{F}_5)$, then we would speak of x'' as "being Medium Positive"; otherwise we would speak of x'' as "being Very Positive."

Again, we can formally describe what we have just explained as follows. Given P type-2 fuzzy sets $\tilde{F}_i$ with membership functions $\mu_{\tilde{F}_i}(x,u)$, $i = 1, \ldots, P$. These membership functions are characterized by their FOUs, $FOU(\tilde{F}_i)$, whose upper and lower membership functions, are $\overline{\mu}_{\tilde{F}_i}(x)$ and $\underline{\mu}_{\tilde{F}_i}(x)$ $(i = 1, \ldots, P)$, re-

---

[3]No doubt, other operators than the center of gravity can be used.

spectively. Consider an arbitrary value of x, say $x = x'$, and compute $\max\left[f_{x'}^{cg}(\tilde{F}_1), f_{x'}^{cg}(\tilde{F}_2), \ldots, f_{x'}^{cg}(\tilde{F}_p)\right] \equiv f_{x'}^{cg}(\tilde{F}_m)$, where $f_{x'}^{cg}(\tilde{F}_i)$ is the center of gravity of the secondary membership function $f_{x'}(u), \forall u \in \left[\underline{\mu}_{\tilde{F}_i}(x'), \overline{\mu}_{\tilde{F}_i}(x')\right]$. Again, let $L(x')$ denote the linguistic label associated with x'. Then, $L(x') \equiv \tilde{F}_m$, i.e.,

$$L(x') = \arg\ \max_{\forall \tilde{F}_i}\ \left[f_{x'}^{cg}(\tilde{F}_1), f_{x'}^{cg}(\tilde{F}_2), \ldots, f_{x'}^{cg}(\tilde{F}_p)\right] \tag{3-38}$$

Example 3-19: For interval secondary membership functions, it is easy to compute $f_{x'}^{cg}(\tilde{F}_i)$, as

$$f_{x'}^{cg}(\tilde{F}_i) = \tfrac{1}{2}\left[\overline{\mu}_{\tilde{F}_i}(x') + \underline{\mu}_{\tilde{F}_i}(x')\right] \tag{3-39}$$

For non-interval secondary membership functions, the computations of the $f_{x'}^{cg}(\tilde{F}_i)$ will be more complicated, and will, most likely, have to be done numerically. ∎

Note that when type-2 fuzzy sets reduce to type-1 fuzzy sets, i.e., when $\overline{\mu}_{\tilde{F}_i}(x') = \underline{\mu}_{\tilde{F}_i}(x')$, then (3-38) reduces to (3-37). This is consistent with our basic design requirement that, when all uncertainties disappear, type-2 results must reduce to their well-established type-1 results.

3.5 MULTIVARIABLE MEMBERSHIP FUNCTIONS

All of our discussions in this chapter, so far, have been for fuzzy sets that depend on only one variable. In this section, we describe how to characterize fuzzy sets that depend on up to p variables, $x_1, x_2, \ldots, x_p$

3.5.1 Type-1 membership functions

For two variables, x_1 and x_2, type-1 fuzzy set A_x is defined on the Cartesian product[4] $X_1 \times X_2$, i.e.,

---

[4] Recall that the Cartesian product of two non-fuzzy sets X_1 and X_2, denoted $X_1 \times X_2$, is the non-fuzzy set of all ordered 2-tuples (x_1, x_2) such that $x_1 \in X_1$ and $x_2 \in X_2$, i.e., $X_1 \times X_2 = \left\{(x_1, x_2) \mid x_1 \in X_1, x_2 \in X_2\right\}$.

$$A_{\mathbf{x}} = \left\{ \left((x_1, x_2), \mu_{A_{\mathbf{x}}}(x_1, x_2) \right) \middle| x_1 \in X_1, x_2 \in X_2 \right\} = \left\{ \left(\mathbf{x}, \mu_{A_{\mathbf{x}}}(\mathbf{x}) \right) \middle| \mathbf{x} \in X_1 \times X_2 \right\} \quad (3\text{-}40)$$

where $\mu_{A_{\mathbf{x}}}(x_1, x_2)$ is a general function of x_1 and x_2. When $X_1 \times X_2$ is continuous, then $A_{\mathbf{x}}$ can also be written as

$$A_{\mathbf{x}} = \int_{x_1 \in X_1} \int_{x_2 \in X_2} \mu_{A_{\mathbf{x}}}(x_1, x_2) / (x_1, x_2) \quad (3\text{-}41)$$

or, if $X_1 \times X_2$ is discrete, then $A_{\mathbf{x}}$ can be written as

$$A_{\mathbf{x}} = \sum_{x_1 \in X_1} \sum_{x_2 \in X_2} \mu_{A_{\mathbf{x}}}(x_1, x_2) / (x_1, x_2) \quad (3\text{-}42)$$

When the membership function $\mu_{A_{\mathbf{x}}}(x_1, x_2)$ is *separable*, then it is expressed in terms of $\mu_{A_{x_1}}(x_1)$ and $\mu_{A_{x_2}}(x_2)$, as

$$\mu_{A_{\mathbf{x}}}(x_1, x_2) = \mu_{A_{x_1}}(x_1) \star \mu_{A_{x_2}}(x_2) \quad (3\text{-}43)$$

where $\star$ denotes a t-norm such as minimum or product. In this book we only use separable membership functions.[5]

The extensions of these two-variable results to more than two variables is straightforward, e.g., for p variables, when the membership function $\mu_{A_{\mathbf{x}}}(x_1, x_2, ..., x_p)$ is separable, then

$$\mu_{A_{\mathbf{x}}}(\mathbf{x}) = \mu_{A_{x_1}}(x_1) \star \mu_{A_{x_2}}(x_2) \star \cdots \star \mu_{A_{x_p}}(x_p) \quad (3\text{-}44)$$

which we frequently write as[6]

$$\mu_{A_{\mathbf{x}}}(\mathbf{x}) = \mu_{X_1}(x_1) \star \mu_{X_2}(x_2) \star \cdots \star \mu_{X_p}(x_p) \quad (3\text{-}45)$$

Using the notation of (3-45), X_i plays a double role as the label of the fuzzy set and as the universe of discourse for x_i. Usually, this does not cause any confusion. Equation (3-45) is widely used in Chapters 5 and 6.

---

[5] See Exercise 3-11 for a situation where a non-separable type-1 membership function of two variables can be treated as two *type-2* membership functions.

[6] See, also, Section 8.6 for an interpretation of (3-44) as a Cartesian product of the type-1 fuzzy sets A_{x_1}, A_{x_2}, ..., A_{x_p}.

3.5.2 Type-2 membership functions

Next let us extend some of these notions to a type-2 fuzzy set, $\tilde{A}_\mathbf{x}$, that is in terms of two variables, x_1 and x_2, where $\mathbf{x} = (x_1, x_2)^T$. When $X_1 \times X_2$ is continuous, then using the first part of (3-6) $\tilde{A}_\mathbf{x}$ can be expressed as

$$\tilde{A}_\mathbf{x} = \int_{x_1 \in X_1} \int_{x_2 \in X_2} \mu_{\tilde{A}_\mathbf{x}}(x_1, x_2) / (x_1, x_2) \tag{3-46}$$

When the secondary membership function $\mu_{\tilde{A}_\mathbf{x}}(x_1, x_2)$ is *separable*, then it can be expressed in terms of $\mu_{\tilde{A}_{x_1}}(x_1)$ and $\mu_{\tilde{A}_{x_2}}(x_2)$, as

$$\mu_{\tilde{A}_\mathbf{x}}(x_1, x_2) = \mu_{\tilde{A}_{x_1}}(x_1) \sqcap \mu_{\tilde{A}_{x_2}}(x_2) \tag{3-47}$$

where $\sqcap$ denotes the meet operation which is associated with computing the intersection of type-2 fuzzy sets, and is discussed in great detail in Chapter 7.

The extensions of these two-variable results to more than two variables is straightforward, e.g., for p variables,

$$\mu_{\tilde{A}_\mathbf{x}}(\mathbf{x}) = \mu_{\tilde{A}_{x_1}}(x_1) \sqcap \mu_{\tilde{A}_{x_2}}(x_2) \sqcap \cdots \sqcap \mu_{\tilde{A}_{x_p}}(x_p) \tag{3-48}$$

which we frequently write as[7]

$$\mu_{\tilde{A}_\mathbf{x}}(\mathbf{x}) = \mu_{\tilde{X}_1}(x_1) \sqcap \mu_{\tilde{X}_2}(x_2) \sqcap \cdots \sqcap \mu_{\tilde{X}_p}(x_p) \tag{3-49}$$

where $\mathbf{x} = (x_1, x_2, ..., x_p)^T$. Note that (3-48) and (3-49) are the generalizations of (3-44) and (3-45), respectively, to type-2 fuzzy sets, and are widely used in Chapters 10-13.

3.6 COMPUTATION

The following M-file, which is found in the folder *interval type-2 fuzzy logic systems*, is useful for making 2-D plots of interval type-2 membership functions:

---

[7]See, also, Section 8.6 for an interpretation of (3-48) as a Cartesian product of the type-2 fuzzy sets $\tilde{A}_{x_1}$, $\tilde{A}_{x_2}$,..., $\tilde{A}_{x_p}$.

plot2d1.m: Function to plot 2-D representation of the FOU of an interval type-2 fuzzy set (e.g., Figure 3-8). The area between the upper and lower membership functions is shaded uniformly to indicate that all the secondary grades are unity.

EXERCISES

3-1: Express $\tilde{A}$ in Example 3-1 as in (3-7), being sure to establish numerical values for M_1, ..., M_5.

3-2: Determine the FOU for a triangular membership function (see Figure 3-7) when $b - \sigma_b < a + \sigma_a$.

3-3: Determine the FOU when *center location* and *interval length* information are requested for a phrase. Consider the two cases, when: (a) uncertainty interval for the center location does not overlap with the uncertainty intervals for the interval end-points; and (b) uncertainty interval for the center location overlaps with the uncertainty intervals for the interval end-points.

3-4: Develop some FOUs for a trapezoidal membership function.

3-5: Determine the FOU for a Gaussian primary membership function with uncertain mean *and* standard deviation.

3-6: Sketch the FOU for

$$x \in \left\{ s \exp\left\{ -\tfrac{1}{2}\left(\frac{x-m}{\sigma} \right)^2 \right\}, \exp\left\{ -\tfrac{1}{2}\left(\frac{x-m}{\sigma} \right)^2 \right\} \right\}$$

when $0 < s < 1$.

3-7: Consider the combined case of Examples 3-10 and 3-11 (Exercise 3-5), i.e., a Gaussian primary membership function with uncertain mean *and* standard deviation. Determine expressions for the upper and lower membership functions for this case.

3-8: For Example 3-15, show that

$$\partial N(m_1, \sigma; x) / \partial m_1 = (x - m_1) N(m_1, \sigma; x) / \sigma^2$$

and

$$\partial N(m_1,\sigma;x)/\partial\sigma = (x-m_1)^2 N(m_1,\sigma;x)/\sigma^3 .$$

3-9: (a) Sketch five more embedded type-2 sets for the type-2 membership function that is depicted in Figure 3-3. (b) For the five sets in part (a), enumerate their embedded type-1 sets.

3-10: Sketch four embedded type-2 sets for the type-2 membership function that is depicted in Figure 3-9.

3-11: Some people prefer to initially think in terms of a *non-separable* 2D type-1 membership function (obtained, perhaps, as a result of a clustering procedure); but, they then create rules using the projections of those membership functions onto each of its axes. There are uncertainties about the parameters of the 2D membership function, just as there are uncertainties about the parameters of a 1D membership function. For example, if the 2D membership function is a 2D Gaussian, then there can be uncertainty about its orientation in the 2D space of its two variables. (a) Show that the projections of an uncertain *non-separable* 2D type-1 membership function onto the axes of the two variables can be handled by working with a type-2 membership function for each of the variables that is of the kind in Example 3-11. (b) Doesn't this mean that the use of a non-separable 2D type-1 membership function as described earlier can be replaced at the onset by type-2 membership functions for each of the two variables?

3-12: (a) What is the counterpart to (3-40) for a non-separable type-2 fuzzy set $\tilde{A}_x$, where $\mathbf{x} = (x_1, x_2)^T$? (b) What is the counterpart to (3-42) in this case? (c) How many dimensions are needed to characterize $\tilde{A}_x$?

CHAPTER 4

Case Studies

4.1 INTRODUCTION

FL has been applied in many fields and to many applications. Frequently, one must already be an expert in a particular field to understand the details of the application. While it is tempting to provide the reader with many diverse applications, to demonstrate the wide-range of applicability for type-2 FLSs, I have chosen not to do this. By now, it is already well established that FL is widely applicable, so I don't need to further demonstrate this. Also, I don't want the reader who is unfamiliar with the details of an application to feel left out. So, I have chosen two applications, which I treat as *case studies*, that I believe can be easily understood by all readers. These applications are used throughout the rest of this book, and are *forecasting of time-series* and *knowledge mining using surveys*. Other applications are described in Chapter 14.

4.2 FORECASTING OF TIME-SERIES

Let $s(k)$ $(k = 1, 2, \ldots, N)$ be a time series, such as daily temperatures of Sante Fe, New Mexico, or hourly measurements of the Dow-Jones stock index. Measured values of $s(k)$ are denoted $x(k)$, where $x(k) = s(k) + n(k)$ and $n(k)$ denotes measurement errors—noise. The problem of forecasting a time-series (i.e., prediction) is:

> Given a window of p past measurements of $s(k)$, namely $x(k - p + 1)$, $x(k - p + 2)$, ..., $x(k)$, determine an estimate of a future value of s, $\hat{s}(k + l)$,

where p and l are fixed positive integers.

Note that if the measurements are noise-free (i.e., perfect), then $x(k-p+1)$, $x(k-p+2)$, ..., $x(k)$ in this problem statement are replaced by $s(k-p+1)$, $s(k-p+2)$, ..., $s(k)$.

Forecasting is a very important problem that appears in many disciplines. Better weather forecasts can, for example, save lives in the event of a catastrophic hurricane; better financial forecasts can improve the return on an investment; etc.

When $l = 1$, we obtain the single-stage forecaster of s, when $l = 2$ we obtain the two-stage forecaster of s, and, in general, for arbitrary values of l, we obtain an l-stage forecaster. For illustrative purposes, we shall focus our attention on the case of $l = 1$.

Suppose that we are given a collection of N data points, $x(1), x(2),...,x(N)$. Then, as is commonly done when neural networks are used to forecast a time-series, we shall partition this data set into two subsets: a *training* data subset with D data points, $x(1), x(2),...,x(D)$, and a *testing* data subset with $N - D$ data points, $x(D+1), x(D+2),...,x(N)$. Because we will use a window of p data points to forecast the next data point, there are at most $D-p$ training pairs, $\mathbf{x}^{(1)}, \mathbf{x}^{(2)},...,\mathbf{x}^{(D-p)}$, where

$$
\begin{aligned}
\mathbf{x}^{(1)} &= [x(1), x(2),...,x(p), x(p+1)]^T \\
\mathbf{x}^{(2)} &= [x(2), x(3),...,x(p+1), x(p+2)]^T \\
&\cdots \\
\mathbf{x}^{(D-p)} &= [x(D-p), x(D-p+1),...,x(D-1), x(D)]^T
\end{aligned}
\tag{4-1}
$$

In (4-1), the first p elements of $\mathbf{x}^{(t)}$ are the inputs to the forecaster and the last element of $\mathbf{x}^{(t)}$ is the desired output of the forecaster, i.e.,

$$
\mathbf{x}^{(t)} = [p \times 1 \text{ input, desired output}]^T = [x_1^{(t)}, x_2^{(t)},...,x_p^{(t)}, x_{p+1}^{(t)}]^T
\tag{4-2}
$$

where $t = 1, 2,..., D-p$. The training data are used in a fuzzy logic system (FLS) forecaster to establish its rules.

There are at least three ways to extract rules from the numerical training data:

1. Let the data establish the centers of the fuzzy sets that appear in the antecedents and consequents of the rules.

2. Pre-specify fuzzy sets for the antecedents and consequents and then associate the data with these fuzzy sets.

3. Establish the architecture of a FLS and use the data to optimize its parameters.

We briefly describe these approaches next.

Because a predicted value of s will depend on p past values of x, there will be p antecedents in each rule. Let these p antecedents be denoted $x_1, x_2, ..., x_p$. The interesting feature of time-series forecasting is that, although each rule has p antecedents, these antecedents are all associated with the *same* variable, e.g., daily temperature in Sante Fe, and so is the consequent.

4.2.1 Extracting rules from the data

Method 1: *Let the data establish the centers of the fuzzy sets that appear in the antecedents and consequents of the rules.*

For purposes of single-stage forecasting, here are $D-p$ rules that we can extract from the $D-p$ training pairs, $\mathbf{x}^{(1)}, \mathbf{x}^{(2)}, ..., \mathbf{x}^{(D-p)}$ [Mendel (1995)]:

R^1: IF x_1 is F_1^1 and x_2 is F_2^1 and $\cdots$ and x_p is F_p^1 , THEN y is G^1

In this rule, which is obtained from $\mathbf{x}^{(1)}$, F_1^1 is a fuzzy set whose membership function is centered at $x(1)$, F_2^1 is a fuzzy set whose membership function is centered at $x(2)$, ..., F_p^1 is a fuzzy set whose membership function is centered at $x(p)$, and G^1 is a fuzzy set whose membership function is centered at $x(p + 1)$.

R^2: IF x_1 is F_1^2 and x_2 is F_2^2 and $\cdots$ and x_p is F_p^2 , THEN y is G^2

In this rule, which is obtained from $\mathbf{x}^{(2)}$, F_1^2 is a fuzzy set whose membership function is centered at $x(2)$, F_2^2 is a fuzzy set whose membership function is centered at $x(3)$, ..., F_p^2 is a fuzzy set whose membership function is centered at $x(p + 1)$, and G^2 is a fuzzy set whose membership function is centered at $x(p + 2)$.

• • • • • • • • • •

$$R^{D-p}: \text{ IF } x_1 \text{ is } F_1^{D-p} \text{ and } x_2 \text{ is } F_2^{D-p} \text{ and } \cdots \text{ and } x_p \text{ is } F_p^{D-p}, \text{ THEN } y \text{ is } G^{D-p}$$

In this rule, which is obtained from $\mathbf{x}^{(D-p)}$, F_1^{D-p} is a fuzzy set whose membership function is centered at $x(D - p)$, F_2^{D-p} is a fuzzy set whose membership function is centered at $x(D - p + 1)$, ..., F_p^{D-p} is a fuzzy set whose membership function is centered at $x(D - 1)$, and G^{D-p} is a fuzzy set whose membership function is centered at $x(D)$.

In this first approach to obtaining rules from numerical data, we see that the centers of the antecedent and consequent membership functions are completely determined by the data that are used to create the rules. Usually, all other membership function parameters (e.g., the standard deviation of a Gaussian membership function) are specified ahead of time by the designer.

Method 2: *Pre-specify fuzzy sets for the antecedents and consequents and then associate the data with these fuzzy sets.*

In this second approach ([Wang (1992a, 1994)], [Wang and Mendel (1992c)]), we begin by establishing fuzzy sets for all the antecedents and the consequent. This is done by first establishing domain intervals for all input and output variables. For the example of time-series forecasting, these domain intervals are all the same, because $x_1, x_2, ..., x_p$ and y are all sampled values of the measured time series, $x(k)$ ($k = 1, 2, ...$). Let us assume that, by examining the measured time-series, we establish that $x(k) \in [X^-, X^+]$ for $\forall k$. Next, we divide this domain interval into a pre-specified number of overlapping regions, where the lengths of these overlapping regions can be equal or unequal. Each overlapping region is then labeled and is assigned a membership function. Resolution in forecasting can be controlled by the coarseness of the fuzzy sets that are associated with $x(k)$. Measured values of $x(k)$ are permitted to lie outside of its domain interval, because if $x(k) > X^+$ then $\mu_X(x(k)) = 1$, or if $x(k) < X^-$ then $\mu_X(x(k)) = 0$.

Fuzzy rules are generated from the given data pairs using the following three-step procedure [Wang and Mendel (1992c)]:

1. Determine the degrees (i.e., the membership function values) of the elements of $\mathbf{x}^{(t)}$. As an example, in Figure 4-1 we consider the case when $p = 5$. We see that $x_1^{(t)}$ has degree 0.45 in $B2$ and 0.75 in $B1$, $x_2^{(t)}$ has degree 0.2 in $S1$ and 0.75 in $S2$, $x_3^{(t)}$ has degree 0.45 in $S2$ and 0.6 in $S3$, $x_4^{(t)}$ has degree 0.4 in $S1$ and 0.75 in CE, $x_5^{(t)}$ has degree 1.0 in $S1$ and 0.2 in CE, and $x_6^{(t)}$ has

degree 0.3 in *B3* and 0.6 in *B2*.

2. Assign each variable to the region with maximum degree, e.g., $x_1^{(t)}$ is considered to be *B1*, $x_2^{(t)}$ is considered to be *S2*, $x_3^{(t)}$ is considered to be *S3*, $x_4^{(t)}$ is considered to be *CE*, $x_5^{(t)}$ is considered to be *S1*, and $x_6^{(t)}$ is considered to be *B2*.

3. Obtain one rule from one pair of input–output data, e.g.,

IF $x_1^{(t)}$ is *B1* and $x_2^{(t)}$ is *S2* and $x_3^{(t)}$ is *S3* and $x_4^{(t)}$ is *CE* and $x_5^{(t)}$ is *S1*,

THEN $y^{(t)}$ is *B2*

This three-step procedure is repeated for the *D–p* training pairs in equation (4-1), i.e., $t = 1, ..., D\text{-}p$.

Because there can be lots of data, it is quite likely that there will be some *conflicting rules*, i.e., rules with the same antecedents but different consequents. We resolve this by assigning a degree, $D(R^t)$, to each rule and accept only the rule from a conflict group that has maximum degree, where

$$D(R^t) \equiv \mu_X(x_1^{(t)})\mu_X(x_2^{(t)})\cdots\mu_X(x_p^{(t)})\mu_X(y^{(t)}) ; \qquad (4\text{-}3)$$

hence, there will be *at most D–p* linguistic rules of the form just obtained for $R^{(t)}$ in step 3. For our example, we find, from step 1 of our three-step procedure, that $D(R^j) = 0.75 \times 0.75 \times 0.60 \times 0.75 \times 1.0 \times 0.60 = 0.1519$.

A generalized version of this procedure is described in Chapter 5 as the "one-pass method." By "one-pass" we mean that the data are used just one time to obtain all of the rules. Note that, according to this definition, Method 1 can also be referred to as a one-pass method.

Method 3: *Establish the architecture for a FLS and then use the data to optimize its parameters.*

In this third approach, we fix the architecture of the FLS ahead of time, e.g., we fix the number of rules, the number of rule-antecedents, the shapes of the antecedent and consequent membership functions, the inference method, the t-norm, the kind of fuzzification, and the kind of defuzzifier. The resulting FLS has parameters associated with it that have to be specified. These parameters are optimized by using the data. Sometimes the data are only used one time to do this, in which case even this method could be called "one-pass;" however, many times the data are used multiple times to obtain the best possible performance, in which case this is a multiple-pass method.

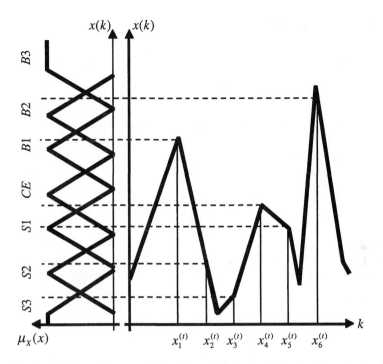

Figure 4-1: Construction to determine degrees of the elements of $\mathbf{x}^{(t)}$ for a representative time-series. The time-series is in the right-hand plot. Membership functions for seven fuzzy sets are in the left-hand plot. Each dashed line projects from a value of the sampled time-series to its intersections with one or two fuzzy sets, which provide the membership function values for that point.

4.2.2 Mackey–Glass chaotic time-series

In the rest of this book (except for Chapters 13 and 14), we shall direct our attention at single-stage forecasting for a specific time-series, one that is chaotic and obtained from the Mackey–Glass equation.

Today, chaos is having an impact on many different fields including physics, biology, chemistry, economics, and medicine (e.g., [Casdagli (1992)], [Farmer (1982)], and [Rasband (1990)]). Very briefly, chaotic behavior can be described as bounded fluctuations of the output of a *non-linear* system with high degree of sensitivity to *initial conditions* [Casdagli (1992)], i.e., trajectories with nearly identical initial conditions can differ a lot from each other. A system exhibiting chaotic dynamics evolves in a *deterministic* manner; however, the correlation of observations from such a system appears to be limited, so the observations appear to be uncorrelated; thus, forecasting for such a system is particularly difficult [Rasband (1990)].

In 1977 Mackey and Glass published an important paper in which they "associate the onset of disease with bifurcations in the dynamics of first-order differential-delay equations which model physiological systems." Equation (4b) of that paper has become known as the *Mackey–Glass equation*. It is a non-linear delay differential equation, one form of which is

$$\frac{ds(t)}{dt} = \frac{0.2s(t-\tau)}{1+s^{10}(t-\tau)} - 0.1s(t) \tag{4-4}$$

For $\tau > 17$ (4-4) is known to exhibit chaos.

To demonstrate the qualitative nature of the Mackey–Glass equation, we display representative portions of the associated Mackey–Glass time series [i.e., the solution of (4-4)] for two values of τ in Figure 4-2 (a) and (b). We also depict the corresponding two-dimensional phase plots in Figure 4-2 (c) and (d). From these plots we are able to distinguish periodic behavior for small values of τ and chaotic behavior for larger values of τ.

The Mackey–Glass time series (for $\tau > 17$) has become one of the benchmark problems for time-series prediction in both the neural network and fuzzy logic fields (e.g., [Lapedus and Farber (1987)], [Moody (1989)], [Moody and Darkin (1989)], [Jones et al. (1990)], [Sanger (1991)], [Wang (1994)], [Hohenson and Mendel (1996)], and [Jang et al. (1997)]).

As we mentioned earlier, all of the single-stage forecasters that we shall design in the rest of this book (except for Chapter 13), using different kinds of FLSs, are based on $D - p$ training pairs. These training pairs are obtained by simulating (4-4) for $\tau = 30$, which we did by converting (4-4) to a discrete-time equation by using Euler's method with a step size equal to 1 [Quinney (1985)]. Because of the 30 time-unit delay, the resulting discrete-time equation requires 31 initial values. These first 31 values of $s(k)$ (i.e., $s(1), s(2), ..., s(31)$) were chosen randomly a number of times until a time series was obtained that looked interesting (see Figure 5-11a). Thereafter, the same 31 initial values were used to produce a deterministic (albeit, chaotic) time series that is used in the forecasting studies that are described in Chapters 5, 6, and 10–12.

One of the important features of time-series forecasting is that it can be used to illustrate *all* of the FLSs that are covered in the rest of this book. Table 4-1 summarizes six situations that are covered in later chapters. These situations are distinguished from one another by the natures of the signal, additive meas-

urement noise, training and testing data, and measurements after the design of
the forecaster is completed.

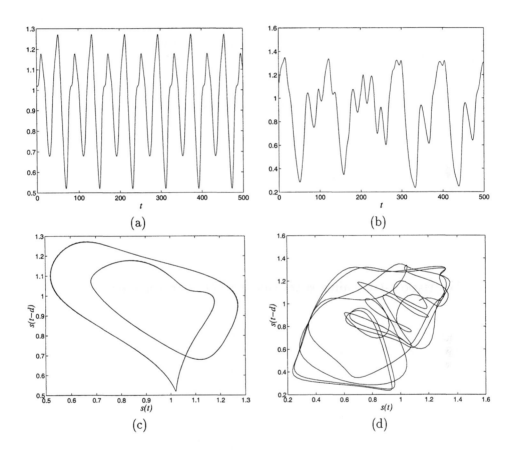

(a)

(b)

(c)

(d)

Figure 4-2: (a) and (b) are representative samples of the Mackey–Glass
time-series after letting transients relax. (c) and (d) are the corresponding
phase plots of the time segments depicted in (a) and (b). Note that "d" in
$s(t-d)$ on the vertical axis denotes the delay used in the Mackey–Glass
equation; it is 13 for (c) and 30 for (d).

Table 4-1: Forecasters covered in later chapters of this book. Measurements = signal + noise.

Name of Forecaster	Chapter	Distinguishing Features			
		Signal	Measurement Noise	Training and Testing Data	Measurements After the Design is Completed
Singleton type-1	5	Deterministic	None	Noise free	Noise free
Non-singleton type-1	6	Deterministic	Stationary	Noisy	Noisy
Singleton type-2	10	Deterministic	Stationary	Noisy	Noise free
Non-singleton type-2 with type-1 inputs	11	Deterministic	Stationary	Noisy	Noisy
Non-singleton type-2 with type-2 inputs	12	Deterministic	Non-stationary	Noisy	Noisy
TSK	13	Random	None	Noise free	Noise free

4.3 KNOWLEDGE MINING USING SURVEYS

Knowledge mining,[1] as used in this book, means extracting information in the form of IF–THEN rules from people. These rules can be modeled using a FLS, which can then be used as a fuzzy logic advisor (FLA) to make decisions or judgments. By "judgment" we mean an assessment of the *level* of a variable of interest. For example, in everyday social interaction, each of us is called upon to make judgments about the meaning of another's behavior (e.g., kindness, generosity, flirtation, harassment). Such judgments are far from trivial, since they often affect the nature and direction of the subsequent social interaction and communications. Although a variety of factors may enter into our decision, behavior (e.g., touching, eye contact) is apt to play a critical role in assessing the level of the variable of interest.

As an engineering example, consider one of the traffic control functions for an asynchronous transfer mode network, called *connection admission control* (CAC).[2] CAC decides whether to accept or reject a telephone call based on the availability of network capacity required to support its quality of service. Here the judgment is associated with the variable CAC. For example, if the total

---

[1] Another term for this is *knowledge engineering*.
[2] CAC is described in more detail in Section 14.7.

average input rate of real-time voice and video traffic is moderately high and the total average input rate of non-real-time data traffic (e.g., fax) is low, then the confidence of accepting a call is a moderate amount.

4.3.1 Methodology for knowledge mining

In developing a FLA for engineering or social variables, it is useful to adopt the following methodology [Mendel et al. (1999)]:

1. *Identify the behavior of interest.* This step, although obvious, is highly application dependent. For social judgments, we have already mentioned the behaviors of kindness, generosity, flirtation, and harassment; other social variables of interest might be level of violence or amount of sexually explicit material in a television program (leading to, perhaps, a FL V-chip). For engineering judgments, we have mentioned connection admission control; other engineering variables of interest might include toxicity, video quality, sound quality, environmental contamination level, etc.

2. *Determine the indicators of the behavior of interest.* This sometimes requires:

   a. Establishing a list of candidate indicators (e.g., for flirtation [Mendel et al. (1999)], six candidate indicators are touching, eye contact, acting witty, primping, smiling, and complementing).

   b. Conducting a survey in which a representative population is asked to rank-order in importance the indicators on the list of candidate indicators. In some applications it may already be known what the relative importance of the indicators is, in which case a survey is not necessary.

   c. Choosing a meaningful subset of the indicators, because not all of them may be important. In Step 6, where people are asked to provide consequents for a collection of IF–THEN rules by means of a survey, the survey must be kept manageable, because most people do not like to answer lots of questions; hence, it is very important to focus on the truly significant indicators. Factor analysis, from statistics, can be used to help establish the relative significance of indicators.

3. *Establish scales for each indicator and the behavior of interest.* If an indicator is a physically measurable quantity (e.g., temperature, pressure), then the scale is associated with the expected range between the minimum and maximum values for that quantity. On the other hand, many indicators are not measurable by means of instrumentation (e.g., touching, flirtation, harassment, video quality, etc.). Such indicators need to have a scale associated with them, or else it will not be possible to design or activate a FLA. Commonly used scales are 1 through 5, 0 through 5, 0 through 10, etc.

4. *Establish names and interval information for each of the indicator's fuzzy sets and behavior of interest's fuzzy sets.* The issues here are:

   a. What names should be used for the fuzzy sets so that each indicator's scale and the behavior of interest's scale are completely covered by the fuzzy sets?

   b. What are the numerical intervals that a representative group (who will later take the survey in Step 6) associate with the named fuzzy sets?

   c. What is the smallest number of fuzzy sets that should be used for each indicator and behavior of interest?

Surveys can be used to provide answers to each of these questions. We have already demonstrated in Chapter 2 that words can mean different things to different people; hence, the results of this step's surveys can be used to provide the FOUs for all of the fuzzy sets that will be used in the FLA.

5. *Establish the rules.* Rules are the heart of the FLA; they link the indicators of a behavior of interest to that behavior. The following issues need to be addressed:

   a. How many antecedents will the rules have? As mentioned earlier, people generally do not like to answer complicated questions; so, we advocate using rules that have either one or two antecedents. An interesting (non-engineering) interpretation for a two-antecedent rule is that it provides the correlation effect that exists in the mind of the survey respondent between the two antecedents. Using only one or two antecedents does not mean that a person does not use more than this number of indicators to make a judgment; it means that a person uses the indicators one or two at a time (this should be viewed as a *conjecture*).

   b. How many rule bases need to be established? Each rule base leads to its own FLA. When there is more than one rule base, each of the advisors is a FL *sub-advisor*, and the outputs of these sub-advisors can be combined to create the structure of the overall FLA. If, e.g., we had established that four indicators were equally important for the judgment of flirtation, then there could be up to four single-antecedent rule bases as well as six two-antecedent rule bases. A decision must be made about which of the rule bases would actually be used. This can be done by means of another survey in which the respondents are asked to rank-order the rule bases in order of importance. Later, when (and if) the outputs of the different rule bases are combined, they can be weighted using the results of this step.

6. *Survey people (experts) to provide consequents for the rules.* If, e.g., a single antecedent has five fuzzy sets associated with it, then respondents would be asked five questions. For two-antecedent rules, where each antecedent is again described by five fuzzy sets, there would be 25 questions. The order of the questions should be randomized so that respondents don't correlate their answers from one question to the next. In Step 4 earlier, the names of the consequent fuzzy sets were established. Each rule is associated with a question of the form:

IF antecedent 1 is (state one of antecedent 1's fuzzy sets) and antecedent 2 is (state one of antecedent 2's fuzzy sets), THEN there is _____ of the behavior.

The respondent is asked to choose one of the given names for the consequent's fuzzy sets. The rule base surveys will lead to rule consequent histograms, because everyone will not answer a question the same way.

4.3.2 Survey results

Here we present survey results that will be used in later chapters of this book to design FLAs. We do this for a generic behavior, to illustrate our design procedures, so as not to get lost in the details of a specific social or engineering behavior. Based on the results described in Chapter 2, we used the following five terms for antecedents and consequent: *none to very little, some, a moderate amount, a large amount,* and *a maximum amount.* Table 4-2, which is a repeat of Table 2-3, summarizes the data collected from the Step 4 survey for these labels.

Table 4-2: Processed survey results for labels of fuzzy sets.

		Mean		Standard Deviation	
		Start	End	Start	End
No.	Range Label	(a)	(b)	(σ_a)	(σ_b)
1	*None to very little* (NVL)	0	1.9850	0	0.8104
2	*Some* (S)	2.5433	5.2500	0.9066	1.3693
3	*A moderate amount* (MOA)	3.6433	6.4567	0.8842	0.8557
4	*A large amount* (LA)	6.4833	8.7500	0.7484	0.5981
5	*A maximum amount* (MAA)	8.5500	10	0.7468	0

We limited our FLA to rule bases for one- and two-antecedent rules. In the spirit of generic results, we use x_1 and x_2 to denote the generic antecedents and y to denote the generic consequent for these rules. Tables 4-3 through 4-5 provide the data collected from 47 respondents to the Step 6 surveys. The antecedents for each rule appear in the parentheses after the rule number.

Table 4-3: Histogram of survey responses for single-antecedent rules between indicator x_1 and consequent y. Entries denote the number of respondents out of 47 that chose the consequent.

	Consequent				
Rule No.	**None to Very Little (NVL)**	**Some (S)**	**A Moderate Amount (MOA)**	**A Large Amount (LA)**	**A Maximum Amount (MAA)**
1 (NVL)	42	3	2	0	0
2 (S)	33	12	0	2	0
3 (MOA)	12	16	15	3	1
4 (LA)	3	6	11	25	2
5 (MAA)	3	6	8	22	8

Table 4-4: Histogram of survey responses for single-antecedent rules between indicator x_2 and consequent y. Entries denote the number of respondents out of 47 that chose the consequent.

	Consequent				
Rule No.	**None to Very Little (NVL)**	**Some (S)**	**A Moderate Amount (MOA)**	**A Large Amount (LA)**	**A Maximum Amount (MAA)**
1 (NVL)	36	7	4	0	0
2 (S)	26	17	4	0	0
3 (MOA)	2	16	27	2	0
4 (LA)	1	3	11	22	10
5 (MAA)	0	3	7	17	20

4.3.3 Methodology for designing a FLA

In Chapter 5 we design a singleton type-1 FLA in which all uncertainties from the surveys, which are summarized in Tables 4-2 through 4-5, are ignored. In Chapter 10, on the other hand, we design a singleton type-2 FLA in which all of the uncertainties from the surveys are accounted for. From the results in Tables 4-2 through 4-5, we see that two sources of uncertainties that were discussed in Chapter 2 are indeed present, namely uncertainties about the words used for the antecedents and consequents (Table 4-2) and uncertainties about the rule consequents (Tables 4-3 through 4-5). Why we will limit our attention just to singleton designs (i.e., to designs in which the FLA is activated by crisp measurements) is clarified next, when we explain how one would make use of a FLA after it is designed.

Table 4-5: Histogram of survey responses for two-antecedent rules between indicators x_1 and x_2 and consequent y. Entries denote the number of respondents out of 47 that chose the consequent.

Rule No.	None to Very Little (NVL)	Some (S)	A Moderate Amount (MOA)	A Large Amount (LA)	A Maximum Amount (MAA)
1 (NVL/NVL)	38	7	2	0	0
2 (NVL/S)	33	11	3	0	0
3 (NVL/MOA)	6	21	16	4	0
4 (NVL/LA)	0	12	26	8	1
5 (NVL/MAA)	0	9	16	19	3
6 (S/NVL)	31	11	4	1	0
7 (S/S)	17	23	7	0	0
8 (S/MOA)	0	19	19	8	1
9 (S/LA)	1	8	23	13	2
10 (S/MAA)	0	7	17	21	2
11 (MOA/NVL)	7	23	16	1	0
12 (MOA/S)	5	22	20	0	0
13 (MOA/MOA)	2	7	22	15	1
14 (MOA/LA)	1	4	13	17	12
15 (MOA/MAA)	0	4	12	24	7
16 (LA/NVL)	7	13	21	6	0
17 (LA/S)	3	11	23	10	0
18 (LA/MOA)	0	3	18	18	8
19 (LA/LA)	0	1	9	17	20
20 (LA/MAA)	1	2	6	11	27
21 (MAA/NVL)	2	16	18	11	0
22 (MAA/S)	2	9	22	13	1
23 (MAA/MOA)	0	3	15	18	11
24 (MAA/LA)	0	1	7	17	22
25 (MAA/MAA)	0	2	3	12	30

4.3.4 How to use a FLA

Each FLA that we shall design can be referred to as a *consensus* FLA, because it is obtained by using survey results from a population of people. In this section we describe how one can use the resulting FLAs.

Figure 4-3 depicts one way to use a FLA to advise an individual about a social judgment. It assumes that an individual is given the same questionnaire that was used in Step 6 of the knowledge mining process, which led to the consensus FLA. Their completed questionnaire can be interpreted as the individual's FLA, and its output can be plotted on the same plot as the output of the consensus FLA. These outputs can then be compared, and if some or all of the individual's outputs are "far" from those of the consensus FLA, then some action could be taken to sensitize the individual about these differences. Figure 4-4 depicts this for a type-1 consensus FLA, whereas Figure 4-5 depicts this for a type-2 consensus FLA.

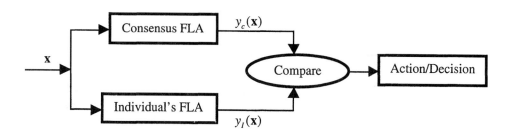

Figure 4-3: One way to use the FLA for a social judgment.

We immediately see a problem with the type-1 comparisons, namely, how "far" must the differences be between the individual FLA and the consensus FLA before some action (e.g., sensitivity training) is taken? This can be difficult to establish when we are comparing two functions, especially since "far" is in itself a fuzzy term.

This problem is handled directly with the type-2 comparisons in Figure 4-5. Note that the individual's FLA is still type-1, and has not changed from Figure 4-4 to 4-5. It is treated as type-1 because the individual takes the survey only one time; hence, there is no uncertainty associated with his or her consequents. The type-2 consensus FLA is represented on Figure 4-5 by two curves, $y_{c2,L}(x)$ and $y_{c2,R}(x)$. These represent the left-hand and right-hand curves, respectively, for the type-reduced sets (which are described in Chapters 9 and 10) of the type-2 consensus FLA. The difference between these curves represents a measure of the uncertainties due to the words used in the surveys as well as the consensus consequents. Observe from Figure 4-5 that the individual's FLA curve falls within the bounds of the type-reduced set; hence, no actions need to be taken. This conclusion is quite different from the one that might have been reached by examining the curves in Figure 4-4 where it appears that there is a significant difference between the individual's behavior level and the consensus FLA's behavior level for larger values of x. How to design the type-1 and type-2 FLAs will be described in Chapters 5 and 10, respectively.

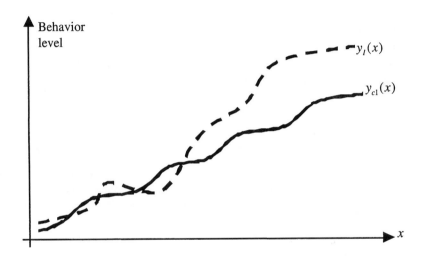

Figure 4-4: Comparison of a type-1 consensus FLA behavior level and an individual's FLA behavior level.

Another way to use a FLA is depicted in Figure 4-6. After the consensus FLA has been designed, it is exposed to a situation, say $x = x'$ (in this discussion **x** is assumed to be a scalar indicator, x), for which it provides the consensus output $y_c(x')$. Then some action or decision occurs. The problem that was associated with the type-1 FLA for a social judgment is the same for an engineering judgment, namely, we would have to take an action or make a decision based only on a point value. This is again resolved by using a type-2 consensus FLA, as depicted in Figure 4-7. Now the region defined by the type-reduced set (i.e., the "uncertain" region) is one where the designer is free to make a decision. For any $y_{c2,L}(x) < f(x) < y_{c2,R}(x)$, using a different decision boundary will lead to different engineering judgment. For example, if we use $y_{c2,L}(x)$ we accept a call when $x = x''$, or, on the other hand, if we use $y_{c2,R}(x)$ we reject the call when

$x = x''$. This kind of soft decision has the potential to be used in network control, signal detection and classification, communication receivers, etc.

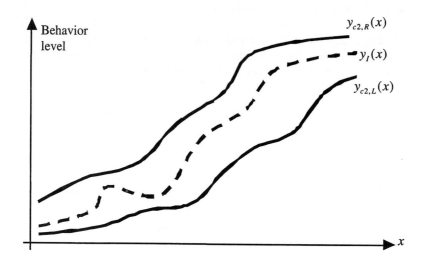

Figure 4-5: Comparison of a type-2 consensus FLA behavior level and an individual's FLA behavior level.

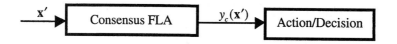

Figure 4-6: A way to use the FLA for an engineering judgment.

EXERCISES

4-1: The way in which we have established the training data to forecast a time-series is to ensure maximum overlap between successive training elements. Many other ways can be created to use the training data that either do not have so much overlap, or do not have any overlap at all between successive training elements.

(a) For the same N data points, create a training set that advances two points to the right, from one element in the training set to the next, instead of just one point to the right [as in (4-1)]. Suppose that the training set is to consist of 50% of all the data. What are the rules for this set of training data? How many rules will there be? What are the testing elements?

(b) For the same N data points, create a training set that has no overlap from one element in the training set to the next. As in part (a), suppose that the training set is to consist of 50% of all the data. What are the rules for this set of training data? How many rules will there be? What are the testing elements?

4-2: Explain some other ways to use a FLA for:

(a) social judgments

(b) engineering judgments

4-3: Suppose that the FLA is comprised of 3 FL sub-advisors. Explain how to use this FLA to make: (a) a social judgment decision, or (b) an engineering judgment decision or action.

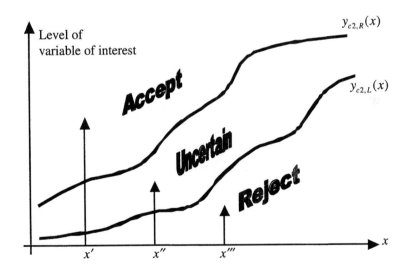

Figure 4-7: A way to use the FLA for an engineering judgment. The judgments are to accept when $x = x'$, reject when $x = x'''$, and must be further clarified when $x = x''$.

Part 2— Type-1 FLSs

CHAPTER 5

Singleton Type-1 Fuzzy Logic Systems: No Uncertainties

5.1 INTRODUCTION

In this chapter we explore many aspects of the basic singleton type-1 FLS that was introduced in Chapter 1. Recall that this FLS is also known as a Mamdani FLS[1] (or fuzzy-rule-based system, fuzzy expert system, fuzzy model, fuzzy system, FL controller [Jang and Sun (1995)], [Jang, et al. (1997)]). We focus on the case when there are no uncertainties, for which all fuzzy sets are type-1 and measurements are perfect and treated as crisp values, i.e., as singletons. We do this to provide a baseline for other types of FLSs that handle various types of uncertainties—and those FLSs, which are the main subjects of this book, are described in Chapters 6, 10, and 11–13.

We begin by discussing the four elements of the Figure 5-1 FLS, which is the same as Figure 1-1 (except that the Output Processor block has been replaced by the Defuzzifier block), so that we can write a mathematical formula that relates the output of the FLS to its inputs. We then briefly describe some design procedures for determining the free parameters of the FLS and for optimizing its performance. Finally, we illustrate the design of a singleton FLS for

---

[1]All of the FLSs considered in Chapters 5, 6, and 10–12 are Mamdani; hence, we just refer to them as a "FLS." In Chapter 13, however, where we must distinguish between Mamdani and TSK FLSs, we restore the Mamdani prefix to the FLSs of these earlier chapters.

our two Chapter 4 case studies.

To begin, we focus on the Figure 5-1 block labeled *Rules*.

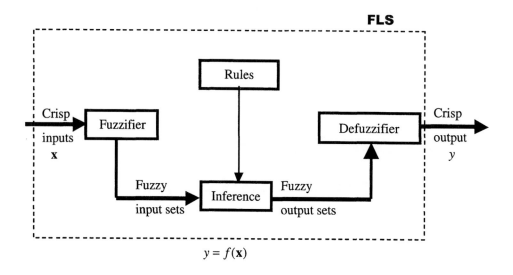

$$y = f(\mathbf{x})$$

Figure 5-1: Type-1 FLS.

5.2 RULES

Consider a type-1 FLS having p inputs $x_1 \in X_1,...,x_p \in X_p$ and one output $y \in Y$. Let us suppose that it has M rules, where the lth rule has the form

$$R^l: \text{IF } x_1 \text{ is } F_1^l \text{ and } \cdots \text{ and } x_p \text{ is } F_p^l, \text{ THEN } y \text{ is } G^l \quad l = 1,...,M \tag{5-1}$$

This rule represents a type-1 fuzzy relation between the input space $X_1 \times \cdots \times X_p$ and the output space, Y, of the FLS.

It is well known that a multiple-antecedent multiple-consequent rule can always be considered as a group of multi-input single-output rules [Lee, Part II, p. 426 (1990)], which is why we shall concentrate on multi-input single-output rules. It is also possible to cast "non-obvious" rules into the form of (5-1). Six such rules are summarized next, because it is very important for the reader to understand the power and flexibility of the generic rule structure in (5-1). The first five are adapted from Wang (1994).

1. *Incomplete IF Rules*: Suppose that we have created a rule base where there are p inputs, but some rules have antecedents that are only a subset of the p inputs, e.g.,

$$\text{IF } x_1 \text{ is } F_1 \text{ and } \cdots \text{ and } x_m \text{ is } F_m, \text{ THEN } y \text{ is } G$$

   Such rules are called *incomplete IF rules* and apply regardless of $x_{m+1}, ..., x_p$. They can be put into the format of the complete IF rule (5-1) by treating the unnamed antecedents (e.g., $x_{m+1}, ..., x_p$) as elements of the fuzzy set IN-COMPLETE (IN for short) where, by definition $\mu_{IN}(x) = 1$ for all $x \in X$, i.e.,

$$(\text{IF } x_1 \text{ is } F_1 \text{ and } \cdots \text{ and } x_m \text{ is } F_m, \text{ THEN } y \text{ is } G\ )$$
$$\Leftrightarrow (\text{IF } x_1 \text{ is } F_1 \text{ and } \cdots \text{ and } x_m \text{ is } F_m \text{ and } x_{m+1} \text{ is } IN$$
$$\cdots \text{ and } x_p \text{ is } IN, \text{ THEN } y \text{ is } G\ )$$

2. *Mixed Rules*: Not all rules use the "and" connective; some use the "or" connective and some use a mixture of both. The latter rules are called *mixed rules*. These rules can be decomposed into a collection of equivalent rules, using standard techniques from crisp logic. Suppose, for example, we have the rule:

$$\text{IF } (x_1 \text{ is } F_1 \text{ and } \cdots \text{ and } x_m \text{ is } F_m) \text{ or } (x_{m+1} \text{ is } F_{m+1} \text{ and } \cdots \text{ and } x_p \text{ is } F_p\ ),$$
$$\text{THEN } y \text{ is } G$$

   This rule can be expressed as the following two rules:

$$R^1: \text{IF } x_1 \text{ is } F_1 \text{ and } \cdots \text{ and } x_m \text{ is } F_m, \text{ THEN } y \text{ is } G$$

$$R^2: \text{IF } x_{m+1} \text{ is } F_{m+1} \text{ and } \cdots \text{ and } x_p \text{ is } F_p, \text{ THEN } y \text{ is } G$$

   Observe that both of these rules are Incomplete IF rules. See Vadiee and Jamshidi (1993) for related discussions on nesting of rules.

3. *Fuzzy Statement Rules*: Some rules do not appear to have any antecedents; they are statements involving fuzzy sets. Hence, they are called *fuzzy statement rules*. For example, "y is G" is such a rule. Clearly, this is an extreme case of an incomplete IF rule, and can therefore be formulated as:

IF x_1 is *IN* and $\cdots$ and x_p is *IN*, THEN y is G

4. *Comparative Rules*: Some rules are comparative, e.g.,

The smaller the x the bigger the y.

Such rules must first be reformulated as IF–THEN rules; this takes some experience. The preceding rule can be expressed as

IF x is S, THEN y is B

where S is a fuzzy set representing *smaller* and B is a fuzzy set representing *bigger*.

5. *Unless Rules*: Rules are sometimes stated using the connective "unless"; such rules are called *unless rules* and can be put into the format of (5-1) by using logical operations, including De Morgan's Laws. For example, the rule

y is G unless x_1 is F_1 and $\cdots$ and x_p is F_p

can first be expressed as

IF not $\left(x_1 \text{ is } F_1 \text{ and } \cdots \text{ and } x_p \text{ is } F_p \right)$, THEN y is G

Using De Morgan's Law, $\overline{A \cap B} = \overline{A} \cup \overline{B}$, this can be re-expressed as

IF x_1 is not F_1 or $\cdots$ or x_p is not F_p, THEN y is G

We treat " not F_i " as a fuzzy set and then decompose this rule into a collection of p *incomplete IF rules* each of the form

IF x_i is not F_i , THEN y is G, $i = 1, ..., p$

Although De Morgan's Laws are always valid in crisp set theory and logic, they may not be valid in fuzzy set theory and logic. For example, they are valid for maximum t-conorm and minimum t-norm, but are invalid for maximum t-conorm and product t-norm. See Section 7.6.1 and Appendix B for discussions about this.

6. *Quantifier Rules*: Rules sometimes include the quantifiers "some" or "all"; such rules are called *quantifier rules*. Because of the duality between pro-

positional logic and set theory, rules with the quantifier "some" mean that we have to apply the union operator to the antecedents or consequents to which the "some" applies, whereas rules with the quantifier "all" mean we have to apply the intersection operator to the antecedents or consequents to which the "all" applies.

Of course, in practical applications, it is possible to have rules that combine non-obvious IF–THEN rules 1–6 in all sorts of interesting ways.

5.3 FUZZY INFERENCE ENGINE

In the fuzzy inference engine (which is labeled *Inference* in Figure 5-1), fuzzy logic principles are used to combine fuzzy IF–THEN rules from the fuzzy rule base into a mapping from fuzzy input sets in $X_1 \times \cdots \times X_p$ to fuzzy output sets in Y. Each rule is interpreted as a fuzzy implication. With reference to (5-1), let $F_1^l \times \cdots \times F_p^l = A^l$; then, (5-1) can be re-expressed as

$$R^l: F_1^l \times \cdots \times F_p^l \to G^l = A^l \to G^l \quad l = 1, ..., M \tag{5-2}$$

R^l is described by the membership function $\mu_{R^l}(\mathbf{x}, y)$, where

$$\mu_{R^l}(\mathbf{x}, y) = \mu_{A^l \to G^l}(\mathbf{x}, y) \tag{5-3}$$

and $\mathbf{x} = (x_1, ..., x_p)^T$. Consequently, $\mu_{R^l}(\mathbf{x}, y) = \mu_{R^l}(x_1, ..., x_p, y)$ and

$$
\begin{aligned}
\mu_{R^l}(\mathbf{x}, y) &= \mu_{A^l \to G^l}(\mathbf{x}, y) = \mu_{F_1^l \times \cdots \times F_p^l \to G^l}(\mathbf{x}, y) \\
&= \mu_{F_1^l \times \cdots \times F_p^l}(\mathbf{x}) \star \mu_{G^l}(y) \\
&= \mu_{F_1^l}(x_1) \star \cdots \star \mu_{F_p^l}(x_p) \star \mu_{G^l}(y) \\
&= \left[T_{i=1}^p \mu_{F_i^l}(x_i) \right] \star \mu_{G^l}(y)
\end{aligned}
\tag{5-4}
$$

where it has been assumed that Mamdani implications are used, multiple antecedents are connected by *and*—by t-norms—[as in (3-45)], and T is short for a t-norm. As discussed in Section 1.11.2, Mamdani implications are the most commonly used implications in engineering applications of fuzzy logic, and are the ones that we adhere to throughout most of this book. We leave it to the reader to explore other t-norms and implications both for type-1 and type-2 FLSs.

The p-dimensional input to R^l is given by the fuzzy set A_x whose membership function is [see (3-45)]

$$\mu_{A_x}(\mathbf{x}) = \mu_{X_1}(x_1) \star \cdots \star \mu_{X_p}(x_p) = T_{i=1}^p \mu_{X_i}(x_i) \tag{5-5}$$

Each rule R^l determines a fuzzy set $B^l = A_x \circ R^l$ in Y such that

$$\mu_{B^l}(y) = \mu_{A_x \circ R^l}(y) = \sup_{\mathbf{x} \in X} \left[\mu_{A_x}(\mathbf{x}) \star \mu_{A^l \to G^l}(\mathbf{x}, y) \right], \quad y \in Y \tag{5-6}$$

This equation is the input–output relationship in Figure 5-1 between the fuzzy set that excites a one-rule inference engine and the fuzzy set at the output of that engine. This sup-star composition is a highly non-linear mapping from the input vector $\mathbf{x}$ into a scalar output fuzzy set $\mu_{B^l}(y)$.

We can interpret the fuzzy inference engine as a *system*, one that maps fuzzy sets into fuzzy sets by means of the sup-star composition in (5-6). This is depicted in Figure 5-2.

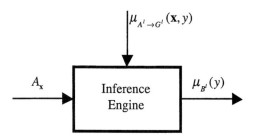

Figure 5-2: Interpretation of fuzzy inference engine as a system.

Substituting (5-4) and (5-5) into (5-6), we see that

$$\mu_{B^l}(y) = \sup_{\mathbf{x} \in X} \left[\mu_{A_x}(\mathbf{x}) \star \mu_{A^l \to G^l}(\mathbf{x}, y) \right]$$

$$= \sup_{\mathbf{x} \in X} \left[T_{i=1}^p \mu_{X_i}(x_i) \star \left[T_{i=1}^p \mu_{F_i^l}(x_i) \right] \star \mu_{G^l}(y) \right]$$

$$= \sup_{\mathbf{x} \in X} \left\{ \left[T_{i=1}^p \mu_{X_i}(x_i) \star \mu_{F_i^l}(x_i) \right] \star \mu_{G^l}(y) \right\}$$

$$\mu_{B^l}(y) = \mu_{G^l}(y) \star \left\{ \left[\sup_{x_1 \in X_1} \mu_{X_1}(x_1) \star \mu_{F_1^l}(x_1) \right] \star \right.$$

$$\left. \cdots \star \left[\sup_{x_p \in X_p} \mu_{X_p}(x_p) \star \mu_{F_p^l}(x_p) \right] \right\}, \quad y \in Y \tag{5-7}$$

This is a very important sequence of calculations and result. The last line follows from the commutativity of a t-norm and the fact that $\mu_{X_i}(x_i) \star \mu_{F_i^l}(x_i)$ is only a function of x_i, so that each supremum in (5-7) is over just a scalar variable.

The final fuzzy set, B, is determined by all M rules, and is obtained by combining B^l and its associated membership function $\mu_{B^l}(y)$ for all $l = 1, ..., M$, i.e.,

$$B = A_{\mathbf{x}} \circ [R^1, \cdots, R^M]. \tag{5-8}$$

Zadeh (1973) connects rules using the word "else," one of whose definitions is *otherwise*. Lee (1990) uses the connective "also" and has a discussion about a number of studies that were performed to determine the best way to connect rules. Many people connect rules using a t - conorm—the fuzzy union—i.e., $B = B^1 \oplus \cdots \oplus B^M$.

Lee (1990) provides a rigorous proof that the sup-min or sup-product compositions and connective "also," interpreted as a maximum t-conorm, are commutative, i.e.,

$$A_{\mathbf{x}} \circ [R^1, \cdots, R^M] = \bigcup_{i=1}^{M} A_{\mathbf{x}} \circ R^i \tag{5-9}$$

For additional discussions on connecting rules, see: [Dubois and Prade (1985)], [Kiska et al. (1985a, b, c)], [Lin and Lee (1996)], [Mizumoto (1987)], [Stachowicz and Kochanska (1987)], [Wang (1997)], and [Yen and Langari (1999)].

There does not appear to be a unique or compelling theoretical reason for combining rules using a t-conorm. In fact, some people prefer to combine rules before defuzzification [e.g., as in (5-9)], whereas other people prefer to combine them as part of defuzzification. For example, combining rules additively [Kosko (1992, 1997)], by adding fired rule membership functions, is a way to combine rules before defuzzification. Figure 5-3 depicts the additive combiner. It resembles an adaptive filter whose inputs are the output fuzzy sets. The weights of the combiner, $w_1,...,w_M$, can be thought of as providing degrees of belief to each rule. It is conceivable that we know that some rules are more reliable than others, in which case such rules would be assigned a larger weight than less reliable rules. If such information is not known ahead of time, then we either set all the weights equal to unity or we use a training procedure to learn optimal values for the weights. In Section 5.5 we show that the additive combiner is somewhat unique in that it is also equivalent to combining rules as part of defuzzification; so, it's use resolves the issue of combining before or as part of defuzzification.

We will return to the question of how to combine rules later, when we discuss the defuzzifier block of Figure 5-1.

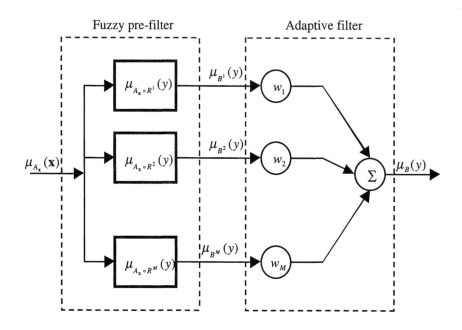

Figure 5-3: An additive combiner that can be interpreted as an adaptive filter activated by fuzzy sets that are the output of a fuzzy pre-filter (Mendel, 1995a, © 1995, IEEE).

5.4 FUZZIFICATION AND ITS EFFECT ON INFERENCE

In the FLS of Figure 5-1, crisp inputs are first fuzzified into fuzzy input sets that then activate the inference block. In this section, we explain singleton fuzzification and the effect of such fuzzification on the inference engine.

5.4.1 Fuzzifier

The *fuzzifier* maps a crisp point $\mathbf{x} = (x_1, ..., x_p)^T \in X_1 \times X_2 \times \cdots \times X_p \equiv \mathbf{X}$ into a fuzzy set $A_{\mathbf{x}}$ in $\mathbf{X}$. The most widely used fuzzifier is the *singleton fuzzifier* which is nothing more than a fuzzy singleton, i.e.,

> $A_{\mathbf{x}}$ is a *fuzzy singleton* with support $\mathbf{x}'$ if $\mu_{A_{\mathbf{x}}}(\mathbf{x}) = 1$ for $\mathbf{x} = \mathbf{x}'$ and
> $\mu_{A_{\mathbf{x}}}(\mathbf{x}) = 0$ for all other $\mathbf{x} \in \mathbf{X}$ with $\mathbf{x} \neq \mathbf{x}'$

We shall interpret this to mean that *each* of the separable components of $\mu_{A_{\mathbf{x}}}(\mathbf{x})$ is a fuzzy singleton, i.e., we shall assume that $\mu_{X_i}(x_i') = 1$ for $x_i = x'$ and $\mu_{X_i}(x_i) = 0$ for $\forall x_i \in X_i$ and $x_i \neq x_i'$.

This chapter focuses on singleton fuzzification. Non-singleton fuzzification is the subject of Chapter 6.

5.4.2 Fuzzy inference engine

For singleton fuzzification the supremum operation in the sup-star composition (5-7) is very easy to evaluate because $\mu_{X_i}(x_i)$ is non-zero only at one point, $x_i = x_i'$; hence,

$$
\begin{aligned}
\mu_{B'}(y) &= \mu_{G'}(y) \star \left\{ \left[\sup_{x_1 \in X_1} \mu_{X_1}(x_1) \star \mu_{F_1^l}(x_1) \right] \star \right. \\
&\qquad \left. \cdots \star \left[\sup_{x_p \in X_p} \mu_{X_p}(x_p) \star \mu_{F_p^l}(x_p) \right] \right\} \\
&= \mu_{G'}(y) \star \left\{ \left[\mu_{X_1}(x_1') \star \mu_{F_1^l}(x_1') \right] \star \right. \qquad\qquad (5\text{-}10) \\
&\qquad \left. \cdots \star \left[\mu_{X_p}(x_p') \star \mu_{F_p^l}(x_p') \right] \right\} \\
&= \mu_{G'}(y) \star \left[\mu_{F_1^l}(x_1') \star \cdots \star \mu_{F_p^l}(x_p') \right], \quad y \in Y
\end{aligned}
$$

where we have used the fact that $\mu_{X_i}(x_i') \star \mu_{F_i^l}(x_i') = 1 \star \mu_{F_i^l}(x_i') = \mu_{F_i^l}(x_i')$, which is true for minimum or product t-norms. The term in the bracket on the last line of (5-10) is referred to as the *firing level*. Note that $\mu_{B'}(y)$ depends on $\mathbf{x} = \mathbf{x}'$; change $\mathbf{x}'$ and $\mu_{B'}(y)$ changes. A notation like $\mu_{B'}(y \mid \mathbf{x} = \mathbf{x}')$ might be more accurate; but, no one uses it, so we will adhere to the accepted notation, $\mu_{B^l}(y)$.

At each value of $y \in Y$, say y', $\mu_{B^l}(y')$ is a crisp number. Because $y \in Y$ and $\mu_{B^l}(y)$ are a function of y, (5-10) must be evaluated at $\forall y \in Y$, and it then is a membership function.

It is the (tremendous) simplification of the sup-star composition in (5-10) that is (in my opinion) the reason for the popularity of singleton fuzzification; however, singleton fuzzification may not always be adequate, e.g., when data are corrupted by measurement noise. Non-singleton fuzzification provides a means for handling such uncertainties totally within the framework of a type-1 FLS, and is the subject of Chapter 6.

Example 5-1: Here we consider a pictorial description of (5-10) for the minimum and product t-norms. We do this because FL designers are all familiar with such pictorial descriptions of a type-1 FLS, since they provide them with a good understanding of some of the operations of such a system. We also do this because we will provide comparable pictorial descriptions for type-2 FLSs in later chapters, which can then be contrasted with the figures of this example to better understand the flow of uncertainties through type-2 FLSs.

Figure 5-4 depicts input and antecedent operations [the terms in the bracket in (5-10)] for a two-antecedent–single consequent rule, singleton fuzzification, and minimum or product t-norms. Note that μ_1^l and μ_2^l are short for $\mu_{F_1^l}(x_1')$ and $\mu_{F_2^l}(x_2')$, respectively; and, μ^l is short for $\mu_{F_1^l}(x_1') \star \mu_{F_2^l}(x_2')$. In all cases, the firing level is a number equal to $\mu_{F_1^l}(x_1') \star \mu_{F_2^l}(x_2')$. Observe, for example, that $\mu_{F_1^l}(x_1')$ occurs at the intersection of the vertical line at x_1' with $\mu_{F_1^l}(x_1)$. For minimum t-norm $\mu_{F_1^l}(x_1') \star \mu_{F_2^l}(x_2') = \min[\mu_{F_1^l}(x_1'), \mu_{F_2^l}(x_2')]$, whereas for product t-norm $\mu_{F_1^l}(x_1') \star \mu_{F_2^l}(x_2') = \mu_{F_1^l}(x_1') \times \mu_{F_2^l}(x_2')$. The main thing to observe from these figures is that regardless of the t-norm, the result of input and antecedent operations is a number—the *firing level* (μ^l).

Figure 5-5 depicts $\mu_{B^l}(y)$ for a two-rule ($l = l_1, l_2$) FLS. It is obtained by t-norming the firing-level term in (5-10) with $\mu_{G^l}(y)$ for all $y \in Y$ (the dashed curves) and for each rule. Observe that $\mu_{B^l}(y)$ for minimum t-norm is a clipped version of $\mu_{G^l}(y)$, where the clipping level equals the firing level for that rule. On the other hand, $\mu_{B^l}(y)$ for product t-norm is a scaled version of $\mu_{G^l}(y)$, where the scaling level equals the firing level for that rule.

Figure 5-6 depicts the combined output set, $\mu_B(y)$, for the two-rule FLS, where the fired output sets are combined as in (5-9) using the maximum for the union. The results are fairly similar for both t-norms. ■

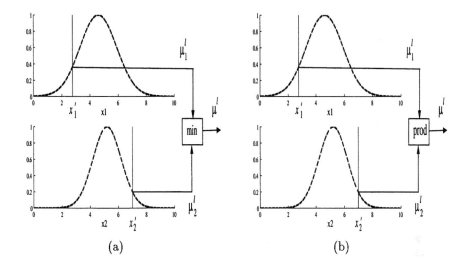

Figure 5-4: Pictorial description of input and antecedent operations for a type-1 FLS. (a) Singleton fuzzification with minimum t-norm, and (b) singleton fuzzification with product t-norm.

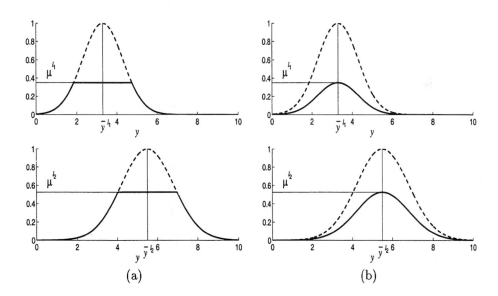

Figure 5-5: Pictorial description of consequent operations for a type-1 FLS. (a) Fired output sets with minimum t-norm, and (b) fired output sets with product t-norm.

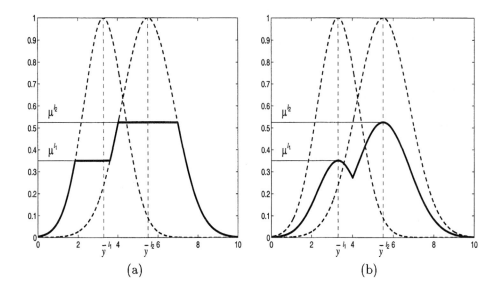

Figure 5-6: Pictorial description of (a) combined output sets for the two fired output sets depicted in Figure 5-5 (a), and (b) combined output sets for the two fired output sets depicted in Figure 5-5 (b).

5.5 DEFUZZIFICATION

Defuzzification produces a crisp output for our FLS from the fuzzy sets that appear at the output of the inference block in Figure 5-1. Many defuzzifiers have been proposed in the literature. Because we are interested in engineering applications of FL, one criterion for the choice of a defuzzifier is *computational simplicity*. This criterion has led to numerous candidates for defuzzifiers, including: maximum, mean-of-maxima, centroid, center-of-sums, height, modified height, and center-of-sets.

The *maximum defuzzifier* examines the fuzzy set B and chooses as its output the value of y for which $\mu_B(y)$ is a maximum. The *mean-of-maxima defuzzifier* examines the fuzzy set B and first determines the values of y for which $\mu_B(y)$ is a maximum. It then computes the mean of these values as its output. If the maximum value of $\mu_B(y)$ only occurs at a single point, then the mean-of-maxima defuzzifier reduces to the maximum defuzzifier.

Both of these defuzzifiers can lead to peculiar results. For example, the maximum defuzzifier completely ignores the fact that $\mu_B(y)$ is distributed over a range of y-values, and the mean-of-maxima defuzzifier may provide a zero mean value even though $\mu_B(y)$ is non-zero over most of its range. Even though these defuzzifers may be useful in some applications, we will not use them in this book.

In the rest of this section we provide brief descriptions of centroid, center-of-sums, height, modified height, and center-of-sets defuzzifiers, since they are the ones that are used in the rest of this book.

5.5.1 Centroid defuzzifier

The centroid defuzzifier combines the output type-1 fuzzy sets using union (i.e., a t-conorm, e.g., maximum) and then finds the centroid of this set. If the composite output fuzzy set B is

$$B = \bigcup\nolimits_{l=1}^{M} B^l \tag{5-11}$$

with associated membership function $\mu_B(y)$, and $\mu_{B^l}(y)$ is the membership function of the lth rule [given in (5-10)], then the centroid defuzzifier is given as:

$$y_c(\mathbf{x}) = \frac{\sum_{i=1}^{N} y_i \mu_B(y_i)}{\sum_{i=1}^{N} \mu_B(y_i)} \tag{5-12}$$

where the membership function for the output set B has been discretized into N points. In (5-12) we show $y_c(\mathbf{x})$ as an explicit function of $\mathbf{x}$ because $\mu_B(y_i)$ is a function of FLS input $\mathbf{x}$ [see the discussion after (5-10)]. For each FLS input $\mathbf{x}$ we can get a different value of $y_c(\mathbf{x})$.

Unfortunately, the centroid defuzzifier is usually difficult to compute because of first having to compute the union in (5-11). This has led to the introduction of other defuzzifiers.

5.5.2 Center-of-sums defuzzifier

The center-of-sums defuzzifier [Driankov et al. (1996)] combines the output type-1 fuzzy set membership functions by adding them, i.e.,

$$\mu_B(y) = \sum\nolimits_{l=1}^{M} \mu_{B^l}(y) \quad \forall y \in Y \tag{5-13}$$

and then finds the centroid of this set. The center-of-sums defuzzifier can be expressed as

$$y_a(\mathbf{x}) = \frac{\sum_{l=1}^{M} c_{B^l} a_{B^l}}{\sum_{l=1}^{M} a_{B^l}} \tag{5-14}$$

where c_{B^l} denotes the centroid of the lth output set and a_{B^l} denotes the area of that set. The subscript a on y indicates the "additive" combining. Note that the areas of overlapping membership functions, if this occurs, are accounted for more than once by additive combining; but, computing $y_a(\mathbf{x})$ is much easier to do than is computing $y_c(\mathbf{x})$.

If we use product inference, the output sets will be scaled versions of the consequent sets (see Figure 5-5 (b)). In that case, c_{B^l} equals the centroid of the lth consequent set, c_{G^l}, and a_{B^l} equals the area, a_{G^l}, of the lth consequent set multiplied by the degree of firing of the lth consequent set, $T_{i=1}^{p}\mu_{F_i^l}(x_i)$; therefore, (5-14) can be expressed as

$$y_a(\mathbf{x}) = \frac{\sum_{l=1}^{M} c_{G^l} a_{G^l} T_{i=1}^{p}\mu_{F_i^l}(x_i)}{\sum_{l=1}^{M} a_{G^l} T_{i=1}^{p}\mu_{F_i^l}(x_i)} \tag{5-15}$$

Since c_{G^l} and a_{G^l} ($l = 1,...,M$) can be precomputed, this $y_a(\mathbf{x})$ is easy to compute.

Closely related to the center-of-sums defuzzifier is Kosko's (1997) *Standard Additive Model* (SAM), which, as depicted in Figure 5-3, uses a weighted additive combining of the output sets. It also uses product implication and product t-norm [this means that *all* the t-norms in (5-10) are products, which is *not* a requirement in the general center-of-sums defuzzifier in (5-14)]. The output of the SAM for input $\mathbf{x}$ is

$$y_{SAM}(\mathbf{x}) = \frac{\sum_{l=1}^{M} w_l c_{G^l} a_{G^l} T_{i=1}^{p}\mu_{F_i^l}(x_i)}{\sum_{l=1}^{M} w_l a_{G^l} T_{i=1}^{p}\mu_{F_i^l}(x_i)} \tag{5-16}$$

Observe that (5-16) is the same as (5-15) except for the weights w_l. Observe, also, that since $w_l a_{G^l}$ always appears as a product, one really does not have two degrees of freedom in (5-16). The weights can be absorbed into the areas or vice-versa. So, without loss of generality, we can set $w_l = 1$ for all l in (5-16), in which case $y_{SAM}(\mathbf{x}) = y_a(\mathbf{x})$. In summary, $y_a(\mathbf{x})$ is more general than $y_{SAM}(\mathbf{x})$;

however, when product implication and product t-norm are used, as we frequently do in this book, then $y_a(\mathbf{x}) = y_{SAM}(\mathbf{x})$.

5.5.3 Height defuzzifier

The height defuzzifier [Driankov et al. (1996)] (also called the *center average defuzzifier* [Wang (1994, 1997)]) replaces each rule output fuzzy set by a singleton at the point having maximum membership in that output set, and then calculates the centroid of the type-1 set comprised of these singletons. The output of a height defuzzifier is given as

$$y_h(\mathbf{x}) = \frac{\sum_{l=1}^{M} \bar{y}^l \mu_{B^l}(\bar{y}^l)}{\sum_{l=1}^{M} \mu_{B^l}(\bar{y}^l)} \tag{5-17}$$

where: $\bar{y}^l$ is the point having maximum membership in the *l*th output set (if there is more than one such point, their average can be taken as $\bar{y}^l$), and its membership grade in the *l*th output set is $\mu_{B^l}(\bar{y}^l)$. For singleton fuzzification, it follows from (5-10) that

$$\mu_{B^l}(\bar{y}^l) = \mu_{G^l}(\bar{y}^l) \star \left[\mu_{F_1^l}(x_1') \star \cdots \star \mu_{F_p^l}(x_p') \right] \tag{5-18}$$

Equation (5-17) is easily derived from calculus applied to the situation that is depicted in Figure 5-7. Note, also, that although (5-17) and (5-12) look alike, they are quite different. Usually, $M \ll N$, so it is much easier to compute $y_h(\mathbf{x})$ than it is to compute $y_c(\mathbf{x})$.

It is very easy to use (5-17) because the centers of gravity of commonly used membership functions are known ahead of time. For example, regardless of whether minimum or product inference are used, the center of gravity of B^l for:

1. A symmetric triangular consequent membership function is at the apex of the triangle.
2. A Gaussian consequent membership function is at the center value of the Gaussian function.
3. A symmetric trapezoidal membership function is at the midpoint of its support.

Although (5-17) is easy to use, it suffers from a deficiency that may not be so obvious. Whereas $y_h(\mathbf{x})$ makes use of the entire shape of each antecedent's

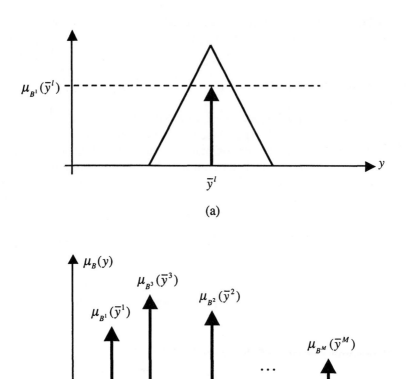

(a)

(b)

Figure 5-7: (a) Spike of height $\mu_{B^l}(\bar{y}^l)$ located at $\bar{y}^l$, and (b) discrete masses that are located at the centroids of the membership functions for each rule; each mass equals the peak value of the activated consequent membership function for R^l, $\mu_{B^l}(\bar{y}^l)$; an unactivated rule has zero value for $\mu_{B^l}(\bar{y}^l)$; centroids do not have to appear in chronological order.

membership function [because this information is embodied in $\mu_{B^l}(\bar{y}^l)$], it does not make use of the entire shape of the consequent membership function. It only uses the center of the support, $\bar{y}^l$, of the consequent membership function. Regardless of whether or not the consequent membership function is very narrow, which can be interpreted as indicating a very strong belief in that rule, or is very broad, which can be interpreted as indicating much less belief in that rule, the height defuzzifier gives the same result. This has led to the next defuzzifier, the modified height defuzzifier.

5.5.4 Modified height defuzzifier

The modified height defuzzifier [Mendel (1995)] (also called the *modified center average defuzzifier* [Wang (1994)]) is very similar to the height defuzzifier, the only difference being that the modified height defuzzifier scales each $\mu_{B^l}(\bar{y}^l)$ by the inverse of the square of the spread (or some measure of the spread) of the *l*th consequent set. Its output can be expressed as

$$y_{mh}(\mathbf{x}) = \frac{\sum_{l=1}^{M} \bar{y}^l \mu_{B^l}(\bar{y}^l) / \delta^{l2}}{\sum_{l=1}^{M} \mu_{B^l}(\bar{y}^l) / \delta^{l2}} \qquad (5\text{-}19)$$

where δ^l is some measure of the spread of the *l*th consequent set, and $\bar{y}^l$ and $\mu_{B^l}(\bar{y}^l)$ have the same meaning as in (5-17). For triangular and trapezoidal membership functions, δ^l could be the support of the triangle or trapezoid, whereas for Gaussian membership functions, δ^l could be its standard deviation. The modified height defuzzifier is also easy to use, although the δ^l parameters must be specified in addition to $\bar{y}^l$ and $\mu_{B^l}(\bar{y}^l)$.

5.5.5 Center-of-sets defuzzifier

In center-of-sets defuzzification ([Sugeno and Yasakuwa (1993)], [Karnik and Mendel (1998b)]), we replace each rule consequent set by a singleton situated at its centroid, whose amplitude equals the firing level, and then find the centroid of the type-1 set comprised of these singletons. The expression for the output is given as

$$y_{\cos}(\mathbf{x}) = \frac{\sum_{l=1}^{M} c^l T_{i=1}^{p} \mu_{F_i^l}(x_i)}{\sum_{l=1}^{M} T_{i=1}^{p} \mu_{F_i^l}(x_i)} \qquad (5\text{-}20)$$

where c^l is the centroid of the lth consequent set (for notational simplicity, we use c^l instead of c_{G^l}). Observe that if each consequent is symmetric, normal, and convex, then $c^l = \bar{y}^l$ and [in (5-18)] $\mu_{G^l}(\bar{y}^l) = 1$ for $l = 1, ..., M$; consequently, in this case, $y_{cos}(\mathbf{x}) = y_h(\mathbf{x})$. It is when the consequents are not all symmetric that the center-of-sets defuzzifer gives results that are different from those obtained from the height defuzzifier. In that sense, it may be a more appropriate kind of defuzzification than the height defuzzifier.

Example 5-2: Consider a type-1 FLS having consequent fuzzy sets as shown in Figure 5-8 (a). Suppose that for some particular input $\mathbf{x}$ the fired outputs are as shown in Figure 5-8 (b) (assuming product inference). The numbers 0.9, 0.8, and 0.2 indicate the degree of firing of each of the consequent sets. The outputs of our five defuzzifiers for this example are:

$$y_c = 2.4289, \ y_a = 2.4429, \ y_h = 2.7368, \ y_{mh} = 3.1429, \ \text{and} \ y_{cos} = 2.7259$$

For the modified height defuzzifier, δ^l was set equal to the standard deviation of the lth consequent set, which for the three fired consequent sets are 0.4, 0.2, and 0.2, respectively. Observe that for the consequent set centered at 5, $\bar{y}^5 = 5$ but $c^5 = 4.8436$; therefore, the outputs of the height and center-of-sets defuzzifiers for this example are slightly different. ■

5.5.6 An interesting fact

In Section 5.3 we pointed out that some people prefer to combine rules before defuzzification, whereas others prefer to combine them as part of defuzzification. The center-of-sums defuzzifier does the former whereas the modified height defuzzifier does the latter. Under product implication we obtain the following interesting result:

Theorem 5-1: *Under product implication and t-norm, the center-of-sums (SAM) defuzzifier and modified height defuzzifier are equivalent.* ■

We leave the proof of this result to the reader (Exercise 5-3). The significance of the result in Theorem 5-1 is that, in this case, it doesn't matter whether we conceptually think about combining rules before or as part of defuzzification, since the results are the same. A limitation of the theorem is that it is only true when product inference and t-norm are used in the center-of-sums defuzzifier, but these are very popular choices in engineering applications of FLSs.

For additional discussions on defuzzifiers, see [Filev and Yager (1991)],

[Hellendoorn and Thomas (1993)], [Terano et al. (1992)], and [Yager and Filev (1994a, b)].

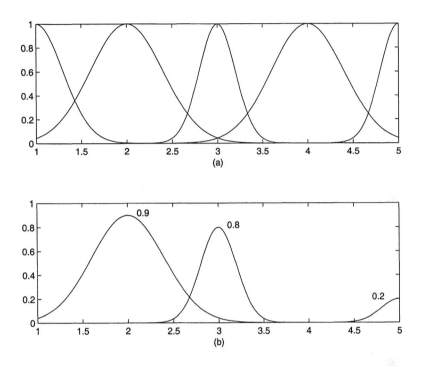

Figure 5-8: (a) Consequent sets for Example 5-2. (b) Fired consequent sets for some input **x**.

5.6 POSSIBILITIES

From our detailed discussions about the four elements that comprise the Figure 5-1 FLS, we see that there are many possibilities to choose from. Figure 5-9 summarizes some of the possibilities that we have discussed so far. We must decide on the kind of fuzzification (singleton or non-singleton), functional forms for membership functions (triangular, trapezoidal, Gaussian, piece-wise linear), parameters of membership functions (fixed ahead of time or tuned during a training procedure), composition (max-min, max-product), implication (minimum, product), and defuzzifier (centroid, center-of-sums, height, modified height, center-of-sets). Just choosing among the parenthetical possibilities leads to $2^{17} = 131{,}072$ different FLSs. This demonstrates the richness of FLSs and that there is no such thing as *the* FLS.

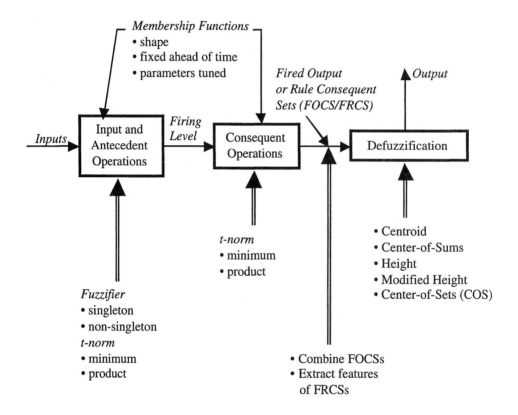

Figure 5-9: Choices that need to be made to specify or design a type-1 FLS.

Observe, in Fig. 5-9, that prior to defuzzification we also need to decide on whether we are going to combine fired output consequent sets (using union of the sets or addition of the membership functions) or are going to extract features of the fired rule consequent sets. The latter are: center of gravity, area, peak location, and spread. One or more are used by a defuzzifier, e.g., the modified height defuzzifer uses the peak location and spread of the fired rule consequent sets.

5.7 FUZZY BASIS FUNCTIONS

The pictorial interpretation we have provided for the inference block of our FLS, in Figures 5-4–5-6, is informative; however, it does not provide us with a complete description of our FLS. For such a description, we need a mathematical formula that maps a crisp input $\mathbf{x}$ into a crisp output $y = f(\mathbf{x})$. From Figure 5-1, we see that such a formula can be obtained by following the signal $\mathbf{x}$ through the fuzzifier, where it is converted into the fuzzy set A_x, into the inference block, where it is converted into the fuzzy sets B^l ($l = 1, \ldots, M$) and possibly B, and finally into the defuzzifier, where it is converted into $f(\mathbf{x})$. To write such a formula, we must make specific choices for fuzzifier, membership functions, composition, implication, t-norm, and defuzzifier.

Example 5-3: When we choose singleton fuzzification, max-product composition, product implication,[2] and height defuzzification, leaving the choice of membership functions open, it is easy to show that

$$y(\mathbf{x}) = f_s(\mathbf{x}) = \frac{\sum_{l=1}^{M} \bar{y}^l \prod_{i=1}^{p} \mu_{F_i^l}(x_i)}{\sum_{l=1}^{M} \prod_{i=1}^{p} \mu_{F_i^l}(x_i)} \qquad (5\text{-}21)$$

We use the subscript "s" on $f_s(\mathbf{x})$ to remind us that this is a singleton FLS. To obtain (5-21), we started with (5-17) and substituted for $\mu_{B^l}(\bar{y}^l)$ from (5-18), i.e.,

$$\mu_{B^l}(\bar{y}^l) = \left[\prod_{i=1}^{p} \mu_{F_i^l}(x_i') \right] \times \mu_{G^l}(\bar{y}^l) = \prod_{i=1}^{p} \mu_{F_i^l}(x_i') \qquad (5\text{-}22)$$

where we have assumed that membership functions are normalized, so that $\mu_{G^l}(\bar{y}^l) = 1$. Additionally, for notational simplicity, we have relabeled x_i' to x_i, so that we write $f_s(\mathbf{x}')$ as $f_s(\mathbf{x})$. ∎

Example 5-4: When we choose singleton fuzzification, max-min composition, minimum implication,[2] and height defuzzification, again leaving the choice of membership functions open, it is easy to show that

$$y(\mathbf{x}) = f_s(\mathbf{x}) = \frac{\sum_{l=1}^{M} \bar{y}^l \min_{i=1,\ldots,p} \left\{ \mu_{F_i^l}(x_i) \right\}}{\sum_{l=1}^{M} \min_{i=1,\ldots,p} \left\{ \mu_{F_i^l}(x_i) \right\}} \qquad ∎ \qquad (5\text{-}23)$$

---

[2]Fixing the composition and implication, as we have done, also fixes the t-norm.

The FLSs in (5-21) and (5-23) can be represented more generally as

$$y(\mathbf{x}) = f_s(\mathbf{x}) = \sum_{l=1}^{M} \overline{y}^l \phi_l(\mathbf{x}) \tag{5-24}$$

where $\phi_l(\mathbf{x})$ is called a *fuzzy basis function* (FBF) [Wang and Mendel (1992a)] that is given, in the case of (5-21), as

$$\phi_l(\mathbf{x}) = \frac{\prod_{i=1}^{p} \mu_{F_i^l}(x_i)}{\sum_{l=1}^{M} \prod_{i=1}^{p} \mu_{F_i^l}(x_i)} \quad l = 1, \ldots, M \tag{5-25}$$

or, in the case of (5-23), as

$$\phi_l(\mathbf{x}) = \frac{\min_{i=1,\ldots,p}\left\{\mu_{F_i^l}(x_i)\right\}}{\sum_{l=1}^{M} \min_{i=1,\ldots,p}\left\{\mu_{F_i^l}(x_i)\right\}} \quad l = 1, \ldots, M \tag{5-26}$$

We can now refer to our FLS as a *FBF expansion*. Doing this is very useful, because it places a FLS into the more global perspective of function approximation. Remember though that the FBFs in (5-25) and (5-26) are valid only for very specific choices made about fuzzifier, composition, implication, and defuzzifier. Change any of these and (5-25) and (5-26) are no longer valid; but, the interpretation of a FLS as a FBF expansion still is valid (except for centroid defuzzification). Formulas that are comparable to these can be derived for many other possibilities.

Although the index l on the FBF seems to be associated with a rule number, i.e., $l = 1, \ldots, M$, each FBF is affected by all of the rules because of the denominator in $\phi_l(\mathbf{x})$; hence, it is only partially correct to associate the jth FBF just with the jth rule. Of course, if we add or remove a rule, thereby increasing or decreasing M, then we add or remove a FBF from the FBF expansion. It is in that sense that it is correct to associate the jth FBF with the jth rule.

The relationships between FBFs and other basis functions have been extensively studied by Kim and Mendel (1995). They are more general than radial basis functions, generalized radial basis functions, and hyper-basis functions [Poggio and Girosi (1990)]. For very special choices of their parameters and singleton fuzzification, they bear structural resemblance to generalized regression neural networks [Specht (1991)] and Gaussian sum approximations [Alspach and Sorenson (1972)]. The latter two begin by assuming that the measured data are random and that an estimate is desired of another random quantity. This bears no resemblance to our starting point for a FLS where no assumption about randomness has been made.

The denominator in (5-25), which is a result of the height defuzzifier, serves to normalize the numerators of the FBFs. The numerators are radially symmetric; hence, one could also refer to our FBFs as normalized radial basis functions. Such basis functions were originally suggested by Moody and Darkin (1989) as a means for sharing information across radial basis functions. Tao (1993) compared normalized and un-normalized radial basis functions, and demonstrated, by means of examples, the superiority of the former over the latter. It is important to note that FBFs are normalized not by abstraction, as in [Moody and Darkin (1989)], but rather by design of the overall FLS.

Many mathematical basis functions are orthogonal; but, not all basis functions have to be. FBFs are not, nor are the radial basis functions (e.g., [Haykin (1996)]) that are widely used in neural networks.

Example 5-5: [Mendel (1995)] What do the FBFs in (5-25) look like? We shall consider two situations, equally spaced and unequally spaced Gaussian antecedent membership functions. To visualize the FBFs on a two-dimensional plot, we choose dim $\mathbf{x} = p = 1$, so that $\phi_l(\mathbf{x}) = \phi_l(x)$. We also choose the number of rules, M, equal to 5. Standard deviations for all Gaussian antecedent membership functions are set equal to 10. In this case,

$$\mu_{F^l}(x) = \exp\left\{-\tfrac{1}{2}\left(\frac{x - m_{F^l}}{10}\right)^2\right\} \qquad l = 1, \ldots, 5 \qquad (5\text{-}27)$$

and

$$\phi_l(\mathbf{x}) = \frac{\exp\left\{-\tfrac{1}{2}\left[(x - m_{F^l})/10\right]^2\right\}}{\sum_{l=1}^{5}\exp\left\{-\tfrac{1}{2}\left[(x - m_{F^l})/10\right]^2\right\}} \qquad l = 1, \ldots, 5 \qquad (5\text{-}28)$$

In the equally spaced situation, we choose $m_{F^1} = 20$, $m_{F^2} = 35$, $m_{F^3} = 50$, $m_{F^4} = 65$ and $m_{F^5} = 80$. Figure 5-10 (a) depicts the five FBFs. Observe that the three interior FBFs are radially symmetric, whereas the two exterior FBFs are sigmoidal. These FBFs seem to combine the advantages of radial basis functions, which are good at characterizing local properties and sigmoidal neural networks, which are good at characterizing global properties.

Lest one believe that radial symmetry must occur for interior FBFs, we next consider the non-equally spaced situation, where we choose $m_{F^1} = 20$, $m_{F^2} = 25$, $m_{F^3} = 50$, $m_{F^4} = 62$ and $m_{F^5} = 80$. Figure 5-10 (b) depicts the five FBFs. Observe that the three interior FBFs are no longer radially symmetric, whereas the two exterior FBFs are still approximately sigmoidal. These figures should dispel the notion that fuzzy basis functions are radial basis functions. They are not; they are nonlinear functions of radial basis functions.

Equally spaced FBFs are possible only if the mean values (centers) of the antecedent membership functions can be fixed ahead of time by the designer. If these values are designed by means of a tuning procedure (as described in Section 5.9), so that they adapt to the data that is associated with the rules, then unequally spaced FBFs are the norm rather than the exception. ■

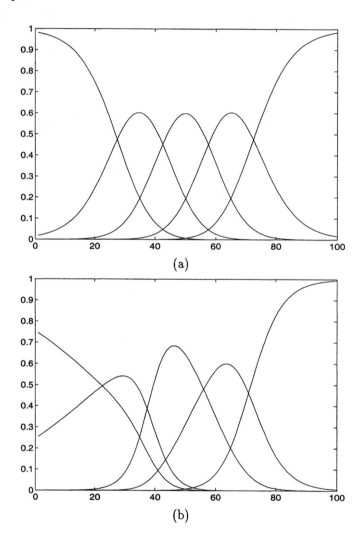

(a)

(b)

Figure 5-10: Fuzzy basis functions for five rules in singleton FLSs. (a) Equally spaced, and (b) unequally spaced Gaussian antecedent membership functions (Mendel, 1995a, © 1995, IEEE).

Rules can come from numerical data or they can come from expert linguistic knowledge. Each rule contributes a basis function to the FBF expansion. It is convenient, therefore, to decompose $f_s(\mathbf{x})$ into the sum of two terms, one associated with FBFs that are associated with rules that come from numerical data and the other associated with rules that come from linguistic information, i.e., $y(\mathbf{x}) = f_s(\mathbf{x}) = f_{s,N}(\mathbf{x}) + f_{s,L}(\mathbf{x})$. If we have a higher degree of belief in one set of rules over the other, then we can combine $f_{s,N}(\mathbf{x})$ and $f_{s,L}(\mathbf{x})$ in the following way:

$$y(\mathbf{x}) = f_s(\mathbf{x}) = \alpha f_{s,N}(\mathbf{x}) + (1 - \alpha) f_{s,L}(\mathbf{x}) \quad 0 \le \alpha \le 1 \tag{5-29}$$

When $\alpha = 0$, then $y(\mathbf{x}) = f_{s,L}(\mathbf{x})$, which means, of course, that we are only using linguistic information. On the other hand, if $\alpha = 1$, then $y(\mathbf{x}) = f_{s,N}(\mathbf{x})$, which means we are only using numerical information. It is only when $0 < \alpha < 1$ that we are combining linguistic and numerical information.

This is not the only way that we can combine linguistic and numerical information. One deficiency in using (5-29) is that it does not produce a strong coupling between the linguistic and numerical FBFs. Such coupling occurs when the denominators of all the basis functions are made dependent on *both* linguistic and numerical information. We illustrate how to do this next for singleton fuzzification, max-product composition, product implication, product t-norm, and height defuzzification. We begin by rewriting (5-24) as

$$y(\mathbf{x}) = f_s(\mathbf{x}) = \sum_{l=1}^{M} \bar{y}^l \phi_l(\mathbf{x}) = \sum_{i=1}^{M_N} \bar{y}_N^i \phi_{N,i}(\mathbf{x}) + \sum_{j=1}^{M_L} \bar{y}_L^j \phi_{L,j}(\mathbf{x}) \tag{5-30}$$

where there are M_N FBFs associated with numerical data and M_L FBFs associated with linguistic information, and $M_N + M_L = M$. The FBFs are given by:

$$\phi_{N,i}(\mathbf{x}) = \frac{\prod_{s=1}^{p} \mu_{F_s^i}(x_s)}{\sum_{l=1}^{M} \prod_{s=1}^{p} \mu_{F_s^l}(x_s)} \quad i = 1, \ldots, M_N \tag{5-31}$$

$$\phi_{L,j}(\mathbf{x}) = \frac{\prod_{s=1}^{p} \mu_{F_s^j}(x_s)}{\sum_{l=1}^{M} \prod_{s=1}^{p} \mu_{F_s^l}(x_s)} \quad j = 1, \ldots, M_L \tag{5-32}$$

Observe that the FBFs in (5-31) and (5-32) are normalized by information that is associated with both numerical and linguistic information, because their denominators depend on M, where $M = M_N + M_L$.

We have shown, therefore, that a large number of FLSs have the structure of a function approximator in which the basis functions of the approximator derive from either numerical or linguistic information. Each numerical rule leads to a FBF, as does each linguistic rule. To date, FBFs are the only basis functions that can include linguistic information as well as numerical information; this makes them quite unique among all function approximation techniques.

5.8 FLSs Are Universal Approximators

How well does a FLS approximate an unknown function? This is an important question that is asked about all types of function approximations, including the popular feedforward neural network (FFNN). Cybenko (1989), Hornik et al. (1989), Hornik (1993), as well as others (e.g., [Blum and Li (1991)]) demonstrated that a FFNN is a universal approximator, which means that a FFNN can uniformly approximate any real continuous non-linear function to arbitrary degree of accuracy. Hornik et al. (1989) used the Stone–Weirstrass theorem from real analysis to prove this result.

The same result has been proven, using the Stone–Weirstrass theorem, by Wang and Mendel (1992a) and Wang (1992b) for a singleton FLS that uses product composition, product implication, Gaussian membership functions, and height defuzzification. Kosko (1992, 1994) proved a similar result for an additive FLS, one that uses singleton fuzzification, centroid defuzzification, product composition, and product implication (i.e., the SAM), using the concept of *fuzzy patches*. There is now a very large literature about different kinds of FLSs that are universal approximators, all of which are summarized very well by Kreinovich et al. (1998).

A universal approximation theorem is an existence theorem. It helps to explain why a FLS is so successful in engineering applications; however, it does not tell us how to specify a FLS. The same is true for FFNN universal approximation theorems, which do not indicate how many layers of neurons should be used, how many neurons should be used in each layer, or how interconnected the neurons should be. Universal approximation theorems imply that by using *enough* layers, *enough* neurons in each layer, and *enough* interconnectivity, the FFNN can uniformly approximate any real continuous non-linear function to arbitrary degree of accuracy.

We have already seen the enormous number of possibilities for a FLS. The design degrees of freedom that control the *accuracy* of a FLS are: number of inputs, number of rules, and number of fuzzy sets for each input variable. Consider the ith input variable x_i, where $x_i \in X_i = [X_i^-, X_i^+]$. It is intuitively obvious that dividing the interval $[X_i^-, X_i^+]$ into 100 overlapping regions will lead to greater resolution, and consequently greater accuracy than dividing the interval $[X_i^-, X_i^+]$ into say 10 overlapping regions.

If there are p input variables, each of which is divided into r overlapping regions, then a complete FLS must contain p^r rules. As resolution parameter r increases, the size of the FLS becomes enormous (complex), i.e., there is an explosion in the number of rules—*rule explosion*. There must, therefore, be a practical tradeoff between resolution and complexity. In actual practice, one almost never needs a complete FLS of p^r rules. The reason for this is that in practical applications of a FLS, there are large regions of the input space that are never seen during the actual operation of a system; hence, rules are usually not needed for such regions. In short, one important way to achieve high resolution and low complexity is to *design* the FLS using *representative data* that are collected for a specific application. It is also possible to reduce the number of rules as part of the design of a FLS, as we explain in Section 5.9.4. Finally, it is possible to reduce the number of rules by making use of uncertainty, as we have explained in Section 2.2; but, this can only be done within the framework of type-2 FLSs.

5.9 Designing FLSs

Because of the large number of possibilities for FLSs, some guidelines are necessary for their practical designs. Linguistic rules are easily converted into their subset of FBFs, using FL, as we have explained earlier. Numerical rules and their associated FBFs must be extracted from numerical training data. Ultimately, after we have chosen the type of fuzzification, composition, implication, t-norm, defuzzification, and membership functions, we must fix the parameters of the membership functions. Prior to 1992, all FLSs reported in the open literature fixed these parameters somewhat arbitrarily, e.g., the locations and spreads of the membership functions were chosen by the designer independent of the numerical training data. Then, at the first IEEE Conference on Fuzzy Systems, held in San Diego in 1992, three different groups of researchers ([Horikowa et al. (1992)], [Jang (1992)], and [Wang and Mendel (1992b)]) presented the same idea: *tune the parameters of a FLS using the numerical training data*. Since that time, quite a few adaptive training procedures have been published. Because tuning of free parameters had been done in FFNNs long before it was done in a FLS, a tuned FLS has also come to be known as a *neural–fuzzy system*.

Designing a FLS [Mendel and Mouzouris (1997)] can be viewed as approximating a function or fitting a complex surface in a multi-dimensional high-dimensional space. Given a set of input–output pairs, tuning is essentially equivalent to determining a system that provides an optimal fit to the input–output pairs, with respect to a cost function. In addition, the system produced by the tuning algorithm should be able to generalize to certain regions of the multi-dimensional space where no training data are given, i.e., it must be able to interpolate the given input–output data. Within the framework of approximation and interpolation theory, it is common in many approximation /interpolation methods to generate the desired surface using a linear combination of basis functions (typically non-linear transformations of the input). We have already seen that a FLS can be expressed as such a linear combination of FBFs.

There exists a multitude of design methods that can be used to construct FLSs that have different properties and characteristics.[3] Some of these design methods are data-intensive, some are aimed at computational simplicity, some are recursive (thus giving the FLS an adaptive nature), some are offline, and some are application-specific. The textbook by Lin and Lee (1996) has a very good summary of many of these methods.

Our goal in this section is *not* to describe the different design approaches in complete detail. We shall briefly outline some of them in connection with the following problem:

> We are given a collection of N input–output numerical data *training* pairs, $(\mathbf{x}^{(1)}:y^{(1)}),(\mathbf{x}^{(2)}:y^{(2)}),\ldots,(\mathbf{x}^{(N)}:y^{(N)})$, where $\mathbf{x}$ is the vector input and y is the scalar output of a FLS. Our goal is to completely specify the FLS using the training data.

For illustrative purposes, all designs in this chapter assume singleton fuzzification, Gaussian membership functions, *product* implication and t-norm, and height defuzzification; hence, this FLS is described by (5-24) and (5-25). Note that the basic principles used in each design procedure carry over to many other FLSs.

To begin, we must explain how the training data can be interpreted as a collection of IF–THEN rules. Each rule is of the form given in (5-1), where F_i^l are fuzzy sets described by Gaussian membership functions, i.e.,

---

[3]For example: [Bardossy and Duckstein (1995)], [Berenji and Khedkar (1992)], [Chen and Chang (1996)], [Chen and Chen (1993)], [Cho et al. (1998)], [Cooper (1995)], [Daley and Gill (1986)], [Dickerson and Kosko (1993, 1994)], [Figueiredo and Gomide (1999)], [Gonzalez and Perez (1995)], [Hasan et al. (1994)], [Hohenson and Mendel (1994, 1996)], [Hsu and Chen (1990)], [Jang (1992)], [Jang and Sun (1995)], [Langari and Wang (1995)], [Larkin (1985)], [Lin and Lin (1995)], [Linkens and Nyongesa (1995a, b)], [Liu and Huang (1994)], [Mancuso et al. (1995)], [Mendel and Mouzouris (1997)], [Momoh et al. (1995)], [Mori and Kobayashi (1996)], [Nawa and Furuhashi (1999)], [Pedrycz (1992)], [Rahmoun and Benmohamed (1998)], [Shi et al. (1999)], [Tong (1985)], [Vidal-Verdu and Rodriguez-Vazquez (1995)], [Wang (1999)], [Wu and Chen (1999)], [Yasunobu and Miyamota (1985)], [Zhang and Kandel (1998)], [Zhang and Morris (1995)], and [Zheng and Singh (1997)].

$$\mu_{F_i^l}(x_i) = \exp\left\{-\frac{1}{2}\left(\frac{x_i - m_{F_i^l}}{\sigma_{F_i^l}}\right)^2\right\} \tag{5-33}$$

where $i = 1, \ldots, p$ and $l = 1, \ldots, M$. Each design method establishes how to specify the parameters $m_{F_i^l}$ and $\sigma_{F_i^l}$ of these membership functions, as well as the centers of the consequent membership functions, the $\bar{y}^l$ in (5-24), using the training pairs $(\mathbf{x}^{(1)}:y^{(1)}),(\mathbf{x}^{(2)}:y^{(2)}),\ldots,(\mathbf{x}^{(N)}:y^{(N)})$.

How many rules there can be in the FLS depends on the design method that is used to construct it. If no tuning of the FLS parameters is done, then there can be as many as $M = N$ rules. If tuning is used, and we abide by the commonly used design principle that there must be fewer tuned design parameters than training pairs, then we must use less than N rules.

Example 5-6: Let us enumerate how many design parameters there can be in the just-stated design:

- Antecedent parameters $m_{F_i^l}$ and $\sigma_{F_i^l}$: 2 per antecedent, p antecedents, and M rules, for a total of $2pM$ parameters.
- Consequent parameter $\bar{y}^l$: 1 per consequent and M rules, for a total of M parameters.

Consequently, the maximum number of design parameters is $2pM + M$. We say "maximum" because in some design methods all of these parameters are not tuned, i.e., some are fixed ahead of time. In other design approaches the number of parameters may be reduced. For example, in Jang (1993) and Jang and Sun (1995), each rule has p antecedents and each antecedent has a fixed number (s) of fuzzy sets that are common to all M rules, and it is assumed that each of the M rule's common antecedent membership functions are characterized by the *same* two parameters; hence, there will only be $2ps$ antecedent parameters—and $2ps \ll 2pM$.

From our discussion just before this example, we see that if no tuning of FLS parameters is done, then there can be as many as $2pN + N$ parameters that are pre-specified; however, if tuning is used, then there is the following design constraint:

$$2pM + M < N \tag{5-34}$$

Usually, the number of antecedents, p, is fixed ahead of time; so, this inequality can be used to choose M or N. For example, if we are given a fixed number of training samples, $N = N'$, then

$$M < N'/(2p+1) \tag{5-35}$$

which constrains the number of rules that can be used. Because M must be an integer, we choose $M = M'$ as an integer that is smaller than $N'/(2p + 1)$. ∎

At a very high level, we can think of three designs associated with the preceding formulation:

1. Fix the shapes and parameters of all the antecedent and consequent membership functions ahead of time. The data establish the rules and no tuning is used.
2. Fix the shapes and parameters of the antecedent membership functions ahead of time. Use the training data to tune the consequent parameters [the $\bar{y}^l$ in (5-24)]. Because the FLS is linear in the consequent parameters [see (5-24)], this leads to an easy optimization problem.
3. Fix the shapes of all the antecedent and consequent membership functions ahead of time. Use the training data to tune the antecedent and consequent parameters. Because the FLS is non-linear in the antecedent parameters [see (5-25)], this leads to a more difficult optimization problem than in the second design.

Naturally, other even more complicated design problems can be formulated that try to answer questions such as: (a) what shape membership functions should be used, (b) how many and which antecedents should be used (e.g., can p be reduced?), and (c) how many and which rules should be used (e.g., can M be reduced?)? Evolutionary optimization algorithms can be used to address the first of these questions, systematic trial and error or evolutionary optimization algorithms are viable approaches to answering the second question, and singular-value decomposition techniques can be used to answer the third question. Because answers to the second and third questions can reduce the complexity of the FLS, these questions should not be ignored.

In the rest of this section we briefly describe some design methods that can be used for the three designs just formulated, and also for rule-reduction.

5.9.1 One-pass methods

Two one-pass methods were described in Section 4.2.1. Recall that in Method 1 we let the data establish the centers of the fuzzy sets that appear in the antecedents and consequent of the rules. This method leads to a FLS with exactly $M = N$ rules, and is the one-pass method that we shall use below when we design a FLS for forecasting the chaotic Mackey–Glass time-series.

In Method 2 we pre-specify fuzzy sets for the antecedents and consequents, and then associate the data with the fuzzy sets. This method, which leads to a FLS with $M \le N$ rules, which is also known as the *Wang–Mendel Method*

[Cox (1995)], was briefly described in Chapter 4 in the context of the time-series case study. Because it is widely used in many other contexts, we expand on its description here.

Given a set of training data, or input–output pairs

$$(\mathbf{x}^{(1)}:y^{(1)}),(\mathbf{x}^{(2)}:y^{(2)}),\ldots,(\mathbf{x}^{(N)}:y^{(N)}) = \left\{ x_1^{(t)},x_2^{(t)},\ldots,x_p^{(t)}:y^{(t)} \right\}_{t=1}^{N} \qquad (5\text{-}36)$$

where $x_1,x_2,\ldots,x_p$ are inputs and y is the output, we proceed as follows to construct a FLS:

1. Let $[X_1^-,X_1^+],[X_2^-,X_2^+],\ldots,[X_p^-,X_p^+],[Y^-,Y^+]$ be the domain intervals of the input and output variables, respectively, where domain interval implies the interval the variable is most likely to lie in. We divide each domain interval into $2L + 1$ regions, where L can be different for each variable. Then, we assign membership functions to the regions, labeled SL (Small L), ..., $S1$(Small 1), CE (Center), $B1$(Big 1), ..., and BL (Big L). Of course, other label names can be used instead of these names.

2. Because of overlapping membership functions, it frequently happens that $x_k^{(t)}$ is in more than one fuzzy set. We therefore evaluate the membership of each input–output point in regions where it may occur, and assign the given $x_1^{(t)},x_2^{(t)},\ldots x_p^{(t)}$, or $y^{(t)}$ to the region with maximum membership.

3. To resolve conflicting rules, i.e., rules with the same antecedent membership functions and different consequent membership functions, we assign a degree to each rule as follows: let $\mu_{X_k}(x_k^{(t)})$ denote the membership of the kth input variable in the region $\left[X_k^-,X_k^+ \right]$ with maximum membership, and let $\mu_Y(y^{(t)})$ denote the membership of the output variable in the region $\left[Y^-,Y^+ \right]$ with maximum membership, where X_k and Y are labels from their corresponding sets SL, ..., $S1$, CE, $B1$, ..., BL. Then, the degree for the tth rule, R^t, is defined as

$$D(R^t) = \left[\prod_{k=1}^{p} \mu_{X_k}(x_k^{(t)}) \right] \mu_Y(y^{(t)}) \qquad t = 1,\ldots,N \qquad (5\text{-}37)$$

In the event of conflicting rules, the rule with the highest degree, $D(R^t)$, is kept in the rule-base, and all other conflicting rules are discarded.

4. We generate a combined rule-base comprised both of numerically generated fuzzy rules (as described earlier) and linguistic information provided by experts.

5. After the combined rule-base is generated, we employ a defuzzification

method—in the present case, the height defuzzifier—to obtain the crisp output of the FLS.

Steps 1-3 extract the rules from the data. Step 4 joins all the rules together as in (5-1). Step 5 completes the description of the FLS. Knowing the antecedents and the consequent for all rules, as well as their membership functions, it is straightforward to translate this information into a FBF expansion, as in (5-24). Note that all of the parameters of this FLS have been specified during this one-pass design.

The simplicity of this method has led to its use and recommendation by others (e.g, [Lin and Lee (1996)], [Cox (1995)]); however, it does have some shortcomings, namely: (1) how to choose the parameters of the antecedent and consequent membership functions is left as an open issue, and (2) it can lead to a FLS that has too many rules.

5.9.2 Least-squares method

In the least-squares method ([Wang (1992a, 1994)], [Wang and Mendel (1992a)]), all of the antecedent parameters, i.e., the FBFs, are fixed by the designer, and only the centers of the consequent membership functions, the $\bar{y}^l$ in (5-24), are tuned. The number of FBFs (i.e., the number of rules), M, must also be specified subject to the design constraint $M < N$ (since there are only M design parameters). Then, a standard least-squares optimization problem can be formulated (e.g., [Mendel (1995b)]), leading to a straightforward least-squares solution for the $\bar{y}^l$.

Example 5-7: Here we illustrate the least-squares formulation and solution. Beginning with (5-24), which we repeat here for the convenience of the reader, but using the notation for the elements in our training set, we have

$$y(\mathbf{x}^{(i)}) = f_s(\mathbf{x}^{(i)}) = \sum_{l=1}^{M} \bar{y}^l \phi_l(\mathbf{x}^{(i)}) \quad i = 1,...,N \tag{5-38}$$

Collecting the N equations, they can be expressed in vector-matrix format as:

$$\mathbf{y} = \Phi\theta \tag{5-39}$$

where

$$\mathbf{y} = [y^{(1)},...,y^{(N)}]^T = [y(\mathbf{x}^{(1)}),...,y(\mathbf{x}^{(N)})]^T \tag{5-40}$$

$$\mathbf{x} = [x_1, x_2, ..., x_p]^T \tag{5-41}$$

$$\theta = [\bar{y}^1, ..., \bar{y}^M]^T \tag{5-42}$$

and

$$\Phi = \begin{pmatrix} \phi_1(\mathbf{x}^{(1)}) & \cdots & \phi_M(\mathbf{x}^{(1)}) \\ \vdots & \ddots & \vdots \\ \phi_1(\mathbf{x}^{(N)}) & \cdots & \phi_M(\mathbf{x}^{(N)}) \end{pmatrix} \tag{5-43}$$

where $\phi_l(\mathbf{x})$ ($l = 1, ..., M$) are defined in (5-25). Matrix Φ is called a *fuzzy basis function matrix*. The least-squares design for θ, θ_{LS}, is obtained by minimizing

$$J(\theta) = \tfrac{1}{2}[\mathbf{y} - \Phi\theta]^T[\mathbf{y} - \Phi\theta] \tag{5-44}$$

with respect to θ. Doing this minimizes the sum of the squared errors between the left- and right-hand sides of (5-38) for all $i = 1, ..., N$. The solution to this optimization problem can be expressed as

$$[\Phi^T\Phi]\theta_{LS} = \Phi^T\mathbf{y} \tag{5-45}$$

which is a linear system of equations (known as the *normal equations*) that has to be solved for θ_{LS}. The most numerically sound methods for doing this involve orthogonal transformations (e.g., [Golub and Van Loan (1989)]). Another numerically sound method for finding θ_{LS} is SVD. It does not solve (5-45) directly; instead, it is based on the SVD of Φ (e.g., see Lesson 4 in [Mendel (1995b)]). ∎

Drawbacks to the least-squares method are: (1) how to choose the parameters of the antecedent membership functions is left as an open issue, and (2) how to choose the number of FBFs, M, is also left as an open issue. Usually, each variable is broken up into "enough" fuzzy sets so as to cover its domain interval with "enough" resolution. The centers of the Gaussian membership functions can be located at the centers of the intervals associated with each variable's fuzzy sets. The standard deviations can be chosen so that the membership functions have "sufficient" overlap.

An orthogonal least-squares (OLS) procedure can be used to select the most significant FBFs (i.e., for rule-reduction). The detailed formulas for the OLS procedure can be found in [Wang (1994)] and [Wang and Mendel (1992a)], and are based on the works of [Chen et al. (1989, 1991)]. Linguistic information can be incorporated as a subset of the FBFs. The OLS procedure then establishes the simultaneous significance of linguistically and data-based FBFs. Unfortunately, the OLS procedure is somewhat of a brute-force method for determining M because it requires choosing $M = 1, 2, ..., M_{max}$ and solving a least-squares optimization design problem for each value of M. The design stops when a value for M has been reached—say M^*, where $M^* \leq M_{max}$—for which there is no longer an appreciable decline in the value of $J(\theta)$.

5.9.3 Back-propagation (steepest descent) method

In the back-propagation method none of the antecedent or consequent parameters are fixed ahead of time. They are all tuned using a steepest descent method that we briefly describe in this section. We begin by recalling that

$$y(\mathbf{x}^{(i)}) = f_s(\mathbf{x}^{(i)}) = \sum_{l=1}^{M} \bar{y}^l \phi_l(\mathbf{x}^{(i)})$$

$$= \frac{\sum_{l=1}^{M} \bar{y}^l \prod_{k=1}^{p} \exp\left(-\frac{\left(x_k^{(i)} - m_{F_k^l}\right)^2}{2\sigma_{F_k^l}^2}\right)}{\sum_{l=1}^{M} \prod_{k=1}^{p} \exp\left(-\frac{\left(x_k^{(i)} - m_{F_k^l}\right)^2}{2\sigma_{F_k^l}^2}\right)} \qquad i = 1, ..., N \qquad (5\text{-}46)$$

Given an input–output training pair $(\mathbf{x}^{(i)} : y^{(i)})$, we now wish to design the FLS in (5-46) such that the following error function is minimized:

$$e^{(i)} = \tfrac{1}{2}[f_s(\mathbf{x}^{(i)}) - y^{(i)}]^2 \qquad i = 1, ..., N \qquad (5\text{-}47)$$

It is evident from (5-46) that f_s is completely characterized by $\bar{y}^l$, $m_{F_k^l}$ and $\sigma_{F_k^l}$ ($l = 1, ..., M$ and $k = 1, ..., p$). Using a steepest descent algorithm to minimize $e^{(i)}$, it is straightforward (see Exercise 5-9) to obtain the following recursions to update all the design parameters of this FLS ($k = 1, ..., p$, $l = 1, ..., M$ and $i = 0, 1, ...$):

$$m_{F_k^l}(i+1) = m_{F_k^l}(i) - \alpha_m [f_s(\mathbf{x}^{(i)}) - y^{(i)}][\bar{y}^l(i) - f_s(\mathbf{x}^{(i)})]$$
$$\times \frac{\left[x_k^{(i)} - m_{F_k^l}(i)\right]}{\sigma_{F_k^l}^2(i)} \phi_l(\mathbf{x}^{(i)}) \qquad (5\text{-}48)$$

$$\bar{y}^l(i+1) = \bar{y}^l(i) - \alpha_{\bar{y}}[f_s(\mathbf{x}^{(i)}) - y^{(i)}]\phi_l(\mathbf{x}^{(i)}) \qquad (5\text{-}49)$$

and

$$\sigma_{F_k^l}(i+1) = \sigma_{F_k^l}(i) - \alpha_\sigma[f_s(\mathbf{x}^{(i)}) - y^{(i)}]\left[\bar{y}^l(i) - f_s(\mathbf{x}^{(i)})\right]$$

$$\times \frac{\left[x_k^{(i)} - m_{F_k^l}(i)\right]^2}{\sigma_{F_k^l}^3(i)}\phi_l(\mathbf{x}^{(i)}) \qquad (5\text{-}50)$$

In (5-50), we update $\sigma_{F_k^l}$ instead of $\sigma_{F_k^l}^2$, because $\sigma_{F_k^l}^2$ must be positive (i.e., $\sigma_{F_k^l}^2$ is constrained) whereas $\sigma_{F_k^l}$ can be positive or negative (i.e., $\sigma_{F_k^l}$ is unconstrained). We then square up $\sigma_{F_k^l}$ to obtain $\sigma_{F_k^l}^2$. Values for $m_{F_k^l}(0)$, $\bar{y}^l(0)$ and $\sigma_{F_k^l}(0)$ must be provided to initialize (5-48)–(5-50). How to do this is application-dependent and is discussed in Section 5.10.2. Because $\bar{y}^l$, $m_{F_k^l}$, and $\sigma_{F_k^l}$ are parameters associated with membership functions for physically meaningful quantities, it is usually possible to obtain very good initial values for them. About the worst way to initialize these parameters is to choose them randomly. Doing this will cause the back-propagation algorithm to converge very slowly. Choosing them smartly will cause this algorithm to converge much faster (see [Chu and Mendel (1994)]).

The learning parameters, α_m, $\alpha_{\bar{y}}$, and α_σ must also be chosen with some care. Frequently, they are chosen to be the same, say α. Choosing too large a value for α can cause the algorithm not to converge, whereas choosing too small a value for α can cause the algorithm to take a very long time to converge. In practice, one often must develop a schedule for how to choose α. One schedule is to choose it larger for the early iterations of the algorithm and to then let it become smaller for later iterations of the algorithm.

Let one *epoch* be defined as the collection of N training data. We have just described a back-propagation algorithm in which each element of the training set is used only one time, and the FLS parameters are updated using an error function, (5-47) that depends only on one data point at a time. Training occurs for only one epoch. Other variations are possible, including:

1. Apply (5-48)–(5-50) within an epoch and then for many epochs until convergence occurs.
2. Define a squared error function that depends on all N training data. Redevelop (5-48)–(5-50) for this new error function and apply the modified back-propagation algorithm until convergence occurs.

Recall that a FFNN is a layered architecture, and that when its parameters (weights) are optimized using the method of steepest descent, the resulting algorithm is called a *back-propagation algorithm*. In that algorithm, the output error is propagated in a backward direction from the output layer down into lower layers, hence the name *back-propagation*. Wang (1992a) was the first to show that the FLS described by (5-24) and (5-25) could also be viewed as a layered architecture, one with three layers. Equations (5-48)–(5-50) are therefore referred to as a *back-propagation algorithm* because of their dependence on the error $f_s(\mathbf{x}^{(i)}) - y^{(i)}$, which propagates from the output layer of the FLS down into lower layers.

A drawback to the back-propagation method is that how to choose the number of FBFs, M, is left as an open issue. Our next method can be used to resolve this drawback.

5.9.4 SVD–QR method

Rule explosion is a major disadvantage of a FLS. Some design methods have been proposed to eliminate it. Wang and Mendel (1992a) proposed an OLS method to select the most important FBFs, each of which is associated with a specific rule. Yen and Wang (1999) used an eigenvalue decomposition method to construct a reduced fuzzy model. Mouzouris and Mendel (1996, 1997) used a SVD–QR method to extract the most important fuzzy rules from a given rule base. Yen and Wang (1996) proposed using a direct SVD method to determine the number and positions of the most significant fuzzy rules. Yam et al. (1999) also used the SVD for rule reduction. Because the SVD is widely used in signal processing (e.g., [Haykin (1996)] and [Mendel (1995b)]), we focus here on the SVD–QR method.

The SVD of a matrix is a very powerful tool in numerical linear algebra. Among its important uses are the determination of the rank of a matrix and numerical solutions of linear least-squares problems. It can be applied to square or rectangular matrices, whose elements are either real or complex. According to Klema and Laub (1980, p. 166),

> The SVD was established for real square matrices in the 1870s by Beltrami and Jordan (see, e.g., [MacDuffee (1933), p. 78]), for complex square matrices by Autonne (1902), and for general rectangular matrices by Eckart and Young (1939) (the Autonne–Eckart–Young theorem).

The SVD is presently one of the major computational tools in signal processing.

Let $\mathbf{H}$ be a $K \times M$ matrix, and $\mathbf{U}$ and $\mathbf{V}$ be two $K \times K$ and $M \times M$ unitary matrices, respectively. The SVD of $\mathbf{H}$ is:

$$\mathbf{H} = \mathbf{U}\left[\begin{array}{c|c}\Sigma & \mathbf{0} \\ \hline \mathbf{0} & \mathbf{0}\end{array}\right]\mathbf{V} \qquad (5\text{-}51)$$

where

$$\Sigma = \mathrm{diag}(\sigma_1, \sigma_2, \ldots, \sigma_r) \qquad (5\text{-}52)$$

and

$$\sigma_1 \ge \sigma_2 \ge \cdots \ge \sigma_r > 0 \qquad (5\text{-}53)$$

The σ_is are the *singular values* of $\mathbf{H}$ and r is the rank of $\mathbf{H}$. This decomposition is true for both the over-determined ($K > M$) and under-determined ($K < M$) cases.

There are many excellent sources for comprehensive discussions about the SVD, including its derivation and how to compute it (e.g., [Stewart (1973)], [Golub and Van Loan (1989)], [Haykin (1996)], and [Mendel (1995b)]). We do not present any of those details here since doing so would take us too far afield from our main purpose for this section, which is to explain how the SVD can be used to choose the most important of the M FBFs in (5-24).

The SVD provides a natural way to separate a space into dominant and sub-dominant subspaces. If we view the FBF matrix Φ in (5-43) as a span of the input subspace, then the SVD of Φ decomposes the span into an equivalent orthogonal span, from which we can identify the dominant and subdominant spans [Vaccaro (1991)], i.e., we can identity which FBFs contribute the most to the FLS, and how many of them are needed to effectively represent it. The FBFs that contribute the least can be discarded, and a reduced parsimonious FLS can be designed. Note that the SVD approach only reorders the original FBFs to form a set of independent FBFs; thus, it preserves the meaning of linguistic information initially incorporated into the system.

The steps of the SVD–QR algorithm ([Mouzouris and Mendel (1996, 1997)], [Yen and Wang (1996, 1999)]) are:

1. Calculate the SVD of the FBF matrix Φ given in (5-43). Computer programs for doing this are widely available, e.g., MATLAB® (MATLAB is a registered trademark of The MathWorks, Inc.).

2. Estimate the numerical rank of Φ by examining the singular values of this matrix. A common choice for the numerical rank is the number of singular values that are above a small threshold that must be pre-specified.

3. Keep that part of the SVD of Φ associated with the estimated numerical rank of Φ.

4. Using a QR algorithm (e.g., [Golub and Van Loan (1989)]), rank-order the

FBFs that are associated with the rank-ordered singular values that are above the small threshold. Doing this leads to another FBF matrix, $\Phi_{M'}$, where

$$\Phi_{M'} = \begin{pmatrix} \phi_1'(\mathbf{x}^{(1)}) & \cdots & \phi_{M'}'(\mathbf{x}^{(1)}) \\ \vdots & \ddots & \vdots \\ \phi_1'(\mathbf{x}^{(N)}) & \cdots & \phi_{M'}'(\mathbf{x}^{(N)}) \end{pmatrix} \tag{5-54}$$

in which $M' < M$ and the primed FBFs denote the fact that they have been re-ordered. The FBF expansion in (5-24) now is:

$$y(\mathbf{x}^{(i)}) = f_s(\mathbf{x}^{(i)}) = \sum_{l=1}^{M'} \bar{y}^l \phi_l'(\mathbf{x}) \tag{5-55}$$

5. Re-normalize the denominators of the M' FBFs using the firing levels for just those FBFs. If this step is not performed, then the FBFs will still be normalized by the firing levels of the original M FBFs, which defeats the purpose of the SVD–QR method (see, also [Hohenson and Mendel (1994, 1996)]).

6. Determine the M' $\bar{y}^l$ parameters in (5-55) using the least-squares method described earlier.

We illustrate this design method at the end of Chapter 12, where we apply SVD–QR methods to the designs of five FLSs, two type-1 and three type-2.

Although the SVD–QR design method provides optimal values for $\bar{y}^l$ in a least-squares sense, it does not provide any values for the remaining design parameters of the FLS. The antecedent membership function parameters must be pre-specified to use the SVD-QR design method.[4]

5.9.5 Iterative design method

By combining the SVD–QR method with the back-propagation method, we can design all of the parameters of the FLS including the number of the most significant FBSs, M'. The following iterative design method can be very successful:

1.   Fix the number of FBFs, M, at a reasonable value.

---

[4]Very recently, Setnes and Hellendoorn (2000) considered a pivoted QR decomposition to order and select fuzzy rules. They point out that rank-revealing methods that are based on the SVD do not produce an "importance ordering" of the rules. Our use of the SVD in the SVD–QR method does not attempt to determine the rank of a matrix. We simply use a pre-specified small number to compare the singular values, accepting those above that number and rejecting the others. In that way, we are assured that the kept rules contain all the important ones, although they may not be in the order of importance.

2. Use the back-propagation method to design all the antecedent and consequent parameters.

3. Apply the SVD–QR method to the results of the back-propagation method to determine $M' < M$ and the associated FBFs.

4. If performance is acceptable, STOP. Otherwise, return to Step 2 for a retuning of the antecedent and consequent parameters.

5.10 CASE STUDY: FORECASTING OF TIME-SERIES

We have described the problem of forecasting a time-series in Section 4.2. Here we examine two designs of singleton type-1 FLS forecasters for the Mackey–Glass time-series. One design is based on the one-pass method (Method 1) and the other is based on the back-propagation method. Both designs are based on the following noise-free 1,000 data points: $s(1001), s(1002), \ldots, s(2000)$. Note that we use the notation $s(k)$ here instead of $x(k)$ to emphasize the fact that our measurements are noise-free; hence, they are of the signal itself. Later, we shall also be interested in noise-corrupted versions of $s(k)$, which we denote as $x(k)$, i.e.,

$$x(k) = s(k) + n(k) \quad k = 1001, 1002, \ldots, 2000 \tag{5-56}$$

where $n(k)$ is the additive measurement noise. We used the first 504 data, $s(1001), s(1002), \ldots, s(1504)$, for designing the FLS forecasters, whereas the remaining 496 data, $s(1505), s(1502), \ldots, s(2000)$, were used for testing the designs. We depict the noise-free Mackey-Glass time-series, $s(1001), s(1002), \ldots, s(2000)$, in Figure 5-11a.

We used four antecedents for forecasting, namely $s(k-3)$, $s(k-2)$, $s(k-1)$, and $s(k)$ to predict $s(k+1)$. Gaussian membership functions were used in both designs, and we evaluated the performance of both designs using the following root mean-squared error (RMSE):

$$RMSE_s = \sqrt{\tfrac{1}{496} \sum_{k=1504}^{1999} \left[s(k+1) - f_s(\mathbf{s}^{(k)}) \right]^2} \tag{5-57}$$

where $\mathbf{s}^{(k)} = [s(k-3), s(k-2), s(k-1), s(k)]^T$ and the subscript "s" on RMSE reminds us that this is a singleton design .

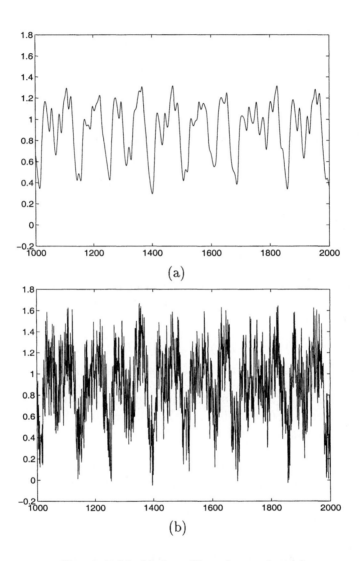

Figure 5-11: Mackey–Glass time-series. (a) noise-free data, $s(1001)$, $s(1002)$, ..., $s(2000)$, and (b) one realization of 0dB uniformly-distributed noisy data, $x(1001)$, $x(1002)$, ..., $x(2000)$.

5.10.1 One-pass design

We used the Method-1 (Section 4.2.1) one-pass design to construct 500 rules from $s(1001), s(1002), \ldots, s(1504)$. The antecedent and consequent membership functions were centered at the noise-free measurements in each one of the 500 rules, and the standard deviation of the Gaussians was set equal to 0.1. This established the singleton FLS $f_s(\mathbf{s})$. Then we used $s(1505), s(1502), \ldots, s(2000)$ to compute the one-pass RMSE in (5-57). Its value is $RMSE_s(OP) = 0.0438$.

Although this design is very simple, it leads to a FLS with 500 rules, which seems rather excessive. Our next design demonstrates better RMSE performance using only 16 rules.

5.10.2 Back-propagation design

As in Jang (1993), we used only two fuzzy sets (which is as small a number as one can use in a FLS) for each of the four antecedents; hence, the number of rules is very small and equals $2^4 = 16$. Each rule is characterized by eight antecedent membership function parameters (the mean and standard deviation for each of the four Gaussian membership functions) and one consequent parameter, $\bar{y}$. The *initial* location of each Gaussian antecedent membership function was based on the mean, m_s, and the standard deviation, σ_s, of the data in the 504 training samples, $s(1001), s(1002), \ldots, s(1504)$. More specifically, we initially chose the mean of each and every antecedent's two Gaussian membership functions as $m_s - 2\sigma_s$ or $m_s + 2\sigma_s$, respectively, and their standard deviations as $2\sigma_s$. We used the height defuzzifier and initially chose the center of each consequent's membership function, $\bar{y}^i$ ($i = 1, \ldots, 16$), to be a random number from the interval [0, 1]. After training using the back-propagation method, as described in Section 5.9.3, in which the learning parameter $\alpha = 0.2$, the FLS forecaster was fixed. Its performance was then evaluated using the RMSE in (5-57).

The initial values of the centers of the Gaussian antecedent membership functions as well as of all $\bar{y}^i$ are given in Table 5-1. The initial values of the standard deviations of these Gaussian membership functions were all set equal to the same value of 0.5240. The final values of all these parameters after six epochs of tuning are given in Tables 5-2 and 5-3.

The back-propagation RMSE, $RMSE_s(BP)$, for each of the six epochs of tuning are:

$$RMSE_s(BP) = \{0.0548, 0.0431, 0.0322, 0.0261, 0.0237, 0.0232\} \qquad (5\text{-}58)$$

Table 5-1: Initial values for the centers of the Gaussian antecedent membership functions and the centroid of the consequent set. Note that $m_s - 2\sigma_s = 0.3793$ and $m_s + 2\sigma_s = 1.4272$.

Rule Number	Initial Value for Centers of the Four Antecedent Membership Functions				Initial Value for $\bar{y}^l$
1	0.3793	0.3793	0.3793	0.3793	0.5314
2	0.3793	0.3793	0.3793	1.4272	0.3831
3	0.3793	0.3793	1.4272	0.3793	0.0159
4	0.3793	0.3793	1.4272	1.4272	0.8181
5	0.3793	1.4272	0.3793	0.3793	0.6931
6	0.3793	1.4272	0.3793	1.4272	0.1209
7	0.3793	1.4272	1.4272	0.3793	0.4647
8	0.3793	1.4272	1.4272	1.4272	0.9975
9	1.4272	0.3793	0.3793	0.3793	0.9522
10	1.4272	0.3793	0.3793	1.4272	0.6991
11	1.4272	0.3793	1.4272	0.3793	0.2673
12	1.4272	0.3793	1.4272	1.4272	0.7625
13	1.4272	1.4272	0.3793	0.3793	0.6460
14	1.4272	1.4272	0.3793	1.4272	0.6483
15	1.4272	1.4272	1.4272	0.3793	0.3887
16	1.4272	1.4272	1.4272	1.4272	0.8687

These values were obtained by tuning for one epoch and then testing the design on the testing data, $s(1505), s(1502), \ldots, s(2000)$; then, tuning for a second epoch and again testing on the testing data, and so forth, for six epochs. There is a substantial reduction in the RMSE from the first epoch to the sixth epoch, and we can see a leveling off of the RMSE at around the fifth epoch, so stopping the tuning after the sixth epoch is reasonable.

Recall that $RMSE_s(OP) = 0.0438$, whereas $RMSE_s(BP) = 0.0232$ for our final back-propagation design. It is rather amazing that a FLS with only 16 rules vastly outperforms the 500-rule FLS. This confirms our earlier comment that although the one-pass method is simple it leads to a FLS with too many rules (basis functions).

Table 5-2: Final values for the centers of the Gaussian antecedent membership functions and the centroid of the consequent set, after six epochs of tuning.

Rule Number	Final Value for Centers of the Four Antecedent Membership Functions				Final Value for $\bar{y}^l$
1	0.4001	0.3613	0.3076	0.1694	0.4986
2	0.3075	0.2707	0.1988	1.5524	0.3860
3	0.4273	0.3821	1.3487	0.2121	0.0035
4	0.2586	0.3205	1.3205	1.3434	0.8631
5	0.3451	1.5229	0.3352	0.3297	0.6929
6	0.2942	1.5375	0.2316	1.4938	0.1211
7	0.3473	1.4700	1.4523	0.2704	0.4622
8	0.5727	1.1876	1.2624	1.3675	1.2695
9	1.5721	0.3604	0.3790	0.3960	0.9506
10	1.4782	0.2994	0.2817	1.4598	0.7021
11	1.4265	0.4093	1.3689	0.3367	0.2556
12	1.4560	0.2404	1.4518	1.4497	0.7644
13	1.4698	1.4427	0.3778	0.3500	0.6403
14	1.4748	1.4641	0.2593	1.4445	0.6486
15	1.4555	1.4210	1.3917	0.3730	0.3868
16	1.3964	1.4352	1.4933	1.6955	0.8715

5.10.3 A change in the measurements

Suppose we now have the following situation: we have just designed (in Section 5.10.2) two FLS forecasters based on perfect measurements, expecting that they will operate in the same noise-free environment; but, instead, the environment changes and they must now operate in a noisy measurement environment. How robust are the just-designed type-1 FLS forecasters to this noisy measurement environment? To answer this question we tested our final FLS forecasters on noisy testing data, i.e., $x(k) = s(k) + n(k)$, $k = 1505, 1506, \ldots, 2000$, where $n(k)$ is 0 dB uniformly distributed noise [Figure 5-11 (b)]. We did this for a Monte-Carlo set of 50 realizations. Figure 5-12 depicts the outputs of our two singleton type-1 FLS forecasters for the 50 Monte-Carlo realizations (i.e., each part of Figure 5-12 is the superimposition of 50 plots). Observe that the 500-rule one-pass-designed forecaster is more robust to the unexpected noise than is the 16-rule back-propagation-designed forecaster. Its standard deviation (i.e., the thickness of the superimposed plots) is visibly smaller than that of the back-propagation design. Having more rules makes the one-pass designed forecaster less susceptible to the additive measurement noise.

Table 5-3: Final values for the standard deviations of the Gaussian antecedent membership functions after six epochs of tuning.

Rule Number	Final Value for Standard Deviations			
1	0.5649	0.5254	0.4571	0.2268
2	0.4646	0.4094	0.2630	0.3728
3	0.5403	0.5075	0.7142	0.1399
4	0.3043	0.4044	0.6618	0.5931
5	0.5109	0.3561	0.4589	0.4267
6	0.4224	0.3640	0.2616	0.4736
7	0.4987	0.4718	0.5109	0.2772
8	0.6775	0.7240	0.6280	0.3527
9	0.2497	0.5214	0.5362	0.5489
10	0.4766	0.4106	0.3519	0.4872
11	0.4682	0.5493	0.6171	0.2966
12	0.5154	0.2404	0.5106	0.5082
13	0.4408	0.4884	0.5000	0.4111
14	0.4754	0.4926	0.2648	0.5216
15	0.4618	0.5299	0.5777	0.3553
16	0.5861	0.5408	0.4678	0.1198

Note that we are in no way advocating the use of a one-pass or a back-propagation designed singleton FLS forecaster in a noisy measurement environment. In fact, if we know that only noisy measurements will be used in the FLS forecaster, then such measurements should be accounted for and used during the design of the forecaster. This can be done in a number of different ways, and we shall explore all of them in later chapters of this book.

❀❀❀❀❀❀❀❀❀❀

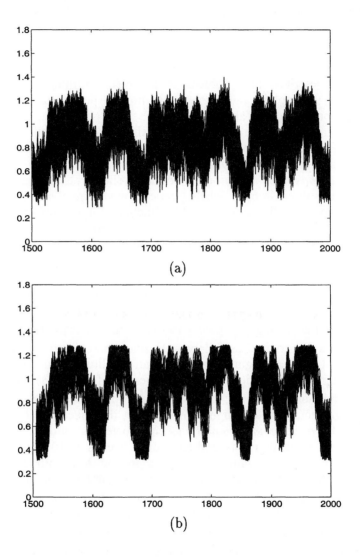

Figure 5-12: Outputs of the: (a) back-propagation-designed type-1 singleton FLS forecaster, and (b) one-pass-designed type-1 singleton FLS forecaster. In both cases, there are 50 Monte-Carlo realizations and the data from time-point 1504 to 2000 are corrupted by additive uniformly distributed noise with *SNR* = 0dB.

5.11 CASE STUDY: KNOWLEDGE MINING USING SURVEYS

We have described the problem of knowledge mining using surveys in Chapter 4. Here we explain and demonstrate how to design fuzzy logic advisors using the data presented in Tables 4-2–4-5.

First, we must associate type-1 membership functions with the Table 4-2 interval data. Figure 5-13 depicts the membership functions we have chosen for the five linguistic labels (*none to very little, some, a moderate amount, a large amount*, and *a maximum amount*). We have chosen triangular membership functions for the three interior labels (*some, a moderate amount*, and *a large amount*) and piecewise-linear membership functions for the left-most and right-most labels (*none to very little* and *a maximum amount*). These choices were made because it is relatively easy, as we explain next, to go from the data in Table 4-2 to them.

The triangular membership functions were constructed as follows (values for all symbols are given in Table 4-2): (1) their apex was located at $(a+b)/2$; (2) their left-end base point was located at $a-\sigma_a$, and (3) their right-end base point was located at $b+\sigma_b$. The piecewise-linear membership function for *none to very little* was constructed as follows: (1) since there is no uncertainty about its left-hand end point, it begins at zero with an amplitude of unity; (2) the unity amplitude continues to the right until it reaches $b = 1.9850$; (3) the point $b+\sigma_b$ is located on the horizontal axis; and (4) the two points established in Steps (2) and (3) are connected by a straight line. Finally, the piecewise linear membership function for *a maximum amount* was constructed as follows: (1) since there is no uncertainty about its right-hand end point, it ends at 10 with an amplitude of unity; (2) the unity amplitude continues to the left until it reaches $a = 8.5500$; (3) the point $a-\sigma_a$ is located on the horizontal axis; and, (4) the two points established in Steps (2) and (3) are connected by a straight line.

There is uncertainty associated with our use of $a-\sigma_a$ and $b+\sigma_b$; e.g. why not use $a-0.5\sigma_a$ or $a-2\sigma_a$, instead of $a-\sigma_a$, and $b+0.5\sigma_b$ or $b+1.5\sigma_b$ instead of $b+\sigma_b$? This uncertainty cannot be captured using type-1 fuzzy sets; however, as we explain in Chapter 10, it can be captured using type-2 fuzzy sets.

The centroids of the five fuzzy sets, which are used below in (5-60), are:

$$c_1 = c_{NVL} = 1.1811, \; c_2 = c_S = 4.0507, \; c_3 = c_{MOA} = 5.0402,$$
$$c_4 = c_{LA} = 7.5666, \; c_5 = c_{MAA} = 9.1015 \tag{5-59}$$

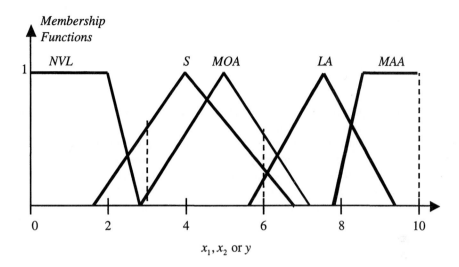

Figure 5-13: Membership functions for the five linguistic labels *none to very little* (*NVL*), *some* (*S*), *a moderate amount* (*MOA*), *a large amount* (*LA*), and *a maximum amount* (*MAA*).

Results from three surveys are summarized in Tables 4-3–4-5. The two single-antecedent surveys asked questions of the form " IF x_1 is F^i, THEN what is y?" ($i = 1, ..., 5$) or " IF x_2 is F^j , THEN what is y?" ($j = 1, ..., 5$), whereas the two-antecedent survey asked questions of the form " IF x_1 is F^i and x_2 is F^j, THEN what is y?" ($i, j, = 1, ..., 5$). Tables 4-3–4-5 reveal that each rule has a histogram of responses, which raises the question "what should be done with this information?" Three possibilities come to mind:

1. Keep the response chosen by the largest number of experts. So, for example, the consequent used for Rule 4 in Table 4-3 would be *a large amount*.

2. Find a weighted average of the rule consequents for each rule. In this case, the consequent of each rule is treated as a number, c_{avg}^l (e.g., a two-antecedent rule is now interpreted as IF x_1 is F^i and x_2 is F^j, THEN $y = c_{avg}^l$), where

$$c_{avg}^l = \frac{\sum_{i=1}^{5} c_i w_i^l}{\sum_{i=1}^{5} w_i^l}$$

(5-60)

in which c_i is the centroid of the ith consequent set and w_i^l is the weight associated with the ith consequent for the lth rule. The entries in Tables 4-3–4-5 are the weights.

3. Preserve the distributions of the expert-responses for each rule.

Obviously, preserving the distributions of the expert responses for each rule makes maximum use of the uncertainties associated with rule consequents; however, it is computationally very costly. We discuss this strategy some more later. Keeping the response chosen by the largest number of experts completely ignores the uncertainties associated with rule consequents; hence, we shall not adopt this strategy. Finally, finding a weighted average of the rule consequents for each rule uses some aspects of the uncertainties associated with rule consequents and does not lead to exessive computations. It is the strategy that we shall adopt. In this chapter, however, we do not make use of any of the uncertainties associated with the weighted average. In Chapter 10 we show how to account for these uncertainties.

5.11.1 Averaging the responses

To begin, we must compute c_{avg}^l for the results in Tables 4-3–4-5. These results are summarized in Tables 5-4–5-6. Note that c_{avg}^l plays the role of $\bar{y}^l$ in the FBF expansion (5-24). From Tables 5-4–5-6 and (5-24), it is straightforward to

Table 5-4: Histogram of survey responses for single-antecedent rules between indicator x_1 and consequent y. Entries denote the number of respondents out of 47 (w_i^l) that chose the consequent. c_{avg}^l is the weighted average of the responses, given by (5-60).

	Consequent					
Rule No.	None to Very Little	Some	A Moderate Amount	A Large Amount	A Maximum Amount	c_{avg}^l
1 (NVL)	42	3	2	0	0	1.5285
2 (S)	33	12	0	2	0	2.1855
3 (MOA)	12	16	15	3	1	3.9657
4 (LA)	3	6	11	25	2	6.1842
5 (MAA)	3	6	8	22	8	6.5414

Table 5-5: Histogram of survey responses for single-antecedent rules between indicator x_2 and consequent y. Entries denote the number of respondents out of 47 (w_i^l) that chose the consequent. c_{avg}^l is the weighted average of the responses, given by (5-60).

	Consequent					
Rule No.	None to Very Little	Some	A Moderate Amount	A Large Amount	A Maximum Amount	c_{avg}^l
1 (NVL)	36	7	4	0	0	1.9369
2 (S)	26	17	4	0	0	2.5475
3 (MOA)	2	16	27	2	0	4.6466
4 (LA)	1	3	11	22	10	6.9416
5 (MAA)	0	3	7	17	20	7.6191

compute the three consensus FLAs $y_{c1}(x_1)$, $y_{c1}(x_2)$ and $y_{c1}(x_1, x_2)$ (where the subscript "c1" denotes "consensus type-1"), as:

$$y_{c1}(x_1) = \sum_{l=1}^{5} c_{avg}^l \phi_l(x_1) = \sum_{l=1}^{5} c_{avg}^l \left[\frac{\mu_{F_1^l}(x_1)}{\sum_{l=1}^{5} \mu_{F_1^l}(x_1)} \right], \qquad (5\text{-}61)$$

$$c_{avg}^l \text{ from Table 5-4}$$

$$y_{c1}(x_2) = \sum_{l=1}^{5} c_{avg}^l \phi_l(x_2) = \sum_{l=1}^{5} c_{avg}^l \left[\frac{\mu_{F_1^l}(x_2)}{\sum_{l=1}^{5} \mu_{F_1^l}(x_2)} \right], \qquad (5\text{-}62)$$

$$c_{avg}^l \text{ from Table 5-5}$$

$$y_{c1}(x_1, x_2) = \sum_{l=1}^{25} c_{avg}^l \phi_l(x_1, x_2)$$

$$= \sum_{l=1}^{25} c_{avg}^l \left[\frac{\mu_{F_1^l}(x_1) \times \mu_{F_2^l}(x_2)}{\sum_{l=1}^{25} \mu_{F_1^l}(x_1) \times \mu_{F_2^l}(x_2)} \right], \qquad (5\text{-}63)$$

$$c_{avg}^l \text{ from Table 5-6}$$

Table 5-6: Histogram of survey responses for two-antecedent rules between indicators x_1 and x_2 and consequent *y*. Entries denote the number of respondents out of 47 (w_i^l) that chose the consequent. c_{avg}^l is the weighted average of the responses, given by (5-60).

| | Consequent | | | | | |
Rule No.	None to Very Little	Some	A Moderate Amount	A Large Amount	A Maximum Amount	c_{avg}^l
1 (NVL/NVL)	38	7	2	0	0	1.7727
2 (NVL/S)	33	11	3	0	0	2.0990
3 (NVL/MOA)	6	21	16	4	0	4.3204
4 (NVL/LA)	0	12	26	8	1	5.3040
5 (NVL/MAA)	0	9	16	19	3	6.1313
6 (S/NVL)	31	11	4	1	0	2.3170
7 (S/S)	17	23	7	0	0	3.1601
8 (S/MOA)	0	19	19	8	1	5.1566
9 (S/LA)	1	8	23	13	2	5.6613
10 (S/MAA)	0	7	17	21	2	6.1945
11 (MOA/NVL)	7	23	16	1	0	4.0350
12 (MOA/S)	5	22	20	0	0	4.1665
13 (MOA/MOA)	2	7	22	15	1	5.6213
14 (MOA/LA)	1	4	13	17	12	6.8246
15 (MOA/MAA)	0	4	12	24	7	6.8509
16 (LA/NVL)	7	13	21	6	0	4.5143
17 (LA/S)	3	11	23	10	0	5.0998
18 (LA/MOA)	0	3	18	18	8	6.6359
19 (LA/LA)	0	1	9	17	20	7.6612
20 (LA/MAA)	1	2	6	11	27	7.8403
21 (MAA/NVL)	2	16	18	11	0	5.1304
22 (MAA/S)	2	9	22	13	1	5.4717
23 (MAA/MOA)	0	3	15	18	11	6.8951
24 (MAA/LA)	0	1	7	17	22	7.8340
25 (MAA/MAA)	0	2	3	12	30	8.2354

Plots of $y_{c1}(x_1)$, $y_{c1}(x_2)$, and $y_{c1}(x_1, x_2)$ are depicted in Figures 5-14, 5-15, and 5-16, respectively.

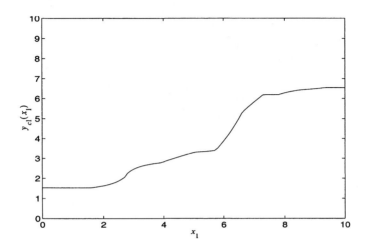

Figure 5-14: FLA $y_{c1}(x_1)$.

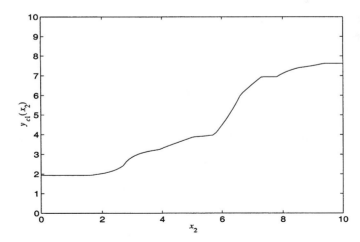

Figure 5-15: FLA $y_{c1}(x_2)$.

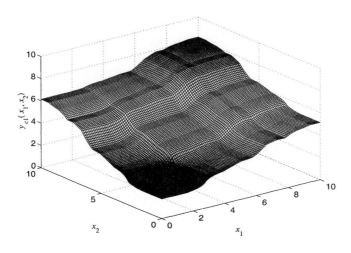

Figure 5-16: FLA $y_{c1}(x_1, x_2)$.

Example 5-8: We show a sample calculation of $y_{c1}(x_1, x_2)$ when $(x_1, x_2) = (3, 6)$. Observe, from Figure 5-13, that when $x_1 = 3$ two subsets are fired, S and MOA, and their firing degrees are 0.6032 and 0.1052 respectively. When $x_2 = 6$ three subsets are fired, S, MOA, and LA, and their firing degrees are 0.2275, 0.5801, and 0.1409, respectively. It follows, therefore, that the rules whose antecedent pairs are (S, S), (S, MOA), (S, LA), (MOA, S), (MOA, MOA), and (MOA, LA) are the ones fired. From Table 5-6, we see that these are Rules 7, 8, 9, 12, 13, and 14. The firing degree for each of these rules is obtained by multiplying the rule's respective antecedent firing degrees, e.g., the firing degree for R^8 is $0.6032 \times 0.5801 = 0.3499$. Consequently, we can compute $y_{c1}(3, 6)$ using (5-63), as

$$
\begin{aligned}
y_{c1}(3,6) = & \left[\frac{1}{(0.1372 + 0.3499 + 0.0850 + 0.0239 + 0.0610 + 0.0148)} \right] \\
& \times [0.1372 \times 3.1601 + 0.3499 \times 5.1566 + 0.0850 \times 5.6613 \\
& + 0.0239 \times 4.1665 + 0.0610 \times 5.6213 + 0.0148 \times 6.8246] \quad \text{(5-64)} \\
= & \ 3.2629 / 0.6719 \\
= & \ 4.8564
\end{aligned}
$$

■

Note that single-antecedent FLAs for x_1 and x_2 implicitly assume independence between x_1 and x_2, whereas a zero value for either x_1 or x_2 in the two-antecedent FLA is not equivalent to independence between x_1 and x_2; hence, $y_{c1}(x_1,0) \neq y_{c1}(x_1)$ and $y_{c1}(0,x_2) \neq y_{c1}(x_2)$.

Now that the three FLAs have been designed, it may be useful for the reader to reread Section 4.3.4 to recall the main limitation of a type-1 FLA, namely, that no uncertainties have been incorporated into it, so that its output is only a point value. We rectify this in Chapter 10.

5.11.2 Preserving all the responses

Each possible response to every question can be considered to form one rule of a FLA, and since one rule in a FLA can have only one consequent, different responses to the same question can be considered as rules from different FLAs. All the expert responses taken together can be viewed as a collection of many different type-1 FLAs, each corresponding to one combination of expert responses. For each of the single-antecedent results in Tables 5-4 and 5-5, there are $5^5 = 3,125$ possible type-1 FLAs. For the two-antecedent results in Table 5-6, there are $5^{25} = 9,765,625$ possible type-1 FLAs. Each possible consequent for every rule can be assigned a weight that is equal to the percentage of experts who voted in favor of it; hence, each rule in every one of the 3,125 or 9,765,625 FLAs can be assigned the weight of its consequent, and each FLA can be assigned a weight equal to the t-norm of the weight of its 5 or 25 rules. Consequently, one survey can be represented as a collection of many different type-1 FLAs, each having this weight associated with it. While this may be somewhat practical for our single-antecedent survey results, it is impractical for our two-antecedent survey results. For additional discussions about this approach, see Karnik and Mendel (1998b).

5.12 A Final Remark

When no uncertainties are present, then singleton type-1 FLSs, as explained in this chapter, can provide excellent results. Input (type-1) measurement uncertainties, in the absence of linguistic uncertainties, are better handled using non-singleton type-1 FLSs, as described in Chapter 6, whereas linguistic uncertainties, in the absence or in the presence of input measurement uncertainties, are better handled using type-2 FLSs, which are described in Chapters 10–12.

5.13 COMPUTATION

The following M-files, which are found in the folder *type-1 FLSs*, are useful for designing a singleton type-1 FLS:

> **sfls_type1.m:** Compute the output(s) of a singleton type-1 FLS when the antecedent membership functions are Gaussian.
>
> **train_sfls_type1.m:** Tune the parameters of a singleton type-1 FLS when the antecedent membership functions are Gaussian, using some input–output training data.
>
> **svd_qr_sfls_type1.m:** Rule-reduction of a singleton type-1 FLS when the antecedent membership functions are Gaussian, using some input–output training data.

EXERCISES

5-1: Create a graphical example of $\mu_B(y)$ for which the mean-of-maxima defuzzifier provides a zero value even though $\mu_B(y)$ is non-zero over most of its range.

5-2: Derive (5-16) by beginning with the additive combiner depicted in Figure 5-3, assuming product implication and product t-norm, and formally determining the center of gravity of its output $\mu_B(y) = \sum_{l=1}^{M} w_l \mu_{B^l}(y)$ [Hint: $c_{G^l} = \int_{-\infty}^{\infty} y\mu_{G^l}(y) \Big/ \int_{-\infty}^{\infty} \mu_{G^l}(y) = \int_{-\infty}^{\infty} y\mu_{G^l}(y) \Big/ a_{G^l}$]. Kosko (1997) refers to the result in (5-16) as the "Standard Additive Model (SAM) Theorem." Does this result hold for product implication, but minimum t-norm between $\mu_{G^l}(y)$ and the firing level in (5-10)?

5-3: Prove Theorem 5-1 [Hint: $\mu_{G^l}(\bar{y}^l) = 1$].

5-4: Which *features* of a fired-rule consequent set are used by the center-of-sums, height, and center-of-sets defuzzifiers?

5-5: Repeat Example 5-5 for the FBFs in (5-26).

5-6: Suppose that triangles are used for all the interior membership functions and piecewise linear functions are used for the two shoulder (exterior) membership functions. Enumerate the design parameters for this case.

5-7: Derive the normal equations in (5-45).

5-8: Suppose one of the antecedent variables has for its domain [0, 10], and is broken into five overlapping fuzzy sets. Explain where to locate the centers of the Gaussian membership functions, and how to choose a common standard deviation for them.

5-9: A steepest descent algorithm to minimize $J(\theta)$ has the following general structure $\theta(i+1) = \theta(i) - \alpha \mathrm{grad}_\theta [J(\theta)]\big|_i$ where α is a positive step size, and $[\ ]_i$ indicates that, after taking the gradient of $J(\theta)$ with respect to θ, we must replace all remaining θ values by $\theta(i)$. Based on this structure, and $J(\theta) = e^{(i)}$ in (5-47), derive Equations (5-48)–(5-50).

5-10: Define a squared error function that depends on all N training data, and redevelop (5-48)–(5-50) for this new error function.

5-11: Show that the FLS described by (5-24) and (5-25) can be viewed as a three-layered architecture.

5-12: Establish all of the numerical values that are needed to completely specify the five membership functions depicted in Figure 5-13.

5-13: Explain how to go from the data in Table 4-2 to Gaussian membership functions for all five labels.

5-14: As in Example 5-8, compute $y_{cl}(2,4)$.

5-15: Examine Figure 5-13 and explain why it is possible for a single-antecedent FLA to fire 1, 2, or 3 rules, and for a two-antecedent FLA to fire 1, 2, 3, 4, 6, or 9 rules.

Non-Singleton Type-1 Fuzzy Logic Systems

6.1 INTRODUCTION

A non-singleton type-1 FLS is a type-1 FLS whose inputs are modeled as type-1 fuzzy numbers; hence, it can be used to handle uncertainties that occur when uncertain inputs (e.g., noisy measurements), which are modeled as such numbers, are applied to a type-1 FLS. Note that we are not in any way advocating that this is the only or the best way to handle such uncertainties. In fact, it is not, and in later chapters we show that a better way to do this is to use a type-2 FLS. Some people, however, may still prefer to use a type-1 FLS; hence, our objective in this chapter is to explain how it is possible to improve performance within the framework of a type-1 FLS when uncertain inputs are applied to such systems, even though better results can be obtained using a type-2 FLS.

A non-singleton type-1 FLS is described by the same diagram as is a singleton type-1 FLS (Figure 5-1) which we repeat here as Figure 6-1, for the convenience of the readers. The rules of a non-singleton type-1 FLS are the same as those for a singleton type-1 FLS. What is different is the fuzzifier, which treats the inputs as type-1 fuzzy sets, and the effect of this on the inference block. The output of the inference block will again be a type-1 fuzzy set. So, the defuzzifiers that we described for a singleton type-1 FLS apply as well to a non-singleton type-1 FLS.

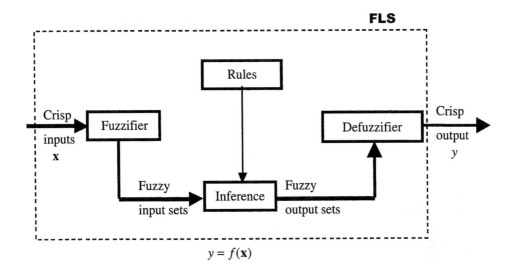

Figure 6-1: Type-1 FLS, singleton or non-singleton.

6.2 FUZZIFICATION AND ITS EFFECT ON INFERENCE

In the FLS of Figure 6-1, as in the FLS of Figure 5-1, crisp inputs are first fuzzi-fied into fuzzy input sets that then activate the inference block. In this section, we explain non-singleton fuzzification and the effect of such fuzzification on the inference engine.

6.2.1 Fuzzifier

In non-singleton fuzzification, measurement $x_i = x_i'$ is mapped into a fuzzy number [Kaufman and Gupta (1991)]; i.e. a membership function is associated with it. More specifically:

> a *non-singleton fuzzifier* is one for which $\mu_{X_i}(x_i') = 1$ $(i = 1,...,p)$ and $\mu_{X_i}(x_i)$ decreases from unity as x_i moves away from x_i'.

Conceptually, the non-singleton fuzzifier implies that the given input value x_i' is the most likely value to be the correct one from all the values in its immediate neighborhood; however, because the input is corrupted by noise, neighboring points are also likely to be the correct value, but to a lesser degree.

It is up to the designer to determine the shape of the membership function $\mu_{X_i}(x_i)$ based on an estimate of the kind and quantity of noise present. It seems logical, though, for this membership function to be symmetric about x_i' since the effect of noise is most likely to be equivalent on all points. Examples of such membership functions are:

1. Gaussian: $\mu_{X_i}(x_i) = \exp\left[-(x_i - x_i')^2 / 2\sigma^2\right]$

2. Triangular: $\mu_{X_i}(x_i) = \max\left(0, 1 - |(x_i - x_i')/c|\right)$

3. Unnamed: $\mu_{X_i}(x_i) = 1/\left(1 + |(x_i - x_i')/c|^n\right)$

where x_i' is the center value of the fuzzy sets and $\sigma(c)$ is the spread of these sets. Larger values of the spread for these membership functions imply that more noise is anticipated to exist in the data.

6.2.2 Fuzzy Inference Engine

The reader should review the section in Chapter 5 that has the same name as this section, because we pick up its story here with Equation (5-7), i.e.,

$$\mu_{B^l}(y) = \mu_{G^l}(y) \star \left\{ \left[\sup_{x_1 \in X_1} \mu_{X_1}(x_1) \star \mu_{F_1^l}(x_1)\right] \star \right.$$
$$\left. \cdots \star \left[\sup_{x_p \in X_p} \mu_{X_p}(x_p) \star \mu_{F_p^l}(x_p)\right] \right\}, \quad y \in Y \tag{6-1}$$

where $l = 1, \ldots, M$. Recall that, for singleton fuzzification, (6-1) simplifies to (5-10) in which all of the suprema are very easy to evaluate because each $\mu_{X_i}(x_i)$ is non-zero only at the single point $x_i = x_i'$. Unfortunately, the same simplification does not occur for non-singleton fuzzification.

We define

$$\mu_{Q_k^l}(x_k) \equiv \mu_{X_k}(x_k) \star \mu_{F_k^l}(x_k) \tag{6-2}$$

where $k = 1, \ldots, p$ and $l = 1, \ldots, M$, and let the value of x_k at which the supremum of $\mu_{Q_k^l}(x_k)$ occurs[1] be denoted $x_{k,\max}^l$. Then, (6-1) can be re-expressed as:

$$\mu_{B^l}(y) = \mu_{G^l}(y) \star \left[T_{k=1}^p \mu_{Q_k^l}(x_{k,\max}^l) \right] \tag{6-3}$$

where $y \in Y$ and $l = 1,\dots,M$. This is the fundamental equation for a non-singleton type-1 FLS. The bracketed term is the *firing level* for a non-singleton type-1 FLS.

Comparing (6-3) and (5-10), we see that a non-singleton FLS first *pre-filters* its input **x**, transforming it to $\mathbf{x}_{\max}^l$. This is depicted in Figure 6-2. Doing this accounts for the effects of the input measurement uncertainty. This pre-filtering is a direct result of the sup-star composition and occurs naturally within the existing framework of a FLS. Interestingly enough, no such pre-filtering occurs naturally within the framework of neural networks.

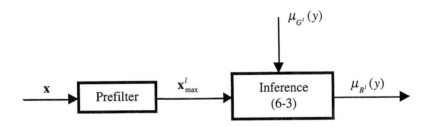

Figure 6-2: Prefiltering of the input to a non-singleton FLS.

Example 6-1: Here, analogous to Example 5-1, we consider a pictorial description of (6-3) for the minimum and product t-norms. Figure 6-3 depicts input and antecedent operations—the bracketed term in (6-3)—for a two-antecedent–single-consequent rule, non-singleton fuzzification, and minimum or product t-norms. The reader again should be sure that he or she understands how these figures were obtained from the bracketed term in (6-3). As in Figure 5-4, the main thing to observe from these figures is that regardless of the t-norm, the result of input and antecedent operations is again a number—the *firing level*. Consequently, the results depicted in Figures 5-5 [$\mu_{B^l}(y)$ for a two-rule FLS] and 5-6 (combined output set for a two-rule FLS) remain the same for a non-singleton type-1 FLS. The only difference between a type-1 non-singleton and singleton FLS is the *numerical value* of the firing level. For a non-singleton type-1 FLS this value includes the effects of input uncertainties, whereas for a singleton type-1 FLS it does not. ∎

---

[1] We are, of course, assuming that the supremum occurs at only a single point.

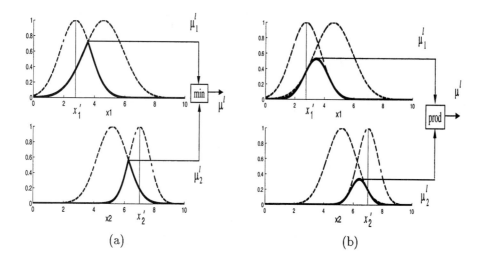

(a)   (b)

Figure 6-3: Pictorial description of input and antecedent operations for a non-singleton type-1 FLS. (a) Minimum t-norm and (b) product t-norm.

Example 6-2: Here we quantify the results that were presented in Example 6-1. When the t-norm is the product and all membership functions are Gaussian, then it is straightforward to carry out the supremum computations of (6-1). The kth input fuzzy set and the corresponding rule antecedent fuzzy sets are assumed to have the following membership functions:

$$\mu_{X_k}(x_k) = \exp\left\{-\frac{1}{2}\left[\frac{x_k - m_{X_k}}{\sigma_{X_k}}\right]^2\right\} \tag{6-4}$$

where $k = 1, \ldots, p$, and

$$\mu_{F_k^l}(x_k) = \exp\left\{-\frac{1}{2}\left[\frac{x_k - m_{F_k^l}}{\sigma_{F_k^l}}\right]^2\right\} \tag{6-5}$$

where $k = 1, \ldots, p$ and $l = 1, \ldots, M$. By maximizing the function in (6-2), i.e.,

$$\mu_{Q_k^l}(x_k) = \mu_{X_k}(x_k)\mu_{F_k^l}(x_k) \tag{6-6}$$

we find (Exercises 1-27 and 6-1) that it is maximum at [Mouzouris and Mendel (1997)]

$$x^l_{k,\max} = \frac{\sigma^2_{X_k} m_{F^l_k} + \sigma^2_{F^l_k} m_{X_k}}{\sigma^2_{X_k} + \sigma^2_{F^l_k}} \tag{6-7}$$

where $k = 1, \ldots, p$ and $l = 1, \ldots, M$, at which value of x_k

$$\mu_{Q^l_k}(x^l_{k,\max}) = \exp\left\{-\frac{1}{2}\frac{\left(m_{X_k} - m_{F^l_k}\right)^2}{\sigma^2_{X_k} + \sigma^2_{F^l_k}}\right\} \tag{6-8}$$

where $k = 1, \ldots, p$ and $l = 1, \ldots, M$. In the special but important case when all input points for each input variable have the same level of uncertainty (e.g., as in time-series forecasting), the spreads of the input sets will be the same, in which case $\sigma^2_{X_k}$ in (6-7) and (6-8) is a constant. Also, we usually choose the mean of the fuzzy input sets, m_{X_k}, as the crisp input x'_k. Under these conditions, (6-7) and (6-8) simplify to:

$$x^l_{k,\max} = \frac{\sigma^2_X m_{F^l_k} + \sigma^2_{F^l_k} x'_k}{\sigma^2_X + \sigma^2_{F^l_k}} \tag{6-9}$$

where $k = 1, \ldots, p$ and $l = 1, \ldots, M$, and

$$\mu_{Q^l_k}(x^l_{k,\max}) = \exp\left\{-\frac{1}{2}\frac{\left(x'_k - m_{F^l_k}\right)^2}{\sigma^2_X + \sigma^2_{F^l_k}}\right\} \tag{6-10}$$

where $k = 1, \ldots, p$ and $l = 1, \ldots, M$. This result means that, in the special case of Gaussian membership functions and product t-norm, it is possible to interpret the non-singleton FLS as a singleton FLS. The membership functions of the latter are given by (6-10) [or (6-8)]. Comparing (6-10) with (6-5), we see that the uncertainty about the measurements, contained in σ^2_X, causes the membership functions in the equivalent singleton FLS to become broader; i.e., $\sigma^2_{F^l_k}$ is replaced by $\sigma^2_{F^l_k} + \sigma^2_X$.

Comparing (6-10) and (6-5), observe that $\mu_{Q^l_k}(x^l_{k,\max}) > \mu_{F^l_k}(x_k)$, which means that the firing level is larger in the non-singleton case than it is in the singleton case. We provide a FBF interpretation for this in Example 6-5.

Note that when the uncertainty of the input becomes zero (i.e., $\sigma^2_X = 0$), then (6-9) reduces to the singleton case; i.e., $x^l_{k,\max} = x'_k$, for which (6-4) (in which we have already set

$m_{X_k} = x_k'$) becomes

$$\mu_{X_k}(x_{k,\max}^l = x_k') = \exp\left\{-\tfrac{1}{2}\left(\frac{x_k' - x_k'}{\sigma_{X_k}}\right)^2\right\} = 1 \tag{6-11}$$

where $k = 1, ..., p$, so that [from (6-6)]

$$\mu_{Q_k^l}(x_{k,\max}^l) = \mu_{F_k^l}(x_{k,\max}^l) = \mu_{F_k^l}(x_k') \tag{6-12}$$

where $k = 1, ..., p$ and $l = 1, ..., M$, which agrees with the third line of (5-10).

For minimum t-norm, $\mu_{Q_k^l}(x_k) = \min\left[\mu_{X_k}(x_k), \mu_{F_k^l}(x_k)\right]$, and it is easy to show that when all membership functions are Gaussian (Exercises 1-28 and 6-2),

$$x_{k,\max}^l = \frac{\sigma_{X_k} m_{F_k^l} + \sigma_{F_k^l} m_{X_k}}{\sigma_{X_k} + \sigma_{F_k^l}} \tag{6-13}$$

where $k = 1, ..., p$ and $l = 1, ..., M$. ■

Unfortunately, it is very difficult to repeat the analytical calculations given in Example 6-2 for other types of membership functions. In general, the supremum operations in (6-2) have to be performed numerically, and this is very time-consuming. Although formulas for $x_{k,\max}^l$ are given in Mouzouris and Mendel (1997) for the case when all membership functions are triangles, these formulas are, in my opinion, too complicated to be used in design situations where, for example, derivatives of membership functions must be computed with respect to their parameters—as in the back-propagation design method. For this reason, we advocate the use of Gaussian membership functions throughout a design. After a design is completed, the Gaussian membership functions can be replaced by triangles to simplify online computations, if one wants to do this.

We reiterate the statement made at the end of Section 6.1, that the defuzzifiers we described for a singleton type-1 FLS apply as well to a non-singleton type-1 FLS; hence, we refer the reader to Chapter 5 for discussions about centroid, center-of-sums, height, modified height, and center-of-sets defuzzifiers.

❀❀❀❀❀❀❀❀❀❀

6.3 POSSIBILITIES

Section 5.6 (see, also, Figure 5-9) enumerated all of the possible design choices that have to be made by a designer of a type-1 singleton FLs. That section also applies as is for a non-singleton type-1 FLS. What is new for a non-singleton type-1 FLS is the need for the designer to choose membership functions for the input measurements, something that wasn't necessary for a singleton type-1 FLS. If, for example, the designer chooses a Gaussian membership function for each input, then the mean and standard deviation need to be specified for each function. These represent the additional new possibilities for a non-singleton type-1 FLS.

6.4 FBFs

As in Section 5.7, we note that the pictorial interpretations we have provided for the inference block of a non-singleton type-1 FLS, in Figures 6-3, 5-5 and 5-6, while informative, do not provide us with a complete description of the FLS. From Figure 6-1, we see that a formula for $y = f(\mathbf{x})$ can be obtained by following the signal $\mathbf{x}$ through the fuzzifier, where it is converted into the fuzzy set $A_{\mathbf{x}}$, into the inference block, where it is converted into the fuzzy sets B^l or set B, and finally into the defuzzifier, where it is converted into $f(\mathbf{x})$. To write such a formula, we must again make specific choices for fuzzifier, membership functions, composition, implication, and defuzzifier.

Example 6-3: This example parallels Example 5-3. When we choose non-singleton fuzzification, max-product composition, product implication, and height defuzzification, leaving the choice of membership functions open, it is easy to show that

$$y(\mathbf{x}) = f_{ns}(\mathbf{x}) = \frac{\sum_{l=1}^{M} \bar{y}^l \prod_{k=1}^{p} \mu_{Q_k^l}(x_{k,\max}^l)}{\sum_{l=1}^{M} \prod_{k=1}^{p} \mu_{Q_k^l}(x_{k,\max}^l)} \tag{6-14}$$

We use the subscript "ns" on $f_{ns}(\mathbf{x})$ to remind us that this is a non-singleton FLS. To obtain (6-14), we started with (5-17) and substituted for $\mu_{B^l}(\bar{y}^l)$ from (6-3), i.e.,

$$\mu_{B^l}(\bar{y}^l) = \left[\prod_{k=1}^{p} \mu_{Q_k^l}(x_{k,\max}^l)\right] \times \mu_{G^l}(\bar{y}^l) = \prod_{k=1}^{p} \mu_{Q_k^l}(x_{k,\max}^l) \tag{6-15}$$

where we have again assumed that membership functions are normalized, so that

$\mu_{G^l}(\bar{y}^l) = 1.$ ∎

Example 6-4: This example parallels Example 5-4. When we choose non-singleton fuzzification, max-min composition, minimum implication, and height defuzzification, again leaving the choice of membership functions open, it is easy to show that

$$y(\mathbf{x}) = f_{ns}(\mathbf{x}) = \frac{\sum_{l=1}^{M} \bar{y}^l \min_{k=1,\ldots,p}\left\{\mu_{Q_k^l}(x_{k,\max}^l)\right\}}{\sum_{l=1}^{M} \min_{k=1,\ldots,p}\left\{\mu_{Q_k^l}(x_{k,\max}^l)\right\}} \quad ∎ \tag{6-16}$$

The FLSs in (6-14) and (6-16) can also be represented as

$$y(\mathbf{x}) = f_{ns}(\mathbf{x}) = \sum_{l=1}^{M} \bar{y}^l \phi_l(\mathbf{x}) \tag{6-17}$$

where $\phi_l(\mathbf{x})$ is a FBF, given, in the case of (6-14), as

$$\phi_l(\mathbf{x}) = \frac{\prod_{k=1}^{p} \mu_{Q_k^l}(x_{k,\max}^l)}{\sum_{l=1}^{M} \prod_{k=1}^{p} \mu_{Q_k^l}(x_{k,\max}^l)} \quad l = 1, \ldots, M \tag{6-18}$$

or, in the case of (6-16), as

$$\phi_l(\mathbf{x}) = \frac{\min_{k=1,\ldots,p}\left\{\mu_{Q_k^l}(x_{k,\max}^l)\right\}}{\sum_{l=1}^{M} \min_{k=1,\ldots,p}\left\{\mu_{Q_k^l}(x_{k,\max}^l)\right\}} \quad l = 1, \ldots, M \tag{6-19}$$

Example 6-5: [Mendel (1995)] This example parallels Example 5-5. What do the FBFs in (6-18) look like? We shall again consider two situations—equally spaced and unequally spaced Gaussian antecedent membership functions and Gaussian fuzzy numbers. To visualize the FBFs in two dimensions, we again choose dim $\mathbf{x} = p = 1$, so that $\phi_l(\mathbf{x}) = \phi_l(x)$. We again also choose the number of rules, M, equal to 5. Standard deviations for all Gaussian antecedent membership functions, as well as for the fuzzy input, are set equal to 10. In this case, when the input is x', we set $m_X = x'$, so that

$$\mu_{F^l}(x) = \exp\left\{-\frac{1}{2}\left(\frac{x - m_{F^l}}{10}\right)^2\right\} \quad l = 1, \ldots, 5 \tag{6-20}$$

$$\mu_X(x) = \exp\left\{-\frac{1}{2}\left(\frac{x - x'}{10}\right)^2\right\} \tag{6-21}$$

$$\mu_{Q^l}(x^l_{max}) = \exp\left\{-\frac{1}{2}\frac{\left(x' - m_{F^l}\right)^2}{200}\right\} \quad l = 1, ..., 5 \tag{6-22}$$

and

$$\phi_l(x) = \frac{\mu_{Q^l_k}(x^l_{max})}{\sum_{l=1}^{5}\mu_{Q^l_k}(x^l_{max})} \quad l = 1, ..., 5 \tag{6-23}$$

In the equally spaced situation, as in Example 5-5, we chose $m_{F^1} = 20$, $m_{F^2} = 35$, $m_{F^3} = 50$, $m_{F^4} = 65$, and $m_{F^5} = 80$. Figure 6-4 (a) depicts the five non-singleton FBFs as well as the five singleton FBFs [which were plotted in Figure 5-10 (a)]. Observe that the FBFs for non-singleton fuzzification have longer tails and are broader than their singleton counterparts. This means that more of them will be activated in the non-singleton case than in the singleton case for a specific input value. For example, a vertical line at $x = 30$ in Figure 6-4 (a) intersects three of the singleton FBFs and four of the non-singleton FBFs. *Input uncertainty may activate more FBFs*, which means that decisions are more distributed in the non-singleton case than in the singleton case.

In the non-equally-spaced situation, we again chose $m_{F^1} = 20$, $m_{F^2} = 25$, $m_{F^3} = 50$, $m_{F^4} = 62$, and $m_{F^5} = 80$. Figure 6-4 (b) depicts the five non-singleton FBFs as well as the five singleton FBFs [which were plotted in Figure 5-10 (b)]. Note that a vertical line at $x = 40$ intersects four of the singleton FBFs and all five of the non-singleton FBFs. Even in the non-equally-spaced situation, *input uncertainty may activate more FBFs*. ■

6.5 NON-SINGLETON FLSS ARE UNIVERSAL APPROXIMATORS

Utilizing concepts from real analysis, Mouzouris and Mendel (1997) have proven that a non-singleton FLS can uniformly approximate any continuous function on a compact set. Their proof includes the case first considered by Wang and Mendel (1992a) as a special case. For discussions about this result, as well as many more results about universal approximation, we again refer the reader to the article by Kreinovich et al. (1998).

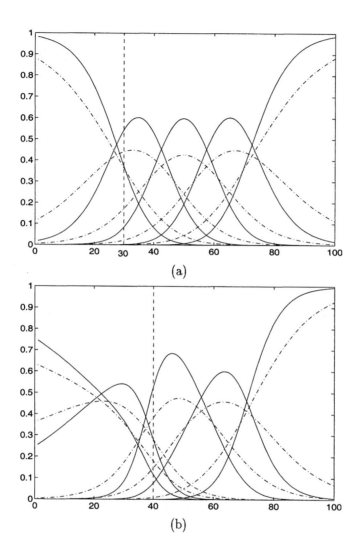

Figure 6-4: FBFs for five rules in non-singleton (dash-dotted lines) and singleton (solid lines) FLSs. (a) Equally spaced and (b) unequally spaced Gaussian antecedent membership functions and input Gaussian fuzzy numbers (Mendel, 1995a, © 1995, IEEE).

As mentioned in Section 5.8, a universal approximation theorem is an existence result, one that gives us assurance that there exists a non-singleton FLS capable of uniformly approximating any continuous function on a compact set. Although the Mouzouris and Mendel proof of universal approximation provides some insight, it does not tell us how to choose the parameters of the non-singleton FLS, nor does it tell us how many basis functions will be needed to achieve such performance. The latter are accomplished through design.

6.6 DESIGNING NON-SINGLETON FLSs

The design of a non-singleton FLS is associated with the following problem:

> We are given a collection of N input–output *noisy* numerical data *training* pairs, $(\mathbf{x}^{(1)}: y^{(1)}), (\mathbf{x}^{(2)}: y^{(2)}), \ldots, (\mathbf{x}^{(N)}: y^{(N)})$, where $\mathbf{x}$ is the vector *noisy* input and y is the scalar (possibly) *noisy* output of a non-singleton FLS. Our goal is to completely specify the non-singleton FLS using the training data.

For illustrative purposes, all designs assume Gaussian membership functions, product implication and t-norm, and height defuzzification; hence, our FLS is described by (6-17) and (6-18).

As in Section 5.9, we must first explain how the training data can be interpreted as a collection of IF–THEN rules. Each rule is still of the form given in (5-1), where F_i^l are fuzzy antecedent sets that are associated with the elements of $\mathbf{x}$ and are described by Gaussian membership functions, i.e.,

$$\mu_{F_i^l}(x_i) = \exp\left\{-\tfrac{1}{2}\left[\frac{x_i - m_{F_i^l}}{\sigma_{F_i^l}}\right]^2\right\} \qquad (6\text{-}24)$$

where $i = 1, \ldots, p$ and $l = 1, \ldots, M$. In addition, each input to the FLS is modeled as a Gaussian fuzzy number whose membership function is

$$\mu_{X_k}(x_k) = \exp\left\{-\tfrac{1}{2}\left[\frac{x_k - m_{X_k}}{\sigma_X}\right]^2\right\} \qquad (6\text{-}25)$$

where $k = 1, \ldots, p$ and $m_{X_k} = x'$. We are assuming, for illustrative purposes, that the uncertainty about each input is the same. If this is not the case, then simply replace σ_X in (6-25) by σ_{X_k}. Each design method establishes how to specify the parameters $m_{F_i^l}, \sigma_{F_i^l}$, and σ_X of these membership functions, as well as the centers of the consequent membership functions, the $\bar{y}^l$ in (6-17), using the training pairs $(\mathbf{x}^{(1)}:y^{(1)}),(\mathbf{x}^{(2)}:y^{(2)}),...,(\mathbf{x}^{(N)}:y^{(N)})$.

Example 6-6: As in Example 5-6, let us enumerate how many design parameters there can be in the just-stated design:

- Antecedent parameters $m_{F_i^l}$ and $\sigma_{F_i^l}$: 2 per antecedent, p antecedents, and M rules, for a total of $2pM$ parameters
- Consequent parameter $\bar{y}^l$: 1 per consequent and M rules, for a total of M parameters
- Measurement parameters σ_X: 1 additional parameter [if each input membership function has a different standard deviation, σ_{X_k} $(k = 1,...,p)$, there will be p additional parameters]

So, the number of design parameters is $2pM + M + 1$. Note that in some design methods all of these parameters are not tuned (i.e., some are fixed ahead of time). In other designs, the number of parameters may be reduced. In yet other designs, in which it is more appropriate to assume a different standard deviation for each of the p inputs, then there could be as many as $2pM + M + p$ design parameters.

Our discussions about requiring more training elements than design parameters, given in Example 5-6, hold here as well, except that now (5-34) and (5-35) become

$$2pM + M + 1 < N \tag{6-26}$$

and

$$M < \left[\frac{N' - 1}{2p + 1} \right] \tag{6-27}$$

respectively. ∎

At a very high level, we can think of four designs associated with the preceding formulation:

1. Fix the shapes and parameters of all the antecedent, consequent, and input measurement membership functions ahead of time. The data estab-

lish the rules and the standard deviation of the measurements, and no tuning is used.

2. Fix the shapes and parameters of the antecedent and input measurement membership functions ahead of time. Use the training data to tune the consequent parameters. Because the FLS is linear in the consequent parameters [see (6-17)], this leads to an easy optimization problem.

3. Fix the shapes and parameters of all the antecedent and consequent membership functions ahead of time. Fix the shape but not the parameter(s) of the input measurement membership function(s) ahead of time. Use the training data to tune the parameter(s) of the input measurement membership function(s). Because the FLS is non-linear in this (these) parameter(s), this leads to a more difficult optimization problem than in the second design.

4. Fix the shapes of all the antecedent, consequent, and input measurement membership functions ahead of time. Use the training data to tune the antecedent, consequent, and input measurement parameters. Because the FLS is non-linear in both the antecedent and input measurement membership function parameters, this leads to an even more difficult optimization problem than in the third design.

As we pointed out in Section 5.9, other even more complicated design problems can be formulated that try to answer questions such as: (a) what shape membership functions—including the input measurement membership function(s)—should be used?, (b) how many and which antecedents should be used (e.g., can p be reduced)?, and, (c) how many and which rules should be used (e.g., can M be reduced)? Evolutionary optimization algorithms can again be used to address the first of these questions, systematic trial and error or evolutionary optimization algorithms can again be used to answer the second question, and, SVD techniques can again be used to answer the third question.

Before we briefly touch on the design methods that were described in Section 5.9, let us note that there can be two very different *approaches to the tuning of a non-singleton FLS*:

1. **Partially dependent approach:** In this approach, one first designs the best possible singleton FLS, by tuning all of its parameters, and then updates the design by: (a) keeping all of the parameters that are shared by the singleton and non-singleton FLSs fixed at the values obtained from the best possible singleton FLS, and (b) tuning only the new parameter(s) of the non-singleton FLS. In the present case, only the standard deviation, σ_X, would be tuned.

2. **Totally independent approach:** In this approach, all of the parameters of the non-singleton FLS are tuned. If, by chance, a singleton FLS has already been designed, then its parameters can be used as the *initial parameters* for the tuning algorithms of the parameters that are shared by the singleton and non-singleton FLSs.

One would expect the best performance to be obtained by the totally independent approach; however, sometimes it is very useful to use the partially dependent approach to observe the incremental improvement that can be obtained from the previous design to the new design.

In the rest of this section, we focus on *differences* in Section 5.9 that occur because of the non-singleton nature of the FLS considered in this chapter. We do not repeat the discussions given in that section; so, this would be a good time for the reader to review its design methods.

6.6.1 One-pass methods

There are no changes to these methods, since they are based entirely on the training data. Following the procedures given in Section 5.9.1, one can again easily design up to N rules from the now noisy training data. To complete these designs, one must also determine a value for σ_X. This requires that the variance of the additive measurement noise be known ahead of time or that it can be estimated from the data; otherwise, one should use another design method in which σ_X can be tuned.

6.6.2 Least-squares method

In the least-squares method, as described in Section 5.9.2, all of the antecedent parameters, i.e., the FBFs, are fixed by the designer, and only the centers of the consequent membership functions, the $\bar{y}^l$ in (6-17), are tuned (i.e., computed using a least-squares method). Now the standard deviation of the input measurements, σ_X, must also be known ahead of time, or else the FBFs in (6-18) cannot be computed. The number of FBFs (i.e., the number of rules), M, must also be specified. If it is not possible to determine σ_X ahead of time or from the data, then one should use another design method in which σ_X can be tuned.

6.6.3 Back-propagation (steepest descent) method

In the back-propagation method, some or all of the antecedent, consequent, or input measurement membership function parameters are *not* fixed ahead of time. These parameters are tuned using a steepest descent method that we will briefly describe in this section. For illustrative purposes, we assume that *all* of the antecedent, consequent, or input measurement membership function's parameters are to be tuned. While the results in this section are similar to those in Section 5.9.3, many of the associated equations are somewhat different; hence, we provide more details for this tuning method than we have for the other methods.

We begin by recalling, from (6-17), (6-18), and (6-10), that

$$y(\mathbf{x}^{(i)}) = f_{ns}(\mathbf{x}^{(i)}) = \frac{\sum_{l=1}^{M} \bar{y}^l \prod_{k=1}^{p} \mu_{Q_k^l}(x_{k,max}^{l,(i)})}{\sum_{l=1}^{M} \prod_{k=1}^{p} \mu_{Q_k^l}(x_{k,max}^{l,(i)})}$$

$$= \frac{\sum_{l=1}^{M} \bar{y}^l \prod_{k=1}^{p} \exp\left[-\frac{1}{2}\frac{\left(x_k^{(i)} - m_{F_k^l}\right)^2}{\sigma_X^2 + \sigma_{F_k^l}^2}\right]}{\sum_{l=1}^{M} \prod_{k=1}^{p} \exp\left[-\frac{1}{2}\frac{\left(x_k^{(i)} - m_{F_k^l}\right)^2}{\sigma_X^2 + \sigma_{F_k^l}^2}\right]} \qquad (6\text{-}28)$$

where $i = 1, \ldots, N$. As in Section 5.9.3, given an input–output training pair $(\mathbf{x}^{(i)}:y^{(i)})$, we wish to design the FLS in (6-28) such that the following error function is minimized:

$$e^{(i)} = \tfrac{1}{2}[f_{ns}(\mathbf{x}^{(i)}) - y^{(i)}]^2 \qquad i = 1, \ldots, N \qquad (6\text{-}29)$$

It is evident from (6-28) that f_{ns} is completely characterized by $\bar{y}^l$, $m_{F_k^l}$, $\sigma_{F_k^l}$, and σ_X ($l = 1, \ldots, M$ and $k = 1, \ldots, p$). Using a steepest descent algorithm to minimize $e^{(i)}$, it is straightforward (see Exercise 6-5) to obtain the following recursions to update all the design parameters of this FLS ($k = 1, \ldots, p$, $l = 1, \ldots, M$, and $i = 0, 1, \ldots$):

$$m_{F_k^l}(i+1) = m_{F_k^l}(i) - \alpha_m [f_{ns}(\mathbf{x}^{(i)}) - y^{(i)}][\bar{y}^l(i) - f_{ns}(\mathbf{x}^{(i)})]$$
$$\times \left[\frac{x_k^{(i)} - m_{F_k^l}(i)}{\sigma_X^2(i) + \sigma_{F_k^l}^2(i)}\right]\phi_l(\mathbf{x}^{(i)}) \qquad (6\text{-}30)$$

$$\bar{y}^l(i+1) = \bar{y}^l(i) - \alpha_{\bar{y}}[f_{ns}(\mathbf{x}^{(i)}) - y^{(i)}]\phi_l(\mathbf{x}^{(i)}) \qquad (6\text{-}31)$$

$$\sigma_{F_k^l}(i+1) = \sigma_{F_k^l}(i) - \alpha_\sigma [f_{ns}(\mathbf{x}^{(i)}) - y^{(i)}][\overline{y}^l(i) - f_{ns}(\mathbf{x}^{(i)})]$$

$$\times \sigma_{F_k^l}(i) \left[\frac{x_k^{(i)} - m_{F_k^l}(i)}{\sigma_X^2(i) + \sigma_{F_k^l}^2(i)} \right]^2 \phi_l(\mathbf{x}^{(i)}) \qquad (6\text{-}32)$$

and

$$\sigma_X(i+1) = \sigma_X(i) - \alpha_X [f_{ns}(\mathbf{x}^{(i)}) - y^{(i)}][\overline{y}^l(i) - f_{ns}(\mathbf{x}^{(i)})]$$

$$\times \sigma_X(i) \left[\frac{x_k^{(i)} - m_{F_k^l}(i)}{\sigma_X^2(i) + \sigma_{F_k^l}^2(i)} \right]^2 \phi_l(\mathbf{x}^{(i)}) \qquad (6\text{-}33)$$

As in Section 5.9.3, we update $\sigma_{F_k^l}$ and σ_X instead of $\sigma_{F_k^l}^2$ and σ_X^2, because $\sigma_{F_k^l}^2$ and σ_X^2 must be positive whereas $\sigma_{F_k^l}$ and σ_X can be positive or negative. We then square up $\sigma_{F_k^l}$ and σ_X to obtain $\sigma_{F_k^l}^2$ and σ_X^2. Note, also, that (6-30)–(6-33) need to be initialized by $m_{F_k^l}(0)$, $\overline{y}^l(0)$, $\sigma_{F_k^l}(0)$, and $\sigma_X(0)$. See the discussions about this in Section 5.9.3, as well as the discussions on how to choose the learning parameters $\alpha_m, \alpha_{\overline{y}}$, and α_σ. Learning parameter α_X is chosen in a similar manner.

If $x_{k,\max}^l$ cannot be computed in closed form (being able to do this depends on the specific choice made for the membership functions), in which case the explicit dependence of $y(\mathbf{x}^{(i)})$ on $\overline{y}^l$, $m_{F_k^l}$, $\sigma_{F_k^l}$, and σ_X will not be known, then a different kind of optimization algorithm must be used to minimize $e^{(i)}$ in (6-29) (e.g., a random search algorithm).

6.6.4 SVD–QR method

The six-step SVD–QR algorithm given in Section 5.9.4 remains the same for a non-singleton FLS. What does change, however, is the construction of the FBF matrix in (5-43), because the M FBFs are now given by (6-18). See Sections 12.5.2 and 12.5.3 for illustrations of this method.

6.6.5 Iterative design method

As in Section 5.9.5, by combining the SVD–QR method with the back-propagation method, we can design some or all of the parameters of the FLS including the number of the most significant FBFs, M'. The following iterative design method can be very successful:

1. Fix the number of non-singleton FBFs, M, at a reasonable value.
2. Use the back-propagation method to design some or all of the antecedent, consequent, and input measurement membership function parameters.
3. Apply the SVD–QR method to the results of the back-propagation method to determine $M' < M$ and the associated non-singleton FBFs.
4. If performance is acceptable, STOP. Otherwise, return to Step 2 for a re-tuning of the antecedent, consequent, and input measurement membership function parameters.

6.7 CASE STUDY: FORECASTING OF TIME-SERIES

We have described the problem of forecasting a time-series in Section 4.2. Here, we examine two designs of non-singleton type-1 FLS forecasters for the Mackey–Glass time-series. One design is based on a one-pass method (Method 1) and the other is based on the back-propagation method. Both designs are based on the following 1,000 *noisy* data points: $x(1001), x(1002),...,x(2000)$. The first 504 noisy data, $x(1001), x(1002),...,x(1504)$, are used for training (i.e., for the designs of the FLS forecasters), whereas the remaining 496 noisy data, $x(1505)$, $x(1506),..., x(2000)$, are used for testing the designs. The noise-free Mackey–Glass time-series is depicted in Figure 5-11 (a). We assumed that the noise-free sampled time-series, $s(k)$, is corrupted by uniformly-distributed stationary additive noise, $n(k)$, so that

$$x(k) = s(k) + n(k) \quad k=1001, \ 1002,...., \ 2000 \tag{6-34}$$

and that $SNR = 0\text{dB}$. One realization of $x(1001), x(1002),...,x(2000)$ is depicted in Figure 5-11 (b). The difference between the designs in this section and those in Section 5.10 is that here we design each FLS using noisy training data, whereas in Section 5.10 we designed each FLS using perfect training data.

As in Section 5.10, we used four antecedents for forecasting, namely, $x(k-3)$, $x(k-2)$, $x(k-1)$, and $x(k)$, to predict $x(k+1)$. Gaussian membership functions were used in both designs, and we again evaluated the performance of the two designs using a RMSE, namely,

$$RMSE_{ns} = \sqrt{\tfrac{1}{496} \sum\nolimits_{k=1504}^{1999} \left[s(k+1) - f_{ns}(\mathbf{x}^{(k)}) \right]^2} \tag{6-35}$$

where $\mathbf{x}^{(k)} = [x(k-3), x(k-2), x(k-1), x(k)]^T$.

6.7.1 One-pass design

We used the Method 1 (Section 4.2.1) one-pass design to construct 500 rules from $x(1001), x(1002), \ldots, x(1504)$. The antecedent and consequent membership functions were centered at the noisy measurements in each one of the 500 rules, and the standard deviation of the Gaussians was set equal to 0.1. Using the fact that signal-to-noise ratio $(SNR) = 10 \log_{10}(\sigma_s^2 / \sigma_n^2)$, from which it follows that $\sigma_n = \sigma_s / 10^{SNR/20}$, we set[2] $\sigma_X = \sigma_n$. Once σ_X was set, this completely established the non-singleton FLS $f_{ns}(\mathbf{x})$. Then we used $x(1505), x(1506), \ldots, x(2000)$ to compute the one-pass $RMSE_{ns}$ in (6-35). This entire process was repeated 50 times using 50 independent sets of 1,000 data points, at the end of which we had 50 $RMSE_{ns}(OP)$ values. The average value and standard deviation for these 50 $RMSE_{ns}$ values are $\overline{RMSE}_{ns}(OP) = 0.1304$ and $\sigma_{RMSE_{ns}(OP)} = 0.0064$.

How does this one-pass-designed non-singleton FLS forecaster compare with a one-pass-designed singleton FLS forecaster? The 500 rules for both designs are exactly the same for each of the 50 realizations of the data; however, the non-singleton FLS forecaster includes the effect of the noisy measurements by means of its pre-filter (Figure 6-2), whereas the singleton FLS forecaster does not. The $RMSE_s$ for each of the one-pass-designed singleton FLS forecasters was computed using

$$RMSE_s = \sqrt{\tfrac{1}{496} \sum\nolimits_{k=1504}^{1999} \left[s(k+1) - f_s(\mathbf{x}^{(k)}) \right]^2} \tag{6-36}$$

The average value and standard deviation for these 50 $RMSE_s(OP)$ values are $\overline{RMSE}_s(OP) = 0.1882$ and $\sigma_{RMSE_s(OP)} = 0.0079$. Observe that $\overline{RMSE}_s(OP)$ is more

---

[2]Note that, because this was a simulation, we had access to the noise-free signal, $s(k)$; hence, it was possible for us to compute σ_s, and since SNR was also assumed known, we could evaluate σ_X. In practice, however, we would not have access to $s(k)$, nor would we know the SNR. In the back-propagation method, described following, we estimate σ_X directly from the data. The more realistic case, when σ_s and SNR are unknown is covered in Sections 10.11 and 11.5.

than 40% larger than $\overline{RMSE}_{ns}(OP)$. So, accounting for the noise by using non-singleton fuzzification can result in a substantial improvement in RMSE performance, even for a one-pass design.

Figure 6-5 depicts this more vividly. It depicts the output of our two one-pass-designed type-1 FLS forecasters for 50 Monte-Carlo realizations (i.e., each part of Figure 6-5 is the superimposition of 50 plots). Clearly, the 500-rule one-pass-designed non-singleton type-1 FLS forecaster has a smaller standard deviation (i.e., the thickness of the superimposed plots) than the 500-rule one-pass-designed singleton type-1 FLS forecaster. The pre-filtering by the non-singleton type-1 FLS forecaster makes a substantial difference.

6.7.2 Back-propagation design

Here we compare a non-singleton type-1 FLS with a singleton type-1 FLS when both are designed using the back-propagation method. Because the non-singleton FLS shares most of the same parameters as the singleton FLS, we shall use the partially dependent design approach that was explained earlier.

As in the Section 5.10.2 back-propagation design, we used only two fuzzy sets for each of the four antecedents, so that there are only 16 rules. Each rule is characterized by eight antecedent membership function parameters (the mean and standard deviation for each of the four Gaussian membership functions) and one consequent parameter, $\bar{y}$. The *initial* location of each Gaussian antecedent membership function was based on the mean, m_x, and the standard deviation, σ_x, of the data in the 504 training samples, $x(1001), x(1002),...,x(1504)$. More specifically, we initially chose the mean of each and every antecedent's two Gaussian membership functions as $m_x - 2\sigma_x$ or $m_x + 2\sigma_x$, respectively, and the standard deviations of these membership functions as $2\sigma_x$. We used the center-of-sets defuzzifier and initially chose the center of each consequent's membership function, $\bar{y}^i$ ($i = 1, ..., 16$), to be a random number from the interval $[0, 1]$.

For the non-singleton type-1 FLS, we modeled each of the four noisy input measurements using a Gaussian membership function. Two choices are possible: (1) use a different standard deviation for each of the four input measurement membership functions, or (2) use the same standard deviation for each of the four input measurement membership functions. We tried both approaches and got very similar results. Because the additive noise is stationary, using the same standard deviation for each of the four input measurement membership functions should suffice; hence, we only present results for that choice.

Each FLS was tuned using a steepest descent algorithm in which all of the learning parameters were set equal to the same $\alpha = 0.2$. Training and testing

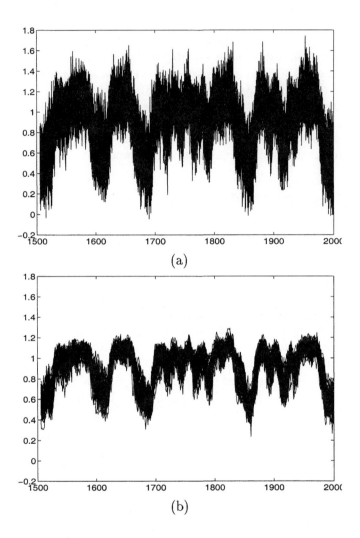

Figure 6-5: Outputs of the: (a) one-pass-designed singleton FLS forecaster, and (b) one-pass-designed non-singleton FLS forecaster. In both cases, there are 50 Monte-Carlo realizations and the data from time point 1504 to 2000 are corrupted by additive uniformly distributed noise with $SNR = 0$dB.

were carried out for six epochs. After each epoch we used the testing data to see how each FLS performed, by computing $RMSE_s(BP)$ using (6-36) and $RMSE_{ns}(BP)$ using (6-35). This entire process was repeated 50 times using 50 independent sets of 1,000 data points,[3] at the end of which we had 50 $RMSE_s(BP)$ and 50 $RMSE_{ns}(BP)$ values. The average values and standard deviations of $RMSE_s(BP)$ and $RMSE_{ns}(BP)$ are plotted in Figure 6-6 for each of the six epochs. Observe that the type-1 non-singleton FLS always outperforms the type-1 singleton FLS, *although not by much*, as a careful examination of the scales on the two plots reveals. In fact, after six epochs of training the performances of the two designs are just about the same; i.e., their final RMSE's are both close to 0.15. Note that the minimum value of the average RMSE is just about reached after the first epoch by the non-singleton FLS, whereas it takes five epochs for the singleton FLS to reach this value. This suggests that the non-singleton type-1FLS could be used in a real-time adaptive environment, whereas the singleton type-1 FLS should not be.

It is possible to explain why the back-propagation-designed singleton and non-singleton FLSs achieved the same final performance. Just below (6-10), we explained that a non-singleton FLS that uses Gaussian membership functions and product t-norm is equivalent to a singleton FLS, one whose membership functions are given in (6-10). Observe, from (6-10), that σ_X^2 and $\sigma_{F_k^l}^2$ always occur as a sum, $\sigma_{F_k^l}^2 + \sigma_X^2$; hence, tuning them individually (as we have done) cannot be expected to give better results than tuning their sum, as is essentially done in the type-1 design. Consequently, in this case, the tuned singleton and non-singleton FLSs should lead to the same results.

In a one-pass design, on the other hand, there is no tuning. Fixing σ_X^2 in the non-singleton one-pass design can cause that design to outperform the singleton one-pass design because in a one-pass design σ_X^2 and $\sigma_{F_k^l}^2$ are set separately.

Comparing the final *RMSE* of the back-propagation design with the RMSE of the one-pass designs (Section 6.7.1), we see that:

1. The back-propagation-designed 16-rule singleton FLS outperforms the one-pass-designed 500-rule singleton FLS; i.e., $\overline{RMSE_s}(BP) \approx 0.15$ and $\overline{RMSE_s}(OP) = 0.1882$.

2. The back-propagation-designed 16-rule non-singleton FLS underperforms the one-pass-designed 500-rule non-singleton FLS; i.e., $\overline{RMSE_{ns}}(BP)$

---

[3]We do not include tables like Tables 5-1–5-3 here, or in later chapters, because when the training data are noisy we perform 50 Monte-Carlo designs, and we would need to show three tables for each of the 50 designs.

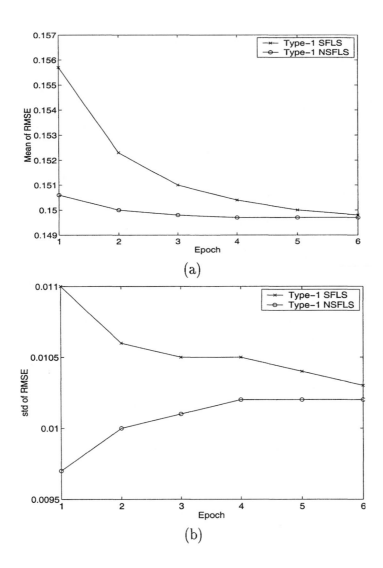

Figure 6-6: The mean and standard deviations of $RMSE_s(BP)$ and $RMSE_{ns}(BP)$, averaged over 50 Monte-Carlo designs. Tuning was performed in each realization for six epochs. (a) mean values, and (b) standard deviation values.

≈ 0.15 and $\overline{RMSE}_{ns}(OP) = 0.1304$.

3. The best design of those considered so far is the 500-rule one-pass-designed non-singleton FLS; i.e., $\overline{RMSE}_{ns}(OP) = 0.1304$.

6.8 A FINAL REMARK

The reason for the not-so-spectacular improvement in performance by the type-1 non-singleton FLS is that we have not accounted for all of the uncertainties as they should be accounted for. The training data are noisy, but there is no way to account for this in the antecedent membership functions of a type-1 FLS. The best we can do using a type-1 non-singleton FLS is to account for the noise in the measurements that excite the fully designed non-singleton FLS through the filtering action of non-singleton fuzzification; but, that is just not good enough! We return to this case study in Chapter 10, where for the first time we will be able to handle the noisy training data correctly.

6.9 COMPUTATION

The following M-files, which are found in the folder *type-1 fuzzy logic systems*, are useful for designing a non-singleton type-1 FLS:

nsfls_type1.m: Compute the output(s) of a non-singleton type-1 FLS when the antecedent membership functions are Gaussian and the input sets are Gaussian.

train_nsfls_type1.m: Tune the parameters of a non-singleton type-1 FLS when the antecedent membership functions are Gaussian, and the input sets are Gaussian, using some input–output training data.

svd_qr_nsfls_type1.m: Rule-reduction of a non-singleton type-1 FLS when the antecedent membership functions are Gaussian, and the input sets are Gaussian, using some input–output training data.

EXERCISES

6-1: Derive (6-7) and (6-8).

6-2: Derive (6-13). What is $\mu_{Q_k^l}(x_{k,\max}^l)$ in this case?

6-3: Repeat Example 6-5 for the FBF expansion in (6-16).

6-4: Demonstrate that the results of Example 5-7, for a least-squares design, apply as well for a non-singleton FLS.

6-5: As in Exercise 5-9, derive Equations (6-30)–(6-33). Demonstrate that they reduce to (5-48)–(5-50) when $\sigma_X = 0$.

6-6: As in Exercise 5-10, define a squared error function that depends on all N training data, and redevelop (6-30)–(6-33) for this new error function.

6-7: In Section 6.6 we stated four designs (e.g., Fix the shapes and parameters of all the antecedent, consequent, and input measurement membership functions ahead of time. The data establish the rules and the standard deviation of the measurements, and no tuning is used.). Explain how to use one or more of the design methods that are described in Section 6.6 for each of these four designs.

Part 3—

Type-2 Fuzzy Sets

CHAPTER 7

Operations on and Properties of Type-2 Fuzzy Sets

7.1 INTRODUCTION

In this chapter we examine set theoretic operations on and properties of type-2 fuzzy sets. After reviewing operations for type-1 fuzzy sets and providing some more discussions about the Extension Principle (since it is the basis for all of the type-2 set theoretic operations), we structure the rest of the chapter as follows:

> Operations—set theoretic and arithmetic—on *general* type-2 fuzzy sets
> Operations—set theoretic and arithmetic—on *interval* type-2 fuzzy sets

A summary of where to locate important set theoretic and algebraic operations for interval type-2 fuzzy sets is given in Table 7-1 and for general type-2 fuzzy sets is given in Table 7-2, both of which are in Section 7.5.

To begin, we recall some facts about type-1 fuzzy sets. Suppose that we have two type-1 fuzzy sets F_1 and F_2 that are characterized by membership functions $\mu_{F_1}(y)$ and $\mu_{F_2}(y)$; i.e.,

$$F_1 = \int_{y \in Y} \mu_{F_1}(y)/y \qquad (7\text{-}1)$$

and

$$F_2 = \int_{y \in Y} \mu_{F_2}(y)/y \qquad (7\text{-}2)$$

Using maximum t-conorm and minimum t-norm, the membership functions of the union, intersection, and complement of these sets are given as [(1-12)–(1-14)]:

$$\mu_{F_1 \cup F_2}(y) = \max[\mu_{F_1}(y), \mu_{F_2}(y)] \quad \forall y \in Y \qquad (7\text{-}3)$$

$$\mu_{F_1 \cap F_2}(y) = \min[\mu_{F_1}(y), \mu_{F_2}(y)] \quad \forall y \in Y \qquad (7\text{-}4)$$

$$\mu_{\bar{F}_1}(y) = 1 - \mu_{F_1}(y) \quad \forall y \in Y \qquad (7\text{-}5)$$

$$\mu_{\bar{F}_2}(y) = 1 - \mu_{F_2}(y) \quad \forall y \in Y \qquad (7\text{-}6)$$

Algebraic product is another popular t-norm operation, especially in engineering applications of fuzzy sets and logic (see Section 1.10.7). In this case,

$$\mu_{F_1 \cap F_2}(y) = \mu_{F_1}(y) \times \mu_{F_2}(y) \quad \forall y \in Y \qquad (7\text{-}7)$$

Because F_1 and F_2 are type-1 fuzzy sets, their membership grades $\mu_{F_1}(y)$ and $\mu_{F_2}(y)$ are crisp numbers and, at each y, $\mu_{F_1 \cup F_2}(y)$, $\mu_{F_1 \cap F_2}(y)$, $\mu_{\bar{F}_1}(y)$ and $\mu_{\bar{F}_2}(y)$ are also crisp numbers.

7.2 EXTENSION PRINCIPLE

In this chapter we are interested in the case of type-2 fuzzy sets, $\tilde{F}_i \ (i = 1, ..., r)$, whose secondary membership functions are type-1 fuzzy sets. To compute the union, intersection, and complement of type-2 fuzzy sets, we need to extend the binary operations of minimum (or product) and maximum, and the unary operation of negation, from crisp numbers to type-1 fuzzy sets, because at each y, $\mu_{\tilde{F}_i}(y, u)$ is a *function* [unlike the type-1 case, where $\mu_{F_i}(y)$ is a crisp number].

The tool for computing the union, intersection, and complement of type-2 fuzzy sets is Zadeh's Extension Principle ([Zadeh (1975)], [Dubois and Prade (1980)]), which we described in Section 1.10.13 for one and two variables, and which we now re-examine for more than two variables.

The Cartesian product of r arbitrary non-fuzzy sets $X_1, X_2, ..., X_r$, denoted by $X_1 \times X_2 \times \cdots \times X_r$, is the non-fuzzy set of all ordered r-tuples $(x_1, x_2, ..., x_r)$ such that $x_i \in X_i$ for $i \in \{1, 2, ..., r\}$; i.e., [Rudin (1966)]

$$X_1 \times \cdots \times X_r = \{(x_1, ..., x_r) \mid x_1 \in X_1, ..., x_r \in X_r\}.$$

Let **X** be a Cartesian product of universes $X_1, X_2, ..., X_r$ (i.e.,

$$\mathbf{X} = X_1 \times X_2 \times \cdots \times X_r)$$

and let f be a mapping from **X** to a universe Y such that $y = f(x_1, ..., x_r) \in Y$.

Next, let $A_1, A_2, ..., A_r$ be type-1 fuzzy sets in $X_1, X_2, ..., X_r$, respectively. Then, Zadeh's Extension Principle allows us to induce from the r type-1 fuzzy sets $A_1, A_2, ..., A_r$ a type-1 fuzzy set B on Y, through f, i.e., $B = f(A_1, A_2, ..., A_r)$, such that [see (1-63)][1]

$$\mu_B(y) = \begin{cases} \sup_{(x_1, ..., x_r) \in f^{-1}(y)} \min\{\mu_{A_1}(x_1), ..., \mu_{A_r}(x_r)\} \\ 0 \quad \text{if } f^{-1}(y) = \varnothing \end{cases} \tag{7-8}$$

where $f^{-1}(y)$ denotes the set of all points $x_1 \in X_1, ..., x_r \in X_r$ such that

$$y = f(x_1, ..., x_r).$$

To implement (7-8), we first find the values of $x_1, ..., x_r$ for which $y = f(x_1, ..., x_r)$, after which we compute $\mu_{A_1}(x_1), ..., \mu_{A_r}(x_r)$ at those values and then $\min\{\mu_{A_1}(x_1), ..., \mu_{A_r}(x_r)\}$. If more than one set of $x_1, ..., x_r$ satisfy $y = f(x_1, ..., x_r)$, then we repeat this procedure for all of them and choose the largest of the minima as the choice for $\mu_B(y)$.

Zadeh defined the Extension Principle using minimum t-norm and maximum t-conorm (for the supremum operation). Other t-norms and t-conorms can be used as described, e.g, in Mizumoto and Tanaka (1976) and Dubois and Prade (1980). In this book, we use the maximum t-conorm and either the mini-

---

[1]Equation (7-8) assumes that $x_1, ..., x_r$ are *non-interactive* (e.g., if $x_1 = a$ and $x_2 = a^2$, then x_1 and x_2 are interactive) or that there is no joint constraint on $x_1, ..., x_r$. For a detailed discussion about this, see Zadeh (1975) and Appendix B in Karnik and Mendel (1998b).

mum or product t-norms. Note that when we replace the minimum in (7-8) by another t-norm, we are replacing the sup-min composition by the sup-star composition (see, also, Section 8.4).

When we need to extend an operation of the form $f(x_1,...,x_r)$ to an operation $f(A_1,...,A_r)$, where the A_i are type-1 fuzzy sets, we do not extend the individual operations like multiplication, addition, etc., involved in f. Instead, we use the following definition, which derives directly from (7-8) when the maximum operation is used for the union and a general t-norm ($\star$) is used instead of the minimum operation:

$$f(A_1,...,A_r) = \int_{x_1 \in X_1} \cdots \int_{x_r \in X_r} \mu_{A_1}(x_1) \star \cdots \star \mu_{A_r}(x_r) / f(x_1,...,x_r) \qquad (7\text{-}9)$$

For example, if $f(x_1,x_2) = x_1 x_2 /(x_1 + x_2)$, we write the extension of f to type-1 sets A_1 and A_2 as

$$f(A_1,A_2) = \int_{x_1 \in X_1} \int_{x_2 \in X_2} \mu_{A_1}(x_1) \star \mu_{A_2}(x_2) \bigg/ \frac{x_1 x_2}{x_1 + x_2} \qquad (7\text{-}10)$$

and **not** as $f(A_1,A_2) = A_1 \times A_2 /(A_1 + A_2)$.

To compute $f(A_1,...,A_r)$ using (7-9), we must compute $f(x_1,...,x_r)$ and $\mu_{A_1}(x_1) \star \cdots \star \mu_{A_r}(x_r)$ for $\forall x_1 \in X_1, \ldots, \forall x_r \in X_r$. It is easy to write a computer program to do this.

7.3 OPERATIONS ON GENERAL TYPE-2 FUZZY SETS

Consider two type-2 fuzzy sets $\tilde{A}$ and $\tilde{B}$, i.e.,

$$\tilde{A} = \int_X \mu_{\tilde{A}}(x) / x = \int_X [\int_{J_x^u} f_x(u) / u] / x \quad J_x^u \subseteq [0,1] \qquad (7\text{-}11)$$

and

$$\tilde{B} = \int_X \mu_{\tilde{B}}(x) / x = \int_X [\int_{J_x^w} g_x(w) / w] / x \quad J_x^w \subseteq [0,1] \qquad (7\text{-}12)$$

Observe that in (7-11) and (7-12), u and w are just dummy variables used to differentiate between the different secondary membership functions of x in $\tilde{A}$ and $\tilde{B}$, respectively. In this section we focus on set theoretic and algebraic operations for such general type-2 fuzzy sets

7.3.1 Set theoretic operations

Here we explain how to compute the union, intersection and complement for type-2 fuzzy sets $\tilde{A}$ and $\tilde{B}$.

Union of type-2 fuzzy sets

The union of $\tilde{A}$ and $\tilde{B}$ is another type-2 fuzzy set, just as the union of type-1 fuzzy sets A and B is another type-1 fuzzy set; hence, from (3-6), it follows that

$$\tilde{A} \cup \tilde{B} \Leftrightarrow \mu_{\tilde{A} \cup \tilde{B}}(x,v) = \int_{x \in X} \mu_{\tilde{A} \cup \tilde{B}}(x)/x = \int_{x \in X} \left[\int_{v \in J_x^v \subseteq [0,1]} h_x(v)/v \right] /x \qquad (7\text{-}13)$$

where

$$\int_{v \in J_x^v \subseteq [0,1]} h_x(v)/v = \varphi \left(\int_{u \in J_x^u} f_x(u)/u, \int_{w \in J_x^w} g_x(w)/w \right) = \varphi \left(\mu_{\tilde{A}}(x), \mu_{\tilde{B}}(x) \right) \qquad (7\text{-}14)$$

and φ, which plays the role of f in (7-9), is a t-conorm function of the secondary membership functions, $\mu_{\tilde{A}}(x)$ and $\mu_{\tilde{B}}(x)$, which are type-1 fuzzy sets. φ is a t-conorm function because the union of two type-1 fuzzy sets [see (7-3)] is equivalent to the t-conorm (e.g., maximum) of their membership functions. Note that the right-hand side of (7-3) plays the role of $f(x_1, x_2)$ in the Extension Principle. Following the prescription of the right-hand side of (7-9), we see that

$$\varphi \left(\int_{u \in J_x^u} f_x(u)/u, \int_{w \in J_x^w} g_x(w)/w \right) = \int_{u \in J_x^u} \int_{w \in J_x^w} f_x(u) \star g_x(w)/\varphi(u,w) \qquad (7\text{-}15)$$

When φ is the maximum operation $\vee$, then from (7-13) and (7-15) we find

$$\mu_{\tilde{A} \cup \tilde{B}}(x) = \int_{v \in J_x^v \subseteq [0,1]} h_x(v)/v = \int_{u \in J_x^u} \int_{w \in J_x^w} f_x(u) \star g_x(w)/(u \vee w) \qquad x \in X \qquad (7\text{-}16)$$

In this equation $\star$ indicates minimum or product, and $\iint$ indicates union over $J_x^u \times J_x^w$.

Another way to express (7-16) is in terms of the secondary membership functions of $\tilde{A}$ and $\tilde{B}$, $\mu_{\tilde{A}}(x)$ and $\mu_{\tilde{B}}(x)$, as

$$\mu_{\tilde{A}\cup\tilde{B}}(x) = \int_{u\in J_x^u}\int_{w\in J_x^w} f_x(u)\star g_x(w)/v \equiv \mu_{\tilde{A}}(x)\sqcup\mu_{\tilde{B}}(x) \quad x\in X \qquad (7\text{-}17)$$

where $v \equiv u \vee w$ and $\sqcup$ denotes the so-called *join* operation [Mizumoto and Tanaka (1976)]. The use of the notation $\mu_{\tilde{A}}(x)\sqcup\mu_{\tilde{B}}(x)$ to indicate the join between the secondary membership functions $\mu_{\tilde{A}}(x)$ and $\mu_{\tilde{B}}(x)$ is, of course, a *shorthand notation* for the operations in the middle of (7-17).

What (7-17) says is that to perform the join between two secondary membership functions, $\mu_{\tilde{A}}(x)$ and $\mu_{\tilde{B}}(x)$, $v = u \vee w$ must be performed between every possible pair of primary memberships u and w, such that $u \in J_x^u$ and $w \in J_x^w$ and that the secondary grade of $\mu_{\tilde{A}\cup\tilde{B}}(x)$ must be computed as the t-norm operation between the corresponding secondary grades of $\mu_{\tilde{A}}(x)$ and $\mu_{\tilde{B}}(x)$, $f_x(u)$ and $g_x(w)$, respectively. According to (7-13), this must be done for $\forall x \in X$ to obtain $\mu_{\tilde{A}\cup\tilde{B}}(x,v)$.

If more than one combination of u and w gives the same point $u \vee w$, then in the join we keep the one with the largest membership grade. Suppose, for example, $u_1 \vee w_1 = \theta$ and $u_2 \vee w_2 = \theta$. Then, within the computations of (7-17), we would have the terms

$$f_x(u_1)\star g_x(w_1)/\theta + f_x(u_2)\star g_x(w_2)/\theta$$

where + denotes union. Combining these two terms at the *common* θ is a type-1 computation in which we use a t-conorm for the union. In our work, we choose the maximum t-conorm, as suggested by Zadeh (1975) and Mizumoto and Tanaka (1976).

Intersection of type-2 fuzzy sets

The intersection of $\tilde{A}$ and $\tilde{B}$ is another type-2 fuzzy set, just as the intersection of type-1 fuzzy sets A and B is another type-1 fuzzy set; hence, again from (3-6), it follows that

$$\tilde{A} \cap \tilde{B} \Leftrightarrow \mu_{\tilde{A} \cap \tilde{B}}(x,v) = \int_{x \in X} \mu_{\tilde{A} \cap \tilde{B}}(x) \big/ x \qquad (7\text{-}18)$$

The development of $\mu_{\tilde{A} \cap \tilde{B}}(x)$ is the same as the development of $\mu_{\tilde{A} \cup \tilde{B}}(x)$, except that in the present case φ is the minimum or product function (again, corresponding to the type-1 case), $\wedge$; hence,

$$\mu_{\tilde{A} \cap \tilde{B}}(x) = \int_{u \in J_x^u} \int_{w \in J_x^w} f_x(u) \star g_x(w) \big/ (u \wedge w) \quad x \in X \qquad (7\text{-}19)$$

Another way to express (7-19) is in terms of the secondary membership functions of $\tilde{A}$ and $\tilde{B}$, as

$$\mu_{\tilde{A} \cap \tilde{B}}(x) = \int_{u \in J_x^u} \int_{w \in J_x^w} f_x(u) \star g_x(w) \big/ v \equiv \mu_{\tilde{A}}(x) \sqcap \mu_{\tilde{B}}(x) \quad x \in X \qquad (7\text{-}20)$$

where $v \equiv u \wedge w$ and $\sqcap$ denotes the so-called *meet* operation [Mizumoto and Tanaka (1976)]. The use of the notation $\mu_{\tilde{A}}(x) \sqcap \mu_{\tilde{B}}(x)$ to indicate the meet between the secondary membership functions $\mu_{\tilde{A}}(x)$ and $\mu_{\tilde{B}}(x)$ is another *shorthand notation*, but this time for the operations in the middle of (7-20).

What (7-20) says is that to perform the meet between two secondary membership functions, $\mu_{\tilde{A}}(x)$ and $\mu_{\tilde{B}}(x)$, $v = u \wedge w$ must be performed between every possible pair of primary memberships u and w, such that $u \in J_x^u$ and $w \in J_x^w$, and the secondary grade of $\mu_{\tilde{A} \cap \tilde{B}}(x)$ must be computed as the t-norm operation between the corresponding secondary grades of $\mu_{\tilde{A}}(x)$ and $\mu_{\tilde{B}}(x)$, $f_x(u)$ and $g_x(w)$, respectively. According to (7-18), this must be done for $\forall x \in X$ to obtain $\mu_{\tilde{A} \cap \tilde{B}}(x,v)$.

If more than one combination of u and w gives the same point $u \wedge w$, then in the meet (just as in the join) we keep the one with the largest membership grade.

Complement of a type-2 fuzzy set

The complement of $\tilde{A}$ is another type-2 fuzzy set, just as the complement of type-1 fuzzy set A is another type-1 fuzzy set; hence, again from (3-6), it follows that

$$\bar{\tilde{A}} \Leftrightarrow \mu_{\bar{\tilde{A}}}(x,v) = \int_{x \in X} \mu_{\bar{\tilde{A}}}(x) \big/ x \qquad (7\text{-}21)$$

In this equation $\mu_{\tilde{A}}(x)$ is a secondary membership function; i.e., at each value of x $\mu_{\tilde{A}}(x)$ is a function (unlike the type-1 situation where, at each value of x, $\mu_{\tilde{A}}(x)$ is a point value). Again using the Extension Principle (7-9) and (7-5), we find that

$$\mu_{\overline{\tilde{A}}}(x) = \int_{u \in J_x^u} f_x(u)/(1-u) \equiv \neg \mu_{\tilde{A}}(x) \quad x \in X \tag{7-22}$$

where $\neg$ denotes the so-called *negation* operation [Mizumoto and Tanaka (1976)]. The use of the notation $\neg\mu_{\tilde{A}}(x)$ to indicate the negation of the secondary membership function $\mu_{\tilde{A}}(x)$ is yet another *shorthand notation*, but this time for the operations in the middle of (7-22).

What (7-22) says is that to perform the negation of the secondary membership function $\mu_{\tilde{A}}(x)$, $1-u$ must be computed at $\forall u \in J_x^u$, and the secondary grade of $\mu_{\overline{\tilde{A}}}(x)$ at $1-u$ is the corresponding secondary grade of $\mu_{\tilde{A}}(x)$, $f_x(u)$. According to (7-21), this must be done for $\forall x \in X$ to obtain $\mu_{\overline{\tilde{A}}}(x,v)$.

Discussion

Note that Zadeh (1975) was the first to define the membership function for the intersection of type-2 fuzzy sets $\tilde{A}$ and $\tilde{B}$, whereas Mizumoto and Tanaka (1976) did this for union, intersection, and complement.[2]

Results comparable to those in (7-11)–(7-22) over discrete universes of discourse are obtained by replacing the symbol $\int$ by the symbol Σ.

Note, also, that when product is used for $\wedge$ and $\star$, then (7-17) and (7-20) become:

$$\mu_{\tilde{A} \cup \tilde{B}}(x) = \mu_{\tilde{A}}(x) \sqcup \mu_{\tilde{B}}(x) = \int_{u \in J_x^u} \int_{w \in J_x^w} f_x(u)g_x(w)/(u \vee w) \quad x \in X \tag{7-23}$$

and

---

[2]Our derivations of union, intersection, and complement of type-2 fuzzy sets have relied on the Extension Principle, because that is what was used by Zadeh and Mizumoto and Tanaka. The Extension Principle, however, is somewhat ad hoc, and deriving things using it may therefore be considered problematic. Very recently, while working with Dr. Robert John, we have been able to derive exactly the same formulas for the union, intersection, and complement of type-2 fuzzy sets without having to use the Extension Principle. Our derivation is based on a new decomposition of a type-2 fuzzy set as a union of all embedded type-2 fuzzy sets. Because this work has not yet appeared in any published form, its details are not included here.

$$\mu_{\tilde{A}\cap\tilde{B}}(x) = \mu_{\tilde{A}}(x)\Pi\mu_{\tilde{B}}(x) = \int_{u\in J_x^u}\int_{w\in J_x^w} f_x(u)g_x(w)/(uw) \quad x\in X \qquad (7\text{-}24)$$

Example 7-1: It can easily be shown that the extended operations reduce to the original ones when we deal with type-1 sets. For example, consider the join operation in (7-17) when minimum t-norm is used. In the case of type-1 sets, $f_x(u)$ will have a value equal to 1 at only one value of u, say u_1, and $g_x(w)$ will also have a value equal to 1 at only one value of w, say w_1. The rest of the $f_x(u)$ $(u\neq u_1)$ and $g_x(w)$ $(w\neq w_1)$ will all be zero. When we find the minima between all of the $f_x(u)$ and $g_x(w)$, $u\in J_x^u$ and $w\in J_x^w$, the only pair that will give a non-zero value is $\{f_x(u_1),g_x(w_1)\}$, and its minimum value will be equal to 1. All other minima will be 0. So the union of the two sets will consist of only one element $u_1\vee w_1 = \max\{u_1,\ w_1\}$, which agrees with (7-3). ■

Example 7-2: Here we illustrate [Karnik and Mendel (1998b)] the details of the calculations in (7-17), (7-20), and (7-22) for two type-2 fuzzy sets $\tilde{A}$ and $\tilde{B}$, and for a particular element x for which the secondary membership functions in these two sets are $\mu_{\tilde{A}}(x) = 0.5/0 + 0.7/0.1$ and $\mu_{\tilde{B}}(x) = 0.3/0.4 + 0.9/0.8$. From (7-17), using the minimum t-norm and maximum t-conorm, we have:

$$\mu_{\tilde{A}\cup\tilde{B}}(x) = \mu_{\tilde{A}}(x)\sqcup\mu_{\tilde{B}}(x) = (0.5/0 + 0.7/0.1)\sqcup(0.3/0.4 + 0.9/0.8)$$

$$= \frac{0.5\wedge 0.3}{0\vee 0.4} + \frac{0.5\wedge 0.9}{0\vee 0.8} + \frac{0.7\wedge 0.3}{0.1\vee 0.4} + \frac{0.7\wedge 0.9}{0.1\vee 0.8}$$

$$= 0.3/0.4 + 0.5/0.8 + 0.3/0.4 + 0.7/0.8$$

$$= \max\{0.3,0.3\}/0.4 + \max\{0.5,0.7\}/0.8$$

$$= 0.3/0.4 + 0.7/0.8$$

From (7-20), using the minimum t-norm and maximum t-conorm, we have:

$$\mu_{\tilde{A}\cap\tilde{B}}(x) = \mu_{\tilde{A}}(x)\Pi\mu_{\tilde{B}}(x) = (0.5/0 + 0.7/0.1)\Pi(0.3/0.4 + 0.9/0.8)$$

$$= \frac{0.5\wedge 0.3}{0\wedge 0.4} + \frac{0.5\wedge 0.9}{0\wedge 0.8} + \frac{0.7\wedge 0.3}{0.1\wedge 0.4} + \frac{0.7\wedge 0.9}{0.1\wedge 0.8}$$

$$= 0.3/0 + 0.5/0 + 0.3/0.1 + 0.7/0.1$$

$$= \max\{0.3,0.5\}/0 + \max\{0.3,0.7\}/0.1$$

$$= 0.5/0 + 0.7/0.1$$

Finally, from (7-22), we have:

$$\mu_{\tilde{A}}(x) = \neg\mu_{\tilde{A}}(x) = 0.5/(1-0) + 0.7/(1-0.1)$$
$$= 0.5/1 + 0.7/0.9 \quad \blacksquare$$

Example 7-3: Here we examine the meet between a *type-2 singleton*, $\tilde{A}$, and a *type-2 fuzzy set*, $\tilde{B}$, under minimum and product t-norms. By a type-2 singleton (see Section 3.3.5), we mean a type-2 fuzzy set whose membership function $\mu_{\tilde{A}}(x,v)$ is

$$\mu_{\tilde{A}}(x,v) = \begin{cases} 1/1 & x = x' \\ 1/0 & \forall x \neq x' \end{cases} \tag{7-25}$$

Type-2 fuzzy set $\tilde{B}$ is described by its membership function $\mu_{\tilde{B}}(x,w)$, where

$$\mu_{\tilde{B}}(x,w) = \int_{x\in X} \mu_{\tilde{B}}(x)/x = \int_{x\in X} \left[\int_{w\in J_x^w} g_x(w)/w\right]\bigg/x \quad J_x^w \subseteq [0,1] \tag{7-26}$$

From (7-20), (7-25), (7-26), and (B-15),[3] it follows that, for minimum or product t-norms,

$$\mu_{\tilde{A}}(x)\sqcap\mu_{\tilde{B}}(x) = \begin{cases} (1/1)\sqcap\mu_{\tilde{B}}(x') & x = x' \\ 1/0 & \forall x \neq x' \end{cases}$$
$$= \begin{cases} \int_{w\in J_{x'}^w} g_{x'}(w)/(1 \wedge w) & x = x' \text{ and } J_{x'}^w \subseteq [0,1] \\ 1/0 & \forall x \neq x' \end{cases}$$
$$= \begin{cases} \int_{w\in J_{x'}^w} g_{x'}(w)/w & x = x' \text{ and } J_{x'}^w \subseteq [0,1] \\ 1/0 & \forall x \neq x' \end{cases} \tag{7-27}$$
$$= \begin{cases} \mu_{\tilde{B}}(x') & x = x' \\ 1/0 & \forall x \neq x' \end{cases}$$

Observe that the meet between a type-2 singleton, $\tilde{A}$, and a type-2 fuzzy set, $\tilde{B}$, sifts out a specific vertical slice of $\mu_{\tilde{B}}(x,w)$, namely $\mu_{\tilde{B}}(x')$, where the secondary membership function $\mu_{\tilde{B}}(x')$ is a type-1 fuzzy set. $\blacksquare$

For completeness, Appendix A presents more detailed results for the join and meet of arbitrary type-2 fuzzy sets when minimum or product t-norms and maximum t-conorm are used. We do not include these results in the main body of this book because our emphasis is on interval type-2 fuzzy sets. More detailed

---

[3]Using (B-15) we can show that $(1/0)\sqcap\mu_{\tilde{B}}(x) = 1/0$.

results for join and meet of interval type-2 fuzzy sets are given below in Section 7.4.

7.3.2 Algebraic operations on fuzzy numbers

Convex[4] and normal type-1 fuzzy subsets of the real line are known as *fuzzy numbers* ([Dubois and Prade (1980)], [Kaufman and Gupta (1991)]). Algebraic operations like addition and multiplication of fuzzy numbers can be defined using the Extension Principle in (7-9), just as we defined the meet and join operations. The two operations of most interest to us are addition and multiplication.

Addition of type-1 fuzzy numbers

The addition of two fuzzy numbers $F = \int_{u \in U} f(u)/u$ and $G = \int_{w \in W} g(w)/w$ is defined as (for discrete universes of discourse $\sum \cdot$ replaces $\int \cdot$)

$$F + G = \int_{u \in U} \int_{w \in W} [f(u) \star g(w)]/(u + w) \tag{7-28}$$

where $\star$ indicates the t-norm, minimum, or product.

Example 7-4: Given n type-1 Gaussian fuzzy numbers $F_1, ..., F_n$, with means $m_1, ..., m_n$ and standard deviations $\sigma_1, ..., \sigma_n$, i.e.,

$$F_i = \int_{v \in V} \exp\left[-\frac{1}{2}\left(\frac{v - m_i}{\sigma_i} \right)^2 \right] / v \quad i = 1, ..., n \tag{7-29}$$

their affine combination $\sum_{i=1}^{n} \alpha_i F_i + \beta$, where α_i and β are crisp constants, is also a Gaussian fuzzy number with mean $\sum_{i=1}^{n} \alpha_i m_i + \beta$ and standard deviation Σ', where

$$\Sigma' = \begin{cases} \sqrt{\sum_{i=1}^{n} \alpha_i^2 \sigma_i^2} & \text{if product t - norm is used} \\ \sum_{i=1}^{n} |\alpha_i \sigma_i| & \text{if minimum t - norm is used} \end{cases} \tag{7-30}$$

---

[4]A type-1 fuzzy set A is *convex* (e.g., [Klir and Yuan (1995)]) if and only if $\mu_A(\lambda x_1 + (1-\lambda)x_2) \geq \min(\mu_A(x_1), \mu_A(x_2))$, where $x_1 \in X_1$, $x_2 \in X_2$ and $\lambda \in [0,1]$.

The proofs of these results, which can be found in [Karnik and Mendel (1998b, Appendix C.9)], use the results from Exercises 7-5 and 7-6. ∎

Multiplication of type-1 fuzzy numbers

The product of two fuzzy numbers $F = \int_{u \in U} f(u) / u$ and $G = \int_{w \in W} g(w) / w$ is defined as (for discrete universes of discourse $\sum \cdot$ replaces $\int \cdot$)

$$F \times G = \int_{u \in U} \int_{w \in W} [f(u) \star g(w)] / (u \times w) \qquad (7\text{-}31)$$

where, as usual, $\star$ indicates the t-norm, minimum, or product.

Observe, from (7-20) and (7-31), that under product t-norm, the product of F and G is the same as the meet of F and G; so, all discussions about meet under product t-norm apply to multiplication of fuzzy numbers under product t-norm.

7.4 OPERATIONS ON INTERVAL TYPE-2 FUZZY SETS

In this section we focus on set theoretic and algebraic operations for interval type-2 fuzzy sets because they are used extensively in the rest of this book. From (7-17), (7-20), and (7-22), it is clear that to compute the union, intersection, or complement of type-2 fuzzy sets, we need to compute the join, meet, and negation of secondary membership functions, which are type-1 fuzzy sets; hence, it is those calculations that we focus on here.

7.4.1 Set theoretic operations

It is relatively straightforward to determine the join, meet, and negation of interval type-2 sets, as we demonstrate in this section. Our results are stated for continuous universes of discourse for the secondary membership functions.

Join of interval type-2 fuzzy sets

Theorem 7-1: *The join,* $\sqcup_{i=1}^{n} F_i,$ *of n interval type-1 sets* $F_1, ..., F_n,$ *having domains* $[l_1, r_1], ..., [l_n, r_n],$ *respectively, is an interval set with domain* $[(l_1 \vee l_2 \vee \cdots \vee l_n), (r_1 \vee r_2 \vee \cdots \vee r_n)],$ *where* $\vee$ *denotes maximum.*

Proof: The proof uses mathematical induction. (a) Let F and G be two interval type-1 fuzzy sets with domains $[l_f, r_f]$ and $[l_g, r_g]$, respectively. The join between F and G, under either minimum or product t-norm, can be expressed [using (7-17)] as

$$F \sqcup G = \int_{u \in J_x^u} \int_{w \in J_x^w} 1/(u \vee w) \qquad (7\text{-}32)$$

where $J_x^u = [l_f, r_f]$ and $J_x^w = [l_g, r_g]$. To begin, we show that $r_f \vee r_g$ is the rightmost point in $F \sqcup G$. To see this, note that for any $u \in J_x^u$ and $w \in J_x^w$, since $w \le r_g$ then $u \vee w = \max(u, w) \le u \vee r_g$, and since $u \le r_f$, $u \vee w \le r_f \vee r_g$.

Next, we show that $l_f \vee l_g$ is the left-most point in $F \sqcup G$. To see this, note that for any $u \in J_x^u$ and $w \in J_x^w$, since $w \ge l_g$ then $u \vee w = \max(u, w) \ge u \vee l_g$, and since $u \ge l_f$, $u \vee w \ge l_f \vee l_g$.

In summary, each term in $F \sqcup G$ is equal to $u \vee w$ for some $u \in J_x^u$ and $w \in J_x^w$, the smallest term being $l_f \vee l_g$ and the largest term being $r_f \vee r_g$. Because F and G have continuous domains, $F \sqcup G$ also has a continuous domain; hence, $F \sqcup G$ is an interval type-1 set with domain $[l_f \vee l_g, r_f \vee r_g]$.

(b) Assume that when $n = k$ this theorem is valid, i.e.,

$$F_1 \sqcup F_2 \sqcup \cdots \sqcup F_k = \int_{q \in [(l_1 \vee l_2 \vee \cdots \vee l_k), (r_1 \vee r_2 \vee \cdots \vee r_k)]} 1/q \quad ; \qquad (7\text{-}33)$$

then, when $n = k + 1$,

$$F_1 \sqcup F_2 \sqcup \cdots \sqcup F_{k+1} = (F_1 \sqcup F_2 \sqcup \cdots \sqcup F_k) \sqcup F_{k+1}$$

$$= \left[\int_{q \in [(l_1 \vee l_2 \vee \cdots \vee l_k), (r_1 \vee r_2 \vee \cdots \vee r_k)]} 1/q \right]$$

$$\sqcup \left[\int_{w \in [l_{k+1}, r_{k+1}]} 1/w \right]$$

$$F_1 \sqcup F_2 \sqcup \cdots \sqcup F_{k+1} = \int_{g \in [((l_1 \vee l_2 \vee \cdots \vee l_k) \vee l_{k+1}, (r_1 \vee r_2 \vee \cdots \vee r_k) \vee r_{k+1}]} 1/g$$

$$= \int_{g \in [((l_1 \vee l_2 \vee \cdots \vee l_k \vee l_{k+1}), (r_1 \vee r_2 \vee \cdots \vee r_k \vee r_{k+1})]} 1/g \qquad (7\text{-}34)$$

where we have made use of the fact that the associative law holds for join and t-conorm operations (see Section 7.6.2). Equation (7-34) is what we obtain by setting $n = k + 1$ in the statement of the theorem; hence, this demonstrates that Theorem 7-1 is valid for all n. ∎

Meet of interval type-2 fuzzy sets under minimum or product t-norms

Theorem 7-2: *The meet, $\prod_{i=1}^{n} F_i$, of n interval type-1 sets $F_1, \ldots, F_n$, having domains $[l_1, r_1], \ldots, [l_n, r_n]$, respectively, where $l_i \geq 0$ and $r_i \geq 0$ ($i = 1, \ldots, n$), is an interval type-1 set with domain $[(l_1 \star l_2 \star \cdots \star l_n), (r_1 \star r_2 \star \cdots \star r_n)]$ where $\star$ denotes either minimum or product t-norm.*

Proof: (a) *minimum t-norm*—The proof of Theorem 7-2 in this case is so similar to the proof of Theorem 7-1 (making use of mathematical induction) that we leave it as an exercise for the reader.

(b) *product t-norm*—(b.i) Let F and G be two interval type-1 fuzzy sets with domains $[l_f, r_f]$ and $[l_g, r_g]$, respectively. The meet between F and G, under product t-norm, can be expressed [using (7-20)] as

$$F \sqcap G = \int_{u \in J_x^u} \int_{w \in J_x^w} (1 \times 1)/(uw) \qquad (7\text{-}35)$$

where $J_x^u = [l_f, r_f]$ and $J_x^w = [l_g, r_g]$. Observe from (7-35) that: (1) each term in $F \sqcap G$ is equal to the product uw for some $u \in J_x^u$ and $w \in J_x^w$; (2) since l_f, l_g, r_f, and r_g are greater than or equal to zero, the smallest uw-product is $l_f l_g$ and the largest uw-product is $r_f r_g$; and (3) since both F and G have continuous domains, $F \sqcap G$ also has a continuous domain; hence, $F \sqcap G$ is an interval type-1 set with domain $[l_f l_g, r_f r_g]$.

(b.ii) We leave the rest of this proof to the reader, since it again uses mathematical induction and is very straightforward. ∎

In our later applications of this theorem, it will always be true that

$[l_i, r_i] \subseteq [0,1]$ because the domains of all F_i will correspond to primary membership, which are bounded between 0 and 1. The F_i will correspond to secondary membership functions.

7.4.2 Algebraic operations on interval fuzzy numbers

Addition of type-1 interval fuzzy numbers

Theorem 7-3: *The algebraic sum,* $\sum_{i=1}^{n} F_i$, *of n interval type-1 numbers* $F_1, ..., F_n$, *having domains* $[l_1, r_1], ..., [l_n, r_n]$, *respectively, is an interval type-1 set with domain* $\left[\sum_{i=1}^{n} l_i, \sum_{i=1}^{n} r_i \right]$.

Proof: Again the proof is by mathematical induction. (a) Let F and G be two interval type-1 fuzzy sets with domains $[l_f, r_f]$ and $[l_g, r_g]$, respectively. Using (7-28), the algebraic sum of F and G can be obtained as

$$F + G = \int_{u \in [l_f, r_f]} \int_{w \in [l_g, r_g]} (1 \star 1) / (u + w) \qquad (7\text{-}36)$$

Observe from (7-36) that: (1) each term in $F + G$ is equal to the sum $u + w$ for some $u \in [l_f, r_f]$ and $w \in [l_g, r_g]$, the smallest term being $(l_f + l_g)$ and the largest being $(r_f + r_g)$; and (2) since both F and G have continuous domains, $F+G$ has a continuous domain; hence, $F + G$ is an interval type-1 set with domain $[l_f + l_g, r_f + r_g]$.

(b) The proof of the general result is straightforward, and is left to the reader. ∎

Multiplication of type-1 interval fuzzy numbers

Based on (7-31) and the discussion given in the paragraph just below it, we conclude that Theorem 7-2 also gives the results for the multiplication of n interval type-1 numbers $F_1, ..., F_n$.

Affine combination of type-1 interval fuzzy numbers

Theorem 7-4: *Given* n *interval type-1 fuzzy numbers* $F_1,...,F_n$, *with means* $m_1,...,m_n$ *and spreads* $s_1,...,s_n$, *their affine combination* $\sum_{i=1}^{n}\alpha_i F_i + \beta$, *where* α_i *and* β *are crisp constants, is also an interval fuzzy number with mean* $\sum_{i=1}^{n}\alpha_i m_i + \beta$ *and spread* $\sum_{i=1}^{n}|\alpha_i|s_i$.

Proof: Consider $F_i = [m_i - s_i, m_i + s_i]$. Multiplying F_i by a crisp constant α_i (expressed as $1/\alpha_i$) yields [see (7-31)][5]

$$\alpha_i F_i = \int_{v\in V} 1/(\alpha_i v) \quad V = [m_i - s_i, m_i + s_i] \qquad (7\text{-}37)$$

Adding a crisp constant β (expressed as $1/\beta$) to $\alpha_i F_i$ yields [see (7-36)]

$$\alpha_i F_i + \beta = \int_{v\in V} 1/(\alpha_i v + \beta) \quad V = [m_i - s_i, m_i + s_i] \qquad (7\text{-}38)$$

Substituting $w = \alpha_i v + \beta$ into (7-38), we obtain

$$\alpha_i F_i + \beta = \int_{w\in W} 1/w \quad W = [\alpha_i m_i + \beta - |\alpha_i|s_i, \alpha_i m_i + \beta + |\alpha_i|s_i] \qquad (7\text{-}39)$$

Note that the mean value of $\alpha_i F_i + \beta$ is $\alpha_i m_i + \beta$, and its spread is $|\alpha_i|s_i$.

Next, recall that F_i can be expressed as $[l_i, r_i]$, where $l_i = m_i - s_i$ and $r_i = m_i + s_i$. Observe, therefore, from Theorem 7-3, that

$$\sum_{i=1}^{n} F_i = \left[\sum_{i=1}^{n} m_i - \sum_{i=1}^{n} s_i, \sum_{i=1}^{n} m_i + \sum_{i=1}^{n} s_i\right] \qquad (7\text{-}40)$$

From (7-39) and (7-40), we see that

$$\sum_{i=1}^{n}\alpha_i F_i + \beta = \left[\sum_{i=1}^{n}\alpha_i m_i + \beta - \sum_{i=1}^{n}|\alpha_i|s_i, \sum_{i=1}^{n}\alpha_i m_i \right.$$
$$\left. + \beta + \sum_{i=1}^{n}|\alpha_i|s_i\right] \qquad (7\text{-}41)$$

---

[5]Note that $1\star1 = 1$ regardless of whether the t-norm is minimum or product.

The mean value of this set is $\sum_{i=1}^{n} \alpha_i m_i + \beta$ and the spread is $\sum_{i=1}^{n} |\alpha_i| s_i$. ∎

This theorem will be used in Section 13.3.

7.5 SUMMARY OF OPERATIONS

To see the forest from the trees, so-to-speak, we summarize the operations for interval type-2 fuzzy sets in Table 7-1 and for general type-2 fuzzy sets in Table 7-2. Note that the more detailed results for general type-2 fuzzy sets are stated without proof in Appendix A.

Table 7-1: Operations for interval type-2 fuzzy sets.

Operation	Location of Results
Join	Theorem 7-1
Meet (product or minimum t-norms)	Theorem 7-2
Addition	Theorem 7-3
Multiplication	Theorem 7-2
Affine combination	Theorem 7-4

Table 7-2: Operations for general type-2 fuzzy sets.

Operation	Location of Results
Join	Theorem A-1 and Corollary A-1
Meet (minimum t-norm)	Theorem A-2 and Corollary A-1
Meet (product t-norm)	General results are in (A-9), and approximation for Gaussian type-2 fuzzy sets is in Example A-7
Negation	Theorem A-3
Addition	Equation (7-28)
Product (product or minimum t-norms)	Equation (7-31)
Affine combination of type-1 Gaussian fuzzy numbers	Example 7-4

7.6 PROPERTIES OF TYPE-2 FUZZY SETS

Not only do we perform union, intersection, and complement with type-2 fuzzy sets, but we sometimes also perform other important set-theoretic operations on them using well-known laws; e.g., commutative, associative, distributive, and De Morgan's laws (see Table B-2 for a list of all the laws). An important question that needs to be answered is:

> Are we permitted to use a particular law for type-2 (type-1) fuzzy sets under maximum t-conorm and either minimum or product t-norms?

We focus just on maximum t-conorm and the minimum or product t-norms, because as we explained earlier, these are the most widely used ones in the FLS literature. The question must, of course, be re-examined if one uses other t-conorms and t-norms. Because the studies into the answers to this question, although important, are very technical, we present their details in Appendix B. Here we just state the results and draw some conclusions about them.

7.6.1 Type-1 fuzzy sets

The aforementioned question has already been well studied for type-1 fuzzy sets (see Table B-1). For maximum t-conorm and minimum t-norm all laws are satisfied; however, for maximum t-conorm and product t-norm certain laws are not satisfied, namely (e.g., [Karnik and Mendel (1998b)]):   (1) Idempotent law—second part, (2) Absorption law—first part, (3) Distributive law—second part, and (4) De Morgan's law—both parts. This means that one must be careful when using maximum t-conorm and product t-norm. If, for example, the design of a maximum t-conorm and product t-norm type-1 FLS involves the use of any of these violated laws it will be in error.

7.6.2 Type-2 fuzzy sets

Mizumoto and Tanaka (1976) studied the aforementioned question for maximum t-conorm/minimum t-norm type-2 fuzzy sets. They showed that, as for type-1 fuzzy sets, all laws are satisfied. Karnik and Mendel (1998b) studied this question for maximum t-conorm/product t-norm type-2 fuzzy sets (see Table B-2). They showed that not only are the laws that are listed in the previous subsection for type-1 fuzzy sets not satisfied, but even more laws are not satisfied for type-2 fuzzy sets, namely: (1) Idempotent law—both parts, (2) Absorption law—both parts, (3) Distributive law—both parts, and (4) De Morgan's law—both parts. This means, therefore, that for type-2 fuzzy sets one must be even more careful when using maximum t-conorm and product t-norm. The design of a maximum t-conorm and product t-norm type-2 FLS that involves the use of any of these violated laws will be in error. *Fortunately, one usually does not have to use any of these violated laws in the creation and design of a type-2 FLS.* The same cannot be said, in general, for other applications of type-2 fuzzy sets.

7.7 COMPUTATION

The following M-file is found in the folder *general type-2 fuzzy logic systems* and is useful for combining Gaussian type-1 fuzzy sets:

gaussian_sum.m: Function to compute an affine combination of n Gaussian type-1 sets, as described in Example 7-4.

The following M-files, which are found in the folder *interval type-2 fuzzy logic systems*, are useful for performing some operations on interval type-1 fuzzy sets (see, also, Exercise 7-14):

interval_meet.m: Function to compute the meet (or product) of n interval type-1 sets, as described in Theorem 7-2.

interval_sum.m: Function to compute an affine combination of n interval type-1 sets, as described in Theorem 7-4.

EXERCISES

7-1: Show that the extended operations for meet and negation reduce to the original ones when we deal with type-1 sets.

7-2: Repeat Example 7-2 using the product t-norm and maximum t-conorm.

7-3: Suppose, for a particular element x, that

$$\mu_{\tilde{A}}(x) = 0.6\,/\,0.2 + 0.8\,/\,0.3 + 0.2\,/\,0.4 \quad \text{and} \quad \mu_{\tilde{B}}(x) = 0.7\,/\,0.2 + 0.3\,/\,0.5 + 0.1\,/\,0.8$$

Compute $\mu_{\tilde{A}\cup\tilde{B}}(x)$, $\mu_{\tilde{A}\cap\tilde{B}}(x)$, $\mu_{\overline{\tilde{A}}}(x)$, and $\mu_{\overline{\tilde{B}}}(x)$.

7-4: Here you will examine the meet between a *type-1 fuzzy set*, A, and a *type-2 fuzzy set*, $\tilde{B}$, under minimum and product t-norms. To do this, we first represent A as a type-2 fuzzy set (see Section 3.3.6), i.e.,

$$\mu_{\tilde{A}}(x) = 1/\mu_A(x) \qquad \forall x \in X$$

and recall that type-2 fuzzy set B is described by its membership function $\mu_{\tilde{B}}(x,w)$, where

$$\mu_{\tilde{B}}(x,w) = \int_{x \in X} \mu_{\tilde{B}}(x)/x = \int_{x \in X} \left[\int_{w \in J_x^w} g_x(w)/w \right]/x \qquad J_x^w \subseteq [0,1]$$

In this example we assume that $J_x^w \in K = [l_w, r_w] \subseteq [0,1]$.

(a) For product t-norm, show that

$$\mu_A(x) \sqcap \mu_{\tilde{B}}(x) = \int_{w \in K} g_x(w)/\mu_A(x)w \qquad \mu_A(x) \in [0,1]$$

(b) For minimum t-norm, the evaluation of $\mu_A(x) \sqcap \mu_{\tilde{B}}(x)$ requires considering the three cases that are depicted in Figure 7-1. For case 1, $\mu_A(x) < w$ when $w \in K$; for case 2, $\mu_A(x) \in K$ when $w \in K$; and for case 3, $\mu_A(x) > w$ when $w \in K$. Show that

$$\mu_A(x) \sqcap \mu_{\tilde{B}}(x) = \begin{cases} 1/\mu_A(x) & \text{if } \mu_A(x) < w \text{ and } w \in K \\ \int_{d \in D} g_x(d)/d & \text{if } \mu_A(x) \in K \text{ and } w \in K, \text{ and } D \equiv [l_w, \mu_A(x)] \\ \mu_{\tilde{B}}(x) & \text{if } \mu_A(x) > w \text{ and } w \in K \end{cases}$$

7-5: Given the type-1 Gaussian fuzzy number F_i, with mean m_i and standard deviation σ_i, prove that $\alpha_i F_i + \beta$ is a Gaussian fuzzy number with mean $\alpha_i m_i + \beta$ and standard deviation $|\alpha_i \sigma_i|$. Note that this result does not depend on the kind of t-norm used, since α_i and β are crisp numbers.

7-6: Given n type-1 Gaussian fuzzy numbers $F_1, ..., F_n$, with means $m_1, ..., m_n$ and standard deviations $\sigma_1, ... \sigma_n$, as in (7-29), prove that $\sum_{i=1}^n F_i$ is a Gaussian fuzzy number with mean $\sum_{i=1}^n \alpha_i m_i$ and standard deviation Σ'', where

$$\Sigma'' = \begin{cases} \sqrt{\sum_{i=1}^{n} \sigma_i^2} & \text{if product t - norm is used} \\ \sum_{i=1}^{n} \sigma_i & \text{if minimum t - norm is used} \end{cases}$$

[Hints: (1) First prove the results for two sets and then for three sets; (2) show that the supremum of the minimum of two Gaussians is reached at their point of intersection lying between their means.]

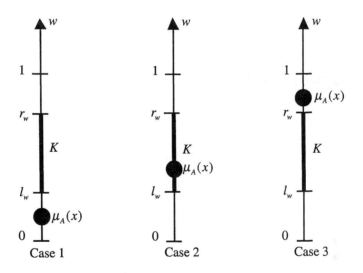

Figure 7-1: Three cases associated with the calculation of $\mu_A(x) \sqcap \mu_{\tilde{B}}(x)$ for minimum t-norm.

7-7: Using the results from Exercises 7-5 and 7-6, prove the results in Example 7-4.

7-8: Evaluate (7-31) under minimum t-norm for Gaussian fuzzy numbers.

7-9: Complete the proofs of parts (a) and (b.ii) of Theorem 7-2.

7-10: Prove that for interval type-2 fuzzy sets and minimum t-norm: (a) if $r_f < l_g$ then $F \sqcap G = F$, and (b) if $r_g < l_f$ then $F \sqcap G = G$. Note that there do not appear to be comparable results for product t-norm.

7-11: Given the three interval sets $F_1 = [0.1, 0.3]$, $F_2 = [0.15, 0.25]$, and $F_3 = [0.2, 0.4]$, compute the following: (a) $F_1 \sqcup F_2 \sqcup F_3$ and (b) $F_1 \sqcap F_2 \sqcap F_3$. Do (b) for both minimum and product t-norms.

7-12: Complete the proof of Theorem 7-3.

7-13: Re-express the results in Theorem 7-4 in terms of l_i and r_i.

7-14: Write an M-file, called **interval_join.m**, to compute the join of n interval type-1 sets, as described in Theorem 7-1.

CHAPTER 8

Type-2 Relations
and Compositions

8.1 INTRODUCTION

In this chapter we examine type-2 fuzzy relations and their compositions. They play an important role in a type-2 FLS.

8.2 RELATIONS IN GENERAL

Let $R(A_1,...,A_n)$ denote a *relation* among the n non-fuzzy (crisp) sets $A_1,...,A_n$. Then $R(A_1,...,A_n)$ is a crisp subset of the Cartesian product $A_1 \times \cdots \times A_n$ and $R(A_1,...,A_n) \subset A_1 \times \cdots \times A_n$. We can use the following membership function to represent a non-fuzzy relation:

$$\mu_R(a_1,...,a_n) = \begin{cases} 1, \text{ if } (a_1,...,a_n) \in R(A_1,...,A_n) \\ 0, \text{ otherwise} \end{cases} \tag{8-1}$$

A *binary relation* is the special case of a relation when $n = 2$ (see Section 1.10.8).

A *type-1 fuzzy relation* $F(A_1,...,A_n)$ is [Lin and Lee (1996)] a type-1 fuzzy set that is defined on the Cartesian product space of crisp sets $A_1,...,A_n$, where tuples $(a_1, a_2, ..., a_n)$ may have varying degrees of membership $\mu_F(a_1, ..., a_n)$ within the relation. More specifically,

$$F(A_1, ..., A_n) = \int_{A_1 \times A_2 \times \cdots \times A_n} \mu_F(a_1, a_2, ..., a_n)/(a_1, a_2, ..., a_n) \quad a_i \in A_i \qquad (8\text{-}2)$$

where type-1 membership function $\mu_F(a_1, ..., a_n) \in [0,1]$. Binary type-1 fuzzy relations were described in Section 1.10.9.

A *type-2 fuzzy relation* $\tilde{F}(A_1, ..., A_n)$ is a type-2 fuzzy set that is also defined on the Cartesian product space of crisp sets $A_1, ..., A_n$. More specifically,

$$\tilde{F}(A_1, ..., A_n) = \int_{A_1 \times A_2 \times \cdots \times A_n} \mu_{\tilde{F}}(a_1, a_2, ..., a_n)/(a_1, a_2, ..., a_n) \quad a_i \in A_i \qquad (8\text{-}3)$$

where $\mu_{\tilde{F}}(a_1, ..., a_n)$ is a secondary membership function; i.e., a type-1 fuzzy set at each $(a_1, ..., a_n)$.

All the previously discussed type-2 operations (Sections 7.3 and 7.4) like join, meet, and negation can be used with type-2 relations.

Example 8-1: [Karnik and Mendel (1998b)] As in Example 1-8, consider the type-1 fuzzy relation between real numbers u and v, namely "u is close to v." Recall, from that example, the membership function chosen for this relation is

$$u_c(|u - v|) = \max\{(5 - |u - v|) / 5, 0\} \qquad (8\text{-}4)$$

This membership function is depicted in Figure 8-1 (a).

If one is not sure of the exact nature of the membership function for this relation, perhaps because of the vagueness of the word "close," one could blur the membership function in Figure 8-1 (a) to reflect this uncertainty. An example of this is depicted in Figure 8-1 (b), where the FOU that is associated with $u_{\tilde{c}}(|u - v|)$ is shown.[1] This FOU has been arbitrarily chosen so that when $|u - v| = 0$ there is no additional fuzziness about "close." Similarly, when $|u - v| = 5$, this is so far from $|u - v| = 0$ that, again, there is no additional fuzziness about it. When $|u - v| = 2.5$ the primary membership is the interval $[0.25, 0.75]$, and the secondary grade reaches unity when the primary membership equals 0.5. Figure 8-1 (c) shows an example of a triangular secondary membership function corresponding to $|u - v| = 2.5$. Other choices are possible for both the FOU and the shape of the secondary membership functions, e.g., we could have used interval secondary membership functions. ∎

---

[1] For $0 \le |u - v| \le 2.5$, at each value of $|u - v|$, $u_{\tilde{c}}(|u - v|)$ is a type-1 fuzzy set with primary membership arbitrarily chosen to be $[1 - 0.3|u - v|, 1 - 0.1|u - v|]$. For $2.5 \le |u - v| \le 5$, at each value of $|u - v|$, $u_{\tilde{c}}(|u - v|)$ is a type-1 fuzzy set with primary membership arbitrarily chosen to be $[0.5 - 0.1|u - v|, 1.5 - 0.3|u - v|]$.

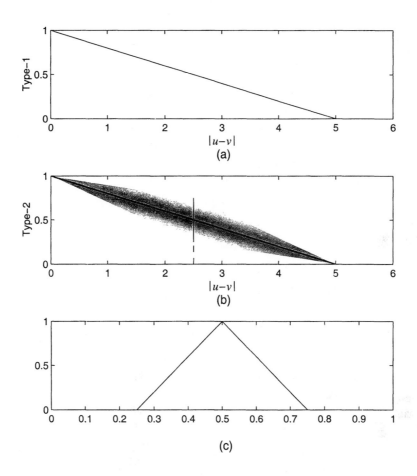

Figure 8-1: Examples of membership functions for (a) type-1 and (b) type-2 fuzzy relations. In (b) the thick dark line shows the primary memberships that have secondary grades equal to 1 (i.e., the principal membership function). The intensity of color in the gray area is approximately proportional to the value of the secondary grades; darker color represents higher secondary grades. The primary membership corresponding to $|u - v| = 2.5$ is also indicated in the figure by the dark vertical line. Figure (c) shows the secondary membership function corresponding to $|u - v| = 2.5$.

8.3 RELATIONS AND COMPOSITIONS ON THE SAME PRODUCT SPACE

Consider two universes of discourse U and V. Let $\tilde{R}(u,v)$ and $\tilde{S}(u,v)$ be two type-2 fuzzy relations that are defined on the same product space. The elements of $\tilde{R}(u,v)$ and $\tilde{S}(u,v)$ are type-1 fuzzy sets (i.e., secondary membership functions). Using (8-3) and (3-6), we can express $\tilde{R}(u,v)$ and $\tilde{S}(u,v)$ in terms of their secondary membership functions, as

$$\tilde{R}(u,v) = \int_{U \times V} \mu_{\tilde{R}}(u,v)/(u,v) = \int_{U \times V} \left[\int_{\alpha \in J_{(u,v)}^{\alpha}} r_{(u,v)}(\alpha)/\alpha \right] \Big/ (u,v) \tag{8-5}$$

and

$$\tilde{S}(u,v) = \int_{U \times V} \mu_{\tilde{S}}(u,v)/(u,v) = \int_{U \times V} \left[\int_{\beta \in J_{(u,v)}^{\beta}} s_{(u,v)}(\beta)/\beta \right] \Big/ (u,v) \tag{8-6}$$

where[2] primary memberships $J_{(u,v)}^{\alpha}, J_{(u,v)}^{\beta} \subseteq [0,1]$. According to (7-13) and (7-18), the union and intersection of $\tilde{R}(u,v)$ and $\tilde{S}(u,v)$ can be expressed in terms of the secondary membership functions $\mu_{\tilde{R}}(u,v)$ and $\mu_{\tilde{S}}(u,v)$. From (7-17) and (7-20), we find

$$\mu_{\tilde{R} \cup \tilde{S}}(u,v) = \mu_{\tilde{R}}(u,v) \sqcup \mu_{\tilde{S}}(u,v)$$
$$= \int_{\alpha \in J_{(u,v)}^{\alpha}} \int_{\beta \in J_{(u,v)}^{\beta}} r_{(u,v)}(\alpha) \star s_{(u,v)}(\beta)/(\alpha \vee \beta) \quad \forall (u,v) \in U \times V \tag{8-7}$$

and

$$\mu_{\tilde{R} \cap \tilde{S}}(u,v) = \mu_{\tilde{R}}(u,v) \sqcap \mu_{\tilde{S}}(u,v)$$
$$= \int_{\alpha \in J_{(u,v)}^{\alpha}} \int_{\beta \in J_{(u,v)}^{\beta}} r_{(u,v)}(\alpha) \star s_{(u,v)}(\beta)/(\alpha \wedge \beta) \quad \forall (u,v) \in U \times V \tag{8-8}$$

Although these formulas look formidable, they are easy to evaluate, as we demonstrate in the following example.

---

[2] α and β are dummy variables that are associated with the primary memberships.

Example 8-2: [Karnik and Mendel (1998b)] As in Example 1-9, consider the two somewhat contradictory fuzzy relations "u is close to v" *and* "u is smaller than v," and also the less-contradictory relations "u is close to v" *or* "u is smaller than v." All relations are on the same product space $U \times V$. Recall that $U = \{u_1, u_2\} = \{2, 12\}$ and $V = \{v_1, v_2, v_3\}$ $= \{1, 7, 13\}$. Here we consider a type-2 version of these two relations; i.e., we assume that there is some uncertainty about the type-1 membership grades. Let the secondary membership functions for the type-2 case be as follows:

$$\mu_{\tilde{c}}(u,v) = \begin{matrix} & v_1 & v_2 \\ u_1 & \left(0.3/0.8 + 1/0.9 + 0.7/1 \right. & 0.7/0.3 + 1/0.4 + 0.1/0.5 \\ u_2 & 0.5/0 + 1/0.1 & 0.7/0.3 + 1/0.4 + 0.1/0.5 \end{matrix}$$

$$\begin{matrix} v_3 \\ 0.5/0 + 1/0.1 \\ 0.3/0.8 + 1/0.9 + 0.7/1 \end{matrix}\Bigg) \tag{8-9}$$

and

$$\mu_{\tilde{s}}(u,v) = \begin{matrix} & v_1 & v_2 \\ u_1 & \left(1/0 + 0.9/0.1 + 0.4/0.5 \right. & 0.8/0.3 + 0.8/0.4 + 0.9/0.5 + 1/0.6 \\ u_2 & 1/0 + 0.1/0.1 + 0.1/0.2 & 1/0 + 0.3/0.1 \end{matrix}$$

$$\begin{matrix} v_3 \\ 0.9/0.9 + 1/1 \\ 1/0.3 + 0.9/0.4 + 0.4/0.5 \end{matrix}\Bigg) \tag{8-10}$$

We have purposely chosen the secondary membership functions so that the primary memberships that correspond to the membership grades in the type-1 case have unity secondary grades in the type-2 case [e.g., element $1/0.9$ in $\mu_{\tilde{c}}(u_1, v_1)$, element $1/0.4$ in $\mu_{\tilde{c}}(u_1, v_2)$, etc.]. This can be interpreted as "perturbing" the membership matrices in (1-29) and (1-30) a little bit. Observe that pairs having the same membership grades in the type-1 case need not necessarily have the same complete secondary membership functions in the type-2 case [e.g., see $\mu_{\tilde{s}}(u_1, v_1)$ and $\mu_{\tilde{s}}(u_2, v_1)$].

The secondary membership functions for the union and intersection of these relations can be found from (8-7) and (8-8) as follows [because in this example U and V are discrete universes, $\int$ in (8-7) is replaced by Σ]:

$$\mu_{\tilde{c} \cup \tilde{s}}(u_i, v_j) = \mu_{\tilde{c}}(u_i, v_j) \sqcup \mu_{\tilde{s}}(u_i, v_j)$$

$$= \sum_{\alpha \in J^{\alpha}_{(u_i,v_j)}} \sum_{\beta \in J^{\beta}_{(u_i,v_j)}} r_{(u_i,v_j)}(\alpha) \star s_{(u_i,v_j)}(\beta) / (\alpha \vee \beta) \tag{8-11}$$

and

$$\mu_{\tilde{c}\cap\tilde{s}}(u_i,v_j) = \mu_{\tilde{c}}(u_i,v_j)\Pi\mu_{\tilde{s}}(u_i,v_j)$$

$$= \sum_{\alpha\in J^{\alpha}_{(u_i,v_j)}}\sum_{\beta\in J^{\beta}_{(u_i,v_j)}} r_{(u_i,v_j)}(\alpha)\star s_{(u_i,v_j)}(\beta)\big/(\alpha\wedge\beta) \tag{8-12}$$

where $i = 1, 2$ and $j = 1, 2, 3$. Using (8-11) and (8-12) with minimum t-norm and maximum t-conorm, it is straightforward to show, for example, that

$$\mu_{\tilde{c}\cup\tilde{s}}(u_1,v_1) = (0.3/0.8 + 1/0.9 + 0.7/1)\sqcup(1/0 + 0.9/0.1 + 0.4/0.5)$$
$$= 0.3/0.8 + 0.3/0.8 + 0.3/0.8 + 1/0.9 + 0.9/0.9$$
$$+ 0.4/0.9 + 0.7/1 + 0.7/1 + 0.4/1 \tag{8-13}$$
$$= 0.3/0.8 + 1/0.9 + 0.7/1$$

and

$$\mu_{\tilde{c}\cap\tilde{s}}(u_1,v_1) = (0.3/0.8 + 1/0.9 + 0.7/1)\Pi(1/0 + 0.9/0.1 + 0.4/0.5)$$
$$= 0.3/0 + 0.3/0.1 + 0.3/0.5 + 1/0 + 0.9/0.1$$
$$+ 0.4/0.5 + 0.7/0 + 0.7/0.1 + 0.4/0.5 \tag{8-14}$$
$$= 1/0 + 0.9/0.1 + 0.4/0.5$$

We leave the calculations of the remaining elements in $\mu_{\tilde{c}\cup\tilde{s}}(u,v)$ and $\mu_{\tilde{c}\cap\tilde{s}}(u,v)$ as an exercise for the reader. The final results are:

$$\mu_{\tilde{c}\cup\tilde{s}}(u,v) = \begin{array}{c} \\ u_1 \\ u_2 \end{array}\left(\begin{array}{ccc} v_1 & v_2 & v_3 \\ 0.3/0.8 + 1/0.9 + 0.7/1 & 0.7/0.3 + 0.8/0.4 + 0.9/0.5 + 1/0.6 & 0.9/0.9 + 1/1 \\ 0.5/0 + 1/0.1 + 0.1/0.2 & 0.7/0.3 + 1/0.4 + 0.1/0.5 & 0.3/0.8 + 1/0.9 + 0.7/1 \end{array}\right) \tag{8-15}$$

and

$$\mu_{\tilde{c}\cap\tilde{s}}(u,v) = \begin{array}{c} \\ u_1 \\ u_2 \end{array}\left(\begin{array}{ccc} v_1 & v_2 & v_3 \\ 1/0 + 0.9/0.1 + 0.4/0.5 & 0.8/0.3 + 1/0.4 + 0.1/0.5 & 0.5/0 + 1/0.1 \\ 1/0 + 0.1/0.1 & 1/0 + 0.3/0.1 & 1/0.3 + 0.9/0.4 + 0.4/0.5 \end{array}\right) \tag{8-16}$$

Comparing the results in (8-15) and (8-16) with those for the type-1 case, in (1-33) and (1-34), respectively, we observe the following:

1. Since we chose secondary membership functions in such a way that the primary memberships corresponding to the membership grades in the type-1 case have unity secondary grades, the memberships of union and intersection also exhibit a similar structure; i.e., primary memberships for the union (intersection) of $\tilde{c}$ and $\tilde{s}$ that correspond to the membership grades for the union (intersection) in the type-1 case have unity secondary grades. For example, $\mu_{c \cap s}(u_1, v_2) = 0.4$ and in $\mu_{\tilde{c} \cap \tilde{s}}(u_1, v_2)$ the secondary grade at the primary membership of 0.4 is 1.

2. The values of primary memberships of the union that have non-zero secondary grades are, in general, higher than those of the intersection of the aforementioned two relations, again indicating that the union (close *or* smaller) of the above two relations is treated with a higher degree of belief than their intersection (close *and* smaller). ∎

8.4 RELATIONS AND COMPOSITIONS ON DIFFERENT PRODUCT SPACES

Consider two different product spaces $U \times V$ and $V \times W$ that share a common set, and let $R(U, V)$ and $S(V, W)$ be two *crisp* relations on these spaces. The composition of these relations is defined (e.g., [Klir and Folger (1988, p. 75)]) as "a subset $T(U, W)$ of $U \times W$ such that $u, w \in T$ if and only if $(u, v) \in R$ and $(v, w) \in S$."[3] This can be expressed as a *max-min, max-product*, or in general, as a *sup-star* composition (where $\star$ indicates any suitable t-norm), i.e.,

$$\mu_{R \circ S}(u, w) = \sup_{v \in V}\left[\mu_R(u, v) \star \mu_S(v, w)\right] \quad u \in U, w \in W \qquad (8\text{-}17)$$

The validity of the sup-star composition for crisp sets is shown in Wang (1997). If, for example, R and S are two crisp relations on $U \times V$ and $V \times W$ respectively, then the membership for any pair (u, w), $u \in U$ and $w \in W$, is 1 if and only if there exists at least one $v \in V$ such that $\mu_R(u, v) = 1$ *and* $\mu_S(v, w) = 1$. In Wang (1997) it is shown that this condition is equivalent to having the sup-star composition equal to 1. See Section 1.10.10 for more discussions and examples about crisp relations and compositions on different product spaces.

---

[3] The condition that $u, w \in T$ is very important because type-1 operations have only been defined for fuzzy sets whose variables share the same space; e.g., see (7-1) and (7-2) in which F_1 and F_2 depend on the same variable y where $y \in Y$. When we state that $u \in U$ and $v \in V$, where $U \neq V$, we interpret U and V as subsets of a common space, T. Doing this permits us to use the defined type-1 operations.

When we enter the fuzzy domain, set memberships belong to the interval [0, 1] rather than just being 0 or 1. We can now think of an element as belonging to a set if it has a non-zero membership in that set. In this respect, the aforementioned condition on the composition of relations can be rephrased for type-1 fuzzy relations as follows:

> If R and S are two type-1 fuzzy relations on $U \times V$ and $V \times W$ respectively, then the membership for any pair[3] (u,w), $u \in U$ and $w \in W$ is non-zero if and only if there exists at least one $v \in V$ such that $\mu_R(u,v) \neq 0$ *and* $\mu_S(v,w) \neq 0$.

It can easily be shown (e.g., [Karnik and Mendel (1998b)]) that this condition is again equivalent to the sup-star composition in (8-17). See Section 1.10.11 for more discussions and examples about type-1 relations and compositions on different product spaces.

If $\tilde{R}$ and $\tilde{S}$ are two type-2 fuzzy relations on $U \times V$ and $V \times W$ respectively, then the membership for any pair[3] (u,w), $u \in U$ and $w \in W$, is non-zero if and only if there exists at least one $v \in V$ such that $\mu_{\tilde{R}}(u,v) \neq 1/0$ *and* $\mu_{\tilde{S}}(v,w) \neq 1/0$; this is equivalent to the following *extended sup-star composition*:

$$\mu_{\tilde{R} \circ \tilde{S}}(u,w) = \bigsqcup_{v \in V} \left[\mu_{\tilde{R}}(u,v) \sqcap \mu_{\tilde{S}}(v,w) \right] \quad u \in U, w \in W \qquad (8\text{-}18)$$

A detailed validation of (8-18) is quite technical and can be found in Karnik and Mendel [(1998b), (2000a)]. Observe that, when type-2 relations reduce to type-1 relations, then (8-18) reduces to (8-17), because in that case we can replace the meet and join operations with the t-norm and t-conorm, respectively. For the t-conorm we use the maximum operation.[4]

Example 8-3: [Karnik and Mendel (1998b)] As in Example 1-12, consider the relation "u is close to v" on $U \times V$, where $U = \{u_1, u_2\} = \{2, 12\}$ and $V = \{v_1, v_2, v_3\} = \{1, 7, 13\}$. Now consider another fuzzy relation "v is much bigger than w" on $V \times W$, where $W = \{w_1, w_2\} = \{4, 8\}$. Here we consider type-2 versions of these two relations obtained by adding some uncertainty to the type-1 relations in (1-29) and (1-46). The secondary membership function $\mu_{\tilde{c}}(u,v)$ is given by (8-9), whereas the secondary membership function $\mu_{\tilde{mb}}(v,w)$ is:

---

[4]Dubois and Prade (1979, 1980) give a formula for the composition of type-2 relations, using the minimum t-norm as an extension of the type-1 sup-min composition. Their formula is the same as (8-18); however, Karnik and Mendel (1998b, 2000a) have demonstrated the validity of (8-18) for product as well as minimum t-norms.

$$
\mu_{\tilde{m}b}(v,w) =
\begin{array}{c}
v_1 \\
v_2 \\
v_3
\end{array}
\left(
\begin{array}{cc}
w_1 & w_2 \\
1/0+0.6/0.1 & 1/0+0.1/0.1 \\
0.4/0.5+1/0.6+0.9/0.7 & 1/0+0.8/0.1+0.2/0.2 \\
0.7/0.9+1/1 & 0.5/0.6+1/0.7+0.7/0.8
\end{array}
\right)
\tag{8-19}
$$

The composition of $\mu_{\tilde{c}}(u,v)$ and $\mu_{\tilde{m}b}(v,w)$ can be found by using (8-18) as follows:

$$
\mu_{\tilde{c}\circ\tilde{m}b}(u_i,w_j) = \left[\mu_{\tilde{c}}(u_i,v_1)\sqcap\mu_{\tilde{m}b}(v_1,w_j)\right]\sqcup\left[\mu_{\tilde{c}}(u_i,v_2)\sqcap\mu_{\tilde{m}b}(v_2,w_j)\right]
$$
$$
\sqcup\left[\mu_{\tilde{c}}(u_i,v_3)\sqcap\mu_{\tilde{m}b}(v_3,w_j)\right]
\tag{8-20}
$$

where $i = 1, 2$ and $j = 1, 2, 3$. For example [using (7-17) and (7-20) in which $\int$ is replaced by Σ],

$$
\mu_{\tilde{c}\circ\tilde{m}b}(u_1,w_1) = \left[(0.3/0.8+1/0.9+0.7/1)\sqcap(1/0+0.6/0.1)\right]
$$
$$
\sqcup[(0.7/0.3+1/0.4+0.1/0.51)
$$
$$
\sqcap(0.4/0.5+1/0.6+0.9/0.7)]
\tag{8-21}
$$
$$
\sqcup[(0.5/0+1/0.1)\sqcap(0.7/0.9+1/1)]
$$
$$
= 0.7/0.3+1/0.4
$$

Doing all the calculations in a similar manner, we get

$$
\mu_{\tilde{c}\circ\tilde{m}b}(u,w) =
\begin{array}{c}
u_1 \\
u_2
\end{array}
\left(
\begin{array}{cc}
w_1 & w_2 \\
0.7/0.3+1/0.4 & 0.5/0+1/0.1+0.2/0.2 \\
0.3/0.8+1/0.9+0.7/1 & 0.5/0.6+1/0.7+0.7/0.8
\end{array}
\right)
\tag{8-22}
$$

Observe that the results in (8-22) are quite similar to the results of the type-1 sup-star composition in (1-49); i.e., in the type-2 results, primary memberships corresponding to the memberships of the type-1 results have unity secondary grades. Equation (8-22) provides additional uncertainty information to account for the uncertainties present in $\mu_{\tilde{c}}(u,v)$ and $\mu_{\tilde{m}b}(v,w)$. ∎

8.5 COMPOSITION OF A SET WITH A RELATION

Consider the case where one of the type-2 relations involved in the extended sup-star composition is just a type-2 fuzzy set. The composition of a type-2 fuzzy set $\tilde{R}$ and a type-2 fuzzy relation $\tilde{S}(U,V)$ is given by the following special case of (8-18) [Karnik and Mendel (1998b), (2000a)]

$$\mu_{\tilde{R}\circ\tilde{S}}(v) = \sqcup_{u\in U}\left[\mu_{\tilde{R}}(u)\sqcap\mu_{\tilde{S}}(u,v)\right] \qquad (8\text{-}23)$$

in which $\mu_{\tilde{R}}(u)$ is the secondary membership function of $\tilde{R}$. This equation plays an important role as the inference mechanism of a rule whose antecedents or consequents are type-2 fuzzy sets, and *is the fundamental inference mechanism for rules in a type-2 FLS*. It is the type-2 version of (1-51).

Example 8-4: As in Example 1-13, consider again the relation "u is close to v" on $U\times V$, where $U=\{2,12\}$ and $V=\{1,7,13\}$. Here, however, we use its type-2 version, whose secondary membership function $\mu_{\tilde{c}}(u,v)$ is given in (8-9). We also consider the type-2 fuzzy set "small" on U, whose secondary membership function is obtained by adding some uncertainty to the membership function of small, given in (1-52) as follows:

$$\mu_{\tilde{s}}(u) = \left(\overset{u_1}{0.5/0.7+1/0.9}\quad \overset{u_2}{1/0.1+0.3/0.4}\right) \qquad (8\text{-}24)$$

The composition of the type-2 set "small" and the type-2 relation "u is close to v" can now be obtained using (8-23) as follows:

$$\mu_{\tilde{s}\circ\tilde{c}}(v_j) = \left[\mu_{\tilde{s}}(u_1)\sqcap\mu_{\tilde{c}}(u_1,v_j)\right]\sqcup\left[\mu_{\tilde{s}}(u_2)\sqcap\mu_{\tilde{c}}(u_2,v_j)\right] \qquad (8\text{-}25)$$

where $j = 1, 2, 3$. Using (8-25) it is again straightforward to show that

$$\mu_{\tilde{s}\circ\tilde{c}}(v) = \left(\overset{v_1}{0.5/0.7+0.3/0.8+1/0.9}\quad \overset{v_2}{0.7/0.3+1/0.4+0.1/0.5}\quad \overset{v_3}{1/0.1+0.3/0.4}\right) \qquad (8\text{-}26)$$

Comparing (8-26) and (1-54), we observe that the type-1 and type-2 results are again quite similar. In the type-2 results, primary memberships corresponding to the membership grades in the type-1 results have unity secondary grades. ∎

8.6 CARTESIAN PRODUCT OF FUZZY SETS

When $A_1, A_2, ..., A_n$ are type-1 fuzzy sets in universes of discourse $X_1, X_2, ..., X_n$, then the Cartesian product of $A_1, A_2, ..., A_n$ is a type-1 fuzzy set in the product space $X_1\times X_2\times\cdots\times X_n$ with membership function [Zadeh (1975)]

$$\mu_{A_1 \times \cdots \times A_n}(x_1,\ldots,x_n) = \mu_{A_1}(x_1) \star \mu_{A_2}(x_2) \star \cdots \star \mu_{A_n}(x_n) \tag{8-27}$$

where $x_1 \in X_1, \ldots, x_n \in X_n$ and $\star$ denotes a t-norm (e.g., minimum or product).

Let $\tilde{A}_1, \tilde{A}_2, \ldots, \tilde{A}_n$ be type-2 fuzzy sets in universes of discourse $X_1, X_2, \ldots, X_n$. The Cartesian product of $\tilde{A}_1, \tilde{A}_2, \ldots, \tilde{A}_n$, $\tilde{A}_1 \times \tilde{A}_2 \times \cdots \times \tilde{A}_n$, is a type-2 fuzzy set in the product space $X_1 \times X_2 \times \cdots \times X_n$ with the membership function

$$\mu_{\tilde{A}_1 \times \cdots \times \tilde{A}_n}(x_1,\ldots,x_n) = \mu_{\tilde{A}_1}(x_1) \sqcap \mu_{\tilde{A}_2}(x_2) \sqcap \cdots \sqcap \mu_{\tilde{A}_n}(x_n) \tag{8-28}$$

where $x_1 \in X_1, \ldots, x_n \in X_n$ and $\sqcap$ denotes the meet operation. In (8-28), $\mu_{\tilde{A}_i}(x_i)$ is the secondary membership function of $\tilde{A}_i$ at x_i, and $\mu_{\tilde{A}_1 \times \cdots \times \tilde{A}_n}(x_1,\ldots,x_n)$ can also be viewed as a secondary membership function (i.e., a type-1 fuzzy set) at $(x_1,\ldots,x_n)$.

Example 8-5: Consider two universes of discourse U and V, where $U = \{u_1, u_2, u_3\}$ and $V = \{v_1, v_2\}$. Let $\tilde{F}$ be a type-2 fuzzy set on U with secondary membership function

$$\mu_{\tilde{F}}(u) = \left(\overset{u_1}{0.9/0.2 + 0.9/0.8 + 0.4/1} \quad \overset{u_2}{0.1/0.4 + 1/0.7 + 1/1} \quad \overset{u_3}{0.6/0 + 0.8/0.2} \right) \tag{8-29}$$

and let $\tilde{G}$ be a type-2 fuzzy set on V with secondary membership function

$$\mu_{\tilde{G}}(v) = \left(\overset{v_1}{0.4/0.5 + 0.3/0.6} \quad \overset{v_2}{0.7/0.6 + 0.6/0.8 + 0.1/0.9} \right) \tag{8-30}$$

The membership function of the Cartesian product of $\tilde{F}$ and $\tilde{G}$ can be obtained as

$$\mu_{\tilde{F} \times \tilde{G}}(u_i, v_j) = \mu_{\tilde{F}}(u_i) \sqcap \mu_{\tilde{G}}(v_j) \quad i = 1, 2, 3 \text{ and } j = 1, 2 \tag{8-31}$$

We leave it to the reader to show that

$$\mu_{\tilde{F} \times \tilde{G}}(u,v) = \begin{array}{c} \\ u_1 \\ u_2 \\ u_3 \end{array} \left(\begin{array}{c} v_1 \\ 0.4/0.2 + 0.4/0.5 + 0.3/0.6 \\ 0.1/0.4 + 0.4/0.5 + 0.3/0.6 \\ 0.4/0 + 0.4/0.2 \end{array} \right.$$

$$\begin{matrix} v_2 \\ 0.7/0.2+0.7/0.6+0.6/0.8+0.1/0.9 \\ 0.1/0.4+0.7/0.6+0.6/0.7+0.6/0.8+0.1/0.9 \\ 0.6/0+0.7/0.2 \end{matrix} \Bigg) \qquad (8\text{-}32)$$

■

8.7 IMPLICATIONS

Just as type-1 FLSs use rules, so do type-2 FLSs (we will have much more to say about this in Chapters 10–13). The good news is that the structure of a rule does not change as we go from a type-1 to a type-2 FLS. All that changes is that (some or all of) the antecedents or consequents in a type-2 rule become type-2 fuzzy sets instead of type-1 fuzzy sets; hence, the structure of the lth type-2 rule is:

$$R^l: \text{IF } x_1 \text{ is } \tilde{F}_1^l \text{ and } x_2 \text{ is } \tilde{F}_2^l \text{ and } \cdots \text{ and } x_p \text{ is } \tilde{F}_p^l \text{ THEN } y \text{ is } \tilde{G}^l \qquad (8\text{-}33)$$

i.e.,

$$R^l: \tilde{F}_1^l \times \cdots \times \tilde{F}_p^l \to \tilde{G}^l = \tilde{A}^l \to \tilde{G}^l \quad l=1,...,M \qquad (8\text{-}34)$$

Recall from Section 5.2 that we view a rule as a *relation* between a collection of p antecedents and a single consequent. We generalize the type-1 implication membership function, given in (5-4) to its type-2 counterpart:

$$\mu_{R^l}(\mathbf{x},y) = \mu_{\tilde{A}^l \to \tilde{G}^l}(\mathbf{x},y) = \mu_{\tilde{F}_1^l}(x_1) \Pi \cdots \Pi \mu_{\tilde{F}_p^l}(x_p) \Pi \mu_{\tilde{G}^l}(y)$$
$$= \left[\Pi_{i=1}^p \mu_{\tilde{F}_i^l}(x_i) \right] \Pi \mu_{\tilde{G}^l}(y) \qquad (8\text{-}35)$$

where in this book the meet will either involve the minimum or the product t-norms. Just as (5-4) made use of the Cartesian product for $\mu_{F_1^l \times \cdots \times F_p^l}(\mathbf{x})$, given in (8-27), (8-35) makes use of the Cartesian product for $\mu_{\tilde{F}_1^l \times \cdots \times \tilde{F}_p^l}(\mathbf{x})$, given in (8-29). Observe that, for each $\mathbf{x}$ and y, $\mu_{R^l}(\mathbf{x},y)$ is a type-1 fuzzy set. To evaluate $\mu_{R^l}(\mathbf{x},y)$ we need to use the results given in Section 7.3 for meet. Equation (8-35) will be used extensively in Chapters 10-12.

EXERCISES

8-1: Complete the calculations to obtain the results in (8-15) and (8-16).

8-2: Complete the calculations to obtain the results in (8-22).

8-3: Redo the calculations in Example 8-3 using product t-norm.

8-4: Carefully show how (8-23) follows from (8-18), when the first relation in the latter equation is just a fuzzy set.

8-5: Complete the calculations to obtain the results in (8-26).

8-6: Explain how to carry out the computations in the extended sup-star composition (8-18) when U, W, and V are continuous universes of discourse.

8-7: Perform the detailed calculations to obtain $\mu_{\tilde{F} \times \tilde{G}}(u, v)$ in (8-32).

Centroid of a Type-2 Fuzzy Set: Type-Reduction

9.1 INTRODUCTION

Many of the most useful defuzzification methods that have been described in Section 5.5 involve computing the centroid of a type-1 fuzzy set. An important calculation for a type-2 FLS is *type reduction*; it is an extension (obtained using the Extension Principle, as described in Section 7.2) of a type-1 defuzzification procedure. Consequently, to implement a type-2 FLS we need a method for computing the centroid of a type-2 fuzzy set. The concept of a centroid of a type-2 fuzzy set is new, and in this chapter we present its definition and ways to compute it. It represents a mapping of a type-2 fuzzy set into a type-1 fuzzy set. We also discuss type-reduction and demonstrate how different type-reduction methods reduce to the calculation of the centroid of *specific* type-2 fuzzy sets. Much of the material in this chapter is from [Karnik and Mendel (1998b)].

9.2 GENERAL RESULTS FOR THE CENTROID

The centroid of a type-1 fuzzy set A, whose domain, $x \in X$, is discretized into N

points, is given as

$$c_A = \frac{\sum_{i=1}^N x_i \mu_A(x_i)}{\sum_{i=1}^N \mu_A(x_i)} \tag{9-1}$$

Similarly, the centroid of a type-2 fuzzy set $\tilde{A} = \left\{ \left(x, \mu_{\tilde{A}}(x)\right) \middle| x \in X \right\}$ whose x-domain is discretized into N points, $x_1, x_2, ..., x_N$, so that [see (3-7)]

$$\tilde{A} = \sum_{i=1}^N \left[\int_{u \in J_{x_i}} f_{x_i}(u)/u \right] \Big/ x_i, \tag{9-2}$$

can be defined using the Extension Principle in (7-9) as follows [Karnik and Mendel (1998b), (1999d)]:

$$C_{\tilde{A}} = \int_{\theta_1 \in J_{x_1}} \cdots \int_{\theta_N \in J_{x_N}} \left[f_{x_1}(\theta_1) \star \cdots \star f_{x_N}(\theta_N) \right] \Big/ \frac{\sum_{i=1}^N x_i \theta_i}{\sum_{i=1}^N \theta_i} \tag{9-3}$$

$C_{\tilde{A}}$ is a type-1 fuzzy set.

Every combination of θ_1, ..., θ_N and its associated secondary grade $f_{x_1}(\theta_1)$ $\star \cdots \star f_{x_N}(\theta_N)$ forms an embedded type-2 set, $\tilde{A}_e$, as in Definition 3-10. Each element of $C_{\tilde{A}}$ is determined by computing the centroid

$$\sum_{i=1}^N x_i \theta_i \Big/ \sum_{i=1}^N \theta_i$$

of the embedded type-1 set A_e that is associated with $\tilde{A}_e$ (see Definition 3-12) and computing the t-norm of the secondary grades associated with $\theta_1, ..., \theta_N$, namely $f_{x_1}(\theta_1) \star \cdots \star f_{x_N}(\theta_N)$. The complete centroid $C_{\tilde{A}}$ is determined by doing this for *all* the embedded type-2 sets in $\tilde{A}$.

Let $\theta = [\theta_1, ..., \theta_N]^T$,

$$a(\theta) \equiv \frac{\sum_{i=1}^N x_i \theta_i}{\sum_{i=1}^N \theta_i} \tag{9-4}$$

and

$$b(\theta) \equiv f_{x_1}(\theta_1) \star \cdots \star f_{x_N}(\theta_N);$$ (9-5)

then $C_{\tilde{A}}$ can also be expressed as

$$C_{\tilde{A}} = \int_{\theta_1 \in J_{x_1}} \cdots \int_{\theta_N \in J_{x_N}} b(\theta)/a(\theta)$$ (9-6)

In terms of $a(\theta)$ and $b(\theta)$, the computation of $C_{\tilde{A}}$ involves computing the tuple $(a(\theta), b(\theta))$ many times (as described following). Suppose, for example, $(a(\theta), b(\theta))$ is computed α times [for α to be finite, $J_{x_1}, \ldots, J_{x_N}$ must also be discretized, as in the second line of (3-7); we do this next]; then, we can view the computation of $C_{\tilde{A}}$ as the computation of the α tuples (a_1, b_1), (a_2, b_2), ..., (a_α, b_α). If two or more combinations of vector θ give the same point in the centroid set, $a(\theta)$, we keep the one with the largest value of $b(\theta)$.

From (9-6), we see that the domain of $C_{\tilde{A}}$ will be an interval $[a_l(\theta), a_r(\theta)]$ where

$$a_l(\theta) = \min_\theta a(\theta)$$ (9-7)

and

$$a_r(\theta) = \max_\theta a(\theta)$$ (9-8)

A practical sequence of computations to obtain $C_{\tilde{A}}$ is as follows:

1. Discretize the x-domain into N points $x_1, \ldots, x_N$.
2. Discretize each J_{x_j} (the primary memberships of x_j) into a suitable number of points, say M_j ($j = 1, \ldots, N$).
3. Enumerate all the embedded type-1 sets; there will be $\prod_{j=1}^{N} M_j$ of them (Definition 3-12).
4. Compute the centroid using (9-6), i.e., compute the α tuples (a_k, b_k), $k = 1, 2, \ldots, \prod_{j=1}^{N} M_j$, where a_k and b_k are given in (9-4) and (9-5), respectively. In this case, $\alpha = \prod_{j=1}^{N} M_j$.

This is depicted in Figure 9-1 for interval type-1 sets.

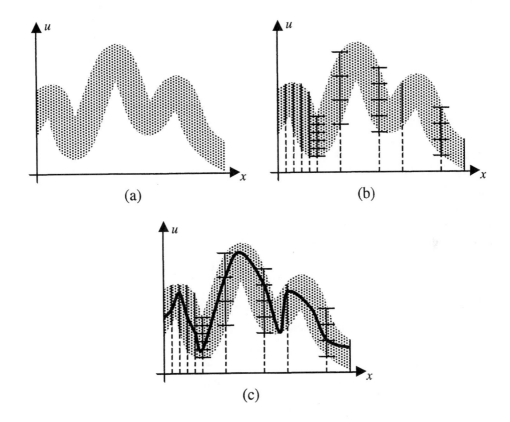

Figure 9-1: Computation of the centroid of an interval type-2 fuzzy set: (a) FOU for the interval type-2 set; (b) sampled independent variable and discretized primary memberships; (c) the solid curve is one embedded type-1 set (the upper and lower membership functions for the FOU are two other embedded type-1 sets; all-in-all, there are $\prod_{j=1}^{N} M_j$ embedded type-1 sets).

In Step 3, $\prod_{j=1}^{N} M_j$ can be very large even for small M_j or N. For interval type-2 sets the exact centroid can be obtained relatively easily by using the computational procedure that is discussed in Sections 9.3 and 9.4.

Unfortunately, there is an unwelcome technical problem hidden in the calculation of the t-norm in (9-5) *when the type-2 fuzzy set has a continuous x-domain and its secondary membership functions are anything but interval sets.* This problem has to do with using the product as the t-norm and the fact that the calculation of $b(\theta)$ in (9-5) is very much dependent on N when product t-norm is used; i.e., changing N changes $b(\theta)$. Recall that we have focused on using either minimum or product t-norm; however, as we explain next, for the centroid calculation under the conditions just stated, we must *not* use the product t-norm.

Technical subtlety: [Karnik and Mendel (1998b), (2000b)] We concentrate on type-2 sets having a continuous domain whose secondary membership functions are such that, for any x-domain point, only one primary membership has a secondary grade equal to 1. Let $\tilde{A}$ be such a type-2 set. In the discussion associated with (9-3) we assumed that the x-domain of $\tilde{A}$ is discretized into N points. The true centroid of $\tilde{A}$ (for $\tilde{A}$ with a continuous x-domain) is the limit of $C_{\tilde{A}}$ in (9-3) as $N \to \infty$. When we use the product t-norm

$$\lim_{N \to \infty} T_{i=1}^{N} f_{x_i}(\theta_i) = \lim_{N \to \infty} \prod_{i=1}^{N} f_{x_i}(\theta_i) = 0 \tag{9-9}$$

unless only a finite number of the $f_{x_i}(\theta_i)$ are less than 1.

When $\forall f_{x_i}(\theta_i) = 1$, the associated embedded type-1 set is for the principal membership function (see Definition 3-5), which we denote as $A_e(principal\ MF)$. This embedded type-1 set contributes the element $1/a(\theta_{prinicpal\ MF})$ to $C_{\tilde{A}}$ because all of its secondary grades equal 1. Karnik and Mendel (1998b) have shown that any embedded type-1 set whose membership function differs from that of $A_e(principal\ MF)$ by only a *finite* number of points also contributes the *same* element[1] $1/a(\theta_{prinicpal\ MF})$ to $C_{\tilde{A}}$. This means that, when $N \to \infty$, there is only one point that has a non-zero membership grade in $C_{\tilde{A}}$ and that grade equals 1. In this case, $C_{\tilde{A}}$ will be equal to a crisp number, namely $1/a(\theta_{prinicpal\ MF})$—the centroid of $A_e(principal\ MF)$. This is unacceptable because such a centroid ignores all of the uncertainties about type-2 fuzzy set $\tilde{A}$.

This problem occurs because, as we just noted, under the product t-norm (9-9) occurs unless only a finite number of the $f_{x_i}(\theta_i)$ are less than one. Fortunately, the minimum t-norm does not cause such a problem, i.e., the calculation of $b(\theta)$ in (9-5) is relatively independent of N when the minimum t-norm is used, because changing N does not change $b(\theta)$ too much and will not cause $b(\theta) \to 0$. Consequently, *we will always use the minimum t-norm to calculate*

---

[1] This has to do with the fact, from real analysis, that if functions $\alpha(x)$ and $\beta(x)$ differ for only a finite number of x-points then $\int_{x \in X} \alpha(x)dx = \int_{x \in X} \beta(x)dx$, where $\int$ is an integral.

the centroid of a type-2 set having a continuous domain. ■

Observe that the centroid of a type-1 fuzzy set in (9-1) is a weighted average of the general form

$$y(z_1,...,z_N,w_1,...,w_N) = \frac{\sum_{l=1}^{N} z_l w_l}{\sum_{l=1}^{N} w_l} \tag{9-10}$$

where z_l are real numbers ($z_l \in \Re$) and $w_l \in [0,1]$ for $l = 1, ..., N$. Thus far we have only considered the extension of (9-10) when w_l becomes a type-1 set, because most of the type-1 defuzzification methods fit this case; however, the extension of the center-of-sets defuzzifier (Section 5.5.5) to the center-of-sets type-reducer requires both w_l and z_l to become type-1 sets; hence, we need to generalize from our previous extension of (9-1) to (9-2) to the extension of (9-10) when both w_l and z_l are type-1 sets. The result of doing this is called a *generalized centroid* [Karnik and Mendel (1998b), (2000b)], which we denote as *GC*.

If each z_l is replaced by a type-1 fuzzy set $Z_l \subset \Re$ with associated membership function $\mu_{Z_l}(z_l)$, and each w_l is replaced by a type-1 fuzzy set $W_l \subseteq [0,1]$ with associated membership function $\mu_{W_l}(w_l)$, then the extension of (9-10)—the *generalized centroid*—is

$$GC = \int_{z_1 \in Z_1} \cdots \int_{z_N \in Z_N} \int_{w_1 \in W_1} \cdots \int_{w_N \in W_N} \left[T_{l=1}^{N} \mu_{Z_l}(z_l) \star T_{l=1}^{N} \mu_{W_l}(w_l) \right] \bigg/ \frac{\sum_{l=1}^{N} z_l w_l}{\sum_{l=1}^{N} w_l} \tag{9-11}$$

where T and $\star$ both indicate the t-norm used (product or minimum). Observe that *GC* is a type-1 fuzzy set.

In this case, we let $\theta = [z_1,...,z_N,w_1,...,w_N]^T$ and re-express $a(\theta)$ and $b(\theta)$ in (9-4) and (9-5) as

$$a(\theta) = \frac{\sum_{l=1}^{N} z_l w_l}{\sum_{l=1}^{N} w_l} \tag{9-12}$$

and

$$b(\theta) = T_{l=1}^{N} \mu_{Z_l}(z_l) \star T_{l=1}^{N} \mu_{W_l}(w_l) \tag{9-13}$$

A practical sequence of computations to obtain GC is as follows:

1. Discretize the domain of each type-1 fuzzy set Z_l into a suitable number of points, say N_l ($l = 1, \ldots, N$).

2. Discretize the domain of each type-1 fuzzy set W_l into a suitable number of points, say M_l ($l = 1, \ldots, N$).

3. Enumerate all the possible combinations $\theta = [z_1, \ldots, z_N, w_1, \ldots, w_N]^T$ such that $z_l \in Z_l$ and $w_l \in W_l$. The total number of combinations will be $\prod_{j=1}^{N} M_j N_j$.

4. Compute the generalized centroid using (9-11); i.e., compute the α tuples (a_i, b_i), $i = 1, 2, \ldots, \prod_{j=1}^{N} M_j N_j$, where a_i and b_i are given in (9-12) and (9-13), respectively. In this case, $\alpha = \prod_{j=1}^{N} M_j N_j$.

Clearly, the centroid and generalized centroid have high computational complexity. Fortunately, however, a type-2 fuzzy set can be thought of as a collection of a large number of embedded type-2 fuzzy sets. As described at the beginning of this section, the centroid $C_{\tilde{A}}$ is a collection of the centroids of all these embedded type-2 fuzzy sets. The centroid or generalized centroid operations for each type-2 set can be processed in parallel. The number of parallel processors equals the number of (a_i, b_i) tuples, α.

Example 9-1: For the type-2 *centroid*, if the x-domain is sampled to N points and the domain of each secondary membership function $\mu_{\tilde{A}}(x_j)$ ($j = 1, \ldots, N$) is sampled to M_j points, then there are $N - 1$ t-norm (minimum) operations, N multiplications, $2(N - 1)$ additions and 1 division, and $\prod_{j=1}^{N} M_j$ parallel processors are required. A similar analysis applies to the generalized centroid. ∎

Example 9-2: [Karnik and Mendel (1998a)] Here we illustrate the centroid computational procedure for a relatively simple type-2 fuzzy set, the one depicted in Figure 9-2 (a). As simple as this type-2 set is, there are $2^{21} = 2,097,152$ embedded type-2 sets for which the centroid computational procedure must be performed. The results of doing this are depicted in Figure 9-2 (b). Observe that, although the domain of the centroid is a finite interval, the centroid is not an interval set (because its amplitude is different from unity over its entire domain), and that the point having unity membership value in the centroid set is at $y = 2.4729$, which corresponds to the centroid of the principal membership function of the type-2 fuzzy set in (a), where the latter corresponds to the upper curve in Figure 9-2 (a). ∎

Presently, parallel processing is not available for most researchers, so the computational complexity of centroid and generalized centroid computations is high. When the secondaries are interval sets, then *exact* results for the centroid or generalized centroid can be determined using a totally different computational procedure, as we explain in the next section. The computational complexity in this case is so low that the centroid and generalized centroid calculations become very practical.

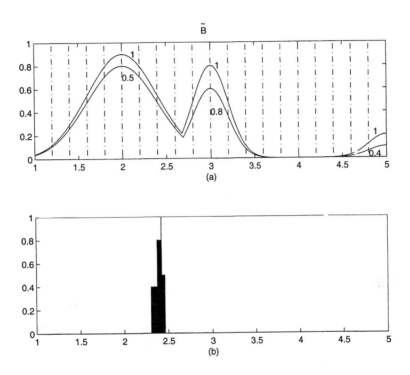

Figure 9-2: (a) A type-2 fuzzy set whose secondary membership functions only have two values, one each for the upper and lower curves. The secondary grades appear as numbers next to the upper and lower curves. The domain of y is discretized into 21 equally spaced values; (b) the centroid of the type-2 fuzzy set in (a). In (a) the vertical axis shows primary memberships of y in type-2 fuzzy set $\tilde{B}$, and in (b) the vertical axis shows memberships of y in the centroid set.

9.3 GENERALIZED CENTROID FOR INTERVAL TYPE-2 FUZZY SETS

Consider the generalized centroid in (9-11). If each Z_l and W_l ($l = 1, ..., N$) is an interval type-1 set, then using the fact that $\mu_{Z_l}(z_l) = \mu_{W_l}(w_l) = 1$, (9-11) can be rewritten as

$$GC = \int_{z_1 \in Z_1} \cdots \int_{z_N \in Z_N} \int_{w_1 \in W_1} \cdots \int_{w_N \in W_N} 1 \Bigg/ \frac{\sum_{l=1}^{N} z_l w_l}{\sum_{l=1}^{N} w_l} = [y_l, y_r] \qquad (9\text{-}14)$$

In this section we present an iterative procedure [Karnik and Mendel (1998b)][2] to compute the generalized centroid GC when each Z_l in (9-14) is an interval type-1 set having center c_l and spread s_l ($s_l \geq 0$), and when each W_l is also an interval type-1 set with center h_l and spread Δ_l ($\Delta_l \geq 0$). Note that, because $W_l \subseteq [0,1]$ [as stated three lines above (9-11)], we assume that $h_l \geq \Delta_l$ so that $w_l \geq 0$ for $l = 1, ..., M$.

Comment: Readers who are familiar with interval arithmetic may be wondering why we cannot get a closed-form expression for $[y_l, y_r]$ in (9-14). For example, in Klir and Folger (1988) the following formula is given for the division of two interval sets:

$$[a,b]/[d,e] = [a,b] \times [1/e, 1/d]$$
$$= [\min(a/d, a/e, b/d, b/e), \max(a/d, a/e, b/d, b/e)]$$

so, it would seem that we could apply this result to determine $[y_l, y_r]$. Unfortunately, we cannot do this, because the derivation of this result assumes that a, b, d, and e are *independent*. Due to the appearance of the w_l in both the numerator and denominator of $\sum_{l=1}^{N} z_l w_l \big/ \sum_{l=1}^{N} w_l$, we do not have the required independence; hence, we cannot use this interesting closed-form result. ∎

---

[2] Our procedure is a special case of computing a fractionally linear function [Kreinovich et al. (1998)]; however, it was developed independently of their work and at about the same time as it.

$$\frac{\partial}{\partial w_k} y(w_1,...,w_N) \underset{\leq}{\overset{\geq}{}} 0 \quad \text{if} \quad z_k \underset{\leq}{\overset{\geq}{}} y(w_1,...,w_N) \tag{9-18}$$

Unfortunately, equating $\partial y/\partial w_k$ to zero does not give us any information about the value of w_k that optimizes $y(w_1,...,w_N)$. When we do this we find:

$$y(w_1,...,w_N) = z_k \Rightarrow \frac{\sum_{l=1}^{N} z_l w_l}{\sum_{l=1}^{N} w_l} = z_k \Rightarrow \frac{\sum_{l\neq k}^{N} z_l w_l}{\sum_{l\neq k}^{N} w_l} = z_k \tag{9-19}$$

Observe that w_k no longer appears in the final expression in (9-19), so the direct calculus approach does not work.

Equation (9-18) does give us the direction in which w_k should be changed in order to increase or decrease $y(w_1,...,w_N)$, i.e.,

$$\left.\begin{array}{ll} \text{If } z_k > y(w_1,...,w_N) & y(w_1,...,w_N) \text{ increases as } w_k \text{ increases} \\ \text{If } z_k < y(w_1,...,w_N) & y(w_1,...,w_N) \text{ increases as } w_k \text{ decreases} \end{array}\right\} \tag{9-20}$$

Recall that the maximum value that w_k can attain is $h_k + \Delta_k$ and the minimum value that it can attain is $h_k - \Delta_k$. Equation (9-20) therefore implies that $y(w_1,...,w_N)$ attains its *maximum value* if:

1. $w_k = h_k + \Delta_k$ for those values of k for which $z_k > y(w_1,...,w_N)$.
2. $w_k = h_k - \Delta_k$ for those values of k for which $z_k < y(w_1,...,w_N)$.

Similarly, we can deduce from (9-10) that $y(w_1,...,w_N)$ attains its *minimum value* if:

1. $w_k = h_k + \Delta_k$ for those values of k for which $z_k < y(w_1,...,w_N)$.
2. $w_k = h_k - \Delta_k$ for those values of k for which $z_k > y(w_1,...,w_N)$.

Theorem 9-1: [Karnik and Mendel (1998a)] *(a) The maximum of $y(w_1,...,w_N)$ can be obtained by the following iterative procedure. Set $z_l = c_l + s_l$ ($l = 1, ..., N$), and without loss of generality assume that the z_l are arranged in ascending order; i.e., $z_1 \leq z_2 \leq \cdots \leq z_N$. Then:*

Returning to (9-14), we make the following observations:

1. Since $Z_1, ..., Z_N, W_1, ..., W_N$ are interval type-1 sets, GC will also be an in type-1 set; i.e., it will be a crisp set, $[y_l, y_r]$. So, to find GC we ne compute just the two end-points of this interval, y_l and y_r.

2. Let $y \equiv \sum_{l=1}^{N} z_l w_l / \sum_{l=1}^{N} w_l$. Since $w_l \geq 0$ for all l, the partial deriv $\partial y / \partial z_k = w_k / \sum_l w_l \geq 0$. Therefore, y always increases with increasing and for any combination of $w_1, ..., w_N$ chosen so that $w_l \in W_l$, y is n mized when $z_l = c_l + s_l$ for $l = 1, ..., N$, and y is minimized $z_l = c_l - s_l$ for $l = 1, ..., N$. y_r is therefore obtained by maximi $\sum_l (c_l + s_l) w_l / \sum_l w_l$ subject to the constraints $w_l \in W_l$ for $l = 1, ..., N$ addition, y_l is obtained by minimizing $\sum_l (c_l - s_l) w_l / \sum_l w_l$ again sub to the constraints $w_l \in W_l$ for $l = 1, ..., N$.

From these two observations, it is clear that to compute GC, we on to consider the problems of maximizing and minimizing y treated as a of $w_1, ..., w_N$; i.e., optimizing

$$y(w_1, ..., w_N) = \frac{\sum_{l=1}^{N} z_l w_l}{\sum_{l=1}^{N} w_l}$$

subject to the constraints

$$w_l \in [h_l - \Delta_l, h_l + \Delta_l] \quad \text{where } l = 1, ..., N$$

and $h_l \geq \Delta_l$. As explained in Observation 2, we set $z_l = c_l + s_l$ ($l = 1, ..., N$) maximizing $y(w_1, ..., w_N)$, and $z_l = c_l - s_l$ ($l = 1, ..., N$) when minim $y(w_1, ..., w_N)$.

Suppose we take the usual calculus approach to optimizing $y(w_1, ...$ Differentiating $y(w_1, ..., w_N)$ with respect to w_k gives us

$$\frac{\partial}{\partial w_k} y(w_1, ..., w_N) = \frac{\partial}{\partial w_k} \left[\frac{\sum_{l=1}^{N} z_l w_l}{\sum_{l=1}^{N} w_l} \right] = \frac{z_k - y(w_1, ..., w_N)}{\sum_{l=1}^{N} w_l} \qquad (9$$

Because $\sum_{l=1}^{N} w_l > 0$, it is easy to see from (9-17) that

1. *Initialize* w_l *by setting* $w_l = h_l$ *for* $l = 1, ..., N,$ *and then compute* $y' = y(h_1,...,h_N)$ *using (9-15).*

2. *Find* k $(1 \le k \le N-1)$ *such that* $z_k \le y' \le z_{k+1}.$

3. *Set* $w_l = h_l - \Delta_l$ *for* $l \le k$ *and* $w_l = h_l + \Delta_l$ *for* $l \ge k + 1,$ *and compute* $y'' = y(h_1 - \Delta_1,...,h_k - \Delta_k, h_{k+1} + \Delta_{k+1},...,h_N + \Delta_N)$ *using (9-15). [The procedure for choosing the* w_l, *which is based on (9-20), guarantees that* $y'' \ge y'$.*]*

4. *Check if* $y'' = y'$. *If yes, stop.* y'' *is the maximum value of* $y(w_1,...,w_N)$. *If no, go to Step 5.*

5. *Set* y' *equal to* y''. *Go to Step 2.*

(b) The minimum of $y(w_1,...,w_N)$ *can be obtained using a procedure similar to the one in (a). Only two changes need to be made:*

1. *Set* $z_l = c_l - s_l$ *for* $= 1, ..., N.$

2. *In step 3, set* $w_l = h_l + \Delta_l$ *for* $l \le k$ *and* $w_l = h_l - \Delta_l$ *for* $l \ge k + 1,$ *and compute* $y'' = y(h_1 + \Delta_1,...,h_k + \Delta_k, h_{k+1} - \Delta_{k+1},...,h_N - \Delta_N)$ *using (9-15).*

(c) This iterative procedure converges in at most N iterations, where one iteration consists of one pass through Steps 2 to 5 (Step 1 is an initialization).

Proof: Parts (a) and (b) follow directly from the extensive discussions prior to the statement of this theorem.

(c) At any iteration let k' be such that $z_{k'} \le y'' \le z_{k'+1}$. Because $y'' \ge y'$, $k' \ge k$. If k' is the same as k, the algorithm converges at the end of the next iteration. This can be explained as follows: $k' = k$ implies both y' and y'' are in $[z_k, z_{k+1}]$. Note it is still possible that $y'' \ne y'$. If this happens, however, observe from step 3 that $y'' = y(h_1 - \Delta_1,...,h_k - \Delta_k, h_{k+1} + \Delta_{k+1}, ...,h_N + \Delta_N)$, and, because of step 5, for the next iteration $y' = y(h_1 - \Delta_1,...,h_k - \Delta_k, h_{k+1} + \Delta_{k+1}, ...,h_N + \Delta_N)$. The index k chosen for the next iteration will, therefore, be the same as the index k chosen for the current iteration $(k' = k)$; consequently, at the end of the next iteration we will have $y'' = y(h_1 - \Delta_1,...,h_k - \Delta_k, h_{k+1} + \Delta_{k+1},...,h_N + \Delta_N) = y'$, and the algorithm will converge. Because k can have at most $N - 1$ values, the algorithm converges in at most $(N - 1) + 1 = N$ iterations. ∎

Note that during the iterative procedure the z_l values are re-ordered in ascending order and the resulting w_l values are associated with the re-ordered z_l

values. At the end of the calculations for y_l and y_r the w_l values must be mapped back into their original order. This is easy to do, because the mapping from the unordered z_l values to the re-ordered z_l values is one-to-one and is invertible.

Not only does this algorithm reduce the computations by an enormous amount—from $\prod_{j=1}^{N} M_j N_j$ calculations to at most $2N$ calculations—but, these $2N$ calculations can be done in parallel by just two processors, one each for the left and right end-points. These calculations are totally independent of one another.

Example 9-3: In this example we compute the generalized centroid for the interval sets that are depicted in Figure 9-3 (a) and (b). Figure 9-3 (a) depicts the interval sets $Z_1, Z_2, ..., Z_{N=9}$ and Figure 9-3 (b) depicts the interval sets $W_1, W_2, ..., W_{N=9}$ that are used in (9-14). We associate N with the number of *rules* in a FLS, which is why the horizontal axes in these plots are labeled "Rule Number."

According to Theorem 9-1, when we compute y_l we must use all the left-hand (lower) values of $Z_1, Z_2, ..., Z_{N=9}$, whereas when we compute y_r we must use all the right-hand (upper) values of $Z_1, Z_2, ..., Z_{N=9}$. The iterative procedure in Theorem 9-1 establishes whether it is the upper or lower value of W_i ($i = 1, ..., 9$) that contributes to the calculation of y_l or y_r. Figure 9-3 (c) and (d) depicts the values of $w \in W_1, W_2, ..., W_{N=9}$, as determined by that procedure, which contribute to either y_l or y_r. Observe that it is possible for the same value of w to be used in the calculations of both y_l and y_r. For this example, using the Theorem 9-1 procedure, we computed $[y_l, y_r] = [3.0194, 7.1702]$. ■

9.4 CENTROID OF AN INTERVAL TYPE-2 FUZZY SET

For an interval type-2 fuzzy set, (9-2) reduces to

$$C_{\tilde{A}} = \int_{\theta_1 \in J_{x_1}} \cdots \int_{\theta_N \in J_{x_N}} 1 \bigg/ \frac{\sum_{i=1}^{N} x_i \theta_i}{\sum_{i=1}^{N} \theta_i} = [c_l, c_r] \qquad (9-21)$$

Let $J_{x_i} \equiv [L_i, R_i]$. To use the computational procedure described in Theorem 9-1, note that: x_i plays the role of c_i; $s_i = 0$ for all i since the x_i are crisp; $(L_i + R_i)/2 = h_i$; and $(R_i - L_i)/2 = \Delta_i$. So computing the centroid of an interval type-2 fuzzy set is just a special case of computing the generalized centroid of interval sets using Theorem 9-1.

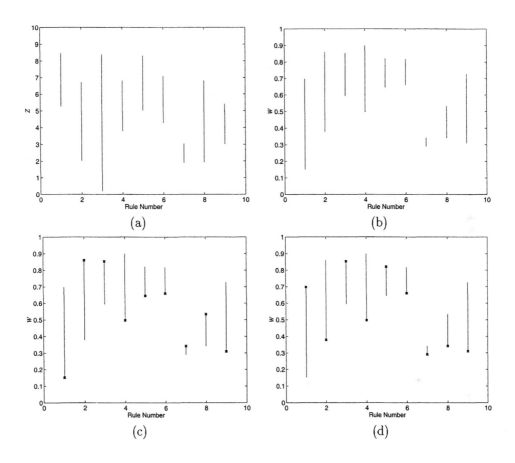

(a)   (b)

(c)   (d)

Figure 9-3: An example that shows generalized centroid results for interval secondary membership functions. (a) and (b) depict the values of $Z_1, Z_2, ..., Z_{N=9}$ and $W_1, W_2, ..., W_{N=9}$, respectively, whereas (c) depicts the values (denoted by the small *ex*) of $w \in W_1, W_2, ..., W_{N=9}$ that contribute to the calculation of y_l, and (d) depicts the values (denoted by the small *ex*) of $w \in W_1, W_2, ..., W_{N=9}$ that contribute to the calculation of y_r.

Example 9-4: In this example, we compute the centroid for the Gaussian primary membership function with uncertain mean $m \in [m_1, m_2]$, whose secondary membership functions are interval sets (see Figure 3-8). Table 9-1 summarizes the results for a range of $m_2 - m_1$ values, including the type-1 case when $m_2 - m_1 = 0$. Karnik and Mendel (1998b) have proven that if $m_2 - m_1$ is small compared to the standard deviation (σ) of each Gaussian, then $[c_l, c_r] \approx [m_2, m_1]$. In this example, $\sigma = 1$ and the results in Table 9-1 support this theoretical result. ■

Table 9-1: Centroid results for a Gaussian primary membership function with uncertain mean, whose secondary membership functions are interval sets.

$[m_1, m_2]$	$m_2 - m_1$	$[c_l, c_r]$	$c_r - c_l$
[5, 5]	0	[5, 5]	0
[4.875, 5.125]	0.25	[4.8750, 5.1250]	0.25
[4.75, 5.25]	0.5	[4.7495, 5.2505]	0.5010
[4.625, 5.375]	0.75	[4.6226, 5.3774]	0.7548
[4.5, 5.5]	1	[4.4928, 5.5072]	1.0144
[4.25, 5.75]	1.5	[4.2168, 5.7832]	1.5664
[4, 6]	2	[3.9070, 6.0930]	2.1860
[3.75, 6.25]	2.5	[3.5519, 6.4481]	2.8962
[3.5, 6.5]	3	[3.1505, 6.8495]	3.6990

Example 9-5: In this example, we compute the centroid for the Gaussian primary membership function with uncertain standard deviation $\sigma \in [\sigma_1, \sigma_2]$, whose secondary membership fiunctions are interval sets (see Figure 3-9). Table 9-2 summarizes the results for a range of $\sigma_2 - \sigma_1$ values, including the type-1 case when $\sigma_2 - \sigma_1 = 0$. In this example, $m = 5$. Observe that $[c_l, c_r]$ is not close to $[\sigma_2, \sigma_1]$, even for small values of $\sigma_2 - \sigma_1$. ■

Table 9-2: Centroid results for a Gaussian primary membership function with uncertain standard deviation, whose secondary membership functions are interval sets.

$[\sigma_1, \sigma_2]$	$\sigma_2 - \sigma_1$	$[c_l, c_r]$	$c_r - c_l$
[1, 1]	0	[5, 5]	0
[0.875, 1.125]	0.25	[4.8005, 5.1995]	0.3990
[0.75, 1.25]	0.5	[4.6008, 5.3992]	0.7984
[0.625, 1.375]	0.75	[4.3985, 5.6015]	1.2030
[0.5, 1.5]	1	[4.1849, 5.8151]	1.6302
[0.375, 1.625]	1.25	[3.9344, 6.0656]	2.1312
[0.25, 1.75]	1.5	[3.5939, 6.4061]	2.8122

Example 9-6: Suppose our domain of interest is the interval [0, 10] and that we associate three terms with that interval whose type-1 membership functions are depicted in Figure 9-4 (a). Note that the centroids of the three type-1 membership functions (F, G, and H) are $c_F = 1.3213$, $c_G = 5$, and $c_H = 8.6787$. Because of uncertainties about where to center these Gaussian membership functions, we obtain the FOUs that are depicted in Figure 9-4 (b). The centroids of these interval type-2 fuzzy sets are depicted in Figure 9-4 (c). Each centroid was calculated separately for each of the three fuzzy sets using the results in Theorem 9-1. $C_{\tilde{F}}$, for example, is the interval set $C_{\tilde{F}} = [1.2058, 1.7617]$. Note that the midpoint of this centroid is 1.4838, which differs from c_F. This demonstrates that *uncertainty leads to results that are different than results obtained when uncertainty is ignored*. This observation is important when we study defuzzification for a type-2 FLS in Section 10.6. ∎

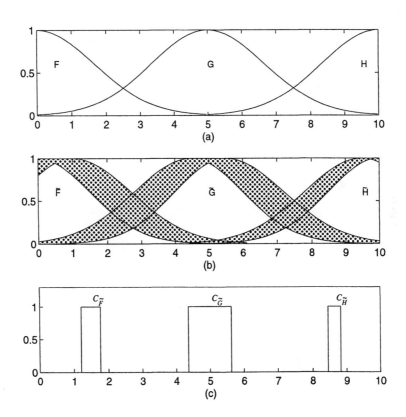

Figure 9-4: (a) Type-1 membership functions, (b) FOUs for their type-2 counterparts, and (c) centroids of the type-2 membership functions.

Example 9-7: Figure 9-5 depicts a FOU for an interval type-2 fuzzy set, and four of its embedded type-1 fuzzy sets. The center of gravity for each of these embedded type-1 sets is: $c_{(a)} = 4.6504$, $c_{(b)} = 4.6860$, $c_{(c)} = 3.9851$, and $c_{(d)} = 5.3695$. By using Theorem 9-1, we established that $c_l = c_{(c)}$ and $c_r = c_{(d)}$; hence, this example should dispel any mistaken belief that the end-points of the centroid of a type-2 fuzzy set are associated with the centroids of its lower- and upper-membership functions, $c_{(a)}$ and $c_{(b)}$. They are associated with embedded type-1 sets that involve segments from both the lower- and upper-membership functions. ■

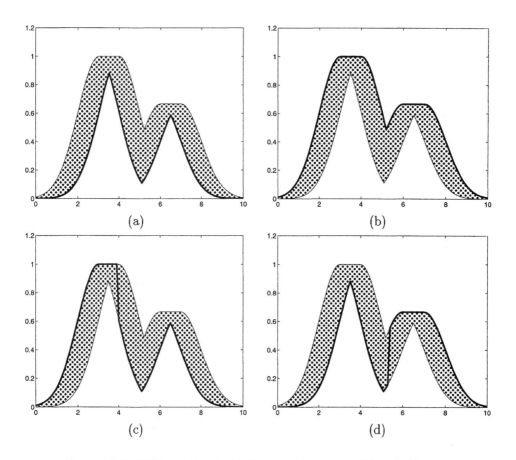

(a)   (b)   (c)   (d)

Figure 9-5: FOU and 4 embedded type-1 fuzzy sets. (a) and (b) correspond to the lower and upper membership functions, respectively; (c) and (d) (which are a result of using the method in Theorem 9-1) are associated with c_l and c_r, respectively.

9.5 TYPE-REDUCTION: GENERAL RESULTS

In a type-1 FLS the output corresponding to each fired rule is a type-1 fuzzy set in the output space (Section 5.2). An example of a type-1 rule is:

$$R^l: \text{IF } x_1 \text{ is } F_1^l \text{ and } x_2 \text{ is } F_2^l \text{ and } \cdots \text{ and } x_p \text{ is } F_p^l, \text{ THEN } y \text{ is } G^l \qquad (9\text{-}22)$$

The defuzzifier combines the output sets corresponding to all the fired rules in some way to obtain a single output set and then finds a crisp number that is representative of this combined output set; e.g., the centroid defuzzifier finds the union of all the output sets and uses the centroid of the union as the crisp output. In all of the defuzzifiers of interest to us in this book, the crisp number is obtained as the centroid of some combined output set.

The output set corresponding to each rule of a type-2 FLS is a type-2 fuzzy set (see Section 10.2). An example of a type-2 rule is:

$$R^l: \text{IF } x_1 \text{ is } \tilde{F}_1^l \text{ and } x_2 \text{ is } \tilde{F}_2^l \text{ and } \cdots \text{ and } x_p \text{ is } \tilde{F}_p^l, \text{ THEN } y \text{ is } \tilde{G}^l \qquad (9\text{-}23)$$

A type-reducer combines all these output sets in some way (just like a type-1 defuzzifier combines the type-1 rule output sets) and then performs a centroid calculation on this type-2 fuzzy set, which leads to a type-1 fuzzy set that we call the *type-reduced set*.

In this section we focus on the type-1 defuzzification methods that were described in Section 5.5 and their associated type-reduction methods. We rely very heavily on the earlier sections of this chapter, since type-reduction is equivalent to computing the centroid of a type-2 fuzzy set. In those earlier sections we showed how to compute the centroid and generalized centroid for an *arbitrary* type-2 fuzzy set. Type-reduction computes the centroid or generalized centroid for very *specific* type-2 fuzzy sets.

The Extension Principle in (7-9) is used to extend each type-1 defuzzification method to the formula for the corresponding type-reduced set. In this way, when all uncertainties disappear, the type-reduced set reduces to a defuzzification formula. This is consistent with our fundamental design requirement (stated in Section 1.4) that when all uncertainties in a type-2 FLS disappear it must reduce to a type-1 FLS.

9.5.1 Centroid type-reduction [Karnik and Mendel (1998b)]

The centroid defuzzifier (Section 5.5.1) combines the output type-1 fuzzy sets using union (e.g., maximum) and then finds the centroid of this set. If we denote the composite output fuzzy set as B, where

$$B = \bigcup_{l=1}^{M} B^l \qquad (9\text{-}24)$$

with associated membership function $\mu_B(y)$, and $\mu_{B^l}(y)$ is the membership function of the output set for the lth rule, then the centroid defuzzifier is given as:

$$y_c(\mathbf{x}) = \frac{\sum_{i=1}^{N} y_i \mu_B(y_i)}{\sum_{i=1}^{N} \mu_B(y_i)} \qquad (9\text{-}25)$$

where the output set B has been discretized into N points. The exact nature of $\mu_{B^l}(y)$ depends on many factors, and formulas for it are given in Sections 5.3 and 6.2. Recall that we show $y_c(\mathbf{x})$ as an explicit function of $\mathbf{x}$ because $\mu_B(y_i)$ is a function of FLS input $\mathbf{x}$. For different FLS inputs we obtain different values of $y_c(\mathbf{x})$.

In a similar manner, the centroid type-reducer combines all the rule-output type-2 fuzzy sets, $\tilde{B}^l$, by finding their union. In Section 7.3.1 we showed that the union of type-2 fuzzy sets requires computing the join of their secondary membership functions; hence, $\bigcup_{l=1}^{M} \tilde{B}^l \equiv \tilde{B}$ has a secondary membership function $\mu_{\tilde{B}}(y)$ given by

$$\mu_{\tilde{B}}(y) = \sqcup_{l=1}^{M} \mu_{\tilde{B}^l}(y) \quad \forall y \in Y \qquad (9\text{-}26)$$

where $\mu_{\tilde{B}^l}(y)$ is the secondary membership function for the lth rule, and the exact nature of $\mu_{\tilde{B}^l}(y)$ also depends on many factors. Explicit formulas for $\mu_{\tilde{B}^l}(y)$ are given in Chapters 10–12.

The centroid type-reducer calculates the centroid of $\tilde{B}$. The expression for the centroid type-reduced set, $Y_c(\mathbf{x})$, is an extended version of (9-25), and following the notation in (9-3), can be expressed as

$$Y_c(\mathbf{x}) = \int_{\theta_1 \in J_{y_1}} \cdots \int_{\theta_N \in J_{y_N}} \left[f_{y_1}(\theta_1) \star \cdots \star f_{y_N}(\theta_N) \right] \bigg/ \frac{\sum_{i=1}^{N} y_i \theta_i}{\sum_{i=1}^{N} \theta_i} \qquad (9\text{-}27)$$

where $i = 1, \ldots, N$. In this equation θ_i, J_{y_i} and f_{y_i} ($\forall i$) are associated with $\mu_{\tilde{B}}(y)$ and we show $Y_c(\mathbf{x})$ as an explicit function of $\mathbf{x}$ because each $\mu_{\tilde{B}^l}(y)$ in (9-26) is a function of FLS input $\mathbf{x}$. For different FLS inputs, we obtain different values of

$Y_c(\mathbf{x})$.

A practical sequence of computations to obtain $Y_c(\mathbf{x})$ is based on the five-step procedure described in Section 9.2, and is:

1. Compute $\mu_{\tilde{B}}(y)$ using (9-26). This is possible because we will have already computed $\mu_{\tilde{B}^l}(y)$ ($l = 1, ..., M$) for all $y \in Y$. For general type-2 fuzzy sets, Theorem A-1 can be used to do this step. For interval type-2 fuzzy sets, we use formulas given in Chapters 10, 11, or 12.

2. Discretize the y-domain into N points $y_1, ..., y_N$.

3. Discretize each J_{y_i} into a suitable number of points, say M_i ($i = 1, ..., N$).

4. Enumerate all the embedded type-1 sets of $\tilde{B}$; there will be $\prod_{i=1}^{N} M_i$ of them.

5. Compute the centroid type-reduced set using (9-27); i.e., compute the centroid of each enumerated embedded type-1 set and assign it a membership grade equal to the t-norm of the secondary grades corresponding to that enumerated embedded type-1 set. We must use the minimum t-norm here, as explained earlier in Section 9.2.

The centroid and membership computations have to be repeated $\prod_{i=1}^{N} M_i$ times and so, in general, will involve an enormous amount of computation. We will have more to say about computational complexity of all type-reducers in Section 9.5.6.

9.5.2 Center-of-sums type-reduction [Karnik and Mendel (1998b)]

The center-of-sums defuzzifier (Section 5.5.2) combines the output type-1 fuzzy sets by adding them, i.e.,

$$\mu_B(y) = \sum_{l=1}^{M} \mu_{B^l}(y) \quad \forall y \in Y \tag{9-28}$$

and then finds the centroid of this set. The center-of-sums defuzzifier can be expressed as

$$y_a(\mathbf{x}) = \frac{\sum_{l=1}^{M} c_{B^l} a_{B^l}}{\sum_{l=1}^{M} a_{B^l}} \tag{9-29}$$

where c_{B^l} denotes the centroid of the lth output set and a_{B^l} denotes the area of that set. The subscript a on y indicates the "additive" combining.

The center-of-sums type-reducer combines the type-2 rule output sets by adding their secondary membership functions and then finds the centroid of the resulting type-2 set; i.e., the center-of-sums type-reduced set $Y_a(\mathbf{x})$. Although (9-29) can be expressed in terms of the centroid and area of the lth consequent fuzzy set [see (5-15)] which simplifies the computation of (9-29), Karnik and Mendel (1998b) have shown that the same is *not* true for the center-of-sums type-reducer. The most straightforward way of computing $Y_a(\mathbf{x})$, therefore, is by finding the centroid of the sum of the output secondary membership functions, just as the centroid type-reducer finds the centroid of the union of the output sets. Equation (9-27) can be used for this purpose, where

$$\mu_{\tilde{B}}(y) = \sum_{l=1}^{M} \mu_{\tilde{B}^l}(y) \quad \forall y \in Y \tag{9-30}$$

and θ_i, J_{y_i}, and f_{y_i} ($\forall i$) are now associated with $\mu_{\tilde{B}}(y)$. At each value of $y \in Y$, (7-28) is used to compute the right-hand side of (9-30). The sequence of computations needed to obtain $Y_a(\mathbf{x})$ is exactly the same as we just described for $Y_c(\mathbf{x})$, except that in Step 1 we compute $\mu_{\tilde{B}}(y)$ for the combined output set in (9-30).

9.5.3 Height type-reduction [Karnik and Mendel (1998b)]

The height defuzzifier (Section 5.5.3) replaces each rule output set by a singleton at the point having maximum membership in that output set, and then calculates the centroid of the type-1 set comprised of these singletons. The output of a height defuzzifier is given as

$$y_h(\mathbf{x}) = \frac{\sum_{l=1}^{M} \bar{y}^l \mu_{B^l}(\bar{y}^l)}{\sum_{l=1}^{M} \mu_{B^l}(\bar{y}^l)} \tag{9-31}$$

where: $\bar{y}^l$ is the point having maximum membership in the lth output set (if there is more than one such point, their average can be taken as $\bar{y}^l$) and its membership grade in the lth output set is $\mu_{B^l}(\bar{y}^l)$, given in (5-18).

The height type-reducer replaces each type-2 output set by a type-2 fuzzy set whose y-domain consists of a single point ($\bar{y}$), the secondary membership function of which is a type-1 fuzzy set. The lth output set is replaced by a singleton situated at $\bar{y}^l$, where $\bar{y}^l$ can be chosen to be the point having the highest primary membership in the principal membership function[3] of the output set $\tilde{B}^l$ (e.g., in Figure 3-4, we would set $\bar{y} = 3$). How to calculate the secondary membership function of $\bar{y}^l$ in the type-2 case will be described in Chapters 10–12; it is denoted $\mu_{\tilde{B}^l}(\bar{y}^l)$.

The expression for the height type-reduced set is obtained as an extension of (9-31), as

$$Y_h(\mathbf{x}) = \int_{\theta_1 \in J_{\bar{y}^1}} \cdots \int_{\theta_M \in J_{\bar{y}^M}} \left[f_{\bar{y}^1}(\theta_1) \star \cdots \star f_{\bar{y}^M}(\theta_M) \right] \bigg/ \frac{\sum_{l=1}^{M} \bar{y}^l \theta_l}{\sum_{l=1}^{M} \theta_l} \tag{9-32}$$

In this equation, θ_l, $J_{\bar{y}^l}$, and $f_{\bar{y}^l}$ ($\forall l$) are associated with $\mu_{\tilde{B}^l}(\bar{y}^l)$.

A practical sequence of computations to obtain $Y_h(\mathbf{x})$ is as follows:

1. Choose $\bar{y}^l$ for each rule output set $\tilde{B}^l$ ($l = 1, \ldots, M$).

2. Discretize the primary membership of each $\mu_{\tilde{B}^l}(\bar{y}^l)$, $J_{\bar{y}^l}$, into a suitable number of points, say M_l ($l = 1, \ldots, M$). The discretization is carried out in a manner similar to that for centroid or center-of-sums type reduction, the only difference is that the number of points on the horizontal axis is now M (the number of rules) instead of N.

3. Enumerate all the possible combinations $\{\theta_1, \ldots, \theta_M\}$ such that $\theta_l \in J_{\bar{y}^l}$; there will be $\prod_{l=1}^{M} M_l$ combinations.

4. Compute the height type-reduced set using (9-32). Since the domain of the combined output set is discrete, we can use product or minimum t-norm in (9-32).

In Step 4, the weighted sum and membership computations in (9-32) have to be repeated $\prod_{l=1}^{M} M_l$ times. Generally, $\prod_{l=1}^{M} M_l \ll \prod_{l=1}^{N} M_l$ (where N is the number of discrete y-points in case of centroid or center-of-sums type-reduction). So, computing the height type-reduced set generally involves much fewer computations than computing the centroid or center-of-sums type-reduced set.

---

[3]If $\tilde{B}^l$ is such that a principal membership function cannot be defined (e.g., see Figure 3-8), one may choose $\bar{y}^l$ as the point having the highest primary membership with a secondary grade equal to 1, or as a point satisfying some similar criterion (e.g., in Figure 3-8, choose $\bar{y}^l = 5$, the midpoint of the interval of uncertainty of the mean).

9.5.4 Modified height type-reduction [Karnik and Mendel (1998b)]

The modified height defuzzifier (Section 5.5.4) is very similar to the height defuzzifier, the only difference being that in the modified height defuzzifier each $\mu_{B^l}(\bar{y}^l)$ is scaled by the inverse of the spread (or some measure of the spread) of the lth consequent set. Its output can be expressed as

$$y_{mh}(\mathbf{x}) = \frac{\sum_{l=1}^{M} \bar{y}^l \mu_{B^l}(\bar{y}^l) / \delta^{l2}}{\sum_{l=1}^{M} \mu_{B^l}(\bar{y}^l) / \delta^{l2}} \tag{9-33}$$

where δ^l is some measure of the spread of the lth consequent set, and $\bar{y}^l$ and $\mu_{B^l}(\bar{y}^l)$ have the same meaning as in (9-31).

    The only difference between the modified height type-reducer and the height type-reducer is that each output set secondary membership function, $\mu_{\bar{B}^l}(\bar{y}^l)$, in the modified height type-reducer is scaled by $1/\delta^{l2}$ (δ^l can, e.g., be taken as the spread of the principal membership function of the lth consequent set). The expression for the modified height type-reduced set is given as

$$Y_{mh}(\mathbf{x}) = \int_{\theta_1 \in J_{\bar{y}^1}} \cdots \int_{\theta_M \in J_{\bar{y}^M}} \left[f_{\bar{y}^1}(\theta_1) \star \cdots \star f_{\bar{y}^M}(\theta_M) \right] \Bigg/ \frac{\sum_{l=1}^{M} \bar{y}^l \theta_l / \delta^{l2}}{\sum_{l=1}^{M} \theta_l / \delta^{l2}} \tag{9-34}$$

where all symbols have the same meaning as in (9-32).

9.5.5 Center-of-sets type-reduction [Karnik and Mendel (1998b)]

In center-of-sets defuzzification (Section 5.5.5) we replace each rule consequent set by a singleton situated at its *centroid* and then find the centroid of the type-1 set comprised of these singletons. The expression for the output is given as

$$y_{cos}(\mathbf{x}) = \frac{\sum_{l=1}^{M} c^l T_{i=1}^p \mu_{F_i^l}(x_i)}{\sum_{l=1}^{M} T_{i=1}^p \mu_{F_i^l}(x_i)} \tag{9-35}$$

where T indicates the chosen t-norm, and c^l is the centroid of the lth consequent set.

The center-of-sets type-reducer replaces each type-2 consequent set, $\tilde{G}^l$, by its centroid, $C_{\tilde{G}^l}$, (which itself is a type-1 set) and, as in (9-35), finds a weighted average of these centroids. The weight associated with the lth centroid is the degree of firing corresponding to the lth rule (this will be discussed in Chapters 10–12), namely $\prod_{i=1}^{p}\mu_{\tilde{F}_i^l}(x_i) \equiv E_l$. Note that E_l is also a type-1 set. The expression for the center-of sets type-reduced set is now that of a generalized centroid, as in (9-11), and is given by the following extension of (9-35):

$$Y_{\cos}(\mathbf{x}) = \int_{d_1 \in C_{\tilde{G}^1}} \cdots \int_{d_M \in C_{\tilde{G}^M}} \int_{e_1 \in E_1} \cdots \int_{e_M \in E_M} T_{l=1}^{M}\mu_{C_{\tilde{G}^l}}(d_l) \star T_{l=1}^{M}\mu_{E_l}(e_l) \Bigg/ \frac{\sum_{l=1}^{M} d_l e_l}{\sum_{l=1}^{M} e_l} \qquad (9\text{-}36)$$

where T and $\star$ indicate the chosen t-norm.

A practical sequence of computations to obtain $Y_{\cos}(\mathbf{x})$ is as follows:

1. Discretize the output space Y into a suitable number of points, and compute the centroid $C_{\tilde{G}^l}$ of each consequent set on the discretized output space using (9-3). These consequent centroid sets can be computed ahead of time and stored for future use.

2. Compute the degree of firing $E_l = \prod_{i=1}^{p}\mu_{\tilde{F}_i^l}(x_i)$ associated with the lth consequent set using Theorem A-1. Note that E_l is a type-1 fuzzy set ($l = 1, \ldots, M$).

3. Discretize the domain of each type-1 fuzzy set $C_{\tilde{G}^l}$ into a suitable number of points, say N_l ($l = 1, \ldots, M$).

4. Discretize the domain of each type-1 fuzzy set E_l into a suitable number of points, say M_l ($l = 1, \ldots, M$).

5. Enumerate all the possible combinations $\{d_1, \ldots, d_M, e_1, \ldots, e_M\}$ such that $d_l \in C_{\tilde{G}^l}$ and $e_l \in E_l$. The total number of combinations will be $\prod_{l=1}^{M} M_l N_l$.

6. Compute the center-of-sets type-reduced set using (9-36). Since there are exactly M $C_{\tilde{G}^l}$ and E_l, where M is the number of rules, we can use product or minimum t-norm in (9-36).

In Step 6 the weighted sum and t-norm operations in (9-36) have to be repeated $\prod_{l=1}^{M} M_l N_l$ times. This number is, in general, larger than that required for height (or modified height) type-reduction, but is less than that required for centroid (or center-of-sums) type-reduction.

If only the consequents are type-2 fuzzy sets (as in function approximation, e.g., Example 10-3), so that all of the degrees of firing are crisp numbers, then $Y_{cos}(\mathbf{x})$ reduces to (Exercise 9-8)

$$Y_{cos}(\mathbf{x}) = \frac{\sum_{l=1}^{M} C_{\tilde{G}^l} T_{i=1}^{p} \mu_{F_i^l}(x_i)}{\sum_{l=1}^{M} T_{i=1}^{p} \mu_{F_i^l}(x_i)} \tag{9-37}$$

Note that this formula derives from $y_{cos}(\mathbf{x})$ in (9-35) in which c^l is replaced by set $C_{\tilde{G}^l}$. When the $C_{\tilde{G}^l}$ are interval sets or Gaussian sets, then $Y_{cos}(\mathbf{x})$ in (9-37) can be computed using Theorem 7-4 or Example 7-4, respectively.

9.5.6 Computational complexity of type-reduction

Clearly, type-reduction for arbitrary type-2 fuzzy sets can be computationally very costly. Figure 9-6 locates our five type reduction methods on a complexity scale. The most costly are the centroid and center-of-sums type-reducers; the least costly are the height and modified height type-reducers; the center-of-sets type-reducer's complexity is somewhere between these two groups.

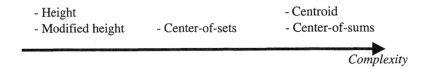

Figure 9-6: Complexity of type-reduction methods.

How can type-reduction be simplified? Clearly, using height and modified height type-reducers will greatly reduce the computational complexity; however, as stated in Exercise 9-9, there can be a problem using these if only one rule fires. The center-of-sets type-reducer is better to use in that case.

When each of the detailed computational procedures for the type-reducers is examined closely, we observe that we also need to compute meet and possibly join for arbitrary type-2 fuzzy sets. In Section 7.3 we learned that this is difficult to do except for interval type-2 sets; so, in Section 9.6 we examine type-reduction for such sets.

9.5.7 Concluding example

Example 9-8: [Karnik and Mendel (1998b)] Consider a type-1 FLS having consequent fuzzy sets whose membership functions are shown in Figure 9-7 (a). Suppose that for some particular input **x** the fired output membership functions are as shown in Figure 9-7 (b) (assuming product inference). The numbers 0.9, 0.8, and 0.2 indicate the degree of firing of each of the consequent sets. The outputs of our five defuzzifiers for this example are listed in Figure 9-7. For the modified height defuzzifier δ^l was set equal to the standard deviation of the lth consequent set. The standard deviations for the three fired consequent sets are equal to 0.4, 0.2, and 0.2, respectively. Note that for the consequent set centered at 5, $\bar{y}^5 = 5$ but $c^5 = 4.8436$; therefore, the outputs of the height and center-of-sets defuzzifiers for this example are slightly different.

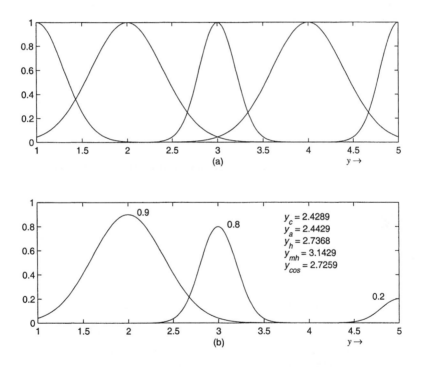

Figure 9-7: (a) Consequent set membership functions for Example 9-8. (b) Membership functions of fired consequent sets for some input **x**. Outputs of different defuzzifiers are listed in (b).

Now suppose that the antecedents are characterized by type-2 fuzzy sets and the consequents are characterized by type-1 fuzzy sets. The membership functions for the latter are the same as shown in Figure 9-7 (a), and are shown again in Figure 9-8 (a). The fired rule output membership functions for some input $\mathbf{x}$ are shown in Figure 9-8 (b) assuming product inference and t-norm. At each point $y \in [1,5]$, $\tilde{B}^1$, e.g., has two primary memberships, one equal to $0.9N(y;2,0.4)$ and the other equal to $0.8N(y;2,0.4)$. The corresponding secondary grades are 1 and 0.5, respectively, as labeled on Figure 9-8 (b). Observe the difference between Figure 9-8 (b) and Figure 9-7 (b) where, in the latter figure, each output has a fixed height. In the rest of this example, we compute the five type-reduced sets for the Figure 9-8 (b) fired rule output membership functions.

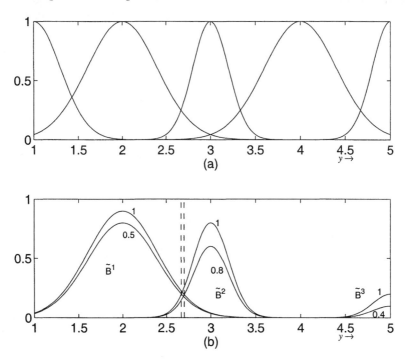

Figure 9-8: (a) Consequent set membership functions for Example 9-8. (b) Type-2 membership functions for fired consequent sets for some input **x**. The fired consequent sets are type-2, because the degrees of firing associated with each of the consequent sets are assumed to be type-1 sets. In (b), the vertical axis shows the primary memberships of *y* in the output sets. Secondary grades are indicated on the figure. The dashed lines show the region within which a point may have more than two primary memberships.

To use a centroid type-reducer, we begin by finding a composite output fuzzy set which equals the union of the individual fired rule output sets. While finding the union of these sets, since $\tilde{B}^3$ does not overlap with any of the other two sets, it will remain exactly as is. Let's see how to compute the union of $\tilde{B}^1$ and $\tilde{B}^2$. For any point y (along the horizontal axis), the secondary membership function of $\tilde{B}^1$, $\mu_{\tilde{B}^1}(y)$, can be expressed as

$$\mu_{\tilde{B}^1}(y) = 0.5/a_1 + 1/a_2 \quad y \in [1,5] \tag{9-38}$$

and the secondary membership function of $\tilde{B}^2$, $\mu_{\tilde{B}^2}(y)$, can be expressed as

$$\mu_{\tilde{B}^2}(y) = 0.8/b_1 + 1/b_2 \quad y \in [1,5] \tag{9-39}$$

where sum indicates logical union. Then, from (7-17) (using product t-norm),

$$\begin{aligned}
\mu_{\tilde{B}^1}(y) \sqcup \mu_{\tilde{B}^2}(y) &= (0.5/a_1 + 1/a_2) \sqcup (0.8/b_1 + 1/b_2) \\
&= (0.5 \times 0.8)/(a_1 \vee b_1) + (0.5 \times 1)/(a_1 \vee b_2) \\
&\quad + (1 \times 0.8)/(a_2 \vee b_1) + (1 \times 1)/(a_2 \vee b_2)
\end{aligned} \tag{9-40}$$

Observe in Figure 9-8(b) that to the left of the two dashed lines each of a_1 and a_2 is greater than either b_1 or b_2, respectively; consequently, in this region (9-40) gives

$$\begin{aligned}
\mu_{\tilde{B}^1}(y) \sqcup \mu_{\tilde{B}^2}(y) &= 0.4/a_1 + 0.5/a_1 + 0.8/a_2 + 1/a_2 \\
&= 0.5/a_1 + 1/a_2 = \mu_{\tilde{B}^1}(y)
\end{aligned} \tag{9-41}$$

Similarly, to the right of the two dashed lines, each of b_1 and b_2 is greater than either a_1 or a_2, respectively; consequently,

$$\mu_{\tilde{B}^1}(y) \sqcup \mu_{\tilde{B}^2}(y) = \mu_{\tilde{B}^2}(y) \tag{9-42}$$

Between the two dashed lines the union will, in general, be different from either $\mu_{\tilde{B}^1}(y)$ or $\mu_{\tilde{B}^2}(y)$. In this region a point may have more than two primary memberships [see (9-40)]; however, since this region is very small compared to the interval [1,5], we assume, for simplicity, that even between the two dashed lines, every point has only two primary memberships. The resulting composite output set $\tilde{B}$ is depicted in Figure 9-2 (a) [in Example 9-2 we did not discuss the origins of $\tilde{B}$ depicted in Figure 9-2 (a); now we know where it came from], and the centroid of $\tilde{B}$ (computed as described earlier) is depicted in Figure 9-2 (b). That centroid is the centroid type-reduced set for this example.

Turning next to the height type-reducer, we replace each fired rule output set by a singleton at the point having highest primary membership in the principal membership function in that output set [see the dashed lines in Figure 9-9 (a)]. In this example there are 3 $\bar{y}^l$

corresponding to the three fired output sets, each $\bar{y}^l$ having two possible primary member-ships. The height type-reducer considers each of the eight possible type-1 embedded sets and performs height defuzzification on them to get points in the type-reduced set. We show the calculation for two points here. First consider the situation where the first, second, and third membership functions for the fired consequent sets have primary memberships equal to 0.9, 0.6 and 0.2, respectively. The corresponding point in the type-reduced set is calculated, us-ing (9-32) and Figure 9-9 (a), as $(1 \times 0.8 \times 1)\big/\left(\frac{0.9 \times 2 + 0.6 \times 3 + 0.2 \times 5}{0.9 + 0.6 + 0.2}\right) = 0.8 / 2.7059$. Next, observe that the point having maximum membership in the type-reduced set is calculated as $(1 \times 1 \times 1)\big/\left(\frac{0.9 \times 2 + 0.8 \times 3 + 0.2 \times 5}{0.9 + 0.8 + 0.2}\right) = 1 / 2.7368$. The complete height type-reduced set is depicted in Figure 9-9 (b).

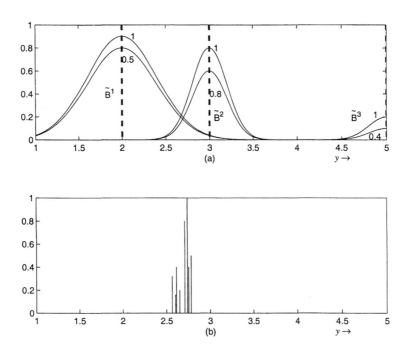

Figure 9-9: Example 9-8 calculations. (a) The $\bar{y}^l$ (lo-cated at the dashed lines) and their output set member-ship functions, and (b) the height type-reduced set. The point having unity membership in the height type-reduced set is equal to 2.7368. In (a), the vertical axis shows the primary memberships of y in the output sets; and in (b) the vertical axis shows the memberships of y in the height type-reduced set.

We leave the details about modified height and center-of-sets type-reduction for the reader to fill in (Exercise 9-10).

Table 9-3 summarizes the results of this example for our five type-reducers. The last column, titled "Centroid," gives the center of gravity of the type-reduced set; it can be used as the defuzzified value of the type-reduced set (see Section 10.6). Just as different defuzzification methods provide different results, different type-reduction methods also provide different results. Which type-reduction method to choose is an open issue, as is which defuzzification method to choose. ∎

Table 9-3: Results for Example 9-8 [Karnik and Mendel (1998b)].

Type-Reduced Set	Left-Most Point	Right-Most Point	Width	Unity Height Point	Centroid[a]
Centroid	2.3403	2.5114	0.1711	2.4729	2.4321
Center-of-sums	2.3167	2.4511	0.1344	2.4172	2.3856
Height	2.5625	2.7778	0.2153	2.7368	2.6985
Modified height	2.9730	3.2000	0.2270	3.1429	3.1125
Center-of-sets	2.5527	2.7604	0.2077	2.7204	2.6832

[a]The centroid is *not* the average of the left- and right-most points. To calculate it, one uses the amplitudes of all points in each type-reduced set [e.g., as in Figures 9-2 (b) and 9-9 (b)].

9.6 TYPE-REDUCTION: INTERVAL SETS

When the secondary membership functions are interval sets, then each of our five type-reducers can be computed using the very efficient iterative procedure given in Theorem 9-1. Here we briefly indicate how to do this.

9.6.1 Centroid type-reduction

The centroid type-reducer combines output sets for different rules by finding their union, so that the membership function of the combined output set, $\tilde{B}$, is given by (9-26). In this case (Theorem 7-1), $\tilde{B}$ is an interval set and $\forall f_{y_i} = 1$ in (9-27). Let the combined output set be discretized into N points, $y_1, ..., y_N$, and let $J_{y_i} \equiv [L_i, R_i]$. To use the computational procedure described in Theorem 9-1, y_i plays the role of c_l, $s_l = 0$ for all l, $(L_i + R_i)/2 = h_l$, and, $(R_i - L_i)/2 = \Delta_l$. Note that in these expressions the dummy variables i and l are treated as the same.

9.6.2 Center-of-sums type-reduction

The center-of-sums type-reducer combines the output sets for different rules by summing their secondary membership functions. The result of doing this is an interval set (Theorem 7-3). The type-reduced set can be computed in exactly the same manner as just described for the centroid type-reducer where $\tilde{B}$ is now the sum of the secondary membership functions.

9.6.3 Height type-reduction

For the height type-reducer, in Theorem 9-1 the $\bar{y}^l$ play the role of the c_l, $s_l = 0$ for all l (because the $\bar{y}^l$ are all crisp), and the output set secondary membership functions, $\mu_{\tilde{B}^l}(\bar{y}^l)$, which are interval sets, play the role of the W_l. If the primary membership of each $\mu_{\tilde{B}^l}(\bar{y}^l)$, $J_{\bar{y}^l}$, is represented as $[L_l, R_l]$, then $h_l = (L_l + R_l)/2$ and $\Delta_l = (R_l - L_l)/2$.

9.6.4 Modified height type-reduction

The computations for a modified height type-reducer are very similar to those for a height type-reducer, the only difference being that each output secondary membership function, $\mu_{\tilde{B}^l}(\bar{y}^l)$, is now multiplied by a factor of $1/\delta^{l2}$, so that in Theorem 9-1 $h_l = (L_l + R_l)/2\delta^{l2}$ and $\Delta_l = (R_l - L_l)/2\delta^{l2}$.

9.6.5 Center-of-sets type-reduction

The center-of-sets type-reduced set is given in (9-36), where $C_{\tilde{G}^l}$ is the centroid of the lth consequent set, $E_l = \prod_{i=1}^{p} \mu_{\tilde{F}_i^l}(x_i)$ is the degree of firing for the lth consequent set, and $l = 1, ..., M$. In this case the iterative procedure in Theorem 9-1 has to be applied in two stages. In the first stage we compute the centroids ($C_{\tilde{G}^l}$) of the interval type-2 consequent sets, and in the next stage we compute the type-reduced set using (9-14). When computing the type-reduced set, $C_{\tilde{G}^l}$ plays the role of Z_l in (9-14). If the domain of type-1 fuzzy set $C_{\tilde{G}^l}$ is the interval $[L_l^c, R_l^c]$, then $c_l = (L_l^c + R_l^c)/2$ and $s_l = (R_l^c - L_l^c)/2$. The degree of firing E_l plays the role of W_l. If the domain of type-1 fuzzy set E_l is the interval $[L_l, R_l]$, then $h_l = (L_l + R_l)/2$ and $\Delta_l = (R_l - L_l)/2$.

9.6.6 Concluding example

Example 9-9: [Karnik and Mendel (1998b)] In this example we illustrate the use of the just-described type-reduction methods for an interval type-2 FLS. We consider a single-input–single-output type-2 FLS using product t-norm and product inference, one that has rules of the form:

$$R^l: \text{IF } x \text{ is } \tilde{F}^l, \text{ THEN } y \text{ is } \tilde{G}^l \tag{9-43}$$

where $x, y \in [0,10]$.

Figures 9-10 (a) and (b) depict the antecedent and consequent type-2 fuzzy set FOUs. Each type-2 set is an interval set that can be described by two Gaussians that have the same mean and standard deviation. The two Gaussians are scaled to different heights. The maximum height reached by the taller Gaussian is unity, whereas that reached by the shorter Gaussian is s. If the mean and standard deviations of the Gaussians are m and s, respectively, then the primary membership of a domain point x' is an interval

$$\left[s\exp\left\{ -0.5\left(\frac{x'-m}{\sigma} \right)^2 \right\}, \exp\left\{ -0.5\left(\frac{x'-m}{\sigma} \right)^2 \right\} \right].$$

The m values for each of the antecedent sets, $\tilde{F}_1$, $\tilde{F}_2$, and $\tilde{F}_3$, are 2, 5, and 8, respectively; the σ values are all the same and are equal to 1; and the s values are 0.8, 0.6, and 0.9, respectively. For the three consequent sets ($\tilde{G}_1$, $\tilde{G}_2$, and $\tilde{G}_3$), the m values are 6, 2, and 9, respectively; the σ values are 1, 1.2, and 1, respectively; and the s values are 0.75, 0.75, and 0.8, respectively.

The applied input is $x = 4$, as shown by the dashed line in Figure 9-10 (a). It has non-zero memberships in two antecedents $\tilde{F}_1$ and $\tilde{F}_2$. For the modified height type-reducer, the δ^l were set equal to the σ values of the consequent sets, i.e., $\delta^1 = 1$, $\delta^2 = 1.2$, and $\delta^3 = 1$.

The type-reduced results for this example, which were obtained as described in Sections 9.6.1–9.6.5, are collected in Table 9-4. In this table we represent each interval type-1 set in terms of its center and spread. Recall that an interval type-1 set with center c' and spread s' has $[c' - s', c' + s']$ as its domain. ∎

9.7 CONCLUDING REMARK

The material in this chapter will be very heavily used in the remaining chapters of this book. The calculations of different type-reducers, which rely on the calculations of either the centroid or generalized centroid of a type-2 fuzzy set, are fundamental to all type-2 FLSs. To perform these calculations, one needs to also compute the meet and possibly the join or sum of type-2 fuzzy sets, and these calculations require an understanding of the material in Sections 7.3 and 7.4.

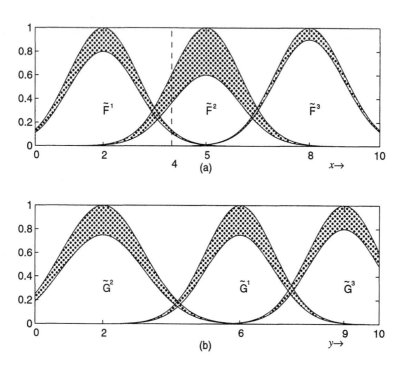

Figure 9-10: Example 9-9, (a) antecedent set FOUs (the vertical axis shows the primary memberships of x in the antecedent sets) and (b) consequent set FOUs (the vertical axis shows the primary memberships of y in the consequent sets). The applied input $(x = 4)$ is shown in (a). (Karnik et al., 1999, © 1999, IEEE).

9.8 COMPUTATION

The following M-file, which is found in the folder *general type-2 fuzzy logic systems*, is useful for computing the generalized centroid or centroid of type-2 fuzzy sets:

> **weighted_avg.m:** Function to extend the weighted average of crisp numbers to the case where all the quantities involved are general type-1 sets. It implements the generalized centroid in (9-11).

The following M-file, which is found in the folder *interval type-2 fuzzy logic systems*, is useful for computing the generalized centroid or centroid of interval type-2 fuzzy sets:

> **interval_wtdavg.m:** Function used to implement the iterative procedure described in Theorem 9-1 to compute the maximum and minimum of a weighted average, where both the z_i and the w_i are interval sets.

Table 9-4: Results for Example 9-9 [Karnik and Mendel (1998b)].

Type-Reduced Set	Center	Spread
Centroid	2.8179	0.4918
Center-of-sums	2.8685	0.4999
Height	2.9026	0.4280
Modified height	3.1607	0.5111
Center-of-sums	2.9462	0.3653

EXERCISES

9-1: Explain why the technical subtlety described in Section 9.2 does not occur when the secondary membership functions are interval sets.

9-2: Figure 9-1 is helpful for understanding the centroid calculation of (9-3). Create a comparable figure to help explain the generalized centroid computation of (9-11).

9-3: Provide a complete derivation of (9-17).

9-4: The FOU for a specific type-2 fuzzy set $\tilde{F}$ is depicted in Figure 9-11. Secondary membership functions are assumed to be symmetrical triangles. (a) Explain how to compute the centroid $C_{\tilde{F}}$. (b) Write a computer program to compute $C_{\tilde{F}}$. (c) Evaluate $C_{\tilde{F}}$ for different discretizations of both y and $\mu_{\tilde{F}}(y)$.

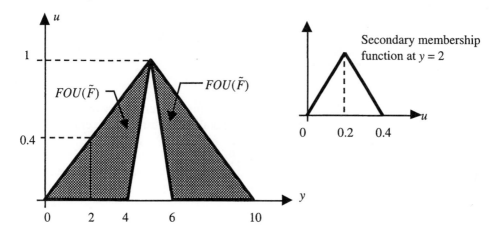

Figure 9-11: FOU for Exercise 9-4, and the secondary membership function at $y = 2$.

9-5: Program the generalized centroid computational procedure that is stated in Theorem 9-1 and apply your program to the data given in Example 9-3, to verify that $[y_l, y_r] = [3.0194, 7.1702]$.

9-6: Assume the same FOU as in Exercise 9-4. Now, however, the secondaries are interval sets. Evaluate $C_{\tilde{F}}$.

9-7: Develop a computation schedule for $Y_{mh}(\mathbf{x})$. How many embedded sets will there be?

9-8: Derive (9-37) by starting from (9-35).

9-9: [Karnik and Mendel (1998b)] (a) Show that when only one rule is fired, corresponding to $l = l'$, then $Y_h(\mathbf{x}) = \bar{y}^{l'}$ and $Y_{cos}(\mathbf{x}) = C_{\tilde{G}^{l'}}$. This means that when a single rule is fired, the height type-reduced set collapses to a single point. In this case no uncertainty is associated with the output, which is generally not true. Uncertainty still affects the center-of-sets type-reducer, although it is only the uncertainty of the consequent set. To get the effects of *both* antecedent and consequent set uncertainties when only one rule fires, one should use either the centroid or center-of-sums type reducers. (b) Explain why this is so.

9-10: Fill in the detailed calculations of modified height and center-of-sets type reduction for Example 9-8.

9-11: In Example 9-8, if the secondary membership functions of the three fired sets each contained three elements, how many possible type-1 embedded sets would there be for the calculation of the height type-reduced set?

Part 4—
Type-2 FLSs

CHAPTER 10

Singleton Type-2 Fuzzy Logic Systems

10.1 INTRODUCTION

This chapter discusses the structure of a singleton type-2 FLS, which is a system that accounts for uncertainties about the antecedents or consequents in rules, but does not explicitly account for input measurement uncertainties. More complicated (but, more versatile) non-singleton type-2 FLSs, which account for both types of uncertainties, are discussed in Chapters 11 and 12.

The tenets of FL do not change from type-1 to type-2 fuzzy sets, and in general, will not change for type-n. A higher type number just indicates a higher degree of fuzziness. Since a higher type changes the nature of the membership functions, the operations that depend on the membership functions change; however, the basic principles of fuzzy logic are independent of the nature of membership functions and hence do not change. Rules of inference, like Generalized Modus Ponens, continue to apply.

A general type-2 FLS is depicted in Figure 10-1. As discussed in Chapter 1, a type-2 FLS is very similar to a type-1 FLS, the major structural difference being that the defuzzifier block of a type-1 FLS is replaced by the *output processing* block in a type-2 FLS. That block consists of type-reduction followed by defuzzification.

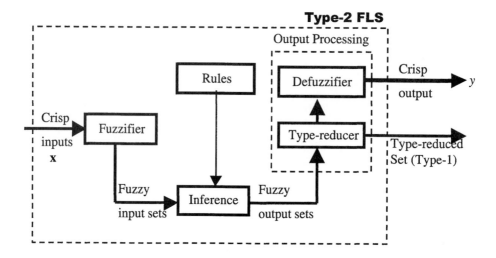

Figure 10-1: Type-2 FLS.

During our development of a type-2 FLS, we assume that *all* the antecedent and consequent sets in rules are type-2; however, this need not necessarily be the case in practice. All results remain valid as long as just one set is type-2. This means that *a FLS is type-2 as long as any one of its antecedent or consequent sets is type-2*. In Chapter 12, we also explain that *a FLS whose type-1 rules are activated by a type-2 input is also a type-2 FLS*.

Wherever possible we shall try to parallel the organization of Chapter 5, so that it will be relatively easy to compare a singleton type-1 FLS with a singleton type-2 FLS.

10.2 RULES

In the type-1 case, we generally have IF–THEN rules of the form (5-1), i.e.,

$$R^l: \text{IF } x_1 \text{ is } F_1^l \text{ and } \cdots \text{ and } x_p \text{ is } F_p^l, \text{ THEN } y \text{ is } G^l \quad l = 1,...,M \qquad (10\text{-}1)$$

As mentioned earlier, the distinction between type-1 and type-2 is associated with the nature of the membership functions, which is not important when forming the rules. Paraphrasing Gertrude Stein, "a rule, is a rule, is a rule." The structure of the rules remains exactly the same in the type-2 case, but now some or all of the sets involved are type-2.

Consider a type-2 FLS having p inputs $x_1 \in X_1, ..., x_p \in X_p$ and one output $y \in Y$. As in the type-1 case, we assume there are M rules; but, in the type-2 case the lth rule has the form

$$R^l: \text{ IF } x_1 \text{ is } \tilde{F}_1^l \text{ and } \cdots \text{ and } x_p \text{ is } \tilde{F}_p^l, \text{ THEN } y \text{ is } \tilde{G}^l \quad l = 1, ..., M \qquad (10\text{-}2)$$

This rule represents a type-2 relation between the input space $X_1 \times \cdots \times X_p$, and the output space, Y, of the type-2 FLS.

10.3 FUZZY INFERENCE ENGINE

In a type-1 FLS the inference engine combines rules and gives a mapping from input type-1 fuzzy sets to output type-1 fuzzy sets. Multiple antecedents in rules are connected by the t-norm. The membership grades in the input sets are combined with those in the output sets using the sup-star composition. Multiple rules may be combined using the t-conorm operation or during defuzzification by weighted summation. In the type-2 case the inference process is very similar. The inference engine combines rules and gives a mapping from input type-2 fuzzy sets to output type-2 fuzzy sets. To do this one needs to compute unions and intersections of type-2 sets (using results from Section 7.3 or Appendix A), as well as compositions of type-2 relations (using results from Section 8.5).

Just as the sup-star composition is the backbone computation for a type-1 FLS, the extended sup-star composition is the backbone computation for a type-2 FLS. Although we shall present a detailed derivation of the input–output relation for type-2 fuzzy inference, when we compare (8-35) with (5-4) and (8-23) with (5-6) we see that it should be possible to go directly from our type-1 results to their type-2 counterparts simply by replacing type-1 membership functions by type-2 membership functions, the sup operation with the join operation, and the t-norm operation with the meet operation. It is as simple as that.

Each rule in (10-2) is interpreted as a type-2 fuzzy implication (Section 8.7). With reference to (10-2), let $\tilde{F}_1^l \times \cdots \times \tilde{F}_p^l = \tilde{A}^l$; then, as in (8-34), (10-2) can be re-expressed as

$$R^l: \tilde{F}_1^l \times \cdots \times \tilde{F}_p^l \to \tilde{G}^l = \tilde{A}^l \to \tilde{G}^l \quad l = 1, ..., M \qquad (10\text{-}3)$$

R^l is described by the membership function $\mu_{R^l}(\mathbf{x}, y) = \mu_{R^l}(x_1, ..., x_p, y)$, where

$$\mu_{R^l}(\mathbf{x}, y) = \mu_{\tilde{A}^l \to \tilde{G}^l}(\mathbf{x}, y) \tag{10-4}$$

We know, from (8-35), that

$$\mu_{R^l}(\mathbf{x}, y) = \mu_{\tilde{A}^l \to \tilde{G}^l}(\mathbf{x}, y) = \mu_{\tilde{F}_1^l}(x_1)\sqcap \cdots \sqcap \mu_{\tilde{F}_p^l}(x_p)\sqcap\mu_{\tilde{G}^l}(y)$$
$$= \left[\sqcap_{i=1}^p \mu_{\tilde{F}_i^l}(x_i)\right]\sqcap\mu_{\tilde{G}^l}(y) \tag{10-5}$$

In this book, we only use the product or minimum t-norms for the meet.

Most generally, the p-dimensional input to R^l is given by the type-2 fuzzy set $\tilde{A}_\mathbf{x}$ whose membership function is (see Section 3.5.2)

$$\mu_{\tilde{A}_\mathbf{x}}(\mathbf{x}) = \mu_{\tilde{X}_1}(x_1)\sqcap\cdots\sqcap\mu_{\tilde{X}_p}(x_p) = \sqcap_{i=1}^p \mu_{\tilde{X}_i}(x_i) \tag{10-6}$$

where $\tilde{X}_i$ ($i = 1,...,p$) are the labels of the fuzzy sets describing the inputs. Each rule R^l determines a type-2 fuzzy set $\tilde{B}^l = \tilde{A}_\mathbf{x} \circ R^l$ such that [see (8-23)]:

$$\mu_{\tilde{B}^l}(y) = \mu_{\tilde{A}_\mathbf{x} \circ R^l}(y) = \sqcup_{\mathbf{x} \in X}\left[\mu_{\tilde{A}_\mathbf{x}}(\mathbf{x})\sqcap\mu_{R^l}(\mathbf{x}, y)\right] \quad y \in Y \, l = 1, ..., M \tag{10-7}$$

This equation is the input–output relation in Figure 10-1 between the type-2 fuzzy set that excites one rule in the inference engine and the type-2 fuzzy set at the output of that engine.

Substituting (10-5) and (10-6) into (10-7), we see that ($l = 1, ..., M$)

$$\mu_{\tilde{B}^l}(y) = \sqcup_{\mathbf{x} \in X}\left[\mu_{\tilde{A}_\mathbf{x}}(\mathbf{x})\sqcap\mu_{R^l}(\mathbf{x}, y)\right]$$
$$= \sqcup_{\mathbf{x} \in X}\left\{\left[\sqcap_{i=1}^p \mu_{\tilde{X}_i}(x_i)\right]\sqcap\left[\sqcap_{i=1}^p \mu_{\tilde{F}_i^l}(x_i)\right]\sqcap\mu_{\tilde{G}^l}(y)\right\}$$
$$= \sqcup_{\mathbf{x} \in X}\left\{\left[\sqcap_{i=1}^p \mu_{\tilde{X}_i}(x_i)\sqcap\mu_{\tilde{F}_i^l}(x_i)\right]\sqcap\mu_{\tilde{G}^l}(y)\right\} \tag{10-8}$$
$$= \mu_{\tilde{G}^l}(y)\sqcap\left\{\left[\sqcup_{x_1 \in X_1}\mu_{\tilde{X}_1}(x_1)\sqcap\mu_{\tilde{F}_1^l}(x_1)\right]\sqcap\right.$$
$$\left.\cdots\sqcap\left[\sqcup_{x_p \in X_p}\mu_{\tilde{X}_p}(x_p)\sqcap\mu_{\tilde{F}_p^l}(x_p)\right]\right\}, \quad y \in Y$$

The last line follows in part from the commutativity of the meet using minimum or product (see Section 7.6.2 and Table B-2) and the fact that

$\mu_{\tilde{X}_i}(x_i)\prod \mu_{\tilde{F}_i^l}(x_i)$ is only a function of x_i, so that each join in the final line of (10-8) is over just a scalar variable. Equation (10-8) is analogous to (5-7).

As in the type-1 case, fired rule sets are combined either before or as part of output processing, in this case during type-reduction. We return to this later. Here we focus on the simplification of (10-8) as a result of singleton fuzzification. Equation (10-8) is also the starting point for Chapters 11 and 12, where more complicated fuzzifications are considered.

10.4 FUZZIFICATION AND ITS EFFECT ON INFERENCE

In the FLS of Figure 10-1, as in the FLS of Figure 5-1, crisp inputs are first fuzzified into fuzzy input sets that then activate the inference block, which in the present case is associated with type-2 fuzzy sets. In this section, we explain singleton fuzzification and the effect of such fuzzification on the inference engine.

10.4.1 Fuzzifier

The *fuzzifier* maps a crisp point $\mathbf{x} = (x_1,...,x_p)^T \in X_1 \times X_2 \times \cdots \times X_p \equiv \mathbf{X}$ into a type-2 fuzzy set $\tilde{A}_\mathbf{x}$ in $\mathbf{X}$. In this chapter we focus on the type-2 singleton fuzzifier. We defined the membership function for a single-variable type-2 singleton in (7-25). It is easy to extend that definition to the multi-variable case, in terms of the secondary membership function of $\tilde{A}_\mathbf{x}$, $\mu_{\tilde{A}_\mathbf{x}}(\mathbf{x})$, i.e.,

> $\tilde{A}_\mathbf{x}$ is a *type-2 fuzzy singleton* if $\mu_{\tilde{A}_\mathbf{x}}(\mathbf{x}) = 1/1$ for $\mathbf{x} = \mathbf{x}'$ and $\mu_{\tilde{A}_\mathbf{x}}(\mathbf{x}) = 1/0$ for all other $\mathbf{x} \neq \mathbf{x}'$

Because we only use separable membership functions in this book, we take this statement to mean that $\mu_{\tilde{X}_i}(x_i) = 1/1$ when $x_i = x_i'$ and $\mu_{\tilde{X}_i}(x_i) = 1/0$ when $x_i \neq x_i'$, for all $i = 1, ..., p$.

❀❀❀❀❀❀❀❀❀❀

10.4.2 Fuzzy inference engine

When type-2 fuzzy input set $\tilde{A}_x$ only contains a single element $\mathbf{x}'$ then the join operations [see (7-17)] in the extended sup-star composition (10-8) are very easy to evaluate because each $\mu_{\tilde{X}_i}(x_i)$ is non-zero only at one point, $x_i = x_i'$; hence,

$$
\begin{aligned}
\mu_{\tilde{B}^l}(y) &= \mu_{\tilde{G}^l}(y)\sqcap\left\{\left[\bigsqcup_{x_1 \in X_1}\mu_{\tilde{X}_1}(x_1)\sqcap\mu_{\tilde{F}_1^l}(x_1)\right]\sqcap\right.\\
&\qquad \left.\cdots\sqcap\left[\bigsqcup_{x_p \in X_p}\mu_{\tilde{X}_p}(x_p)\sqcap\mu_{\tilde{F}_p^l}(x_p)\right]\right\}\\
&= \mu_{\tilde{G}^l}(y)\sqcap\left\{\left[\mu_{\tilde{X}_1}(x_1')\sqcap\mu_{\tilde{F}_1^l}(x_1')\right]\sqcap\cdots\sqcap\left[\mu_{\tilde{X}_p}(x_p')\sqcap\mu_{\tilde{F}_p^l}(x_p')\right]\right\} \qquad (10\text{-}9)\\
&= \mu_{\tilde{G}^l}(y)\sqcap\left\{\left[(1/1)\sqcap\mu_{\tilde{F}_1^l}(x_1')\right]\sqcap\cdots\sqcap\left[(1/1)\sqcap\mu_{\tilde{F}_p^l}(x_p')\right]\right\}\\
&= \mu_{\tilde{G}^l}(y)\sqcap\left[\sqcap_{i=1}^{p}\mu_{\tilde{F}_i^l}(x_i')\right], \quad y \in Y
\end{aligned}
$$

where we have used the fact that $(1/1)\sqcap\mu_{\tilde{F}_i^l}(x_i') = \mu_{\tilde{F}_i^l}(x_i')$, which is true for minimum or product t-norm [see Example 7-3 or (B-13)].

The term in the bracket on the last line of (10-9) is referred to as the *firing set*. Comparing (10-9) to (5-10), we see that a *firing level*—a number—alters the consequent set for a fired rule in a singleton type-1 FLS, whereas a *firing set*—a set—alters the consequent set for a fired rule in a singleton type-2 FLS. The firing set conveys the uncertainties of the antecedents to the consequent set.

At a specific value of $y \in Y$, say y', secondary membership function $\mu_{\tilde{B}^l}(y')$ is a type-1 fuzzy set. To obtain a complete description of $\mu_{\tilde{B}^l}(y)$ using (10-9), it must be computed for $\forall y \in Y$, since $\mu_{\tilde{G}^l}(y)$ is a function of y. Note that $\mu_{\tilde{B}^l}(y)$—just as $\mu_{B^l}(y)$ in Chapter 5—depends on $\mathbf{x} = \mathbf{x}'$; change $\mathbf{x}'$ and $\mu_{\tilde{B}^l}(y)$ changes.

In general, evaluating (10-9) is still difficult, even after the simplification from (10-8), because, as explained in Section 7.3, it is difficult to compute the meet of arbitrary type-2 fuzzy sets.

Example10-1: [Karnik and Mendel (1998b)] Consider a one-rule type-2 FLS that uses Gaussian type-2 antecedent and consequent fuzzy sets. The antecedent and consequent membership function FOUs are depicted in Figures 10-2 (a) and (b), respectively. The input to the system is $x = 4$, for which the value of the principal membership function of the antecedent, shown as the horizontal dashed line in Figure 10-2 (a), is μ. Figure 10-2 (c) depicts the results of the computations in (10-9), which, in this simple case, reduce to $\mu_{\tilde{B}^1}(y) = \mu_{\tilde{G}^1}(y) \sqcap \mu_{\tilde{F}^1}(4)$, $\forall y \in Y$. Observe, from Figure 10-2 (a), that the firing set $\mu_{\tilde{F}^1}(4)$ is the intersection of the vertical dashed line at $x = 4$ with the FOU of the Gaussian membership function.

In this example we compute the meet using minimum t-norm; hence, the meet in $\mu_{\tilde{B}^1}(y) = \mu_{\tilde{G}^1}(y) \sqcap \mu_{\tilde{F}^1}(4)$ is computed using Theorem A-2. Note that this calculation involves finding the meet of the secondary membership function $\mu_{\tilde{F}^1}(4)$ with the secondary membership functions of the consequent function, $\mu_{\tilde{G}^1}(y)$ (as depicted in Figure 10-2 (b)) for $\forall y \in Y$. Observe, from Figure 10-2 (c) that the result of inference is a type-2 fuzzy set. The banded behavior about the output's principal membership function is an indication of combined antecedent and consequent uncertainties.

Results comparable to those given in Figure 10-2 are given in Figure 10-3 for meet using product t-norm. ■

Because of the difficulty in computing (10-9) for arbitrary type-2 fuzzy sets, we shall focus our attention later in this chapter on interval type-2 fuzzy sets, for which it is possible to obtain a closed-form formula for (10-9).

10.5 TYPE-REDUCTION

The type-2 output of the inference engine shown in Figure 10-1 must be processed next by the output processor, the first operation of which is type-reduction. Type-reduction methods have been discussed in Sections 9.5 and 9.6, and include: centroid, center-of-sums, height, modified height, and center-of-sets. Recall that if we use height, modified height, or center-of-sets type-reduction, then we do not have to first combine the fired-output type-2 consequent sets; i.e., these type-reduction methods work directly with $\mu_{\tilde{B}^1}(y)$ in (10-9). If, however, we use the centroid or center-of-sums type-reducers, then we must first combine the M $\mu_{\tilde{B}^1}(y)$ using the join or summation operations, as in (9-26) or (9-30), respectively.

This would be a good time for the reader to review Section 9.5, including Example 9-8, which illustrates the five different type-reducers for general type-2 antecedent fuzzy sets and type-1 consequent sets.

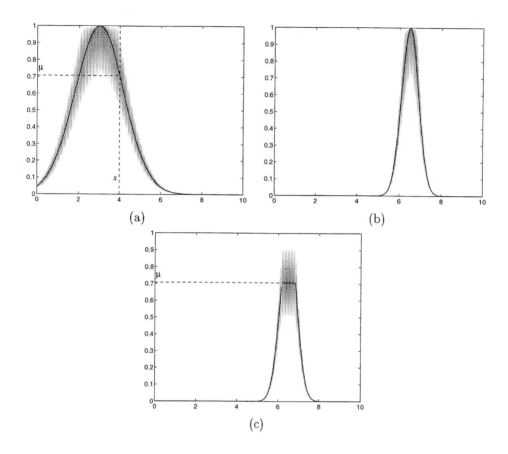

Figure 10-2: Illustration of minimum inference for a single antecedent and single consequent type-2 rule. (a) FOU for a Gaussian type-2 antecedent set; (b) FOU for the Gaussian type-2 consequent set; and, (c) FOU of the clipped consequent set, for $x = 4$, using minimum inference.

Assume for illustrative purposes that we have performed centroid type-reduction. Then [see the discussion following (9-3)] each element of the type-reduced set is the centroid of some embedded type-1 set for the output type-2 set of the FLS. Each of these embedded sets can be thought of as an output set of an associated type-1 FLS, and, correspondingly, the type-2 FLS can be thought of as a collection of many different type-1 FLSs. Each type-1 FLS is *embedded* in the type-2 FLS; hence, the type-reduced set is a collection of the outputs of all of the embedded type-1 FLSs (see Figure 10-4). The type-reduced set lets us represent the output of the type-2 FLS as a fuzzy set rather than as a crisp number, something that cannot be done with a type-1 FLS.

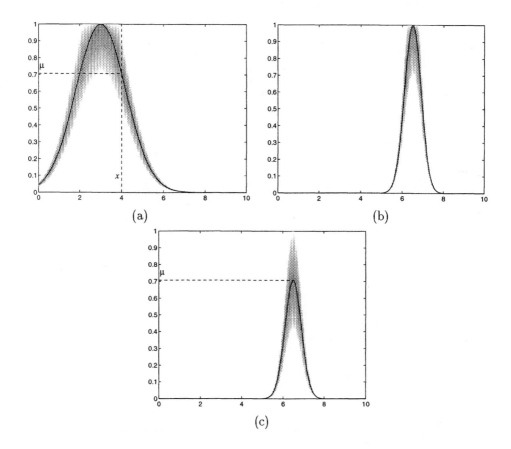

(a)

(b)

(c)

Figure 10-3: Illustration of product inference for a single antecedent and single consequent type-2 rule. (a) FOU for a Gaussian type-2 antecedent set; (b) FOU for the Gaussian type-2 consequent set; and, (c) FOU of the scaled consequent set, for $x = 4$, using product inference.

Referring to Figure 10-4, when the antecedent and consequent membership functions of the type-2 FLS have continuous domains, the number of embedded sets is uncountable. Figure 10-4 has been drawn assuming that the membership functions have discrete (or discretized) domains. The memberships in the type-reduced set,[1] $\mu_Y(y_i)$, represent the level of uncertainty associated with each embedded type-1 FLS. A crisp output can be obtained by aggregating the outputs of all the embedded type-1 FLSs by, e.g., finding the centroid of the type-reduced set. We explain this further in Section 10.6.

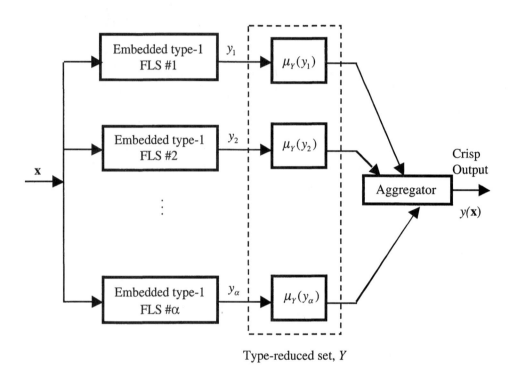

Figure 10-4: A type-2 FLS can be thought of as a collection of a large number of embedded type-1 FLSs (Karnik et al., 1999, © 1999, IEEE).

Although we just discussed, and continue to discuss, the type-reduced set for a centroid type-reducer, these discussions are valid for any other kind of type-reducer. The type-reduced set for *any* type-2 FLS represents a collection of outputs of all the type-1 FLSs embedded in the type-2 FLS.

If all of the type-2 uncertainties were to disappear (e.g., if all the type-2 membership functions in the FLS were to collapse to their principal membership functions), the secondary membership functions for all antecedents and consequents would each collapse to a single point (i.e., to a single-element pri-

---

[1]For example, in centroid type-reduction, these memberships are given by $f_{y_1}(\theta_1)\star\cdots\star f_{y_N}(\theta_N)$ in (9-27).

mary membership), which would have a unity secondary grade. This would cause the type-reduced set to collapse to its unity height point (Exercise 10-4), which shows that all of our results are valid when all the type-2 uncertainties disappear, in which case our type-2 FLS collapses to a type-1 FLS. So, our type-reduction methods fulfill the basic design requirement, stated in Section 1.4, i.e., if all uncertainties disappear our type-2 results must reduce to their type-1 counterparts.

If we think of a type-2 FLS as a "perturbed" version of a type-1 FLS, due to uncertainties in their membership functions, then the type-reduced set of the type-2 FLS can be thought of as representing the uncertainty in the crisp output due to these perturbations. Some measure of the spread of the type-reduced set may then be taken to indicate the possible variation in the crisp output due to these perturbations. This is analogous to using confidence intervals in a stochastic-uncertainty situation. What we have developed so far is only for *linguistic uncertainties*. In Chapters 11 and 12, we extend this to a combination of linguistic and input measurement uncertainties.

10.6 DEFUZZIFICATION

We defuzzify the type-reduced set to get a crisp output from the type-2 FLS. The most natural way to do this seems to be by finding the centroid of the type-reduced set. Finding the centroid is equivalent to finding a weighted average of the outputs of all the type-1 FLSs that are embedded in the type-2 FLS, where the weights correspond to the memberships in the type-reduced set (see Figure 10-4). If the type-reduced set Y for an input $\mathbf{x}$ is discretized or is discrete and consists of α points, then the expression for its centroid is

$$y(\mathbf{x}) = \frac{\sum_{k=1}^{\alpha} y_k \mu_Y(y_k)}{\sum_{k=1}^{\alpha} \mu_Y(y_k)} \qquad (10\text{-}10)$$

If α is large then data storage may be a problem for the computation of (10-10). This equation can, however, be evaluated using parallel processing, in which case data storage will not be a problem. Currently, however, most researchers still depend on software for simulations and cannot make use of parallel processing. We can, however, use a recursive method to vastly reduce the memory required for storing the data that are needed to compute the defuzzified output. Examining (10-10), we compute

$$A(i) = A(i-1) + y_i \mu_Y(y_i) \quad A(0) \equiv 0 \qquad (10\text{-}11)$$

and

$$B(i) = B(i-1) + \mu_Y(y_i) \quad B(0) \equiv 0 \tag{10-12}$$

for $i = 1, \ldots, \alpha$. After the last iteration, the defuzzified output is computed as

$$y(\mathbf{x}) = \frac{A(\alpha)}{B(\alpha)} \tag{10-13}$$

By this means, we just need to store A and B during each iteration. Note that $\mu_Y(y_i)$ in (10-11) and (10-12) is the same as b in (9-5) (Exercise 10-5). Using (10-11) and (10-12) requires that, as each element in the type-reduced set is computed, it is provided to these equations.

If the type-reduced set has only one point in it that has unity membership, and if we wish to reduce computational complexity, we may think that a more straightforward choice for the defuzzified value is the unity membership point in the type-reduced set. Choosing the unity membership point, however, means that we are doing away with all of the type-2 analyses and are choosing the output corresponding to only the principal membership function type-1 FLS that is embedded in the type-2 FLS. Consequently, since the unity height point conveys no information about membership function uncertainties, it does not make sense to use that point as the crisp output, unless the type-reduced set is convex and symmetric, in which case the unity height point is the same as the centroid. In general, for arbitrary type-2 membership functions, the type-reduced set is not symmetrical and the centroid location is different from the location of the unity height point. Table 9-3 for Example 9-8 illustrates these points.

10.7 Possibilities

From our detailed discussions about the five elements that comprise the Figure 10-1 type-2 FLS, we see that there are many possibilities to choose from, even more than for a type-1 FLS. Figure 10-5 summarizes some of the possibilities that we have discussed so far. To begin, we must decide on the kind of fuzzification—singleton or non-singleton—and, if the latter, whether it will be type-1 or type-2 (these two kinds of non-singleton fuzzification are described in Chapters 11 and 12, respectively). We must also choose a FOU for each type-2 membership function, decide on the functional forms (shapes) for both the primary and secondary membership functions, and choose the parameters of the membership functions (fixed ahead of time or tuned during a training procedure). Then we need to choose the composition (max-min, max-product), implication (minimum, product), type-reduction method (centroid, center-of-sums, height, modified height, center-of-sets), and defuzzifier. Clearly, there is an even greater richness among type-2 FLSs then there is among type-1 FLSs. Put another way, there are more design degrees of freedom associated with a type-2 FLS than with a type-1 FLS; hence, a type-2 FLS has the potential to outperform a type-1 FLS because of these extra degrees of freedom.

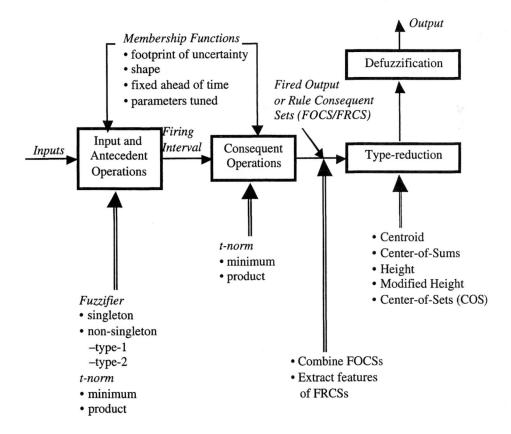

Figure 10-5: Choices that need to be made to specify or design a type-2 FLS.

Observe, in Figure 10-5, that prior to defuzzification we also need to decide on whether we are going to combine fired output secondary membership functions through the join operation or addition, or are going to extract features of the fired rule consequent sets. The latter are centroid, peak location, and spread. One or more of these features are used by the height, modified height, or center-of-sets type-reducers; e.g., the modified height type-reducer uses the peak location and spread of the fired rule consequent sets.

10.8 FBFs: The Lack Thereof

The title of this section gives away the rather disappointing fact that the concept of FBFs, which we found so useful for a singleton FLS, is not useful for *general* type-2 FLSs. The good news, though, is that when we focus our attention, in the next section, on an interval type-2 FLS, FBFs will again become very useful.

Recall, from Section 5.7, that in a type-1 FLS using height or modified height defuzzification, the defuzzified output could be expressed as the following FBF expansion:

$$y(\mathbf{x}) = \sum_{l=1}^{M} \bar{y}^l \phi_l(\mathbf{x})$$

(10-14)

where

$$\phi_l(\mathbf{x}) = \frac{T_{i=1}^p \mu_{F_i^l}(x_i)}{\sum_{l=1}^{M} T_{i=1}^p \mu_{F_i^l}(x_i)}$$

(10-15)

A key point to observe from (10-14) and (10-15) is that there is a partitioning of the antecedent and consequent effects; i.e., all antecedent effects appear in the FBFs, and all the consequent effects appear in the $\bar{y}^l$. This partitioning of the antecedent and consequent effects is very important in a type-1 FBF expansion; e.g., it was needed for the least-squares design method that is described in Section 5.9.2. Unfortunately, as we explain next, such a partitioning does *not* occur in a general type-2 FLS that uses height or modified-height type-reduction.

Consider, e.g., the height type-reducer in (9-32), which we restate here for the convenience of the reader:

$$Y_h(\mathbf{x}) = \int_{\theta_1 \in J_{\bar{y}^1}} \cdots \int_{\theta_M \in J_{\bar{y}^M}} \left[f_{\bar{y}^1}(\theta_1) \star \cdots \star f_{\bar{y}^M}(\theta_M) \right] \Big/ \frac{\sum_{l=1}^{M} \bar{y}^l \theta_l}{\sum_{l=1}^{M} \theta_l}$$

(10-16)

where θ_l, $J_{\bar{y}^l}$, and $f_{\bar{y}^l}$ ($\forall l$) are associated with $\mu_{\tilde{B}^l}(\bar{y}^l)$. From (10-9), we see that

$$\mu_{\tilde{B}^l}(\bar{y}^l) = \mu_{\tilde{G}^l}(\bar{y}^l) \sqcap \left[\sqcap_{i=1}^P \mu_{\tilde{F}_i^l}(x_i') \right] \qquad (10\text{-}17)$$

Observe that $\mu_{\tilde{B}^l}(\bar{y}^l)$ depends on *both* the antecedent-set secondary membership functions and the consequent-set secondary membership function, which means that θ_l in (10-16) will *not* depend just on antecedent effects.

Note that in the type-1 case $\mu_{G^l}(\bar{y}^l) = 1$, so the type-1 version of (10-17) only depends on antecedent effects.

Interestingly enough, in the case of the center-of-sets type-reducer (9-36), which we also repeat here,

$$Y_{\cos}(\mathbf{x}) = \int_{d_1 \in C_{\tilde{G}^1}} \cdots \int_{d_M \in C_{\tilde{G}^M}} \int_{e_1 \in E_1} \cdots \int_{e_M \in E_M} T_{l=1}^M \mu_{C_{\tilde{G}^l}}(d_l) \star T_{l=1}^M \mu_{E_l}(e_l) \Bigg/ \frac{\sum_{l=1}^M d_l e_l}{\sum_{l=1}^M e_l} \qquad (10\text{-}18)$$

where $E_l = \sqcap_{i=1}^P \mu_{\tilde{F}_i^l}(x_i)$ and $C_{\tilde{G}^l}$ is the centroid of the *l*th consequent type-2 set, each term to the right of the slash in (10-18) can be interpreted as a valid FBF expansion. In this case, the e_l depend only on antecedent effects and the d_l depend only on consequent effects. So, every point in the domain of a center-of-sets type-reduced set [i.e., the term to the right of the slash in (10-18)] can be expressed as a FBF expansion similar to the one in (10-14).

Since we can interpret the type-reduced set as a collection of a large number of type-1 FLSs (as in Figure 10-4) *when we use center of sets type-reduction, the output of each embedded type-1 FLS can be expressed as a FBF expansion.* According to the six-step computational procedure that is given just after (9-36), there are $\alpha = \prod_{l=1}^M M_l N_l$ embedded type-1 FLSs associated with the calculation of the center of sets type-reduced set. Assuming that each one of these embedded sets has a FBF expansion associated with it that has the same number of terms, say M, then the center of sets type-reduced set has a total of $M' = M \prod_{l=1}^M M_l N_l$ FBFs associated with it. Unfortunately, this value of M' is too large to be practical.

In the type-1 case the FBF expansion occurs *after* the defuzzification step; however, as we explain next, the same is not true for the defuzzified center-of-sets type-reduced set. As just explained, the center-of-sets type-reduced set, $Y_{\cos}(\mathbf{x})$, is described by α points ($y_1, ..., y_\alpha$); hence, its centroid, obtained during the defuzzification step, is given by (10-10), where each y_k has a FBF associated with it. Although (10-10) is a weighted average of these FBFs, it is *not* a FBF expansion because each y_k and $\mu_Y(y_k)$ depend on both the antecedent and consequent membership functions (Exercise 10-6). In summary, the concept of FBFs exists for center-of-sets type-reduction at the type-reduction stage of output processing; however, it does not exist at the defuzzification stage of output processing. It does not exist at all for the other kinds of type-reduction. So, FBFs do not seem to be so useful for general type-2 FLSs.

10.9 INTERVAL TYPE-2 FLSs

A general type-2 FLS is too complicated, because:

1. Calculating the *meet* operations in (10-9) for each fired rule is prohibitive, especially when product t-norm is used.
2. Type-reduction is prohibitive.
3. We presently have no rational basis for choosing secondary membership functions.

Our approach to simplification is to use interval type-2 fuzzy sets. We have already seen, in Sections 7.4 and 9.6, that it is easy to compute meet and join operations and perform type-reduction when interval type-2 fuzzy sets are used. Using interval sets for secondary membership functions also resolves the third complication; it distributes the uncertainty evenly among all admissible primary memberships. Today, there does not seem to be a rational reason for not choosing interval type-2 fuzzy sets; hence, in the rest of this chapter we focus our attention on interval type-2 FLSs. For additional discussions on the use of interval sets in fuzzy logic, see Hisdal (1981), Schwartz (1985), Turksen (1986), Gorzalezany (1987), Lea et al. (1996), Nguyen et al. (1997), Mabuchi (1997), Kreinovich et al. (1998), and Bustince and Burillo (2000).

10.9.1 Upper and lower membership functions for interval type-2 FLSs

The concepts of upper and lower membership functions, which were introduced in Section 3.3.4, play the central role in simplifying all of the calculations for an interval type-2 FLS. This would, therefore, be a good time for the reader to review that section. Because the notation used in that section was not keyed into rules, we briefly restate some of its results that we will need in the rest of this chapter.

1. *Membership function* $\mu_{\tilde{F}_k^l}(x_k)$: Let $\underline{\mu}_{\tilde{F}_k^l}(x_k)$ and $\overline{\mu}_{\tilde{F}_k^l}(x_k)$ denote the lower and upper membership functions for $\mu_{\tilde{F}_k^l}(x_k)$; then, the secondary membership function $\mu_{\tilde{F}_k^l}(x_k)$ can be represented in terms of them, as [see (3-16)]

$$\mu_{\tilde{F}_k^l}(x_k) = \int_{w^l \in [\underline{\mu}_{\tilde{F}_k^l}(x_k), \overline{\mu}_{\tilde{F}_k^l}(x_k)]} 1/w^l \qquad (10\text{-}19)$$

where $k = 1, \ldots, p$ (the number of antecedents) and $l = 1, \ldots, M$ (the number of rules). Similar results hold for membership functions of other interval type-2 fuzzy sets.

2. *Gaussian primary membership function with uncertain mean* (see Example 3-10): A very useful membership function is the Gaussian primary membership function with uncertain mean, i.e.,

$$\mu_k^l(x_k) = \exp\left[-\tfrac{1}{2}\left(\frac{x_k - m_k^l}{\sigma_k^l}\right)^2\right] \quad m_k^l \in [m_{k1}^l, m_{k2}^l] \qquad (10\text{-}20)$$

where $k = 1, \ldots, p$ (the number of antecedents) and $l = 1, \ldots, M$ (the number of rules). The upper membership function, $\overline{\mu}_k^l(x_k)$, is [see (3-18)]

$$\overline{\mu}_k^l(x_k) = \begin{cases} N(m_{k1}^l, \sigma_k^l; x_k) & x_k < m_{k1}^l \\ 1 & m_{k1}^l \leq x_k \leq m_{k2}^l \\ N(m_{k2}^l, \sigma_k^l; x_k) & x_k > m_{k2}^l \end{cases} \qquad (10\text{-}21)$$

and the lower membership function, $\underline{\mu}_k^l(x_k)$, is [see (3-19)]

$$\underline{\mu}_k^l(x_k) = \begin{cases} N(m_{k2}^l, \sigma_k^l; x_k) & x_k \leq \dfrac{m_{k1}^l + m_{k2}^l}{2} \\ N(m_{k1}^l, \sigma_k^l; x_k) & x_k > \dfrac{m_{k1}^l + m_{k2}^l}{2} \end{cases} \qquad (10\text{-}22)$$

3. *Gaussian primary membership function with uncertain standard deviation* (see Example 3-11): Another very useful membership function is the Gaussian primary membership function with uncertain standard deviation, i.e.,

$$\mu_k^l(x_k) = \exp\left[-\tfrac{1}{2}\left(\frac{x_k - m_k^l}{\sigma_k^l}\right)^2\right] \quad \sigma_k^l \in [\sigma_{k1}^l, \sigma_{k2}^l] \tag{10-23}$$

where $k = 1, \ldots, p$ (the number of antecedents) and $l = 1, \ldots, M$ (the number of rules). The upper membership function, $\overline{\mu}_k^l(x_k)$, is [see (3-20)]

$$\overline{\mu}_k^l(x_k) = N(m_k^l, \sigma_{k2}^l; x_k) \tag{10-24}$$

and the lower membership function, $\underline{\mu}_k^l(x_k)$, is [see (3-21)]

$$\underline{\mu}_k^l(x_k) = N(m_k^l, \sigma_{k1}^l; x_k) \tag{10-25}$$

10.9.2 Fuzzy inference engine revisited

The major result for an interval singleton type-2 FLS is summarized in the following:

Theorem 10-1: [Liang and Mendel (2000c)] *In an interval singleton type-2 FLS with meet under product or minimum t-norm: (a) the result of the input and antecedent operations, which are contained in the firing set* $\prod_{i=1}^{p} \mu_{\tilde{F}_i^l}(x_i') \equiv F^l(\mathbf{x}')$, *is an interval type-1 set, i.e.,*

$$F^l(\mathbf{x}') = [\underline{f}^l(\mathbf{x}'), \overline{f}^l(\mathbf{x}')] \equiv [\underline{f}^l, \overline{f}^l] \tag{10-26}$$

where

$$\underline{f}^l(\mathbf{x}') = \underline{\mu}_{\tilde{F}_1^l}(x_1') \star \cdots \star \underline{\mu}_{\tilde{F}_p^l}(x_p') \tag{10-27}$$

and

$$\overline{f}^l(\mathbf{x}') = \overline{\mu}_{\tilde{F}_1^l}(x_1') \star \cdots \star \overline{\mu}_{\tilde{F}_p^l}(x_p'); \tag{10-28}$$

(b) the rule R^l fired output consequent set, $\mu_{\tilde{B}^l}(y)$ in (10-9), is the type-1 fuzzy set

$$\mu_{\tilde{B}^l}(y) = \int_{b^l \in \left[\underline{f}^l \star \underline{\mu}_{\tilde{G}^l}(y), \overline{f}^l \star \overline{\mu}_{\tilde{G}^l}(y)\right]} 1/b^l, \quad y \in Y \qquad (10\text{-}29)$$

where $\underline{\mu}_{\tilde{G}^l}(y)$ and $\overline{\mu}_{\tilde{G}^l}(y)$ are the lower and upper membership grades of $\mu_{\tilde{G}^l}(y)$.

(c) suppose that N of the M rules in the FLS fire, where $N \le M$, and the combined output type-1 fuzzy set is obtained by combining the fired output consequent sets; i.e., $\mu_{\tilde{B}}(y) = \sqcup_{l=1}^{N} \mu_{\tilde{B}^l}(y) \; y \in Y$; then,

$$\mu_{\tilde{B}}(y) = \int_{b \in \left[\left[\underline{f}^1 \star \underline{\mu}_{\tilde{G}^1}(y)\right] \vee \cdots \vee \left[\underline{f}^N \star \underline{\mu}_{\tilde{G}^N}(y)\right], \left[\overline{f}^1 \star \overline{\mu}_{\tilde{G}^1}(y)\right] \vee \cdots \vee \left[\overline{f}^N \star \overline{\mu}_{\tilde{G}^N}(y)\right]\right]} 1/b, \quad y \in Y \qquad (10\text{-}30)$$

Proof: (a) From Theorem 7-2, it follows that in (10-9)

$$\prod_{i=1}^{P} \mu_{\tilde{F}_i^l}(x_i') = \left[\underline{f}^l, \overline{f}^l\right] \qquad (10\text{-}31)$$

where $\underline{f}^l$ and $\overline{f}^l$ are defined in (10-27) and (10-28), respectively.

(b) Using (10-31) and Theorem 7-2, (10-9) can be expressed as

$$\mu_{\tilde{B}^l}(y) = \mu_{\tilde{G}^l}(y) \sqcap \left[\underline{f}^l, \overline{f}^l\right] \equiv \left[\underline{b}^l(y), \overline{b}^l(y)\right], \quad y \in Y \qquad (10\text{-}32)$$

where

$$\underline{b}^l(y) = \underline{f}^l \star \underline{\mu}_{\tilde{G}^l}(y) \qquad (10\text{-}33)$$

and

$$\overline{b}^l(y) = \overline{f}^l \star \overline{\mu}_{\tilde{G}^l}(y) \qquad (10\text{-}34)$$

Equation (10-29) is a restatement of (10-32)–(10-34).

(c) Using (10-32) and Theorem 7-1, we can express $\mu_{\tilde{B}}(y)$ as

$$\mu_{\tilde{B}}(y) = \sqcup_{l=1}^{N}\mu_{\tilde{B}^l}(y) = \sqcup_{l=1}^{N}\left[\underline{b}^l(y), \overline{b}^l(y)\right] \equiv \left[\underline{b}(y), \overline{b}(y)\right], \quad y \in Y \qquad (10\text{-}35)$$

where

$$\underline{b}(y) = \underline{b}^1(y) \vee \underline{b}^2(y) \vee \cdots \vee \underline{b}^N(y) \qquad (10\text{-}36)$$

and

$$\overline{b}(y) = \overline{b}^1(y) \vee \overline{b}^2(y) \vee \cdots \vee \overline{b}^N(y) \qquad (10\text{-}37)$$

Equation (10-30) is a restatement of (10-35)–(10-37), one that also uses (10-33) and (10-34). ∎

This theorem was rather easy to prove, because of singleton fuzzification. Other versions of it will be re-examined in Chapters 11 and 12.

Example 10-2: Here we consider a pictorial description of parts (a)–(c) of Theorem 10-1 using the minimum and product t-norms. As such, it is similar to Example 5-1, and will let us contrast pictorial descriptions for an interval singleton type-2 FLS with a singleton type-1 FLS. It will also help us to better understand the flow of rule-uncertainties through an interval singleton type-2 FLS.

Figure 10-6 depicts input and antecedent operations [(10-27) and (10-28)] for a two-antecedent–single consequent rule, singleton fuzzification, and minimum or product t-norms. In all cases, the firing strength is an interval type-1 set $[\underline{f}^l, \overline{f}^l]$, where $\underline{f}^l = \underline{\mu}_{\tilde{F}_1^l}(x_1') \star \underline{\mu}_{\tilde{F}_2^l}(x_2')$ and $\overline{f}^l = \overline{\mu}_{\tilde{F}_1^l}(x_1') \star \overline{\mu}_{\tilde{F}_2^l}(x_2')$. Observe, for example, that $\overline{\mu}_{\tilde{F}_1^l}(x_1')$ occurs at the intersection of the vertical line at x_1' with $\overline{\mu}_{\tilde{F}_1^l}(x_1)$. For minimum t-norm,

$$\underline{f}^l = \min\left[\underline{\mu}_{\tilde{F}_1^l}(x_1'), \underline{\mu}_{\tilde{F}_2^l}(x_2')\right] \qquad (10\text{-}38)$$

and

$$\overline{f}^l = \min\left[\overline{\mu}_{\tilde{F}_1^l}(x_1'), \overline{\mu}_{\tilde{F}_2^l}(x_2')\right] \qquad (10\text{-}39)$$

whereas, for product t-norm,

$$\underline{f}^l = \underline{\mu}_{\tilde{F}_1^l}(x_1') \times \underline{\mu}_{\tilde{F}_2^l}(x_2') \tag{10-40}$$

and

$$\overline{f}^l = \overline{\mu}_{\tilde{F}_1^l}(x_1') \times \overline{\mu}_{\tilde{F}_2^l}(x_2') \tag{10-41}$$

The main thing to observe from Figure 10-6 (a) and (b) is that, regardless of the t-norm, the result of input and antecedent operations is an interval—the firing interval.

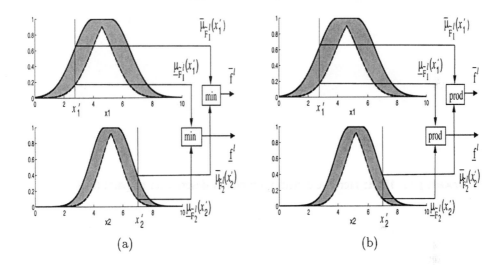

Figure 10-6: Pictorial description of input and antecedent operations for an interval singleton type-2 FLS. (a) minimum t-norm, and (b) product t-norm.

Figure 10-7 depicts $\mu_{\tilde{B}^l}(y)$ for a two-rule ($l = 1, 2$) singleton type-2 FLS. It is obtained by implementing (10-29) at each $y \in Y$. For example, $\overline{f}^l$ is t-normed with the upper membership function $\overline{\mu}_{\tilde{G}^l}(y)$ to give the solid curve $\overline{f}^l \star \overline{\mu}_{\tilde{G}^l}(y)$ for $\forall y \in Y$, and $\underline{f}^l$ is t-normed with the lower membership function $\underline{\mu}_{\tilde{G}^l}(y)$ to give the dashed curve $\underline{f}^l \star \underline{\mu}_{\tilde{G}^l}(y)$ for $\forall y \in Y$. The primary membership of $\mu_{\tilde{B}^l}(y)$ $\forall y \in Y$ [i.e., the $FOU(\tilde{B}^l)$] is the area between these two functions. We have darkened in this area.

Figure 10-8 depicts the combined type-2 output set for the two-rule singleton type-2 FLS, where the fired output sets are combined as in (10-30) using the maximum t-conorm. The upper solid curve corresponds to $\left[\overline{f}^1 \star \overline{\mu}_{\tilde{G}^1}(y)\right] \vee \left[\overline{f}^2 \star \overline{\mu}_{\tilde{G}^2}(y)\right]$ for $\forall y \in Y$, whereas the lower dashed curve corresponds to $\left[\underline{f}^1 \star \underline{\mu}_{\tilde{G}^1}(y)\right] \vee \left[\underline{f}^2 \star \underline{\mu}_{\tilde{G}^2}(y)\right]$ for $\forall y \in Y$. The primary membership of $\mu_{\tilde{B}}(y)$ $\forall y \in Y$ [i.e., the $FOU(\tilde{B})$] is the area between these two functions, which we have darkened in. Type-reduction is applied to $\mu_{\tilde{B}}(y)$ $\forall y \in Y$.

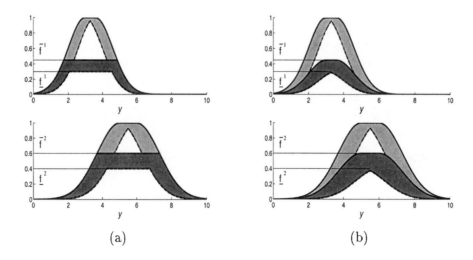

Figure 10-7: Pictorial description of consequent operations for an interval singleton type-2 FLS. (a) fired output sets with minimum t-norm, and (b) fired output sets with product t-norm.

The reader should compare Figures 10-6–10-8 with their respective type-1 counterparts in Figures 5-4–5-6 to fully appreciate the way in which type-2 fuzzy logic has let the uncertainties about antecedent and consequent membership functions flow from the input of the interval singleton type-2 FLS to the output of its inference engine. ■

10.9.3 Type-reduction and defuzzification revisited

From Figure 10-1, we see that a singleton type-2 FLS is a mapping $f_{s2} : \mathfrak{R}^p \to \mathfrak{R}^1$. After fuzzification, fuzzy inference, type-reduction, and defuzzification, we obtain a crisp output. Based on Theorem 10-1, we know that for an interval singleton type-2 FLS that uses either minimum or product t-norm, the result of input and antecedent operations is an interval type-1 set—the firing interval—which is determined by its left-most and right-most points, $\underline{f}^l$ and $\overline{f}^l$, respectively. The fired output consequent set $\mu_{\tilde{B}^l}(y)$ of rule R^l can be obtained from the firing interval using (10-29), and is also an interval set.

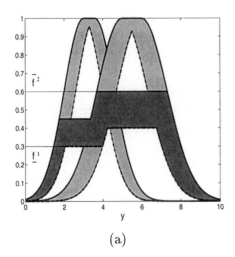
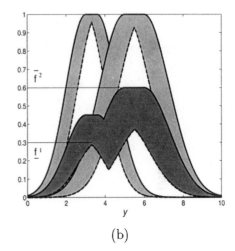

(a)   (b)

Figure 10-8: Pictorial description of (a) combined output sets for the two fired output sets depicted in Figure 10-7 (a), and (b) combined output sets for the two fired output sets depicted in Figure 10-7 (b).

The next step, after fuzzy inference, is type-reduction. Regardless of which type-reduction method we choose, because we are now dealing with interval sets, the type-reduced set is also an interval set, and has the following structure:

$$Y_{TR} = [y_l, y_r] \tag{10-42}$$

For illustrative purposes, let us focus on center-of-sets type reduction, Y_{cos}, which can be expressed as [see (9-36)]

$$Y_{cos}(\mathbf{x}) = [y_l, y_r] = \int_{y^1 \in [y_l^1, y_r^1]} \cdots \int_{y^M \in [y_l^M, y_r^M]} \int_{f^1 \in [\underline{f}^1, \bar{f}^1]} \cdots \int_{f^M \in [\underline{f}^M, \bar{f}^M]} 1 \Bigg/ \frac{\sum_{i=1}^{M} f^i y^i}{\sum_{i=1}^{M} f^i} \tag{10-43}$$

where: $Y_{cos}(\mathbf{x})$ is an interval set determined by its two end-points, y_l and y_r; and $[y_l^i, y_r^i]$ corresponds to the centroid of the type-2 interval consequent set $\tilde{G}^i$, which can be obtained from (9-21), as

$$C_{\tilde{G}^i} = \int_{\theta_1 \in J_{y_1}} \cdots \int_{\theta_N \in J_{y_N}} 1 / \frac{\sum_{i=1}^{N} y_i \theta_i}{\sum_{i=1}^{N} \theta_i} = [y_l^i, y_r^i] \qquad (10\text{-}44)$$

Note that $[y_l^i, y_r^i]$ $(i = 1, \ldots, M)$ must be pre-computed *before* the computation of $Y_{\cos}(\mathbf{x})$.

Clearly, to compute $Y_{\cos}(\mathbf{x})$ we just need to compute its two end-points, y_l and y_r. Let the values of f^i and y^i that are associated with y_l be denoted f_l^i and y_l^i, respectively, and the values of f^i and y^i that are associated with y_r be denoted f_r^i and y_r^i, respectively; hence, from (10-43), we see that

$$y_l = \frac{\sum_{i=1}^{M} f_l^i y_l^i}{\sum_{i=1}^{M} f_l^i} \qquad (10\text{-}45)$$

and

$$y_r = \frac{\sum_{i=1}^{M} f_r^i y_r^i}{\sum_{i=1}^{M} f_r^i} \qquad (10\text{-}46)$$

Note that, although we have not shown it explicitly, y_l, f_l^i, y_r, and f_r^i all depend on FLS input $\mathbf{x}$; i.e., change $\mathbf{x}$ and one obtains different values for these four quantities.

To compute y_l we need to determine $\{f_l^i, i = 1, \ldots, M\}$ and its associated $\{y_l^i, i = 1, \ldots, M\}$, and, to compute y_r we need to determine $\{f_r^i, i = 1, \ldots, M\}$ and its associated $\{y_r^i, i = 1, \ldots, M\}$. This can be done using the exact computational procedure given in Theorem 9-1. Here we briefly provide the computation procedure for y_r.

Without loss of generality, assume that the pre-computed y_r^i are arranged in *ascending order*; i.e., $y_r^1 \le y_r^2 \le \cdots \le y_r^M$. Then,

1. Compute y_r in (10-46) by initially setting $f_r^i = (\underline{f}^i + \overline{f}^i)/2$ for $i = 1, \ldots,$ M, where $\underline{f}^i$ and $\overline{f}^i$ have been previously computed using (10-27) and (10-28), respectively, and let $y_r' \equiv y_r$.

2. Find R $(1 \le R \le M-1)$ such that $y_r^R \le y_r' \le y_r^{R+1}$.

3. Compute y_r in (10-46) with $f_r^i = \underline{f}^i$ for $i \le R$ and $f_r^i = \overline{f}^i$ for $i > R$, and let $y_r'' \equiv y_r$.

4. If $y_r'' \ne y_r'$, then go to Step 5. If $y_r'' = y_r'$, then stop and set $y_r'' \equiv y_r$.

5. Set y_r' equal to y_r'', and return to Step 2.

Recall that this four step iterative procedure (Step 1 is an initialization step) has been proven in Theorem 9-1 to converge to the exact solution in no more than M iterations [here N in (9-15) is replaced by M in (10-46)]. Note that it is not necessary to reorder[2] the f_r^i.

Observe that in this procedure, the number R is very important. For $i \le R$, $f_r^i = \underline{f}^i$, whereas for $i > R$ $f_r^i = \overline{f}^i$; hence, y_r in (10-46) can be represented as

$$y_r = y_r\left(\underline{f}^1,...,\underline{f}^R,\overline{f}^{R+1},...,\overline{f}^M,y_r^1,...,y_r^M\right) \qquad (10\text{-}47)$$

The procedure for computing y_l is very similar to the one just given for y_r. According to part (b) of Theorem 9-1, just replace y_r^i by y_l^i, and, in step 2 find L $(1 \le L \le M-1)$ such that $y_l^L \le y_l' \le y_l^{L+1}$. Additionally, in step 3, we now compute y_l in (10-45) with $f_l^i = \overline{f}^i$ for $i \le L$ and $f_l^i = \underline{f}^i$ for $i > L$. Then y_l in (10-45) can be represented as

$$y_l = y_l\left(\overline{f}^1,...,\overline{f}^L,\underline{f}^{L+1},...,\underline{f}^M,y_l^1,...,y_l^M\right) \qquad (10\text{-}48)$$

This completes type-reduction for an interval singleton type-2 FLS.

Because $Y_{\cos}$ is an interval set, we defuzzify it using the average of y_l and y_r; hence, the defuzzified output of an interval singleton type-2 FLS is

$$y(\mathbf{x}) = f_{s2}(\mathbf{x}) = \frac{y_l + y_r}{2} \qquad (10\text{-}49)$$

Example 10-3: [Karnik and Mendel (1998b)] Here we examine a function approximation example that is different from the usual function approximation examples to which a type-1 FLS has been applied. The function to be approximated is $y = 100 - x^2$

---

[2]We discuss the issue of rule reordering at the end of Section 10.9.4.

where $x \in [-10,10]$. What is novel about this example is that we only have access to noise-corrupted measurements of y. Recognizing this ahead of time, we create an experiment where we collect 10 realizations of each measurement. We do this for nine (x, y) pairs. Each of these pairs includes values of y that are corrupted by additive noise that is uniformly distributed in $[10, 10]$. For each applied input x^i $(i = 1,...,9)$, we then find the minimum (y_{min}^i) and the maximum (y_{max}^i) of the 10 y values. The nine $(x^i,[y_{min}^i, y_{max}^i])$ pairs we obtained are:

$$(x^1,[y_{min}^1, y_{max}^1]) = (-10,[-7.79, 6.49])$$
$$(x^2,[y_{min}^2, y_{max}^2]) = (-7.5,[34.72, 52.93])$$
$$(x^3,[y_{min}^3, y_{max}^3]) = (-5,[66.12, 84.1])$$
$$(x^4,[y_{min}^4, y_{max}^4]) = (-2.5,[84.93, 101.75])$$
$$(x^5,[y_{min}^5, y_{max}^5]) = (0,[93.09, 109.95])$$

$$(x^6,[y_{min}^6, y_{max}^6]) = (2.5,[88.02, 103.53])$$
$$(x^7,[y_{min}^7, y_{max}^7]) = (5,[65.37, 84.32])$$
$$(x^8,[y_{min}^8, y_{max}^8]) = (7.5,[34.14, 50.85])$$
$$(x^9,[y_{min}^9, y_{max}^9]) = (10,[-9.62, 9.62])$$

The FLS function approximator forms one rule from each of these pairs, where each of the nine rules is of the form

$$\text{IF } x \text{ is } A \text{ , THEN } y \text{ is } \tilde{G} \tag{10-50}$$

Observe that, because only the y-values are uncertain in the given input–output pairs, we chose the antecedent fuzzy sets as type-1 and the consequent fuzzy sets as type-2. In this example, we chose the antecedent sets to be type-1 Gaussians and the consequent sets to be Gaussian primary membership functions but with uncertain means (as in Example 3-10, Figure 3-8). The resulting type-2 FLS used singleton fuzzification (since the input x-values could be specified perfectly), maximum t-conorm, product t-norm, product implication, and center-of-sets type-reduction. Exercise 10-8 asks the reader to construct the structure of the singleton type-2 FLS for this special type-2 situation.

Membership functions for the antecedent sets and FOUs for two of the consequent sets are depicted in Figure 10-9. The centers of the Gaussian antecedent membership functions were located at the nine sampled values of x given earlier. Each antecedent set has the same standard deviation, arbitrarily chosen to be 1.25. Each consequent set is an interval type-2 set that was obtained from a Gaussian primary membership function whose mean takes values in the interval $[y_{min}^i, y_{max}^i]$. For illustrative purposes, we chose the standard deviation of the nine consequent sets also to be the same, namely 40. In this way, there is a large overlap in the consequent membership functions for the nine rules.

Figure 10-9 (a) also depicts the antecedent membership function values for a particular input $x' = 5.5$. This x' has non-zero memberships in three antecedent sets: 0.056135 in the set centered at 2.5 (x^6), 0.92312 in the set centered at 5 (x^7), and 0.27804 in the set centered at 7.5 (x^8); consequently, three rules were fired at this x', rules 6, 7, and 8.

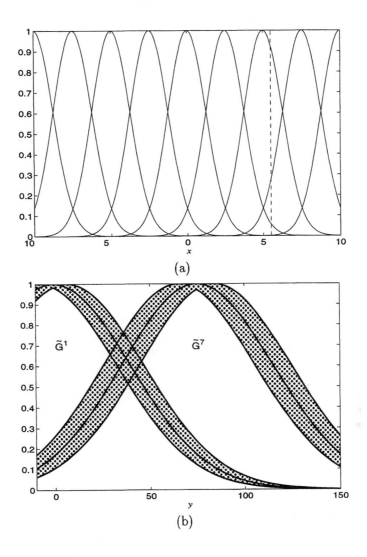

Figure 10-9: (a) Membership functions for the antecedent fuzzy sets of Example 10-3. Figure (b) shows the FOUs for the first and seventh consequent sets. The thick dark line in (b) at the center of each FOU is a Gaussian that is centered at $c^l = (y^l_{min} + y^l_{max})/2$. In (a) the position of a particular input point $x = 5.5$ is also shown.

The center-of-sets type-reducer replaced each consequent set by its centroid and scaled it (because of product implication and t-norm) by the appropriate degree of firing. In this case, the centroids of the three fired consequents (associated with the antecedent sets centered at x^6, x^7 and x^8, respectively) are interval sets whose domains were computed using Theorem 9-1 to be [88.02, 103.53], [65.37, 84.32], and [34.14, 50.85], respectively (Exercise 10-9). The centroids and their respective degrees of firing are shown in Figure 10-10 (a).

The center-of-sets type-reduced set for $x' = 5.5$ is depicted in Figure 10-10 (b). It was calculated using the iterative four-step procedure that was explained earlier. The domain of this type-reduced set is [59.39, 77.70]. We used the mid-point of this interval as the defuzzified output of the FLS. This value is equal to 68.55 and is shown with a dashed line in Figure 10-10 (b). The actual function value at $x' = 5.5$ is 69.75. The two end-points of the domain of the type-reduced set indicate the lower and upper bounds for its crisp output value of 68.55.

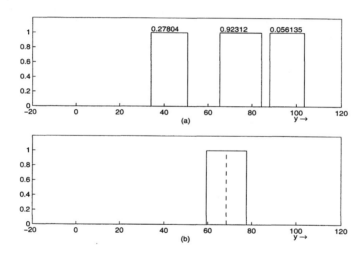

Figure 10-10: The input $x = 5.5$ has non-zero memberships in three antecedent sets. Corresponding to these three sets, three rules are fired. (a) Centroids of the three fired sets and their corresponding degrees of firing and (b) corresponding center-of-sets type-reduced set and the crisp output value (dashed).

Figure 10-11 compares the true function value with the crisp output of the interval singleton type-2 FLS over the entire domain of x, and also shows upper and lower bounds (Exercise 10-10). For each value of x these bounds correspond to the type-reduced set. They give a measure of the uncertainty in the approximation caused by noisy training values, something that could not be obtained just from a type-1 FLS approximation.

We were curious to learn if we could obtain exactly the same defuzzified output that was obtained from the above type-2 FLS using a type-1 FLS. After observing experimentally that this was possible, we obtained the following interesting theoretical result (see also [Zeng and Singh (1997)]):

Theorem 10-2: [Karnik and Mendel (1998b)] *Consider a singleton type-1 FLS that: (a) uses the same antecedent type-1 fuzzy sets as used in an interval singleton type-2 FLS; (b) has type-1 consequent sets having centroids, c^l, where*

$$c^l = \frac{y^l_{min} + y^l_{max}}{2} \tag{10-51}$$

and (c) uses center-of-sets defuzzification.[3] Then, its output is the same as the crisp output of the interval singleton type-2 FLS used in this example in which the consequents are modeled as Gaussian primary membership functions with uncertain means where $m^l \in [y^l_{min}, y^l_{max}]$ and interval secondary membership functions, but, $y^l_{max} - y^l_{min}$ must be small as compared to the standard deviation, σ, of each Gaussian.

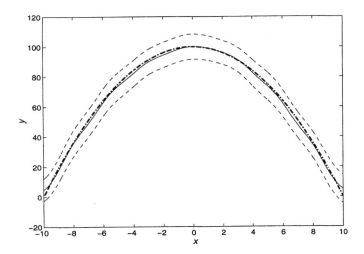

Figure 10-11: The solid line is the crisp output of the interval singleton type-2 FLS; the dash-dotted line is the actual quadratic function; and the dashed lines indicate the upper and lower bounds of the type-reduced set.

---

[3] Height defuzzification can also be used.

Proof: The proof of this theorem uses many of the results we have covered about interval sets. Observe, from (9-37), that when only the consequents are type-2, then $Y_{cos}(\mathbf{x})$ can be expressed as

$$Y_{cos}(\mathbf{x}) = \sum_{l=1}^{M} \frac{T_{i=1}^{p} \mu_{F_i^l}(x_i)}{\sum_{l=1}^{M} T_{i=1}^{p} \mu_{F_i^l}(x_i)} C_{\tilde{G}^l} \tag{10-52}$$

where both the summations indicate algebraic summation. Let

$$\phi_l(\mathbf{x}) = \frac{T_{i=1}^{p} \mu_{F_i^l}(x_i)}{\sum_{l=1}^{M} T_{i=1}^{p} \mu_{F_i^l}(x_i)} \tag{10-53}$$

so that (10-52) can be re-expressed as

$$Y_{cos}(\mathbf{x}) = \sum_{l=1}^{M} \phi_l(\mathbf{x}) C_{\tilde{G}^l} \tag{10-54}$$

Since $y_{max}^l - y_{min}^l$ is small as compared to the standard deviation of the type-2 consequent sets, it follows from Example 9-4 that $C_{\tilde{G}^l} \approx [y_{min}^l, y_{max}^l]$. Using Theorem 7-4 (in which $\phi_l(\mathbf{x})$ is treated as the artificial interval type-1 number $[\phi_l(\mathbf{x}), \phi_l(\mathbf{x})]$), it is easy to show that $\phi_l(\mathbf{x}) C_{\tilde{G}^l} = [\phi_l(\mathbf{x}) y_{min}^l, \phi_l(\mathbf{x}) y_{max}^l]$. Using Theorem 7-3, it then follows that

$$Y_{cos}(x) = \left[\sum_{l=1}^{M} \phi_l(\mathbf{x}) y_{min}^l, \sum_{l=1}^{M} \phi_l(\mathbf{x}) y_{max}^l \right] \tag{10-55}$$

Because the centroid of an interval is its midpoint, the centroid of $Y_{cos}(\mathbf{x})$ can be expressed as

$$\begin{aligned} c_{Y_{cos}} &= \left[\sum_{l=1}^{M} \phi_l(\mathbf{x}) y_{min}^l + \sum_{l=1}^{M} \phi_l(\mathbf{x}) y_{max}^l \right] \Big/ 2 \\ &= \sum_{l=1}^{M} \phi_l(\mathbf{x}) \left[\frac{y_{min}^l + y_{max}^l}{2} \right] \end{aligned} \tag{10-56}$$

We see, from (10-56), that $c_{Y_{cos}}$ is the same as the output of a singleton type-1 FLS [e.g., (5-24)] that uses center-of-sets defuzzification and consequent sets whose centroids, c^l, are $c^l = (y_{min}^l + y_{max}^l)/2$. ◆

Observe that we did not have to use the fact that the number of antecedents, p, is equal to 1 to derive (10-56), which means that this theorem is also applicable to multiple-antecedent rules, even though the rules in (10-50) are single-antecedent ones.

If (10-56) is re-expressed as the sum of two terms, one involving y^l_{min} and the other involving y^l_{max}, we can interpret it in yet another way, as the average output of two type-1 FLSs. One of the type-1 FLSs uses y^l_{min} for its consequent centers or centroid, and the other uses y^l_{max} for its consequent or centroid.

Note that this theorem does not hold if the standard deviations of the consequent Gaussian primary membership functions are not small as compared to the interval over which the means of the Gaussian vary; hence, it is quite limited.

Theorem 10-2 suggests the question: Why do we need to use an interval singleton type-2 FLS approximation instead of a singleton type-1 FLS approximation, since (under the conditions in Theorem 10-2) they both give exactly the same defuzzified outputs? As noted above (prior to the statement of Theorem 10-2), for each value of x the bounds provided by the type-reduced set give a measure of the uncertainty in the approximation caused by noisy training values, something that cannot be obtained just from a type-1 FLS approximation. Just as the standard deviation of the estimate is important in a statistical function approximation method, the bound provided by the type-reduced set is also important. Additionally, Theorem 10-2 requires a rather restrictive constraint between the standard deviation of the consequent Gaussian primary membership functions and the intervals over which their means may vary; so, in general, we will not get the same results when using a singleton type-2 FLS and a singleton type-1 FLS. ■

Before we get carried away with exhuberance about the very good results that we have obtained in Example 10-3 for function approximation, we wish to point out some shortcomings of that example:

1. The quadratic function $y = 100 - x^2$ is a very simple function; it has exactly one extremum, which was (cleverly) located exactly at one of our sample points, namely $x = 0$.

2. The more general function approximation problem is one in which we do not know the function ahead of time; we only have the data $(x^i, [y^i_{min}, y^i_{max}])$, $i = 1, ..., N$. Kosko (1997) has proven that an optimal choice for the x^i is to locate them at the extrema of $y(x)$. He calls this "patching the bumps." Unfortunately, we do not know where to choose the x values ahead of time so as to obtain the extrema. Of course, we could sample the domain of x very finely so as to capture all the extrema; but, doing this could lead to a FLS that has a very large number of rules (although other approaches, such as a back-propagation design, could be used to create and tune a fixed number of rules and then an SVD–QR method could be used to reduce the number of rules). Additionally, when only noisy values of $y(x)$ are available, every value of $y(x)$ may appear to be an extremum.

3. The function we have used depends only on a single variable. Repeating this example for multi-dimensional functions could be quite challenging. For such functions, the sampling issue discussed in Comment 2 is even more severe.

4. The use of a FLS to perform function approximation has been motivated by the universal approximation results for a FLS. For noise-free data there are many excellent methods already available to perform function approximation, so to focus on a FLS to do this may not be so beneficial (noted also in [Kreinovich, et al. (1998)]). For noisy data, one can use a method like stochastic approximation.

From these comments it is clear that, although I have used a function approximation example to *illustrate* the behavior of an interval singleton type-2 FLS, I am not advocating the use of a FLS for function approximation.

10.9.4 FBFs revisited

Equations (10-45) and (10-46) describe the end-points of the type-reduced set. Each has the structure of a FBF expansion; hence, *an interval singleton type-2 FLS is characterized by two FBF expansions.* Next, let us take a closer look at these two FBF expansions.

Equation (10-45) can be expressed as[4]

$$
y_l = \frac{\sum_{i=1}^{M} f_l^i y_l^i}{\sum_{i=1}^{M} f_l^i} = \frac{\sum_{i=1}^{L} \overline{f}^i y_l^i + \sum_{j=L+1}^{M} \underline{f}^j y_l^j}{\sum_{i=1}^{L} \overline{f}^i + \sum_{j=L+1}^{M} \underline{f}^j}
$$
$$
= \sum_{i=1}^{M} y_l^i p_l^i(\mathbf{x}) = \mathbf{y}_l^{\mathrm{T}} \mathbf{p}_l(\mathbf{x})
$$

(10-57)

where $p_l^i(\mathbf{x})$ are the FBFs associated with the calculation of y_l, i.e.,

$$
p_l^i(\mathbf{x}) = \frac{h_l^i}{\sum_{i=1}^{L} \overline{f}^i + \sum_{i=L+1}^{M} \underline{f}^j}
$$

(10-58)

in which

$$
h_l^i = \begin{cases} \overline{f}^i & i = 1,\dots, L(\mathbf{x}) \\ \underline{f}^i & i = L(\mathbf{x})+1,\dots, M \end{cases}
$$

(10-59)

We show the explicit dependence of L on $\mathbf{x}$ to emphasize the fact that for each $\mathbf{x}$ L can change.

---

[4]Remember that, for notational simplicity, we have not shown y_l as $y_l(\mathbf{x})$ and f_l^i as $f_l^i(\mathbf{x})$.

Similarly, (10-46) can be expressed as

$$y_r = \frac{\sum_{i=1}^{M} f_r^i y_r^i}{\sum_{i=1}^{M} f_r^i} = \frac{\sum_{i=1}^{R} \underline{f}^i y_r^i + \sum_{i=R+1}^{M} \overline{f}^i y_r^i}{\sum_{i=1}^{R} \underline{f}^i + \sum_{i=R+1}^{M} \overline{f}^i} \tag{10-60}$$
$$= \sum_{i=1}^{M} y_r^i p_r^i(\mathbf{x}) = \mathbf{y}_r^T \mathbf{p}_r(\mathbf{x})$$

where $p_r^i(\mathbf{x})$ are the FBFs associated with the calculation of y_r, i.e.,

$$p_r^i(\mathbf{x}) = \frac{h_r^i}{\sum_{i=1}^{R} \underline{f}^i + \sum_{i=R+1}^{M} \overline{f}^i} \tag{10-61}$$

in which

$$h_r^i = \begin{cases} \underline{f}^i & i = 1, \dots, R(\mathbf{x}) \\ \overline{f}^i & i = R(\mathbf{x})+1, \dots, M \end{cases} \tag{10-62}$$

There are two problems with the FBF expansions in (10-57) and (10-60) that we are now going to address.

1. Although we have been able to write formulas for y_l and y_r, we cannot actually compute these quantities using these formulas, because we do not know $L(\mathbf{x})$ and $R(\mathbf{x})$ ahead of time. These latter quantities can only be determined using our four-step iterative procedure for computing the center-of-sets type-reduced set (also true for the other kinds of type-reduction). This is very different from the type-1 FBF expansion formulas (5-24) and (6-17), which not only *describe* the type-1 FBF expansions, but can also be used to *compute* them. Note, however, that once $L(\mathbf{x})$ and $R(\mathbf{x})$ are known, then it still may be very useful to organize and describe the calculations of y_l and y_r using (10-57) and (10-60). These formulas will, for example, be used as the bases for the back-propagation design method that is described in Section 10.10.3.

2. The second problem has to do with the re-ordering of the rule-ordered y_l^i or y_r^i, as required by the four-step iterative procedure for computing y_l or y_r. Our Section 5.7 and Section 6.4 FBF expansions have always had an inherent rule-ordering associated with them; i.e., rules $R^1, R^2, \dots, R^M$ always established the first, second, ..., and Mth FBFs. This rule-ordering has been lost in (10-57) and (10-60) and may need to be restored for later use.

Since what we are going to describe next about rule-ordered FBFs applies to the FBF expansions for either y_l or y_r, we shall simplify the notation below by omitting the subscript l or r on y.

Initially, we have a collection of rule-ordered numbers, denoted here as $\{z^1, ..., z^M\}$, which are re-ordered during the iterative computation method for computing y_l and y_r by a rank-ordering process, with the smallest value appearing first and the largest value appearing last. Let $\{y^1, ..., y^M\}$ denote these re-ordered numbers; they correspond, for example, to the y_l^i in (10-57). Collecting $\{z^1, ..., z^M\}$ and $\{y^1, ..., y^M\}$ into two vectors, $\mathbf{z}$ and $\mathbf{y}$, respectively, it is easy to see that they are related by a permutation matrix that depends on $\mathbf{x}$, $\mathbf{Q}(\mathbf{x})$, i.e.,

$$\mathbf{y} = \mathbf{Q}(\mathbf{x})\mathbf{z} \qquad (10\text{-}63)$$

We can re-express (10-57) or (10-60) in vector-matrix format, as $y = \mathbf{y}^T\mathbf{p}(\mathbf{x})$ where $\mathbf{p}(\mathbf{x}) = (p^1(\mathbf{x}), ..., p^M(\mathbf{x}))^T$; hence, using (10-63), we can express y as a function of the original rule-ordered numbers $\{z^1, ..., z^M\}$, as

$$y = \mathbf{y}^T\mathbf{p}(\mathbf{x}) = \mathbf{z}^T[\mathbf{Q}^T(\mathbf{x})\mathbf{p}(\mathbf{x})] \equiv \mathbf{z}^T\phi(\mathbf{x}) \qquad (10\text{-}64)$$

in which $\phi(\mathbf{x})$ is a vector of *rule-ordered FBFs*. So, to obtain a *rule-ordered FBF expansion*, we need to pre-multiply the re-ordered FBFs, $\mathbf{p}(\mathbf{x})$, by the transposition of the permutation matrix, $\mathbf{Q}(\mathbf{x})$; i.e., the rule-ordered FBFs are

$$\phi(\mathbf{x}) = \mathbf{Q}^T(\mathbf{x})\mathbf{p}(\mathbf{x}) \qquad (10\text{-}65)$$

Based on (10-64) and (10-65), we can express (10-57), as $y_l = \mathbf{y}_l^T\mathbf{p}_l(\mathbf{x}) = \mathbf{z}_l^T\phi_l(\mathbf{x})$ where $\phi_l(\mathbf{x}) = \mathbf{Q}_l^T(\mathbf{x})\mathbf{p}_l(\mathbf{x})$, and (10-60) as $y_r = \mathbf{y}_r^T\mathbf{p}_r(\mathbf{x}) = \mathbf{z}_r^T\phi_r(\mathbf{x})$ where $\phi_r(\mathbf{x}) = \mathbf{Q}_r^T(\mathbf{x})\mathbf{p}_r(\mathbf{x})$; hence, *we can think about the FBF expansion in either the rule-ordered format or in the rule re-ordered format without any loss of generality.*

10.10 DESIGNING INTERVAL SINGLETON TYPE-2 FLSS

Our goal in this section is to parallel Section 5.9 to see how, or if, design methods that have already been developed for a type-1 FLS can be extended to a type-2 FLS. As in the Section 5.9 design methods, our type-2 FLS design methods will be associated with the following problem:

We are given a collection of N input–output numerical data *training* pairs, $(\mathbf{x}^{(1)}:y^{(1)}),(\mathbf{x}^{(2)}:y^{(2)}),\ldots,(\mathbf{x}^{(N)}:y^{(N)})$, where $\mathbf{x}$ is the vector input and y is the scalar output of an interval singleton type-2 FLS. Our goal is to completely specify this type-2 FLS using the training data.

For illustrative purposes, all designs assume Gaussian primary membership functions with uncertain mean and interval secondary membership functions (as in Figure 3-8), product implication and t-norm, center-of-sets type-reduction, and defuzzification using the centroid of the type-reduced set; hence, our type-2 FLS is described by the contents of Section 10.9. Note that the basic principles used in each design procedure carry over to many other type-2 FLSs.

To begin, as in Section 5.9, we must explain how the training data can be interpreted as a collection of IF–THEN rules. Each rule is now of the form given in (10-2), where $\tilde{F}_i^l$ are type-2 fuzzy sets that are associated with the elements of $\mathbf{x}^{(t)}$ and are described by the Gaussian primary membership functions with uncertain mean, as in (10-20), i.e.,

$$\mu_i^l(x_i) = \exp\left[-\tfrac{1}{2}\left(\frac{x_i - m_i^l}{\sigma_i^l}\right)^2\right] \quad m_i^l \in [m_{i1}^l, m_{i2}^l] \qquad (10\text{-}66)$$

where $i = 1, \ldots, p$ and $l = 1, \ldots, M$. The consequent sets are also interval Gaussian primary membership functions with uncertain mean, i.e.,

$$\mu^j(y) = \exp\left[-\tfrac{1}{2}\left(\frac{y - m^j}{\sigma^j}\right)^2\right] \quad m^j \in [m_1^j, m_2^j] \quad j = 1, \ldots, M \qquad (10\text{-}67)$$

Note that the centroid of each $\mu^j(y)$, $C_{\tilde{G}^j}$, is an interval type-1 set, i.e.,

$$C_{\tilde{G}^j} = [y_l^j, y_r^j] \quad j = 1, \ldots, M \qquad (10\text{-}68)$$

Each design method establishes how to specify all the parameters of the membership functions in (10-66) and (10-67) using the training pairs $(\mathbf{x}^{(1)}:y^{(1)})$, $(\mathbf{x}^{(2)}:y^{(2)})$, ..., $(\mathbf{x}^{(N)}:y^{(N)})$.

As in Sections 5.9 and 6.6, how many rules there can be in the interval singleton type-2 FLS depends on the design method that is used to construct it. If no tuning of the FLS parameters is done, then there can be as many as $M = N$ rules. If tuning is used, and we again abide by the commonly used design principle that there must be fewer tuned design parameters than training pairs, then we must use less than N rules.

Example 10-4: Let us enumerate how many design parameters there can be in the just-stated design:

- Antecedent parameters m_{i1}^l, m_{i2}^l, and σ_i^l: 3 per antecedent, p antecedents, and M rules, for a total of $3pM$ parameters.

- Consequent parameters m_1^j, m_2^j, and σ^j: 3 per consequent and M rules, for a total of $3M$ parameters. A viable alternative—the one we use—is to treat y_l^j and y_r^j as the consequent parameters, in which case there are a total of $2M$ such parameters.

So, the maximum number of design parameters is $3pM + 2M$. Recall, from Example 5-6, that the maximum number of design parameters for a singleton type-1 FLS is $2pM + M$; hence, we have more degrees of freedom in an interval singleton type-2 FLS, which suggests that we should be able to outperform a singleton type-1 FLS.

From our discussion just before this example, we see that if no tuning of type-2 FLS parameters is done, then there can be as many as $3pN + 2N$ parameters; however, if tuning is used, then there is the following design constraint:

$$3pM + 2M < N \tag{10-69}$$

If we are given a fixed number of training samples, $N = N'$, then

$$M < \left[\frac{N'}{3p + 2} \right] \tag{10-70}$$

which constrains the number of rules that can be used. Because M must be an integer, we choose $M = M'$ as an integer that is smaller than $N'/(3p + 2)$. ∎

At a very high level, there are two designs associated with the preceding formulation:

1. Fix the shapes and parameters of all the antecedent and consequent membership functions ahead of time. Doing this fixes the shape and size of the FOU for each antecedent and consequent membership function. The data establish the rules and no tuning is used.

2. Fix the shapes of all the antecedent and consequent membership functions ahead of time. Doing this fixes the shape of the FOU for each antecedent and consequent membership function. Use the training data to tune the antecedent and consequent parameters. In this way, the size of each FOU adapts to the training data.

For the design of a singleton type-1 FLS there was another high-level approach, namely: fix the shapes and parameters of the antecedent membership functions ahead of time, and use the training data to tune the consequent parameters. Because the singleton type-1 FLS is linear in the consequent parameters [see (5-24)], this leads to an easy optimization problem. Unfortunately, as we explain later, this option is not available to us in designing a singleton type-2 FLS.

Before we describe the design methods, let us note that, just as for the design of a non-singleton type-1 FLS, there can be two very different *approaches to the tuning of an interval singleton type-2 FLS*:

1. **Partially dependent approach:** In this approach, one first designs the best possible type-1 FLS by tuning all of its parameters, and then uses these parameters in some way to *initialize* the parameters of the interval singleton type-2 FLS.

2. **Totally independent approach:** In this approach, all of the parameters of the interval singleton type-2 FLS are tuned without the benefit of a previous type-1 design. In this design the parameters of the interval singleton type-2 FLS are usually initialized in a random manner.

One would expect that good results can be obtained using either approach. Two benefits from the partially dependent approach are: (a) a smart initialization of the parameters of the interval singleton type-2 FLS, and (b) a baseline design whose performance can be compared with that of the interval singleton type-2 FLS.

In the rest of this section we briefly describe some design methods that can be used for the designs just formulated.

10.10.1 One-pass method

Here we explain how the one-pass method (Method 2) that was described in

Section 5.9.1 can be modified for an interval singleton type-2 FLS. Recall that a one-pass method generates a set of IF–THEN rules by using the given training data one time, and then combines the rules in a common rule-base to construct a final FLS. Given a set of training data—input–output pairs—

$$(\mathbf{x}^{(1)}:y^{(1)}),(\mathbf{x}^{(2)}:y^{(2)}),...,(\mathbf{x}^{(N)}:y^{(N)}) = \left\{x_1^{(l)},x_2^{(l)},....,x_p^{(l)}:y^{(l)}\right\}_{l=1}^N \qquad (10\text{-}71)$$

where $x_1, x_2, ..., x_p$ are inputs and y is the output, we proceed as follows to construct a type-2 FLS:

1. Let $[X_1^-, X_1^+], [X_2^-, X_2^+], ..., [X_p^-, X_p^+], [Y^-, Y^+]$ be the domain intervals of the input and output variables, respectively, where domain interval implies the interval the variable is most likely to lie in. We divide each domain interval into $2L + 1$ regions, where L can be different for each variable. Then, we assign interval type-2 membership functions to the regions, labeled SL (Small L), ..., $S1$(Small 1), CE (Center), $B1$(Big 1), ..., and BL (Big L). To do this we first need to decide on a FOU for each type-2 membership function. (See Chapter 3 for some examples.) The choice of a FOU should be related to a careful understanding of the application (see Chapter 14).

2. Because of overlapping FOUs (e.g., see Figure 3-6), it frequently happens that $x_k^{(i)}$ is in more than one type-2 fuzzy set. Therefore, we evaluate the membership of each input–output point in regions where it may occur, and assign the given $x_1^{(i)}, x_2^{(i)}, ... x_p^{(i)}$, or $y^{(i)}$ to the region with maximum membership. We do this using the material in Section 3.4, specifically (3-38), re-expressed here as[5]

$$L(x_k^{(i)}) = \arg \max_{\forall \tilde{F}_k^j, j=1,...,2L+1} \left[f_{x_k^{(i)}}^{cg}(\tilde{F}_k^1), f_{x_k^{(i)}}^{cg}(\tilde{F}_k^2),..., f_{x_k^{(i)}}^{cg}(\tilde{F}_k^{2L+1}) \right] \qquad (10\text{-}72)$$

where $i = 1, ..., N$ and $k = 1, ..., p$.

3. To resolve conflicting rules (rules with the same antecedent membership functions and different consequent membership functions), we assign a degree to each rule as follows: Let

$$\max \left[f_{x_k^{(i)}}^{cg}(\tilde{F}_k^1), f_{x_k^{(i)}}^{cg}(\tilde{F}_k^2),..., f_{x_k^{(i)}}^{cg}(\tilde{F}_k^{2L+1}) \right] \equiv \lambda(x_k^{(i)}) \qquad (10\text{-}73)$$

where $i = 1, ..., N$ and $k = 1, ..., p$, with a comparable definition for $y^{(i)}$, namely $\lambda(y^{(i)})$. Then, the degree for the ith rule, R^i, is defined as

---

[5]See Section 3.4 for a definition of the quantities in (10-72).

$$D(R^i) = \left[\prod_{k=1}^{p} \lambda(x_k^{(i)})\right]\lambda(y^{(i)}) \qquad i = 1, ..., N \qquad (10\text{-}74)$$

In the event of conflicting rules, the rule with the highest degree is kept in the rule-base, and all other conflicting rules are discarded.

4. We generate a combined rule-base comprised both of numerically generated fuzzy rules (as described earlier) and linguistic information provided by experts (Exercise 10-15).

5. After the combined rule-base is generated, we employ a type-reduction method—in the present case, the center-of-sets type-reducer—to obtain the type-reduced set output of the type-2 FLS.

6. Finally, we defuzzify the type-reduced set using (10-49).

Steps 1–3 extract the rules from the data and incorporate antecedent and consequent uncertainties into this process. Step 4 joins all of the rules together as in (10-2). Steps 5 and 6 complete the description of the interval singleton type-2 FLS. Knowing the antecedent and consequent type-2 membership functions for all rules, it is straightforward to translate this information into a completely described interval singleton type-2 FLS. Note that all of the parameters of this type-2 FLS have been specified as part of this one-pass design.

10.10.2 Least-squares method

The starting point for the least-squares method to designing an interval singleton type-1 FLS is a type-1 FBF expansion, such as the one in (5-38). No such FBF expansion exists for a general singleton type-2 FLS. Our discussions in Section 10.9.4 might lead us to conclude that, because we can express FLS output $y(\mathbf{x})$, using (10-49), (10-57), and (10-60), as

$$y(\mathbf{x}) = \tfrac{1}{2}\left[\mathbf{y}_l^T \mathbf{p}_l(\mathbf{x}) + \mathbf{y}_r^T \mathbf{p}_r(\mathbf{x})\right] \qquad (10\text{-}75)$$

then we can use a least-squares method to tune the parameters in $\mathbf{y}_l$ and $\mathbf{y}_r$. Unfortunately, although not immediately obvious from the way we have written $y(\mathbf{x})$ in (10-75), this is incorrect. The problem is that, to know the FBFs $\mathbf{p}_l(\mathbf{x})$ and $\mathbf{p}_r(\mathbf{x})$, we need to *first* know $\mathbf{y}_l$ and $\mathbf{y}_r$, because prior to the very first step of our iterative procedure for determining y_l or y_r [the left and right endpoints of $Y_{\cos}(\mathbf{x})$], the elements of $\mathbf{y}_l$ and $\mathbf{y}_r$ must be rank-ordered. But, if we don't have numerical values for those elements, it is impossible to do this; hence, we can't determine (compute) the FBFs $\mathbf{p}_l(\mathbf{x})$ and $\mathbf{p}_r(\mathbf{x})$ [i.e., we can't compute $p_l^i(\mathbf{x})$ in (10-58) or $p_r^i(\mathbf{x})$ in (10-60)].[6] This situation does not occur for our type-1 FBFs; i.e., the FBFs in (5-38) do not depend on the $\bar{y}^l$.

Our conclusion from this is that, at present, we cannot use a least-squares design method for an interval singleton type-2 FLS.

10.10.3 Back-propagation (steepest descent) method

In the back-propagation method, none of the antecedent or consequent parameters of the interval singleton type-2 FLS are fixed ahead of time. They are all tuned using a steepest descent method that is briefly described in this section [Liang and Mendel (2000c)].

Given an input–output training pair $(\mathbf{x}^{(t)}:y^{(t)})$, we now wish to design an interval singleton type-2 FLS such that the following error function is minimized:

$$e^{(t)} = \tfrac{1}{2}\left[f_{s2}(\mathbf{x}^{(t)}) - y^{(t)}\right]^2 \quad t = 1,...,N \tag{10-76}$$

Based on our discussions and analyses in Section 10.9, we know that only the upper and lower antecedent membership functions and the two end-points of the centroid of each consequent set determine $f_{s2}(\mathbf{x}^{(t)})$; hence, we can conceptually think about minimizing (10-76) with respect to these upper and lower membership functions and the consequent parameters y_l^j and y_r^j. Additionally, for each $\mathbf{x}^{(t)}$ we know that an interval singleton type-2 FLS can be characterized by two FBF expansions which generate the left- and right-hand end-points of the center-of-sets type-reduced set; hence, for each $\mathbf{x}^{(t)}$ we can focus on tuning the parameters of just those two type-1 FLSs. Note that the designs of these type-1 FLSs are *coupled* because $f_{s2}(\mathbf{x}^{(t)})$ in (10-49) depends on both $y_l(\mathbf{x}^{(t)})$ and $y_r(\mathbf{x}^{(t)})$.

Given the N input–output training samples $(\mathbf{x}^{(t)}:y^{(t)})$, $t = 1,...,N$, we wish to update the design parameters so that (10-76) is minimized for E training epochs. A general method for doing this is:

---

[6]A possible way around this would be to choose some initial values for $\mathbf{y}_l$ and $\mathbf{y}_r$, and then compute $\mathbf{p}_l(\mathbf{x})$ and $\mathbf{p}_r(\mathbf{x})$. Then a least-squares method could be used to update $\mathbf{y}_l$ and $\mathbf{y}_r$, after which $\mathbf{p}_l(\mathbf{x})$ and $\mathbf{p}_r(\mathbf{x})$ would be recomputed. This iterative process would be continued until it converges in some sense. Whether or not such an iterative process is successful is an open question.

1. Initialize all of the parameters in the antecedent and consequent membership functions.
2. Set the counter, e, of the training epoch to zero; i.e., $e \equiv 0$.
3. Set the counter, t, of the training data to unity; i.e., $t \equiv 1$.
4. Apply $p \times 1$ input $\mathbf{x}^{(t)}$ to the interval singleton type-2 FLS and compute the total firing interval for each rule; i.e., compute $\underline{f}^i$ and $\overline{f}^i$ $(i = 1,...,p)$ using (10-27) and (10-28).
5. Compute y_l and y_r using the four-step iterative method described on pp. 310–311 [this leads to a re-ordering of the M rules, which are then re-numbered $1,...,M$, as explained in the discussions accompanying (10-63)–(10-65)]. Doing this establishes L and R, so that y_l and y_r can be expressed as in (10-57) and (10-60), respectively, i.e.,

$$y_l = \frac{\sum_{i=1}^{M} f_l^i y_l^i}{\sum_{i=1}^{M} f_l^i} = \frac{\sum_{i=1}^{L} \overline{f}^i y_l^i + \sum_{j=L+1}^{M} \underline{f}^j y_l^j}{\sum_{i=1}^{L} \overline{f}^i + \sum_{j=L+1}^{M} \underline{f}^j}$$

$$= y_l\left(\overline{f}^1,...,\overline{f}^L, \underline{f}^{L+1},...,\underline{f}^M, y_l^1,...,y_l^M\right) \tag{10-77}$$

and

$$y_r = \frac{\sum_{i=1}^{M} f_r^i y_r^i}{\sum_{i=1}^{M} f_r^i} = \frac{\sum_{i=1}^{R} \underline{f}^i y_r^i + \sum_{j=R+1}^{M} \overline{f}^j y_r^j}{\sum_{i=1}^{R} \underline{f}^i + \sum_{j=R+1}^{M} \overline{f}^j}$$

$$= y_r\left(\underline{f}^1,...,\underline{f}^R, \overline{f}^{R+1},...,\overline{f}^M, y_r^1,...,y_r^M\right) \tag{10-78}$$

6. Compute the defuzzified output, $f_{s2}(\mathbf{x}^{(t)})$, of the interval singleton type-2 FLS, as

$$f_{s2}\left(\mathbf{x}^{(t)}\right) = \left[y_l(\mathbf{x}^{(t)}) + y_r(\mathbf{x}^{(t)})\right]/2 \tag{10-79}$$

7. Determine the explicit dependence of y_l and y_r on membership functions. [Because L and R obtained in Step 5 usually change from one t-iteration to the next, the dependence of y_l and y_r on membership functions will also usually change from one t-iteration to the next (see Example 10-5).] To do this, first determine the explicit dependence of $\underline{f}^i$ and $\overline{f}^j$ on membership functions using (10-27) and (10-28); i.e., $\underline{f}^i$ is determined by $\underline{\mu}_{\tilde{F}_1^i}(x_1)$, ...,

$\underline{\mu}_{\tilde{F}_p^i}(x_p)$, and $\overline{f}^j$ is determined by $\overline{\mu}_{\tilde{F}_1^j}(x_1), ..., \overline{\mu}_{\tilde{F}_p^j}(x_p)$. Consequently, from (10-77) and (10-78), we see that

$$
y_l = y_l \Big[\overline{\mu}_{\tilde{F}_1^1}(x_1), ..., \overline{\mu}_{\tilde{F}_p^1}(x_p), ..., \overline{\mu}_{\tilde{F}_1^L}(x_1), ..., \overline{\mu}_{\tilde{F}_p^L}(x_p), \underline{\mu}_{\tilde{F}_1^{L+1}}(x_1),
$$
$$
..., \underline{\mu}_{\tilde{F}_p^{L+1}}(x_p), ..., \underline{\mu}_{\tilde{F}_1^M}(x_1), ..., \underline{\mu}_{\tilde{F}_p^M}(x_p), y_l^1, ..., y_l^M \Big] \tag{10-80}
$$

and

$$
y_r = y_r \Big[\underline{\mu}_{\tilde{F}_1^1}(x_1), ..., \underline{\mu}_{\tilde{F}_p^1}(x_p), ..., \underline{\mu}_{\tilde{F}_1^R}(x_1), ..., \underline{\mu}_{\tilde{F}_p^R}(x_p), \overline{\mu}_{\tilde{F}_1^{R+1}}(x_1),
$$
$$
..., \overline{\mu}_{\tilde{F}_p^{R+1}}(x_p), ..., \overline{\mu}_{\tilde{F}_1^M}(x_1), ..., \overline{\mu}_{\tilde{F}_p^M}(x_p), y_r^1, ..., y_r^M \Big] \tag{10-81}
$$

8. Test each component of $\mathbf{x}^{(t)}$ to determine the *active branches* in $\underline{\mu}_{\tilde{F}_k^i}(x_k)$ and $\overline{\mu}_{\tilde{F}_k^i}(x_k)$ ($k = 1, ..., p$), and represent the active branches as explicit functions of their associated parameters; e.g., use (10-21) and (10-22) for the case of a Gaussian primary membership function with uncertain mean, or use (10-24) and (10-25) for the case of a Gaussian primary membership function with uncertain standard deviation. This step depends on the relative location of each component of $\mathbf{x}^{(t)}$ to the underlying membership functions of its components (see Example 10-5).

9. Tune the parameters of the active branches of the antecedent's membership functions and the parameters associated with the consequent using a steepest descent algorithm for the error function in (10-76). See Examples 3-15 and 3-16 for the calculations of derivatives of upper and lower membership functions with respect to parameters of the active branches.

10. Set $t \equiv t + 1$. If $t = N + 1$, go to Step 11; otherwise, go to Step 4.

11. Set $e = e + 1$. If $e = E$, STOP; otherwise, go to Step 3.

What makes the tuning of the parameters of this interval singleton type-2 FLS challenging and different from the tuning of the parameters in a singleton type-1 FLS is having to first determine which parameters y_l and y_r depend on. This requires (step 8) using $x_k^{(t)}$ ($k = 1, ..., p$) to determine respective active upper and lower antecedent membership functions. As the parameters change, due to their tuning, the dependency of y_l and y_r on these parameters also changes. This does not occur in a type-1 FLS.

Example 10-5: In this example we illustrate some of the major steps in the 11-step design procedure. We do this for an interval singleton type-2 FLS that has only 2 two-antecedent rules, namely:

$$R^1: \text{IF } x_1 \text{ is } \tilde{F}_1^1 \text{ and } x_2 \text{ is } \tilde{F}_2^1 \text{ THEN } y \text{ is } \tilde{G}^1$$

and

$$R^2: \text{IF } x_1 \text{ is } \tilde{F}_1^2 \text{ and } x_2 \text{ is } \tilde{F}_2^2 \text{ THEN } y \text{ is } \tilde{G}^2$$

The antecedent membership functions are Gaussian primaries with uncertain means and interval secondary membership functions [described in (10-20)–(10-22)] whose parameters are m_{k1}^i, m_{k2}^i, and σ_k^i, where $k = 1, 2$ and $i = 1, 2$. The initial forms of these membership functions were chosen arbitrarily and are depicted in Figure 10-12. The centroids of the membership functions $\mu_{\tilde{G}^1}$ and $\mu_{\tilde{G}^2}$, for the two type-2 consequent sets, were assumed for illustrative purposes to be $C_{\tilde{G}^1} = [2.6, 3.9] = [y_l^1, y_r^1]$ and $C_{\tilde{G}^2} = [4.2, 6.4] = [y_l^2, y_r^2]$, respectively [in practice, these centroids would be computed using (9-14)].

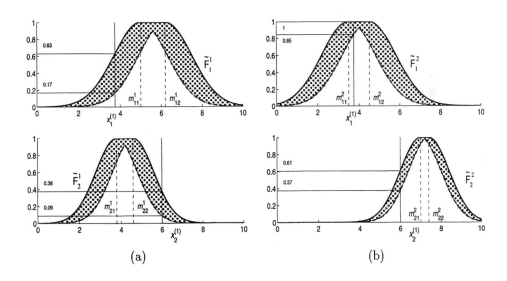

(a)   (b)

Figure 10-12: Illustration of an interval singleton type-2 FLS that has two rules where each rule has two antecedents. (a) FOUs for $\tilde{F}_1^1$ and $\tilde{F}_2^1$ in rule R^1, and (b) FOUs for $\tilde{F}_1^2$ and $\tilde{F}_2^2$ in rule R^2. Also shown are the intersections of $x_1^{(1)}$ and $x_2^{(1)}$ with respective lower and upper membership functions.

The first pair in the training set is $\left(\mathbf{x}^{(1)}:y^{(1)}\right)$, where we assumed that $x_1^{(1)} = 3.75$, $x_2^{(1)} = 6.0$, and $y^{(1)}(x_1^{(1)}, x_2^{(1)}) = 4.6$. Using product t-norm in Step 4, we find that for rule R^1 [see Figure 10-12 (a) for the intersections of the dark vertical lines with the upper and lower membership functions]:

$$\underline{f}^1 = \underline{\mu}_{\tilde{F}_1^1}(x_1^{(1)})\underline{\mu}_{\tilde{F}_2^1}(x_2^{(1)}) = 0.17 \times 0.09 = 0.0153 \tag{10-82a}$$

$$\overline{f}^1 = \overline{\mu}_{\tilde{F}_1^1}(x_1^{(1)})\overline{\mu}_{\tilde{F}_2^1}(x_2^{(1)}) = 0.63 \times 0.38 = 0.2394 \tag{10-82b}$$

and for rule R^2 [see Figure 10-12 (b), also for the intersections of the dark vertical lines with the upper and lower membership functions]:

$$\underline{f}^2 = \underline{\mu}_{\tilde{F}_1^2}(x_1^{(1)})\underline{\mu}_{\tilde{F}_2^2}(x_2^{(1)}) = 0.85 \times 0.37 = 0.3145 \tag{10-83a}$$

$$\overline{f}^2 = \overline{\mu}_{\tilde{F}_1^2}(x_1^{(1)})\overline{\mu}_{\tilde{F}_2^2}(x_2^{(1)}) = 1 \times 0.61 = 0.61 \tag{10-83b}$$

In Step 5, we used the exact four-step iterative procedure to determine y_l and y_r. Doing this, we found that: For y_l, $L = 1$, so that $f_l^1 = \overline{f}^1$ and $f_l^2 = \underline{f}^2$, whereas for y_r, $R = 1$, so that $f_r^1 = \underline{f}^1$ and $f_r^2 = \overline{f}^2$. Next, we numerically evaluated (10-77) and (10-78), as:

$$y_l = \frac{\overline{f}^1 y_l^1 + \underline{f}^2 y_l^2}{\overline{f}^1 + \underline{f}^2} = \frac{0.2394 \times 2.6 + 0.3145 \times 4.2}{0.2394 + 0.3145} = 3.5085 \tag{10-84a}$$

$$y_r = \frac{\underline{f}^1 y_r^1 + \overline{f}^2 y_r^2}{\underline{f}^1 + \overline{f}^2} = \frac{0.0153 \times 3.9 + 0.61 \times 6.4}{0.0153 + 0.61} = 6.3388 \tag{10-84b}$$

This established the type-reduced set for $\left(\mathbf{x}^{(1)}:y^{(1)}\right)$ as $[y_l, y_r] = [3.5085, 6.3388]$, from which we computed the defuzzified output, in Step 6, as

$$f_{s2}(\mathbf{x}^{(1)}) = \frac{y_l + y_r}{2} = 4.9237 \tag{10-85}$$

We know that the desired output is $y^{(1)} = 4.6$; so, we want to get a better fit to it from the interval singleton type-2 FLS than the one in (10-85). To do this, we must tune the parameters of the FLS.

Focusing our attention on Step 7, we find from (10-84a), (10-82b), and (10-83a), that

$$
\begin{aligned}
y_l &= y_l\left(\overline{f}^1, \underline{f}^2, y_l^1, y_l^2\right) \\
&= y_l\left(\overline{\mu}_{\tilde{F}_1^1}(x_1^{(1)}), \overline{\mu}_{\tilde{F}_2^1}(x_2^{(1)}), \underline{\mu}_{\tilde{F}_1^2}(x_1^{(1)}), \underline{\mu}_{\tilde{F}_2^2}(x_2^{(1)}), y_l^1, y_l^2\right)
\end{aligned}
\tag{10-86}
$$

and from (10-84b), (10-82a), and (10-83b), that

$$
\begin{aligned}
y_r &= y_r\left(\underline{f}^1, \overline{f}^2, y_r^1, y_r^2\right) \\
&= y_r\left(\underline{\mu}_{\tilde{F}_1^1}(x_1^{(1)}), \underline{\mu}_{\tilde{F}_2^1}(x_2^{(1)}), \overline{\mu}_{\tilde{F}_1^2}(x_1^{(1)}), \overline{\mu}_{\tilde{F}_2^2}(x_2^{(1)}), y_r^1, y_r^2\right)
\end{aligned}
\tag{10-87}
$$

Next, in Step 8, we must determine the active branches of the upper and lower antecedent membership functions for $\mathbf{x}^{(1)} = (x_1^{(1)}, x_2^{(1)})^{\mathrm{T}} = (3.75, 6.0)^T$. This is where we rely heavily on Figure 10-12 and (3-22)–(3-27); the latter establish which derivatives of $\overline{\mu}_{\tilde{F}_1^1}(x_1^{(1)})$, $\overline{\mu}_{\tilde{F}_2^1}(x_2^{(1)})$, $\underline{\mu}_{\tilde{F}_1^2}(x_1^{(1)})$ and $\underline{\mu}_{\tilde{F}_2^2}(x_2^{(1)})$, or $\underline{\mu}_{\tilde{F}_1^1}(x_1^{(1)})$, $\underline{\mu}_{\tilde{F}_2^1}(x_2^{(1)})$, $\overline{\mu}_{\tilde{F}_1^2}(x_1^{(1)})$ and $\overline{\mu}_{\tilde{F}_2^2}(x_2^{(1)})$ are active. For example, because $x_1^{(1)} < m_{11}^1 < (m_{11}^1 + m_{22}^1)/2$:

- The first line of $\partial\overline{\mu}_{\tilde{F}_1^1}(x_1^{(1)})/\partial m_{11}^1$ in (3-22) is activated.
- $\partial\overline{\mu}_{\tilde{F}_1^1}(x_1^{(1)})/\partial m_{12}^1 = 0$ [from the first line of (3-23)].
- $\partial\underline{\mu}_{\tilde{F}_1^1}(x_1^{(1)})/\partial m_{11}^1 = 0$ [from the first line of (3-25)].
- The first line of $\partial\underline{\mu}_{\tilde{F}_1^1}(x_1^{(1)})/\partial m_{12}^1$ in (3-26) is activated, etc.

Once the active branches of the antecedent's membership functions have been determined, it is relatively straightforward to use this information in Step 9's steepest descent algorithm, e.g.,

$$
\begin{aligned}
m_{11}^1(i+1) &= m_{11}^1(i) - \alpha \left.\frac{\partial e^{(i)}}{\partial m_{11}^1}\right|_i = m_{11}^1(i) \\
&- \alpha\left[\frac{\partial e^i}{\partial f_{s2}(\mathbf{x}^{(i)})}\frac{\partial f_{s2}(\mathbf{x}^{(i)})}{\partial y_l}\frac{\partial y_l}{\partial m_{11}^1} + \frac{\partial e^i}{\partial f_{s2}(\mathbf{x}^{(i)})}\frac{\partial f_{s2}(\mathbf{x}^{(i)})}{\partial y_r}\frac{\partial y_r}{\partial m_{11}^1}\right]\Bigg|_i
\end{aligned}
\tag{10-88}
$$

where $\left.\partial e^{(i)}/\partial f_{s2}(\mathbf{x}^{(i)})\right|_i = f_{s2}(\mathbf{x}^{(i)}) - y^{(i)}$, $\left.\partial f_{s2}(\mathbf{x}^{(i)})/\partial y_l\right|_i = \frac{1}{2}$, and [see (10-86) and (10-87)]

$$\left.\frac{\partial y_l}{\partial m_{11}^1}\right|_i = \left[\frac{\partial y_l}{\partial \overline{\mu}_{\tilde{F}_1^1}(x_1^{(1)})} \; \frac{\partial \overline{\mu}_{\tilde{F}_1^1}(x_1^{(1)})}{\partial m_{11}^1}\right]\Bigg|_i \tag{10-89a}$$

$$\left.\frac{\partial y_r}{\partial m_{11}^1}\right|_i = \left[\frac{\partial y_r}{\partial \underline{\mu}_{\tilde{F}_1^1}(x_1^{(1)})} \; \frac{\partial \underline{\mu}_{\tilde{F}_1^1}(x_1^{(1)})}{\partial m_{11}^1}\right]\Bigg|_i \tag{10-89b}$$

We leave it to the reader (Exercise 10-18) to further develop the right-hand side of (10-89a). Clearly, the term $\partial \overline{\mu}_{\tilde{F}_1^1}(x_1^{(1)})/\partial m_{11}^1$ is needed; but, we have just established that we can obtain it from the first line of (3-22).

Although it is tedious to set up the steepest descent algorithm to update all of the antecedent and consequent parameters, it is not difficult (Exercise 10-18). It just requires a careful use of the chain rule. To write a general computer program for these algorithms, one must incorporate the tests on the antecedent's values that are given in (3-22)–(3-27) (see Section 10.13). ■

10.10.4 SVD–QR method

Recall, from Section 5.9.4, that the SVD–QR method is one that leads to rule reduction. Its starting point for a type-1 FLS is the FBF matrix (5-43). Rule reduction is also needed for a type-2 FLS. A modified version of the Section 5.9.4 SVD–QR method, as described next, will let us accomplish this [Liang and Mendel (2000e)].

The starting points for the SVD–QR method for an interval singleton type-2 FLS are *two* FBF expansions—one for y_l in (10-57) and the other for y_r in (10-60). The result is the following *three-step SVD–QR method*:

1. Create a FBF matrix for y_l, called Φ_l, where

$$\Phi_l = \begin{pmatrix} p_l^1(\mathbf{x}^{(1)}) & \cdots & p_l^M(\mathbf{x}^{(1)}) \\ \vdots & \ddots & \vdots \\ p_l^1(\mathbf{x}^{(N)}) & \cdots & p_l^M(\mathbf{x}^{(N)}) \end{pmatrix} \tag{10-90}$$

and the FBFs—the $p_l^i(\mathbf{x}^{(j)})$—are given by (10-58) and (10-59). Apply the first four steps of the Section 5.9.4 SVD–QR algorithm to Φ_l. This leads to $\hat{r}_l$ rules with rule numbers $J = \{j_1, j_2, ..., j_{\hat{r}_l}\}$, where $j_1, j_2, ..., j_{\hat{r}_l}$ are the rule numbers of the *original M* rules. [Recall that in the first step of the iterative procedure used to compute y_l, the y_l^i are ordered in ascending order, which leads to the order of the original rules being changed. Permutation matrix $\mathbf{Q}_l$ relates the originally numbered and renumbered M rules, as described in the discussion associated with (10-63)–(10-65). Matrix $\mathbf{Q}_l$ is used to establish $j_1, j_2, ..., j_{\hat{r}_l}$.]

2. Create a FBF matrix for y_r, called Φ_r, where

$$\Phi_r = \begin{pmatrix} p_r^1(\mathbf{x}^{(1)}) & \cdots & p_r^M(\mathbf{x}^{(1)}) \\ \vdots & \ddots & \vdots \\ p_r^1(\mathbf{x}^{(N)}) & \cdots & p_r^M(\mathbf{x}^{(N)}) \end{pmatrix} \tag{10-91}$$

and the FBFs—the $p_r^i(\mathbf{x}^{(j)})$—are given by (10-61) and (10-62). Apply the first four steps of the Section 5.9.4 SVD–QR algorithm to Φ_r. This leads to $\hat{r}_r$ rules with rule numbers $K = \{k_1, k_2, ..., k_{\hat{r}_r}\}$, where $k_1, k_2, ..., k_{\hat{r}_r}$ are the rule numbers of the *original M* rules. [Recall, as in Step 1, that in the first step of the iterative procedure used to compute y_r, the y_r^i are ordered in ascending order, which leads to the order of the original rules being changed. Permutation matrix $\mathbf{Q}_r$ relates the originally numbered and renumbered M rules, as described in the discussion associated with (10-63)–(10-65). Matrix $\mathbf{Q}_r$ is used to establish $k_1, k_2, ..., k_{\hat{r}_r}$.]

3. Combine the results from Steps 1 and 2; i.e., keep the rules in $J \cup K$, which is the union of rule-number sets J and K. Note that there will be some common rule numbers in J and K, so the total number of reduced rules, $\hat{r}$, satisfies the following inequalities:

$$\max(\hat{r}_l, \hat{r}_r) \le \hat{r} \le (\hat{r}_l + \hat{r}_r) \tag{10-92}$$

Finally, the $\hat{r}$ rules are renumbered 1, 2, ..., $\hat{r}$.

We shall illustrate this design method in Section 12.5, where we apply SVD–QR methods to the designs of 5 FLSs, two type-1 and three type-2.

10.10.5 Iterative design method

By combining the SVD–QR method with the back-propagation method, we can design all of the parameters of the interval singleton type-2 FLS. The following iterative design method can be very successful:

1. Fix the number of rules, M, at a reasonable value.

2. Use the back-propagation method to design all the antecedent and consequent parameters.

3. Apply the SVD–QR method to the results of the back-propagation method to determine a reduced set of $\hat{r}$ rules.

4. If performance is acceptable, STOP. Otherwise, return to Step 2 for a re-tuning of the antecedent and consequent parameters.

We shall also illustrate this design method in Section 12.5.

10.11 CASE STUDY: FORECASTING OF TIME-SERIES

We have described the problem of forecasting a time-series in Section 4.2. Here we design an interval singleton type-2 FLS forecaster for the Mackey–Glass time-series using the back-propagation method and compare its results with those obtained from back-propagation-designed singleton and non-singleton type-1 FLSs. Our type-2 design uses the *partially dependent approach* that was described above in Section 10.10; i.e., we first designed the best possible singleton and non-singleton type-1 FLSs by tuning their parameters using back-propagation designs, and then we used some of those parameters to initialize the parameters of the interval singleton type-2 FLS.

All designs were based on the following 1,000 *noisy* data points: $x(1001)$, $x(1002)$, ..., $x(2000)$. The first 504 noisy data, $x(1001)$, $x(1002)$, ..., $x(1504)$ were used for training; i.e., for the designs of the FLS forecasters, whereas the remaining 496 noisy data, $x(1505), x(1506),..., x(2000)$, were used for testing the designs. The noise-free Mackey–Glass time-series is depicted in Figure 5-11 (a). As in Section 6.2, we assume that the noise-free sampled time-series, $s(k)$, is corrupted by uniformly distributed stationary additive noise, $n(k)$, so that

$$x(k) = s(k) + n(k) \quad k=1001,\ 1002,....,\ 2000 \tag{10-93}$$

and that $SNR = 0dB$. One realization of $x(1001), x(1002),..., x(2000)$ is depicted in Figure 5-11 (b).

As in Section 6.7, we used four antecedents for forecasting, namely, $x(k-3)$, $x(k-2)$, $x(k-1)$, and $x(k)$, to predict $x(k+1)$, and two fuzzy sets for each antecedent; hence, we used a total of 16 rules. Gaussian membership functions were chosen for the antecedents of the two type-1 FLSs, and Gaussian primary membership functions of uncertain means [see (10-20)] were chosen for the antecedents of the interval singleton type-2 FLS. Each rule of the two type-1 FLSs was characterized by eight antecedent membership function parameters (the mean and standard deviation for each of the four Gaussian membership functions) and one consequent parameter, $\bar{y}^l$. However, each rule of the type-2 FLS was characterized by 12 antecedent membership function parameters (the left- and right-hand bounds on the mean, and the standard deviation for each of the four Gaussian membership functions) and two consequent parameters (the left- and right-hand end-points for the centroid of the consequent type-2 fuzzy set; see Example 10-4). The details of the back-propagation-designed singleton and non-singleton type-1 FLSs can be found in Sections 5.10.2 and 6.7.2. Note that we first designed the singleton type-1 FLS and then designed the non-singleton type-1 FLS using the partially dependent design approach that is described in Section 6.6, so that we were able to observe the marginal improvements in performance obtained by just tuning the "new" parameters.

We again evaluated the performance of all the designs using the following RMSEs:

$$RMSE_{s1}(BP) = \sqrt{\tfrac{1}{496} \sum_{k=1504}^{1999} \left[s(k+1) - f_{s1}(\mathbf{x}^{(k)}) \right]^2} \qquad (10\text{-}94)$$

$$RMSE_{ns1}(BP) = \sqrt{\tfrac{1}{496} \sum_{k=1504}^{1999} \left[s(k+1) - f_{ns1}(\mathbf{x}^{(k)}) \right]^2} \qquad (10\text{-}95)$$

and

$$RMSE_{s2}(BP) = \sqrt{\tfrac{1}{496} \sum_{k=1504}^{1999} \left[s(k+1) - f_{s2}(\mathbf{x}^{(k)}) \right]^2} \qquad (10\text{-}96)$$

For the interval singleton type-2 FLS, we *initially* set the intervals of uncertainty for the means of each of the four antecedent's two fuzzy sets equal to

$$[m_x - 2\sigma_x - 0.25\sigma_n, m_x - 2\sigma_x + 0.25\sigma_n]$$

and

$$[m_x + 2\sigma_x - 0.25\sigma_n, m_x + 2\sigma_x + 0.25\sigma_n],$$

respectively, where m_x and σ_x are the mean and standard deviation, respectively, of the data in the 504 training samples, $x(1001), x(1002), \ldots, x(1504)$. For the standard deviation of the additive noise, σ_n, we initially used the final tuned result for the standard deviation of the input, σ_X, obtained from our non-singleton type-1 FLS design. We also initially chose y_r^i and y_l^j as $\bar{y}^i + \sigma_n$ and $\bar{y}^i - \sigma_n$, respectively, where $\bar{y}^i$ was obtained from the type-1 singleton FLS design.

As stated earlier, the parameters that were tuned during the back-propagation design of the interval singleton type-2 FLS are the left- and right-hand bounds on the mean and the standard deviation for each of the four Gaussian primary membership functions, and the left- and right-hand end-points for the centroid of each consequent type-2 fuzzy set. The total number of parameters tuned in this design is 14 parameters per rule $\times$ 16 rules = 224 parameters.

Each FLS was tuned using a steepest descent algorithm in which the learning parameter $\alpha = 0.2$. Training and testing were carried out for six epochs. After each epoch we used the testing data to see how each FLS performed, by computing $RMSE_{s1}(BP)$, $RMSE_{ns1}(BP)$, and $RMSE_{s2}(BP)$ using (10-94)–(10-96), respectively. This entire process was repeated 50 times using 50 independent sets of 1,000 data points, at the end of which we had 50 $RMSE_{s1}(BP)$, $RMSE_{ns1}(BP)$, and $RMSE_{s2}(BP)$ values. The average values and standard deviations of these $RMSE$s are plotted in Figure 10-13 for each of the six epochs. Observe that:

- The top two curves for the type-1 FLSs are the same as those in Figure 6-6.

- There is a *substantial* improvement in performance (in both the mean and standard deviation of the $RMSE$) for the interval singleton type-2 FLS over its type-1 counterparts.

The reason for this substantial improvement in performance is that for the first time we are incorporating the uncertainties that are in the training data into the rules of the FLS forecaster. Although the reduction in the final average $RMSE$, from around 0.15 to 0.136, only represents a reduction of $9\frac{1}{3}\%$, if this was a financial time-series, a lot of money could be made with a $9\frac{1}{3}\%$ improvement in forecasting performance. The reduction in the standard deviation of the $RMSE$, from around 10.2×10^{-3} to 8.4×10^{-3}, represents a reduction of more than 17%.

Although the interval singleton type-2 FLS forecaster has incorporated the uncertainties that are in the training data into its rules, it still does not account for the input measurement uncertainties because it is using singleton fuzzification. In the next chapter we develop a non-singleton type-2 FLS that will let us account for all of the uncertainties that are present in the forecasting problem.

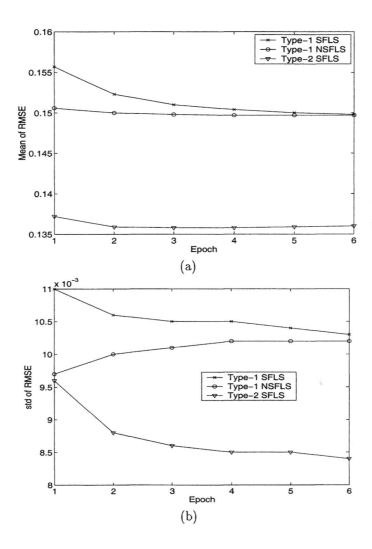

Figure 10-13: The mean and standard deviation of $RMSE_{s1}(BP)$, $RMSE_{ns1}(BP)$, and $RMSE_{s2}(BP)$ averaged over 50 Monte-Carlo designs. Tuning was performed in each realization for six epochs: (a) mean values, and (b) standard deviation values.

10.12 CASE STUDY: KNOWLEDGE MINING USING SURVEYS

We have described the problem of knowledge mining using surveys in Section 4.3. Here we explain and demonstrate how to design interval singleton type-2 FLAs using the data presented in Tables 4-2–4-5. Wherever possible, we parallel the presentation of Section 5.11 so that the reader can compare the type-1 and type-2 FLAs.

First, we must associate type-2 membership functions with the Table 4-2 interval data. To do this we must first decide on a FOU for each of the membership functions. This would be a good time for the reader to review the procedure that was used in Section 5.11 to construct the membership functions depicted in Figure 5-13. In Section 5.11, we stated:

> There is uncertainty associated with our use of $a - \sigma_a$ and $b + \sigma_b$; e.g., why not use $a - 0.5\sigma_a$ or $a - 2\sigma_a$ instead of $a - \sigma_a$, and $b + 0.5\sigma_b$ or $b + 1.5\sigma_b$ instead of $b + \sigma_b$? This uncertainty cannot be captured using type-1 fuzzy sets; however, as we explain in Chapter 10, it can be captured using type-2 fuzzy sets.

This uncertainty is captured in a type-2 fuzzy set by using a *FOU*, as we explain next.

We use the same linguistic labels for the type-2 sets as we did in Section 5.11 for their type-1 counterparts, namely: $\tilde{F}_1$ = *none to very little*, $\tilde{F}_2$ = *some*, $\tilde{F}_3$ = *a moderate amount*, $\tilde{F}_4$ = *a large amount*, and $\tilde{F}_5$ = *a maximum amount*. We use triangular principal membership functions (shown dashed in Figure 10-14) for the three interior labels *some*, *a moderate amount*, and *a large amount*, and piecewise-linear principal membership functions (also shown dashed in Figure 10-14) for the left-most and right-most labels *none to very little* and *a maximum amount*. These choices were made to be consistent with the choices made in Section 5.11, and because it is relatively easy, as we explain next, to go from the data in Table 4-2 to FOUs for each of the principal membership functions. In all cases, we also used interval secondary membership functions.

The FOUs are obtained by specifying upper and lower membership functions for each fuzzy set. Let ρ denote a *fraction of uncertainty*; i.e., $0 \leq \rho \leq 1$. Then, we construct each FOU as follows (see Table 4-2 for values of a, b, σ_a, and σ_b):

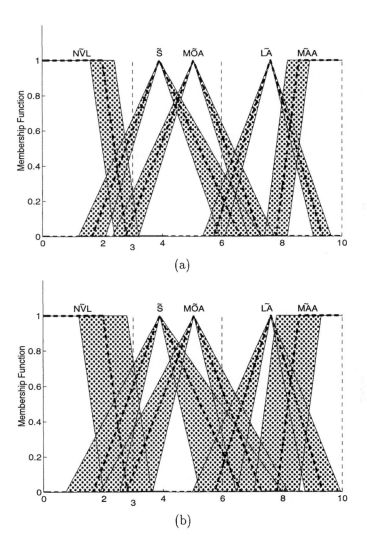

Figure 10-14: The FOUs used to represent the five linguistic labels. The dashed lines denote the type-1 membership functions (see Figure 5-13) that were used to represent the five linguistic labels. (a) $\rho = 0.5$ (50% uncertainty), and (b) $\rho = 1$ (100% uncertainty).

1.   For the *triangle interior membership functions*, the coordinates of the upper membership function are at $(a-(1+\rho)\sigma_a,0)$, $((a+b)/2,1)$ and $(b+(1+\rho)\sigma_b,0)$, and the coordinates of the lower membership function are at $(a-(1-\rho)\sigma_a,0)$, $((a+b)/2,1)$, and $(b+(1-\rho)\sigma_b,0)$.

2.   For the *piecewise-linear membership functions*, the coordinates of the upper membership function are at[7] $(a-(1+\rho)\sigma_a,0)$, $(a-\rho\sigma_a,1)$, $(b+\rho\sigma_b,1)$, and $(b+(1+\rho)\sigma_b,0)$, and the coordinates of the lower membership function are at $(a-(1-\rho)\sigma_a,0)$, $(a+\rho\sigma_a,1)$, $(b-\rho\sigma_b,1)$, and $(b+(1-\rho)\sigma_b,0)$. Note that the slopes of the legs of the piecewise-linear membership functions have been chosen arbitrarily. The slope of the leg of the left piecewise-linear membership function equals $-2/\sigma_b$, whereas the slope of the leg of the right piecewise-linear membership function equals $2/\sigma_b$. Other choices could have been made for these slopes.

Figure 10-14 (a) depicts the FOUs for $\rho=0.5$ (which corresponds to a 50% level of uncertainty) and Figure 10-14 (b) depicts the FOUs for $\rho=1$ (which corresponds to a 100% level of uncertainty). The Figure 10-14 FOUs are used for both the antecedents and consequents of FLA rules. When $\rho=0$, the Figure 10-14 FOUs reduce to the membership functions in Figure 5-13.

Results from three surveys are summarized in Tables 4-3–4-5. In this chapter we associate rules with these surveys in which their antecedents and consequents are type-2 fuzzy sets; i.e., the two single-antecedent surveys are associated with questions of the form "IF x_1 is $\tilde{F}^i$, THEN what is y?" ($i = 1, ..., 5$), or "IF x_2 is $\tilde{F}^j$, THEN what is y?" ($j = 1, ..., 5$), whereas the two-antecedent survey is associated with questions of the form " IF x_1 is $\tilde{F}^i$ and x_2 is $\tilde{F}^j$, THEN what is y" ($i, j = 1, ..., 5$). Note that, regardless of how we model the antecedents and consequents in our fuzzy logic advisors, to the people who answered the survey questions, "a rule is a rule is a rule."

Tables 4-3–4-5 reveal that each rule has a histogram of responses. In Section 5.11 we raised the question "What should be done with this information?" and we described three possibilities: Keep the response chosen by the largest number of experts, find a weighted average of the rule consequents for each rule, or preserve the distributions of the expert-responses for each rule. For reasons explained in Section 5.11 we chose the second possibility. We do the same here; i.e., we *average the responses*.

When we do this, the consequent of each rule is treated as a type-1 fuzzy

---

[7]Note that, for the left piecewise-linear membership function, $a=\sigma_a=0$; so, the first two coordinates of both the upper and lower membership functions are (0, 0) and (0, 1), as they should be.

set, C_{avg}^l (e.g., a two-antecedent rule is now interpreted as " IF x_1 is $\tilde{F}^i$ and x_2 is $\tilde{F}^j$, THEN $y = C_{avg}^l$ "), where

$$C_{avg}^l = \frac{\sum_{i=1}^{M} w_i^l C_{\tilde{G}_i}}{\sum_{i=1}^{M} w_i^l} \equiv \left[\underline{C}_{avg}^l, \overline{C}_{avg}^l \right] \tag{10-97}$$

in which the top sum is an algebraic sum (of interval sets), $C_{\tilde{G}_i}$ is the centroid of the ith consequent set (given in Table 10-1), and w_i^l is the weight associated with the ith consequent for the lth rule. The entries in Tables 4-3–4-5 are the weights. The computation in (10-97) is easy to perform and is done using Theorem 7-4. Tables 10-2–10-4 summarize these calculations and are analogous to Tables 5-4–5-6. Comparing the C_{avg}^l intervals in these tables to their respective c_{avg}^l values in Tables 5-4–5-6, observe that the latter always fall within the former, as expected.

Equations (5-61)–(5-63) describe the three type-1 consensus FLAs, $y_{c1}(x_1)$, $y_{c1}(x_2)$, and $y_{c1}(x_1, x_2)$. Their type-2 counterparts are obtained using (10-57)–(10-62), (10-49), (10-97), (10-27), and (10-28), and for completeness, are stated next.[8]

Table 10-1: Centroids of type-2 consequent fuzzy sets, computed using the iterative procedure described in Section 9.4

Type-2 Con-sequent Set	Centroid	Figure 10-14 (a) Centroid ($\rho = 0.5$)	Figure 10-14 (b) Centroid ($\rho = 1$)
$NVL\ (\tilde{G}_1)$	$C_{\tilde{G}_1}$	[0.9808, 1.3820]	[0.7817, 1.5881]
$S\ (\tilde{G}_2)$	$C_{\tilde{G}_2}$	[3.6717, 4.4320]	[3.2856, 4.8338]
$MOA\ (\tilde{G}_3)$	$C_{\tilde{G}_3}$	[4.7501, 5.3314]	[4.4545, 5.6260]
$LA\ (\tilde{G}_4)$	$C_{\tilde{G}_4}$	[7.3418, 7.7915]	[7.1125, 8.0184]
$MAA\ (\tilde{G}_5)$	$C_{\tilde{G}_5}$	[8.9159, 9.2842]	[8.7136, 9.4651]

---

[8]Note that $\underline{C}_{avg}^i$ and $\overline{C}_{avg}^i$ play the roles of y_l^i and y_r^i, respectively.

Table 10-2: Histogram of survey responses for single-antecedent rules between indicator x_1 and consequent y. Entries denote the number of respondents out of 47 (w_i^l) that chose the consequent. C_{avg}^l is the weighted average of the responses, given by (10-97). For notational simplicity, the tildes have been omitted over the fuzzy set labels.

| | Consequent | | | | | |
Rule No.	None to Very Little	Some	A Moderate Amount	A Large Amount	A Maximum Amount	C_{avg}^l
1 (NVL)	42	3	2	0	0	[1.3130, 1.7447]
2 (S)	33	12	0	2	0	[1.9385, 2.4335]
3 (MOA)	12	16	15	3	1	[3.6747, 4.2580]
4 (LA)	3	6	11	25	2	[5.9277, 6.4413]
5 (MAA)	3	6	8	22	8	[6.2941, 6.7888]

Type-2 consensus FLA for x_1:

$$Y_{c2}(x_1) = [y_{c2,l}(x_1), y_{c2,r}(x_1)] \qquad (10\text{-}98a)$$

$$y_{c2,l}(x_1) = \sum_{i=1}^{5} \underline{C}_{avg}^i \frac{h_l^i}{\sum_{i=1}^{L(x_1)} \overline{f}^i + \sum_{j=L(x_1)+1}^{5} \underline{f}^j}$$

$$= \sum_{i=1}^{5} \underline{C}_{avg}^i \frac{h_l^i}{\sum_{i=1}^{L(x_1)} \overline{\mu}_{\tilde{F}_1^i}(x_1) + \sum_{j=L(x_1)+1}^{5} \underline{\mu}_{\tilde{F}_1^j}(x_1)} \qquad (10\text{-}98b)$$

$$h_l^i = \begin{cases} \overline{\mu}_{\tilde{F}_1^i}(x_1) & i \le L(x_1) \\ \underline{\mu}_{\tilde{F}_1^i}(x_1) & i > L(x_1) \end{cases} \qquad (10\text{-}98c)$$

$$y_{c2,r}(x_1) = \sum_{i=1}^{5} \overline{C}_{avg}^i \frac{h_r^i}{\sum_{i=1}^{R(x_1)} \underline{f}^i + \sum_{j=R(x_1)+1}^{5} \overline{f}^j}$$

$$= \sum_{i=1}^{5} \overline{C}_{avg}^i \frac{h_r^i}{\sum_{i=1}^{R(x_1)} \underline{\mu}_{\tilde{F}_1^i}(x_1) + \sum_{j=R(x_1)+1}^{5} \overline{\mu}_{\tilde{F}_1^j}(x_1)} \qquad (10\text{-}98d)$$

$$h_r^i = \begin{cases} \underline{\mu}_{\tilde{F}_1^i}(x_1) & i \le R(x_1) \\ \overline{\mu}_{\tilde{F}_1^i}(x_1) & i > R(x_1) \end{cases}$$

(10-98e)

$$y_{c2}(x_1) = \frac{y_{c2,l}(x_1) + y_{c2,r}(x_1)}{2}$$

(10-98f)

where $C_{avg}^i = [\underline{C}_{avg}^i, \overline{C}_{avg}^i]$, as given in Table 10-2.

Table 10-3: Histogram of survey responses for single-antecedent rules between indicator x_2 and consequent y. Entries denote the number of respondents out of 47 (w_i^l) that chose the consequent. C_{avg}^l is the weighted average of the responses, given by (10-97). For notational simplicity, the tildes have been omitted over the fuzzy set labels.

	Consequent					
Rule No.	None to Very Little	Some	A Moderate Amount	A Large Amount	A Maximum Amount	C_{avg}^l
1 (NVL)	36	7	4	0	0	[1.7024, 2.1724]
2 (S)	26	17	4	0	0	[2.2749, 2.8213]
3 (MOA)	2	16	27	2	0	[4.3328, 4.9618]
4 (LA)	1	3	11	22	10	[6.7006, 7.1825]
5 (MAA)	0	3	7	17	20	[7.3914, 7.8458]

Type-2 consensus FLA for x_2: Use the equations for the *Type-2 consensus FLA for* x_1 in which x_1 is replaced by x_2, and $C_{avg}^i = [\underline{C}_{avg}^i, \overline{C}_{avg}^i]$ is now given in Table 10-3.

Type-2 consensus FLA for x_1 *and* x_2: Use the equations for the *Type-2 consensus FLA for* x_1 in which: (a) x_1 is replaced by x_1, x_2; (b) $\overline{\mu}_{\tilde{F}_1^i}(x_1)$ is replaced by $\overline{\mu}_{\tilde{F}_1^i}(x_1) \times \overline{\mu}_{\tilde{F}_2^i}(x_2)$; (c) $\underline{\mu}_{\tilde{F}_1^i}(x_1)$ is replaced by $\underline{\mu}_{\tilde{F}_1^i}(x_1) \times \underline{\mu}_{\tilde{F}_2^i}(x_2)$; (d) $L(x_1)$ is replaced by $L(x_1, x_2)$; (e) $R(x_1)$ is replaced by $R(x_1, x_2)$; and, (f) $C_{avg}^i = [\underline{C}_{avg}^i, \overline{C}_{avg}^i]$ is now given in Table 10-4.

Although we have been able to write formulas for $Y_{c2}(x_1)$, $Y_{c2}(x_2)$, and $Y_{c2}(x_1, x_2)$, we cannot actually compute these quantities using them, because (as we explained in Section 10.9.4) we do not know $L(x_1)$, $L(x_2)$, $L(x_1, x_2)$, $R(x_1)$,

Table 10-4: Histogram of survey responses for two-antecedent rules between indicators x_1 and x_2 and consequent y. Entries denote the number of respondents out of 47 (w_i^l) that chose the consequent. C_{avg}^l is the weighted average of the responses, given by (10-97). For notational simplicity, the tildes have been omitted over the fuzzy set labels.

Rule No.	None to Very Little	Some	A Moderate Amount	A Large Amount	A Maximum Amount	C_{avg}^l
			Consequent			
1 (NVL/NVL)	38	7	2	0	0	[1.5420, 2.0043]
2 (NVL/S)	33	11	3	0	0	[1.8512, 2.3479]
3 (NVL/MOA)	6	21	16	4	0	[4.0076, 4.6347]
4 (NVL/LA)	0	12	26	8	1	[5.0045, 5.6046]
5 (NVL/MAA)	0	9	16	19	3	[5.8572, 6.4060]
6 (S/NVL)	31	11	4	1	0	[2.0667, 2.5683]
7 (S/S)	17	23	7	0	0	[2.8590, 3.4628]
8 (S/MOA)	0	19	19	8	1	[4.8439, 5.4706]
9 (S/LA)	1	8	23	13	2	[5.3805, 5.9429]
10 (S/MAA)	0	7	17	21	2	[5.9247, 6.4648]
11 (MOA/NVL)	7	23	16	1	0	[3.7161, 4.3554]
12 (MOA/S)	5	22	20	0	0	[3.8443, 4.4902]
13 (MOA/MOA)	2	7	22	15	1	[5.3449, 5.8986]
14 (MOA/LA)	1	4	13	17	12	[6.5792, 7.0699]
15 (MOA/MAA)	0	4	12	24	7	[6.6022, 7.0998]
16 (LA/NVL)	7	13	21	6	0	[4.2213, 4.8085]
17 (LA/S)	3	11	23	10	0	[4.4085, 5.3922]
18 (LA/MOA)	0	3	18	18	8	[6.3829, 6.8890]
19 (LA/LA)	0	1	9	17	20	[7.4373, 7.8841]
20 (LA/MAA)	1	2	6	11	27	[7.6237, 8.0556]
21 (MAA/NVL)	2	16	18	11	0	[4.8291, 5.4329]
22 (MAA/S)	2	9	22	13	1	[5.1887, 5.7557]
23 (MAA/MOA)	0	3	15	18	11	[6.6488, 7.1413]
24 (MAA/LA)	0	1	7	17	22	[7.6145, 8.0523]
25 (MAA/MAA)	0	2	3	12	30	[8.0250, 8.4443]

$R(x_2)$, or $R(x_1, x_2)$ ahead of time. These latter quantities can *only* be determined by using our four-step iterative procedure for computing the center-of-sets type-reduced set for each FLA. This is very different from the formulas for the three type-1 consensus FLAs, $y_{c1}(x_1)$, $y_{c1}(x_2)$, and $y_{c1}(x_1, x_2)$, in (5-61)–(5-63). Those formulas not only describe the type-1 FLAs, but they could also be used to compute them.

Example10-6: We show a sample calculation of $Y_{c2}(x_1, x_2)$ when (x_1, x_2) $= (3, 6)$ and $\rho = 0.5$. Observe, from the vertical dashed lines in Figure 10-14 (a), that $x_1 = 3$ fires the three type-2 fuzzy sets $N\tilde{V}L$, $\tilde{S}$, and $M\tilde{O}A$ and that $x_2 = 6$ fires the three type-2 fuzzy sets $\tilde{S}$, $M\tilde{O}A$, and $L\tilde{A}$. It follows, therefore, that the rules whose antecedent pairs are

$$(N\tilde{V}L, \tilde{S}), (N\tilde{V}L, M\tilde{O}A), (N\tilde{V}L, L\tilde{A}), (\tilde{S}, \tilde{S}), (\tilde{S}, M\tilde{O}A), (\tilde{S}, L\tilde{A}), (M\tilde{O}A, \tilde{S}),$$

$$(M\tilde{O}A, M\tilde{O}A), \text{ and } (M\tilde{O}A, L\tilde{A})$$

are the ones fired. From Table 10-4, we see that these are rules 2, 3, 4, 7, 8, 9, 12, 13, and 14. The firing interval for each of these rules is obtained by using (10-26)–(10-28). For example, the firing interval, F^8, for R^8 is (use the data in Table 10-5 for $l = 8$)

$$F^8 = [\ \underline{\mu}_{\tilde{F}_1^8}(3) \times \underline{\mu}_{\tilde{F}_2^8}(6), \overline{\mu}_{\tilde{F}_1^8}(3) \times \overline{\mu}_{\tilde{F}_2^8}(6)]$$
$$= [0.5037 \times 0.4822, \ 0.6695 \times 0.6469] = [0.2429, \ 0.4331] \tag{10-99}$$

Using the data in the second and third columns of Table 10-5, we can compute all of the other firing intervals that are needed in order to be able to compute $Y_{c2}(3, 6)$. They are listed in the last column of that table.

Finally, we compute $Y_{c2}(3, 6)$ using the formula in (10-43) for the center-of-sets type reducer:

$$Y_{c2}(3, 6) = \int_{c_2} \cdots \int_{c_{14}} \int_{f_2} \cdots \int_{f_{14}} 1 \bigg/ \frac{\sum_{i \in \Omega} c_i f_i}{\sum_{i \in \Omega} f_i} \qquad \Omega = \{2, 3, 4, 7, 8, 9, 12, 13, 14\} \tag{10-100}$$

where $c_i \in C^i_{avg}$ and the C^i_{avg} are given in the last column of Table 10-4, and $f_i \in F^i$ and the F^i are given in Table 10-5. Using our four-step iterative method to compute $Y_{c2}(3, 6)$, we find that $Y_{c2}(3, 6) = [3.5100, 5.8796]$; hence, $y_{c2}(3, 6) = (3.5100 + 5.8796)/2 = 4.6948$.

Comparing $Y_{c2}(3, 6)$ with its type-1 counterpart in (5-64), $y_{c1}(3, 6) = 4.8564$, we observe that: (a) $y_{c1}(3, 6) \in Y_{c2}(3, 6)$, and (b) $y_{c1}(3, 6) \neq y_{c2}(3, 6)$. The first observation is what we would have expected, but it is reassuring to see that it actually occurs. The second observation means that the type-reduced set, $Y_{c2}(3,6)$, is not symmetrically situated about $y_{c1}(3,6)$. Uncertainties do not necessarily flow in a symmetrical manner about the output of the type-1 FLA. ∎

Table 10-5: Firing intervals needed to compute $Y_{c2}(3,6)$. Note that (to within two significant figures) the primary membership intervals associated with $\mu_{\tilde{F}_1^l}(3)$ and $\mu_{\tilde{F}_2^l}(6)$ can be read directly off of Figure 10-14 (a).

Fired Rule (*l*)	$\mu_{\tilde{F}_1^l}(3)$	$\mu_{\tilde{F}_2^l}(6)$	Firing Interval F^l
2	[0, 0.2475]	[0, 0.3827]	[0, 0.0947]
3	[0, 0.2475]	[0.4822, 0.6469]	[0, 0.1601]
4	[0, 0.2475]	[0, 0.2834]	[0, 0.0701]
7	[0.5037, 0.6695]	[0, 0.3827]	[0, 0.2562]
8	[0.5037, 0.6695]	[0.4822, 0.6469]	[0.2429, 0.4331]
9	[0.5037, 0.6695]	[0, 0.2834]	[0, 0.1897]
12	[0, 0.2499]	[0, 0.3827]	[0, 0.0956]
13	[0, 0.2499]	[0.4822, 0.6469]	[0, 0.1617]
14	[0, 0.2499]	[0, 0.2834]	[0, 0.0708]

Plots of $Y_{c2}(x_1)$, $Y_{c2}(x_2)$, and $Y_{c2}(x_1,x_2)$ are depicted in Figures 10-15–10-17, respectively, for $\rho = 0.5$. The dashed lines on these plots are the defuzzified outputs of the comparable Section 5.11.1 type-1 FLA, namely, $y_{c1}(x_1)$, $y_{c1}(x_2)$ and $y_{c1}(x_1,x_2)$. We have chosen not to display the complete 3D plots of $y_{c2,l}(x_1,x_2)$ and $y_{c2,r}(x_1,x_2)$ on the same graph, because they obscure each other; hence, we have shown the cross-sections of these plots in Figure 10-17. All of these plots reveal that the type-2 FLAs provide a banded output, so that these FLAs can be used as described in Section 4.3.4.

Plots of $Y_{c2}(x_1)$ and $Y_{c2}(x_2)$ for $\rho = 1$ are depicted in Figures 10-18 and 10-19, respectively. Comparing these plots with their respective plots in Figures 10-15 and 10-16, we observe that: (a) the increased uncertainty in the FOUs have indeed propagated all the way through each FLA to its output; i.e., the bands in Figures 10-18 and 10-19 are larger than those in Figures 10-15 and 10-16; and (b) the bands in Figures 10-18 and 10-19 are non-monotonic, something that is undesirable. The regions of non-monotonicity seem to occur in the regions where there is a large overlap among the FOUs [see Figure 10-14 (b)]. Such large overlap does not occur for the $\rho = 0.5$ FOUs [see Figure 10-14 (a)]. In retrospect, a 100% uncertainty level is too large; for, if we were that uncertain we should have chosen the type-1 membership functions—the dashed curves in Figure 10-14—to be associated with the $\pm 2\sigma$ points instead of with the $\pm\sigma$ points as we have done.

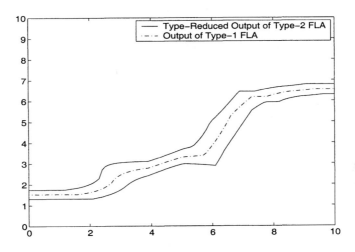

Figure 10-15: Outputs of the (50%) type-2 and type-1 FLAs for indicator x_1.

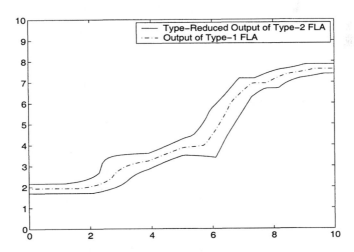

Figure 10-16: Outputs of the (50%) type-2 and type-1 FLAs for indicator x_2.

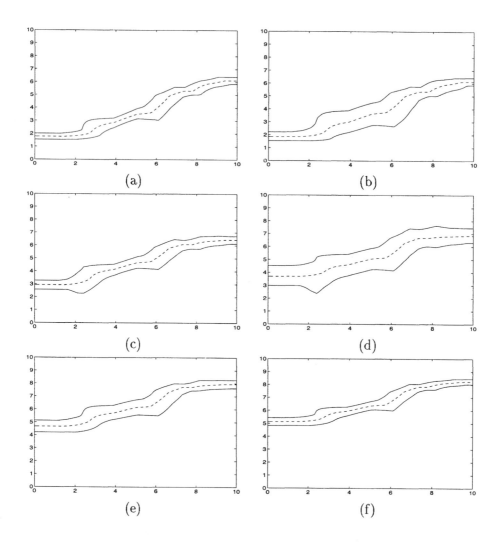

Figure 10-17: Outputs of the (50%) type-2 and type-1 FLAs for indicators x_1 and x_2. (a) $x_1 = 0$, (b) $x_1 = 2$, (c) $x_1 = 4$, (d) $x_1 = 6$, (e) $x_1 = 8$, and (f) $x_1 = 10$. The horizontal axis of each plot is x_2.

This completes our developments of type-1 and type-2 FLAs. Using a type-2 FLA it is now possible to propagate the different kinds of uncertainties that occur in survey-based knowledge-mining, from the inputs of the FLA to its output, something that could not be done using a type-1 FLA.

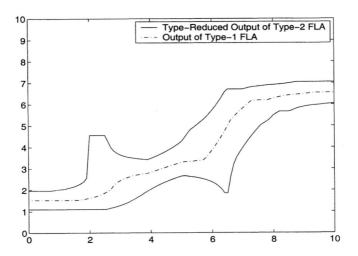

Figure 10-18: Outputs of the (100%) type-2 and type-1 FLAs for indicator x_1.

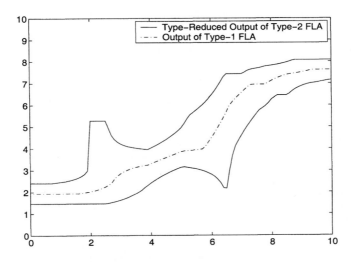

Figure 10-19: Outputs of the (100%) type-2 and type-1 FLAs for indicator x_2.

10.13 COMPUTATION

The following M-files, which are found in the folder *interval type-2 fuzzy logic systems*, are useful for designing an interval singleton type-2 FLS:

> **sfls.m:** Compute the output(s) of an interval singleton type-2 FLS when the antecedent membership functions are Gaussian primary membership functions with uncertain means.
>
> **train_sfls.m:** Tune the parameters of an interval singleton type-2 FLS when the antecedent membership functions are Gaussian primary membership functions with uncertain means, using some input–output training data.
>
> **svd_qr_sfls.m:** Rule-reduction of an interval singleton type-2 FLS when the antecedent membership functions are Gaussian primary membership functions with uncertain means, using some input–output training data.

EXERCISES

10-1: Use Theorem A-2 to compute

$$\mu_{\tilde{B}^1}(y) = \mu_{\tilde{G}^1}(y)\sqcap\mu_{\tilde{F}^1}(1) \text{ and } \mu_{\tilde{B}^1}(y) = \mu_{\tilde{G}^1}(y)\sqcap\mu_{\tilde{F}^1}(3)$$

for the membership functions of Example 10-1. Be sure to handle the clipped nature of $\mu_{\tilde{F}^1}(3)$.

10-2: In Figure 10-3 (a) let the secondary membership function at $x = 4$ in the antecedent be a Gaussian with mean μ and standard deviation Δ, and let the secondary membership function of every domain point of y of the consequent set in Figure 10-3 (b) be a Gaussian with mean $m(y)$ and standard deviation $\sigma(y)$. The Gaussians are contained in [0, 1] and may therefore be clipped. Ignore the effect of this clipping for simplicity. Using the Gaussian approximation in Example A-7, show that $\mu_{\tilde{B}^1}(y)$ is approximately Gaussian

with mean $\mu \times m(y)$ and standard deviation $\sqrt{[\Delta \times m(y)]^2 + [\mu \times \sigma(y)]^2}$ [Karnik and Mendel (1998b)].

10-3: Explain how the height type-reduced set for a type-2 FLS represents a collection of outputs of all the type-1 FLSs that are embedded in the type-2 FLS. What is the formula that describes each output? How many type-reduced sets will there be?

10-4: (a) Using (10-9), show that if all antecedent and consequent secondary membership functions of the type-2 FLS are normal (i.e., have only one point having unity secondary grade), then the output secondary membership function at every $y \in Y$ will also be normal. (b) Show that this means that the type-reduced set will also be normal and will have only one point having unity membership grade, and that this point will correspond to the centroid of the principal membership function of the type-2 output set.

10-5: Explain why $\mu_Y(y_i)$ in (10-11) and (10-12) is the same as b in (9-4).

10-6: Show the details that support the statement that (10-10) is not a FBF expansion for center-of-sets type-reduction.

10-7: Consider the situation when all the type-2 uncertainties disappear. Show that (10-10) reduces to a FBF expansion similar to the one given in (10-14).

10-8: Construct the structure of the singleton type-2 FLS for the special type-2 situation described in Example 10-3.

10-9: Determine the centroids of the three fired consequents that are associated with the Example 10-3 antecedent sets which are centered at x^6, x^7, and x^8. See Example 9-4 for an interpretation of the results.

10-10: Perform the computations needed to obtain the curves in Figure 10-11.

10-11: Redo Example 10-3 for consequent membership functions whose standard deviation equals 20.

10-12: Suppose that we use modified-height type-reduction instead of center-of-sets type-reduction. Everything else is the same. Does this change (10-57)–(10-65)? If not, what does change?

10-13: Provide as detailed a flow chart as possible for the calculations required to implement (10-57)–(10-62).

10-14: Explain why, in Example 10-4, a viable alternative to using the three consequent parameters m_1^j, m_2^j, and σ^j is to use the 2 parameters y_l^j and y_r^j.

10-15: Create a flow-chart that enumerates all the calculations for the one-pass method, which uses the Gaussian primary membership functions in (10-66) and (10-67), product implication and t-norm, center-of sets type-reduction, and the defuzzification in (10-49).

10-16: Repeat Exercise 10-15 for the primary membership functions depicted in Figure 3-9, product implication and t-norm, height type-reduction, and the defuzzification in (10-49).

10-17: In Example 10-5, for $\mathbf{x}^{(1)} = (3.75, 6.0)^T$, examining Figure 10-12 (a), it is easy to show that $x_2^{(1)} > m_{22}^1 > (m_{21}^1 + m_{22}^1)/2$. Using these inequalities, establish equations for the active values of $\partial \overline{\mu}_{\tilde{F}_1^1}(x_2^{(1)})/\partial m_{11}^1$, $\partial \overline{\mu}_{\tilde{F}_1^1}(x_2^{(1)})/\partial m_{12}^1$, $\partial \underline{\mu}_{\tilde{F}_1^1}(x_2^{(1)})/\partial m_{11}^1$, and $\partial \underline{\mu}_{\tilde{F}_1^1}(x_2^{(1)})/\partial m_{12}^1$.

10-18: (a) Complete the evaluation of (10-89). (b) Using the values of $x_1^{(1)}$ and $x_2^{(1)}$ given in Example 10-5, obtain expressions for the partial derivatives of y_l with respect to all of the parameters that it depends on. (c) Repeat part (b) for y_r. (d) Write out the steepest descent algorithms for all of the antecedent mean-value parameters. (e) Write out the steepest descent algorithms for all of the antecedent standard deviation parameters. Hint: The standard deviations appear in both y_l and y_r; hence, e.g.,

$$\frac{\partial e^{(i)}}{\partial \sigma_1^1} = \frac{\partial e^{(i)}}{\partial f_{s2}(\mathbf{x}^{(i)})} \left[\frac{\partial f_{s2}(\mathbf{x}^{(i)})}{\partial y_l} \frac{\partial y_l}{\partial \sigma_1^1} + \frac{\partial f_{s2}(\mathbf{x}^{(i)})}{\partial y_r} \frac{\partial y_r}{\partial \sigma_1^1} \right]$$

(f) Write out the steepest descent algorithms for consequent parameters y_l^1, y_l^2, y_r^1, and y_r^2.

10-19. Suppose, in Example 10-5, $\mathbf{x}^{(2)} = (x_1^{(2)}, x_2^{(2)})^T = (6.0, 2.0)^T$ and $y^{(2)} = 7.2$. Set up the steepest descent algorithms for all of the parameters of the two-rule singleton type-2 FLS.

10-20: Generalize Example 10-5 to a system of M rules each with p antecedents. Set up the steepest descent algorithms for all of the parameters of the M-rule singleton type-2 FLS. Create a flow-chart for the entire process.

10-21: Using Table 4-2, establish all of the numerical values that are needed to completely specify the five FOUs depicted in Figure 10-14 (a) and (b).

10-22: Using (10-97), compute C_{avg}^l in Tables 10-2 and 10-3 for $l = 1, ..., 5$.

10-23: In Example 10-6, compute $Y_{c2}(2,4)$ and $y_{c2}(2,4)$.

CHAPTER 11

Type-1 Non-Singleton Type-2 Fuzzy Logic Systems

11.1 INTRODUCTION

Recall, from Section 6.1, that a non-singleton FLS is one whose inputs are modeled as fuzzy numbers. In that chapter, which was for a non-singleton *type-1* FLS, we focused only on inputs modeled as *type-1* fuzzy numbers. Within the framework of more general type-2 FLSs, we can expand our viewpoint to include inputs that are modeled as either *type-1* or *type-2* fuzzy numbers. This chapter focuses on the former, whereas the next chapter focuses on the latter. A type-2 FLS whose inputs are modeled as type-1 fuzzy numbers is referred to as a *type-1 non-singleton type-2 FLS*.

A type-1 non-singleton type-2 FLS is described by the same diagram as is a singleton type-2 FLS, Figure 10-1, which we repeat here as Figure 11-1, for the convenience of the readers. The rules of a type-1 non-singleton type-2 FLS are the same as those for a singleton type-2 FLS. What are different is the fuzzifier, which treats the inputs as type-1 fuzzy sets, and the effect of this on the inference block. The output of the inference block will again be a type-2 fuzzy set; so, the type-reducers and defuzzifier that we described for a singleton type-2 FLS apply as well to a type-1 non-singleton type-2 FLS.

This chapter parallels Chapters 6 and 10. To make it fairly self-contained there is some repetition of material from each of these chapters.

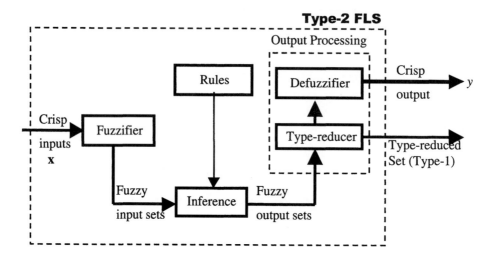

Figure 11-1: Type-2 FLS that is valid regardless of the nature of the input.

11.2 FUZZIFICATION AND ITS EFFECT ON INFERENCE

In the FLS of Figure 11-1, as in the FLS of Figure 10-1, crisp inputs are first fuzzified into fuzzy input sets that then activate the inference block, which in the present case is associated with type-2 fuzzy sets. In this section, we explain type-1 non-singleton fuzzification and the effect of such fuzzification on the inference engine.

11.2.1 Fuzzifier

In type-1 non-singleton fuzzification (described in Section 6.2.1 as "non-singleton fuzzification"), measurement $x_i = x_i'$ is mapped into a fuzzy number; i.e., a membership function is associated with it. More specifically, a type-1 non-singleton fuzzifier is one for which $\mu_{X_i}(x_i') = 1$ ($i = 1, ..., p$) and $\mu_{X_i}(x_i)$ decreases from unity as x_i moves away from x_i'. Conceptually, the type-1 non-singleton fuzzifier implies that the given input value x_i' is the most likely value to be the correct one from all the values in its immediate neighborhood. Section

6.2.1 discussions about the shape of $\mu_{X_i}(x_i)$ (Gaussian, triangular, unnamed) are unchanged for the present chapter.

11.2.2 Fuzzy inference engine

The reader should review Section 10.3, because we pick up its story here with Equation (10-8), i.e.,

$$
\mu_{\tilde{B}^l}(y) = \mu_{\tilde{G}^l}(y) \sqcap \left\{ \left[\sqcup_{x_1 \in X_1} \mu_{\tilde{X}_1}(x_1) \sqcap \mu_{\tilde{F}_1^l}(x_1) \right] \sqcap \right.
$$
$$
\left. \cdots \sqcap \left[\sqcup_{x_p \in X_p} \mu_{\tilde{X}_p}(x_p) \sqcap \mu_{\tilde{F}_p^l}(x_p) \right] \right\}, \quad y \in Y
\tag{11-1}
$$

where $l = 1, \ldots, M$. Recall that, for singleton fuzzification, (11-1) simplified to (10-9) in which all of the joins were very easy to evaluate because $\mu_{\tilde{X}_i}(x_i)$ is non-zero only at one point, $x_i = x_i'$. Unfortunately, the same simplification does not occur for type-1 non-singleton fuzzification.

For type-1 non-singleton fuzzification, (11-1) can be expressed as

$$
\mu_{\tilde{B}^l}(y) = \mu_{\tilde{G}^l}(y) \sqcap \left\{ \left[\sqcup_{x_1 \in X_1} \mu_{X_1}(x_1) \sqcap \mu_{\tilde{F}_1^l}(x_1) \right] \sqcap \right.
$$
$$
\left. \cdots \sqcap \left[\sqcup_{x_p \in X_p} \mu_{X_p}(x_p) \sqcap \mu_{\tilde{F}_p^l}(x_p) \right] \right\}, \quad y \in Y
\tag{11-2}
$$

in which we have replaced the type-2 input sets by their type-1 counterparts. Paralleling our developments in Chapter 6, we let

$$
\mu_{\tilde{Q}_k^l}(x_k) \equiv \mu_{X_k}(x_k) \sqcap \mu_{\tilde{F}_k^l}(x_k)
\tag{11-3}
$$

where $k = 1, \ldots, p$ and $l = 1, \ldots, M$, so that

$$
\mu_{\tilde{B}^l}(y) = \mu_{\tilde{G}^l}(y) \sqcap \left\{ \left[\sqcup_{x_1 \in X_1} \mu_{\tilde{Q}_1^l}(x_1) \right] \sqcap \cdots \sqcap \left[\sqcup_{x_p \in X_p} \mu_{\tilde{Q}_p^l}(x_p) \right] \right\}
$$
$$
= \mu_{\tilde{G}^l}(y) \sqcap \left\{ \sqcup_{x \in X} \left[\sqcap_{k=1}^p \mu_{\tilde{Q}_k^l}(x_k) \right] \right\}, \quad y \in Y
\tag{11-4}
$$

For later use. we define

$$\mu_{\tilde{Q}^l}(\mathbf{x}) \equiv \prod_{k=1}^{p} \mu_{\tilde{Q}_k^l}(x_k) \tag{11-5}$$

and[1]

$$F^l(\mathbf{x}') \equiv \sqcup_{\mathbf{x} \in X} \left[\prod_{k=1}^{p} \mu_{\tilde{Q}_k^l}(x_k) \right] = \sqcup_{\mathbf{x} \in X} \mu_{\tilde{Q}^l}(\mathbf{x}) \tag{11-6}$$

so that $\mu_{\tilde{B}^l}(y)$ in (11-4) can be re-expressed as

$$\mu_{\tilde{B}^l}(y) = \mu_{\tilde{G}^l}(y) \prod F^l(\mathbf{x}'), \quad y \in Y \tag{11-7}$$

This is the fundamental equation for a type-1 non-singleton type-2 FLS. The term $F^l(\mathbf{x}')$ is the *firing set* for a type-1 non-singleton type-2 FLS.

The general material in Sections 10.5–10.8 apply as well to a type-1 non-singleton type-2 FLS, so we refer the reader to them. Regarding "possibilities," what is new for a type-1 non-singleton type-2 FLS is the need for the designer to choose membership functions for the input measurements, something that wasn't necessary for a singleton type-2 FLS. If, e.g., the designer chooses a Gaussian membership function for each input, then the mean and standard deviation need to be specified for each function. These represent the additional new possibilities for a type-1 non-singleton type-2 FLS.

In general, it is very difficult to compute (11-7) for arbitrary type-2 fuzzy sets; so, as in Chapter 10, we focus our attention on interval type-2 fuzzy sets, for which it is possible to obtain a closed-form formula for (11-7).

11.3 INTERVAL TYPE-1 NON-SINGLETON TYPE-2 FLSs

Justification for using interval type-2 fuzzy sets has been given in Section 10.9. This justification is equally valid for a type-1 non-singleton type-2 or a singleton type-2 FLS; hence, it will not be repeated here. In Section 10.9.1, we also found that the concepts of *upper and lower membership functions* for an interval type-2 FLS were very useful for obtaining closed-form formulas for (10-9). That section's descriptions of upper and lower membership functions remain

---

[1]Although input $\mathbf{x}'$ does not appear explicitly on the right-hand side of (11-6), it is contained in each $\mu_{\tilde{Q}_k^l}(x_k)$ through the latter's dependence on the input membership function $\mu_{X_k}(x_k)$. If, e.g., $\mu_{X_k}(x_k)$ is a Gaussian function, then its mean value is chosen to be x'_k.

unchanged for an interval type-1 non-singleton type-2 FLS; i.e., their definitions do not depend on the nature of the inputs to the FLS; hence, we will not repeat them here.

The major result for an interval type-1 non-singleton type-2 FLS is summarized in the following:

Theorem 11-1: [Liang and Mendel (2000c)] *In an interval type-1 nonsingleton type-2 FLS with meet under product or minimum t-norm: (a) the result of the input and antecedent operations, which are contained in the firing set $F^l(\mathbf{x}')$ in (11-6), is an interval type-1 set, i.e.,*

$$F^l(\mathbf{x}') = \left[\underline{f}^l(\mathbf{x}'), \overline{f}^l(\mathbf{x}') \right] \equiv \left[\underline{f}^l, \overline{f}^l \right] \tag{11-8}$$

where

$$\underline{f}^l(\mathbf{x}') = \sup_{\mathbf{x}} \int_{x_1 \in X_1} \cdots \int_{x_p \in X_p} \left[\left[\mu_{X_1}(x_1) \star \underline{\mu}_{\tilde{F}_1^l}(x_1) \right] \star \right.$$
$$\left. \cdots \star \left[\mu_{X_p}(x_p) \star \underline{\mu}_{\tilde{F}_p^l}(x_p) \right] \right] / \mathbf{x} \tag{11-9}$$

and

$$\overline{f}^l(\mathbf{x}') = \sup_{\mathbf{x}} \int_{x_1 \in X_1} \cdots \int_{x_p \in X_p} \left[\mu_{X_1}(x_1) \star \overline{\mu}_{\tilde{F}_1^l}(x_1) \right] \star$$
$$\cdots \star \left[\mu_{X_p}(x_p) \star \overline{\mu}_{\tilde{F}_p^l}(x_p) \right] / \mathbf{x} \tag{11-10}$$

and the supremum is attained when each term in brackets attains its supremum;

(b) the rule R^l fired output consequent set, $\mu_{\tilde{B}^l}(y)$ in (11-7), is a type-1 fuzzy set, where

$$\mu_{\tilde{B}^l}(y) = \int_{b^l \in \left[\underline{f}^l \star \underline{\mu}_{\tilde{G}^l}(y), \overline{f}^l \star \overline{\mu}_{\tilde{G}^l}(y) \right]} 1/b^l, \quad y \in Y \tag{11-11}$$

where $\underline{\mu}_{\tilde{G}^l}(y)$ and $\overline{\mu}_{\tilde{G}^l}(y)$ are the lower and upper membership grades of $\mu_{\tilde{G}^l}(y)$; and,

(c) suppose that N of the M rules in the FLS fire, where $N \leq M$, and the combined type-1 output fuzzy set is obtained by combining the fired output consequent sets; i.e., $\mu_{\tilde{B}}(y) = \sqcup_{l=1}^{N} \mu_{\tilde{B}^l}(y)$ $y \in Y$; then,

$$\mu_{\tilde{B}}(y) = \int_{b \in \left[\left[\underline{f}^1 \star \underline{\mu}_{\tilde{G}^1}(y)\right] \vee \cdots \vee \left[\underline{f}^N \star \underline{\mu}_{\tilde{G}^N}(y)\right], \left[\overline{f}^1 \star \overline{\mu}_{\tilde{G}^1}(y)\right] \vee \cdots \vee \left[\overline{f}^N \star \overline{\mu}_{\tilde{G}^N}(y)\right]\right]} 1/b, \quad y \in Y \quad (11\text{-}12)$$

Proof: (a) To compute $F^l(\mathbf{x}')$ using (11-6), we first compute $\mu_{\tilde{Q}_k^l}(x_k)$ using (11-3) and then compute $\mu_{\tilde{Q}^l}(\mathbf{x})$ using (11-5). Applying Theorem 7-2 to (11-3) for an interval type-1 non-singleton type-2 FLS, and using the facts that

$$\mu_{X_k}(x_k) = \left[\underline{\mu}_{X_k}(x_k), \overline{\mu}_{X_k}(x_k)\right]\Big|_{\underline{\mu}_{X_k}(x_k) = \overline{\mu}_{X_k}(x_k)} \quad (11\text{-}13)$$

and

$$\mu_{\tilde{F}_k^l}(x_k) = \int_{w^l \in \left[\underline{\mu}_{\tilde{F}_k^l}(x_k), \overline{\mu}_{\tilde{F}_k^l}(x_k)\right]} 1/w^l, \quad (11\text{-}14)$$

we find that

$$\mu_{\tilde{Q}_k^l}(x_k) = \mu_{X_k}(x_k) \sqcap \mu_{\tilde{F}_k^l}(x_k)$$
$$= \int_{q^l \in \left[\mu_{X_k}(x_k) \star \underline{\mu}_{\tilde{F}_k^l}(x_k), \mu_{X_k}(x_k) \star \overline{\mu}_{\tilde{F}_k^l}(x_k)\right]} 1/q^l \quad (11\text{-}15)$$
$$= \left[\mu_{X_k}(x_k) \star \underline{\mu}_{\tilde{F}_k^l}(x_k), \mu_{X_k}(x_k) \star \overline{\mu}_{\tilde{F}_k^l}(x_k)\right] \quad \forall x_k \in X_k$$

So, the meet between an input type-1 set and an antecedent type-2 set just involves the t-norm operation between the input membership function and the lower and upper membership functions of the antecedent. From (11-15), we see that the lower and upper membership functions of $\mu_{\tilde{Q}_k^l}(x_k)$ are

$$\underline{\mu}_{\tilde{Q}_k^l}(x_k) = \int_{x_k \in X_k} \left[\mu_{X_k}(x_k) \star \underline{\mu}_{\tilde{F}_k^l}(x_k) \right] / x_k \qquad (11\text{-}16)$$

and

$$\overline{\mu}_{\tilde{Q}_k^l}(x_k) = \int_{x_k \in X_k} \left[\mu_{X_k}(x_k) \star \overline{\mu}_{\tilde{F}_k^l}(x_k) \right] / x_k \qquad (11\text{-}17)$$

Next, we turn to (11-5), from which we note that its meet operations are in a p-dimensional Cartesian product space; hence, the meet operation is over all points $x_k \in X_k$, $k = 1, \dots, p$. Based on Theorem 7-2, we know that the upper membership function of $\mu_{\tilde{Q}^l}(\mathbf{x})$, $\overline{\mu}_{\tilde{Q}^l}(\mathbf{x})$ (which is a type-1 membership function) is obtained from $\overline{\mu}_{\tilde{Q}_1^l}(x_1) \star \cdots \star \overline{\mu}_{\tilde{Q}_p^l}(x_p)$; hence, using (11-17) in this expression, we find

$$\overline{\mu}_{\tilde{Q}^l}(\mathbf{x}) = \int_{x_1 \in X_1} \cdots \int_{x_p \in X_p} \left[\mu_{X_1}(x_1) \star \overline{\mu}_{\tilde{F}_1^l}(x_1) \right] \star$$
$$\cdots \star \left[\mu_{X_p}(x_p) \star \overline{\mu}_{\tilde{F}_p^l}(x_p) \right] / \mathbf{x} \qquad (11\text{-}18)$$

The lower membership function of $\mu_{\tilde{Q}^l}(\mathbf{x})$, $\underline{\mu}_{\tilde{Q}^l}(\mathbf{x})$ (which is also a type-1 membership function) is obtained from $\underline{\mu}_{\tilde{Q}_1^l}(x_1) \star \cdots \star \underline{\mu}_{\tilde{Q}_p^l}(x_p)$; hence, using (11-16) in this expression, we find

$$\underline{\mu}_{\tilde{Q}^l}(\mathbf{x}) = \int_{x_1 \in X_1} \cdots \int_{x_p \in X_p} \left[\mu_{X_1}(x_1) \star \underline{\mu}_{\tilde{F}_1^l}(x_1) \right] \star$$
$$\cdots \star \left[\mu_{X_p}(x_p) \star \underline{\mu}_{\tilde{F}_p^l}(x_p) \right] / \mathbf{x} \qquad (11\text{-}19)$$

Finally, we turn to (11-6), where we observe that its join operation is over all points $\mathbf{x} \in \mathbf{X}$. Based on Theorem 7-1, we know that the right-most point of the join of p interval type-1 sets is the maximum value of all the right-most points in the p interval type-1 sets; hence, the right-most point of $F^l(\mathbf{x}')$, $\overline{f}^l(\mathbf{x}')$, comes from the maximum value (supremum) of $\overline{\mu}_{\tilde{Q}^l}(\mathbf{x})$; consequently, from (11-18), we find

$$\overline{f}^{\,l}(\mathbf{x}') = \sup_{\mathbf{x}} \int_{x_1 \in X_1} \cdots \int_{x_p \in X_p} \left[\mu_{X_1}(x_1) \star \overline{\mu}_{\tilde{F}_1^l}(x_1)\right] \star$$
$$\cdots \star \left[\mu_{X_p}(x_p) \star \overline{\mu}_{\tilde{F}_p^l}(x_p)\right] \Big/ \mathbf{x} \tag{11-20}$$

Similarly, the left-most point of $F^l(\mathbf{x}')$, $f^l(\mathbf{x}')$, comes from the maximum value (supremum) of $\underline{\mu}_{\tilde{Q}^l}(\mathbf{x})$; hence, from (11-19), we find

$$\underline{f}^{\,l}(\mathbf{x}') = \sup_{\mathbf{x}} \int_{x_1 \in X_1} \cdots \int_{x_p \in X_p} \left[\mu_{X_1}(x_1) \star \underline{\mu}_{\tilde{F}_1^l}(x_1)\right] \star$$
$$\cdots \star \left[\mu_{X_p}(x_p) \star \underline{\mu}_{\tilde{F}_p^l}(x_p)\right] \Big/ \mathbf{x} \tag{11-21}$$

The suprema in (11-20) and (11-21) are over all $\mathbf{x} \in \mathbf{X}$. By the monotonicity property of a t-norm (e.g., [Zimmerman (1991)]), the supremum is attained when each term in brackets attains its supremum.

(b) Using (11-8) and Theorem 7-2, (11-7) can be expressed as in (10-32); hence, the rest of the proof is the same as that of part (b) of Theorem 10-1.

(c) The proof is the same as the proof of part (c) of Theorem 10-1. ∎

Observe, from the details of the proof of Theorem 11-1, that it differs from the proof of Theorem 10-1 only in its first part, because the nature of the input—singleton or type-1–non-singleton—only affects the computation of the firing set, which is now a firing interval.

In evaluating (11-9) and (11-10), the supremum is attained when each term in brackets attains its supremum; hence, in the inference mechanism block of a type-1 non-singleton type-2 FLS we will examine

$$\underline{f}_k^l(x_k') \equiv \sup_{x_k} \int_{x_k \in X_k} \left[\mu_{X_k}(x_k) \star \underline{\mu}_{\tilde{F}_k^l}(x_k)\right] \Big/ x_k = \sup_{x_k} \underline{\mu}_{\tilde{Q}_k^l}(x_k) \tag{11-22}$$

and

$$\overline{f}_k^l(x_k') \equiv \sup_{x_k} \int_{x_k \in X_k} \left[\mu_{X_k}(x_k) \star \overline{\mu}_{\tilde{F}_k^l}(x_k)\right] \Big/ x_k = \sup_{x_k} \overline{\mu}_{\tilde{Q}_k^l}(x_k) \tag{11-23}$$

where $k = 1, \ldots, p$, and we have used (11-16) and (11-17).

Let $\underline{x}_{k,\max}^l$ and $\overline{x}_{k,\max}^l$ denote the values of x_k that are associated with $\sup_{x_k} \underline{\mu}_{\tilde{Q}_k^l}(x_k)$ and $\sup_{x_k} \overline{\mu}_{\tilde{Q}_k^l}(x_k)$, respectively, so that

$$\underline{f}^l_k(x'_k) = \underline{\mu}_{\tilde{Q}^l_k}(\underline{x}^l_{k,\max}) \tag{11-24}$$

and

$$\overline{f}^l_k(x'_k) = \overline{\mu}_{\tilde{Q}^l_k}(\overline{x}^l_{k,\max}) \tag{11-25}$$

This means, of course, that $\underline{f}^l(\mathbf{x}')$ and $\overline{f}^l(\mathbf{x}')$ in (11-9) and (11-10) can be re-expressed as

$$\underline{f}^l(\mathbf{x}') = T^p_{k=1}\underline{f}^l_k(x'_k) = T^p_{k=1}\underline{\mu}_{\tilde{Q}^l_k}(\underline{x}^l_{k,\max}) \tag{11-26}$$

and

$$\overline{f}^l(\mathbf{x}') = T^p_{k=1}\overline{f}^l_k(x'_k) = T^p_{k=1}\overline{\mu}_{\tilde{Q}^l_k}(\overline{x}^l_{k,\max}) \tag{11-27}$$

To see the forest from the trees, so-to-speak, we summarize all of this as a procedure to compute $F^l(\mathbf{x}')$ in (11-8):

1. Choose a t-norm (product or minimum) and create the functions $\underline{\mu}_{\tilde{Q}^l_k}(x_k)$ and $\overline{\mu}_{\tilde{Q}^l_k}(x_k)$ using (11-16) and (11-17), respectively.

2. Compute $\underline{x}^l_{k,\max}$ and $\overline{x}^l_{k,\max}$ by maximizing $\underline{\mu}_{\tilde{Q}^l_k}(x_k)$ and $\overline{\mu}_{\tilde{Q}^l_k}(x_k)$, respectively.

3. Evaluate $\underline{f}^l_k(x'_k)$ and $\overline{f}^l_k(x'_k)$ using (11-24) and (11-25), respectively.

4. Compute $\underline{f}^l(\mathbf{x}')$ and $\overline{f}^l(\mathbf{x}')$ using (11-26) and (11-27), respectively.

Example 11-1: Here we consider a pictorial description of this four-step procedure using the minimum and product t-norms. As such, it is similar to Example 10-2, and will let us contrast pictorial descriptions for an interval type-1 non-singleton type-2 FLS with an interval singleton type-2 FLS. It will also help us to better understand the flow of rule-uncertainties combined with type-1 input uncertainties through an interval type-1 non-singleton type-2 FLS.

Figure 11-2 depicts input and antecedent operations [(11-22)–(11-27)] for a two-antecedent single-consequent rule, type-1 non-singleton fuzzification, and minimum or product t-norms. In all cases, the firing strength is an interval type-1 set $[\underline{f}^l, \overline{f}^l]$, where $\underline{f}^l = \underline{f}^l_1 \star \underline{f}^l_2$ and $\overline{f}^l = \overline{f}^l_1 \star \overline{f}^l_2$. According to (11-22), $\underline{f}^l_k$ is the supremum of the firing strength between the t-norm of $\mu_{X_k}(x_k)$ and the lower membership function $\underline{\mu}_{\tilde{F}_k^l}(x_k)$, and according to (11-23) $\overline{f}_k^l$ is the supremum of the firing strength between the t-norm of $\mu_{X_k}(x_k)$ and the upper membership function $\overline{\mu}_{\tilde{F}_k^l}(x_k)$ $(k = 1, 2)$. Note that $\mu_{X_k}(x_k)$ is centered at $x_k = x_k'$. These t-norms are shown as heavy curves in Figure 11-2 (a) and (b). From these heavy curves it is easy to pick off their suprema.

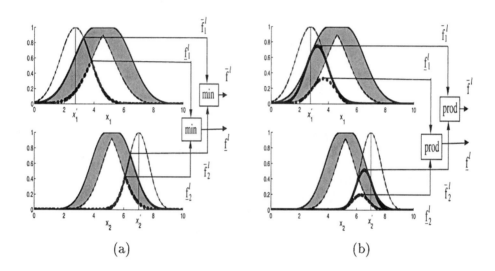

(a)   (b)

Figure 11-2: Pictorial description of input and antecedent operations for an interval type-1 non-singleton type-2 FLS. (a) minimum t-norm, and (b) product t-norm.

The main thing to observe from Figure 11-2 (a) and (b) is that, regardless of the t-norm, the result of input and antecedent operations is an interval—the *firing interval*. Consequently, the results depicted in Figures 10-7 [$\mu_{\tilde{B}^l}(y)$, $y \in Y$, for a two-rule FLS] and 10-8 (combined output set for a two-rule FLS) remain the same for an interval type-1 non-singleton type-2 FLS. The only difference between an interval type-1 non-singleton type-2 FLS and an interval singleton type-2 FLS is their firing intervals. The present case of type-1 non-singleton fuzzification leads to a firing interval that includes the *additional uncertainty* of the type-1 non-singleton inputs. In Examples 11-2 and 11-3, we quantify the firing intervals so that the reader will be able to observe *exactly* how the additional uncertainty of the type-1 non-singleton inputs affects these firing intervals. ■

Example 11-2: Here we quantify the results that were presented in Example 11-1, but for the case when the antecedent membership functions are Gaussian primary membership functions with uncertain standard deviations (as in Figure 3-9) and the inputs are modeled as Gaussian fuzzy numbers. We shall compute $\overline{f}_k^l$ and $\underline{f}_k^l$ for this case.

To begin, we state the membership functions for the inputs and antecedents. In this case,

$$\mu_{X_k}(x_k) = \exp\left[-\frac{1}{2}\left(\frac{x_k - x_k'}{\sigma_{X_k}}\right)^2\right]. \qquad (11\text{-}28)$$

and each $\mu_{\tilde{F}_k^l}(x_k)$ is described in terms of its Gaussian primary membership function

$$\mu_k^l(x_k) = \exp\left[-\frac{1}{2}\left(\frac{x_k - m_k^l}{\sigma_k^l}\right)^2\right] \quad \sigma_k^l \in [\sigma_{k1}^l, \sigma_{k2}^l] \qquad (11\text{-}29)$$

The lower and upper antecedent set membership functions are $\underline{\mu}_{\tilde{F}_k^l}(x_k)$ and $\overline{\mu}_{\tilde{F}_k^l}(x_k)$, respectively (see Example 3-14).

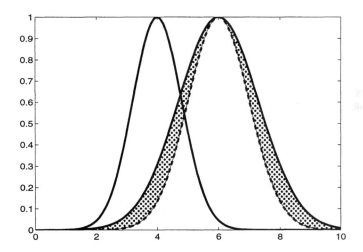

Figure 11-3: The membership functions for Example 11-2. The thick solid line denotes the upper membership function and the thick dashed line denotes the lower membership function. The shaded region is the FOU for the antecedent membership function. The membership function for the input is centered at x_k'.

The input membership function and antecedent FOU are depicted in Figure 11-3. Observe, from (11-23), that $\overline{f}_k^l$ requires the calculation of the supremum of a product or minimum of the two Gaussians $\mu_{X_k}(x_k)$ and $\overline{\mu}_{\tilde{F}_k^l}(x_k)$. Such a calculation has been carried out in Example 6-2 for the product t-norm and in Exercise 6-2 for the minimum t-norm. For convenience of the reader, we restate the results here. In the type-1 non-singleton case, the value of x_k at which

$$\sup_{x_k}\int_{x_k \in X_k}\left[\mu_{X_k}(x_k)\star\mu_{F_k^l}(x_k)\right]\big/x_k$$

is achieved is denoted $x_{k,\max}^l$. For product t-norm,

$$x_{k,\max}^l = \frac{\sigma_{X_k}^2 m_{F_k^l} + \sigma_{F_k^l}^2 x_k'}{\sigma_{X_k}^2 + \sigma_{F_k^l}^2} \tag{11-30}$$

whereas, for minimum t-norm,

$$x_{k,\max}^l = \frac{\sigma_{X_k} m_{F_k^l} + \sigma_{F_k^l} x_k'}{\sigma_{X_k} + \sigma_{F_k^l}} \tag{11-31}$$

Denoting the value of x_k at which the supremum in (11-23) occurs as $\overline{x}_{k,\max}^l$, it follows from (11-23) and Figure 11-3, that for product t-norm

$$\overline{x}_{k,\max}^l = \frac{\sigma_{X_k}^2 m_k^l + \sigma_{k2}^{l2} x_k'}{\sigma_{X_k}^2 + \sigma_{k2}^{l2}} \tag{11-32}$$

Similarly, $\underline{f}_k^l$ requires the calculation of the supremum of a product or minimum of the two Gaussians $\mu_{X_k}(x_k)$ and $\underline{\mu}_{\tilde{F}_k^l}(x_k)$. Denoting the value of x_k at which the supremum in (11-22) occurs as $\underline{x}_{k,\max}^l$, it follows from (11-22) and Figure 11-3, that for product t-norm

$$\underline{x}_{k,\max}^l = \frac{\sigma_{X_k}^2 m_k^l + \sigma_{k1}^{l2} x_k'}{\sigma_{X_k}^2 + \sigma_{k1}^{l2}} \tag{11-33}$$

From these results it is straightforward to compute $\underline{f}_k^l$ using (11-24) and (11-16), and $\overline{f}_k^l$ using (11-25) and (11-17); i.e., [see also (6-10)]

$$\underline{f}^l_k = \mu_{\tilde{Q}^l_k}(\underline{x}^l_{k,\max}) = \mu_{X_k}(\underline{x}^l_{k,\max})\underline{\mu}_{\tilde{F}^l_k}(\underline{x}^l_{k,\max}) = \exp\left\{-\tfrac{1}{2}\frac{\left(m^l_k - x'_k\right)^2}{\sigma^2_{X_k} + \sigma^{l^2}_{k1}}\right\} \qquad (11\text{-}34)$$

and

$$\overline{f}^l_k = \overline{\mu}_{\tilde{Q}^l_k}(\overline{x}^l_{k,\max}) = \mu_{X_k}(\overline{x}^l_{k,\max})\overline{\mu}_{\tilde{F}^l_k}(\overline{x}^l_{k,\max}) = \exp\left\{-\tfrac{1}{2}\frac{\left(m^l_k - x'_k\right)^2}{\sigma^2_{X_k} + \sigma^{l^2}_{k2}}\right\} \qquad ■ \qquad (11\text{-}35)$$

Example 11-3: [Liang and Mendel (2000c)] Here we quantify the results that were presented in Example 11-1 for which the antecedent membership functions were shown as Gaussian primary membership functions with uncertain means (as in Figure 3-8) and the inputs were modeled as Gaussian fuzzy numbers. This is a very important case because we have found it to be very useful for forecasting time-series, and in fact, we shall use its results in Section 11.5. As in Example 11-2, we focus on the computation of $\underline{f}^l_k$ and $\overline{f}^l_k$.

However, because the present case (in which we treat the input measurements as type-1 fuzzy sets) is a special case of the case when the inputs are treated as type-2 fuzzy sets, and the latter is presented in Chapter 12, we defer the details of the computations until that chapter, specifically to Example 12-4. Here we just state the results in Tables 11-1–11-3. Note that these results are keyed into Figure 11-4.

Table 11-1: $\overline{x}^l_{k,\max}$ for Example 11-3.

Cases	x'_k Locations	Product t-Norm	Minimum t-Norm
1. Figure 11-4 (a)	$x'_k \leq m^l_{k1}$	$\overline{x}^l_{k,\max} = \dfrac{\sigma^2_{X_k} m^l_{k1} + \sigma^{l^2}_k x'_k}{\sigma^2_{X_k} + \sigma^{l^2}_k}$	$\overline{x}^l_{k,\max} = \dfrac{\sigma_{X_k} m^l_{k1} + \sigma^l_k x'_k}{\sigma_{X_k} + \sigma^l_k}$
2. (Figure 11-4 (b) – (d))	$x'_k \in [m^l_{k1}, m^l_{k2}]$	$\overline{x}^l_{k,\max} = x'_k$	$\overline{x}^l_{k,\max} = x'_k$
3. Figure 11-4 (e)	$x'_k \geq m^l_{k2}$	$\overline{x}^l_{k,\max} = \dfrac{\sigma^2_{X_k} m^l_{k2} + \sigma^{l^2}_k x'_k}{\sigma^2_{X_k} + \sigma^{l^2}_k}$	$\overline{x}^l_{k,\max} = \dfrac{\sigma_{X_k} m^l_{kl} + \sigma^l_k x'_k}{\sigma_{X_k} + \sigma^l_k}$

This is a more difficult case than the one considered in Example 11-2, because the upper and lower membership functions depend on the relative location of x'_k to m^l_{k1} and m^l_{k2}.

Here is how the results in Tables 11-1–11-3 can be used in practice. Figure 11-4, which was used to establish the results in Tables 11-1–11-3, clearly demonstrates that there are five possible situations that need to be distinguished. To be consistent with the labeling of that figure, we shall refer to these five situations as state(1), state(2),..., state(5), where:

state(1): $\underline{x}_{k,\max}^l$ is in case 1 (Tables 11-2 or 11-3) and $\overline{x}_{k,\max}^l$ is in case 1 (Table 11-1)

state(2): $\underline{x}_{k,\max}^l$ is in case 1 (Tables 11-2 or 11-3) and $\overline{x}_{k,\max}^l$ is in case 2 (Table 11-1)

state(3): $\underline{x}_{k,\max}^l$ is in case 2 (Tables 11-2 or 11-3) and $\overline{x}_{k,\max}^l$ is in case 2 (Table 11-1)

state(4): $\underline{x}_{k,\max}^l$ is in case 3 (Tables 11-2 or 11-3) and $\overline{x}_{k,\max}^l$ is in case 2 (Table 11-1)

state(5): $\underline{x}_{k,\max}^l$ is in case 3 (Tables 11-2 or 11-3) and $\overline{x}_{k,\max}^l$ is in case 3 (Table 11-1)

Note that these results were obtained by pairing up the respective (a), (b), ..., (e) in the first columns of Tables 11-1 and 11-2 (or 11-3). Table 11-4 summarizes $\underline{f}_k^l(x_k') = \underline{\mu}_{\tilde{Q}_k^l}(\underline{x}_{k,\max}^l)$ and $\overline{f}_k^l(x_k') = \overline{\mu}_{\tilde{Q}_k^l}(\overline{x}_{k,\max}^l)$ for these five states under product t-norm. Its entries were obtained by evaluating (11-16) and (11-17) for each state.

The results in Table 11-4 are very useful in the design of a type-1 non-singleton type-2 FLS whose parameters are tuned using steepest descent algorithms. This is discussed in Section 11.4.3. ■

Table 11-2: $\underline{x}_{k,\max}^l$ for Example 11-3 based on product t-norm.

Cases	x_k' Locations	Product t-Norm
1. Figure 11-4 (a) and (b)	$x_k' < \dfrac{m_{k1}^l + m_{k2}^l}{2} - \dfrac{\sigma_{X_k}^2\left(m_{k2}^l - m_{k1}^l\right)}{2\sigma_k^{l2}}$	$\underline{x}_{k,\max}^l = \dfrac{\sigma_{X_k}^2 m_{k2}^l + \sigma_k^{l2} x_k'}{\sigma_{X_k}^2 + \sigma_k^{l2}}$
2. Figure 11-4 (c)	$x_k' \in \left[\dfrac{m_{k1}^l + m_{k2}^l}{2} - \dfrac{\sigma_{X_k}^2\left(m_{k2}^l - m_{k1}^l\right)}{2\sigma_k^{l2}}, \right.$ $\left. \dfrac{m_{k1}^l + m_{k2}^l}{2} + \dfrac{\sigma_{X_k}^2\left(m_{k2}^l - m_{k1}^l\right)}{2\sigma_k^{l2}}\right]$	$\underline{x}_{k,\max}^l = \dfrac{m_{k1}^l + m_{k2}^l}{2}$
3. Figure 11-4 (d) and (e)	$x_k' > \dfrac{m_{k1}^l + m_{k2}^l}{2} + \dfrac{\sigma_{X_k}^2\left(m_{k2}^l - m_{k1}^l\right)}{2\sigma_k^{l2}}$	$\underline{x}_{k,\max}^l = \dfrac{\sigma_{X_k}^2 m_{k1}^l + \sigma_k^{l2} x_k'}{\sigma_{X_k}^2 + \sigma_k^{l2}}$

Based on the statements made toward the end of the Introduction to this chapter, that type-reduction and defuzzification apply as well to type-1 non-singleton and singleton type-2 FLSs, we conclude that: *except for the calcula-*

tions of $\underline{f}^l_k$ and $\overline{f}^l_k$ all the calculations described in Chapter 10 apply as well to this chapter.

Table 11-3: $x^l_{k,\max}$ for Example 11-3 based on minimum t-norm.

Cases	x'_k Locations	Minimum t-Norm
1. Figure 11-4 (a) and (b)	$x'_k < \dfrac{m^l_{k1}+m^l_{k2}}{2} - \dfrac{\sigma_{X_k}\left(m^l_{k2}-m^l_{k1}\right)}{2\sigma^l_k}$	$\underline{x}^l_{k,\max} = \dfrac{\sigma_{X_k}m^l_{k2}+\sigma^l_k x'_k}{\sigma_{X_k}+\sigma^l_k}$
2. Figure 11-4 (c)	$x'_k \in \left[\dfrac{m^l_{k1}+m^l_{k2}}{2} - \dfrac{\sigma_{X_k}\left(m^l_{k2}-m^l_{k1}\right)}{2\sigma^l_k},\right.$ $\left.\dfrac{m^l_{k1}+m^l_{k2}}{2} + \dfrac{\sigma_{X_k}\left(m^l_{k2}-m^l_{k1}\right)}{2\sigma^l_k}\right]$	$\underline{x}^l_{k,\max} = \dfrac{m^l_{k1}+m^l_{k2}}{2}$
3. Figure 11-4 (d) and (e)	$x'_k > \dfrac{m^l_{k1}+m^l_{k2}}{2} + \dfrac{\sigma_{X_k}\left(m^l_{k2}-m^l_{k1}\right)}{2\sigma^l_k}$	$\underline{x}^l_{k,\max} = \dfrac{\sigma_{X_k}m^l_{k1}+\sigma^l_k x'_k}{\sigma^2_{X_k}+\sigma^l_k}$

Table 11-4: $\underline{\mu}_{\tilde{Q}^l_k}(\underline{x}^l_{k,\max})$ and $\overline{\mu}_{\tilde{Q}^l_k}(\overline{x}^l_{k,\max})$ under product t-norm.

State	$\underline{\mu}_{\tilde{Q}^l_k}(\underline{x}^l_{k,\max})$	$\overline{\mu}_{\tilde{Q}^l_k}(\overline{x}^l_{k,\max})$
(1)	$\exp\left[-\tfrac{1}{2}\left(m^l_{k2}-x'_k\right)^2\big/\left(\sigma^2_{X_k}+\sigma^{l2}_k\right)\right]$	$\exp\left[-\tfrac{1}{2}\left(m^l_{k1}-x'_k\right)^2\big/\left(\sigma^2_{X_k}+\sigma^{l2}_k\right)\right]$
(2)	$\exp\left[-\tfrac{1}{2}\left(m^l_{k2}-x'_k\right)^2\big/\left(\sigma^2_{X_k}+\sigma^{l2}_k\right)\right]$	1
(3)	$\exp\left[-\tfrac{1}{2}\left(m^l_{k2}+m^l_{k1}-2x'_k\right)^2\big/4\sigma^2_{X_k}\right.$ $\left.-\tfrac{1}{2}\left(m^l_{k2}-m^l_{k1}\right)^2\big/4\sigma^{l2}_k\right]$	1
(4)	$\exp\left[-\tfrac{1}{2}\left(m^l_{k1}-x'_k\right)^2\big/\left(\sigma^2_{X_k}+\sigma^{l2}_k\right)\right]$	1
(5)	$\exp\left[-\tfrac{1}{2}\left(m^l_{k1}-x'_k\right)^2\big/\left(\sigma^2_{X_k}+\sigma^{l2}_k\right)\right]$	$\exp\left[-\tfrac{1}{2}\left(m^l_{k2}-x'_k\right)^2\big/\left(\sigma^2_{X_k}+\sigma^{l2}_k\right)\right]$

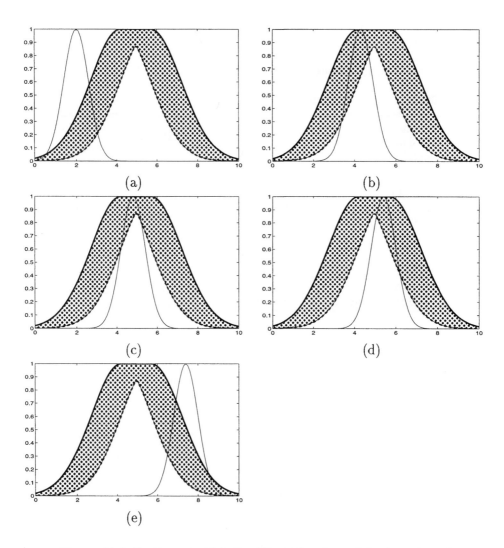

Figure 11-4: For Example 11-3, the different locations of the input type-1 Gaussian membership function in relation to the antecedent FOU. The membership function for the input is centered at x'_k.

11.4 DESIGNING INTERVAL TYPE-1 NON-SINGLETON TYPE-2 FLSS

Just as all the calculations described in Section 10.9 apply to the present case of an interval type-1 non-singleton type-2 FLS (except for the calculations of $\overline{f}_k^l$ and $\underline{f}_k^l$), the Section 10.10 discussions about designing interval singleton type-2 FLSs also apply to this chapter. So, this is a good place for the reader to review the material in Section 10.10. As in that section's design methods, our interval type-1 non-singleton type-2 FLS design methods are associated with the following problem:

> We are given a collection of N input–output numerical data *training* pairs, $(\mathbf{x}^{(1)}:y^{(1)}),(\mathbf{x}^{(2)}:y^{(2)}),\ldots,(\mathbf{x}^{(N)}:y^{(N)})$, where $\mathbf{x}$ is the vector input and y is the scalar output of an interval type-1 non-singleton type-2 FLS. Our goal is to completely specify this type-2 FLS using the training data.

Additionally, for illustrative purposes, all designs assume Gaussian primary membership functions with uncertain mean and interval secondary membership functions (as in Figure 3-8), product implication and t-norm, center-of-sets type-reduction, and defuzzification using the centroid of the type-reduced set. In this chapter, the type-1 nature of the input measurement is described by a Gaussian membership function that is centered at the measurement value. Our type-2 FLS is described by the contents of Section 11.3. Note, again, that the basic principles used in each design procedure carry over to many other interval type-1 non-singleton type-2 FLSs.

To begin, as in Section 10.10, we must explain how the training data can be interpreted as a collection of IF–THEN rules. Each rule is still in the form given in (10-2), where $\tilde{F}_i^l$ are interval type-2 fuzzy sets that are associated with the elements of $\mathbf{x}^{(t)}$ and are described by the interval type-2 Gaussian primary membership functions with uncertain mean, as in (10-20), i.e.,

$$\mu_i^l(x_i) = \exp\left[-\frac{1}{2}\left(\frac{x_i - m_i^l}{\sigma_i^l}\right)^2\right] \quad m_i^l \in [m_{i1}^l, m_{i2}^l] \qquad (11\text{-}36)$$

where $i = 1, \ldots, p$ and $l = 1, \ldots, M$. The consequent sets are also Gaussian primary membership functions with uncertain mean and interval secondary membership functions, i.e.,

$$\mu^j(y) = \exp\left[-\tfrac{1}{2}\left(\frac{y-m^j}{\sigma^j}\right)^2\right] \quad m^j \in [m_1^j, m_2^j] \quad j = 1, \ldots, M \quad (11\text{-}37)$$

Note that the centroid of each $\mu^j(y)$, $C_{\tilde{G}^j}$, is an interval type-1 set, i.e.,

$$C_{\tilde{G}^j} = [y_l^j, y_r^j] \quad j = 1, \ldots, M \quad (11\text{-}38)$$

In addition, the inputs are type-1 Gaussian fuzzy numbers whose membership functions are given in (11-28).

Each design method establishes how to specify all the parameters of the membership functions in (11-36), (11-37), and (11-28), using the training pairs $(\mathbf{x}^{(1)}:y^{(1)}), (\mathbf{x}^{(2)}:y^{(2)}), \ldots, (\mathbf{x}^{(N)}:y^{(N)})$.

As in Sections 5.9, 6.6, and 10.10, how many rules there can be in the interval type-1 non-singleton type-2 FLS depends on the design method that is used to construct it. If no tuning of the FLS parameters is done, then there can be as many as $M = N$ rules. If tuning is used, and we continue to abide by the commonly used design principle that there must be fewer tuned design parameters than training pairs, then we must use less than N rules.

Example 11-4: Let us enumerate how many design parameters there can be in the just-stated design:

- Antecedent parameters m_{i1}^l, m_{i2}^l, and σ_i^l: 3 per antecedent, p antecedents, and M rules, for a total of $3pM$ parameters.

- Consequent parameters m_1^j, m_2^j, and σ^j: 3 per consequent and M rules, for a total of $3M$ parameters. A viable alternative—the one we use (as we did in Section 10.10)—is to treat y_l^j and y_r^j as the consequent parameters, in which case there are a total of $2M$ such parameters.

- Measurement parameters σ_{X_k}: 1 per input and p inputs, for a total of p parameters [if each input membership function has the same standard deviation, σ_X ($k = 1, \ldots, p$), there will only be 1 additional parameter].

So, the maximum number of design parameters is $3pM + 2M + p$. Recall, from Example 10-4, that the maximum number of design parameters for an interval singleton type-2 FLS is $3pM + 2M$; hence, we again have more degrees of freedom in an interval type-1 non-singleton type-2 FLS than in an interval singleton type-2 FLS, which suggests that we should be able to outperform an interval singleton type-2 FLS.

From our discussion just before this example, we see that if no tuning of type-2 FLS parameters is done, then there can be as many as $3pN + 2N + p$ parameters; however, if tuning is used, then there is the following design constraint:

$$3pM + 2M + p < N \qquad (11\text{-}39)$$

If we are given a fixed number of training samples, $N = N'$, then

$$M < \left\lceil \frac{N' - p}{3p + 2} \right\rceil \qquad (11\text{-}40)$$

which constrains the number of rules that can be used. Because M must be an integer, we choose $M = M'$ as an integer that is smaller than $(N' - p)/(3p + 2)$. ∎

At a very high level, we can think of three designs associated with the preceding formulation:

1. Fix the shapes and parameters of all the antecedent, consequent and input measurement membership functions ahead of time. Doing this fixes the shape and size of the FOU for each antecedent and consequent membership function. The data establish the rules and the standard deviation of the measurements, and no tuning is used.

2. Fix the shapes and parameters of all the antecedent and consequent membership functions ahead of time. Fix the shape but not the parameters of the input measurement membership function ahead of time. Doing this fixes the shape and size of the FOU for each antecedent and consequent membership function. Use the training data to tune the parameters of the input measurement membership functions. In this way, the input measurement parameters adapt to the training data.

3. Fix the shapes of all the antecedent, consequent, and input measurement membership functions ahead of time. Doing this fixes the shape of the FOU for each antecedent and consequent membership function. Use the training data to tune the antecedent, consequent, and input measurement parameters. In this way, the size of each FOU, as well as the input measurement parameters, adapt to the training data.

Before we briefly touch upon the design methods that were described in Section 10.10, let us note that there can be two very different *approaches to the tuning of an interval type-1 non-singleton type-2 FLS*.

1. **Partially-dependent approach:** In this approach, one first designs the best possible interval singleton type-2 FLS, by tuning all of its parameters, and then updates the design by: (a) keeping all of the parameters that are shared by the singleton and type-1 non-singleton type-2 FLSs fixed at the values obtained from the best possible singleton type-2 FLS; and, (b) tuning only the new parameter(s) of the type-1 non-singleton type-2 FLS. In the present

case, only the standard deviations, σ_{X_k}, would be tuned.

2. **Totally independent approach:** In this approach, all of the parameters of the interval type-1 non-singleton type-2 FLS are tuned. If, perchance, an interval singleton type-2 FLS has already been designed, then its parameters can be used as the *initial parameters* for the tuning algorithms of the parameters that are shared by the interval singleton and non-singleton FLSs.

One would expect the best performance to be obtained by the totally independent approach; however, as mentioned in Sections 6.6 and 10.10, sometimes it is very useful to use the partially dependent approach to observe the incremental improvement that can be obtained from the previous design to the new design.

In the rest of this section, we focus on *differences* in Section 10.10 that occur because of the type-1 non-singleton nature of the FLS considered in this chapter. We do not repeat the discussions given in that section; so if the reader has not already done it, this would be a good time for the reader to review its design methods.

11.4.1 One-pass method

There are no changes to this method, since it is based entirely on the training data. Following the procedure given in Section 10.10.1, one can again easily design up to N rules from the now noisy training data. To complete this design, one must also determine values for σ_{X_k} ($k = 1, ..., p$). This requires the variance of the additive measurement noise on each measured input be known ahead of time, or that it can be estimated from the data; otherwise, one should use another design method in which σ_{X_k} can be tuned.

11.4.2 Least-squares method

For the same reasons given in Section 10.10.2, we conclude that, at present, we cannot use a least-squares design method for an interval type-1 non-singleton type-2 FLS.[2]

---

[2]See footnote 6 in Chapter 10.

11.4.3 Back-propagation (steepest descent) method

In the back-propagation method some or all of the antecedent, consequent, or input measurement membership function parameters are *not* fixed ahead of time. These parameters are tuned using a steepest descent method that we briefly describe in this section. For illustrative purposes, we assume that *all* of the antecedent, consequent, and input measurement membership function's parameters are to be tuned. The results in this section are very similar to those in Section 10.10.3 where an 11-step design procedure was stated and discussed; hence, here we focus on the differences to that method caused by the inputs in the present chapter being type-1 non-singleton. For completeness, we restate all 11 steps.

Given the N input–output training samples $(\mathbf{x}^{(t)}:y^{(t)})$, $t=1,...,N$, we wish to update the design parameters so that the following error function is minimized for E training epochs:

$$ e^{(t)} = \tfrac{1}{2}\left[f_{ns2-1}(\mathbf{x}^{(t)}) - y^{(t)} \right]^2 \qquad t=1,...,N \qquad (11\text{-}41) $$

A general method for doing this is:

1. Initialize all of the parameters in the antecedent and consequent membership functions. Choose the means of the Gaussian fuzzy numbers [in (11-28)] to be centered at the measurements; i.e., set $x'_k = x_k^{(t)}$, $k = 1, ..., p$, for $t = 1$; and initialize the standard deviations of these numbers.

2. Set the counter, e, of the training epoch to zero; i.e., $e \equiv 0$.

3. Set the counter, t, of the training data to unity; i.e., $t \equiv 1$.

4. Apply $p \times 1$ input $\mathbf{x}^{(t)}$ to the interval type-1 non-singleton type-2 FLS and compute the total firing interval for each rule; i.e., compute $\underline{f}^i$ and $\overline{f}^i$ ($i = 1, ..., p$) using (11-22)–(11-27). This requires using the results in Table 11-4.

5. Compute y_l and y_r using the four-step iterative method described on pp. 310–311 [this leads to a re-ordering of the M rules, which are then re-numbered 1, ..., M, as explained in the discussions accompanying (10-63)–(10-65)]. Doing this establishes L and R, so that y_l and y_r can be expressed as in (10-57) and (10-60), respectively, i.e.,

$$y_l = \frac{\sum_{i=1}^{M} f_l^i y_l^i}{\sum_{i=1}^{M} f_l^i} = \frac{\sum_{i=1}^{L} \overline{f}^i y_l^i + \sum_{j=L+1}^{M} \underline{f}^j y_l^j}{\sum_{i=1}^{L} \overline{f}^i + \sum_{j=L+1}^{M} \underline{f}^j} \tag{11-42}$$

$$= y_l\left(\overline{f}^1, ..., \overline{f}^L, \underline{f}^{L+1}, ..., \underline{f}^M, y_l^1, ..., y_l^M\right)$$

and

$$y_r = \frac{\sum_{i=1}^{M} f_r^i y_r^i}{\sum_{i=1}^{M} f_r^i} = \frac{\sum_{i=1}^{R} \underline{f}^i y_r^i + \sum_{j=R+1}^{M} \overline{f}^j y_r^j}{\sum_{i=1}^{R} \underline{f}^i + \sum_{j=R+1}^{M} \overline{f}^j} \tag{11-43}$$

$$= y_r\left(\underline{f}^1, ..., \underline{f}^R, \overline{f}^{R+1}, ..., \overline{f}^M, y_r^1, ..., y_r^M\right)$$

6. Compute the defuzzified output, $f_{ns2-1}(\mathbf{x}^{(t)})$, of the interval type-1 non-singleton type-2 FLS, as

$$f_{ns2-1}\left(\mathbf{x}^{(t)}\right) = \left[y_l(\mathbf{x}^{(t)}) + y_r(\mathbf{x}^{(t)})\right]/2 \tag{11-44}$$

7. Determine the explicit dependence of y_l and y_r on membership functions. [Because L and R obtained in Step 5 usually change from one iteration to the next, the dependence of y_l and y_r on membership functions will also usually change from one iteration to the next]. To do this, first determine the explicit dependence of $\underline{f}^l$ and $\overline{f}^l$ on membership functions using (11-26) and (11-27); i.e., $\underline{f}^l$ is determined by $T_{k=1}^p \underline{\mu}_{\tilde{Q}_k^l}(\underline{x}_{k,max}^l)$ and $\overline{f}^l$ is determined by $T_{k=1}^p \overline{\mu}_{\tilde{Q}_k^l}(\overline{x}_{k,max}^l)$. Consequently, from (11-42) and (11-43), we see that

$$y_l = y_l\Big[T_{k=1}^p \overline{\mu}_{\tilde{Q}_k^1}(\overline{x}_{k,max}^1), ..., T_{k=1}^p \overline{\mu}_{\tilde{Q}_k^L}(\overline{x}_{k,max}^L), T_{k=1}^p \underline{\mu}_{\tilde{Q}_k^{L+1}}(\underline{x}_{k,max}^{L+1}),$$
$$..., T_{k=1}^p \underline{\mu}_{\tilde{Q}_k^M}(\underline{x}_{k,max}^M), y_l^1, ..., y_l^M\Big] \tag{11-45}$$

Similarly,

$$y_r = y_r\Big[T_{k=1}^p \underline{\mu}_{\tilde{Q}_k^1}(\underline{x}_{k,max}^1), ..., T_{k=1}^p \underline{\mu}_{\tilde{Q}_k^R}(\underline{x}_{k,max}^R), T_{k=1}^p \overline{\mu}_{\tilde{Q}_k^{R+1}}(\overline{x}_{k,max}^{R+1}),$$
$$..., T_{k=1}^p \overline{\mu}_{\tilde{Q}_k^M}(\overline{x}_{k,max}^M), y_r^1, ..., y_r^M\Big] \tag{11-46}$$

8. Test each component of $\mathbf{x}^{(t)}$ to determine which of the five possible states—the *active state*—it is in ($k = 1, \ldots, p$), and use the results in Table 11-4 to express y_l and y_r as explicit functions of the underlying membership function parameters.

9. Tune the parameters of the active state established in Step 8, using a steepest descent algorithm, for the error function in (11-41). Partial derivatives of $\underline{\mu}_{\tilde{Q}_k^l}(\underline{x}_{k,\max}^l)$ or $\overline{\mu}_{\tilde{Q}_k^l}(\overline{x}_{k,\max}^l)$ with respect to specific design parameters are easy to compute using the results given in Table 11-4.

10. Set $t \equiv t + 1$. If $t = N + 1$, go to Step 11; otherwise, go to Step 4.

11. Set $e = e + 1$. If $e = E$, STOP; otherwise, go to Step 3.

As in Section 10.10.3, what makes the tuning of the parameters of this type-1 non-singleton type-2 FLS challenging and different from the tuning of the parameters in a singleton type-1 FLS is having to first determine which parameters y_l and y_r depend on. This requires (Step 8) using $x_k^{(t)}$ ($k = 1, \ldots, p$) to determine which one of the five possible states is active. As the parameters change, due to their tuning, the dependency of y_l and y_r on these parameters also changes. This does not occur in a type-1 FLS.

Of course, the steepest descent algorithms needed in Step 9 will be slightly different than those in Section 10.10.3 because of the additional input measurement parameters that must be determined for an interval type-1 non-singleton type-2 FLS. We leave the details for the reader (Exercise 11-6).

Note: Step 4 can be carried out even if we cannot compute $\underline{x}_{k,\max}^l$ and $\overline{x}_{k,\max}^l$ in closed-form. It can be done numerically along the lines of our discussions in Example 11-1 (see Figure 11-2). Step 7, however, can only be carried out if $\underline{x}_{k,\max}^l$ and $\overline{x}_{k,\max}^l$ can be computed in closed form, so that $\underline{\mu}_{\tilde{Q}_k^l}(\underline{x}_{k,\max}^l)$ and $\overline{\mu}_{\tilde{Q}_k^l}(\overline{x}_{k,\max}^l)$ can be determined as explicit functions of $\underline{x}_{k,\max}^l$ and $\overline{x}_{k,\max}^l$. If $\underline{x}_{k,\max}^l$ and $\overline{x}_{k,\max}^l$ cannot be computed in closed form, it is not possible to complete Step 8. And in this case, it is not possible to use a steepest descent algorithm in Step 9, because the partial derivatives, with respect to membership function parameters, which are needed by such an algorithm, cannot be computed. If $\underline{x}_{k,\max}^l$ and $\overline{x}_{k,\max}^l$ cannot be computed in closed form, then a different kind of optimization algorithm must be used to solve this design problem; e.g., a random search algorithm. The same sort of situation occurred for a non-singleton type-1 FLS in Section 6.6.3.

❀❀❀❀❀❀❀❀❀❀❀

11.4.4 SVD–QR method

The SVD–QR method that was described in Section 10.10.4 is directly applicable to the design of interval type-1 non-singleton type-2 FLSs. We shall illustrate this design method in Section 12.5, where we apply SVD–QR methods to the designs of 5 FLSs, two type-1 and three type-2.

11.4.5 Iterative design method

The four-step iterative design method that was described in Section 10.10.5 is directly applicable to the design of interval type-1 non-singleton type-2 FLSs. We also illustrate this design method in Section 12.5.

11.5 CASE STUDY: FORECASTING OF TIME-SERIES

We have described the problem of forecasting a time-series in Section 4.2. Here we design an interval type-1 non-singleton type-2 FLS forecaster for the Mackey–Glass time-series using the back-propagation method and compare its results with those obtained from back-propagation-designed singleton and non-singleton type-1 FLSs and an interval singleton type-2 FLS. The interval type-1 non-singleton type-2 FLS forecaster represents, for the first time, a FLS that accounts for *all* of the uncertainties that are present, namely, rule uncertainties due to training with noisy data and measurement uncertainties due to noisy measurements that are used during actual forecasting.

Our interval type-1 non-singleton type-2 FLS design uses the *partially dependent approach* that was described in Section 11.4; i.e., we first designed the best possible interval singleton type-2 FLS by tuning its parameters using a back-propagation design. Then, we kept all of the parameters shared by the interval singleton and type-1 non-singleton type-2 FLSs fixed at the values obtained from the best possible interval singleton type-2 FLS. Finally, we tuned only the new parameters of the interval type-1 non-singleton type-2 FLS. In the present case, there is only one new parameter, namely, σ_X; i.e., we used the same standard deviation for each of the four input measurement membership functions, because the inputs are delayed versions of one another.

All designs were based on the following 1,000 *noisy* data points: $x(1001)$, $x(1002)$, ..., $x(2000)$. The first 504 noisy data, $x(1001)$, $x(1002)$, ..., $x(1504)$, were used for training; i.e., for the designs of the FLS forecasters, whereas the remaining 496 noisy data, $x(1505), x(1506), ..., x(2000)$, were used for testing the designs. The noise-free Mackey–Glass time-series is depicted in Figure 5-11 (a).

As in Sections 6.7 and 10.11, we assume that the noise-free sampled time-series, $s(k)$, is corrupted by uniformly distributed stationary additive noise, $n(k)$, so that

$$x(k) = s(k) + n(k) \quad k{=}1001,\ 1002,\dots,\ 2000 \qquad (11\text{-}47)$$

and that $SNR = 0\text{dB}$. One realization of $x(1001), x(1002),\dots,x(2000)$ is depicted in Figure 5-11 (b).

As in Sections 5.10, 6.7, and 10.11, we used four antecedents for forecasting, namely, $x(k-3)$, $x(k-2)$, $x(k-1)$, and $x(k)$, to predict $x(k+1)$, and two fuzzy sets for each antecedent; hence, we used a total of 16 rules. Gaussian membership functions were chosen for the antecedents of the two type-1 FLSs, and Gaussian primary membership functions of uncertain means [(11-36)] were chosen for the antecedents of the interval singleton and interval type-1 non-singleton type-2 FLSs. Each rule of the two type-1 FLSs was characterized by eight antecedent membership function parameters (the mean and standard deviation for each of the four Gaussian membership functions) and one consequent parameter, $\bar{y}^l$; however, each rule of the two type-2 FLSs was characterized by 12 antecedent membership function parameters (the left- and right-hand bounds on the mean, and the standard deviation for each of the four Gaussian membership functions) and two consequent parameters (the left- and right-hand endpoints for the centroid of the consequent type-2 set; see Examples 10-4 and 11-4).

The details of the back-propagation-designed singleton and non-singleton type-1 FLSs can be found in Sections 5.10.2 and 6.7.2. The details of the back-propagation-designed interval singleton type-2 FLS can be found in Section 10.11. Note that we first designed the singleton type-1 FLS and then designed the non-singleton type-1 FLS using the partially dependent design approach that is described in Section 6.6, so that we were able to observe the marginal improvements in performance obtained by just tuning the "new" parameters. As mentioned in the first paragraph of this section, we did the same for the interval type-1 non-singleton type-2 FLS.

We again evaluated the performance of all the designs using RMSEs. Not only did we use the 3 RMSEs defined in (10-94)–(10-96), for the singleton type-1, non-singleton type-1, and interval singleton type-2 designs, but we also used the following RMSE for the interval type-1 non-singleton type-2 FLS:

$$RMSE_{ns2\text{-}1}(BP) = \sqrt{\tfrac{1}{496} \sum\nolimits_{k=1504}^{1999} \left[s(k+1) - f_{ns2\text{-}1}(\mathbf{x}^{(k)}) \right]^2} \qquad (11\text{-}48)$$

For the interval type-1 non-singleton type-2 FLS, we *initially* set the intervals of uncertainty (as we did in Section 10.11) for the means of each of the

4 antecedent's two fuzzy sets equal to $[m_x - 2\sigma_x - 0.25\sigma_n, m_x - 2\sigma_x + 0.25\sigma_n]$ and $[m_x + 2\sigma_x - 0.25\sigma_n, m_x + 2\sigma_x + 0.25\sigma_n]$, respectively, where m_x and σ_x are the mean and standard deviation, respectively, of the data in the 504 training samples, $x(1001), x(1002), \ldots, x(1504)$. For the standard deviation of the additive noise, σ_n, we initially used the final tuned result for the standard deviation of the input, σ_x, obtained from our non-singleton type-1 FLS design. This value was also used to initialize σ_x in the interval type-1 non-singleton type-2 FLS design. We also initially chose y_l^i and y_r^i as $\bar{y}^i - \sigma_n$ and $\bar{y}^i + \sigma_n$, respectively, where $\bar{y}^i$ was obtained from the type-1 singleton FLS design.

As stated earlier, the parameters that were tuned during the back-propagation design of the interval type-1 non-singleton type-2 FLS are the left- and right-hand bounds on the mean and the standard deviation for each of the four Gaussian primary membership functions, the left- and right-hand end-points for the centroid of each consequent type-2 set, and the standard deviation of the measurement noise. The total number of parameters tuned in this design is 14 parameters per rule × 16 rules + 1 = 225 parameters.

Each FLS was tuned using a steepest descent algorithm in which the learning parameter $\alpha = 0.2$. Training and testing were carried out for six epochs. After each epoch we used the testing data to see how each FLS performed, by computing $RMSE_{s1}(BP)$, $RMSE_{ns1}(BP)$, $RMSE_{s2}(BP)$, and $RMSE_{ns2-1}(BP)$, using (10-94)–(10-96) and (11-48), respectively. This entire process was repeated 50 times using 50 independent sets of 1,000 data points, at the end of which we had 50 $RMSE_{s1}(BP)$, $RMSE_{ns1}(BP)$, $RMSE_{s2}(BP)$, and $RMSE_{ns2-1}(BP)$ values. The average values and standard deviations of these $RMSE$s are plotted in Figure 11-5 for each of the six epochs. Observe, that:

1. The top three curves for the two type-1 FLSs and the interval singleton type-2 FLS are the same as those in Figure 10-13.

2. After six epochs of training, there is only a small improvement in performance (in both the mean and standard deviation of the $RMSE$) for the interval type-1 non-singleton type-2 FLS over its singleton counterpart.

3. The minimum values of both the mean and standard deviation of $RMSE_{ns2-1}(BP)$ occur at the first epoch, and there is a substantially lower value for the standard deviation of $RMSE_{ns2-1}(BP)$ at the first epoch than the value of the standard deviation of $RMSE_{s2}(BP)$.

The last observation *strongly* suggests that the interval type-1 non-singleton type-2 FLS can be used in a real-time adaptive environment.

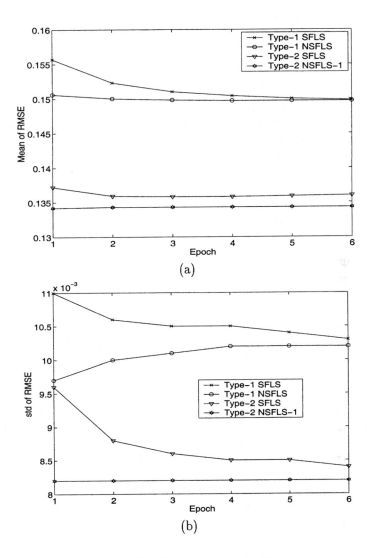

Figure 11-5: The mean and standard deviation of $RMSE_{s1}(BP)$, $RMSE_{ns1}(BP)$, $RMSE_{s2}(BP)$, and $RMSE_{ns2-1}(BP)$ averaged over 50 Monte-Carlo designs. Tuning was performed in each realization for six epochs. (a) mean values, and (b) standard deviation values.

11.6 FINAL REMARK

As mentioned in the first paragraph of Section 11.5, the type-1 non-singleton type-2 FLS forecaster represents, for the first time, a FLS that accounts for *all* of the uncertainties that are present, namely, rule uncertainties due to training with noisy data and measurement uncertainties due to noisy measurements that are used during actual forecasting. Accounting for all the sources of uncertainties has led to a design that performs almost optimally after just one epoch of training. Our earlier designs, which do not account for all of the sources of uncertainties, do not have this property.

The next and final level of uncertainty occurs when the additive measurement noise is non-stationary. In this case, modeling the measurements as type-2 fuzzy numbers is more appropriate than modeling them as type-1 fuzzy numbers. Chapter 12 describes this situation.

11.7 COMPUTATION

The following M-files, which are found in the folder *interval type-2 fuzzy logic systems*, are useful for designing an interval type-1 non-singleton type-2 FLS:

nsfls1.m: Compute the output(s) of an interval type-1 non-singleton type-2 FLS when the antecedent membership functions are Gaussian primary membership functions with uncertain means and the input sets are type-1 Gaussian.

train_nsfls1.m: Tune the parameters of an interval type-1 non-singleton type-2 FLS when the antecedent membership functions are Gaussian primary membership functions with uncertain means and the input sets are type-1 Gaussian, using some input–output training data.

svd_qr_sfls1.m: Rule-reduction of an interval type-1 non-singleton type-2 FLS when the antecedent membership functions are Gaussian primary membership functions with uncertain means and the input sets are type-1 Gaussian, using some input–output training data.

EXERCISES

11-1: Repeat the calculations of Example 11-2 using minimum t-norm.

11-2: Obtain the results given in Table 11-4.

11-3: Suppose that $m_{\tilde{F}_k^l} = m_{X_k}$ in Example 11-2 or Exercise 11-1; then, show that $\overline{f}_k^l = \underline{f}_k^l = 1$.

11-4: Provide as detailed a flow chart as possible for the calculations required to implement (11-42) and (11-43), assuming that the antecedent membership functions and the input membership functions are the ones given in Example 11-3.

11-5: Describe some ways to reduce the number of parameters in an interval type-1 nonsingleton type-2 FLS.

11-6: Develop the steepest descent algorithms for all of the parameters that need to be tuned in the Section 11.4 interval type-1 non-singleton type-2 FLS.

11-7: Explain the conditions under which (11-45) and (11-46) reduce to (10-80) and (10-81), respectively.

11-8: Explain how Step 4 in the 11-step back-propagation procedure can be carried out even if $\underline{x}_{k,max}^l$ and $\overline{x}_{k,max}^l$ cannot be computed in closed-form.

11-9: Create a counterpart to Example 10-5, using Figure 10-12, but for an interval type-1 non-singleton type-2 FLS.

Type-2 Non-Singleton
Type-2 Fuzzy Logic Systems

12.1 INTRODUCTION

In Chapter 11 we focused on inputs modeled as *type-1* fuzzy numbers. In this chapter we expand our viewpoint to include inputs modeled as *type-2* fuzzy numbers. This situation can occur, e.g., in time-series forecasting when the additive measurement noise is non-stationary. A type-2 FLS whose inputs are modeled as type-2 fuzzy numbers is referred to as a *type-2 non-singleton type-2 FLS*.

A type-2 non-singleton type-2 FLS is described by the same diagram as is a type-1 non-singleton type-2 FLS, Figure 11-1. The rules of a type-2 non-singleton type-2 FLS are the same as those for a type-1 non-singleton type-2 FLS, which are the same as those for a singleton type-2 FLS. What is different is the fuzzifier, which treats the inputs as type-2 fuzzy sets, and the effect of this on the inference block. The output of the inference block will again be a type-2 fuzzy set; so, the type-reducers and defuzzifier that we described for a type-1 non-singleton type-2 FLS apply as well to a type-2 non-singleton type-2 FLS.

This chapter parallels Chapter 11 (which can be viewed as a special case of this chapter, as can Chapter 10). To make it fairly self-contained there is some repetition of material from that chapter.

12.2 FUZZIFICATION AND ITS EFFECT ON IN-FERENCE

In the FLS of Figure 11-1, crisp inputs are first fuzzified into fuzzy input sets that then activate the inference block, which in the present case is associated with type-2 fuzzy sets. In this section, we explain type-2 non-singleton fuzzification and the effect of such fuzzification on the inference engine.

12.2.1 Fuzzifier

In type-2 non-singleton fuzzification measurement, $x_i = x'_i$ is mapped into a type-2 fuzzy number; i.e., a type-2 membership function is associated with it. Possible membership functions are: Gaussian with uncertain standard deviation (Figure 3-9) whose mean is located at x'_i; Gaussian with an uncertain mean (Figure 3-8) that is located in some range about x'_i; Gaussian with uncertain mean and standard deviation, where the mean is also located in some range about x'_i; and so forth.

12.2.2 Fuzzy inference engine

The reader should review Section 11.2.2, because we pick up its story here with Equation (11-1), i.e.,

$$\mu_{\tilde{B}^l}(y) = \mu_{\tilde{G}^l}(y) \sqcap \left\{ \left[\sqcup_{x_1 \in X_1} \mu_{\tilde{X}_1}(x_1) \sqcap \mu_{\tilde{F}_1^l}(x_1) \right] \sqcap \right.$$
$$\left. \cdots \sqcap \left[\sqcup_{x_p \in X_p} \mu_{\tilde{X}_p}(x_p) \sqcap \mu_{\tilde{F}_p^l}(x_p) \right] \right\}, \quad y \in Y \tag{12-1}$$

where $l = 1, \ldots, M$. Let

$$\mu_{\tilde{Q}_k^l}(x_k) \equiv \mu_{\tilde{X}_k}(x_k) \sqcap \mu_{\tilde{F}_k^l}(x_k) \tag{12-2}$$

where $k = 1, \ldots, p$ and $l = 1, \ldots, M$, so that

$$\mu_{\tilde{B}^l}(y) = \mu_{\tilde{G}^l}(y) \sqcap \left\{ \left[\sqcup_{x_1 \in X_1} \mu_{\tilde{Q}_1^l}(x_1) \right] \sqcap \cdots \sqcap \left[\sqcup_{x_p \in X_p} \mu_{\tilde{Q}_p^l}(x_p) \right] \right\}$$

$$\mu_{\tilde{B}^l}(y) = \mu_{\tilde{G}^l}(y)\sqcap\left\{\sqcup_{\ x\in X}\left[\sqcap_{k=1}^p \mu_{\tilde{Q}_k^l}(x_k)\right]\right\}, \quad y\in Y \qquad (12\text{-}3)$$

At this point it is instructive to compare (12-1) with (11-2), (12-2) with (11-3), and (12-3) with (11-4). Observe that:

1. The type-1 input sets in (11-2) and (11-3) have been replaced by type-2 input sets in (12-1) and (12-2).
2. Equations (12-3) and (11-4) are identical in structure.

This suggests that the results in the present chapter can be obtained from those in Section 11.2.2 simply by letting $X_k \to \tilde{X}_k$. Unfortunately, it is not quite that simple because (11-13) (in the proof of Theorem 11-1) suppresses the identities of the lower and upper membership functions of the input, and for a type-2 input, those membership functions need to re-emerge. For completeness, therefore, we provide all the details in this chapter.

As in Section 11.2.2, we define

$$\mu_{\tilde{Q}^l}(\mathbf{x}) \equiv \sqcap_{k=1}^p \mu_{\tilde{Q}_k^l}(x_k) \qquad (12\text{-}4)$$

and[1]

$$F^l(\mathbf{x}') \equiv \sqcup_{\ x\in X}\left[\sqcap_{k=1}^p \mu_{\tilde{Q}_k^l}(x_k)\right] = \sqcup_{\ x\in X}\mu_{\tilde{Q}^l}(\mathbf{x}) \qquad (12\text{-}5)$$

so that $\mu_{\tilde{B}^l}(y)$ in (12-3) can be re-expressed as

$$\mu_{\tilde{B}^l}(y) = \mu_{\tilde{G}^l}(y)\sqcap F^l(\mathbf{x}'), \quad y\in Y \qquad (12\text{-}6)$$

As in Section 11.2.2, this is the fundamental equation for a type-2 non-singleton type-2 FLS. The term $F^l(\mathbf{x}')$ is the *firing set* for a type-2 non-singleton type-2 FLS. It not only includes the effects of antecedent uncertainties, as in Section 11.2.2, but it also includes the effects of the additional input measurement uncertainties.

The general material in Sections 10.5–10.8 applies as well to a type-2 non-singleton type-2 FLS, so we refer the reader to those sections. Regarding "possi-

---

[1]Although input $\mathbf{x}'$ does not appear explicitly in the right-hand side of (12-5), it is contained in each $\mu_{\tilde{Q}^l}(\mathbf{x})$ through the latter's dependency on the FOU of the input. If, for example, the membership function of input x_i is a Gaussian with uncertain standard deviation, then this Gaussian is centered at x_i'.

bilities," what is new for a type-2 non-singleton type-2 FLS is the need for the designer to choose *type-2* membership functions for the input measurements, something that wasn't necessary for a type-1 non-singleton type-2 FLS. If, for example, the designer chooses a Gaussian primary membership function with uncertain standard deviation for the input, then an interval for the standard deviation needs to be specified for that function. The interval end-points represent the additional new possibilities for a type-2 non-singleton type-2 FLS.

In general, it is very difficult to compute (12-6) for arbitrary type-2 fuzzy sets; so, as in Chapters 10 and 11, we shall focus our attention on interval type-2 non-singleton type-2 FLSs for which it is possible to obtain a closed-form formula for (12-6).

12.3 INTERVAL TYPE-2 NON-SINGLETON TYPE-2 FLSs

The major result for an interval type-2 non-singleton type-2 FLS is summarized in the following:

Theorem 12-1: [Liang and Mendel (2000c)] *In an interval type-2 non-singleton type-2 FLS with meet under product or minimum t-norm: (a) the result of the input and antecedent operations, which are contained in the firing set $F^l(\mathbf{x}')$ in (12-6), is an interval type-1 set, i.e.,*

$$F^l(\mathbf{x}') = \left[\underline{f}^l(\mathbf{x}'), \overline{f}^l(\mathbf{x}')\right] \equiv \left[\underline{f}^l, \overline{f}^l\right] \tag{12-7}$$

where

$$\underline{f}^l(\mathbf{x}') = \sup_{\mathbf{x}} \int_{x_1 \in X_1} \cdots \int_{x_p \in X_p} \left[\underline{\mu}_{\tilde{X}_1}(x_1) \star \underline{\mu}_{\tilde{F}_1^l}(x_1)\right] \star$$
$$\cdots \star \left[\underline{\mu}_{\tilde{X}_p}(x_p) \star \underline{\mu}_{\tilde{F}_p^l}(x_p)\right] \bigg/ \mathbf{x} \tag{12-8}$$

and

$$\overline{f}^l(\mathbf{x}') = \sup_{\mathbf{x}} \int_{x_1 \in X_1} \cdots \int_{x_p \in X_p} \left[\overline{\mu}_{\tilde{X}_1}(x_1) \star \overline{\mu}_{\tilde{F}_1^l}(x_1) \right] \star$$

$$\cdots \star \left[\overline{\mu}_{\tilde{X}_p}(x_p) \star \overline{\mu}_{\tilde{F}_p^l}(x_p) \right] \Big/ \mathbf{x} \qquad (12\text{-}9)$$

and the supremum is attained when each term in brackets attains its supremum;

(b) the rule R^l fired output consequent set, $\mu_{\tilde{B}^l}(y)$ in (12-3), is a type-1 fuzzy set, where

$$\mu_{\tilde{B}^l}(y) = \int_{b^l \in \left[\underline{f}^l \star \underline{\mu}_{\tilde{G}^l}(y), \overline{f}^l \star \overline{\mu}_{\tilde{G}^l}(y) \right]} 1/b^l, \quad y \in Y \qquad (12\text{-}10)$$

where $\underline{\mu}_{\tilde{G}^l}(y)$ and $\overline{\mu}_{\tilde{G}^l}(y)$ are the lower and upper membership grades of $\mu_{\tilde{G}^l}(y)$; and,

(c) suppose that N of the M rules in the FLS fire, where $N \leq M$ and the combined output type-1 fuzzy set is obtained by combining the fired output consequent sets; i.e., $\mu_{\tilde{B}}(y) = \sqcup_{l=1}^{N} \mu_{\tilde{B}^l}(y)$ $y \in Y$; then,

$$\mu_{\tilde{B}}(y) = \int_{b \in \left[\left[\underline{f}^1 \star \underline{\mu}_{\tilde{G}^1}(y) \right] \vee \cdots \vee \left[\underline{f}^N \star \underline{\mu}_{\tilde{G}^N}(y) \right], \left[\overline{f}^1 \star \overline{\mu}_{\tilde{G}^1}(y) \right] \vee \cdots \vee \left[\overline{f}^N \star \overline{\mu}_{\tilde{G}^N}(y) \right] \right]} 1/b, \quad y \in Y \qquad (12\text{-}11)$$

Comparing Theorems 12-1 and 11-1, we see that they differ only in the formulas for $\underline{f}^l(\mathbf{x}')$ and $\overline{f}^l(\mathbf{x}')$. Equation (11-9) uses $\mu_{X_i}(x_i)$ to compute $\underline{f}^l(\mathbf{x}')$, whereas (12-8) uses $\underline{\mu}_{\tilde{X}_i}(x_i)$ to do this. Equation (11-10) also uses $\mu_{X_i}(x_i)$ to compute $\overline{f}^l(\mathbf{x}')$, whereas (12-9) uses $\overline{\mu}_{\tilde{X}_i}(x_i)$ to do this.

Proof: (a) To compute $F^l(\mathbf{x}')$ using (12-5), we first compute $\mu_{\tilde{Q}_k^l}(x_k)$ using (12-2) and then compute $\mu_{\tilde{Q}^l}(\mathbf{x})$ using (12-4). Applying Theorem 7-2 to (12-2) for an interval type-2 non-singleton type-2 FLS, and using the facts that

$$\mu_{\tilde{X}_k}(x_k) = \int_{v \in \left[\underline{\mu}_{\tilde{X}_k}(x_k), \overline{\mu}_{\tilde{X}_k}(x_k) \right]} 1/v \qquad (12\text{-}12)$$

and

$$\mu_{\tilde{F}_k^l}(x_k^{'}) = \int_{w^l \in \left[\underline{\mu}_{\tilde{F}_k^l}(x_k), \overline{\mu}_{\tilde{F}_k^l}(x_k) \right]} 1/w^l \qquad (12\text{-}13)$$

we find that

$$\mu_{\tilde{Q}_k^l}(x_k) = \mu_{\tilde{X}_k}(x_k) \sqcap \mu_{\tilde{F}_k^l}(x_k)$$

$$= \int_{q^l \in \left[\underline{\mu}_{\tilde{X}_k}(x_k) \star \underline{\mu}_{\tilde{F}_k^l}(x_k), \overline{\mu}_{\tilde{X}_k}(x_k) \star \overline{\mu}_{\tilde{F}_k^l}(x_k) \right]} 1/q^l \qquad (12\text{-}14)$$

$$= \left[\underline{\mu}_{\tilde{X}_k}(x_k) \star \underline{\mu}_{\tilde{F}_k^l}(x_k), \overline{\mu}_{\tilde{X}_k}(x_k) \star \overline{\mu}_{\tilde{F}_k^l}(x_k) \right] \qquad \forall x_k \in X_k$$

So, the meet between an input type-2 set and an antecedent type-2 set just involves the t-norm operations between the points in the two lower and upper membership functions. From (12-14), we see that the lower and upper membership functions of $\mu_{\tilde{Q}_k^l}(x_k)$ are

$$\underline{\mu}_{\tilde{Q}_k^l}(x_k) = \int_{x_k \in X_k} \left[\underline{\mu}_{\tilde{X}_k}(x_k) \star \underline{\mu}_{\tilde{F}_k^l}(x_k) \right] \Big/ x_k \qquad (12\text{-}15)$$

and

$$\overline{\mu}_{\tilde{Q}_k^l}(x_k) = \int_{x_k \in X_k} \left[\overline{\mu}_{\tilde{X}_k}(x_k) \star \overline{\mu}_{\tilde{F}_k^l}(x_k) \right] \Big/ x_k \qquad (12\text{-}16)$$

Next, we turn to (12-4), from which we note that its meet operations are in a p-dimensional Cartesian product space; hence, the meet operation is over all points $x_k \in X_k$, $k = 1, ..., p$. Based on Theorem 7-2, we know that the upper membership function of $\mu_{\tilde{Q}^l}(\mathbf{x})$, $\overline{\mu}_{\tilde{Q}^l}(\mathbf{x})$ (which is a type-1 membership function) is obtained from $\overline{\mu}_{\tilde{Q}_1^l}(x_1) \star \cdots \star \overline{\mu}_{\tilde{Q}_p^l}(x_p)$. Hence, using (12-16) in this expression, we find

$$\overline{\mu}_{\tilde{Q}^l}(\mathbf{x}) = \int_{x_1 \in X_1} \cdots \int_{x_p \in X_p} \left[\overline{\mu}_{\tilde{X}_1}(x_1) \star \overline{\mu}_{\tilde{F}_1^l}(x_1) \right] \star$$
$$\cdots \star \left[\overline{\mu}_{\tilde{X}_p}(x_p) \star \overline{\mu}_{\tilde{F}_p^l}(x_p) \right] \Big/ \mathbf{x} \qquad (12\text{-}17)$$

The lower membership function of $\mu_{\tilde{Q}^l}(\mathbf{x})$, $\underline{\mu}_{\tilde{Q}^l}(\mathbf{x})$ (which is also a type-1 membership function) is obtained from $\underline{\mu}_{\tilde{Q}_1^l}(x_1)\star\cdots\star\underline{\mu}_{\tilde{Q}_p^l}(x_p)$. Hence, using (12-15) in this expression, we find

$$\underline{\mu}_{\tilde{Q}^l}(\mathbf{x}) = \int_{x_1 \in X_1}\cdots\int_{x_p \in X_p}\left[\underline{\mu}_{\tilde{X}_1}(x_1)\star\underline{\mu}_{\tilde{F}_1^l}(x_1)\right]\star$$
$$\cdots\star\left[\underline{\mu}_{\tilde{X}_p}(x_p)\star\underline{\mu}_{\tilde{F}_p^l}(x_p)\right]\Big/\mathbf{x} \qquad (12\text{-}18)$$

Finally, we turn to (12-5), where we observe that its join operation is over all points $\mathbf{x} \in \mathbf{X}$. Based on Theorem 7-1, we know that the right-most point of the join of p interval type-1 sets is the maximum value of all the right-most points in the p interval sets; hence, the right-most point of $F^l(\mathbf{x})$, $\overline{f}^l(\mathbf{x})$, comes from the maximum value (supremum) of $\overline{\mu}_{\tilde{Q}^l}(\mathbf{x})$. Consequently, from (12-17), we find

$$\overline{f}^l(\mathbf{x}') = \sup_{\mathbf{x}}\int_{x_1 \in X_1}\cdots\int_{x_p \in X_p}\left[\overline{\mu}_{\tilde{X}_1}(x_1)\star\overline{\mu}_{\tilde{F}_1^l}(x_1)\right]\star$$
$$\cdots\star\left[\overline{\mu}_{\tilde{X}_p}(x_p)\star\overline{\mu}_{\tilde{F}_p^l}(x_p)\right]\Big/\mathbf{x} \qquad (12\text{-}19)$$

Similarly, the left-most point of $F^l(\mathbf{x}')$, $\underline{f}^l(\mathbf{x}')$, comes from the maximum value (supremum) of $\underline{\mu}_{\tilde{Q}^l}(\mathbf{x})$. Hence, from (12-18), we find

$$\underline{f}^l(\mathbf{x}') = \sup_{\mathbf{x}}\int_{x_1 \in X_1}\cdots\int_{x_p \in X_p}\left[\underline{\mu}_{\tilde{X}_1}(x_1)\star\underline{\mu}_{\tilde{F}_1^l}(x_1)\right]\star$$
$$\cdots\star\left[\underline{\mu}_{\tilde{X}_p}(x_p)\star\underline{\mu}_{\tilde{F}_p^l}(x_p)\right]\Big/\mathbf{x} \qquad (12\text{-}20)$$

The suprema in (12-19) and (12-20) are over all $\mathbf{x} \in \mathbf{X}$. By the monotonicity property of a t-norm (e.g., [Zimmerman (1991)]), the supremum is attained when each term in brackets attains its supremum.

(b) Using (12-7) and Theorem 7-2, (12-6) can be expressed as in (10-32). Hence, the rest of the proof is the same as that of part (b) of Theorem 10-1.

(c) The proof is the same as the proof of part (c) of Theorem 10-1. ∎

In evaluating (12-8) and (12-9), the supremum is attained when each term in brackets attains its supremum. Hence, in the inference mechanism block of a type-2 non-singleton type-2 FLS we will examine

$$\underline{f}_k^l(x_k') \equiv \sup_{x_k} \int_{x_k \in X_k} \left[\underline{\mu}_{\tilde{X}_k}(x_k) \star \underline{\mu}_{\tilde{F}_k^l}(x_k) \right] / x_k = \sup_{x_k} \underline{\mu}_{\tilde{Q}_k^l}(x_k) \qquad (12\text{-}21)$$

and

$$\overline{f}_k^l(x_k') \equiv \sup_{x_k} \int_{x_k \in X_k} \left[\overline{\mu}_{\tilde{X}_k}(x_k) \star \overline{\mu}_{\tilde{F}_k^l}(x_k) \right] / x_k = \sup_{x_k} \overline{\mu}_{\tilde{Q}_k^l}(x_k) \qquad (12\text{-}22)$$

where $k = 1, \ldots, p$, and we have used (12-15) and (12-16).

Let $\underline{x}_{k,\max}^l$ and $\overline{x}_{k,\max}^l$ denote the values of x_k that are associated with $\sup_{x_k} \underline{\mu}_{\tilde{Q}_k^l}(x_k)$ and $\sup_{x_k} \overline{\mu}_{\tilde{Q}_k^l}(x_k)$, respectively, so that

$$\underline{f}_k^l(x_k') = \underline{\mu}_{\tilde{Q}_k^l}(\underline{x}_{k,\max}^l) \qquad (12\text{-}23)$$

and

$$\overline{f}_k^l(x_k') = \overline{\mu}_{\tilde{Q}_k^l}(\overline{x}_{k,\max}^l) \qquad (12\text{-}24)$$

This means, of course, that, as in Section 11.3, $\underline{f}^l(\mathbf{x}')$ and $\overline{f}^l(\mathbf{x}')$ in (12-8) and (12-9) can be re-expressed as

$$\underline{f}^l(\mathbf{x}') = T_{k=1}^p \underline{f}_k^l(x_k') = T_{k=1}^p \underline{\mu}_{\tilde{Q}_k^l}(\underline{x}_{k,\max}^l) \qquad (12\text{-}25)$$

and

$$\overline{f}^l(\mathbf{x}') = T_{k=1}^p \overline{f}_k^l(x_k') = T_{k=1}^p \overline{\mu}_{\tilde{Q}_k^l}(\overline{x}_{k,\max}^l) \qquad (12\text{-}26)$$

The procedure to compute $F^l(\mathbf{x}')$ in (12-7) is:

1. Choose a t-norm (product or minimum) and create the functions $\underline{\mu}_{\tilde{Q}_k^l}(x_k)$ and $\overline{\mu}_{\tilde{Q}_k^l}(x_k)$ using (12-15) and (12-16), respectively.

2. Compute $\underline{x}_{k,\max}^l$ and $\overline{x}_{k,\max}^l$ by maximizing $\underline{\mu}_{\tilde{Q}_k^l}(x_k)$ and $\overline{\mu}_{\tilde{Q}_k^l}(x_k)$, respectively.

3. Evaluate $\underline{f}_k^l(x_k')$ and $\overline{f}_k^l(x_k')$ using (12-23) and (12-24), respectively.

4. Compute $\underline{f}^l(\mathbf{x}')$ and $\overline{f}^l(\mathbf{x}')$ using (12-25) and (12-26), respectively.

Example 12-1: Here we consider a pictorial description of parts (a)–(c) of Theorem 12-1 using the minimum and product t-norms. As such, it is very similar to Example 11-1, and will let us contrast pictorial descriptions for an interval type-2 non-singleton type-2 FLS with both interval singleton type-2 and interval type-1 non-singleton type-2 FLSs. It will also help us to better understand the flow of rule uncertainties combined with type-2 input uncertainties through an interval type-2 non-singleton type-2 FLS.

Figure 12-1 depicts input and antecedent operations [(12-21)–(12-26)] for a two-antecedent single-consequent rule, type-2 non-singleton fuzzification, and minimum or product t-norms. In all cases, the firing strength is an interval type-1 set $[\underline{f}^l, \overline{f}^l]$, where

$\underline{f}^l = \underline{f}_1^l \star \underline{f}_2^l$ and $\overline{f}^l = \overline{f}_1^l \star \overline{f}_2^l$. According to (12-21), $\underline{f}_k^l$ is the supremum of the firing strength between the t-norm of the lower membership functions $\underline{\mu}_{\tilde{X}_k}(x_k)$ and $\underline{\mu}_{\tilde{F}_k^l}(x_k)$, and

according to (12-22), $\overline{f}_k^l$ is the supremum of the firing strength between the t-norm of the upper membership functions $\overline{\mu}_{\tilde{X}_k}(x_k)$ and $\overline{\mu}_{\tilde{F}_k^l}(x_k)$ ($k = 1, 2$). Note that the FOU for $\mu_{\tilde{X}_k}(x_k)$ is centered at $x_k = x_k'$. These t-norms are shown as heavy curves in Figure 12-1 (a) and (b). From these heavy curves it is easy to pick off their suprema.

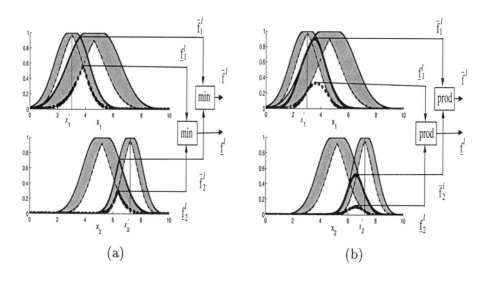

(a)   (b)

Figure 12-1: Pictorial description of input and antecedent operations for an interval type-2 non-singleton type-2 FLS. (a) minimum t-norm, and (b) product t-norm.

The main thing to observe from Figure 12-1 (a) and (b) is that, regardless of the t-norm, the result of input and antecedent operations is an interval—the *firing interval*. Consequently, the results depicted in Figures 10-7 [$\mu_{\tilde{B}^l}(y)$, $y \in Y$, for a two-rule FLS] and 10-8 (combined output set for a two-rule FLS) remain the same for an interval type-2 non-singleton type-2 FLS. The only difference between an interval type-2 non-singleton type-2 FLS and an interval type-1 non-singleton type-2 FLS is their firing intervals. The present case of type-2 non-singleton fuzzification leads to a firing interval that includes the *additional uncertainties* of the type-2 non-singleton inputs. ∎

Example 12-2: We have presented pictures like the ones in Figure 12-1 for five different situations in this book: singleton type-1 (Chapter 5), non-singleton type-1 (Chapter 6), interval singleton type-2 (Chapter 10), interval type-1 non-singleton type-2 (Chapter 11), and interval type-2 non-singleton type-2 (this chapter). It is instructive to compare these results; hence, we collect these results for product t-norm in Figure 12-2. The comparisons for minimum t-norm are similar. Observe that *uncertainties increase either the firing level* [compare Figure 12-2 (a) and (b)] *or the firing interval* [compare Figure 12-2 (c)–(d)]. For the type-2 cases, *as more uncertainties are included* (i.e., in going from an interval singleton type-2 to an interval type-1 non-singleton to an interval type-2 non-singleton FLS), *the larger the firing interval becomes.* ∎

In the next two examples we quantify the firing intervals so that the reader will be able to observe *exactly* how the additional uncertainty of the type-2 non-singleton inputs affects these firing intervals.

Example 12-3: This example is a generalization of Example 11-2. Here we quantify the results that were just presented in Example 12-1 for the case when the antecedent membership functions are Gaussian primary membership functions with uncertain standard deviations (as in Figure 3-9) and the inputs are modeled as type-2 Gaussian fuzzy numbers also of uncertain standard deviations. We shall compute $\overline{f}_k^l$ and $\underline{f}_k^l$ for this case.

To begin, we state the membership functions for the inputs and antecedents. In this case, the primary membership function for each input is

$$\mu_k(x_k) = \exp\left[-\frac{1}{2}\left(\frac{x_k - x_k'}{\sigma_k}\right)^2\right] \qquad \sigma_k \in \left[\sigma_{k1}, \sigma_{k2}\right] \tag{12-27}$$

and, as in Example 11-2, the primary membership function for each antecedent is

$$\mu_k^l(x_k) = \exp\left[-\frac{1}{2}\left(\frac{x_k - m_k^l}{\sigma_k^l}\right)^2\right] \qquad \sigma_k^l \in [\sigma_{k1}^l, \sigma_{k2}^l] \tag{12-28}$$

The lower and upper membership functions of the input membership functions are $\underline{\mu}_{\tilde{X}_k}(x_k)$ and $\overline{\mu}_{\tilde{X}_k}(x_k)$ [given in (3-21) and (3-20)], whereas the lower and upper membership functions of the antecedent membership functions are $\underline{\mu}_{\tilde{F}_k^l}(x_k)$ and $\overline{\mu}_{\tilde{F}_k^l}(x_k)$ [also given in (3-21) and (3-20)].

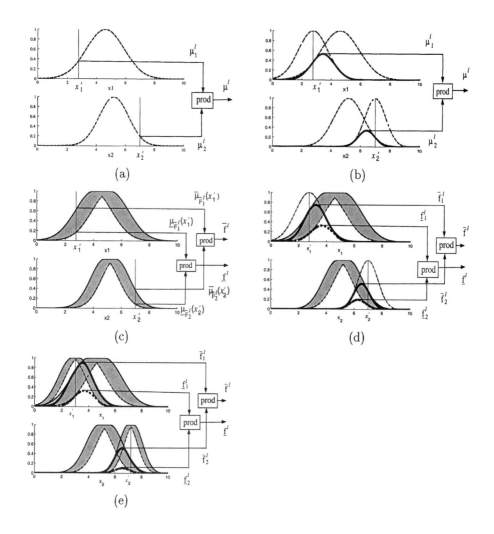

Figure 12-2: Pictorial description of input and antecedent operations using product t-norm, and: (a) singleton type-1, (b) non-singleton type-1, (c) interval singleton type-2, (d) interval type-1 non-singleton type-2, and (e) interval type-2 non-singleton type-2 FLSs.

The input and antecedent FOUs are depicted in Figure 12-3. Observe, from (12-22), that $\bar{f}_k^l$ requires the calculation of the suprema of a product or minimum of the two Gaussians $\bar{\mu}_{\tilde{X}_k}(x_k)$ and $\bar{\mu}_{\tilde{F}_k^l}(x_k)$. Such a calculation was carried out in Example 6-2 for the product t-norm and in Exercise 6-2 for the minimum t-norm, and was restated in Example

11-2 in (11-30) and (11-31). Denoting the value of x_k at which the supremum in (12-22) occurs as $\bar{x}^l_{k,\max}$, it follows from (11-30) and Figure 12-3, that for product t-norm

$$\bar{x}^l_{k,\max} = \frac{\sigma^2_{k2}m^l_k + \sigma^{l^2}_{k2}x'_k}{\sigma^2_{k2} + \sigma^{l^2}_{k2}} \tag{12-29}$$

Similarly, $\underline{f}^l_k$ requires the calculation of the suprema of a product or minimum of the two Gaussians $\mu_{\underline{\tilde{X}}_k}(x_k)$ and $\underline{\mu}_{\tilde{F}^l_k}(x_k)$. Denoting the value of x_k at which the supremum in (12-21) occurs as $\underline{x}^l_{k,\max}$, it follows from (11-30) and Figure 12-3, that for product t-norm

$$\underline{x}^l_{k,\max} = \frac{\sigma^2_{k1}m^l_k + \sigma^{l^2}_{k1}x'_k}{\sigma^2_{k1} + \sigma^{l^2}_{k1}} \tag{12-30}$$

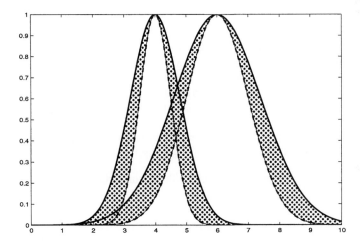

Figure 12-3: The membership functions for Example 12-3. The membership function with the larger variance is for the antecedent, whereas the other is for the input. The thick solid lines denote the upper membership functions, and the thick dashed lines denote the lower membership functions. The shaded regions are the FOUs for both membership functions.

From these results it is straightforward to compute $\underline{f}_k^l$ using (12-23) and (12-15), and to compute $\overline{f}_k^l$ using (12-24) and (12-16); i.e., [see also (6-10)]

$$\underline{f}_k^l = \underline{\mu}_{\tilde{Q}_k^l}(\underline{x}_{k,\max}^l) = \underline{\mu}_{\tilde{X}_k}(\underline{x}_{k,\max}^l)\underline{\mu}_{\tilde{F}_k^l}(\underline{x}_{k,\max}^l) = \exp\left\{-\tfrac{1}{2}\frac{\left(m_k^l - x_k'\right)^2}{\sigma_{k1}^2 + \sigma_{k1}^{l2}}\right\} \qquad (12\text{-}31)$$

and

$$\overline{f}_k^l = \overline{\mu}_{\tilde{Q}_k^l}(\overline{x}_{k,\max}^l) = \overline{\mu}_{\tilde{X}_k}(\overline{x}_{k,\max}^l)\overline{\mu}_{\tilde{F}_k^l}(\overline{x}_{k,\max}^l) = \exp\left\{-\tfrac{1}{2}\frac{\left(m_k^l - x_k'\right)^2}{\sigma_{k2}^2 + \sigma_{k2}^{l2}}\right\} \qquad (12\text{-}32)$$

These results should be compared with those in (11-34) and (11-35), respectively. Because $\sigma_{k1}^2 < \sigma_{X_k}^2$ and $\sigma_{k2}^2 > \sigma_{X_k}^2$, $\underline{f}_k^l\big|_{(12\text{-}31)} < \underline{f}_k^l\big|_{(11\text{-}34)}$ and $\overline{f}_k^l\big|_{(12\text{-}32)} > \overline{f}_k^l\big|_{(11\text{-}35)}$, which proves the statement made at the end of Example 12-2, that as more uncertainties are included, the larger the firing interval becomes. ∎

Example 12-4: [Liang and Mendel (2000c)] This example is a generalization of Example 11-3. Here we quantify the results that were presented in Example 12-1 for which the antecedent membership functions were shown as Gaussian primary membership functions with uncertain means (as in Figure 3-8) and the inputs were modeled as type-2 Gaussian fuzzy numbers with uncertain standard deviations (as in Figure 3-9). This is a very important case because we have found it to be very useful for forecasting time-series in which the measurements are corrupted by additive *non-stationary* noise, and, in fact, we shall use its results in Section 12.5. As in Example 11-3, we focus on the computation of $\underline{f}_k^l$ and $\overline{f}_k^l$. However, here we provide the details for these computations. Our results are summarized in Tables 12-1–12-3. Note that these results are keyed into Figure 12-4.

To begin, we state the membership functions for the inputs and antecedents. In this case, $\mu_k(x_k)$ is given in (12-27), and the primary membership function for each antecedent is

$$\mu_k^l(x_k) = \exp\left[-\tfrac{1}{2}\left(\frac{x_k - m_k^l}{\sigma_k^l}\right)^2\right] \qquad m_k^l \in \left[m_{k1}^l, m_{k2}^l\right] \qquad (12\text{-}33)$$

The upper and lower membership functions for the antecedent membership functions are given in (10-21) and (10-22), respectively, whereas the upper and lower membership functions for the input membership functions are given in (10-24) and (10-25), respectively.[2] In

---

[2]Because $\mu_k(x_k)$ does not depend on rule-index l, we do not need the l-superscripts that appear in (10-24) and (10-25).

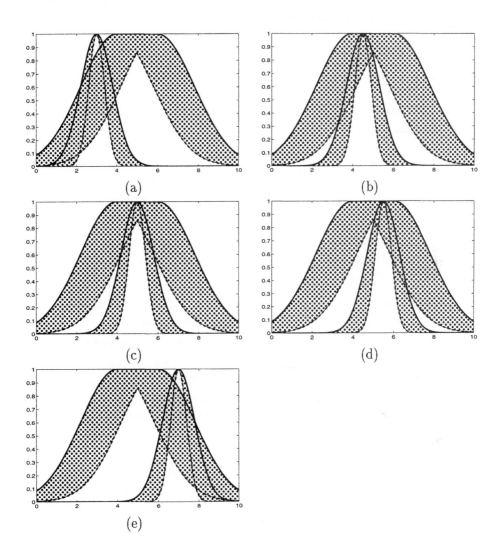

Figure 12-4: For Example 12-4, the different locations of the input FOU in relation to the antecedent FOU. The larger FOU is for the antecedent, whereas the other FOU is for the input. The thick solid lines denote the upper membership functions, and the thick dashed lines denote the lower membership functions. The FOU for the input is centered at x'_k.

this example, we assume that $\sigma_{k2} \leq \sigma'_k$, which means that uncertainty in each input set is never more than the uncertainty in its associated antecedent.

In determining $\bar{x}^l_{k,\max}$ and $\underline{x}^l_{k,\max}$, we need the calculation of the supremum of a product or minimum of two type-1 Gaussian membership functions. As noted in Example 12-3, such a calculation was carried out in Example 6-2 for the product t-norm and in Exercise 6-2 for the minimum t-norm, and was restated in Example 11-2 in (11-30) and (11-31).

Determination of $\bar{x}^l_{k,\max}$: To determine $\bar{x}^l_{k,\max}$, we need to consider three cases of different x'_k locations.

1. $x'_k \leq m^l_{k1}$: This case is depicted in Figure 12-4 (a) (the solid lines). As we see from (10-21), the active branch in the upper membership function of the antecedent comes from $\exp\left[-\frac{1}{2}\left(x_k - m^l_{k1}/\sigma'_k\right)^2\right]$. Hence, it is very straightforward to obtain $\bar{x}^l_{k,\max}$ by using this active antecedent branch and the expression for the upper membership function of the input [as in 10-24)] directly in (11-30) or (11-31). The result for $\bar{x}^l_{k,\max}$ is given in Case 1 of Table 12-1. It is easy to verify that $\bar{x}^l_{k,\max} \leq m^l_{k1}$, as required.

2. $x'_k \in [m^l_{k1}, m^l_{k2}]$: This case is depicted in Figure 12-4 (b)–(d). Note that, although these three possible cases are needed to determine $\underline{x}^l_{k,\max}$, as we explain next, all three cases lead to the same result for $\bar{x}^l_{k,\max}$. In all three cases the active branch in the upper membership function of the antecedent, $\bar{\mu}_{\tilde{F}^l_k}(x_k)$, is associated with the constant membership function $\mu^l_k(x_k) = 1$. And, the maximum value of the upper membership function of the input, $\bar{\mu}_{\tilde{X}_k}(x_k)$, occurs when $x_k = x'_k$, in which case $\bar{x}^l_{k,\max} = x'_k$ and $\bar{\mu}_{\tilde{X}_k}(x'_k) = 1$. In this case

$$\bar{f}^l_k = \bar{\mu}_{\tilde{X}_k}(\bar{x}^l_{k,\max})\bar{\mu}_{\tilde{F}^l}(\bar{x}^l_{k,\max}) = 1$$

This result for $\bar{x}^l_{k,\max}$ is given in Case 2 of Table 12-1.

3. $x'_k \geq m^l_{k2}$: This case is depicted in Figure 12-4 (e). Because the analysis for this case is so similar to that of Case 1, we just state its result as Case 3 in Table 12-1.

Determination of $\underline{x}^l_{k,\max}$: To determine $\underline{x}^l_{k,\max}$, we again need to consider three cases of different x'_k locations, and we also need to consider product and minimum t-norms separately. Regardless of the t-norm, we see from (10-22) that when $x'_k \leq (m^l_{k1} + m^l_{k2})/2$, the active branch of the lower membership function of the antecedent is $N(m^l_{k2}, \sigma^l_k; x_k)$, whereas

Table 12-1: $\bar{x}^l_{k,\max}$ for Example 12-4.

Cases	x'_k Locations	Product t-Norm	Minimum t-Norm
1. Figure 12-4 (a)	$x'_k \leq m^l_{k1}$	$\bar{x}^l_{k,\max} = \dfrac{\sigma^2_{k2} m^l_{k1} + \sigma^{l^2}_k x'_k}{\sigma^2_{k2} + \sigma^{l^2}_k}$	$\bar{x}^l_{k,\max} = \dfrac{\sigma_{k2} m^l_{k1} + \sigma^l_k x'_k}{\sigma_{k2} + \sigma^l_k}$
2. Figure 12-4 (b)–(d)	$x'_k \in [m^l_{k1}, m^l_{k2}]$	$\bar{x}^l_{k,\max} = x'_k$	$\bar{x}^l_{k,\max} = x'_k$
3. Figure 12-4 (e)	$x'_k \geq m^l_{k2}$	$\bar{x}^l_{k,\max} = \dfrac{\sigma^2_{k2} m^l_{k2} + \sigma^{l^2}_k x'_k}{\sigma^2_{k2} + \sigma^{l^2}_k}$	$\bar{x}^l_{k,\max} = \dfrac{\sigma_{k2} m^l_{k2} + \sigma^l_k x'_k}{\sigma_{k2} + \sigma^l_k}$

when $x'_k \geq (m^l_{k1} + m^l_{k2})/2$, the active branch of the lower membership function of the antecedent is $N(m^l_{k1}, \sigma^l_k; x_k)$. Because the steps for obtaining $\underline{x}^l_{k,\max}$ in the case of minimum t-norm are identical to the steps for obtaining $\underline{x}^l_{k,\max}$ in the case of product t norm, we only present the details for the latter.

1. For the cases depicted in Figure 12-4 (a) and (b), $\underline{x}^l_{k,\max}$ involves the lower membership function of the input and $N(m^l_{k2}, \sigma^l_k; x_k)$ [since $x'_k \leq (m^l_{k1} + m^l_{k2})/2$], with the result for $\underline{x}^l_{k,\max}$ that is given in Case 1 in the third column of Table 12-2. We now need to establish when Case 1 occurs. For $\underline{x}^l_{k,\max}$ to be to the left of $(m^l_{k1} + m^l_{k2})/2$, it must be true that

$$\frac{\sigma^2_{k1} m^l_{k2} + \sigma^{l^2}_k x'_k}{\sigma^2_{k1} + \sigma^{l^2}_k} < \frac{m^l_{k1} + m^l_{k2}}{2} \tag{12-34}$$

from which we can solve for x'_k to establish that Case 1 occurs when

$$x'_k < \frac{m^l_{k1} + m^l_{k2}}{2} - \frac{\sigma^2_{k1}\left(m^l_{k2} - m^l_{k1}\right)}{2\sigma^{l^2}_k} \tag{12-35}$$

2. For the cases depicted in Figure 12 (d) and (e), $\underline{x}^l_{k,\max}$ involves the lower membership function of the input and $N(m^l_{k1}, \sigma^l_k; x_k)$ [since $x'_k \geq (m^l_{k1} + m^l_{k2})/2$]. The analysis for this case is very similar to that for Case 1, so we provide its results, without derivation, as Case 3 in Table 12-2.

3. Based on our results for Cases 1 and 3, we see that, for the case depicted in Figure 12-4 (c), it must be true that

$$\frac{m_{k1}^l + m_{k2}^l}{2} - \frac{\sigma_{k1}^2\left(m_{k2}^l - m_{k1}^l\right)}{2\sigma_k^{l2}} \leq x_k' \leq \frac{m_{k1}^l + m_{k2}^l}{2} + \frac{\sigma_{k1}^2\left(m_{k2}^l - m_{k1}^l\right)}{2\sigma_k^{l2}} \tag{12-36}$$

In this case, the supremum point of the product between the lower membership function of the input and $N(m_{k2}^l, \sigma_k^l; x_k)$ is located to the right of or at $(m_{k1}^l + m_{k2}^l)/2$; but, $N(m_{k2}^l, \sigma_k^l; x_k)$ is active only when $x_k' \leq (m_{k1}^l + m_{k2}^l)/2$. Because the product of two Gaussians is convex and is also monotonically increasing to the left of the supremum point, the supremum point of the product of the lower membership function of the input and $N(m_{k2}^l, \sigma_k^l; x_k)$ must occur at $(m_{k1}^l + m_{k2}^l)/2$.

Additionally, the supremum point of the product between the lower membership function of the input and $N(m_{k1}^l, \sigma_k^l; x_k)$ is located to the left of or at $(m_{k1}^l + m_{k2}^l)/2$. Hence, using similar reasoning to that in the previous paragraph, we conclude that the supremum point of the product between the lower membership function of the input and $N(m_{k1}^l, \sigma_k^l; x_k)$ also occurs at $(m_{k1}^l + m_{k2}^l)/2$.

From these two results, we finally conclude that

$$\underline{x}_{k,\max}^l = \frac{m_{k1}^l + m_{k2}^l}{2} \tag{12-37}$$

which appears as Case 2 in Table 12-2.

Here is how the results in Tables 12-1–12-3 can be used in practice. Figure 12-4, which was used to establish the results in Tables 12-1–12-3, clearly demonstrates that there are only five possible situations that need to be distinguished to do this. To be consistent with the labeling of that figure, we refer to these five situations, as we did in Section 11.3, as state(1), state(2),…, state(5), where:

state(1): $\underline{x}_{k,\max}^l$ is in case 1 (Tables 12-2 or 12-3) and $\bar{x}_{k,\max}^l$ is in case 1 (Table 12-1)

state(2): $\underline{x}_{k,\max}^l$ is in case 1 (Tables 12-2 or 12-3) and $\bar{x}_{k,\max}^l$ is in case 2 (Table 12-1)

state(3): $\underline{x}_{k,\max}^l$ is in case 2 (Tables 12-2 or 12-3) and $\bar{x}_{k,\max}^l$ is in case 2 (Table 12-1)

state(4): $\underline{x}_{k,\max}^l$ is in case 3 (Tables 12-2 or 12-3) and $\bar{x}_{k,\max}^l$ is in case 2 (Table 12-1)

state(5): $\underline{x}^l_{k,\max}$ is in case 3 (Tables 12-2 or 12-3) and $\bar{x}^l_{k,\max}$ is in case 3 (Table 12-1)

Note that these results were obtained by pairing up the respective (a), (b), ..., (e) in the first columns of Tables 12-1 and 12-2 (or 12-3). Table 12-4 summarizes $\underline{f}^l_k(x'_k) = \underline{\mu}_{\tilde{Q}^l_k}(\underline{x}^l_{k,\max})$ and $\bar{f}^l_k(x'_k) = \bar{\mu}_{\tilde{Q}^l_k}(\bar{x}^l_{k,\max})$ for these five states under product t-norm. Its entries were obtained by evaluating (12-16) and (12-17) for each state.

The results in Table 12-4 are very useful in the design of a type-2 non-singleton type-2 FLS whose parameters are tuned using steepest descent algorithms. This is discussed in Section 12.4.3. ∎

Table 12-2: $\underline{x}^l_{k,\max}$ for Example 12-4 based on product t-norm.

Cases	x'_k Locations	Product t-Norm
1. Figure 12-4 (a) and (b)	$x'_k < \dfrac{m^l_{k1}+m^l_{k2}}{2} - \dfrac{\sigma^2_{k1}\left(m^l_{k2}-m^l_{k1}\right)}{2\sigma^{l^2}_k}$	$\underline{x}^l_{k,\max} = \dfrac{\sigma^2_{k1}m^l_{k2}+\sigma^{l^2}_k x'_k}{\sigma^2_{k1}+\sigma^l_k}$
2. Figure 12-4 (c)	$x'_k \in \left[\dfrac{m^l_{k1}+m^l_{k2}}{2} - \dfrac{\sigma^2_{k1}\left(m^l_{k2}-m^l_{k1}\right)}{2\sigma^{l^2}_k},\right.$ $\left.\dfrac{m^l_{k1}+m^l_{k2}}{2} + \dfrac{\sigma^2_{k1}\left(m^l_{k2}-m^l_{k1}\right)}{2\sigma^{l^2}_k}\right]$	$\underline{x}^l_{k,\max} = \dfrac{m^l_{k1}+m^l_{k2}}{2}$
3. Figure 12-4 (d) and (e)	$x'_k > \dfrac{m^l_{k1}+m^l_{k2}}{2} + \dfrac{\sigma^2_{k1}\left(m^l_{k2}-m^l_{k1}\right)}{2\sigma^{l^2}_k}$	$\underline{x}^l_{k,\max} = \dfrac{\sigma^2_{k1}m^l_{k1}+\sigma^{l^2}_k x'_k}{\sigma^2_{k1}+\sigma^l_k}$

Based on the statements made toward the end of Section 12.1, that type-reduction and defuzzification apply as well to type-2 non-singleton, type-1–non-singleton type-2, and singleton type-2 FLSs, we conclude, as we did in Section 11.3, that: *except for the calculations of $\underline{f}^l_k$ and $\bar{f}^l_k$, all the calculations described in Section 10.9 apply as well to the present chapter.*

Example 12-5: In this example, we demonstrate that type-1 rules that are excited by a type-2 input lead to a type-2 FLS. In this case,

$$\underline{\mu}_{\tilde{F}^l_k}(x_i) = \bar{\mu}_{\tilde{F}^l_k}(x_i) \equiv \mu_{F^l_k}(x_i) \tag{12-39}$$

Table 12-3: $\underline{x}^l_{k,\max}$ for Example 12-4 based on minimum t-norm.

Cases	x'_k Locations	Minimum t-Norm
1. Figure 12-4 (a) and (b)	$x'_k < \dfrac{m^l_{k1}+m^l_{k2}}{2} - \dfrac{\sigma_{k1}\left(m^l_{k2}-m^l_{k1}\right)}{2\sigma^l_k}$	$\underline{x}^l_{k,\max} = \dfrac{\sigma_{k1}m^l_{k2}+\sigma^l_k x'_k}{\sigma_{k1}+\sigma^l_k}$
2. Figure 12-4 (c)	$x'_k \in \left[\dfrac{m^l_{k1}+m^l_{k2}}{2} - \dfrac{\sigma_{k1}\left(m^l_{k2}-m^l_{k1}\right)}{2\sigma^l_k}\right.,$ $\left.\dfrac{m^l_{k1}+m^l_{k2}}{2} + \dfrac{\sigma_{k1}\left(m^l_{k2}-m^l_{k1}\right)}{2\sigma^l_k}\right]$	$\underline{x}^l_{k,\max} = \dfrac{m^l_{k1}+m^l_{k2}}{2}$
3. Figure 12-4 (d) and (e)	$x'_k > \dfrac{m^l_{k1}+m^l_{k2}}{2} + \dfrac{\sigma_{k1}\left(m^l_{k2}-m^l_{k1}\right)}{2\sigma^l_k}$	$\underline{x}^l_{k,\max} = \dfrac{\sigma_{k1}m^l_{k1}+\sigma^l_k x'_k}{\sigma_{k1}+\sigma^l_k}$

Table 12-4: $\underline{\mu}_{\tilde{Q}^l_k}(\underline{x}^l_{k,\max})$ and $\overline{\mu}_{\tilde{Q}^l_k}(\overline{x}^l_{k,\max})$ under product t-norm.

State	$\underline{\mu}_{\tilde{Q}^l_k}(\underline{x}^l_{k,\max})$	$\overline{\mu}_{\tilde{Q}^l_k}(\overline{x}^l_{k,\max})$
(1)	$\exp\left[-\tfrac{1}{2}\left(m^l_{k2}-x'_k\right)^2 \big/ \left(\sigma^2_{k1}+\sigma^{l^2}_k\right)\right]$	$\exp\left[-\tfrac{1}{2}\left(m^l_{k1}-x'_k\right)^2 \big/ \left(\sigma^2_{k2}+\sigma^{l^2}_k\right)\right]$
(2)	$\exp\left[-\tfrac{1}{2}\left(m^l_{k2}-x'_k\right)^2 \big/ \left(\sigma^2_{k1}+\sigma^{l^2}_k\right)\right]$	1
(3)	$\exp\left[-\tfrac{1}{2}\left(m^l_{k2}+m^l_{k1}-2x'_k\right)^2 \big/ 4\sigma^2_{k1}\right.$ $\left.-\tfrac{1}{2}\left(m^l_{k2}-m^l_{k1}\right)^2 \big/ 4\sigma^{l^2}_k\right]$	1
(4)	$\exp\left[-\tfrac{1}{2}\left(m^l_{k1}-x'_k\right)^2 \big/ \left(\sigma^2_{k1}+\sigma^{l^2}_k\right)\right]$	1
(5)	$\exp\left[-\tfrac{1}{2}\left(m^l_{k1}-x'_k\right)^2 \big/ \left(\sigma^2_{k1}+\sigma^{l^2}_k\right)\right]$	$\exp\left[-\tfrac{1}{2}\left(m^l_{k2}-x'_k\right)^2 \big/ \left(\sigma^2_{k2}+\sigma^{l^2}_k\right)\right]$

so that $\underline{f}^l(\mathbf{x}')$ and $\overline{f}^l(\mathbf{x}')$ in (12-8) and (12-9) simplify to

$$\underline{f}^l(\mathbf{x}') = \sup_{\mathbf{x}} \int_{x_1 \in X_1} \cdots \int_{x_p \in X_p} \left[\underline{\mu}_{\tilde{X}_1}(x_1) \star \mu_{F^l_1}(x_1)\right] \star$$
$$\cdots \star \left[\underline{\mu}_{\tilde{X}_p}(x_p) \star \mu_{F^l_p}(x_p)\right] \Big/ \mathbf{x} \qquad (12\text{-}40)$$

and

$$
\begin{aligned}
\overline{f}^{l}(\mathbf{x}') = \sup_{\mathbf{x}} \int_{x_{1} \in X_{1}} \cdots \int_{x_{p} \in X_{p}} \left[\overline{\mu}_{\tilde{X}_{1}}(x_{1}) \star \mu_{F_{1}^{l}}(x_{1}) \right] \star \\
\cdots \star \left[\overline{\mu}_{\tilde{X}_{p}}(x_{p}) \star \mu_{F_{p}^{l}}(x_{p}) \right] \Big/ \mathbf{x}
\end{aligned}
\tag{12-41}
$$

Observe that $\underline{f}^{l}(\mathbf{x}') \neq \overline{f}^{l}(\mathbf{x}')$, so that in this special case of a type-2 input applied to type-1 rules a firing interval occurs instead of just a single firing level; hence, the overall FLS is a type-2 FLS.

In retrospect, the results of this example should not have been a surprise, because we have already demonstrated that uncertainties are propagated all the way through a type-2 FLS, and that a type-1 FLS is a special case of a type-2 FLS. ■

12.4 DESIGNING INTERVAL TYPE-2 NON-SINGLETON TYPE-2 FLSs

Just as all the calculations described in Section 10.9 apply to the present case of an interval type-2 non-singleton type-2 FLS (except for the calculations of $\underline{f}_{k}^{l}$ and $\overline{f}_{k}^{l}$), the Section 10.10 discussions about designing interval singleton type-2 FLSs also apply to this chapter. So, this is again a good place for the reader to review the material in that section. As in that section's design methods, our interval type-2 non-singleton type-2 FLS design methods are associated with the following problem:

> We are given a collection of N input–output numerical data *training* pairs, $(\mathbf{x}^{(1)}: y^{(1)}), (\mathbf{x}^{(2)}: y^{(2)}), ..., (\mathbf{x}^{(N)}: y^{(N)})$, where $\mathbf{x}$ is the vector input and y is the scalar output of an interval type-2 non-singleton type-2 FLS. Our goal is to completely specify this type-2 FLS using the training data.

Additionally, for illustrative purposes, all designs assume that the antecedent and consequent membership functions are Gaussian primary membership functions, with uncertain mean and interval secondary membership functions (as in Figure 3-8), product implication and t-norm, center-of-sets type-reduction, and defuzzification using the centroid of the type-reduced set. In this chapter, however, the type-2 nature of the input measurement is described by the Gaussian primary membership function with uncertain standard deviation and interval secondary membership functions depicted in Figure 3-9. Our type-2 FLS is described by the contents of Section 12.3. Note, as in Sections 10.10 and 11.4, the basic principles used in each design procedure carry over to many other interval type-2 non-singleton type-2 FLSs.

To begin, as in Sections 10.10 and 11.4, we must explain how the training data can be interpreted as a collection of IF–THEN rules. Each rule is still in the form given in (10-2), where $\tilde{F}_i^l$ are interval type-2 fuzzy sets that are associated with the elements of $\mathbf{x}^{(t)}$ and are described by the primary membership functions in (10-20), i.e.,

$$\mu_i^l(x_i) = \exp\left[-\frac{1}{2}\left(\frac{x_i - m_i^l}{\sigma_i^l}\right)^2\right] \quad m_i^l \in [m_{i1}^l, m_{i2}^l] \qquad (12\text{-}42)$$

where $i = 1, \ldots, p$ and $l = 1, \ldots, M$. The consequent sets are also described by Gaussian primary membership functions with uncertain mean and interval secondary membership functions, i.e.,

$$\mu^j(y) = \exp\left[-\frac{1}{2}\left(\frac{y - m^j}{\sigma^j}\right)^2\right] \quad m^j \in [m_1^j, m_2^j] \quad j = 1, \ldots, M \qquad (12\text{-}43)$$

Note that the centroid of each $\mu^j(y)$, $C_{\tilde{G}^j}$, is an interval type-1 set, i.e.,

$$C_{\tilde{G}^j} = [y_l^j, y_r^j] \quad j = 1, \ldots, M \qquad (12\text{-}44)$$

In addition, the inputs are now type-2 Gaussian fuzzy numbers whose primary membership functions are

$$\mu_k(x_k) = \exp\left[-\frac{1}{2}\left(\frac{x_k - x_k'}{\sigma_k}\right)^2\right] \quad \sigma_k \in [\sigma_{k1}, \sigma_{k2}] \qquad (12\text{-}45)$$

where $k = 1, \ldots, p$, and whose secondary membership functions are interval sets.

Each design method establishes how to specify all the parameters of the membership functions in (12-42), (12-43), and (12-45) using the training pairs $(\mathbf{x}^{(1)}:y^{(1)}), (\mathbf{x}^{(2)}:y^{(2)}), \ldots, (\mathbf{x}^{(N)}:y^{(N)})$.

As in Sections 5.9, 6.6, 10.10, and 11.4, how many rules there can be in the interval type-2 non-singleton type-2 FLS depends on the design method that is used to construct it. If no tuning of the FLS parameters is done, then there can be as many as $M = N$ rules. If tuning is used, and we continue to abide by the commonly used design principle that there must be fewer tuned design parameters than training pairs, then we must use less than N rules.

Example 12-6: Let us enumerate how many design parameters there can be in the just-stated design:

- Antecedent parameters m_{i1}^l, m_{i2}^l, and σ_i^l: 3 per antecedent, p antecedents, and M rules, for a total of $3pM$ parameters.
- Consequent parameters m_1^j, m_2^j, and σ^j: 3 per consequent and M rules, for a total of $3M$ parameters. A viable alternative—the one we use (as we did in Sections 10.10 and 11.4)—is to treat y_l^j and y_r^j as the consequent parameters, in which case there are a total of $2M$ such parameters.
- Measurement parameters σ_{k1} and σ_{k2}: 2 per input and p inputs, for a total of $2p$ parameters. If each input membership function has the same standard deviation parameters, $\sigma_{k1} = \sigma_1$ and $\sigma_{k2} = \sigma_2$ $(k = 1, \ldots, p)$, there will only be 2 additional parameters.

So, the maximum number of design parameters is $3pM + 2M + 2p$. Recall, from Example 11-4, the maximum number of design parameters for an interval type-1 non-singleton type-2 FLS is $3pM + 2M + p$. Hence, we again have more degrees of freedom in an interval type-2 non-singleton type-2 FLS than in an interval type-1 non-singleton type-2 FLS, which suggests we should be able to outperform an interval type-1 non-singleton type-2 FLS.

For the convenience of the reader we collect the parameters and their numbers for all five of our FLS designs in Table 12-5.

From our discussion just before this example, we see that if no tuning of type-2 FLS parameters is done, then there can be as many as $3pN + 2N + 2p$ parameters; however, if tuning is used, then there is the following design constraint:

$$3pM + 2M + 2p < N \tag{12-46}$$

If we are given a fixed number of training samples, $N = N'$, then

$$M < \left\lfloor \frac{N' - 2p}{3p + 2} \right\rfloor \tag{12-47}$$

which constrains the number of rules that can be used. Because M must be an integer, we choose $M = M'$ as an integer that is smaller than $(N' - 2p)/(3p + 2)$. ∎

As in Section 11.4, at a very high level, we can think of three designs associated with the preceding formulation:

1. Fix the shapes and parameters of all the antecedent, consequent, and input measurement membership functions ahead of time. Doing this fixes the shape and size of the FOU for each antecedent, consequent, and input measurement

membership function. The data establish the rules and the range on the standard deviation of the measurements, and no tuning is used.

2. Fix the shapes and parameters of all the antecedent and consequent membership functions ahead of time. Doing this fixes the shape and size of the FOU for each antecedent and consequent membership function. Fix the shape but not the parameters of the input-measurement type-2 membership function ahead of time. Use the training data to tune the parameters of the input measurement membership function. In this way, the size of the input FOU adapts to the training data.

3. Fix the shapes of all the antecedent, consequent, and input measurement membership functions ahead of time. Doing this fixes the shape of the FOU for each antecedent, consequent, and input membership function. Use the training data to tune the antecedent, consequent, and input measurement parameters. In this way, the size of each FOU adapts to the training data.

Table 12-5: The parameters and numbers of parameters in 5 different FLSs (with M rules and p antecedents in each rule, i.e., $i = 1, ..., M$ and $k = 1, ..., p$); P is short for *parameters*.

FLS	P in One Input Set	P in One Antecedent	P in One Consequent	Total # of P
Type-1 SFLS	N/A	$m_{F_k^i}, \sigma_{F_k^i}$	$\bar{y}^i$	$2pM + M$
Type-1 NSFLS	σ_{X_k}	$m_{F_k^i}, \sigma_{F_k^i}$	$\bar{y}^i$	$2pM + M + p$
Type-2 SFLS	N/A	$m_{k1}^i, m_{k2}^i, \sigma_k^i$	y_l^i, y_r^i	$3pM + 2M$
Type-2 NSFLS-1	σ_{X_k}	$m_{k1}^i, m_{k2}^i, \sigma_k^i$	y_l^i, y_r^i	$3pM + 2M + p$
Type-2 NSFLS-2	σ_{k1}, σ_{k2}	$m_{k1}^i, m_{k2}^i, \sigma_k^i$	y_l^i, y_r^i	$3pM + 2M + 2p$

Let us note that, just as in Section 11.4, there can be two very different *approaches to the tuning of an interval type-2 non-singleton type-2 FLS.*

1. **Partially dependent approach:** In this approach, one first designs the best possible interval type-1 non-singleton type-2 FLS, by tuning all of its parameters, and then updates the design by: (a) keeping all of the parameters that are shared by the interval type-1 non-singleton and type-2 non-singleton type 2 FLSs fixed at the values obtained from the best possible interval type-1 non-singleton type-2 FLS; and (b) tuning only the new parameter(s) of the interval type-2 non-singleton type-2 FLS. In the present case, only the standard deviations, σ_{k1}^l and σ_{k2}^l, would be tuned.

2. **Totally independent approach:** In this approach, all of the parameters of the interval type-2 non-singleton type-2 FLS are tuned. If, perchance, an in-

terval type-1 non-singleton type-2 FLS has already been designed, then its parameters can be used as the *initial parameters* for the tuning algorithms of the parameters that are shared by the interval type-1 non-singleton and type-2 non-singleton type-2 FLSs.

One would expect the best performance to be obtained by the totally independent approach; however, as mentioned in Sections 6.6, 10.10, and 11.4, sometimes it is very useful to use the partially dependent approach to observe the incremental improvement that can be obtained from the previous design to the new design.

In the rest of this section, we focus on *differences* in Section 10.10 that occur because of the type-2 non-singleton nature of the FLS considered in the present chapter. The differences are very similar to the ones described in Section 11.4 for an interval type-1 non-singleton type-2 FLS. We do not repeat the discussions given in Section 10.10; so, if the reader has not already done it, this would be a good time for the reader to review its design methods.

12.4.1 One-pass method

There are no changes to this method, since it is based entirely on the training data. Following the procedure given in Section 10.10.1, one can again easily design up to N rules from the now noisy training data. To complete this design, one must also determine values for σ_{k1}^l and σ_{k2}^l ($k = 1, ..., p$ and $l = 1, ..., M$). This requires that a range for the variance of the additive measurement noise on each measured antecedent be known ahead of time, or that it can be estimated from the data; otherwise, one should use another design method in which σ_{k1}^l and σ_{k2}^l can be tuned.

12.4.2 Least-squares method

For the same reasons given in Section 10.10.2, we conclude that, at present, we cannot use a least-squares design method for an interval type-2 non-singleton type-2 FLS.[3]

---

[3] See footnote 6 in Chapter 10.

12.4.3 Back-propagation (steepest descent) method

In the back-propagation method some or all of the antecedent, consequent, or input measurement membership function parameters are *not* fixed ahead of time. These parameters are tuned using a steepest descent method that we briefly describe in this section. For illustrative purposes, we assume that *all* of the antecedent, consequent, and input measurement function parameters are to be tuned. The results in this section are very similar to those in the Section 11.4.3, where an 11-step design procedure was stated and discussed (that method built on the one described in Section 10.10.3). Hence, here we focus on the differences to that method caused by the inputs in the present chapter being type-2 non-singleton. As in Section 11.4.3, for completeness, we restate all 11 steps.

Given the N input–output training samples $(\mathbf{x}^{(t)}, y^{(t)})$, $t = 1,...,N$, we wish to update the design parameters so that the following error function is minimized for E training epochs:

$$e^{(t)} = \tfrac{1}{2}\left[f_{ns2-2}(\mathbf{x}^{(t)}) - y^{(t)}\right]^2 \qquad t = 1,...,N \qquad (12\text{-}48)$$

A general method for doing this is:

1. Initialize all of the parameters in the antecedent and consequent membership functions. Choose the means of the type-2 Gaussian fuzzy numbers [in (12-45)] to be centered at the measurements, i.e., set $x'_k = x_k^{(t)}$, $k = 1,...,p$, for $t = 1$; and initialize the standard deviation interval end-points of these numbers.

2. Set the counter, e, of the training epoch to zero; i.e., $e \equiv 0$.

3. Set the counter, t, of the training data to unity; i.e., $t \equiv 1$.

4. Apply $p \times 1$ input $\mathbf{x}^{(t)}$ to the interval type-2 non-singleton type-2 FLS and compute the total firing interval for each rule; i.e., compute $\underline{f}^i$ and $\overline{f}^i$ ($i = 1, ..., p$) using (12-21)–(12-26). This requires using the results in Table 12-4.

5. Compute y_l and y_r using the four-step iterative method described on pp. 310–311 [this leads to re-ordering of the M rules, which are then re-numbered $1,..., M$, as explained in the discussions accompanying (10-63)–(10-65)]. Doing this establishes L and R, so that y_l and y_r can be expressed as in (10-57) and (10-60), respectively, i.e.,

$$y_l = \frac{\sum_{i=1}^{M} f_l^i y_l^i}{\sum_{i=1}^{M} f_l^i} = \frac{\sum_{i=1}^{L} \overline{f}^i y_l^i + \sum_{j=L+1}^{M} \underline{f}^j y_l^j}{\sum_{i=1}^{L} \overline{f}^i + \sum_{j=L+1}^{M} \underline{f}^j}$$

$$= y_l\left(\overline{f}^1, ..., \overline{f}^L, \underline{f}^{L+1}, ..., \underline{f}^M, y_l^1, ..., y_l^M\right) \tag{12-49}$$

and

$$y_r = \frac{\sum_{i=1}^{M} f_r^i y_r^i}{\sum_{i=1}^{M} f_r^i} = \frac{\sum_{i=1}^{R} \underline{f}^i y_r^i + \sum_{j=R+1}^{M} \overline{f}^j y_r^j}{\sum_{i=1}^{R} \underline{f}^i + \sum_{j=R+1}^{M} \overline{f}^j}$$

$$= y_r\left(\underline{f}^1, ..., \underline{f}^R, \overline{f}^{R+1}, ..., \overline{f}^M, y_r^1, ..., y_r^M\right) \tag{12-50}$$

6. Compute the defuzzified output, $f_{ns2-2}(\mathbf{x}^{(t)})$, of the interval type-2 non-singleton type-2 FLS, as

$$f_{ns2-2}(\mathbf{x}^{(t)}) = \left[y_l(\mathbf{x}^{(t)}) + y_r(\mathbf{x}^{(t)})\right]/2 \tag{12-51}$$

7. Determine the explicit dependence of y_l and y_r on membership functions. [Because L and R obtained in Step 5 usually change from one iteration to the next, the dependence of y_l and y_r on membership functions will also usually change from one iteration to the next.] To do this, first determine the explicit dependence of $\underline{f}^l$ and $\overline{f}^l$ on membership functions using (12-23) and (12-24); i.e., $\underline{f}^l$ is determined by $T_{k=1}^{P} \underline{\mu}_{\tilde{Q}_k^l}(\overline{x}_{k,max}^l)$ and $\overline{f}^l$ is determined by $T_{k=1}^{P} \overline{\mu}_{\tilde{Q}_k^l}(\overline{x}_{k,max}^l)$. Consequently, from (12-49) and (12-50), we see that

$$y_l = y_l\Big[T_{k=1}^{P} \overline{\mu}_{\tilde{Q}_k^1}(\overline{x}_{k,max}^1), ..., T_{k=1}^{P} \overline{\mu}_{\tilde{Q}_k^L}(\overline{x}_{k,max}^L), T_{k=1}^{P} \underline{\mu}_{\tilde{Q}_k^{L+1}}(\underline{x}_{k,max}^{L+1}),$$

$$..., T_{k=1}^{P} \underline{\mu}_{\tilde{Q}_k^M}(\underline{x}_{k,max}^M), y_l^1, ..., y_l^M\Big] \tag{12-52}$$

Similarly,

$$y_r = y_r\Big[T_{k=1}^{P} \underline{\mu}_{\tilde{Q}_k^1}(\underline{x}_{k,max}^1), ..., T_{k=1}^{P} \underline{\mu}_{\tilde{Q}_k^R}(\underline{x}_{k,max}^R), T_{k=1}^{P} \overline{\mu}_{\tilde{Q}_k^{R+1}}(\overline{x}_{k,max}^{R+1}),$$

$$..., T_{k=1}^{P} \overline{\mu}_{\tilde{Q}_k^M}(\overline{x}_{k,max}^M), y_r^1, ..., y_r^M\Big] \tag{12-53}$$

8. Test each component of $\mathbf{x}^{(t)}$ to determine which of the five possible states—the *active state*—it is in ($k = 1, \ldots, p$), and use the results in Table 12-4 to express y_l and y_r as explicit functions of the underlying membership function parameters.

9. Tune the parameters of the active state established in Step 8 using a steepest descent algorithm for the error function in (12-48). Partial derivatives of $\underline{\mu}_{\tilde{Q}_l^i}(\underline{x}_{k,\max}^l)$ or $\overline{\mu}_{\tilde{Q}_l^i}(\overline{x}_{k,\max}^l)$ with respect to specific design parameters are easy to compute using the results given in Table 12-4.

10. Set $t \equiv t + 1$. If $t = N + 1$, go to Step 11; otherwise, go to Step 4.

11. Set $e \equiv e + 1$. If $e = E$, STOP; otherwise, go to Step 3.

As in Section 10.10.3, what makes the tuning of the parameters of this type-2 non-singleton type-2 FLS challenging and different from the tuning of the parameters in a singleton type-1 FLS is having to first determine which parameters y_l and y_r depend on. This requires (Step 8) using $x_k^{(t)}$ ($k = 1, \ldots, p$) to determine which of the five possible states is active. As the parameters change, due to their tuning, the dependency of y_l and y_r on these parameters also changes. This does not occur in a type-1 FLS.

Of course, the steepest descent algorithms needed in Step 9 will be slightly different than those in Section 11.4.3 because of the additional input measurement parameters that must be determined for an interval type-2 non-singleton type-2 FLS. We leave the details for the reader (Exercise 12-7).

Note: The note at the end of Section 11.4.3, about not being able to use a steepest descent algorithm if $\underline{x}_{k,\max}^l$ and $\overline{x}_{k,\max}^l$ cannot be determined in closed form, applies here as well.

12.4.4 SVD–QR method

The SVD–QR method that was described in Section 10.10.4 is directly applicable to the design of interval type-2 non-singleton type-2 FLSs. We illustrate its use below in Section 12.5.

12.4.5 Iterative design method

The four-step iterative design method that was described in Section 10.10.5 is directly applicable to the design of interval type-2 non-singleton type-2 FLSs. It is also illustrated in the next section.

12.5 CASE STUDY: FORECASTING OF TIME-SERIES

We have described the problem of forecasting a time-series in Section 4.2. In actual time-series, such as the price curve for the U. S. dollar versus the German mark, market volatility can change noticeably over the course of time, so the variance of the noise component, which is related to volatility, need not be constant [Magdon-Ismail et al. (1998)]. In that case, the additive measurement noise is non-stationary. In this section we assume that measurements of a time-series are corrupted by additive zero-mean noise, whose signal-to-noise ratio (SNR) varies in an unknown manner from 0dB (with standard deviation $\sigma_{n_{0dB}}$) to 10dB (with standard deviation $\sigma_{n_{10dB}}$). It is the non-stationary nature of the noise that distinguishes the material in this section from the studies in Sections 5.10, 6.7, 10.11, and 11.5.

To begin, let us explain why a type-2 non-singleton type-2 FLS model is appropriate for the case of non-stationary additive noise. In Section 6.7.1 we started with the following well-known formula for SNR

$$SNR = 10 \log_{10}\left(\frac{\sigma_s^2}{\sigma_n^2}\right) \qquad (12\text{-}54)$$

where σ_s^2 is the variance of the signal and σ_n^2 is the variance of the noise, and we solved it for σ_n, as

$$\sigma_n = \frac{\sigma_s}{10^{SNR/20}} \qquad (12\text{-}55)$$

There are two sources of uncertainty in this equation, σ_s and SNR. Because we do not know the signal ahead of time—we're trying to estimate it—we do not know σ_s. All we know about SNR is that it varies over a range of values. These uncertainties suggest that a useful way to model each input measurement in the FLS is as a Gaussian that is centered at the measurement and whose standard deviation varies over an interval of values; i.e., as a type-2 fuzzy set.

12.5.1 Six-epoch back-propagation design

Here we compare the designs of five FLS forecasters for the Mackey–Glass time-series using the back-propagation method. They are: singleton type-1, non-singleton type-1, interval singleton type-2, interval type-1 non-singleton type-2, and interval type-2 non-singleton type-2. All designs are based on the following 1,000 *noisy* data points: $x(1001), x(1002), ..., x(2000)$. The first 504 noisy data, $x(1001), x(1002), ..., x(1504)$, are used for training; i.e., for the designs of the FLS forecasters, whereas the remaining 496 noisy data, $x(1505)$, $x(1506)$, ..., $x(2000)$, are used for testing the designs. The noise-free Mackey –Glass time-series is depicted in Figure 12-5 (a). We assume that the noise-free sampled time-series, $s(k)$, is corrupted by uniformly distributed non-stationary additive noise, $n(k)$, so that

$$x(k) = s(k) + n(k) \quad k=1001, 1002, ..., 2000 \quad (12\text{-}56)$$

and that $0dB \le SNR \le 10dB$ so that $\sigma_{n_{0dB}} \le \sigma_n \le \sigma_{n_{10dB}}$. At each value of k, σ_n was assumed to be uniformly distributed in the interval $\left[\sigma_{n_{0dB}}, \sigma_{n_{10dB}}\right]$ that was broken into 100 levels. One realization of $x(1001)$, $x(1002)$, ..., $x(2000)$ is depicted in Figure 12-5 (b). It may be interesting for the reader to compare Figures 12-5 (b) and 5-11 (b). The latter is also one realization of $x(1001)$, $x(1002)$, ..., $x(2000)$ but for stationary noise at 0dB. The differences between the two noisy time-series are quite noticeable.

As in Sections 5.10, 6.7, 10.11, and 11.5, we used four antecedents for forecasting, namely, $x(k-3)$, $x(k-2)$, $x(k-1)$, and $x(k)$, to predict $x(k+1)$, and two fuzzy sets for each antecedent; hence, we used a total of 16 rules. Gaussian membership functions were chosen for the antecedents of the two type-1 FLSs, and Gaussian primary membership functions of uncertain means [as in (11-36)] were chosen for the antecedents of the three interval type-2 FLSs. Gaussian membership functions were chosen for the input measurements in the type-1 non-singleton cases, whereas a Gaussian primary membership function with uncertain standard deviation was chosen for the input measurements in the type-2 non-singleton case. The parameters as well as the number of parameters that characterize each of the 5 FLSs are summarized in Table 12-5. To use the results in that table, set $p = 4$ and $M = 16$.

All five designs used the *totally independent approach* that was described in Section 12.4; i.e., all of the parameters were tuned independently for each design. For details on how to actually do this, see Sections 5.9.3, 6.6.3, 10.10.3, and 11.4.3, and Section 12.4.3.

Initial values for the parameters in each of the five designs are summarized in Table 12-6. Note that m_x and σ_x are the mean and standard deviation, respectively, of the data in the 504 training samples, $x(1001)$, $x(1002)$, ..., $x(1504)$, and

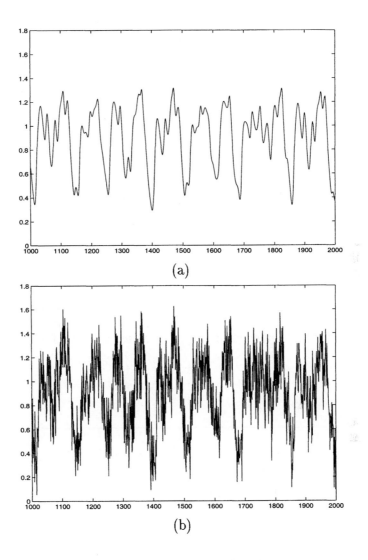

Figure 12-5: Mackey–Glass time-series. (a) noise-free data $s(1001)$, $s(1002)$, ..., $s(2000)$, and (b) one realization of non-stationary uniformly distributed noisy data, $x(1001)$, $x(1002)$, ..., $x(2000)$, where $\sigma_{n_{0dB}} \leq \sigma_n \leq \sigma_{n_{10dB}}$.

$$\sigma_n \equiv \frac{\hat{\sigma}_{n_{0dB}} + \hat{\sigma}_{n_{10dB}}}{2} \tag{12-57}$$

where $\hat{\sigma}_{n_{0dB}}$ and $\hat{\sigma}_{n_{10dB}}$ are guesstimates of $\sigma_{n_{0dB}}$ and $\sigma_{n_{10dB}}$, respectively.

Table 12-6: Initial values of the parameters in five FLSs; $x_k' = x_k^{(t)}$ for all NSFLS designs, and each antecedent is described by two fuzzy sets ($i = 1, ..., M$ and $k = 1, ..., p$).

FLS	Input	For Each Antecedent	Consequent
Type-1 SFLS	N/A	mean: $m_x - 2\sigma_x$ or $m_x + 2\sigma_x$, $\sigma_{F_k^i} = 2\sigma_x$	$\bar{y}^i \in [0,1]$
Type-1 NSFLS	$\sigma_{X_k} = \sigma_n$	mean: $m_x - 2\sigma_x$ or $m_x + 2\sigma_x$, $\sigma_{F_k^i} = 2\sigma_x$	$\bar{y}^i \in [0,1]$
Type-2 SFLS	N/A	mean: $[m_x - 2\sigma_x - 0.25\sigma_n, m_x - 2\sigma_x + 0.25\sigma_n]$ or $[m_x + 2\sigma_x - 0.25\sigma_n, m_x + 2\sigma_x + 0.25\sigma_n]$ $\sigma_k^i = 2\sigma_x$	$y_l^i = \bar{y}^i - \sigma_n$ $y_r^i = \bar{y}^i + \sigma_n$
Type-2 NSFLS-1	$\sigma_{X_k} = \sigma_n$	mean: $[m_x - 2\sigma_x - 0.25\sigma_n, m_x - 2\sigma_x + 0.25\sigma_n]$ or $[m_x + 2\sigma_x - 0.25\sigma_n, m_x + 2\sigma_x + 0.25\sigma_n]$ $\sigma_k^i = 2\sigma_x$	$y_l^i = \bar{y}^i - \sigma_n$ $y_r^i = \bar{y}^i + \sigma_n$
Type-2 NSFLS-2	$\sigma_{k1} = \hat{\sigma}_{n_{10dB}}$ $\sigma_{k2} = \hat{\sigma}_{n_{0dB}}$	mean: $[m_x - 2\sigma_x - 0.25\sigma_n, m_x - 2\sigma_x + 0.25\sigma_n]$ or $[m_x + 2\sigma_x - 0.25\sigma_n, m_x + 2\sigma_x + 0.25\sigma_n]$ $\sigma_k^i = 2\sigma_x$	$y_l^i = \bar{y}^i - \sigma_n$ $y_r^i = \bar{y}^i + \sigma_n$

We again evaluated the performance of all the designs using RMSEs. Not only did we use the three RMSEs defined in (10-94)–(10-96), for the singleton type-1, non-singleton type-1, and interval singleton type-2 designs, and the RMSE defined in (11-48) for the interval type-1 non-singleton type-2 design, but we also used the following RMSE for the interval type-2 non-singleton type-2 design:

$$RMSE_{ns2-2}(BP) = \sqrt{\tfrac{1}{496} \sum_{k=1504}^{1999} \left[s(k+1) - f_{ns2-2}(\mathbf{x}^{(k)}) \right]^2} \tag{12-58}$$

Each FLS was tuned using a steepest descent algorithm in which the learning parameter $\alpha = 0.4$. Training and testing were carried out for six epochs. After each epoch we used the testing data to see how each FLS performed, by computing $RMSE_{s1}(BP)$, $RMSE_{ns1}(BP)$, $RMSE_{s2}(BP)$, $RMSE_{ns2-1}(BP)$, and $RMSE_{ns2-2}(BP)$, using (10-94)–(10-96), (11-48), and (12-58), respectively. This entire process was repeated 50 times using 50 independent sets of 1,000 data points, at the end of which we had 50 of the 5 $RMSE(BP)$ values. The average values and standard deviations of these $RMSE$s are plotted in Figure 12-6 for each of the six epochs. Observe that:

1. Type-2 FLSs outperform the type-1 FLSs. The interval type-2 non-singleton type-2 FLS performs the best and the interval type-1 non-singleton type-2 FLS also gives very good results. The reason for the latter is because the interval type-1 non-singleton type-2 FLS used σ_n in (12-57) as the initial value for the standard deviation of its input measurement membership functions, and this value of σ_n gives a good approximation to the average value of the standard deviation of the uniform noise.

2. The type-2 FLSs achieve close to their optimal performance almost at the first epoch of tuning. This shows that type-2 FLSs (as compared to type-1 FLSs) are very promising for real-time signal processing where more than one epoch of tuning is not possible.

3. From the standard deviations of the RMSEs, we see that the type-2 FLSs (especially the interval type-1 and type-2 non-singleton type-2 FLSs) have a considerably smaller standard deviation than do the type-1 FLSs, which demonstrates that type-2 FLSs are much more robust to the non-stationary noise than are type-1 FLSs. Hence, type-2 FLSs appear to be promising for use in adaptive filters, such as channel equalizers (e.g., [Liang and Mendel (2000b)], [Patra and Mulgrew (1998)], [Sarwal and Srinath (1995)], and [Wang and Mendel (1993)]), because such equalizers must be robust to additive noise.

12.5.2 One-epoch combined back-propagation and SVD–QR design

In this second design we combined the back-propagation and SVD–QR methods. To do this we used the back-propagation method for just one epoch of training after which we applied the SVD–QR method to its results. As in the previous section we designed five FLSs: singleton type-1, non-singleton type-1, interval singleton type-2, interval type-1 non-singleton type-2, and interval type-2 non-singleton type-2. All of the previous section's discussions about number of data points, training points, testing points, number of rule antecedents, number of fuzzy sets for each antecedent, number of rules, choices for antecedent, consequent and input measurement membership functions, initial choices for membership function parameters (using the totally independent

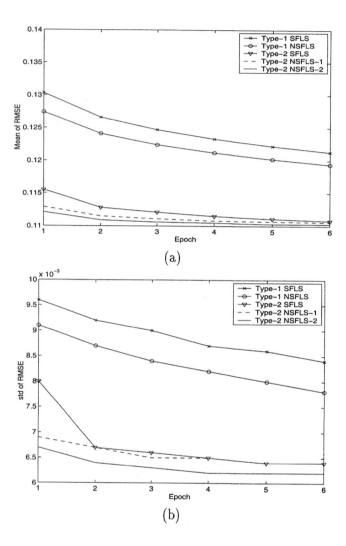

Figure 12-6: The mean and standard deviation of $RMSE_{s1}(BP)$, $RMSE_{ns1}(BP)$, $RMSE_{s2}(BP)$, $RMSE_{ns2-1}$ (BP), and $RMSE_{ns2-2}(BP)$, averaged over 50 Monte-Carlo designs. Tuning was performed in each realization for six epochs; (a) mean values, and (b) standard deviation values.

design approach), and evaluation by means of RMSE formulas remain the same for the present design.

For each of the five designs we ran 50 Monte-Carlo realizations, and for each realization the FLS was tuned before rule-reduction using a simple steepest descent algorithm, but only for one epoch. Each FLS was then rule-reduced using the appropriate SVD–QR method (see discussions about SVD–QR designs in Sections 5.9.4, 6.6.4, 10.10.4, 11.4.4, and in Section 12.4.4). The number of rules to be retained was established by using a threshold, θ, for the singular values that were computed for the SVD of a FBF matrix [e.g., (10-90) and (10-91)]. Let λ_j denote those singular values; then $\hat{r}$ was chosen such that $\lambda_{\hat{r}} \geq \theta$. We arbitrarily set $\theta = 1$.

RMSEs were computed both before and after rule-reduction. Results are summarized in Tables 12-7 and 12-8. Observe, from Table 12-8 that there is a very substantial reduction in the number of rules, from 16 to anywhere from 4 to 9. Unfortunately, there is an accompanying degradation in RMSE performance, as can be seen from the entries in Table 12-7. In our next design, we attempt to improve the rule-reduced RMSEs and to further reduce the number of rules.

12.5.3 Six-epoch iterative combined back-propagation and SVD–QR design

Next, we compare the designs of five FLS forecasters for the Mackey–Glass time-series using an iterative version of combined back-propagation and SVD–QR methods. As in the previous sections, the five designs are: singleton type-1, non-singleton type-1, interval singleton type-2, interval type-1 non-singleton type-2, and interval type-2 non-singleton type-2. Additionally, all of Section 12.5.1's discussions about number of data points, training points, testing points, number of rule antecedents, number of fuzzy sets for each antecedent, number of rules, choices for antecedent, consequent and input measurement membership functions, initial choices for membership function parameters (using the totally independent design approach), and evaluation by means of RMSE formulas remain the same for the present design.

In epoch #1 we tuned the parameters of a 16-rule FLS and then reduced these 16 rules to $\hat{r}_1$ rules using the appropriate SVD–QR method. As in the previous design, we used a threshold of 1 for the singular values and $\hat{r}$ was chosen such that $\lambda_{\hat{r}} \geq 1$. In epoch #2 we tuned the parameters of the $\hat{r}_1$ rule FLS and then reduced these $\hat{r}_1$ rules to $\hat{r}_2$ rules, again using the appropriate SVD–QR method and a threshold of 1 for the singular values. After six epochs, we had a FLS with $\hat{r}_6$ rules.

Table 12-7: Mean and standard deviation (SD) values for RMSEs (for the test data) for the five FLS designs averaged over 50 Monte-Carlo realizations. Tuning was performed in each realization for just one epoch. Information about $\hat{r}$ is given in Table 12-8.

Rules	Type-1 FLS		Type-1 NSFLS	
	Mean	SD	Mean	SD
16 rules	0.1323	0.0098	0.1287	0.0088
$\hat{r}$ rules	0.1626	0.0272	0.1674	0.0295

Rules	Type-2 FLS		Type-2 NSFLS-1		Type-2 NSFLS-2	
	Mean	SD	Mean	SD	Mean	SD
16 rules	0.1154	0.0082	0.1132	0.0071	0.1130	0.0070
$\hat{r}$ rules	0.1536	0.0261	0.1519	0.0256	0.1509	0.0246

Table 12-8: Reduced rules, their range, mean and standard deviations (SD).

Type-1 FLS			Type-1 NSFLS		
Range	Mean	SD	Range	Mean	SD
[4,6]	5.2	0.6389	[4,6]	5.12	0.6273

Type-2 FLS			Type-2 NSFLS-1			Type-2 NSFLS-2		
Range	Mean	SD	Range	Mean	SD	Range	Mean	SD
[4,9]	6.18	1.1726	[4,9]	6.2	1.1066	[4,9]	6.22	1.2171

We summarize the mean and standard deviation of the five rule-reduced RMSEs for each epoch and each design in Figure 12-7 (a) and (b), and the mean and standard deviation of the number of rules for each epoch and design in Figures 12-8 (a) and (b). Observe, from these figures, that:

1. Combining back-propagation and SVD–QR iteratively has indeed improved the rule-reduced RMSE.

2. The rule-reduced type-2 FLSs all perform better than the rule-reduced type-1 FLSs. Additionally, the former are more robust than the latter because of their lower RMSE standard deviations.

3. The rule-reduced type-2 RMSEs either decrease or increase slightly from ep-och-to-epoch, as the average number of their rules decreases from epoch-to-epoch. Meanwhile, rule-reduced type-1 RMSEs increase from epoch-to-epoch, as the average number of their rules decreases from epoch-to-epoch.

4. A rule-reduced type-2 FLS has, on average, one more rule than does a rule-reduced type-1 FLS after the six epochs. However, comparing the perform-ance difference of the rule-reduced type-2 FLS to that of the rule-reduced type-1 FLS, we believe that this gain is worthwhile.

5. The final RMSE performances of the three type-2 FLSs are about the same. Hence, we would choose to implement the simpler of these FLSs, namely the singleton type-2 FLS.

This last design demonstrated that the initial number of rules—16—can be greatly reduced, but with a small loss of overall RMSE performance (compare the six-epoch RMSE values in Figure 12-7 with those in Figure 12-6). So, we see that there is a tradeoff between accuracy and complexity to achieve rule-reduction through design.[4]

For this final case study, in which the additive noise was non-stationary, it is clear that the type-2 FLS models better represent this situation than do the type-1 FLSs.

12.6 COMPUTATION

The following M-files, which are found in the folder *interval type-2 fuzzy logic systems*, are useful for designing an interval type-2 non-singleton type-2 FLS:

nsfls2.m: Compute the output(s) of an interval type-2 non-singleton type-2 FLS when the antecedent membership functions are Gaussian primary membership functions with uncertain means and the input membership functions are Gaus-sian primary membership functions with uncertain standard deviations.

train_nsfls2.m: Tune the parameters of an interval type-2 non-singleton type-2 FLS when the antecedent membership functions are Gaussian primary member-ship functions with uncertain means and input membership functions are Gaus-sian primary membership functions with uncertain standard deviations, using some input–output training data.

---

[4] If we had chosen parameter $\theta < 1$, then our rule-reduced designs would have contained more rules, and would have achieved even smaller RMSEs than in the present designs.

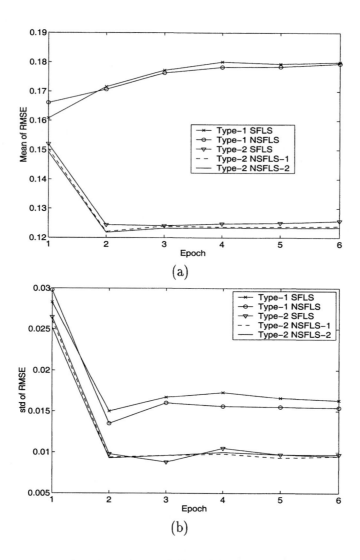

Figure 12-7: The mean and standard deviation of the rule-reduced RMSEs (for the test data) for the five FLS designs, averaged over 50 Monte-Carlo realizations. Tuning was performed in each realization for six epochs; (a) mean values, and (b) standard deviations.

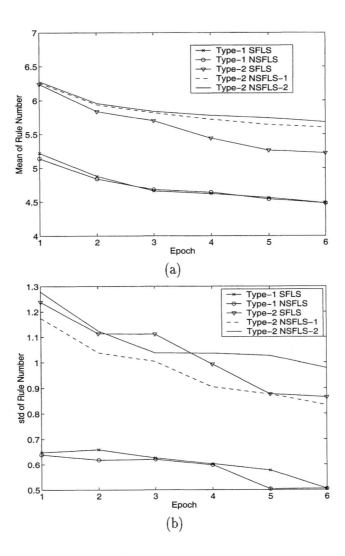

Figure 12-8: The mean and standard deviation of rules after rule-reduction in each epoch using combined back-propagation tuning and an SVD–QR method.

svd_qr_sfls2.m: Rule-reduction of an interval type-2 non-singleton type-2 FLS when the antecedent membership functions are Gaussian primary membership functions with uncertain means and input membership functions are Gaussian primary membership functions with uncertain standard deviations, using some input–output training data.

EXERCISES

12-1: Repeat the calculations of Example 12-3 using minimum t-norm.

12-2: Repeat the analyses given in Example 12-4, but for minimum t-norm, thereby verifying the results that are summarized in Table 12-3.

12-3: Demonstrate that the results given in Tables 12-1–12-4 reduce to those given in Tables 11-1–11-4 when $\tilde{X}_k \Rightarrow X_k$.

12-4: Provide as detailed a flow chart as possible for the calculations required to implement (12-49) and (12-50), assuming that the antecedent membership functions and the input membership functions are the ones given in Example 12-4.

12-5: Determine $\bar{x}^l_{k,\max}$, $\underline{x}^l_{k,\max}$, $\underline{\mu}_{\tilde{Q}^l_k}(\underline{x}^l_{k,\max})$, and $\overline{\mu}_{\tilde{Q}^l_k}(\bar{x}^l_{k,\max})$ for the case of input membership functions that are modeled as Gaussian primary membership functions with uncertain standard deviations (as in Example 12-4), and whose antecedent and consequent membership functions are modeled as Gaussian primary membership functions with *both* uncertain means and standard deviations. (a) Do this for product t-norm. (b) Do this for minimum t-norm.

12-6: Describe some ways to reduce the number of parameters in an interval type-2 non-singleton type-2 FLS.

12-7: Develop the steepest descent algorithms for all of the parameters that need to be tuned in the Section 12.4 interval type-2 non-singleton type-2 FLS.

12-8: Create a counterpart to Example 10-5, using Figure 10-12, but for an interval type-2 non-singleton type-2 FLS.

TSK Fuzzy Logic Systems

13.1 INTRODUCTION

In Section 1.6 we mentioned that the two most popular FLSs used by engineers today are the Mamdani and TSK FLSs. Prior to this chapter,[1] all of our FLSs were Mamdani, even though we did not refer to them as such. In this chapter, where we will need to distinguish between the two kinds of FLSs, we refer to our earlier FLSs as "Mamdani" FLSs. Both kinds of FLS are characterized by IF–THEN rules and have the same antecedent structures. They differ in the structures of their consequents. The consequent of a Mamdani rule is a fuzzy set, whereas the consequent of a TSK rule is a function. When all of the fuzzy sets used in a Mamdani FLS are type-1, then, as we have seen in Sections 5.3 and 6.2.2, the output of the inference engine is a type-1 fuzzy set, and defuzzification is used to obtain a type-0 set. On the other hand, when all of the fuzzy sets used in a TSK FLS are type-1, then its output is (as we demonstrate in the next section) a type-0 set, and this occurs without a defuzzification step.

A type-1 TSK FLS was proposed by Takagi and Sugeno (1985) and Sugeno and Kang (1988) in an effort to develop a systematic approach to generating fuzzy rules from a given input–output data set. In the 1985 article, Takagi and Sugeno used the least-squares method to design the consequent parameters of a TSK model. In the 1988 article, Sugeno and Kang extended this method by adding an unbiasedness constraint. In the extended method the premise structure, premise parameters, consequent structure, and consequent parameters were tuned recursively. Type-1 TSK FLSs have been widely used in control and other applications (e.g., [Terano et al. (1994)]).

---

[1]This chapter was co-authored by Dr. Qilian Liang.

There does not seem to be any mention of a non-singleton TSK FLS in the literature; hence, this chapter focuses exclusively on singleton TSK FLSs—TSK FLSs, for short. Not being able to compensate for uncertain measurements, as we can do in a non-singleton Mamdani FLS, limits the applicability of TSK FLSs to situations where there either is no uncertainty (e.g., as in the design of deterministic TSK FL controllers) or all of the uncertainty can be accounted for just in the antecedent membership functions.[2]

13.2 TYPE-1 TSK FLSs

This section describes the most popular and widely used type-1 TSK FLS, as well as some design methods for it.

13.2.1 First-order type-1 TSK FLS

Consider a type-1 TSK FLS having p inputs $x_1 \in X_1$, ..., $x_p \in X_p$ and one output $y \in Y$. A type-1 TSK FLS is described by fuzzy IF–THEN rules that represent input–output relations of a system. In a *first-order* type-1 TSK model with a rule base of M rules, each having p antecedents, the ith rule can be expressed as

$$R^i: \text{IF } x_1 \text{ is } F_1^i \text{ and } \cdots \text{ and } x_p \text{ is } F_p^i,$$
$$\text{THEN } y^i(\mathbf{x}) = c_0^i + c_1^i x_1 + c_2^i x_2 + \cdots + c_p^i x_p \tag{13-1}$$

where $i = 1,...,M$, c_j^i ($j = 0, 1, ..., p$) are the consequent parameters, $y^i(\mathbf{x})$ is the output of the ith rule, and F_k^i ($k = 1, ..., p$) are type-1 antecedent fuzzy sets.

Although higher than-first-order type-1 TSK models have been described in the literature (e.g., [Buckley (1985, 1993)], [Filev (1990,1991)], [Jang and Sun (1995)]), we focus exclusively on first-order type-1 TSK models, because they are the most widely used and are easily extended to type-2 TSK models, as we demonstrate following. Consequently, whenever we refer to a type-1 TSK FLS it is to be understood that we are referring to a first-order type-1 TSK FLS.

Observe in (13-1) that membership functions are only associated with a rule's antecedents; there is no consequent membership function; i.e., the type-1 TSK rule's consequent is an algebraic function of the p antecedent values. Hence, the rule also acts as the inference mechanism for a type-1 TSK FLS. This means that it is not necessary to use the sup-star composition to obtain the

---

[2]See Section 13.4 for additional remarks about this second situation.

output of a fired type-1 TSK rule, which is quite different than what happens in a type-1 singleton Mamdani FLS.

The output, $y_{TSK,1}(\mathbf{x})$, of a type-1 TSK FLS is obtained by combining the outputs from the M rules in the following prescribed way:

$$
\begin{aligned}
y_{TSK,1}(\mathbf{x}) &\equiv \frac{\sum_{i=1}^{M} f^i(\mathbf{x}) y^i(\mathbf{x})}{\sum_{i=1}^{M} f^i(\mathbf{x})} \\
&= \frac{\sum_{i=1}^{M} f^i(\mathbf{x}) \left(c_0^i + c_1^i x_1 + c_2^i x_2 + \cdots + c_p^i x_p\right)}{\sum_{i=1}^{M} f^i(\mathbf{x})}
\end{aligned}
\tag{13-2}
$$

where the $f^i(\mathbf{x})$ are rule *firing levels* (strengths), defined as

$$
f^i(\mathbf{x}) \equiv T_{k=1}^{p} \mu_{F_k^i}(x_k)
\tag{13-3}
$$

in which T denotes a t-norm, usually minimum or product. In (13-2) and (13-3), $\mathbf{x}$ denotes a specific input that is applied to the type-1 TSK FLS.[3]

The type-1 TSK FLS defined by (13-1)–(13-3) is sometimes referred to as a *normalized* type-1 TSK FLS, because of the normalization of the weighted rule outputs in (13-2) by $\sum_{i=1}^{M} f^i(\mathbf{x})$. An *unnormalized* type-1 TSK FLS ([Tanaka et al. (1995)], [Tanaka and Sugeno (1998)]) has for its output

$$
y_{TSK,1}(\mathbf{x}) \equiv \sum_{i=1}^{M} f^i(\mathbf{x}) y^i(\mathbf{x})
\tag{13-4}
$$

13.2.2 A connection between type-1 TSK and Mamdani FLSs

In (13-1), if $y^i(\mathbf{x}) = c_0$, then

$$
y_{TSK,1}(\mathbf{x}) \equiv \frac{\sum_{i=1}^{M} c_0^i f^i(\mathbf{x})}{\sum_{i=1}^{M} f^i(\mathbf{x})} = \frac{\sum_{i=1}^{M} c_0^i T_{k=1}^{p} \mu_{F_k^i}(x_k)}{\sum_{i=1}^{M} T_{k=1}^{p} \mu_{F_k^i}(x_k)}
\tag{13-5}
$$

---

[3]Because no inference mechanism is associated with the statements of (13-2) and (13-3), the issue of fuzzification does not appear. Hence, unlike Chapter 5, where we used $\mathbf{x}'$ to denote the measured value of input $\mathbf{x}$, no such distinction needs to be made between $\mathbf{x}$ and $\mathbf{x}'$ for a TSK FLS.

This is a very special kind of type-1 TSK FLS, one that does not exploit the full potential of the more general consequent function of (13-1). Comparing (13-5) with (5-15), (5-17), (5-19), or (5-20), we see that this special kind of type-1 TSK FLS is exactly the same as a type-1 Mamdani FLS that uses either center-of-sums, height, modified height, or center-of-sets defuzzification. Although some people refer to (13-5) as a TSK FLS, most people, including myself, do not. The latter prefer to reserve the name "TSK FLS" for the FLS that uses the more general consequent function of (13-1).

13.2.3 TSK FLSs are universal approximators

Universal approximation and its importance have been discussed in Section 5.8. Just as Mamdani FLSs have been proven to be universal approximators, so have TSK FLSs (e.g., [Buckley (1993)]). For a comprehensive review of universal approximation in a wide range of FLSs, see [Kreinovich et al. (1998)].

13.2.4 Designing type-1 TSK FLSs

Next, we briefly outline some design approaches for a type-1 TSK FLS in connection with the same design problem that was stated in Section 5.9 (see also [Jang and Sun (1995)]). For the convenience of the reader, we restate that design problem here:

> We are given a collection of N input–output numerical data *training* pairs, $(\mathbf{x}^{(1)}:y^{(1)}),(\mathbf{x}^{(2)}:y^{(2)}),\ldots,(\mathbf{x}^{(N)}:y^{(N)})$, where $\mathbf{x}$ is the vector input and y is the scalar output of a type-1 TSK FLS. Our goal is to completely specify this TSK FLS using the training data.

For illustrative purposes, all designs in this section assume Gaussian membership functions and product implication and t-norm; hence, this type-1 TSK FLS is described by (13-1)–(13-3). Note that the basic principles used in each design procedure carry over to many other TSK FLSs.

To begin, we must explain how the training data can be interpreted as a collection of IF–THEN TSK rules. Each rule is of the form given in (13-1), where F_k^l are type-1 fuzzy sets described by Gaussian membership functions, i.e.,

$$\mu_{F_k^i}(x_k) = \exp\left\{-\tfrac{1}{2}\left(\frac{x_k - m_{F_k^i}}{\sigma_{F_k^i}}\right)^2\right\} \qquad (13\text{-}6)$$

where $k = 1, ..., p$ and $i = 1, ..., M$. Each design method establishes how to specify the parameters $m_{F_k^i}$ and $\sigma_{F_k^i}$ of the membership functions in (13-6), as well as the coefficients of the consequent membership functions, the c_j^i in (13-1), using the training pairs $(\mathbf{x}^{(1)} : y^{(1)})$, $(\mathbf{x}^{(2)} : y^{(2)})$, ..., $(\mathbf{x}^{(N)} : y^{(N)})$. Because the design methods that we describe next all use tuning, the number of rules, M, must be chosen ahead of time so that there are more training data, N, than parameters, or else we will have an underdetermined design.

Example 13-1: Let us enumerate the number of design parameters there can be in the just-stated design:

- Antecedent parameters m_{F^i} and σ_{F^i}: 2 per antecedent, p antecedents, and M rules, for a total of $2pM$ parameters
- Consequent parameters $c_0^i, c_1^i, ..., c_p^i$: $p + 1$ per consequent and M rules, for a total of $(p + 1)M$ parameters

Consequently, the total number of design parameters is $3pM + M$. Comparing this with the results in Example 5-6, we see that a type-1 TSK FLS has more parameters in it than does a type-1 singleton Mamdani FLS. The latter has, at most, $2pM + M$ design parameters. This suggests that a type-1 TSK FLS that has the same number of rules as a type-1 singleton Mamdani FLS can outperform the latter because the former has more design degrees of freedom than the latter.

As always, we abide by the principle that there should be fewer design parameters than training data; hence, when all the TSK parameters are tuned,

$$(3p + 1)M < N \tag{13-7}$$

If we are given a fixed number of training samples, $N = N'$, then

$$M < \left[\frac{N'}{3p + 1} \right] \tag{13-8}$$

which constrains the number of rules that can be used. Because M must be an integer, we choose $M = M'$ as an integer that is smaller than $N' / (3p + 1)$. ∎

At a very high level, we can think of the following two designs for a type-1 TSK FLS:

1. Fix the shapes and parameters of all the antecedent membership functions, and use the training data to tune the consequent parameters. Because the type-

1 TSK FLS is linear in its consequent parameters, this leads to a relatively easy least-squares optimization problem.

2. Fix the shapes of all antecedent membership functions ahead of time. Use the training data to tune the antecedent and consequent parameters. This can be done in a number of different ways, including back-propagation and iterative methods.

Least-squares method: In the least-squares method, all of the antecedent parameters are fixed by the designer and only the coefficients of the consequents are tuned. The number of rules, M, must be specified, and because there will be $(p+1)M$ parameters, we know, from Example 13-1, that there must be at least $(p+1)M$ training samples.

The starting point for the least-squares method is (13-2), re-expressed as

$$
\begin{aligned}
y_{TSK,1}(\mathbf{x}) = g_0^1(\mathbf{x})c_0^1 &+ g_1^1(\mathbf{x})c_1^1 + g_2^1(\mathbf{x})c_2^1 + \cdots + g_p^1(\mathbf{x})c_p^1 + \cdots \\
&+ g_0^M(\mathbf{x})c_0^M + g_1^M(\mathbf{x})c_1^M + g_2^M(\mathbf{x})c_2^M + \cdots + g_p^M(\mathbf{x})c_p^M
\end{aligned}
\tag{13-9}
$$

where

$$
g_j^i(\mathbf{x}) = \frac{f^i(\mathbf{x})x_j}{\sum_{i=1}^{M} f^i(\mathbf{x})}
\tag{13-10}
$$

where $i = 1, \ldots, M, j = 0, 1, \ldots, p$, and, $x_0 \equiv 1$. Equation (13-9) can be written more compactly as

$$
y_{TSK,1}(\mathbf{x}) = \mathbf{g}^T(\mathbf{x})\mathbf{c}
\tag{13-11}
$$

where $\mathbf{g}(\mathbf{x})$ and $\mathbf{c}$ are $(p+1)M \times 1$ vectors, whose elements are easily deduced from (13-9).

We use (13-11) for each of the N elements in the training set, i.e.,

$$
y_{TSK,1}(\mathbf{x}^{(t)}) = \mathbf{g}^T(\mathbf{x}^{(t)})\mathbf{c} \quad t = 1, \ldots, N
\tag{13-12}
$$

Collecting the N equations, they can be expressed in vector-matrix format as:

$$
\mathbf{y}_{TSK,1} = \mathbf{G}\mathbf{c}
\tag{13-13}
$$

where the structures of $\mathbf{y}_{TSK,1}$ and $\mathbf{G}$ are also easily deduced from (13-12). Note that $\mathbf{G}$ is an $N \times (p+1)M$ matrix, where[4] $N > (p+1)M$; i.e., it has more rows than columns. This means that (13-13) is an over-determined system of equations.

The least-squares design for $\mathbf{c}$, $\mathbf{c}_{LS}$, is obtained by minimizing

$$J(\mathbf{c}) = \tfrac{1}{2}[\mathbf{y}_{TSK,1} - \mathbf{Gc}]^T [\mathbf{y}_{TSK,1} - \mathbf{Gc}] \tag{13-14}$$

with respect to $\mathbf{c}$. The solution to this optimization problem can be expressed as

$$[\mathbf{G}^T \mathbf{G}] \mathbf{c}_{LS} = \mathbf{G}^T \mathbf{y}_{TSK,1} \tag{13-15}$$

which is a linear system of $(p+1)M$ equations that has to be solved for $\mathbf{c}_{LS}$. See Example 5-7 for some discussions on how to do this.

Back-propagation (steepest descent) method: In the back-propagation method none of the antecedent or consequent parameters are fixed ahead of time. They are all tuned using a steepest descent method. In this case, we again begin with (13-9) and (13-10), but now we make more use of the following detailed structure of $g_j^i(\mathbf{x}^{(t)})$ [which derives from (13-10), (13-3), and (13-6)]:

$$g_j^i(\mathbf{x}^{(t)}) = \frac{x_j^{(t)} \prod_{k=1}^{p} \exp\left(-\dfrac{\left(x_k^{(t)} - m_{F_k^i}\right)^2}{2\sigma_{F_k^i}^2}\right)}{\sum_{i=1}^{M} \prod_{k=1}^{p} \exp\left(-\dfrac{\left(x_k^{(t)} - m_{F_k^i}\right)^2}{2\sigma_{F_k^i}^2}\right)} \tag{13-16}$$

where $j = 0, 1, \ldots, p$ and $i = 1, \ldots, M$. Given an input–output training pair $(\mathbf{x}^{(t)} : y^{(t)})$, we now wish to design the type-1 TSK FLS in (13-9) and (13-16) such that the following error function is minimized:

$$e^{(t)} = \tfrac{1}{2}[y_{TSK,1}(\mathbf{x}^{(t)}) - y^{(t)}]^2 \quad t = 1, \ldots, N \tag{13-17}$$

---

[4]From Example 13-1, when only the consequent parameters are design parameters, (13-7) becomes $N > (p+1)M$.

It is evident from (13-16) and (13-9) that $y_{TSK,1}(\mathbf{x})$ is completely characterized by the $3pM + M$ parameters that have already been enumerated in Example 13-1. Because the development of the recursive steepest descent algorithms for minimizing $e^{(t)}$ is so similar to what we did in Section 5.9.3, we leave the details for the reader (Exercise 13-1).

The discussions that appear in the third paragraph below Equation (5-50) about minimizing $e^{(t)}$ within an epoch and then for many epochs until convergence occurs, versus defining a squared error function that depends on all N training data and then developing a steepest descent algorithm for it, apply here as well.

Iterative design method:[5] By combining the least-squares method with the back-propagation method, we can simplify the latter. The following iterative design method can be very successful:

1. Fix the number of rules, M, at a reasonable value, subject to the constraint in (13-8).

2. Initialize all of the antecedent parameters.

3. Use the least-squares method to design the consequent parameters, and then compute the sum of the squared errors over *all* the N training data. If this value is not less than the previous computed sum of the squared errors over *all* the N training data by at least an amount equal to ε (where ε is prespecified), then stop and accept the previous design (this test is not performed during the first iteration, since there is no "previous design" at that point).

4. Fix the consequent parameters at the values determined in Step 3, and use the back-propagation method to design the antecedent parameters. Only accept a solution from this step if the sum of the squared errors over *all* the N training data using the new antecedent parameters is less than the sum of the squared errors over *all* the N training data computed in Step 3 by at least an amount equal to ε (where ε is pre-specified). If this cannot be achieved, then accept the previous design.

5. Otherwise, repeat Steps 3 and 4 until performance is acceptable.

By this method, the number of design parameters that have to be optimized using the back-propagation method is reduced from $(3p+1)M$ to $2pM$. Note that Steps 3 and 4 guarantee that the overall sum of the squared errors will continue to be reduced as one iterates through these steps.

---

[5]This method is also known as Adaptive Neuro-Fuzzy Inference Systems (ANFIS). ANFIS was developed by J.-S. Roger Jang (e.g., [Jang (1993)] and [Jang et al. (1997)]) and is implemented in The MathWorks' Fuzzy Logic Toolbox.

13.3 TYPE-2 TSK FLSs

This section extends the first-order type-1 TSK FLS to its type-2 counterpart, with emphasis on interval sets.

13.3.1 First-order type-2 TSK FLS

Consider a type-2 TSK FLS having p inputs $x_1 \in X_1$, ..., $x_p \in X_p$ and one output $y \in Y$. A type-2 TSK FLS is also described by fuzzy IF–THEN rules that represent input–output relations of a system. In a general first-order type-2 TSK model with a rule base of M rules, each having p antecedents, the ith rule can be expressed as

$$R^i: \text{ IF } x_1 \text{ is } \tilde{F}_1^i \text{ and } \cdots \text{ and } x_p \text{ is } \tilde{F}_p^i,$$
$$\text{THEN } Y^i = C_0^i + C_1^i x_1 + C_2^i x_2 + \cdots + C_p^i x_p \tag{13-18}$$

where $i = 1,...,M$; C_j^i ($j = 0, 1, ..., p$) are consequent type-1 fuzzy sets; Y^i, the output of the ith rule, is also a type-1 fuzzy set (because it is a linear combination of type-1 fuzzy sets); and $\tilde{F}_k^i$ ($k = 1, ..., p$) are type-2 antecedent fuzzy sets. These rules let us simultaneously account for uncertainty about antecedent membership functions and consequent *parameter* values. Note that the latter is not the same as being able to account for uncertainty about a *linguistic* consequent, as can be done in a Mamdani FLS.

Special cases of (13-18) occur when the antecedents are type-2 fuzzy sets but the consequents are crisp numbers (i.e., type-0 sets), and when both the antecedents and consequents are type-1 fuzzy sets. These cases are treated in Examples 13-2 and 13-3.

We assume that the C_j^i ($j = 0, 1, ..., p$) are convex and normal type-1 fuzzy subsets of the real line, so that they are fuzzy numbers. These assumptions let us perform algebraic operations on the C_j^i, using the results in Sections 7.3.2 and 7.4.2.

In a type-2 TSK FLS, the firing set of the ith rule is $F^i(\mathbf{x})$, where, as in Section 10.3,

$$F^i(\mathbf{x}) = \prod_{k=1}^{p} \mu_{\tilde{F}_k^i}(x_k) \tag{13-19}$$

The output of a type-2 TSK FLS is obtained by applying the Extension Principle in (7-9) to (13-2), where now both $f^i(\mathbf{x})$ and $y^i(\mathbf{x})$ are replaced by type-1 fuzzy sets, i.e.,

$$Y_{TSK,2}(\mathbf{x}) = \int_{y^1 \in Y^1} \cdots \int_{y^M \in Y^M} \int_{f^1 \in F^1} \cdots \int_{f^M \in F^M} \left[T_{i=1}^M \mu_{Y^i}(y^i) \right.$$

$$\left. \star T_{i=1}^M \mu_{F^i}(f^i) \right] \Big/ \frac{\sum_{i=1}^M f^i y^i}{\sum_{i=1}^M f^i} \qquad (13\text{-}20)$$

where $Y^i = C_0^i + C_1^i x_1 + C_2^i x_2 + \cdots + C_p^i x_p$ is a type-1 fuzzy set. We refer to $Y_{TSK,2}(\mathbf{x})$ as the *extended output* of a type-2 TSK FLS. It reveals the uncertainty at the output of a type-2 TSK FLS due to antecedent or consequent parameter uncertainties.

Although (13-20) resembles the center-of-sets type-reduced set for a singleton type-2 Mamdani FLS, there is no type-reduction needed for a type-2 TSK FLS, just as there is no defuzzification needed for a type-1 TSK FLS.

Discussions on how to compute (13-20) are given in Section 9.2, following (9-11). Because these computations can be very complicated, except for interval type-2 fuzzy sets, we focus on this case in the sequel.

13.3.2 Interval type-2 TSK FLSs

When interval type-2 fuzzy sets are used for the antecedents, and interval type-1 fuzzy sets are used for the consequent sets of a type-2 TSK rule, then $\mu_{\tilde{F}_k^i}(x_k)$ and C_j^i are interval sets, i.e.,

$$\mu_{\tilde{F}_k^i}(x_k) = [\underline{\mu}_{\tilde{F}_k^i}(x_k), \overline{\mu}_{\tilde{F}_k^i}(x_k)] \qquad k = 1, \ldots, p \qquad (13\text{-}21)$$

and

$$C_j^i = [c_j^i - s_j^i, c_j^i + s_j^i] \qquad (13\text{-}22)$$

where c_j^i denotes the center (mean) of C_j^i and s_j^i denotes the spread of C_j^i ($i = 1, \ldots, M$ and $j = 0, 1, \ldots, p$). In this case, we are able to easily compute the firing set and rule-consequent of the type-2 TSK FLS.

Theorem 13-1: [Liang and Mendel (2000f)] *(a) In an interval type-2 TSK FLS with meet under product or minimum t-norm, the firing set, $F^i(\mathbf{x})$, of rule R^i in (13-18) is an interval type-1 set, i.e.,*

$$F^i(\mathbf{x}) = [\underline{f}^i(\mathbf{x}), \overline{f}^i(\mathbf{x})] \tag{13-23}$$

where

$$\underline{f}^i(\mathbf{x}) = \underline{\mu}_{\tilde{F}_1^i}(x_1) \star \cdots \star \underline{\mu}_{\tilde{F}_p^i}(x_p) \tag{13-24}$$

and

$$\overline{f}^i(\mathbf{x}) = \overline{\mu}_{\tilde{F}_1^i}(x_1) \star \cdots \star \overline{\mu}_{\tilde{F}_p^i}(x_p) \tag{13-25}$$

(b) The consequent of rule R^i, Y^i, is also an interval set; i.e., $Y^i = [y_l^i, y_r^i]$, where

$$y_l^i = \sum_{k=1}^{p} c_k^i x_k + c_0^i - \sum_{k=1}^{p} |x_k| s_k^i - s_0^i \tag{13-26}$$

and

$$y_r^i = \sum_{k=1}^{p} c_k^i x_k + c_0^i + \sum_{k=1}^{p} |x_k| s_k^i + s_0^i \tag{13-27}$$

Proof: (a) This follows directly from Theorem 7-2, and is analogous to the proof of part (a) of Theorem 10-1.

(b) This follows directly from Theorem 7-4, (13-22), and the consequent expression in rule R^i in (13-18). ∎

Directing our attention to (13-20), we see that because $F^i(\mathbf{x})$ and Y^i ($i = 1,$ ..., M) are now interval type-1 fuzzy sets, $\mu_{Y^i}(y^i) = 1$ and $\mu_{F^i}(f^i) = 1$, this equation simplifies to

$$Y_{TSK,2}(\mathbf{x}) = [y_l, y_r] = \int_{y^1 \in [y_l^1, y_r^1]} \cdots \int_{y^M \in [y_l^M, y_r^M]} \int_{f^1 \in [\underline{f}^1, \overline{f}^1]} \cdots \int_{f^M \in [\underline{f}^M, \overline{f}^M]} 1 \Bigg/ \frac{\sum_{i=1}^{M} f^i y^i}{\sum_{i=1}^{M} f^i} \quad (13\text{-}28)$$

where $\underline{f}^i$, $\overline{f}^i$, y_l^i, and y_r^i are computed using (13-24)–(13-27). Hence, $Y_{TSK,2}(\mathbf{x})$ is an interval type-1 set. To compute $Y_{TSK,2}(\mathbf{x})$, we therefore only need to compute its two end-points y_l and y_r. These computations are identical to those for center-of-sets type-reduction of a type-2 singleton Mamdani FLS, and are described in Section 10.9.3; e.g., compare (13-28) with (10-43) to see that they are the same.

In an interval type-2 TSK FLS, Y is an interval type-1 fuzzy set; so, as we did in Section 10.6, we defuzzify it using the average of y_l and y_r; hence, the defuzzified output of any interval type-2 TSK FLS is

$$y_{TSK,2}(\mathbf{x}) = \frac{y_l + y_r}{2} \quad (13\text{-}29)$$

Example 13-2: [Liang and Mendel (2000f)] Here we consider the special case of an interval type-2 TSK FLS when its antecedents are type-2 fuzzy sets but its consequents are crisp numbers (type-0 sets). To distinguish this case from the more general one, we refer to it as the A2-C0 case, where "A" and "C" are short for antecedent and consequent, respectively.[6] In the A2-C0 case, the rules in (13-18) simplify to

$$R^i:\ \text{IF } x_1 \text{ is } \tilde{F}_1^i \text{ and } \cdots \text{ and } x_p \text{ is } \tilde{F}_p^i, \text{ THEN } y^i = c_0^i + c_1^i x_1 + c_2^i x_2 + \cdots + c_p^i x_p \quad (13\text{-}30)$$

where $i = 1, \dots, M$. Such rules have been used by Liang and Mendel [(2000b), (2000d)] for Bayesian equalization of a time-varying digital communication channel.

When interval type-2 sets are used for the antecedents: (a) Theorem 13-1 (a) is still applicable to the A2-C0 case; (b) part (b) of that theorem is not applicable to the A2-C0 case; (c) (13-28) simplifies to

$$Y_{TSK,2}(\mathbf{x}) = [y_l, y_r] = \int_{f^1 \in [\underline{f}^1, \overline{f}^1]} \cdots \int_{f^M \in [\underline{f}^M, \overline{f}^M]} 1 \Bigg/ \frac{\sum_{i=1}^{M} f^i y^i}{\sum_{i=1}^{M} f^i}; \quad (13\text{-}31)$$

and (d) the procedure to compute y_l and y_r is the same as for the A2-C1 case, except that in the present A2-C0 case, $y_l^i = y_r^i = y^i$. Note that, in the iterative method for computing y_l and y_r, $R \neq L$ even though $y_l^i = y_r^i = y^i$ (Exercise 13-4). ∎

---

[6]The general case could be referred to as the A2-C1 case.

Example 13-3: [Liang and Mendel (2000f)] Here we consider the special case of an interval type-2 TSK FLS when its consequent sets are type-1 fuzzy sets but its antecedents are only type-1 fuzzy sets. To distinguish this case from the more general one, we refer to it as the A1-C1 case. In this case, the rules in (13-18) simplify to

$$R^i: \text{IF } x_1 \text{ is } F_1^i \text{ and } \cdots \text{ and } x_p \text{ is } F_p^i, \text{ THEN } Y^i = C_0^i + C_1^i x_1 + C_2^i x_2 + \cdots + C_p^i x_p \quad (13\text{-}32)$$

where $i = 1, ..., M$. These rules are for the case when all the uncertainties are in the consequent sets. In this case, the firing strength of the ith rule is a crisp number, i.e.,

$$f^i(\mathbf{x}) = T_{k=1}^p \mu_{F_k^i}(x_k) \quad (13\text{-}33)$$

When interval type-1 sets are used in the consequents, the output of this A1-C1 case is a special case of (13-28), where each F^i is now a crisp value, f^i, i.e.,

$$Y_{TSK,2}(\mathbf{x}) = [y_l, y_r] = \int_{y^1 \in [y_l^1, y_r^1]} \cdots \int_{y^M \in [y_l^M, y_r^M]} 1 \bigg/ \frac{\sum_{i=1}^M f^i y^i}{\sum_{i=1}^M f^i} \quad (13\text{-}34)$$

In this case: (a) Theorem 13-1 (b) is still applicable; (b) (13-34) can be expressed in closed form, as (Exercise 13-5)

$$Y = \left[\frac{\sum_{i=1}^M f^i y_l^i}{\sum_{i=1}^M f^i}, \frac{\sum_{i=1}^M f^i y_r^i}{\sum_{i=1}^M f^i} \right] \quad (13\text{-}35)$$

where y_l^i and y_r^i are given in (13-26) and (13-27), respectively; and, (c) $y_{TSK,2}(\mathbf{x})$ in (13-29) can be expressed as (Exercise 13-5)

$$y_{TSK,2}(\mathbf{x}) = \frac{\sum_{i=1}^M f^i \left(\sum_{k=1}^p c_k^i x_k + c_0^i \right)}{\sum_{i=1}^M f^i} \quad (13\text{-}36)$$

where c_k^i is the center of C_k^i, $k = 0, 1, ..., p$.

Comparing (13-36) and (13-2), we see the output of an interval A1-C1 type-2 TSK FLS is the same as the output of a type-1 TSK FLS whose consequent parameters are the centers of the consequent sets of the interval A1-C1 type-2 TSK FLS. Consequently, if someone is only interested in the defuzzified output of the interval A1-C1 type-2 TSK FLS, he or she may just as well use a type-1 TSK FLS directly, because they both provide identical results. If, however, someone is also interested in the extended output, given by (13-35), then it will provide additional information about the uncertainties that are associated with

$y_{TSK,2}(\mathbf{x})$, and this information can only be obtained by working with the interval A1-C1 type-2 TSK FLS. ■

13.3.3 Unnormalized interval type-2 TSK FLSs

Normalizing the output of a TSK FLS increases its complexity and has been shown to be unnecessary in some cases (e.g., [Tanaka et al. (1995)] and [Tanaka and Sugeno (1998)]). In a general unnormalized interval type-2 TSK FLS, Theorem 13-1 is still applicable. Its extended output is simpler than (13-28), and because of (13-4) is given by

$$Y_{TSK,2}(\mathbf{x}) = [y_l, y_r] = \int_{y^1 \in [y_l^1, y_r^1]} \cdots \int_{y^M \in [y_l^M, y_r^M]} \int_{f^1 \in [\underline{f}^1, \bar{f}^1]} \cdots \int_{f^M \in [\underline{f}^M, \bar{f}^M]} 1 / \sum_{i=1}^{M} f^i y^i \quad (13\text{-}37)$$

Because $Y_{TSK,2}(\mathbf{x})$ is an interval type-1 set, we again just need to compute the end-points y_l and y_r.

Theorem 13-2: *In an unnormalized interval type-2 TSK FLS with output $Y_{TSK,2}(\mathbf{x}) = [y_l, y_r]$: (a) y_l can be generated from an unnormalized type-1 TSK FLS, whose antecedent membership functions are the lower membership functions of the type-2 TSK FLS and whose consequent is y_l^i, where*

$$y_l^i = \sum_{k=1}^{P} c_k^i x_k + c_0^i - \sum_{k=1}^{P} |x_k| s_k^i - s_0^i \quad (13\text{-}38)$$

and (b) y_r can be generated from an unnormalized type-1 TSK FLS whose antecedent membership functions are the upper membership functions of the type-2 TSK FLS, and whose consequent is y_r^i, where

$$y_r^i = \sum_{k=1}^{P} c_k^i x_k + c_0^i + \sum_{k=1}^{P} |x_k| s_k^i + s_0^i \quad (13\text{-}39)$$

Proof: From (13-37), we see that, for any $y \in Y_{TSK,2}(\mathbf{x})$, y can be represented as

$$y = \sum_{i=1}^{M} f^i y^i \quad (13\text{-}40)$$

The maximum value of this y is y_r, whereas the minimum value of this y is y_l. From (13-40) we see that y is a monotonically increasing function of y^i and f^i. Hence, y_l is associated only with y_l^i and $\underline{f}^i(\mathbf{x})$, and, y_r is associated only with y_r^i and $\overline{f}^i(\mathbf{x})$. This means that

$$y_l = \sum_{i=1}^{M} \underline{f}^i(\mathbf{x})y_l^i \qquad (13\text{-}41)$$

and

$$y_r = \sum_{i=1}^{M} \overline{f}^i(\mathbf{x})y_r^i \qquad (13\text{-}42)$$

Equation (13-42) demonstrates that y_l can be generated from an unnormalized type-1 TSK FLS, whose antecedent membership functions are the lower membership functions of the type-2 TSK FLS and whose consequent is y_l^i, and (13-42) demonstrates that y_r can be generated from an unnormalized type-1 TSK FLS whose antecedent membership functions are the upper membership functions of the type-2 TSK FLS, and whose consequent is y_r^i. ∎

There is no doubt that the unnormalized interval type-2 TSK FLS is the simplest of all the type-2 FLSs that we have presented. Whether it achieves the same performance as the normalized TSK or Mamdani type-2 FLSs is application dependent.

13.3.4 Further comparisons of TSK and Mamdani FLSs

We have constructed new type-2 TSK FLSs that contain lots of design parameters. In this section we illustrate and compare the number of design parameters in TSK and Mamdani type-1 and type-2 FLSs. Table 13-1 summarizes these results. Note that:

1. For the type-1 Mamdani and TSK FLSs, antecedent membership functions are assumed to be

$$\mu_{F_k^i}(x_k) = \exp\left[-\frac{1}{2}\left(\frac{x_k - m_k^i}{\sigma_k^i}\right)^2\right] \qquad (13\text{-}43)$$

where $k = 1, \ldots, p$ and $i = 1, \ldots, M$; note that m_k^i and σ_k^i are short for $m_{F_k^i}^i$ and $\sigma_{F_k^i}^i$, respectively.

2. As in Example 5.6, we have assumed height defuzzification for the type-1 Mamdani FLS, so that each rule's consequent is characterized only by $\bar{y}^i$.

3. For each antecedent of the interval type-2 Mamdani and TSK FLSs, we used the Gaussian primary membership function, $\mu_k^i(x_k)$ in (10-20), for which σ_k^i is fixed but m_k^i is uncertain, and has values in $[m_{k1}^i, m_{k2}^i]$, as in Figure 3-8.

4. Each consequent type-1 set C_j^i of a type-2 TSK FLS is defined by its center, c_j^i, and spread, s_j^i, where $j = 0, 1, \ldots, p$.

5. y_l^i and y_r^i denote the parameters of the centroids of Gaussian interval consequent membership functions for the type-2 Mamdani FLS.

6. The number of parameters in each FLS depends on the number of antecedents and rules; e.g., in the type-2 TSK FLS A2-C1, five parameters depend on the number of antecedents that are associated with each rule, namely, m_{k1}^i, m_{k2}^i, σ_k^i, c_k^i, and s_k^i ($k = 1, \ldots, p$, and, $i = 1, \ldots, M$). And, there are also two parameters associated with the constant term (C_0^i) in each consequent that depend only on the number of rules, namely, c_0^i and s_0^i; so the total number of parameters in this FLS is $(5p + 2)M$.

7. The results in Table 13-1 hold for both the normalized and unnormalized TSK FLSs.

Table 13-1: The number of free design parameters for different FLSs. Each rule has p antecedents, and there are $i = 1, \ldots, M$ rules. Additionally, $k = 1, \ldots, p$, and $j = 0, 1, \ldots, p$. The Mamdani FLSs are singleton type-1 and type-2.

FLS Category	Number of Design Parameters	Design Parameters
Type-1 Mamdani FLS	$(2p+1)M$	$m_k^i, \sigma_k^i, \bar{y}^i$
Type-1 TSK FLS	$(3p+1)M$	m_k^i, σ_k^i, c_j^i
Type-2 Mamdani FLS	$(3p+2)M$	$m_{k1}^i, m_{k2}^i, \sigma_k^i, y_l^i, y_r^i$
Type-2 TSK FLS: A2-C1	$(5p+2)M$	$m_{k1}^i, m_{k2}^i, \sigma_k^i, c_j^i, s_j^i$
Type-2 TSK FLS: A2-C0	$(4p+1)M$	$m_{k1}^i, m_{k2}^i, \sigma_k^i, c_j^i$
Type-2 TSK FLS: A1-C1	$(4p+2)M$	$m_k^i, \sigma_k^i, c_j^i, s_j^i$

8. If, for each antecedent of the interval type-2 Mamdani and TSK FLSs, we used the Gaussian primary membership function in (10-23) for which m_k^i is fixed but σ_k^i is uncertain, and has values in $[\sigma_{k1}^i, \sigma_{k2}^i]$, as in Figure 3-9, then in rows 3-5 of Table 13-1 we would replace m_{k1}^i, m_{k2}^i, and σ_k^i by $\sigma_{k1}^i, \sigma_{k2}^i$, and m_k^i, respectively. Note that, in this case, the numbers of design parameters are unchanged from the numbers listed in Table 13-1.

Finally, observe from Table 13-1 that the type-2 TSK FLS A2-C1 has the largest number of design parameters for each rule, namely $5p + 2$. It is possible though that a TSK FLS will require fewer rules (M) than a Mamdani FLS. Hence, it is possible for a type-2 TSK FLS to have fewer design parameters than a type-2 Mamdani FLS. This, of course, is *problem dependent*.

13.3.5 Designing interval type-2 TSK FLSs using a back-propagation (steepest descent) method

The design problem is the one stated in Section 13.2.4, except that our goal in this section is to completely specify a type-2 TSK FLS. We focus exclusively on a back-propagation design method for the interval type-2 TSK FLS A2-C1, because we cannot use a least-squares design method for it, just as we could not do this for an interval type-2 Mamdani FLS (see Section 10.10.2).

For illustrative purposes, our design in this section assumes Gaussian primary membership functions each of the form depicted in Figure 3-8, product implication and product t-norm; hence, this type-2 TSK FLS is described by (13-23)–(13-29). Note that the basic principles used in our design procedure carry over to many other TSK FLSs.

To begin, as always, we must explain how the training data can be interpreted as a collection of IF–THEN TSK rules. Each rule is of the form given in (13-18), where $\tilde{F}_i^l$ are type-2 fuzzy sets associated with the elements of $\mathbf{x}^{(t)}$ and are described by the Gaussian primary membership functions in (10-20), i.e.,

$$\mu_k^i(x_k) = \exp\left[-\tfrac{1}{2}\left(\frac{x_k - m_k^i}{\sigma_k^i}\right)^2\right] \quad m_k^i \in [m_{k1}^i, m_{k2}^i] \qquad (13\text{-}44)$$

where $k = 1, \ldots, p$ and $i = 1, \ldots, M$. In addition, the consequent parameters, C_j^i, are interval sets given in (13-22).

Our back-propagation method establishes how to specify the parameters m_{k1}^i, m_{k2}^i, σ_k^i, c_j^i, and s_j^i (see Table 13-1) of the type-2 TSK FLS A2-C1 using the training pairs $(\mathbf{x}^{(1)}:y^{(1)}), (\mathbf{x}^{(2)}:y^{(2)}), \ldots, (\mathbf{x}^{(N)}:y^{(N)})$.

Example 13-4: From Table 13-1, we see that the total number of design parameters is $(5p + 2)M$. As always, we abide by the principle that there should be fewer design parameters than training data. Hence, when all the type-2 TSK parameters are tuned, then

$$(5p + 2)M < N \tag{13-45}$$

For example, if we are given a fixed number of training samples, $N = N'$, then

$$M < \left[\frac{N'}{5p + 2} \right] \tag{13-46}$$

which constrains the number of rules that can be used. Because M must be an integer, we choose $M = M'$ as an integer that is smaller than $N'/(5p + 2)$. ∎

At a very high level, we can think of the following two designs for a type-2 TSK FLS:

1. Fix the shapes and parameters of all the antecedent membership functions, and use training data to tune the parameters of consequent sets. Doing this fixes the shape and size of the FOU for each antecedent membership function. The data establish the rules and tuning is used only for the parameters of the consequent sets.
2. Fix the shapes of all antecedent membership functions ahead of time. Doing this fixes the shape of the FOU for each antecedent membership function. Use the training data to tune the antecedent and consequent-set parameters. In this way, the size of the FOU for each antecedent membership function, as well as the parameters of the consequent sets, adapts to the training data.

Before we describe the back-propagation method, let us note that, just as for the design of a singleton Mamdani type-2 FLS, there can be two very different *approaches to the tuning of type-2 TSK FLSs*:

1. **Partially dependent approach:** In this approach, one first designs the best possible type-1 TSK FLS, by tuning all of its parameters, and then uses these parameters in some way to *initialize* the parameters of the type-2 TSK FLS.
2. **Totally independent approach:** In this approach, all of the parameters of the type-2 TSK FLS are tuned without the benefit of a previous type-1 de-

sign. Hence, the parameters of the type-2 TSK FLS are usually initialized in a random manner.

One would expect that good results can be obtained using either approach. As mentioned in earlier chapters, two benefits from the partially dependent approach are: (a) a smart initialization of the parameters of the type-2 TSK FLS, and (b) a baseline design whose performance can be compared with that of the type-2 TSK FLS.

For illustrative purposes, in the rest of this section we assume that all of the parameters of the interval type-2 TSK FLS A2-C1 are tuned. The results in this section are very similar to those in Section 10.10.3, where an 11-step design procedure was stated and discussed. For completeness, we restate all 11 steps.

Given the N input–output training samples $(\mathbf{x}^{(t)}:y^{(t)})$, $t = 1,...,N$, we wish to update the design parameters so that (13-17), in which $\mathbf{y}_{TSK,1}(\mathbf{x}^{(t)})$ is replaced by $\mathbf{y}_{TSK,2}(\mathbf{x}^{(t)})$, is minimized for E training epochs. A general method for doing this is:

1. Initialize all of the parameters in the antecedent and consequent membership functions.
2. Set the counter, e, of the training epoch to zero; i.e., $e \equiv 0$.
3. Set the counter, t, of the training data to unity; i.e., $t \equiv 1$.
4. Apply $p \times 1$ input $\mathbf{x}^{(t)}$ to the interval type-2 TSK FLS and compute the total firing interval and consequent for each rule; i.e., compute $\underline{f}^j$ and $\overline{f}^i$ $(i = 1,...,p)$ using (13-24) and (13-25), and compute y_l^i and y_r^i using (13-26) and (13-27).
5. Compute y_l and y_r using the four-step iterative method described pp. 310–311 [this leads to a re-ordering of the M rules, which are then re-numbered 1,..., M, as explained in the discussions accompanying (10-63)–(10-65)]. Doing this establishes L and R, so that y_l and y_r can be expressed as in (10-57) and (10-60), respectively, i.e.,

$$y_l = \frac{\sum_{i=1}^{M} f_l^i y_l^i}{\sum_{i=1}^{M} f_l^i} = \frac{\sum_{i=1}^{L} \overline{f}^i y_l^i + \sum_{j=L+1}^{M} \underline{f}^j y_l^j}{\sum_{i=1}^{L} \overline{f}^i + \sum_{j=L+1}^{M} \underline{f}^j}$$

$$= y_l\left(\overline{f}^1,...,\overline{f}^L, \underline{f}^{L+1},...,\underline{f}^M, y_l^1,...,y_l^M\right)$$

(13-47)

and

$$y_r = \frac{\sum_{i=1}^{M} f_r^i y_r^i}{\sum_{i=1}^{M} f_r^i} = \frac{\sum_{i=1}^{R} \underline{f}^i y_r^i + \sum_{j=R+1}^{M} \overline{f}^j y_r^j}{\sum_{i=1}^{R} \underline{f}^i + \sum_{j=R+1}^{M} \overline{f}^j} \tag{13-48}$$

$$= y_r\left(\underline{f}^1, ..., \underline{f}^R, \overline{f}^{R+1}, ..., \overline{f}^M, y_r^1, ..., y_r^M\right)$$

6. Compute the defuzzified output, $y_{TSK,2}(\mathbf{x}^{(t)})$, of the interval type-2 TSK FLS, as

$$y_{TSK,2}(\mathbf{x}^{(t)}) = \left[y_l(\mathbf{x}^{(t)}) + y_r(\mathbf{x}^{(t)})\right]/2 \tag{13-49}$$

7. Determine the explicit dependence of y_l and y_r on membership functions. [Because L and R obtained in Step 5 usually change from one iteration to the next, the dependence of y_l and y_r on membership functions will also usually change from one iteration to the next (see Example 10-5)]. To do this, first determine the explicit dependence of f^i and $\overline{f}^j$ on membership functions using (13-24) and (13-25); i.e., $\underline{f}^i$ is determined by $\underline{\mu}_{\tilde{F}_1^i}(x_1), ..., \underline{\mu}_{\tilde{F}_p^i}(x_p)$, and $\overline{f}^j$ is determined by $\overline{\mu}_{\tilde{F}_1^j}(x_1), ..., \overline{\mu}_{\tilde{F}_p^j}(x_p)$. Recall, also, that *both* y_l^i and y_r^i are determined by c_j^i and s_j^i ($j = 0, 1, ..., p$). Consequently, from (13-47) and (13-48), we see that

$$y_l = y_l\left[\overline{\mu}_{\tilde{F}_1^1}(x_1), ..., \overline{\mu}_{\tilde{F}_p^1}(x_p), ..., \overline{\mu}_{\tilde{F}_1^L}(x_1), ..., \overline{\mu}_{\tilde{F}_p^L}(x_p), \underline{\mu}_{\tilde{F}_1^{L+1}}(x_1),\right.$$
$$..., \underline{\mu}_{\tilde{F}_p^{L+1}}(x_p), ..., \underline{\mu}_{\tilde{F}_1^M}(x_1), ..., \underline{\mu}_{\tilde{F}_p^M}(x_p), c_0^1, ..., c_p^1, ..., c_0^M, \tag{13-50}$$
$$\left. ..., c_p^M, s_0^1, ..., s_p^1, ..., s_0^M, ..., s_p^M\right]$$

and

$$y_r = y_r\left[\underline{\mu}_{\tilde{F}_1^1}(x_1), ..., \underline{\mu}_{\tilde{F}_p^1}(x_p), ..., \underline{\mu}_{\tilde{F}_1^R}(x_1), ..., \underline{\mu}_{\tilde{F}_p^R}(x_p), \overline{\mu}_{\tilde{F}_1^{R+1}}(x_1),\right.$$
$$..., \overline{\mu}_{\tilde{F}_p^{R+1}}(x_p), ..., \overline{\mu}_{\tilde{F}_1^M}(x_1), ..., \overline{\mu}_{\tilde{F}_p^M}(x_p), c_0^1, ..., c_p^1, ..., c_0^M, \tag{13-51}$$
$$\left. ..., c_p^M, s_0^1, ..., s_p^1, ..., s_0^M, ..., s_p^M\right]$$

Although the dependence of y_l and y_r on their activated upper and lower membership functions and consequent parameters have been shown, the exact formulas for y_l and y_r need to be worked out so that partial derivatives of y_l and y_r with respect to parameters can be determined.

8. Test each component of $\mathbf{x}^{(t)}$ to determine the *active branches* in $\underline{\mu}_{\tilde{F}_k^l}(x_k)$ and $\overline{\mu}_{\tilde{F}_k^l}(x_k)$ $(k = 1, \ldots, p)$, and represent the active branches as explicit functions of their associated parameters; e.g., use (10-21) and (10-22) for the case of a Gaussian primary membership function with uncertain mean. This step depends on the relative location of each component of $\mathbf{x}^{(t)}$ to the underlying membership functions of its components (see Example 10-5).

9. Tune the parameters of the active branches of the antecedent's membership functions and the parameters in the consequents using a steepest descent algorithm, using the error function in (13-17), in which $\mathbf{y}_{TSK,1}(\mathbf{x}^{(t)})$ is replaced by $\mathbf{y}_{TSK,2}(\mathbf{x}^{(t)})$. See Examples 3-15 and 3-16 for the calculations of derivatives of upper and lower membership functions with respect to parameters of the active branches. Observe that the parameters in the consequents are shared by *both* y_l and y_r, so consequent parameter updates need to be connected to *both* y_l and y_r using chain rules.

10. Set $t \equiv t + 1$. If $t = N + 1$, go to Step 11; otherwise, go to Step 4.

11. Set $e = e + 1$. If $e = E$, STOP; otherwise, go to Step 3.

13.4 EXAMPLE: FORECASTING OF COMPRESSED VIDEO TRAFFIC

In Section 13.1 we mentioned that not being able to compensate for uncertain measurements, as we can do in a non-singleton Mamdani FLS, limits the applicability of a TSK FLS to situations where there either is no uncertainty or all of the uncertainty appears only in the rule antecedents. Consequently, a TSK FLS is not applicable to as many kinds of time-series forecasting problems as is a Mamdani FLS.

One kind of time-series forecasting problem for which a TSK FLS is applicable is the *random-signal and perfect-measurement* case. Because the Mackey–Glass model, which has been the basis for all of our previous forecasting studies (in Chapters 5, 6, and 10–12), is based on a *deterministic* signal that is then measured in the presence of additive stationary or non-stationary noise, it is not in this class of time-series forecasting problems. Hence, we will not use it in this chapter. Instead, we shall use a time-series that is associated with MPEG-1 compressed video traffic.

13.4.1 Introduction to MPEG video traffic

Moving Picture Expert Group (MPEG) is a standard for digital video compression coding that has been extensively used to overcome the problem of storage of prerecorded video on digital storage media, because of the high compression ratios it achieves. MPEG video traffic is composed of a Group of Pictures (GoP) that contains the following encoded frames: intracoded (I), predicted (P), and bidirectional (B). I frames are coded with respect to the current frame using a two-dimensional discrete cosine transform; they have a relatively low compression ratio. P frames are coded with reference to previous I or P frames using interframe coding; they can achieve a better compression ratio than I frames. B frames are coded with reference to the next and previous I or P frame; they can achieve the highest compression ratio of the three frame types. The use of these three types of frames allows MPEG to be both robust (I frames permit error recovery) and efficient (B and P frames have high compression ratio).

Oliver Rose [Rose (1995)], of the University of Wurzburg, has made 20 MPEG-1 video traces available on-line.[7] He compressed the videos using an MPEG-1 encoder using a pattern with GoP size 12—IBBPBBPBBPBB. Observe that in this GoP there is one I frame, three P frames, and eight B frames. Each of his MPEG video streams consists of 40,000 video frames (3,333 I frames, 10,000 P frames, and 26,667 B frames) which, at 25 frames/sec, represents about 30 minutes of real-time full motion video.

Using these 20 compressed video traces, Rose (1995) analyzed their statistical properties and observed that the frame and GoP sizes (i.e., bits per frame or bits per GoP) can be approximated by Gamma or Lognormal distributions. Additionally, Manzoni et al. (1999) studied the workload models of variable bit rate (VBR) video traffic, Adas (1998) used adaptive linear prediction to forecast the VBR video for dynamic bandwidth allocation, and Krunz et al. (1995) found that the lognormal distribution is the best match for the frame sizes of all I/P/B frames; i.e., if the I, P, or B frame size at time j is s_j, then

$$\log_{10} s_j \approx N(\log_{10} s_j; m, \sigma^2) \tag{13-52}$$

Example 13-5: Liang and Mendel (2000h) modeled the logarithm of the frame size of all I/P/B frames to see if a Gaussian function with constant mean and variance can indeed match each kind of frame size. They did this for all 20 of Rose's MPEG-1 compressed videos. Results for the movie *Jurassic Park* are given in Table 13-2. These results were obtained as follows:

---

[7]FTP://ftp-info3.informatik.uni-wuerzburg.de/pub/MPEG/

1. The first 6000 frames (which included 500 I frames, 1,500 P frames, and 4,000 B frames) were decomposed into five non-overlapping segments (each of which included 100 I frames, 300 P frames, and 800 B frames).

2. The mean, $m_i(F)$, and standard deviation, $\sigma_i(F)$, of the logarithm of the frame size of the ith segment ($i = 1, ..., 5$) were computed for I/P/B frames ($F = I, P, B$). These statistics are summarized in the rows of Table 13-2 labeled "Segment 1," ..., and "Segment 5."

3. The mean, $m(F)$, and standard deviation, $\sigma(F)$, of all 500 I frames, 1,500 P frames and 4,000 B frames were computed (next to last row in Table 13-2; $F = I, P, B$).

4. The normalized mean, $m_i(F) / m(F)$, and standard deviation, $\sigma_i(F) / \sigma(F)$, were then computed for the five non-overlapping segments of I/P/B frames ($F = I, P, B$).

5. The standard deviation of the normalized mean, $\sigma_m(F)$, and of the normalized standard deviation, $\sigma_{std}(F)$ ($F = I, P, B$), were computed from $m_i(F) / m(F)$ and $\sigma_i(F) / \sigma(F)$ ($i = 1, ..., 5$), respectively (last row in Table 13-2).

Table 13-2: Mean and standard deviation (SD) values for 5 non-overlapping segments of the first 6000 frames of *Jurassic Park* MPEG-1 video traffic and their normalized standard deviation. Segment 1 is for frames 1-1200, segment 2 is for frames 1201-2400, etc.

Video Data	I Frame		P Frame		B Frame	
	Mean	SD	Mean	SD	Mean	SD
Segment 1	4.7359	0.0910	4.2338	0.1982	3.9195	0.1748
Segment 2	4.7491	0.1052	4.1734	0.2342	3.8738	0.1998
Segment 3	4.7861	0.0597	4.1186	0.2616	3.8291	0.2069
Segment 4	4.7181	0.0755	4.0556	0.2515	3.7504	0.1981
Segment 5	4.6477	0.0820	3.8252	0.3503	3.5892	0.2942
Entire segment	4.7274	0.0954	4.0813	0.2990	3.7924	0.2474
Normalized SD*	$\sigma_m(I)$	$\sigma_{SD}(I)$	$\sigma_m(P)$	$\sigma_{SD}(P)$	$\sigma_m(B)$	$\sigma_{SD}(B)$
	0.0108	0.1780	0.0386	0.1885	0.0342	0.1860

*Short for SD of normalized mean or standard deviation.

Observe, from the entries in Table 13-2, that:

- Both the means and standard deviations vary from segment to segment for I/P/B frames.

- The variations of the standard deviations are much greater than the variations in the means; e.g., from the last row of Table 13-2, observe that $\sigma_{std}(F) \gg \sigma_m(F)$ ($F = I, P, B$). ∎

Example 13-5 demonstrates that a Gaussian function whose mean and variance are constants *cannot* match the logarithm of each kind of frame size, and suggests that the logarithm of the I, P, or B frame sizes is more appropriately modeled as a Gaussian whose standard deviation varies. This also suggests that we should use a Gaussian primary membership function with a fixed mean and an uncertain standard deviation (as in Figure 3-9) to model the frame size of the compressed video traffic.

Our purpose for presenting Example 13-5, with its analysis of the statistics of the I, P, and B frame sizes, was to determine an appropriate FOU for the respective frame sizes, since the first step to using a type-2 FLS—TSK or Mamdani—is to choose an appropriate type-2 membership function. This example also demonstrates that MPEG-1 coded video traffic can be modeled as a *random-signal and perfect-measurement* time series,[8] so that it is appropriate to forecast it using a TSK FLS.

Forecasting video traffic is very important so that a telecommunication network can forecast its future traffic. By doing this, network bandwidth can be dynamically allocated using connection admission control (see Section 14.7), in such a way that bandwidth utilization and cell loss ratio are effectively traded off.

13.4.2 Forecasting I frame sizes: General information

In the rest of this section we focus on the problem of forecasting I frame sizes (i.e., the number of bits/frame) for a specific video product, namely *Jurassic Park*. All of our methodologies for doing this apply as well to forecasting P and B frame sizes and can also be applied to other video products.

Here we examine four designs of FLS forecasters based on the logarithm of the first 1000 I frame sizes of *Jurassic Park*, $s(1)$, $s(2)$, ..., $s(1000)$ (see Figure 13-1). Those designs are: type-1 TSK FLS, type-2 TSK FLS A2-CO, singleton type-1 Mamdani FLS, and singleton type-2 Mamdani FLS. We used the first 504 data $[s(1), s(2), ..., s(504)]$ for tuning the parameters of these forecasters, and the remaining 496 data $[s(505), s(502), ..., s(1000)]$ for testing after tuning.

---

[8] The "perfect" measurements are random due to the random nature of the compressed data, but no additional random measurement noise is present. Therefore, it is correct to refer to such random measurements as *perfect measurements*.

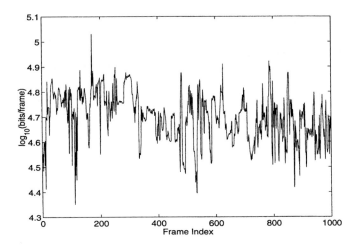

Figure 13-1: The first 1000 I frame sizes of
Jurassic Park MPEG-1 video data.

1. **Type-1 TSK FLS:** The rules of this FLS forecaster are $(i = 1, ..., M)$

   $$R^i: \text{IF } s(k-3) \text{ is } F_1^i \text{ and } s(k-2) \text{ is } F_2^i \text{ and } s(k-1) \text{ is } F_3^i$$
   $$\text{and } s(k) \text{ is } F_4^i \text{ THEN } \hat{s}^i(k+1) = c_0^i + c_1^i s(k-3) \tag{13-53}$$
   $$+ c_2^i s(k-2) + c_3^i s(k-1) + c_4^i s(k)$$

   We initially chose F_j^i to be the same for all i and j, and used a Gaussian membership function for them, one whose initial mean and standard deviation were chosen from the first 500 I frames as (see "Entire segment" row of Table 13-2) $m = 4.7274$ and $\sigma = 0.0954$. According to Table 13-1, the number of design parameters for this type-1 TSK FLS is $(3p+1)M = 13M$.

2. **Type-2 TSK FLS A2-C0:** The rules of this FLS forecaster (see Example 13-2) are $(i = 1, ..., M)$

   $$R^i: \text{IF } s(k-3) \text{ is } \tilde{F}_1^i \text{ and } s(k-2) \text{ is } \tilde{F}_2^i \text{ and } s(k-1) \text{ is } \tilde{F}_3^i$$
   $$\text{and } s(k) \text{ is } \tilde{F}_4^i \text{ THEN } \hat{s}^i(k+1) = c_0^i + c_1^i s(k-3) \tag{13-54}$$
   $$+ c_2^i s(k-2) + c_3^i s(k-1) + c_4^i s(k)$$

   We initially chose $\tilde{F}_j^i$ to be the same for all i and j, and used a Gaussian primary membership function for them, one with a fixed mean and an uncertain standard deviation. As we did for the type-1 TSK FLS, we chose the initial mean from the first 500 I frames (see "Entire segment" row of Table 13-2) as $m = 4.7274$; however, in this case, for which $\sigma \in [\sigma_1, \sigma_2]$, we divided the 500 I frames into five 100-frame segments and then computed the initial values of σ_1^i and σ_2^i ($i = 1, ..., M$) using the standard deviations for the jth segment, σ^j, (see "SD" column under "I Frame" in Table 13-2, for "Segment 1," ..., and "Segment 5") as

$$\sigma_1^i = \min_{j=1,2,...,5} \sigma^j = 0.0597 \tag{13-55}$$

$$\sigma_2^i = \max_{j=1,2,...,5} \sigma^j = 0.1052 \tag{13-56}$$

According to Table 13-1, the number of design parameters for this type-2 TSK FLS A2-C0 is $(4p+1)M = 17M$.

3. **Singleton type-1 Mamdani FLS:** The rules of this FLS forecaster are ($i = 1, ..., M$)

$$R^i: \text{IF } s(k-3) \text{ is } F_1^i \text{ and } s(k-2) \text{ is } F_2^i \text{ and } s(k-1) \text{ is } F_3^i$$
$$\text{and } s(k) \text{ is } F_4^i \text{ THEN } \hat{s}^i(k+1) \text{ is } G^i \tag{13-57}$$

We used height defuzzification. As we did for the type-1 TSK FLS, we initially chose F_j^i to be the same for all i and j, and used a Gaussian membership function for them, one whose initial mean and standard deviation were chosen from the first 500 I frames, as described earlier, as $m = 4.7274$ and $\sigma = 0.0954$. According to Table 13-1, the number of design parameters for this singleton type-1 Mamdani FLS is $(2p+1)M = 9M$.

4. **Singleton type-2 Mamdani FLS:** The rules of this FLS forecaster are ($i = 1, ..., M$)

$$R^i: \text{IF } s(k-3) \text{ is } \tilde{F}_1^i \text{ and } s(k-2) \text{ is } \tilde{F}_2^i \text{ and } s(k-1) \text{ is } \tilde{F}_3^i$$
$$\text{and } s(k) \text{ is } \tilde{F}_4^i \text{ THEN } \hat{s}^i(k+1) \text{ is } \tilde{G}^i \tag{13-58}$$

We used height type-reduction, and we initially chose the $\tilde{F}_j^i$ as just described for the type-2 TSK FLS A2-C0. We also used the same kind of Gaussian primary membership function for $\tilde{G}^i$; i.e., one with a fixed mean and an uncertain standard deviation. However, because we used height type-reduction (see Section 9.5.3), the consequent membership functions are only characterized by $\bar{y}^i$ instead of by interval end-points, as would have been the case if we had used center-of-sets type-reduction. According to Table 13-1, the number of design parameters[9] for this singleton type-2 Mamdani FLS is $(3p+1)M = 13M$.

13.4.3 Forecasting I frame sizes: Using the same number of rules

In this first approach to designing the four FLS forecasters, we fixed the number of rules at five in all of them; i.e., $M = 5$. Doing this means that the type-1 TSK FLS is described by 65 design parameters, the type-2 TSK FLS A2-C0 is described by 85 design parameters, the singleton type-1 Mamdani FLS is described by 45 design parameters, and the singleton type-2 Mamdani FLS is described by 65 design parameters. Steepest descent algorithms (as described in Sections 5.9.3 and 10.10.3 for the Mamdani FLSs, and in Sections 13.2.4 and 13.3.5 for the TSK FLSs) were used to tune all of these parameters. In these algorithms, we used step sizes of $\alpha = 0.001$ and $\alpha = 0.01$ for the TSK and Mamdani FLSs, respectively.

We have already explained how we chose initial values for the membership function parameters. All of the remaining parameters were initialized randomly, as follows:

- Consequent parameters, $c_j^i (i = 1,...,5; j = 0,1,...,4)$, of the two TSK FLSs were each chosen randomly in [0, 0.2] with uniform distribution.
- Consequent parameters, $\bar{y}^i (i = 1,...,5)$, of the two Mamdani FLSs were chosen randomly in [0, 5] with uniform distribution.

Because we chose the initial values of the consequent parameters randomly, we ran 50 Monte-Carlo realizations for each of the 4 designs.[10] For each realization, each of the four FLSs was tuned for 10 epochs on the 504 training data. All designs were then evaluated on the remaining 496 testing data using the following *RMSE*:

$$RMSE = \sqrt{\tfrac{1}{496} \sum_{k=504}^{999} \left[s(k+1) - f_{FLS}(\mathbf{s}^{(k)}) \right]^2} \qquad (13\text{-}59)$$

---

[9]Table 13-1 was prepared by assuming the use of center-of-sets type-reduction for the type-2 Mamdani FLS. As just explained, there is one less design parameter when height type-reduction is used. This is why we have $(3p + 1)M$ design parameters instead of the $(3p + 2)M$ design parameters that are listed in Table 13-1.
[10]In Chapters 5, 6, and 10–12, Monte-Carlo simulations were run to average out the effects of additive measurement noise. Here they are run to average out the effects of random initial consequent parameter values.

where $\mathbf{s}^{(k)} = [s(k-3), s(k-2), s(k-1), s(k)]^T$. The average value and standard deviations of these *RMSE*s are plotted in Figure 13-2 for each of the 10 epochs. Observe, from Figure 13-2(a), that:

1. The type-2 TSK FLS outperforms the type-1 TSK FLS at each epoch.
2. The type-2 Mamdani FLS outperforms the type-1 Mamdani FLs at each epoch.
3. The type-2 Mamdani FLS performs the best at the end of the first epoch. It outperforms the type-2 TSK FLS by $[(0.1124-0.0912)/0.1124] \times 100 \cong 19\%$, and outperforms the type-1 TSK FLS by $[(0.1336-0.0912)/0.1336] \times 100 \cong 32\%$. This again demonstrates that a type-2 Mamdani FLS is very promising for adaptive signal processing where more than one epoch of tuning is not possible.
4. After 10 epochs of tuning, the average *RMSE* of the 4 FLS forecasters is:

   - Type-1 TSK FLS: 0.0779
   - Type-2 TSK FLS: 0.0687
   - Singleton type-1 Mamdani FLS: 0.0808
   - Singleton type-2 Mamdani FLS: 0.0746

Observe, from Figure 13-2(b), that:

1. The type-2 Mamdani FLS has the smallest RMSE standard deviation at the end of the first epoch.
2. After 10 epochs of training, the type-2 TSK FLS has the smallest RMSE standard deviation.

In conclusion, after 10 epochs of tuning the type-2 TSK FLS gives the best performance of all four designs.

13.4.4 Forecasting I frame sizes: Using the same number of design parameters

Because a five-rule TSK FLS always has more parameters (design degrees of freedom) to tune than does a comparable five-rule Mamdani FLS, we modified the previous approach to designing the four FLSs. We did this by fixing the rules used by both TSK FLSs at five and by then choosing the number of rules used by both Mamdani FLSs so that their total number of design parameters approximately equals the number for the respective TSK FLS. Doing this led us to use seven rules for the two Mamdani FLSs. The designs of the resulting four FLSs

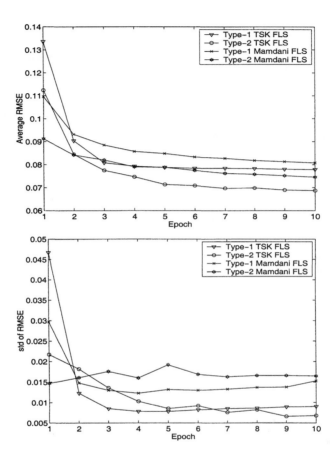

Figure 13-2: The mean and standard deviations of RMSE (using the test data) for the four five-rule FLS forecasters, averaged over 50 Monte-Carlo designs. Tuning was performed in each design for 10 epochs. (a) Mean values, and (b) standard deviations.

proceeded exactly as described in the preceding section. All designs were again evaluated using the *RMSE* in (13-59). The average value and standard deviations of these *RMSE*s are plotted in Figure 13-3 for each of the 10 epochs. Observe that:

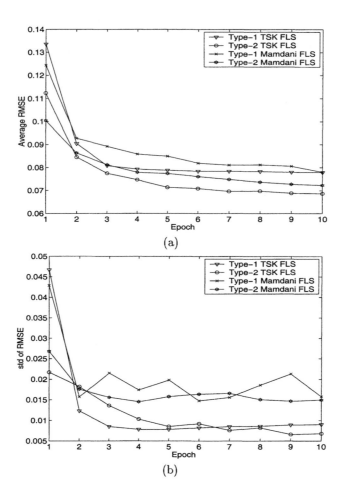

Figure 13-3: The mean and standard deviations of RMSE (using the test data) for four FLS forecasters, averaged over 50 Monte-Carlo designs. The type-1 TSK and Mamdani FLSs have approximately the same number of design parameters, as did the type-2 TSK and Mamdani FLSs. Tuning was performed in each design for 10 epochs. (a) Mean values, and (b) standard deviations.

1. The results are similar to the ones depicted in Figure 13-2; so, at least for this example, equalizing the numbers of design parameters in the Mamdani and TSK FLSs does not seem to be so important.

2. The type-2 Mamdani and TSK FLSs still outperform their type-1 counterparts.

3. After only one epoch of tuning the type-2 Mamdani FLS still performs the best, after 10 epochs of tuning the type-2 TSK FLS performs the best.

13.4.5 Conclusion

It is not our intention in this example to recommend one FLS architecture over another. Stepping back from the details of the two simulations, we can see that the type-2 TSK and Mamdani FLSs outperformed their type-1 counterparts, supporting our contention that uncertainties can be handled by type-2 FLSs.

13.5 FINAL REMARK

Some people prefer a TSK FLS over a Mamdani FLS or vice-versa. We leave that choice to the designer who, as always, must be guided by a specific application. We do wish to point out, however, that, at present, Mamdani FLSs seem to be applicable to a broader range of problems than are TSK FLSs because they are able to handle more kinds of uncertainties. When both kinds of FLSs are applicable, as in the case of forecasting a random-signal and perfect-measurement time-series, the designer can carry out a comparative performance analysis between the two architectures, as we have just done.

13.6 COMPUTATION

The following M-files, which are found in the folder *type-1 fuzzy logic systems*, are useful for designing a type-1 TSK FLS:

tsk_type1.m: Compute the output(s) of a type-1 TSK FLS (type-1 antecedents and type-0 consequent) when the antecedent membership functions are Gaussian.

train_tsk_type1.m: Tune the parameters of a type-1 TSK FLS (type-1 antecedents and type-0 consequent) when the antecedent membership functions are Gaussian, using some input–output training data.

The following M-files, which are found in the folder *interval type-2 fuzzy logic systems*, are useful for designing a type-2 TSK FLS:

tsk_type2.m: Compute the output(s) of an interval type-2 TSK FLS A2-C1 (type-2 antecedents and type-1 consequent) when the antecedent membership functions are Gaussian primary membership functions with uncertain means.

train_tsk_type2.m: Tune the parameters of an interval type-2 TSK FLS A2-C1 when the antecedent membership functions are Gaussian primary membership functions with uncertain means, using some input–output training data.

EXERCISES

13-1: Based on $e^{(t)}$ in (13-17), $y_{TSK,1}(\mathbf{x})$ in (13-9), and $g_j^i(\mathbf{x}^{(t)})$ in (13-16), derive the back-propagation algorithms for all of the antecedent and consequent parameters in the type-1 TSK FLS.

13-2: Define a squared error function that depends on all N training data, and derive the back-propagation algorithms for all of the antecedent and consequent parameters in the type-1 TSK FLS for this new error function.

13-3: Develop an SVD–QR design based on $\mathbf{G}$ in (13-13). Interpret this design in terms of (13-1) and (13-2); i.e., explain what is being reduced by it.

13-4: At the end of Example 13-2, it is stated that in the iterative method for computing y_l and y_r, $R \ne L$, even though $y_l^i = y_r^i = y^i$. Explain why this is so.

13-5: Derive (13-35) and (13-36).

13-6: Review Example 10-3, which was for function approximation, and then explain: (a) how an interval A1-C1 type-2 TSK FLS can be used for function approximation, and (b) under what conditions the interval A1-C1 type-2 TSK FLS, whose output is in (13-36), gives exactly the same results as an interval Mamdani type-2 singleton FLS [Hint: see (10-56)].

13-7: Derive the back-propagation algorithms in Step 9 of the Section 13.3.5 11-step procedure for all of the antecedent and consequent parameters.

13-8: In this exercise you will be asked to illustrate some of the major steps in the 11-step Section 13.3.5 design procedure for an interval type-2 TSK FLS that only has 2 two-antecedent rules, namely:

$$R^1: \text{ IF } x_1 \text{ is } \tilde{F}_1^1 \text{ and } x_2 \text{ is } \tilde{F}_2^1 \text{ THEN } Y^1 = C_0^1 + C_1^1 x_1 + C_2^1 x_2$$

and

$$R^2: \text{ IF } x_1 \text{ is } \tilde{F}_1^2 \text{ and } x_2 \text{ is } \tilde{F}_2^2 \text{ THEN } Y^2 = C_0^2 + C_1^2 x_1 + C_2^2 x_2$$

As in Example 10-5, the antecedent membership functions are Gaussian primary membership functions with uncertain means [described in (10-20)–(10-22)] whose parameters are m_{k1}^i, m_{k2}^i, and σ_k^i, where $k = 1, 2$ and $i = 1, 2$. The initial forms of these membership functions were chosen arbitrarily and are depicted in Figure 10-12. The mean, c_j^i, and spread, s_j^i, of the consequent type-1 sets, C_j^i (where $j = 0, 1, 2$ and $i = 1, 2$) are chosen for illustrative purposes to be:

$$c_0^1 = 2.80, \ c_1^1 = -1.56, \ c_2^1 = 1.05, \ s_0^1 = 0.20, \ s_1^1 = 0.04, \ s_2^1 = 0.05$$
$$c_0^2 = 2.75, \ c_1^2 = 1.80, \ c_2^2 = 1.55, \ s_0^2 = 0.05, \ s_1^2 = 0.20, \ s_2^2 = 0.05$$

Finally, as in Example 10-5, the first pair in the training set is $\left(\mathbf{x}^{(1)} : y^{(1)} \right)$, where $x_1^{(1)} = 3.75$, $x_2^{(1)} = 6.0$ and $y^{(1)}(x_1^{(1)}, x_2^{(1)}) = 4.6$.

(a) Explain why the lower and upper firing levels in (13-24) and (13-25) are the same as the ones in (10-82a) and (10-82b) for R^1, and (10-83a) and (10-83b) for R^2.

(b) Show that $[y_l^1, y_r^1] = [2.6, 3.9] = C_{\tilde{G}^1}$ and $[y_l^2, y_r^2] = [4.2, 6.4] = C_{\tilde{G}^2}$, where $C_{\tilde{G}^1}$ and $C_{\tilde{G}^2}$ are defined in Example 10-5. Explain why we get the same results for $C_{\tilde{G}^1}$ and $C_{\tilde{G}^2}$ in both examples.

(c) How much of the rest of Example 10-5 is directly applicable to this exercise?

(d) Write out the steepest descent algorithms for all of the interval type-2 TSK parameters.

13-9: Suppose, in Exercise 13-8, $\mathbf{x}^{(2)} = (x_1^{(2)}, x_2^{(2)})^{\text{T}} = (6.0, 2.0)^T$ and $y^{(2)} = 7.2$. Set up the steepest descent algorithms for all of the parameters of the two-rule type-2 TSK FLS.

CHAPTER 14

Epilogue

14.1 INTRODUCTION

We have presented a tour through type-1 and type-2 FLSs and have demonstrated that a type-2 FLS is a natural generalization of a type-1 FLS. Our type-2 FLSs have been constructed so that when all sources of uncertainty disappear, they reduce to type-1 FLSs. This is analogous to what happens in probability theory when random uncertainties disappear, in which case a probability density function collapses to a point value, and random analysis reduces to deterministic analysis.

Going from type-1 fuzzy sets to type-2 fuzzy sets means going from a two-dimensional membership function for a type-1 fuzzy set to a three-dimensional membership function for a type-2 fuzzy set. It is this new dimension for fuzzy sets—the third dimension—that lets us handle—model —uncertainties totally within the framework of fuzzy sets and FL. Naturally, it may be possible to create and use even higher order fuzzy sets, in much the same way that people use higher-than-second-order statistics (e.g. [Nikias and Mendel (1993)], [Mendel (1991)]),[1] and we look forward to their development.

The extension of a type-1 FLS to a type-2 FLS has required a number of new concepts, namely: FOU, lower and upper membership functions, active branch of a lower or upper membership function, the extended sup-star compo-

---

[1]Higher order statistics are useful and popular when the data are known to be non-Gaussian, in which case there is more information contained in the data than can be revealed by just the first- and second-order statistics. These higher order statistics are either third- and higher-order moments or cumulants.

sition, centroid of a type-2 fuzzy set, embedded type-2 and type-1 fuzzy sets, and type-reduction. I mention this here to remind the reader that the extension of a type-1 FLS to a type-2 FLS is built on solid principles, some of which are new.

Although we have presented a very general framework for a type-2 FLS—a framework that is valid for general type-2 fuzzy sets—we have focused very heavily on interval type-2 fuzzy sets. We did this because: (a) calculating the meet operations for each fired rule is computationally prohibitive when general type-2 fuzzy sets are used, especially if the product t-norm is used (and we emphasize the use of this t-norm); (b) type-reduction is also computationally prohibitive when general type-2 fuzzy sets are used; and (c) we presently have no rational basis for not choosing interval secondary membership functions.

We have tried to balance theory and design methodologies for type-1 and type-2 FLSs. It should be evident to the reader that design methodologies for a type-2 FLS are very natural extensions of those for a type-1 FLS. This is in keeping with our fundamental design requirement, which states that when all sources of uncertainty disappear, a type-2 FLS must reduce to a type-1 FLS. This does not mean that one can use a type-1 FLS design method as is. In fact, the design of an interval type-2 FLS—the type-2 FLS that we have stressed—is more challenging than the design of a type-1 FLS, since it is characterized by *two* FBF expansions, whereas a type-1 FLS is characterized by only one FBF expansion. What it does mean is that the more challenging type-2 design methods must reduce to their simpler type-1 design methods when all sources of uncertainty disappear.

We have provided access to software that is available online so that the reader will immediately be able to use the results in this book. Although the software that is appropriate to each chapter is listed and described at the end of each chapter, we have collected all of these descriptions together in Appendix C, so that the reader may see the forest from the trees.

Finally, our two case studies, which we have carried throughout the book wherever it was possible, have demonstrated potential benefits to using a type-2 FLS over using a type-1 FLS. Later in this chapter, I describe four real-world applications in which the performance of a type-1 FLS is compared to that of a type-2 FLS. I do this so that the reader will be further convinced of the merits of using a type-2 FLS, and so that the reader will see the potential importance of a type-2 FLS to the fields of classification, mobile communications, and computer networks.

14.2 TYPE-2 VERSUS TYPE-1 FLSS

Table 14-1 summarizes the similarities and differences between type-1 and type-2 singleton and non-singleton FLSs. To reiterate, a type-2 FLS can model a broad range of uncertainties, namely: uncertainty about the meanings of the words that are used in rules, uncertainty about the consequent that is used in a rule, uncertainty about the measurements that activate the FLS, and uncertainty about the data that are used to tune the parameters of a FLS.

Table 14-1: Comparisons of type-1 and type-2 singleton and non-singleton FLSs [Mendel (2000)].

	Type-1 FLS	**Type-2 FLS**
Singleton fuzzification	• No uncertainties about antecedents or consequents	• Uncertainties about antecedents or consequents are accounted for (the FOU)
	• No uncertainties on measurements that activate the FLS	• No uncertainties on measurements that activate the FLS
	• Only a point output is obtained	• Both a type-reduced set and a point output are obtained
Non-singleton fuzzification	• No uncertainties about antecedents or consequents	• Uncertainties about antecedents or consequents are accounted for (the FOU)
	• There are uncertainties on measurements that activate the FLS; they are modeled by treating the measurements as type-1 fuzzy numbers	• There are uncertainties on measurements that activate the FLS; they are modeled by treating the measurements as type-1 or type-2 fuzzy numbers
	• Only a point output is obtained	• Both a type-reduced set and a point output are obtained

A type-1 FLS can only model the uncertainty about the measurements that activate the FLS, and then in a more restricted way than can a type-2 FLS, restricted in the sense that it can only model measurements as type-1 fuzzy sets, whereas a type-2 FLS has the ability to model measurements as either type-1 or type-2 fuzzy sets. Consequently, type-2 FLSs are much richer than type-1 FLSs. They include more design parameters (degrees of freedom), which provide them with the potential for outperforming their type-1 counterparts.

Some people may object to using a type-2 FLS because they are more complicated than a type-1 FLS. If there is a benefit to account for uncertainties within the framework of FL, then there must be a tradeoff between performance improvement and additional complexity. This sort of performance–complexity tradeoff is common to all design situations. Note that we have already greatly simplified a type-2 FLS by emphasizing an interval type-2 FLS, which has only about twice the complexity of a type-1 FLS (e.g. two FBF expansions versus one FBF expansion). Using parallel computing, it should be possible to run an interval type-2 FLS in about the same time as it takes to run a type-1 FLS.

14.3 APPROPRIATE APPLICATIONS FOR A TYPE-2 FLS

It is important to have some guidance about the kinds of situations that seem to be most appropriate for using type-2 FLSs. So far, in my own applications of them, I have found they are very suitable when:

- *Measurement noise is non-stationary*, but the nature of the non-stationarity cannot be expressed ahead of time mathematically (e.g. the variable SNR measurements used in Section 12.5)

- A *data-generating mechanism is time-varying*, but the nature of the time-variations cannot be expressed ahead of time mathematically (e.g. equalization of non-linear and time-varying digital communication channels as described in Section 14-5; or, reduction of co-channel interference (CCI) for non-linear and time-varying digital communication channels as described in Section 14-6)

- *Features are described by statistical attributes that are non-stationary*, but the nature of the non-stationarity cannot be expressed ahead of time mathematically (e.g. rule-based classification of video traffic, as described in Section 14-4)

- *Knowledge is mined* from experts using IF–THEN questionnaires (e.g. connection admission control for ATM networks, as described in Section 14-7)

In the next four sections of this chapter I describe the applications just mentioned. Here, I wish to emphasize that the starting point for all applications of type-2 FLSs is *choosing appropriate FOUs for it*. This is presently done in any one of the following ways, by:

- Analyzing the available data using statistical techniques and examining the variations of the appropriate statistics

- Analyzing the natures of the uncertainties by understanding the problem being solved

- Collecting surveys about the words that will be used in knowledge-mining questionnaires

- Deciding on the natures of the uncertainties of the measurements that activate a FLS (e.g. type-0, type-1, or type-2)

We look forward to new techniques for doing this as type-2 FLSs are applied to many new situations by the readers of this book.

14.4 RULE-BASED CLASSIFICATION OF VIDEO TRAFFIC

Pattern recognition usually involves [Duda (1994), p. 4][2] "the extraction of significant, characterizing features followed by classification on the basis of the values of the features." There are many approaches to pattern recognition, including deterministic, statistical, neural network, and, more recently, rule-based. In this section, we explain the rule-based approach to a high-level video classification problem.

For a brief introduction to MPEG video traffic, see Section 13.4.1. The problem that we examine in the present section is the direct classification of compressed (MPEG-1) video traffic without decompressing it. This is for high-level classification, e.g. classify a video as a movie or a sports program, or as a movie or documentary. It is not for content-based classification, because content (e.g. the gunfighter in movie A, the ballerina in movie B, the Eiffel Tower in movie C, etc.) is part of a video frame, whereas it is the entire frame that is available in compressed form. In this section we focus on the two-class problem (i.e., classifying a video as either a movie or a sports program), leaving the more general case to the reader.

There can be two approaches to rule-based classification from compressed video traffic:

1. Decompress the video traffic, followed by classification
2. Classify the compressed video traffic directly

The first approach has the following disadvantages: it requires a decoder, which

---

[2]This chapter was originally published in *Adaptive, Learning and Pattern Recognition Systems*, edited by J. M. Mendel and K. S. Fu, in 1970, by Academic Press. It was reprinted in 1994 by Prentice Hall and is dedicated to K. S. Fu, after his untimely death in the 1980s.

has a cost associated with it; decoding takes time, which introduces latency; and the decompressed video requires a lot of storage. The second approach—the one taken here—has the following advantages: it requires no decoder, so that no decoding time is needed and no additional storage is needed. Consequently, direct classification of compressed video traffic can save time and money.

Given a collection of MPEG-1 compressed movies and sports program videos, we shall use a subset of them to create (i.e., design and test) a rule-based classifier (RBC) in the framework of FL. We shall develop type-1 and type-2 classifiers and compare them to see which provides the best performance. Our overall approach is to:

1. Choose appropriate features that act as the antecedents in a RBC
2. Establish the FOUs for the features
3. Establish rules using the features
4. Establish the FOUs for the measurements
5. Optimize the rule design-parameters using a tuning procedure
6. Evaluate the performance of the optimized RBC using testing

The first four steps of this procedure are relatively straightforward. The fifth step requires that we establish the computational formulas for the FL-based classifiers, in much the same way that we established such formulas for the FLSs of Chapters 5, 6, and 10-12. We do this following. The sixth step requires that we also baseline our FL classifiers. We do this using the accepted standard of a Bayesian classifier, one whose structure we also explain following.

14.4.1 Selected features

MPEG-1 compression produces three kinds of frames—I, P, and B. Bits per I, P, and B frames are available as measurements. We use the logarithm of bits per I, P, and B frame as the three features of our RBCs. Since these features are used as the antecedents in rules, it is imperative to associate a measurement with its proper antecedent. Figure 14-1 depicts these three kinds of frame sizes for the movie Terminator II.[3] Observe that I frames have more bits/frame than P frames, which have more bits/frame than B frames. This observation is important, because it lets us classify a measurement into one of the three features, so that it is possible to associate a measurement with its proper antecedent.

---

[3]As explained in Section 13.4.1, this video was compressed using a GoP size 12—IBBPBBPBBPBB. A total of 40,000 video frames of Terminator II were available. To plot 3,000 I, P, and B frame sizes, the first 36,000 frames were used for the I frame size plot in Figure 14-1 (a); the first 12,000 frames were used for the P frame size plot in Figure 14-1 (b); and, the first 4,500 frames were used for the B frame size plot in Figure 14-1 (c).

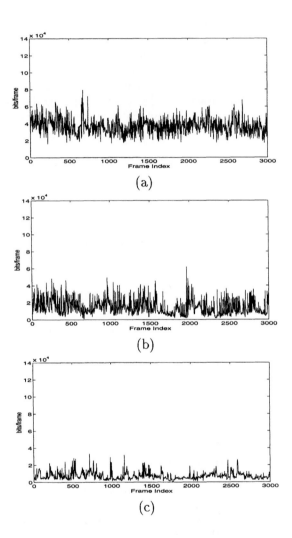

Figure 14-1: Portions of I/P/B frame sizes of *Terminator II* movie: (a) I frame, (b) P frame, and (c) B frame.

14.4.2 FOUs for the features

In Section 13.4.1, we mentioned that Krunz et al. (1995) found that the lognormal distribution is the best match for the frame sizes of all I/P/B frames, and in Example 13-5, we demonstrated (as shown by [Liang and Mendel (2000h)]) that the logarithm of I, P, or B frame sizes are more appropriately modeled as Gaussians each of whose mean is a constant, but whose standard deviation varies. This suggests that we should use a Gaussian membership function with a fixed mean and an uncertain standard deviation to model each frame size of the compressed video. This statistical analysis of real data has led us to use the FOU that is depicted in Figure 3-9. We also use interval secondary membership functions.

14.4.3 Rules

Rules for a RBC of compressed video traffic use the three selected features as their antecedents and have one consequent. The antecedents are: logarithm of bits/I frame, logarithm of bits/P frame, and logarithm of bits/B frame. The consequent is +1 if the video is a movie and −1 if it is a sports program. Observe that there is nothing fuzzy about a rule's consequent in rule-based classification; i.e., each rule's consequent is assigned a numerical value, +1 or −1.

Each rule in a *type-1 fuzzy logic rule-based classifier* (FL RBC) has the following structure:[4]

$$R^l: \text{IF I frame is } F_1^l \text{ and P frame is } F_2^l \text{ and B frame is } F_3^l \text{ , THEN the product is} \quad (14\text{-}1)$$
$$\text{a movie (+1) or a sports program (-1)}$$

whereas it has the following structure in a *type-2 FL RBC*:

$$R^l: \text{IF I frame is } \tilde{F}_1^l \text{ and P frame is } \tilde{F}_2^l \text{ and B frame is } \tilde{F}_3^l \text{ , THEN the product is} \quad (14\text{-}2)$$
$$\text{a movie (+1) or a sports program (-1)}$$

Observe that these rules are a special case of a Mamdani FLS rule, one in which the consequent is a singleton.

We use a very small number of rules, namely one per video product, e.g. if our training set contains four movies and four sports programs, we use just eight rules.

---

[4]See also Kuncheva (2000) for an excellent introduction to RBCs.

14.4.4 FOUs for the measurements

Within the framework of a FL-based classifier we have a lot of flexibility in how we choose to model the measurements that activate it. If the measurements are perfect, then we would model them as type-0 fuzzy sets; if they are uncertain, but stationary, then we would model them as type-1 fuzzy sets; and, if they are uncertain, but non-stationary, then we would model them as type-2 fuzzy sets.

In this application, each measurement came from a window of 600 frames that contained 50 I frames, 150 P frames, and 400 B frames. For each measurement's type-1 fuzzy set we used a Gaussian membership function whose mean was located at the measurement's value and whose standard deviation parameter was estimated using a window of frames. For each measurement's type-2 fuzzy set we used the Figure 3-9 FOU, where, as in the type-1 case, its mean was located at the measurement's value. However, there are now two standard deviation parameters (σ_1 and σ_2) that were estimated by sub-dividing each window of frames into five smaller windows, each with its own estimated standard deviation. σ_1 was chosen as the minimum value of the five estimated standard deviations, whereas σ_2 was chosen as the maximum value of the five estimated standard deviations.

14.4.5 Design parameters in a FL RBC

In our simulations below we shall design five FL RBCs: singleton type-1 FL RBC, non-singleton type-1 FL RBC, interval singleton type-2 FL RBC, interval type-1 non-singleton type-2 FL RBC, and interval type-2 non-singleton type-2 FL RBC. The design results will establish which classifier provides the best performance.

For the type-1 FL RBCs, each antecedent membership function has two design parameters, its mean and standard deviation; hence, there are six design parameters per rule. For the type-2 FL RBCs each antecedent membership function has three design parameters, its mean and two standard deviation parameters; hence, there are nine design parameters per rule.

Depending on how the measurements are modeled, there can be from zero to two additional design parameters.

Optimum values for all design parameters are determined during a tuning process; but, before such a process can be programmed, we must first establish computational formulas for the FL RBCs.

14.4.6 Computational formulas for type-1 FL RBCs

We have already mentioned that the rules in (14-1) are a special case of a Mamdani FLS rule, one in which the consequent is a singleton. Rule consequent, y^l, is treated as a crisp set; i.e. $y^l = 1$ for a movie, and $y^l = -1$ for a sports program. The membership function $\mu_{G^l}(y)$ for this crisp set is

$$\mu_{G^l}(y) = \begin{cases} 1 & y = y^l \\ 0 & \text{otherwise} \end{cases} \tag{14-3}$$

where $l = 1, \ldots, M$. Using (5-7), we see that the membership function of each three-antecedent fired rule, $\mu_{B^l}(y)$, can be expressed

$$\mu_{B^l}(y) = \mu_{G^l}(y) \star \left\{ \left[\sup_{x_1 \in X_1} \mu_{X_1}(x_1) \star \mu_{F_1^l}(x_1) \right] \star \left[\sup_{x_2 \in X_2} \mu_{X_2}(x_2) \star \mu_{F_2^l}(x_2) \right] \right.$$
$$\left. \star \left[\sup_{x_3 \in X_3} \mu_{X_3}(x_3) \star \mu_{F_3^l}(x_3) \right] \right\} \tag{14-4}$$

Applying (14-3) to this result, we find that

$$\mu_{B^l}(y) = \begin{cases} \left[\sup_{x_1 \in X_1} \mu_{X_1}(x_1) \star \mu_{F_1^l}(x_1) \right] \star \left[\sup_{x_2 \in X_2} \mu_{X_2}(x_2) \star \mu_{F_2^l}(x_2) \right] \\ \quad \star \left[\sup_{x_3 \in X_3} \mu_{X_3}(x_3) \star \mu_{F_3^l}(x_3) \right] \end{cases} \quad \begin{matrix} y = y^l \\ \\ y \neq y^l \end{matrix} \tag{14-5}$$

For a *singleton type-1 FL RBC*, (14-5) reduces further to

$$\mu_{B^l}(y) = \begin{cases} T_{k=1}^3 \mu_{F_k^l}(x_k') \\ 0 \end{cases} \equiv \begin{cases} f^l & y = y^l \\ 0 & y \neq y^l \end{cases} \tag{14-6}$$

For a non-singleton type-1 FL RBC, (14-5) reduces to

$$\mu_{B^l}(y) = \begin{cases} T_{k=1}^3 \sup_{x_k \in X_k} \left[\mu_{X_k}(x_k) \star \mu_{F_k^l}(x_k) \right] & y = y^l \\ 0 & y \neq y^l \end{cases} \tag{14-7}$$

In light of our discussions in Section 6.2.2, (14-7) can be expressed as

$$\mu_{B^l}(y) = \begin{cases} T_{k=1}^3 \left[\mu_{X_k}(x_{k,\max}^l) \star \mu_{F_k^l}(x_{k,\max}^l) \right] \\ 0 \end{cases} \equiv \begin{cases} f^l & y = y^l \\ 0 & y \neq y^l \end{cases} \tag{14-8}$$

See Example 6-2 for explicit formulas for $x_{k,\max}^l$, when the membership functions for both $\mu_{X_k}(x_k)$ and $\mu_{F_k^l}(x_k)$ are Gaussians, and the t-norm is product or minimum. We use the product t-norm in the rest of this section.

Using the height defuzzifier (Section 5. 5.3), the output of a type-1 RB FLC can be expressed as

$$y_{RBC,1}(\mathbf{x}) = \frac{\sum_{l=1}^M f^l y^l}{\sum_{l=1}^M f^l} \tag{14-9}$$

in which $y^l = \pm 1$. We make a final decision that the measurements correspond to a movie or a sports program based on the sign of the defuzzified output, i.e.

$$\begin{aligned} &\text{IF } y_{RBC,1}(\mathbf{x}) > 0 \quad \text{decide movie} \\ &\text{IF } y_{RBC,1}(\mathbf{x}) < 0 \quad \text{decide sports program} \end{aligned} \tag{14-10}$$

If $y_{RBC,1}(\mathbf{x}) = 0$, we flip a fair coin to decide whether the measurements correspond to a movie or a sports program.

Observe, from (14-9), that the normalization operation does not change the sign of $y_{RBC,1}(\mathbf{x})$: hence, for two-category classification, (14-9) can be simplified. To that end, we use the following unnormalized output for the FLS in (14-10),

$$y_{RBC,1}(\mathbf{x}) = \sum_{l=1}^M f^l y^l \tag{14-11}$$

14.4.7 Computational formulas for type-2 FL RBCs

Using (10-8), we see that the secondary membership function $\mu_{\tilde{B}^l}(y)$ of each three-antecedent fired rule in (14-2) can be expressed as:

$$\mu_{\tilde{B}^l}(y) = \mu_{\tilde{G}^l}(y) \sqcap \left\{ \left[\sqcup_{x_1 \in X_1} \mu_{\tilde{X}_1}(x_1) \sqcap \mu_{\tilde{F}_1^l}(x_1) \right] \sqcap \left[\sqcup_{x_2 \in X_2} \mu_{\tilde{X}_2}(x_2) \sqcap \mu_{\tilde{F}_2^l}(x_2) \right] \right.$$

$$\Pi\left[\sqcup_{x_3 \in X_3} \mu_{\tilde{X}_3}(x_3) \Pi \mu_{\tilde{F}_3^l}(x_3)\right]\right\}, \quad y \in Y \tag{14-12}$$

where $l = 1, \ldots, M$. Applying (14-3) to this result, we find that

$$\mu_{\tilde{B}^l}(y) = \begin{cases} \left\{ \left[\sqcup_{x_1 \in X_1} \mu_{\tilde{X}_1}(x_1) \Pi \mu_{\tilde{F}_1^l}(x_1)\right] \Pi \left[\sqcup_{x_2 \in X_2} \mu_{\tilde{X}_2}(x_2) \Pi \mu_{\tilde{F}_2^l}(x_2)\right] \right. \\ \qquad \left. \Pi \left[\sqcup_{x_3 \in X_3} \mu_{\tilde{X}_3}(x_3) \Pi \mu_{\tilde{F}_3^l}(x_3)\right] \right\} & y = y^l \\ 0 & y \neq y^l \end{cases} \tag{14-13}$$

which can also be expressed as

$$\mu_{\tilde{B}^l}(y) \equiv \begin{cases} F^l(\mathbf{x}') & y = y^l \\ 0 & y \neq y^l \end{cases} \tag{14-14}$$

When the input and antecedent sets are interval type-2 fuzzy sets, $F^l(\mathbf{x}')$ is an interval type-1 set, i.e.

$$F^l(\mathbf{x}') = [\underline{f}^l(\mathbf{x}'), \overline{f}^l(\mathbf{x}')] \tag{14-15}$$

where, from Theorem 12-1,

$$\underline{f}^l(\mathbf{x}') = \sup_{\mathbf{x}} \int_{x_1 \in X_1} \int_{x_2 \in X_2} \int_{x_3 \in X_3} \left[\underline{\mu}_{\tilde{X}_1}(x_1) \star \underline{\mu}_{\tilde{F}_1^l}(x_1)\right] \star \left[\underline{\mu}_{\tilde{X}_2}(x_2) \star \underline{\mu}_{\tilde{F}_2^l}(x_2)\right] \\ \star \left[\underline{\mu}_{\tilde{X}_3}(x_3) \star \underline{\mu}_{\tilde{F}_3^l}(x_3)\right] \Big/ \mathbf{x} \tag{14-16}$$

and

$$\overline{f}^l(\mathbf{x}') = \sup_{\mathbf{x}} \int_{x_1 \in X_1} \int_{x_2 \in X_2} \int_{x_3 \in X_3} \left[\overline{\mu}_{\tilde{X}_1}(x_1) \star \overline{\mu}_{\tilde{F}_1^l}(x_1)\right] \star \left[\overline{\mu}_{\tilde{X}_2}(x_2) \star \overline{\mu}_{\tilde{F}_2^l}(x_2)\right] \\ \star \left[\overline{\mu}_{\tilde{X}_3}(x_3) \star \overline{\mu}_{\tilde{F}_3^l}(x_3)\right] \Big/ \mathbf{x} \tag{14-17}$$

and the supremum is attained when each term in the brackets attains its supremum. See Example 12-3 for the calculations of the bracketed suprema when the antecedent membership functions are Gaussian primary membership functions with uncertain standard deviations and the inputs are modeled as type-2 Gaussian fuzzy numbers also of uncertain standard deviations. Comparable results can be found in Example 11-2 for the case when the antecedent membership functions are Gaussian primary membership functions with uncertain standard deviations and the inputs are modeled as type-1 Gaussian fuzzy numbers. These results are needed to design a specific type-2 FL RBC.

Applying the Extension Principle to (14-11), we obtain the extended output of a type-2 FL RBC as

$$Y_{RBC,2}(\mathbf{x}') = [y_l, y_r] = \int_{f^1 \in [\underline{f}^1, \overline{f}^1]} \cdots \int_{f^M \in [\underline{f}^M, \overline{f}^M]} 1 \bigg/ \sum_{i=1}^{M} f^i y^i \qquad (14\text{-}18)$$

Because $f^i \in F^i = [\underline{f}^i, \overline{f}^i]$ and y^i is a crisp value, we find that

$$y_l = \sum_{i=1}^{M} \underline{f}^i y^i \qquad (14\text{-}19)$$

and

$$y_r = \sum_{i=1}^{M} \overline{f}^i y^i \qquad (14\text{-}20)$$

The defuzzified output of the type-2 FL RBC is $y_{RBC,2}(\mathbf{x}') = (y_l + y_r)/2$, i.e.

$$y_{RBC,2}(\mathbf{x}') = \sum_{i=1}^{M} y^i \left(\underline{f}^i + \overline{f}^i \right) \bigg/ 2 \qquad (14\text{-}21)$$

We use this value of $y_{RBC,2}(\mathbf{x}')$ in decision rule (14-10).

Although we have provided the detailed formulas for the interval type-2 non-singleton type-2 FL RBC, it is straightforward to simplify these formulas to obtain the corresponding formulas for the interval type-1 non-singleton type-2 FL RBC and the interval singleton type-2 FL RBC (Exercise 14-2). Note, also, that although we have provided computational formulas for type-1 and type-2 FL RBCs within the context of a three-antecedent rule, it is trivial to modify them for classifiers that have fewer than or more than three antecedents.

14.4.8 Optimization of rule design-parameters

In our simulation results discussed in Section 14.4.10, we begin with five movies and five sports programs and, by way of illustration, design FL RBCs using four movie rules and four sports program rules; i.e. each classifier has eight rules. Each one of the five FL RBCs is optimized using very simple modifications of the tuning procedures that are described in Sections 5.9.3, 6.6.3, 10.10.3, 11.4.3, and 12.4.3. The modifications are due to using an unnormalized output. We leave it to the reader to develop the details of these tuning procedures. The online M-files (see Appendix C) *train_sfls_type1.m*, *train_nsfls_type1.m*, *train_sfls.m*, *train_nsfls1.m*, and *train_nsfls2.m*, which are for tuning normalized type-1 and type-2 FLSs, are easily adapted to the present situations.

14.4.9 Testing the FL RBCs

After the tuning of each FL RBC is completed, that classifier is tested on the remaining unused products. Its false alarm rate[5] (FAR) is the performance measure that is used to evaluate it and to compare it against the other classifiers. In addition, the FL RBCs are base-lined against a Bayesian classifier, whose structure we describe next.

It is well known that Bayesian decision theory (e.g. [Duda and Hart (1973)]) provides the optimal solution to a general decision-making problem. To begin, we assume that each video product (movie or sports program) v_i is given a numerical label (the five movies are labeled 1, 2, ..., 5 and the five sports programs are labeled 6, 7, ..., 10) and is equiprobable; i.e. $p(v_i) = 1/10$, where $i \in \{1,...,10\}$. Hypothesis H_1 is associated with a *movie*, whereas hypothesis H_2 is associated with a *sports program*, and $p(H_1) = p(H_2) = 0.5$.

We also assume that each component of the frame size vector $\mathbf{s}_i \equiv (s_i^I, s_i^P, s_i^B)^T$ is a lognormal function of the I, P, and B frames of the *i*th video product, $i = 1, ..., 10$, and that $\mathbf{x}_i \equiv \log \mathbf{s}_i$; hence,

$$p(\mathbf{x}_i \mid v_i) = \frac{1}{(2\pi)^{3/2} |\Sigma_i|^{1/2}} \exp\left[-\tfrac{1}{2}(\mathbf{x}_i - \mathbf{m}_i)^T \Sigma_i^{-1}(\mathbf{x}_i - \mathbf{m}_i)\right] \qquad (14\text{-}22)$$

where $\mathbf{m}_i \equiv (m_i^I, m_i^P, m_i^B)^T$ and $\Sigma_i \equiv diag(\sigma_i^{I^2}, \sigma_i^{P^2}, \sigma_i^{B^2})$ are the mean vector (3×1) and covariance matrix (3×3) of $\mathbf{x}_i$, respectively, and $\mathbf{m}_i$ and Σ_i are estimated from the training data.

In this case,

$$p(\mathbf{x} \mid H_1) = \sum_{i=1}^{5} p(\mathbf{x} \mid v_i) p(v_i) \qquad (14\text{-}23)$$

and

---

[5]A *false alarm* occurs when an incorrect decision is made, i.e., when the classifier decides the video is a movie when it actually is a sports program, or when it decides the video is a sports program when it actually is a movie.

$$p(\mathbf{x} \mid H_2) = \sum_{i=6}^{10} p(\mathbf{x} \mid v_i) p(v_i) \qquad (14\text{-}24)$$

Because $p(H_1) = p(H_2) = 0.5$, the Bayes decision rule is:

The video traffic is a *movie* if $\quad p(\mathbf{x} \mid H_1) > p(\mathbf{x} \mid H_2)$

The video traffic is a *sports program* if $\quad p(\mathbf{x} \mid H_1) < p(\mathbf{x} \mid H_2)$ (14-25)

The video traffic is a movie or a *sports program* if $\quad p(\mathbf{x} \mid H_1) = p(\mathbf{x} \mid H_2)$

14.4.10 Results and conclusions

So as not to get lost in the many details associated with the designs of the 5 FL RBCs, we refer the reader to Liang and Mendel (2000e) for them. Here we focus on one set of results for so-called *out-of-product classification*. "Out-of-product" means that we use *some* of the compressed data from *some* of the *available* video products to establish the rules and to optimize (tune) the resulting classifiers, and we test the classifiers on the unused video products. As mentioned earlier, we used eight video products out of a total of 10 available products—four movies and four sports programs—to design each RBC. The first 24,000 (out of 40,000) compressed frames of each of the eight video products were used to establish and design five eight-rule FL RBCs. The first 37,500 compressed frames of the remaining two videos were then used for testing. An exhaustive study of the 25 possible designs was conducted. Average FAR (averaged aver the 25 possible designs) for the five FL RBCs as well as for the Bayesian classifier are:

- singleton type-1 FL RBC: FAR = 9.41%
- non-singleton type-1 FL RBC: FAR = 9.17%
- singleton type-2 FL RBC: FAR = 13.65%
- type-1 non-singleton type-2 FL RBC: FAR = 8.43%
- type-2 non-singleton type-2 FL RBC: FAR = 8.03%
- Bayesian classifier: FAR = 14.29%

From these results, we see that the type-2 non-singleton type-2 FL RBC provides the best performance, and has 44% fewer false alarms than does the Bayesian classifier. This is because the type-2 non-singleton type-2 FL RBC allows for variations in the standard deviations of I, P, and B frame sizes whereas the Bayesian classifier does not. Additional simulation studies that use 20 video products (10 movies and 10 sports programs) have been performed and support these conclusions.

In summary, we have demonstrated that it is indeed possible to perform high-level classification of movies and sports programs working directly with compressed data. This seems to be possible because a type-2 FL RBC allows the uncertainties about the variable standard deviations of the logarithm of the frame sizes to be handled within the framework of type-2 fuzzy sets. These uncertainties are not only accounted for by the FOUs of the rule-antecedents, but are also accounted for by modeling the measurements as type-2 fuzzy numbers.

14.5 EQUALIZATION OF TIME-VARYING NON-LINEAR DIGITAL COMMUNICATION CHANNELS

When a message (e.g., speech) gets confused because of the transmitting and receiving media (e.g., telephone system) as well as by objects that may interfere with it (e.g., tall buildings, mountains), we say that there is inter-symbol interference (ISI). For the message to be understood at the receiving end, inter-symbol interference must be undone. This is accomplished at the receiving end by hardware and software and is known as *equalization*.[6]

The block diagram for a baseband communication system subject to ISI[7] and additive Gaussian noise (AGN) is depicted in Figure 14-2, where $s(k)$ is the symbol to be transmitted, $e(k)$ is the AGN, the channel order is n (i.e. there are $n + 1$ taps), and time-varying tap coefficients are $a_i(k)$ ($i = 0, 1, ..., n$). The measured channel output $r(k)$ can be represented as

$$r(k) = \hat{r}(k) + e(k) = \sum_{i=0}^{n} a_i(k)s(k-i) + e(k) \qquad (14\text{-}26)$$

Here we assume that $s(k)$ is binary, either +1 or −1 with equal probability. The goal in channel equalization is to recover the input sequence $s(k)$ ($k = 1, 2, ...$) based on a sequence of $r(k)$ values without knowing or estimating the channel coefficients. This is accomplished with the equalizer block, whose output can be expressed as

$$\hat{s}(k-d) = sign\left(f(window\ of\ past\ measurements)\right) = \begin{cases} +1 & \text{If } f(\cdot) \geq 0 \\ -1 & \text{If } f(\cdot) < 0 \end{cases} \qquad (14\text{-}27)$$

---

[6]The material in this section is taken from [Karnik et al. (1999)] and [Liang and Mendel (2000d)].
[7]Definitions of the terms used in this section can be found in any standard textbook on communication theory, e.g. [Proakis (1989)].

where d is a decision delay, and $f(\cdot)$ denotes some non-linear operation on a window of past measurements. Usually, $f(\cdot)$ is referred to as the *equalizer*.

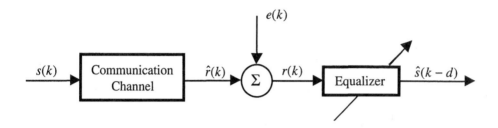

Figure 14-2: Block diagram of a baseband communication system that is subject to ISI and AGN (Karnik et al., 1999, ©1999, IEEE).

Most of the work that has been done in the area of adaptive equalization over the past few decades has focused on time-invariant channels (e.g. see [Proakis (1989)] and the many references therein, and, [Chen et al. (1993a, 1993b, 1995)], [Cowan and Semnani (1998)], [Lee (1996)], [Moon and Jeon (1998)], [Patra and Mulgrew (1998)], [Sarwal and Srinath (1995)], [Savazzi, et al. (1998)], and [Wang and Mendel (1993)]). In today's communication environment (e.g. mobile communications), the channels are time-varying because of fading. The classical equalizers do not perform well for rapidly fading channels.

We interpret the time-varying nature of a channel as uncertainties in its coefficients. Such uncertainties motivated us to use a type-2 FLS as an adaptive equalizer for time-varying channels. We shall refer to such an equalizer as a *fuzzy adaptive filter* (FAF).

Before we can provide the structure of our FAF, we need to provide some preliminaries and additional motivation for why type-2 FAFs are more appropriate then type-1 FAFs.

14.5.1 Preliminaries for channel equalization

A very popular architecture for the equalizer $f(\cdot)$ is that of a transversal equalizer, for which the window of past measurements is $r(k)$, $r(k-1)$, ..., $r(k-p+1)$, where p is the order of the equalizer (i.e., the number of its taps). In this section we limit our discussions to transversal equalizers. We denote

$$\mathbf{r}(k) \equiv [r(k), r(k-1), ..., r(k-p+1)]^T \qquad (14\text{-}28)$$

and observe, from (14-26), that $\mathbf{r}(k)$ depends on the channel input sequence $s(k), s(k-1), ..., s(k-n-p+1)$, which we collect into the following $(n+p) \times 1$ vector

$$\mathbf{s}(k) = [s(k), s(k-1), ..., s(k-n-p+1)]^T \qquad (14\text{-}29)$$

Because $s(k)$ can be $+1$ or -1, there are $n_s = 2^{n+p}$ possible combinations of the channel input sequence.

In Figure 14-2, the noise-free signal is $\hat{r}(k)$, where

$$\hat{r}(k) = \sum_{i=0}^n a_i(k)s(k-i) \qquad (14\text{-}30)$$

We let

$$\hat{\mathbf{r}}(k) \equiv [\hat{r}(k), \hat{r}(k-1), ..., \hat{r}(k-p+1)]^T \qquad (14\text{-}31)$$

where $\hat{\mathbf{r}}(k)$ is called the *channel state* [Chen et al. (1993b)]. Observe, from (14-31) and (14-30), that each of the $n_s = 2^{n+p}$ combinations of the channel input-sequence $\mathbf{s}(k)$ generates one $\hat{\mathbf{r}}(k)$, which we denote as $\hat{\mathbf{r}}_i(k)$, where

$$\hat{\mathbf{r}}_i(k) \equiv [\hat{r}_i(k), \hat{r}_i(k-1), ..., \hat{r}_i(k-p+1)]^T \quad i = 1, ..., n_s \qquad (14\text{-}32)$$

Hence, each channel state has a probability of occurrence equal to $1/n_s$.

A correct decision by the equalizer occurs if

$$\hat{s}(k-d) = s(k-d) \qquad (14\text{-}33)$$

Based on the category of $s(k-d)$ (i.e. ± 1), the channel states $\hat{\mathbf{r}}(k)$ can be partitioned into two classes [Chen et al. (1993b)]

$$R^+ = \{\hat{\mathbf{r}}(k) | s(k-d) = 1\} \qquad (14\text{-}34)$$

$$R^- = \{\hat{\mathbf{r}}(k) | s(k-d) = -1\} \qquad (14\text{-}35)$$

The number of elements in R^+ and R^- are denoted n_s^+ and n_s^-, respectively. Because $s(k-d)$ has equal probability to be $+1$ or -1, it follows that $n_s^+ = n_s^- = n_s/2 = 2^{n+p-1}$. The channel states in R^+ and R^- are denoted $\hat{\mathbf{r}}_i^+$ $(i = 1, ..., n_s^+)$ and $\hat{\mathbf{r}}_i^-$ $(i = 1, ..., n_s^-)$, respectively.

Example 14-1: Consider the following time-invariant non-linear channel model that was used by Wang and Mendel (1993):

$$r(k) = a_1 s(k) + a_2 s(k-1) - 0.9\left[a_1 s(k) + a_2 s(k-1)\right]^3 + e(k) \qquad (14\text{-}36)$$

where $a_1 = 1$ and $a_2 = 0.5$, as shown in Figure 14-3 (a). Here we assume that the decision delay $d = 0$. From Table 14-2, we see that there are eight channel states and that $s(k)$ determines which category ($+1$ or -1) $\hat{\mathbf{r}}(k)$ belongs to. Observe that $[\hat{r}(k), \hat{r}(k-1)]$ in the first four rows of Table 14-2 have category $+1$ [as determined by (14-34) for $s(k-d) = s(k)$], and $[\hat{r}(k), \hat{r}(k-1)]$ in the last four rows of Table 14-2 have category -1 [as determined by (14-35) for $s(k-d) = s(k)$]. The channel states are plotted in Figure 14-3 (b) when $a_1 = 1$ and $a_2 = 0.5$. To construct that figure, we assumed no additive noise was present, so that $\hat{r}(k) = r(k)$ and $\hat{r}(k-1) = r(k-1)$. ∎

Table 14-2: Channel states for the channel model in (14-36) with binary symbols: $d = 0$ and $p = 2$ ([Karnik et al. (1999)] and [Liang and Mendel (2000d)]).

			Channel States	
s(k)	s(k-1)	s(k-2)	$\hat{r}(k)$	$\hat{r}(k-1)$
1	1	1	$a_1(k)+a_2(k)-0.9\left[a_1(k)+a_2(k)\right]^3$	$a_1(k)+a_2(k)-0.9\left[a_1(k)+a_2(k)\right]^3$
1	1	-1	$a_1(k)+a_2(k)-0.9\left[a_1(k)+a_2(k)\right]^3$	$a_1(k)-a_2(k)-0.9\left[a_1(k)-a_2(k)\right]^3$
1	-1	1	$a_1(k)-a_2(k)-0.9\left[a_1(k)-a_2(k)\right]^3$	$-a_1(k)+a_2(k)-0.9\left[-a_1(k)+a_2(k)\right]^3$
1	-1	-1	$a_1(k)-a_2(k)-0.9\left[a_1(k)-a_2(k)\right]^3$	$-a_1(k)-a_2(k)-0.9\left[-a_1(k)-a_2(k)\right]^3$
-1	1	1	$-a_1(k)+a_2(k)-0.9\left[-a_1(k)+a_2(k)\right]^3$	$a_1(k)+a_2(k)-0.9\left[a_1(k)+a_2(k)\right]^3$
-1	1	-1	$-a_1(k)+a_2(k)-0.9\left[-a_1(k)+a_2(k)\right]^3$	$a_1(k)-a_2(k)-0.9\left[a_1(k)-a_2(k)\right]^3$
-1	-1	1	$-a_1(k)-a_2(k)-0.9\left[-a_1(k)-a_2(k)\right]^3$	$-a_1(k)+a_2(k)-0.9\left[-a_1(k)+a_2(k)\right]^3$
-1	-1	-1	$-a_1(k)-a_2(k)-0.9\left[-a_1(k)-a_2(k)\right]^3$	$-a_1(k)-a_2(k)-0.9\left[-a_1(k)-a_2(k)\right]^3$

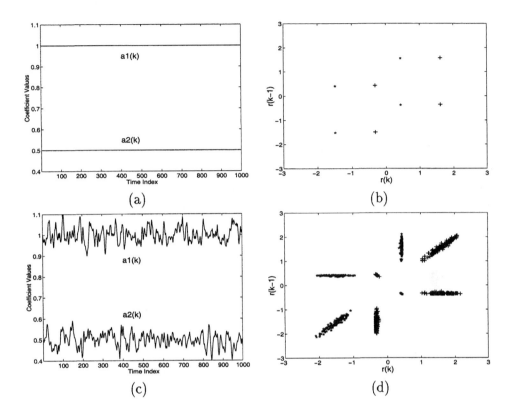

Figure 14-3: For the channels in (14-36) and (14-43): (a) time-invariant channel coefficients, $a_1 = 1$ and $a_2 = 0.5$; (b) channel states (noise-free) of time-invariant channel, where * denotes the category $\hat{r}(k) = +1$ and + denotes the category $\hat{r}(k) = -1$; (c) an example of time-varying channel coefficients when $\beta = 0.1$; and (d) channel states (noise-free) of the time-varying channel whose coefficients are the ones in (c) (Karnik et al., 1999, ©1999, IEEE).

Chen et al. (1993b) have shown that the decision output of a Bayesian equalizer can be expressed as

$$\hat{s}(k-d) = \text{sgn}\big(f(\mathbf{r}(k))\big) = \begin{cases} +1 & f(\mathbf{r}(k)) \geq 0 \\ -1 & f(\mathbf{r}(k)) < 0 \end{cases} \tag{14-37}$$

where $f(\mathbf{r}(k))$ is given by

$$f(\mathbf{r}(k)) = \sum_{i=1}^{n_s^+} (2\pi\sigma_e^2)^{-m/2} \exp\left[-\frac{\|\mathbf{r}(k) - \hat{\mathbf{r}}_i^+\|^2}{2\sigma_e^2}\right]$$
$$-\sum_{i=1}^{n_s^-} (2\pi\sigma_e^2)^{-m/2} \exp\left[-\frac{\|\mathbf{r}(k) - \hat{\mathbf{r}}_i^-\|^2}{2\sigma_e^2}\right] \qquad (14\text{-}38)$$

in which σ_e denotes the standard deviation of the AGN $e(k)$. Because only the sign of $f(\mathbf{r}(k))$ is used to make the decision in (14-38), the scaling term $(2\pi\sigma_e^2)^{-m/2}$ in (14-38) can be ignored.

Let

$$w_i \equiv \begin{cases} +1 & \hat{\mathbf{r}}(k) \in R^+ \\ -1 & \hat{\mathbf{r}}(k) \in R^- \end{cases} \qquad (14\text{-}39)$$

then (14-38) can be re-expressed as

$$f(\mathbf{r}(k)) = \sum_{i=1}^{n_s} w_i \exp\left[-\frac{\|\mathbf{r}(k) - \hat{\mathbf{r}}_i\|^2}{2\sigma_e^2}\right] \qquad (14\text{-}40)$$

Based on properties of the squared norm and the exponential function, (14-40) can be rewritten as:

$$f(\mathbf{r}(k)) = \sum_{i=1}^{n_s} \prod_{l=0}^{p-1} w_i \exp\left\{-\frac{[r(k-l) - \hat{r}_i(k-l)]^* [r(k-l) - \hat{r}_i(k-l)]}{2\sigma_e^2}\right\} \qquad (14\text{-}41)$$

where $*$ denotes the complex conjugate operation. For a binary input sequence, $r(k-l)$ and $\hat{r}_i(k-l)$ are real, so that the conjugate operation can be ignored, i.e.

$$f(\mathbf{r}(k)) = \sum_{i=1}^{n_s} \prod_{l=0}^{p-1} w_i \exp\left\{-\frac{1}{2}\left(\frac{r(k-l) - \hat{r}_i(k-l)}{\sigma_e}\right)^2\right\} \qquad (14\text{-}42)$$

It is easy to show that (14-42) is identical to (14-11), when Gaussian membership functions are used for the rule-antecedents, singleton fuzzification is used, and the f^l are chosen as in (14-6). This means, of course, that equalization of binary signals is equivalent to two-category classification, and that an unnormalized output singleton type-1 FL RBC can be used to implement a Bayesian equalizer for a time-invariant channel.

Why not just implement (14-42) directly without connecting it to FL? Equation (14-42) is based on a probability model—the Gaussian density function for the AGN noise—whereas (14-11) is model free. As we have noted earlier in this book, a shortcoming to model-based statistical signal processing is the assumed probability model, for which model-based statistical signal processing results will be good if the data agree with the model, but may not be so good if the data do not.

14.5.2 Why a type-2 FAF is needed

When a channel's coefficients are time-varying, as we illustrate next, the channel's states are no longer simple points, but are instead clusters.

Example 14-2: Here we generalize the results of Example 14-1 to the time-varying version of the channel in (14-36), i.e. to

$$r(k) = a_1(k)s(k) + a_2(k)s(k-1) - 0.9\left[a_1(k)s(k) + a_2(k)s(k-1)\right]^3 + e(k) \qquad (14\text{-}43)$$

where a_1 and a_2 are time-varying coefficients, each simulated, as in [Cowan and Semnani (1998)], by using a second-order Markov model in which a white Gaussian noise source drives a second-order Butterworth low-pass filter. Note that we centered $a_1(k)$ about 1 and $a_2(k)$ about 0.5, and that the white Gaussian input to the Butterworth filter has a standard deviation equal to β.

Realizations of the time-varying coefficients and channel states are plotted in Figure 14-3 (c) and (d), respectively, for a moderate noise level of $\beta = 0.1$. The results in (d) are based on $\hat{r}(k)$ and $\hat{r}(k-1)$ given in Table 14-2. Observe that the channel states are now eight clusters instead of eight individual points. These clusters illustrate that $\hat{r}_i$ is uncertain for all $i = 1, ..., 8$ when the coefficients of the channel are time-varying. ■

For a type-1 FAF we chose type-1 Gaussian membership functions that are centered at the single-channel states for rule antecedents, as we explained just after (14-42). For a type-2 FAF we chose type-2 membership functions for rule antecedents, namely Gaussian primary membership functions with uncertain means, given in (10-20), where $\sigma_k^l \equiv \sigma_e$. The latter choice was motivated by the projections of the channel state clusters onto each of their two axes. By understanding the nature of the channel states when a channel's coefficients are varying we are again led to a specific FOU.

14.5.3 Designing the FAFs

Here we illustrate the design of singleton type-1 and singleton type-2 FAFs for the non-linear time-varying channel in (14-43). Each FAF has eight rules, one per channel state. The rules in a *singleton type-1 FAF* have the following structure ($l = 1, \ldots, 8$):

$$R^l: \text{IF } r(k) \text{ is } F_1^l \text{ and } r(k-1) \text{ is } F_2^l, \text{ THEN } y^l = w_l \qquad (14\text{-}44)$$

whereas they have the following structure in a *singleton type-2 FAF* ($l = 1, \ldots, 8$):

$$R^l: \text{IF } r(k) \text{ is } \tilde{F}_1^l \text{ and } r(k-1) \text{ is } \tilde{F}_2^l, \text{ THEN } y^l = w_l \qquad (14\text{-}45)$$

In these rules, w_l is a crisp value of $+1$ or -1, as determined by (14-39). For the type-1 rules, as we just mentioned, we used Gaussian membership functions for F_1^l and F_2^l; and, for the type-2 rules, we used the Gaussian primary membership functions in (10-20) for $\tilde{F}_1^l$ and $\tilde{F}_2^l$, where $\sigma_k^l \equiv \sigma_e$. As just explained, the range of the mean of the primary membership function for antecedent $\tilde{F}_1^l$ ($\tilde{F}_2^l$) corresponds to the horizontal (vertical) projection of the lth cluster depicted in Figure 14-3 (d).

Because of the isomorphism between equalization and classification, the computational formulas for type-1 and type-2 FAF's are easily obtained from Sections 14.4.6 and 14.4.7, respectively.

In Karnik et al. (1999) and Liang and Mendel (2000d), the mean-value parameters of all membership functions were estimated using a clustering procedure [Chen et al. (1993a)] that was applied to some training data, because such a procedure is computationally simple. We use this same procedure following. An alternative to doing this is to use a tuning procedure. To complete the specification of the membership functions, a value is also needed for the standard deviation, σ_e, of the AGN $e(k)$. Chen et al. (1995) showed that equalizer performance is not very sensitive to the value of σ_e; hence, in the following simulations we assumed that the value of σ_e is known exactly. Of course, σ_e could also have been estimated during a tuning process using some training data.

14.5.4 Simulations and conclusions

Here we compare singleton type-1 and singleton type-2 FAFs and a K-nearest neighbor classifier (NNC) [Savazzi et al. (1998)] for equalization of the time-varying non-linear channel in (14-43). Comparable results for a different channel can be found in [Mendel (2000)]. In our simulations, we chose the number of taps of the equalizer, p, equal to the number of taps of the channel, $n+1$, where $n = 1$; i.e. $p = n + 1 = 2$. The number of rules equaled the number of clusters; i.e. $2^{p+n} = 8$. We used a sequence $s(k)$ of length 1000 for our experiments. The first 121 symbols[8] were used for training (i.e. clustering) and the remaining 879 were used for testing. The training sequence established the parameters of the antecedent membership functions, as described in Section 14.5.3. After training, the parameters of the type-1 and type-2 FAFs were fixed and then testing was performed.

In our first experiment, we fixed SNR at 20dB and ran simulations for eight different values of noise level β, ranging from $\beta = 0.04$ to $\beta = 0.32$ (at equal increments of 0.04), and we set $d = 0$. We performed 100 Monte-Carlo simulations for each value of β, where in each realization the channel coefficients and the AGN were uncertain. The mean values and standard deviations of the bit error rate (BER) for the 100 Monte-Carlo realizations are plotted in Figure 14-4 (a) and (b), respectively.

In a second experiment, we fixed $\beta = 0.1$ and ran simulations for five different SNR values, ranging from $SNR = 15$dB to $SNR = 25$dB (at equal increments of 5dB), and we again set $d = 0$. We performed 100 Monte-Carlo simulations for each value of SNR, where in each realization the channel coefficients and the AGN were uncertain. The mean values and standard deviations of the bit error rate (BER) for the 100 Monte-Carlo realizations are plotted in Figure 14-5 (a) and (b), respectively. Observe, from Figures 14-4 and 14-5, that:

- In terms of the mean values of BER, the type-2 FAF performs better than both the type-1 FAF and NNC (see Figures 14-4 (a) and 14-5 (a)).

- When $SNR = 20$dB and $\beta \geq 0.12$, the NNC performs about the same as the type-1 FAF, but the type-1 FAF performs better than the NNC when $\beta < 0.12$. However, regardless of β, the type-2 FAF always performs better than the NNC (see Figure 14-4 (a)).

- In terms of the standard deviation of BER, the type-2 FAF is more robust to the AGN than are the other two equalizers; and, the type-1 FAF is also more robust than the NNC (see Figures 14-4 (b) and 14-5 (b)).

---

[8]In the K-NNC, if the number of training prototypes is N, then $K = \sqrt{N}$ is the optimal choice for K. It is required that N be an odd integer; hence, the choice of $N = 121$.

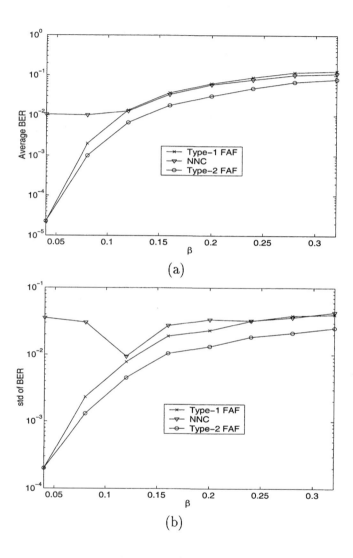

Figure 14-4: Performance of type-1 FAF, NNC, and type-2 FAF versus β when $SNR = 20$dB and the number of training proto-types is 121. (a) average BER, and (b) standard deviation (std) of BER for 100 Monte-Carlo realizations.

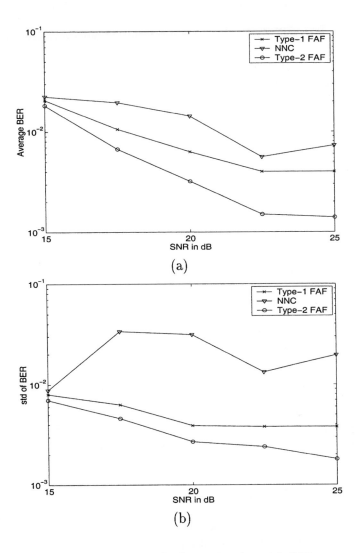

Figure 14-5: Performance of type-1 FAF, NNC, and type-2 FAF versus SNR when $\beta = 0.1$ and the number of training prototypes is 121. (a) average BER, and (b) standard deviation (std) of BER for 100 Monte-Carlo realizations.

These observations suggest that a type-2 FAF, as just designed, looks very promising as a good transversal equalizer for time-varying non-linear channels. This is because a type-2 FAF allows uncertainties about the uncertain nature of the channel states to be modeled within the framework of type-2 fuzzy sets. As in the previous FL RBC application, these uncertainties can be accounted for by the FOUs of the rule antecedents. We also conjecture that even better performance could have been obtained had we modeled the measurements using type-2 fuzzy sets, as we did for our type-2 FL RBC.

14.6 Overcoming CCI and ISI for Digital Communication Channels

Cellular mobile communication systems rely on an intelligent allocation and re-use of channels throughout a coverage region. The reuse of channels is realized by frequency reuse. Frequency reuse implies that in a given coverage area there are several cells that use the same frequencies. These cells are called co-channel cells, and the interference between signals from these cells is called CCI [Rappaport (1996)].[9]

With the limitation of available signal spectrum, one way to incorporate more subscribers is to increase frequency reuse by reducing cell size, which introduces more CCI. For cellular communication systems, the radio link is usually limited by interference rather than noise, and therefore by CCI. The effect of CCI on the radio link performance depends on the ability of the radio receiver to reject it [Stuber (1998)].

Chen and Mulgrew (1992) used an adaptive radial basis function network to overcome CCI; Xiang et al. (1994) used polynomial perceptrons to equalize fading channels and to suppress CCI; Lo et al. (1995) used an adaptive fractionally spaced decision feedback equalizer (DFE), which exploits the correlation of the cyclo-stationary interference, to eliminate CCI in a fading channel environment; Chen et al. (1996) used a Bayesian DFE to overcome CCI; Hussain et al. (1997) used a functional-link neural network-based DFE to overcome CCI; and Patra and Mulgrew (1998) used a type-1 FAF to eliminate CCI.

All statistical signal processing-based approaches to overcoming CCI are based on an assumed probability model for the additive noise, whereas a FAF approach is model free. In this section, we assume that the co-channel models are time-varying and that the number of co-channels is larger than 1 and we design type-1 and type-2 FAFs to simultaneously overcome ISI and CCI. Our approach is to assume that CCI can be interpreted as an uncertain disturbance that

---

[9]The material in this section is taken from Liang and Mendel (2000g).

is added to the channel states. Theoretical analysis shows that this interpretation again matches the reason of existence for a type-2 FAF—namely, to handle unknown uncertainties—and motivates us to use a type-2 FAF to overcome ISI and CCI.

14.6.1 Communication system with ISI and CCI

The discrete-time model of a communication system that is subject to CCI, ISI, and AGN is shown in Figure 14-6, where (as in Section 14.5) $s(k)$ is the symbol to be transmitted, $e(k)$ is the AGN, the CCI comes from the N co-channels, the channel order is n (i.e. there are $n + 1$ taps), and time-varying tap coefficients are $a_i(k)$ ($i = 0, 1, \ldots, n$). The measured channel output $r(k)$ can be represented as

$$r(k) = \hat{r}(k) + u(k) + e(k) = \sum_{i=0}^{n} a_i(k)s(k-i) + u(k) + e(k) \qquad (14\text{-}46)$$

As in Section 14.5, we assume that $s(k)$ is binary, either +1 or −1 with equal probability. The goal in overcoming CCI and ISI is to recover the input sequence $s(k)$ ($k = 1, 2, \ldots$) based on a sequence of $r(k)$ values without knowing or estimating the channel coefficients and without knowing or estimating the co-channels. This is accomplished using an equalizer whose output can be expressed as in (14-27).

As in Section 14.5.1, assuming the number of taps of the equalizer is p, we define the channel state as in (14-31). The discussions in Section 14.5.1, prior to Example 14-1, all apply to the present case of ISI and CCI. What is different is that here we now have CCI and ISI, whereas in Section 14.5.1 we only had ISI.

Assume the order of the jth co-channel is n_j (i.e. the jth co-channel has $n_j + 1$ taps), and the time-varying co-channel coefficients are $b_{ij}(k)$; then the CCI, $u(k)$, can be expressed as

$$u(k) = \sum_{j=1}^{N} u_j(k) = \sum_{j=1}^{N} \sum_{i=0}^{n_j} b_{ij}(k)s_j(k-i) \qquad (14\text{-}47)$$

where the co-channel filter inputs s_j are also binary, but unlike the symbols $s(k)$, the s_j are always blind to the equalizer, even during training. As in (14-31), the co-channel states of the jth co-channel are

$$\mathbf{u}_j(k) \equiv \left[u_j(k), u_j(k-1), \ldots, u_j(k-p+1) \right]^T \qquad (14\text{-}48)$$

From (14-47) and (14-48), it is easy to see that there are 2^{n_j+p} of these states in the jth co-channel. The total co-channel state is (see Figure 14-6)

$$\mathbf{u}(k) \equiv [u(k), u(k-1), ..., u(k-p+1)]^T = \sum_{j=1}^{N} \mathbf{u}_j(k) \qquad (14\text{-}49)$$

where $\mathbf{u}_j(k)$ ($j = 1, 2, ..., N$) are independent; hence, the total number of co-channel states is

$$n_{co} = \prod_{j=1}^{N} 2^{n_j+p} = 2^{pN + \sum_{j=1}^{N} n_j} \qquad (14\text{-}50)$$

When N is large, there is an enormous number of co-channel states. Because of this, it is not possible to perform an exact analysis of them.

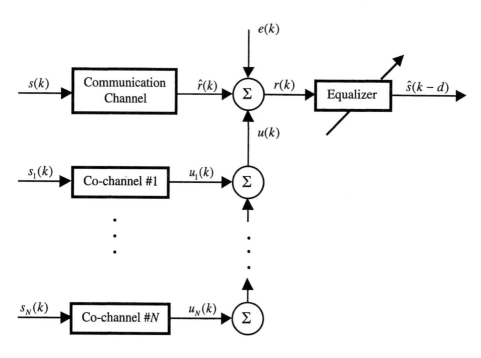

Figure 14-6: Discrete-time model of a communication system subject to CCI, ISI, and AGN.

Example 14-3: Suppose that there are six co-channels (i.e. $N = 6$) and each co-channel has three taps (i.e. $n_j = 2$) and the equalizer has two taps (i.e. $p = 2$). Then, there will be $2^{24} = 16,777,216$ co-channel states, and of course, in this case it is not possible to view these states as we did in Section 14.5 (e.g. Figure 14-3). ■

Analogous to (14-42), when both ISI and CCI are present, the discriminant function of the Bayesian equalizer is

$$f(\mathbf{r}(k)) = \sum_{i=1}^{n_s} \sum_{m=0}^{n_{co}} \prod_{l=0}^{p-1} w_i \exp\left\{-\tfrac{1}{2}\frac{\left[r(k-l) - \hat{r}_i(k-l) + u^m(k-l)\right]^2}{\sigma_e^2 + \sigma_u^2}\right\} \quad (14\text{-}51)$$

where $u^m(k-l)$ is the lth element of the mth co-channel state and $n_s = 2^{n+p}$. Before simplifying this expression, we pause to introduce three measures that are associated with the present problem.

These measures are the traditional SNR, the signal-to-interference ratio (SIR), and the signal-to-interference noise ratio (SINR), where:

$$SNR = 10\log_{10}\left(\sigma_{\hat{r}}^2/\sigma_e^2\right) \quad (14\text{-}52)$$

$$SIR = 10\log_{10}\left(\sigma_{\hat{r}}^2/\sigma_u^2\right) \quad (14\text{-}53)$$

$$SINR = 10\log_{10}\left[\sigma_{\hat{r}}^2/\left(\sigma_e^2 + \sigma_u^2\right)\right] \quad (14\text{-}54)$$

in which σ_e and σ_u denote the standard deviations of the AGN $e(k)$ and the CCI $u(k)$, respectively.

Returning to (14-51), we note that n_{co} is a very large number when $N \gg 1$. To simplify things, we assume that SIR is high, in which case the term $-\hat{r}_i(k-l) + u^m(k-l)$ in (14-51) is an uncertain value that is dominated by $-\hat{r}_i(k-l)$; hence, when SIR is high, (14-51) can be approximated by

$$f(\mathbf{r}(k)) \approx \sum_{i=1}^{n_s} \prod_{l=0}^{p-1} w_i \exp\left\{-\tfrac{1}{2}\frac{\left[r(k-l) - \hat{r}_i(k-l)\right]^2}{\sigma_e^2 + \sigma_u^2}\right\} \quad (14\text{-}55)$$

where $\hat{r}_i(k-l)$ is uncertain. This point of view motivates us to use a type-2 FAF for overcoming CCI and ISI, because a type-2 FAF can handle uncertainties. Additionally, the channel states are time-varying, which is another reason to treat $\hat{r}_i(k-l)$ as an uncertain value. From (14-55), we see that a Gaussian membership function with an uncertain mean, as in (10-20), is an appropriate choice for the membership functions in a type-2 FAF for overcoming CCI and ISI.

Example 14-4: Here, as in Example 14-2, our channel is the time-varying one in (14-43), which we repeat here for the convenience of the reader:

$$r(k) = a_1(k)s(k) + a_2(k)s(k-1) - 0.9\left[a_1(k)s(k) + a_2(k)s(k-1)\right]^3 + e(k) \qquad (14\text{-}56)$$

where a_1 and a_2 are time-varying coefficients, centered about 1 and 0.5, respectively, each simulated as explained in Example 14-2.

We also assumed that the communication system has five co-channels (i.e. $N = 5$), whose z-transform transfer functions are:[10]

$$H_{co1}(z) = \lambda\left[b_{11}(k) + b_{12}(k)z^{-1}\right] \qquad (14\text{-}57)$$

$$H_{co2}(z) = \lambda\left[b_{21}(k) + b_{22}(k)z^{-1} + b_{23}(k)z^{-2}\right] \qquad (14\text{-}58)$$

$$H_{co3}(z) = \lambda\left[b_{31}(k) + b_{32}(k)z^{-1} - b_{33}(k)z^{-2}\right] \qquad (14\text{-}59)$$

$$H_{co4}(z) = \lambda\left[b_{41}(k) + b_{42}(k)z^{-1} + b_{43}(k)z^{-2}\right] \qquad (14\text{-}60)$$

$$H_{co5}(z) = \lambda\left[b_{51}(k) + b_{52}(k)z^{-1} + b_{53}(k)z^{-2}\right] \qquad (14\text{-}61)$$

In our simulations, we assumed that the co-channel coefficients are also time-varying about the following nominal values: $b_{11}(k) = 1$, $b_{12}(k) = 0.2$; $b_{21}(k) = 0.4084$, $b_{22}(k) = 0.8164$, $b_{23}(k) = 0.4084$; $b_{31}(k) = 0.407$, $b_{32}(k) = 0.815$, $b_{33}(k) = 0.407$; $b_{41}(k) = 0.3482$, $b_{42}(k) = 0.8704$, $b_{43}(k) = 0.3482$; and $b_{51}(k) = 0.5$, $b_{52}(k) = 0.81$, $b_{53}(k) = 0.31$. All of these coefficients were simulated in the same way as the channel coefficients $a_1(k)$ and $a_2(k)$ were. The standard deviation of the white Gaussian noise that was used to generate the co-channel coefficients was fixed at 0.1, and λ was determined by the SIR. ∎

---

[10]Strictly speaking, a transfer function cannot have time-varying functions in it. Our use of time-varying coefficients in these transfer functions merely denotes the fact that the coefficients change from time to time.

14.6.2 Designing the FAFs

Recall that in Section 14.5.3, FAFs were designed that had as many rules as channel states. It is tempting to argue that in the case of CCI and ISI we should design FAFs that have as many rules as either $n_s + n_{co}$ or $n_s \times n_{co}$. This is not possible, because we never can know n_{co} ahead of time, since it changes from one environment to another; hence, as in Section 14.5.3, we shall design FAFs that will have as many rules as channel states. It is the tuning of the FAF's parameters, which in the present case will be based on training data that contain CCI, that will permit these FAFs to overcome CCI and ISI. Hence, this section is very similar to Section 14.5.3.

We illustrate the designs of singleton type-1 and singleton type-2 FAFs for the non-linear time-varying channel in (14-56). As just explained, each FAF has eight rules, one per channel state. The rules in a *singleton type-1 FAF* have the following structure ($l = 1, ..., 8$):

$$R^l: \text{IF } r(k) \text{ is } F_1^l \text{ and } r(k-1) \text{ is } F_2^l, \text{ THEN } y^l = w_l \qquad (14\text{-}62)$$

whereas they have the following structure in a *singleton type-2 FAF* ($l = 1, ...,$ 8):

$$R^l: \text{IF } r(k) \text{ is } \tilde{F}_1^l \text{ and } r(k-1) \text{ is } \tilde{F}_2^l, \text{ THEN } y^l = w_l \qquad (14\text{-}63)$$

In these rules, w_l is a crisp value of $+1$ or -1, as determined by (14-39). For the type-1 rules we used Gaussian membership functions for F_1^l and F_2^l; and, for the type-2 rules, we used the Gaussian primary membership functions in (10-20) for $\tilde{F}_1^l$ and $\tilde{F}_2^l$, where $\sigma_k^{l^2} \equiv \sigma_e^2 + \sigma_u^2$.

As in Section 14.5.3, because of the isomorphism between equalization and classification, the computational formulas for type-1 and type-2 FAFs are easily obtained from Sections 14.4.6 and 14.4.7, respectively.

As in Section 14.5.3, the mean-value parameters of all membership functions were estimated using a clustering procedure [Chen et al. (1993a)] that is applied to some training data, because such a procedure is computationally simple. To complete the specification of the membership functions, a value was also needed for $\sigma_e^2 + \sigma_u^2$. Let σ_i^l denote the standard deviation of the ith cluster for the lth rule, where $i = 1, .., p$ and $l = 1, ..., 2^{n+p}$. In our case, $n = 1$ and $p = 2$. We chose $\sqrt{\sigma_e^2 + \sigma_u^2}$ as the average of standard deviations of all clusters, i.e.

$$\sqrt{\sigma_e^2 + \sigma_u^2} \equiv \frac{1}{p2^{n+p}} \sum_{l=1}^{2^{n+p}} \sum_{i=1}^{p} \sigma_i^l \qquad (14\text{-}64)$$

14.6.3 Simulations and conclusions

Here we compare singleton type-1 and singleton type-2 FAFs and a K-NNC [Savazzi et al. (1998)] for overcoming CCI and ISI in the time-varying and non-linear channel (14-56) and the co-channels (14-57)–(14-61). The former FAF is identical to the radial basis function network in [Chen et al. (1993a)]. In our simulations, we chose the number of taps of the equalizer, p, equal to the number of taps of the channel, $n+1$, where $n=1$; i.e. $p=n+1=2$. The number of rules equaled the number of clusters; i.e. $2^{p+n}=8$. As in Section 14.5.4, we used a sequence $s(k)$ of length 1000 for our experiments, and the first 121 symbols were used for training (i.e., clustering) and the remaining 879 were used for testing. The training sequence established the parameters of the antecedent membership functions, as described in Section 14.6.2. After training, the parameters of the type-1 and type-2 FAFs were fixed and then testing was performed. In our simulations, we fixed $SNR = 20\text{dB}$.

In our first experiment, we fixed SIR at 20dB and ran simulations for six different values of noise level β, ranging from $\beta = 0.04$ to $\beta = 0.24$ (at equal increments of 0.04), and we set $d=0$. We performed 100 Monte-Carlo simulations for each value of β, where in each realization the channel coefficients, CCI, and AGN were uncertain. The mean value of the BER for the 100 Monte-Carlo realizations is plotted in Figure 14-7 (a).

In a second experiment, we fixed $\beta = 0.1$ and ran simulations for six different SIR values, ranging from $SIR = 15\text{dB}$ to $SIR = 25\text{dB}$ (at equal increments of 5dB), and we again set $d=0$. We performed 100 Monte-Carlo simulations for each value of SIR, where in each realization the channel coefficients, CCI, and AGN were uncertain. The mean value of the BER for the 100 Monte-Carlo realizations is plotted in Figure 14-7 (b).

To show the robustness of the equalizer in overcoming CCI and ISI, we introduced another co-channel, $H'_{co}(z)$, during the testing period, beginning at time index $k = 500$, and remaining through $k = 1000$, where

$$H'_{co}(z) = \alpha\lambda\left(0.33 - 0.4z^{-1} + 0.5z^{-2} + 0.69z^{-3}\right) \qquad (14\text{-}65)$$

The value of λ is the same as used in (14-57)–(14-61). Changing α changes the CCI strength in $H'_{co}(z)$. In this experiment, we fixed $SNR = 20\text{dB}$ and $SIR = 20\text{dB}$, and ran simulations for six different values of α, ranging from

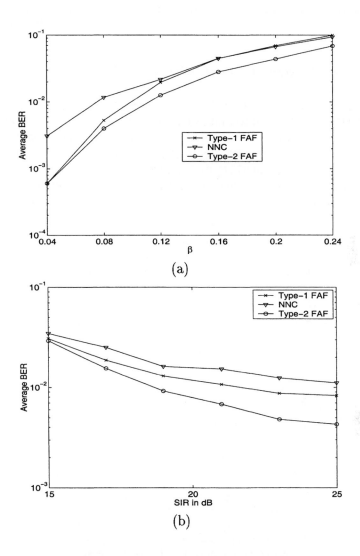

Figure 14-7: Average BER of type-1 FAF, NNC, and type-2 FAF for 100 Monte-Carlo realizations when $SNR = 20$dB and the number of training prototypes is 121. (a) average BER versus β when $SIR = 20$dB, and (b) average BER versus SIR when $\beta = 0.1$.

$\alpha = 0.5$ to $\alpha = 3$ at equal increments of 0.5. We performed 100 Monte-Carlo simulations for each value of α. In Figure 14-8 we plot the average BER for the 100 Monte-Carlo realizations. Observe, from this figure, that all three equalizers are very robust, but that the type-2 FAF maintains better performance than both the type-1 FAF and NNC over the entire range of α values.

From these experiments, we conclude that the type-2 FAF performs better than the type-1 FAF and NNC. This suggests that a type-2 FAF, as just designed, looks very promising as a good transversal equalizer for overcoming CCI and ISI in time-varying non-linear channels. This is because a type-2 FAF allows uncertainties about the nature of the channel states and CCI to be modeled within the framework of type-2 fuzzy sets. As in the previous FL RBC application, these uncertainties can be accounted for by the FOUs of a rule's antecedents. We also conjecture that even better performance could have been obtained had we modeled the measurements using type-2 fuzzy sets, as we did for our type-2 FL RBC.

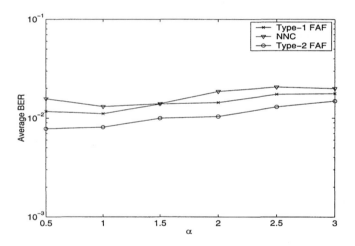

Figure 14-8: Average BER versus α [see (14-65)] for type-1 FAF, NNC, and type-2 FAF using 100 Monte-Carlo realizations when $SNR = 20$dB and $SIR = 20$dB, and the number of training prototypes is 121. The CCI in (14-65) was introduced at time-index 500.

14.7 CONNECTION ADMISSION CONTROL FOR ATM NETWORKS

ATM is the most promising technology for supporting broadband multimedia communication services. The advantages of ATM networks are the flexibility to accommodate a diverse mixture of media traffic that possess different media traffic characteristics and quality of service (QoS) requirements. The ATM technique provides an attractive solution to the problem of integrating different types of services, with widely different bit rates, through common interfaces and switching fabrics. It is a compromise between packet-switching and circuit-switching techniques.[11]

To ensure the QoS of each service and to achieve a high network utilization, the ATM network must provide a set of media traffic control functions. The wide range of service characteristics, such as bit rates, burstiness factors, cell delay constraints (latency), cell-loss tolerance (accuracy), and priority, combined with the need for adaptive and sometimes real-time services, makes the traditional use of control methods very difficult.

Although ATM networks can support a wide variety of transmission rates and provide transmission efficiency by asynchronous multiplexing, a cell might be lost in ATM switches if cells are excessively fed into the networks. To avoid this situation, terminals are required to declare their transmission rates as traffic parameters; e.g. peak cell rate and sustainable cell rate, in advance of transmission. According to these declarations of transmission rates, ATM switches judge whether the required QoS can be achieved. If the QoS can be met without deteriorating the existing cells, the cell is admitted; otherwise, it is rejected. This traffic control function for an ATM system, call *Connection Admission Control* (CAC), decides whether to accept or reject a call based on the available capacity required for support of its QoS. Consequently, an estimate of the QoS is required, one that is based on monitoring traffic patterns and buffer status; this is important in determining the cell loss probability, cell delay, and delay variations.

Taking into consideration factors like the source traffic descriptor, the amount of current network congestion along the path of the incoming call, and QoS requirements of the new and pre-existing calls is a daunting task for any mathematical model. In this section we focus on the type of service class, where by *service* we mean a real-time service, such as voice and video, or a non-real-time service, such as text data. Therefore, we only study two descriptors: *total average input rate of real-time voice and video traffic* and *total average input rate of non-real-time data traffic*.

---

[11]The material in this section is taken from Liang et al. (2000).

Chong and Li (1997) realized CAC using a probabilistic burstiness curve in which each session connection is defined by the buffer space and transmission bandwidth. Zhang et al. (1997) presented a CAC method based on a Chernoff bound that uses a simple novel traffic model that is specified by only a few parameters. Evans and Everitt (1999) focused on CDMA cellular networks and proposed an effective bandwidth-based CAC method.

The decision-making nature of CAC has attracted many researchers to apply FLSs and neural networks to it; e.g. [Delago and Gonzalez (1993)], [Douligeris and Develekos (1997)], [Habib (1996)], [Habib et al. (1997)], [Yoshinari et al. (1993)], and [Wagenknecht and Hartmann (1988)]. Chang et al. (1997, 1998) proposed a power-spectrum-based neural fuzzy CAC for ATM networks. They constructed a decision hyperplane for the CAC using the parameters of the power spectrum. They devised rules that used the following type-1 fuzzy antecedent sets: *light load*, *medium load*, and *heavy load*. Their rules also used the following type-1 consequent sets: *straightly reject*, *weakly reject*, *weakly accept*, and *straightly accept*. All of their rules were based on knowledge collected just from one expert. However, as we argued in Chapter 2, experts have diverse opinions about the meanings of linguistic labels and they often provide different consequents for the same antecedents, so fuzzy rules based on just one expert show partiality (i.e. they ignore the uncertainties associated with collecting rules from a group of experts).

Uehara and Hirota (1997) studied the possibility distribution of cell loss as a function of the number of cells per class by means of a fuzzy inference scheme that is based on the observed data of cell loss ratio (CLR), and obtained the upper bound for the CLR. They applied fuzzy inference to estimate the possibility distribution of CLR, which they then used for admission control decisions. Mehrvar and Le-Ngoc (1997) also proposed a CAC scheme that uses a type-1 FLS to estimate the level of traffic burstiness; they estimated burst parameters and then used them for CAC in an adaptive environment.

Comparing existing FLS-based CAC approaches and other approaches, the main difference between them is that FLSs can handle expert knowledge and numerical data in a unified framework and they require less computing complexity.

In this section, we treat CAC as a *group decision-making problem*, where *group* means a group of experts. Delgado et al. (1998) introduced a fusion operator that can combine numerical and linguistic information with group decision making problems. Marimin et al. (1998) proposed three ways to improve pair-wise group decision making based on fuzzy preference relations: they observed the disadvantages to using type-1 fuzzy sets and proposed to extend them to type-2 fuzzy sets as part of their future research directions. In addition, Tanaka and Hosaka (1993) observed the difficulties of obtaining appropriate membership functions for efficient communication network control, which further suggests that type-2 membership functions will be a better way to represent the uncertainty present in a network.

In this section we develop a survey-based CAC method using type-2 FLSs, because a type-2 FLS provides a new and powerful framework to represent and handle rule uncertainties. For example, in a type-1 FLS-based CAC method, a typical rule might be:

> IF the total average input rate of real-time voice and video traffic is *a moderate amount*, and the total average input rate of the non-real-time data traffic is *some*, THEN the confidence of accepting the call is *a large amount*.

In this case, a type-2 FLS can effectively provide a natural mechanism to represent the vagueness inherent in the italicized linguistic labels.

14.7.1 Survey-based CAC using a type-2 FLS: Overview

In this section we apply type-2 FLSs to CAC for ATM networks, in which rules are based on a survey regarding the CAC as determined by the input traffic. We chose a type-2 FLS for CAC to give ATM network designers more room to accommodate their own thoughts and preferences, and to let their decisions be more flexible, since requirements about CLR and bandwidth (BW) utilization cannot be mutually satisfied. Lower CLR and higher BW utilization are the desired performance of a CAC; but for a fixed BW allocation scheme, lower CLR means less BW utilization, and higher BW utilization means a higher CLR. A type-1 FLS provides a single decision boundary for CAC, which means a compromise/decision must be made with respect to CLR and BW utilization. On the other hand, as we demonstrate soon, a type-2 FLS provides a region bounded by two decision boundaries, so designers are free to choose a decision boundary to meet their preferences (e.g. higher BW utilization).

Designing a survey-based type-2 FLS includes collecting the knowledge, setting the rules, choosing and defining antecedent and consequent membership functions (including their FOUs), choosing a specific kind of type-reduction, and extracting decision boundaries. Except for extracting decision boundaries, we have explained all of the other items either in Sections 4.3, 5.11, or 10.12. This is, therefore, an appropriate time for the reader to review those sections.

14.7.2 Extracting the knowledge for CAC

As mentioned earlier, in ATM networks input traffic is often classified into two classes: class 1 is real-time voice and video traffic, and class 2 is non-real-time data traffic. Based on this, we therefore used two antecedents for our FLS-based CAC—the total average input rate of real-time voice and video traffic, and the total average rate of non-real-time data traffic.

The linguistic variables used to represent the input rate of media traffic were divided into five levels using the terms and interval statistics that are summarized in Table 2-3: *none to very little* (NVL), *some* (S), *a moderate amount* (MOA), *a large amount* (LA), and *a maximum amount* (MAA). The consequent—the confidence of accepting the call—was also divided into these same five levels.

Rule consequents were obtained by surveying a group of 30 USC Electrical Engineering Ph.D. students, who had taken a course entitled *Broadband Network Architecture*. They played the role of a group of experts. These experts were surveyed using 25 questions, such as:

> IF the total average input rate of real-time voice and video traffic is *a moderate amount*, and the total average input rate of the non-real-time data traffic is *some*, THEN the confidence of accepting the call is _____ .

They were requested to choose a consequent from one of the five linguistic variables. Of course, different experts gave different answers to the questions in the survey.

This same group of experts also established the data that are summarized in Table 2-3, so we were able to capture their uncertainties about the words used in the survey. Table 14-3 summarizes the results obtained for the 25-question survey. The last two columns of Table 14-3 are the weighted-average of the responses, given by (5-60) and (10-97), respectively.

14.7.3 Choosing membership functions for the linguistic labels

FOUs and membership functions for the five linguistic labels were chosen exactly as described in Section 10.12. They are depicted in Figure 10-14 (a) for the *fraction of uncertainty* $\rho = 0.5$, which is what we used in this section.

14.7.4 Survey processing

To see the benefits of a type-2 FLS, we also created the type-1 FLS that is associated with the data in Table 14-3. Our approach for the type-1 FLS is the one that is described in Section 5.11.1 in which the histograms of rule-consequents were averaged to provide an average consequent value for each rule.

Table 14-3: Histogram of survey responses for CAC survey. Entries under "Consequent" denote the number of respondents out of 30 that chose the consequent*.

Rule No. (l)	None to Very Little	Some	A Moderate Amount	A Large Amount	A Maximum Amount	c_{avg}^{l}	C_{avg}^{l}
				Consequent			
1	0	1	0	0	29	8.9331	[8.7411, 9.1224]
2	0	1	2	5	22	8.4066	[8.2010, 8.6101]
3	0	0	1	6	23	8.6591	[8.4622, 8.8539]
4	0	0	5	15	10	7.6572	[7.4346, 7.8790]
5	0	1	13	10	6	6.6616	[6.4112, 6.9120]
6	0	1	6	13	10	7.4558	[7.2258, 7.6850]
7	0	1	11	10	8	6.9324	[6.6889, 7.1755]
8	0	2	14	12	2	6.2556	[5.9926, 6.5190]
9	0	4	11	15	0	6.1715	[5.9022, 6.4415]
10	1	9	11	9	0	5.3726	[5.0784, 5.6680]
11	0	0	14	12	4	6.5923	[6.3422, 6.8425]
12	0	1	12	15	2	6.5412	[6.2877, 6.7950]
13	0	5	12	13	0	5.9701	[5.6934, 6.2475]
14	2	7	13	8	0	5.2258	[4.9383, 5.5143]
15	5	18	7	0	0	3.8033	[3.4748, 4.1335]
16	0	9	9	12	0	5.7539	[5.4632, 6.0456]
17	3	11	6	10	0	5.1336	[4.8417, 5.4267]
18	2	8	15	5	0	4.9401	[4.6432, 5.2383]
19	8	13	7	3	0	4.0030	[3.6951, 4.3122]
20	8	19	3	0	0	3.3844	[3.0620, 3.7086]
21	1	15	9	5	0	4.8379	[4.5172, 5.1601]
22	6	12	7	5	0	4.2936	[3.9968, 4.5918]
23	8	18	4	0	0	3.4174	[3.0979, 3.7386]
24	12	16	2	0	0	2.9688	[2.6672, 3.2720]
25	26	3	1	0	0	1.5967	[1.3756, 1.8186]

*See Table 10-4 for the mapping of Rule No. (l) into a rule's two antecedent labels.

Doing this leads to rules that have the following form:

R^l: IF the total average input rate of real-time voice and video traffic (x_1) is F_1^l and the total average input rate of the non-real-time data traffic (x_2) is F_2^l, THEN the confidence of accepting a call (y) is c_{avg}^l

In this rule c_{avg}^l is given by (5-60), and its value for each of the 25 rules is listed in Table 14-3. The resulting type-1 FLS for CAC is depicted in Figure 14-9. It is computed using (5-63) where c_{avg}^l is given in Table 14-3.

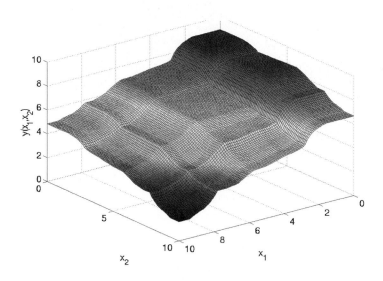

Figure 14-9: The type-1 FLS for CAC. The confidence of accepting the call, $y(x_1, x_2)$, versus x_1 (the total average input rate of real-time voice and video traffic) and x_2 (the total average input rate of the non-real-time data traffic).

Our approach for the type-2 FLS is the one that is described in Section 10.12 in which the histograms of rule-consequents are averaged (this now requires determining the average of type-1 fuzzy sets) to provide an average consequent value for each rule. Doing this leads to rules that have the following form:

R^l : IF the total average input rate of real-time voice and video traffic (x_1) is $\tilde{F}_1^l$ and the total average input rate of the non-real-time data traffic (x_2) is $\tilde{F}_2^l$, THEN the confidence of accepting a call (y) is C_{avg}^l

In this rule C_{avg}^l is given by (10-97), and its value for each of the 25 rules is also listed in Table 14-3. The resulting type-2 FLS for CAC is depicted in Figure 14-10. It is computed using (10-98) where C_{avg}^l is given in Table 14-3.

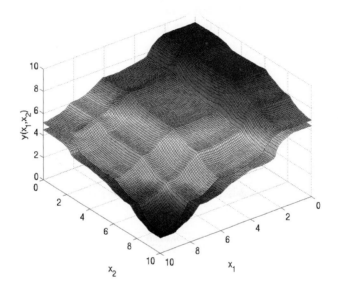

Figure 14-10: The type-2 FLS for CAC. The confidence of accepting the call, $Y(x_1,x_2)$, versus x_1 (the total average input rate of real-time voice and video traffic) and x_2 (the total average input rate of the non-real-time data traffic).

14.7.5 CAC decision boundaries and conclusions

CAC is a binary decision problem—accept or reject—so:

$$\text{the } \textit{confidence of accepting the call} \\ + \text{the } \textit{confidence of rejecting the call} = 10 \tag{14-66}$$

because our two antecedents, as well as the consequent, are on a scale of 0–10. A call will be accepted if the *confidence of accepting the call* > 5. It is then very straightforward to obtain the decision boundary as the *confidence of accepting the call* = 5.

For the type-1 FLS, the decision boundary is $y(x_1, x_2) = 5$ and is plotted in Figure 14-11 as the solid curve. It was obtained from the intersection of $y(x_1, x_2) = 5$ with the three-dimensional surface in Figure 14-9. When a call occurs with input rate of traffic (x_1, x_2) below the decision boundary, then it will be accepted. Similarly, if it occurs above the decision boundary, it will be rejected. As we see, the decision boundary that is generated from a type-1 FLS is a hard-threshold.

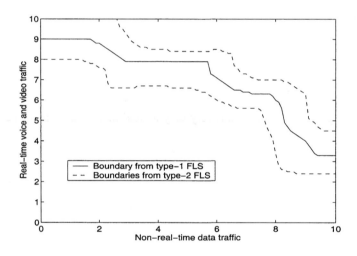

Figure 14-11: The decision boundary generated by the type-1 FLS and the decision boundaries generated by the type-2 FLS.

The decision boundaries for the lower and upper hyper-surfaces for the type-2 FLS output can be represented as $y_l(x_1, x_2) = 5$ and $y_u(x_1, x_2) = 5$, respectively. They are plotted in Figure 14-11 using dashed lines, and were obtained from the intersections of $Y(x_1, x_2) = 5$ with the two three-dimensional surfaces in Figure 14-10. If a designer wishes to increase the BW utilization, he or she can choose the upper decision boundary. In such a case, when a call occurs with input rate of traffic (x_1, x_2) below the upper decision boundary, it will be accepted. On the other hand, if the designer wishes to decrease the CLR, he or she can choose the lower decision boundary. If the designer wishes to achieve a compromise in performance between BW utilization and CLR, he or she can choose any decision boundary between the upper and lower decision boundaries. We see, therefore, that a type-2 FLS provides a soft decision boundary that depends on the preference of the designer; it can be any decision boundary between the lower and upper decision boundaries.

The lower and upper decision boundaries shown in Figure 14-11 are for the FOUs in Figure 10-14 (a) for which the *fraction of uncertainty* $\rho = 0.5$. By varying ρ, we could get families of intervals, each labeled with a different value of ρ. A designer could then make a choice by "thinking" in terms of a level of uncertainty. Finally, note that when $\rho = 0$ the type-2 FLS reduces to the type-1 FLS.

In conclusion, we see that the type-2 FLS CAC method has the following features:

- It combines the input of real-time voice and video traffic and non-real-time data traffic in making decisions about connection admission.

- It combines the experience of lots of experts, so that an acceptable decision boundary can be obtained (it is very easy to fold in the opinions of new experts as they become available, or to weight opinions of different experts differently, based on their presumed degree of expertise).

- It provides an interval decision, so that a soft-decision can be made based on a tradeoff between CLR and BW utilization.

14.8 POTENTIAL APPLICATION AREAS FOR A TYPE-2 FLS

It should be clear to the reader that the potential applicability for type-2 FLSs is enormous. At a very high level, rule-based type-2 FLSs should be applicable to every area where type-1 rule-based FLSs have been applied in which some uncertainty is present. Many of the techniques developed in Chapters 7–9 should also be applicable to non-rule-based applications of fuzzy sets, again if uncertainty is present.

In the rest of this concluding section, we focus on a small number of specific areas, in which there is no doubt that lots of uncertainties are present, and that the payoffs for accounting for them could be very substantial.

14.8.1 Perceptual computing

Zadeh (1996, 1999) coined the phrase "computing with words;" but, in Chapter 2, we argued that "words mean different things to different people," so that computing with words requires type-2 fuzzy sets. Our idea here is to let people interact with a FLS using a vocabulary of words, a vocabulary that can be much larger than the terms used to granulate the antecedents and consequent in the rules of a FLS. The final output of the type-2 FLS can then be converted back into the larger vocabulary of the consequent.

The granulated terms are *perceptions*, so that we can view a type-2 FLS that is activated by words and that provides words at its output as a *perceptual computer*. Figure 14-12 depicts a high-level architecture for a perceptual computer. The *encoder* transforms linguistic perceptions into measurements, $\mathbf{x}_m$, that activate a FLS, whose output(s), which are the numbers y_m, are transformed into output linguistic perceptions by the decoder. The encoder, $\mathbf{g}_{pm}(perceptions)$, is established for a specified vocabulary using surveys that lead to a FOU for each word or phrase in that vocabulary. The FLS is established by means of questionnaires that use a small subset of the terms in the vocabulary, where the subset must cover the domain of interest. The decoder can be based on the method given in Section 3.4 (*Returning to Linguistic Labels*).

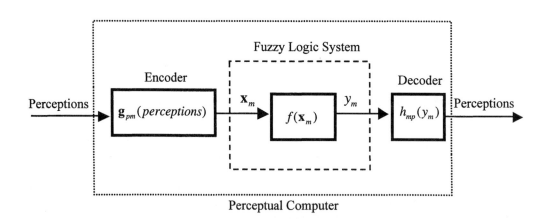

Figure 14-12: The architecture of a perceptual computer.

Perceptual computing has the potential to allow people to interact with devices using a natural language. These devices could be tuned to the people who are going to use them simply by people overriding consensus FOUs with their own FOUs.

14.8.2 FL control

As of the writing of this book, no journal articles have appeared on the applications of type-2 FLSs to FL control. Because FL control is today by far the most widely used application of FL, we can expect to see type-2 FL controllers in the not-so-distant future. They will account for system or input uncertainties in an analogous way that stochastic optimal control or robust control do, all within the framework of FL. By modeling uncertainties using appropriate FOUs, it should be possible to *design for robustness* using type-2 FL controllers.

14.8.3 Diagnostic medicine

FL methods are being used in medicine [Teodorescu (1999)], a field that abounds in uncertainties. Rule-based FLSs (fuzzy logic advisors) that account for all of the kinds of uncertainties that have been described in this book should be able to provide diagnosticians with the same kind of decision-making flexibilities that were explained for our CAC application in Section 14.7. Diagnostic medicine is an application where both linguistic and numerical rules will need to be developed. One of the challenges will be to design hierarchical type-2 FLSs that let low-level decisions be combined in a proper way for making a top-level decision. Perceptual computing could play a very important role, since patients describe things using words—perceptions.

14.8.4 Financial applications

Financial models contain many sources of uncertainties because financial markets change in an unknown manner with time. It will be very interesting to model such changes within the framework of type-2 fuzzy sets—determining appropriate FOUs—for important market indicators and variables, and then developing rule-based FLSs for forecasting and making decisions. This is another application where linguistic and numerical rules will need to be developed, and perceptual computing could play a very important role, since clients describe things using words (expectations, risk aversion) and sometimes numbers (returns).

14.8.5 Perceptual designs of multimedia systems

Multimedia systems that combine different kinds of media, such as video, audio, and data, are usually designed and then evaluated. One of the important ways to evaluate a multimedia product is in terms of human factors, many of which are qualitative (e.g., How does it sound? How does it look?). These factors involve people's *perceptions*, and such perceptions are usually quite uncertain. Designs are then refined until humans are satisfied with them and will purchase the products.

I conjecture that it should be possible to encode people's perceptions by establishing them prior to the design and then designing a product that trades off traditional quantitative performance measures, such as bandwidth, with perceptive measures. Doing this would lead to *perceptual designs* of multimedia systems. The overall design procedure may still be an iterative one, but human factors could be moved closer to the front-end of a design by this methodology of perceptual design.

Of course, this design methodology is not limited to multimedia systems, and could offer a new approach to designing any system that a human being uses. This is possible because of the new methodology of type-2 FLSs.

EXERCISES

14-1: Flowchart and program all of the formulas needed to implement the two type-1 FL RBCs described in Section 14-4.

14-2: (a) Determine the formulas for an interval type-1 non-singleton type-2 FL RBC. (b) Determine the formulas for an interval singleton type-2 FL RBC. (c) Flowchart and program all of the formulas needed to implement the three type-2 FL RBCs.

14-3: Flowchart and program all of the formulas needed to optimize the two type-1 FL RBCs described in Section 14-4.

14-4: Flowchart and program all of the formulas needed to optimize the three type-2 FL RBCs described in Section 14-4.

14-5: Show that (14-42) is identical to (14-11), when Gaussian membership functions are used for the rule-antecedents, singleton fuzzification is used, and the f^l are chosen as in (14-6).

14-6: Explain how the channel state clusters depicted in Figure 14-3 (d) were actually computed.

14-7: Using the isomorphism between equalization and classification, establish the computational formulas for type-1 and type-2 FAFs.

14-8: Derive (14-51).

14-9: Repeat the CAC survey, using a group of local experts, and obtain type-1 and type-2 decision surfaces for your results.

14-10: Describe a new potential application for type-2 FLSs.

Join, Meet, and Negation Operations for Non-Interval Type-2 Fuzzy Sets

A.1 INTRODUCTION

In Chapter 7 we focused our attention primarily on join and meet for interval type-2 sets. In this appendix[1] we provide more general results in the hope that others will be able to use them either for more sophisticated type-2 FLSs or in other applications of type-2 fuzzy sets. Results for join are quite general and are applicable to any kind of secondary membership functions. Results for meet are general for minimum t-norm, but are quite difficult to obtain for product t-norm. When the secondary membership functions are Gaussians, then it is possible to provide an approximation to the meet that preserves the Gaussian nature of the secondaries; i.e. the approximation is *reproducing*.

Recall, from Definition 3.2 and (3-6), that the secondary membership functions of type-2 fuzzy sets are type-1 fuzzy sets; therefore, to perform operations like union and intersection of type-2 fuzzy sets, we need to perform the join and meet operations in (7-17) and (7-20), respectively, that are in terms of these type-1 fuzzy sets. To simplify the notation in this appendix, we therefore present its results for type-1 fuzzy sets; e.g. F and G, having membership func-

---

[1] All of the results (theory and examples) in this appendix are taken from [Karnik and Mendel (1998b) or (2000a)].

tions $f(\theta)$ and $g(\theta)$, respectively. The join of F and G is $F \sqcup G$, and it has membership function $\mu_{F \sqcup G}(\theta)$. The meet of F and G is $F \sqcap G$, and it has membership function $\mu_{F \sqcap G}(\theta)$.

To connect this with join and meet for type-2 fuzzy sets $\tilde{A}$ and $\tilde{B}$ in (7-17) and (7-20), we focus on an arbitrary input x_0 and rename $\mu_{\tilde{A}}(x_0)$ as F, $\mu_{\tilde{B}}(x_0)$ as G, and drop the subscript x_0 on the membership functions $f_{x_0}(\theta)$ and $g_{x_0}(\theta)$. Doing this, we can apply the results given later to compute $\mu_{\tilde{A} \cup \tilde{B}}(x_0)$ and $\mu_{\tilde{A} \cap \tilde{B}}(x_0)$. Of course, this must be done for all values of $x_0 \in X$.

Results are stated here without proof. For the proofs, see [Karnik and Mendel, (1998b) or (2000b)].

A.2 JOIN UNDER MINIMUM OR PRODUCT T-NORMS

The join under minimum or product t-norms can be computed using results in the following:

Theorem A-1: *(a) Suppose that we have two convex, normal, type-1 real fuzzy sets F and G that are characterized by membership functions $f(\theta)$ and $g(\theta)$, respectively. Let v_0 and v_1 be real numbers such that $v_0 \le v_1$ and $f(v_0) = g(v_1) = 1$. Then the membership functions of the join of F and G using maximum t-conorm can be expressed as:*

$$\mu_{F \sqcup G}(\theta) = \begin{cases} f(\theta) \star g(\theta) & \theta < v_0 \\ g(\theta) & v_0 \le \theta \le v_1 \\ f(\theta) \vee g(\theta) & \theta > v_1 \end{cases} \tag{A-1}$$

where $\star$ denotes the t-norm operation used, either minimum or product, and $\vee$ denotes maximum.

(b) Suppose that we have n convex, normal, type-1 real fuzzy sets $F_1, \dots, F_n$ characterized by membership functions $f_1(\theta), \dots, f_n(\theta)$, respectively. Let $v_1, \dots, v_n$ be real numbers such that $v_1 \le v_2 \le \cdots \le v_n$ and $f(v_1) = \cdots = f(v_n) = 1$. Then the membership function of $\sqcup_{i=1}^{n} F_i$ using maximum t-conorm can be expressed as:

$$\mu_{\sqcup_{i=1}^{n} F_i}(\theta) = \begin{cases} T_{i=1}^{n} f_i(\theta) & \theta < v_1 \\ T_{i=k+1}^{n} f_i(\theta) & v_k \leq \theta \leq v_{k+1} \quad 1 \leq k \leq n-1 \\ \vee_{i=1}^{n} f_i(\theta) & \theta > v_n \end{cases} \qquad (A\text{-}2)$$

where T denotes the t-norm operation used, either minimum or product. ■

Note that: (a) the condition " $v_0 \leq v_1$ and $f(v_0) = g(v_1) = 1$" means that the maximum value of $f(\theta)$ occurs either to the left of or at the maximum value of $g(\theta)$; and (b) Dubois and Prade (1978) present the same result given in part (a) of this theorem, but just for the minimum t-norm.

Example A-1: Figure A-1 (b) shows the result of the join operation on the four Gaussian membership functions depicted in Figure A-1 (a) under product t-norm. Figure A-2 (b) shows comparable results for the four Gaussians membership functions depicted in Figure A-2 (a) under minimum t-norm. All results were obtained using (A-2). ■

A.3 MEET UNDER MINIMUM T-NORM

The meet under minimum t-norm can be computed using results in the following:

Theorem A-2: *(a) Suppose that we have two convex, normal, type-1 real fuzzy sets F and G characterized by membership functions $f(\theta)$ and $g(\theta)$, respectively. Let v_0 and v_1 be real numbers such that $v_0 \leq v_1$ and $f(v_0) = g(v_1)$ $= 1$. Then the membership functions of the meet of F and G using maximum t-conorm and minimum t-norm can be expressed as:*

$$\mu_{F \sqcap G}(\theta) = \begin{cases} f(\theta) \vee g(\theta) & \theta < v_0 \\ g(\theta) & v_0 \leq \theta \leq v_1 \\ f(\theta) \wedge g(\theta) & \theta > v_1 \end{cases} \qquad (A\text{-}3)$$

where $\vee$ denotes maximum and $\wedge$ denotes minimum.

(b) Suppose that we have n convex, normal, type-1 real fuzzy sets $F_1,...,F_n$ characterized by membership functions $f_1(\theta),...,f_n(\theta)$, respectively. Let $v_1,...,v_n$ be real numbers such that $v_1 \le v_2 \le \cdots \le v_n$ and $f(v_1) = \cdots = f(v_n) = 1$. Then the membership function of $\prod_{i=1}^n F_i$ using maximum t-conorm and minimum t-norm can be expressed as:

$$\mu_{\prod_{i=1}^n F_i}(\theta) = \begin{cases} \vee_{i=1}^n f_i(\theta) & \theta < v_1 \\ \wedge_{i=1}^k f_i(\theta) & v_k \le \theta \le v_{k+1} \quad 1 \le k \le n-1 \ \blacksquare \\ \wedge_{i=1}^n f_i(\theta) & \theta > v_n \end{cases} \qquad (A\text{-}4)$$

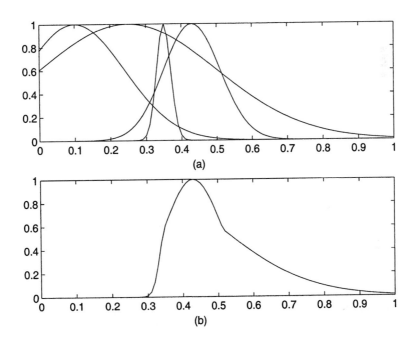

Figure A-1: Illustration of the join operation of (A-2) for (a) four Gaussian secondary membership functions, and (b) join under product t-norm.

Example A-2: Figure A-2 (c) shows the results of the meet operation on the four Gaussian membership functions depicted in Figure A-2 (a) under minimum t-norm. These results were obtained using (A-4). ∎

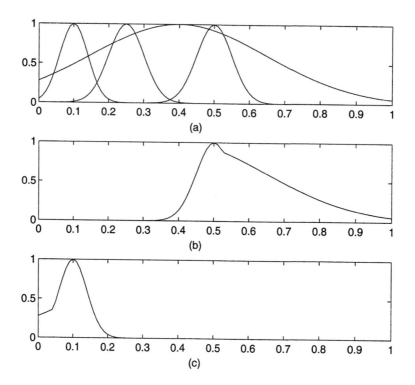

Figure A-2: Illustrations of the join and meet operations of (A-2) and (A-4), respectively, for (a) four Gaussian secondary membership functions, (b) join under minimum t-norm, and (c) meet under minimum t-norm.

Example A-3: Figures A-3 (b) and (c) show examples of union and intersection, under minimum t-norm, of the two Gaussian type-2 fuzzy sets depicted in Figure A-3 (a). In Figure A-3 (a), if we draw a vertical line at any x-value along the horizontal axis we get the secondary membership function of the two participating Gaussian type-2 sets. These secondary membership functions are themselves Gaussian type-1 fuzzy sets confined to the interval [0, 1]. To these type-1 sets we apply Theorems A-1 and A-2 and get the results for the join and meet depicted in Figure A-3 (b) and (c), respectively. Observe that the principal membership function of the result of an operation—union or intersection—can be obtained by performing that operation on the principal membership functions of the participating type-2 fuzzy sets. Consequently, if we replace all the type-2 fuzzy sets by type-1 fuzzy sets whose type-1 membership functions are the principal membership functions of the type-2 fuzzy sets, all our results remain valid. This demonstrates the fact that all of our type-2 operations collapse to the correct type-1 operations. ■

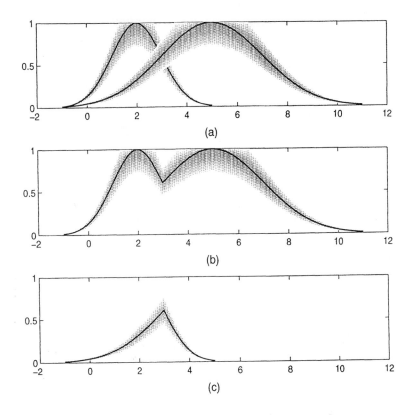

Figure A-3: Union and intersection of Gaussian type-2 fuzzy sets. (a) Participating sets, (b) union, and (c) intersection.

We can combine results from Theorem A-1 (just for minimum t-norm) and Theorem A-2 to obtain the following:

Corollary A-1: *(a) If $f(\theta)$ is the membership function of a convex, normal type-1 real fuzzy set F, and if G is another type-1 set with membership function $f(\theta - k)$, then under minimum t-norm $F \sqcup G = G$ and $F \sqcap G = F$.*

(b) If we have n convex, normal type-1 real fuzzy sets, $F_1, ..., F_n$, characterized by membership functions $f_1(\theta), ..., f_n(\theta)$, respectively, such that $f_i(\theta)$

$= f_1(\theta - k_i)$ *and* $0 = k_1 \le k_2 \le \cdots \le k_n$, *then under minimum t-norm* $\sqcup_{i=1}^{n} F_i = F_n$ *and* $\prod_{i=1}^{n} F_i = F_1$. ∎

Example A-4: Figure A-4 (a) depicts membership functions for type-1 fuzzy sets F and G, where the membership function of G is a right-shifted duplicate of the membership function of F. Using Corollary A-1, it follows that under minimum t-norm $F \sqcup G = G$ and $F \sqcap G = F$, as depicted in Figure A-4 (b) and (c), respectively. ∎

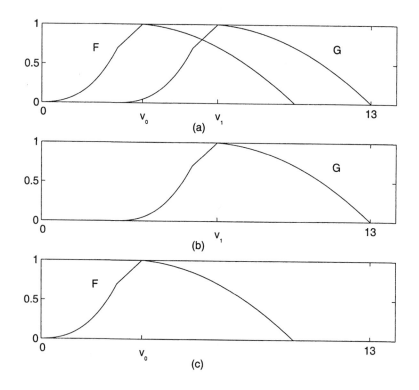

Figure A-4: Illustration of Corollary A-1. (a) Convex type-1 sets F and G, whose membership functions are shifted versions of each other; (b) $F \sqcup G = G$; and (c) $F \sqcap G = F$.

Example A-5: It can be shown [using Theorem A-1 (just for minimum t-norm) and Theorem A-2] that Corollary A-1 is also valid for two type-1 fuzzy sets whose *membership functions don't touch*; in that case, it is also true that $F \sqcup G = G$ and $F \sqcap G = F$.

In the case of membership functions that extend infinitely (e.g. Gaussians), if the two membership functions are far away from each other, then Corollary A-1 approximately holds true, i.e. $F \sqcup G \approx G$ and $F \sqcap G \approx F$. ∎

A.4 MEET UNDER PRODUCT T-NORM

The meet operation between two convex, normal, type-1 real fuzzy sets F and G, that are characterized by membership functions $f(\theta)$ and $g(\theta)$, respectively, under the product t-norm can be represented as [see (7-24)]

$$F \sqcap G = \int_{v \in J^v} \int_{w \in J^w} [f(v)g(w)] / (vw) \tag{A-5}$$

where $J^v \subseteq [0,1]$ and $J^w \subseteq [0,1]$. Observe that this equation involves the product of secondary grades $f(v)$ and $g(w)$ rather than a minimum or maximum operation between them; hence, the analysis of the meet operation under product t-norm is quite different than that of the join or meet operations previously described.

If θ ($\theta \in \mathcal{R}$) is an element of $F \sqcap G$, then the membership grade of θ can be found by finding all the pairs $\{v, w\}$ such that $v \in J^v$, $w \in J^w$, and $vw = \theta$; multiplying the secondary grades of v and w in each pair; and then finding the maximum of these products of secondary grades. The possible admissible $\{v, w\}$ pairs, whose product is θ, are $\{v, \theta / v\}$ ($v \in J^v, v \neq 0$) for $\theta \neq 0$, and $\{v, 0\}$ or $\{0, w\}$ ($v \in J^v$ and $w \in J^w$) for $\theta = 0$. We find the products of the secondary grades of v and w from each such pair and take the maximum of all these products as the membership grade of θ, i.e.

$$\mu_{F \sqcap G}(\theta) = \sup_{v \in J^v, v \neq 0} f(v)g(\theta / v) \qquad \theta \in \mathcal{R} \text{ and } \theta \neq 0 \tag{A-6a}$$

and when $\theta = 0$

$$\mu_{F \sqcap G}(0) = \left[\sup_{v \in J^v} f(v)g(0) \right] \vee \left[\sup_{w \in J^w} f(0)g(w) \right] \tag{A-6b}$$

Observe that

$$\sup_{v \in J^v} f(v)g(0) = g(0) \sup_{v \in J^v} f(v) = g(0) \times 1 = g(0) \tag{A-7}$$

and, similarly

$$\sup_{w \in J^w} f(0)g(w) = f(0) \tag{A-8}$$

In summary, for two convex, normal type-1 fuzzy sets F and G, *the meet under product t-norm can be expressed as*:

$$\mu_{F \sqcap G}(\theta) = \sup_{v \in J^v, v \neq 0} f(v)g(\theta / v) \quad \theta \neq 0 \tag{A-9a}$$

and when $\theta = 0$

$$\mu_{F \sqcap G}(0) = f(0) \vee g(0) \tag{A-9b}$$

Note that, if we substitute $\theta / v = w$ into (A-9a) we get a similar expression in terms of $f(\theta / w)g(w)$. Because the meet operation is commutative (see Table B-2), we get the same result whether we substitute $\theta / w = v$ or $\theta / v = w$.

As is apparent from (A-9), the meet operation under product t-norm is very much dependent on the functions $f(\theta)$ and $g(\theta)$, and does not easily generalize like the join and meet operations under minimum t-norm. Generally it is very difficult to obtain a closed form expression for the result of the meet operation under product t-norm.

Example A-6: Figure A-5 shows an example of the calculation of (A-9a). To determine the membership of a particular point θ in $F \sqcap G$, we find all the pairs $\{v, w\}$ such that $v \in J^v$ and $w \in J^w$ and $vw = \theta$, and multiply the secondary grades of each pair. The membership grade of θ is given by the supremum of the set of all these products. For example, if $\theta = 20$, all the pairs $\{v, w\}$ that give 20 as their product are v and $20 / v$ ($v \in J^v, v \neq 0$). So, the membership grade of 20 is given by the supremum of the set of all the products $f(v)g(20 / v)$ ($v \in J^v, v \neq 0$). Figure A-5 (c) shows how $f(v)g(20 / v)$ looks for F and G in Figure A-5 (a). Clearly, it is no easy matter to represent (A-9a) visually. ∎

Example A-7: One situation where the result of the product operation in (A-9) simplifies considerably is when either F or G is a type-1 fuzzy singleton. For example, assume that F is a type-1 fuzzy singleton, such that $f(v_0) = 1$ and $f(v) = 0$ for $v \neq v_0$. In this case, $f(v)g(\theta / v)$ is non-zero only at $v = v_0$, implying that in (A-9) $\mu_{F \sqcap G}(\theta) = g(\theta / v_0)$. Similarly, if G is a type-1 fuzzy singleton, such that $g(v_1) = 1$ and $g(w) = 0$ for $w \neq v_1$, $f(v)g(\theta / v)$ is non-zero only at $\theta / v = v_1$; i.e. only when $v = \theta / v_1$, implying that $\mu_{F \sqcap G}(\theta) = f(\theta / v_1)$. ∎

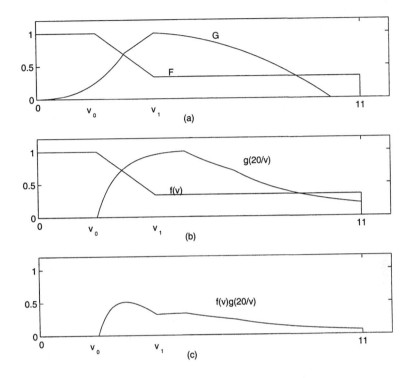

Figure A-5: An example showing how $f(v)g(20/v)$ looks for the membership functions $f(\theta)$ and $g(\theta)$ of the type-1 sets in (a); (b) $f(v)$, which is the same as in Figure (a) and $g(20/v)$; and (c) the product $f(v)g(20/v)$.

Example A-8: Here we focus on Gaussian type-2 fuzzy sets and present an *approximation* for the meet under product t-norm. Recall that the principal membership functions of a Gaussian type-2 fuzzy set can have any shape (e.g., triangular, trapezoidal, Gaussian); it is only the secondary membership functions that must be Gaussian. If, for example, there are n Gaussian type-1 fuzzy sets $F_1, ..., F_n$ with means $m_1, ..., m_n$ and standard deviations $\sigma_1, ..., \sigma_n$, respectively, then the meet under product t-norm of all n Gaussian type-1 fuzzy sets is approximately given by:

$$\mu_{F_1 \sqcap \cdots \sqcap F_n}(\theta) \approx \exp\left[-\frac{1}{2}\left(\frac{\theta - m_1 m_2 \cdots m_n}{\overline{\sigma}}\right)^2\right] \qquad (A\text{-}10)$$

where

$$\bar{\sigma} = \left[\sigma_1^2 \prod_{i:i\neq 1} m_i^2 + \sigma_2^2 \prod_{i:i\neq 2} m_i^2 + \cdots + \sigma_n^2 \prod_{i:i\neq n} m_i^2 \right]^{1/2} \quad i = 1, ..., n \qquad (A-11)$$

Upper and lower error bounds on this approximation are given in Appendix C.8 of [Karnik and Mendel (1998b)]. The approximation in (A-10) preserves the Gaussian natures of the underlying membership functions, regardless of n. This "reproducing" property is very beneficial in practical applications.

Figures A-6 (a)-(f) show some examples of this approximation. In general, if the Gaussians are contained within [0, 1], the results look quite good. In Figure A-6 (f) one of the Gaussians is centered at 1, so only half of this Gaussian (the part lying to the left of the mean) is contained in [0, 1]. Consequently, the result of the meet is much more non-Gaussian than the earlier cases; i.e. the difference between the Gaussian approximation and the actual curve is larger than in the other cases. ■

Results for triangular type-2 fuzzy sets, which are comparable to those just given for Gaussian type-2 sets, can be found in Appendix E of [Karnik (1998)]; i.e. Karnik has developed a reproducing approximation for the meet under product t-norm for symmetrical triangular type-2 fuzzy sets, where the functions that are reproduced remain triangles.

A.5 NEGATION

From the definition of the negation operation in (7-22), it follows that:

Theorem A-3: *If a type-1 fuzzy set F has a membership function* $f(\theta)$ $(\theta \in J^\theta)$, *then* $\neg F$ *has a membership function* $f(1-\theta)$ $(\theta \in J^\theta)$. ■

Example A-9: Figure A-7 shows an example of the complement of a Gaussian type-2 fuzzy set. The result in (b) was obtained by applying Theorem A-3 to the secondary membership functions in (a) for all $\theta \in [0, 5]$. Again, observe that the principal membership function of the result of the complement can be obtained by performing that operation on the principal membership function of the participating type-2 fuzzy set. So, again, if we replace the type-2 set by a type-1 set whose type-1 membership function is the principal membership function of the type-2 set, all our results reduce to the familiar ones for type-1 sets. ■

❀❀❀❀❀❀❀❀❀❀

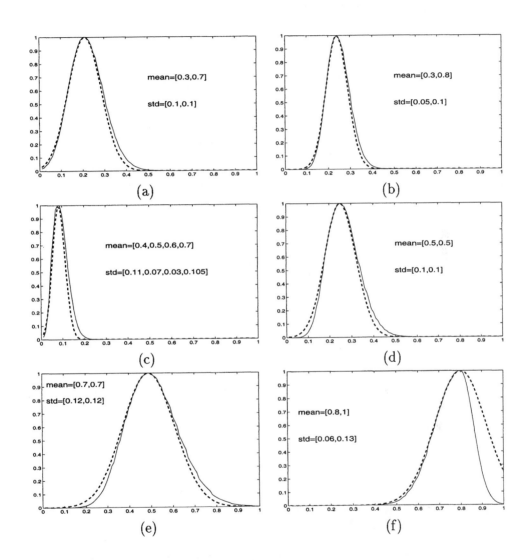

Figure A-6: Actual and approximate results of the meet operation between Gaussian type-1 fuzzy sets under product t-norm. The thin solid line shows the actual result computed numerically. The thick dashed line shows the approximation given in (A-10) and (A-11). Means and standard deviations are as indicated on the figures. In Figures (d) and (e) the two Gaussians are coincident.

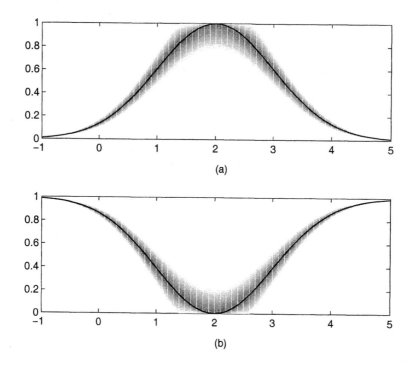

Figure A-7: Complement of a Gaussian type-2 fuzzy set.
(a) Gaussian type-2 set, and (b) complement.

A.6 COMPUTATION

The following M-files, which are found in the folder *general type-2 fuzzy logic systems*, are useful for performing operations on general type-2 fuzzy sets:

join.m: Function to compute the join of n type-1 fuzzy sets under minimum or product t-norms, using Theorem A-1.

meet.m: Function to compute the meet of n type-1 fuzzy sets under minimum t-norm using Theorem A-2.

negation.m: Function to compute the negation of a type-1 fuzzy set using Theorem A-3.

gaussian_meet.m: Function to compute the Gaussian approximation in (A-10) and (A-11) to the meet of n Gaussian type-1 sets under product t-norm.

EXERCISES

A-1: Develop the counterpart to the results shown in Figure A-1(b), using the minimum t-norm.

A-2: Apply (A-2) to the case when the secondary membership functions are interval sets, and check the results obtained with those given in Theorem 7-1.

A-3: Apply (A-4) to the case when the secondary membership functions are interval sets, and check the results obtained with those given in Theorem 7-2.

A-4: In Example A-7, suppose that G is a type-1 fuzzy singleton and F is an interval set. What is $\mu_{F \sqcap G}(\theta)$? What is the domain of θ?

A-5: Figure A-8 depicts an interval type-1 set $g(v)$ and a triangular type-1 set $f(v)$. Note that L, R, A, T, and I stand for left, right, apex, triangle, and interval, respectively. Using (A-9), prove that $\mu_{F \sqcap G}(\theta)$ is given by the trapezoidal function that is depicted in Figure A-9.

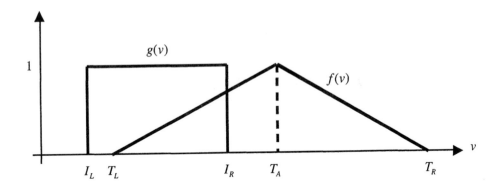

Figure A-8: Interval and triangular type-1 fuzzy sets for Exercise A-5.

❀ ❀ ❀ ❀ ❀ ❀ ❀ ❀ ❀ ❀

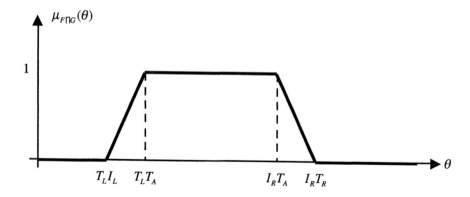

Figure A-9: Solution to Exercise A-5.

Properties of Type-1 and Type-2 Fuzzy Sets

B.1 INTRODUCTION

In this appendix we present details about properties of type-1 and type-2 fuzzy sets. More specifically, we examine the following frequently used laws to see if they remain satisfied under maximum t-conorm and either minimum or product t-norms:

> Reflexive, antisymmetric, transitive, idempotent, commutative, associative, absorption, distributive, involution, De Morgan's, and identity

Before examining type-2 sets, we review which of the above laws are satisfied by membership grades of type-1 sets for maximum t-conorm and *product* t-norm. That they are all satisfied for maximum t-conorm and minimum t-norm (a so-called "dual t-conorm and t-norm pair") is well-known (e.g. [Klir and Yuan, 1995]).

B.2 TYPE-1 FUZZY SETS

The exact nature of all the preceding laws is given in the second column of Table B-1. Reflexive, anti-symmetric, and transitive laws do not make use of any t-norm; hence, they are automatically satisfied for maximum t-conorm and product t-norm. Commutative and associative laws are also satisfied, because both maximum and product operations are commutative and associative; i.e. for $\forall x \in X$:

Table B-1: Summary of set-theoretic laws and whether or not they are satisfied for type-1 fuzzy sets under maximum t-conorm and either minimum or product t-norms* (adapted from Table 1 of [Karnik and Mendel (2000a)).

Set Theoretic Laws		Minimum t-Norm	Product t-Norm
Reflexive	$\mu_A \leq \mu_A$	Yes	Yes
Anti-symmetric	$\mu_A \leq \mu_B, \mu_B \leq \mu_A \Rightarrow \mu_A = \mu_B$	Yes	Yes
Transitive	$\mu_A \leq \mu_B, \mu_B \leq \mu_C \Rightarrow \mu_A \leq \mu_C$	Yes	Yes
Idempotent	$\mu_A \vee \mu_A = \mu_A$	Yes	Yes
	$\mu_A \star \mu_A = \mu_A$	Yes	**NO**
Commutative	$\mu_A \vee \mu_B = \mu_B \vee \mu_A$	Yes	Yes
	$\mu_A \star \mu_B = \mu_B \star \mu_A$	Yes	Yes
Associative	$(\mu_A \vee \mu_B) \vee \mu_C = \mu_A \vee (\mu_B \vee \mu_C)$	Yes	Yes
	$(\mu_A \star \mu_B) \star \mu_C = \mu_A \star (\mu_B \star \mu_C)$	Yes	Yes
Absorption	$\mu_A \star (\mu_A \vee \mu_B) = \mu_A$	Yes	**NO**
	$\mu_A \vee (\mu_A \star \mu_B) = \mu_A$	Yes	Yes
Distributive	$\mu_A \star (\mu_B \vee \mu_C) = (\mu_A \star \mu_B) \vee (\mu_A \star \mu_C)$	Yes	Yes
	$\mu_A \vee (\mu_B \star \mu_C) = (\mu_A \vee \mu_B) \star (\mu_A \vee \mu_C)$	Yes	**NO**
Involution	$\mu_{\bar{\bar{A}}} = \mu_A$	Yes	Yes
De Morgan's Laws	$\overline{\mu_A \vee \mu_B} = \mu_{\bar{A}} \star \mu_{\bar{B}}$	Yes	**NO**
	$\overline{\mu_A \star \mu_B} = \mu_{\bar{A}} \vee \mu_{\bar{B}}$	Yes	**NO**
Identity	$\mu_A \vee 0 = \mu_A$	Yes	Yes
	$\mu_A \star 1 = \mu_A$	Yes	Yes
	$\mu_A \vee 1 = 1$	Yes	Yes
	$\mu_A \star 0 = 0$	Yes	Yes

*Arguments of all membership functions have been omitted; hence, μ_A, for example, is short for $\mu_A(x)$.

- $\mu_A(x) \vee \mu_B(x) = \mu_B(x) \vee \mu_A(x)$
- $\mu_A(x) \times \mu_B(x) = \mu_B(x) \times \mu_A(x)$
- $(\mu_A(x) \vee \mu_B(x)) \vee \mu_C(x) = \mu_A(x) \vee (\mu_B(x) \vee \mu_C(x))$
- $(\mu_A(x) \times \mu_B(x)) \times \mu_C(x) = \mu_A(x) \times (\mu_B(x) \times \mu_C(x))$

Under product t-norm, the second part of the absorption laws is satisfied, because $\mu_A(x) \times \mu_B(x) \leq \mu_A(x)$, so that $\mu_A(x) \vee (\mu_A(x) \times \mu_B(x)) = \mu_A(x)$. The first part of the distributive laws is satisfied; i.e. product is distributive over maximum. The first part of the idempotent laws is also satisfied; i.e. $\mu_A(x) \vee \mu_A(x) = \mu_A(x)$. The involution law is satisfied, since we define complement as $\mu_{\bar{A}}(x) = 1 - \mu_A(x)$. And, all the identity laws are satisfied (i.e. $\mu_A(x) \vee 0 = \mu_A(x)$, $\mu_A(x) \times 1 = \mu_A(x)$, $\mu_A(x) \vee 1 = 1$, and $\mu_A(x) \times 0 = 0$).

None of the other laws are satisfied under product t-norm, because:

- Idempotent laws–second part: $\mu_A(x) \times \mu_A(x) \neq \mu_A(x)$ (B-1)
- Absorption laws–first part: assume, e.g. that $\mu_A(x) > \mu_B(x)$; then,

$$\mu_A(x) \times (\mu_A(x) \vee \mu_B(x)) = \mu_A(x) \times \mu_A(x) = \mu_A^2(x) \neq \mu_A(x) \qquad \text{(B-2)}$$

- Distributive laws–second part: assume, e.g. that $\mu_A(x) > \mu_B(x)$ and $\mu_A(x) > \mu_C(x)$; then,

$$\begin{aligned} \mu_A(x) \vee (\mu_B(x) \times \mu_C(x)) &= \mu_A(x) \\ &\neq (\mu_A(x) \vee \mu_B(x)) \times (\mu_A(x) \vee \mu_C(x)) = \mu_A^2(x) \end{aligned} \qquad \text{(B-3)}$$

- De Morgan's laws:

$$\begin{aligned} \overline{\mu_A(x) \vee \mu_B(x)} &= 1 - (\mu_A(x) \vee \mu_B(x)) \\ &\neq \mu_{\bar{A}}(x) \times \mu_{\bar{B}}(x) = (1 - \mu_A(x)) \times (1 - \mu_B(x)) \end{aligned} \qquad \text{(B-4)}$$

$$\overline{\mu_A(x) \times \mu_B(x)} = 1 - \mu_A(x) \times \mu_B(x)$$
$$\neq \mu_{\bar{A}}(x) \vee \mu_{\bar{B}}(x) = \max\{(1 - \mu_A(x)), (1 - \mu_B(x))\} \tag{B-5}$$

Recall that in Section 1.10.7 we also explained that the Laws of the Excluded Middle and Contradiction are violated for type-1 fuzzy sets.

B.3 TYPE-2 FUZZY SETS

Table B-2 is the type-2 counterpart to Table B-1. Recall that the union and intersection of type-2 fuzzy sets requires computing the join and meet of the secondary membership functions of these sets; hence, set-theoretic laws for type-2 fuzzy sets can be expressed in terms of secondary membership functions. Recall, also, that the join and meet operations in (7-17) and (7-20), respectively, require that a choice be made for a t-norm and t-cornorm. Here we focus exclusively on the maximum t-conorm and product t-norm case.

Recall that all our operations on type-2 fuzzy sets collapse to their type-1 counterparts if we replace all the secondary membership functions by the primary memberships at which the secondary grades are equal to 1. We assume, for simplicity, that the secondary membership functions reach the value 1 at only one point. This means that we can think about a type-1 fuzzy set as a special case of a type-2 fuzzy set; i.e. the case where only one value of the secondary membership function has a secondary grade equal to 1 and all other secondary grades are equal to zero. Consequently, if there are any set-theoretic laws that are not satisfied by type-1 fuzzy sets we can safely say that type-2 fuzzy sets will not satisfy those laws either; however, the converse of this statement may not be true. If any condition is satisfied by type-1 sets, it may or may not be satisfied by type-2 sets. So, next we examine only the set-theoretic laws that are satisfied in the type-1 case.

Consider three type-2 fuzzy subsets, $\tilde{A}$, $\tilde{B}$, and $\tilde{C}$ defined on the same universe of discourse, $X \subseteq [0,1]$, with secondary membership functions as follows for $\forall x \in X$:

$$\mu_{\tilde{A}}(x) = \int_{u \in J_x^u} f_x(u) / u \quad J_x^u \subseteq [0,1] \tag{B-6}$$

$$\mu_{\tilde{B}}(x) = \int_{v \in J_x^v} g_x(v) / v \quad J_x^v \subseteq [0,1] \tag{B-7}$$

Table B-2: Summary of set-theoretic laws and whether or not they are satisfied for type-2 fuzzy sets under maximum t-conorm and either minimum or product t-norms* (adapted from Table 1 of [Karnik and Mendel (2000a)).

Set Theoretic Laws		Minimum t-Norm	Product t-Norm
Reflexive	$\mu_{\tilde{A}} \subseteq \mu_{\tilde{A}}$	Yes	Yes
Anti-symmetric	$\mu_{\tilde{A}} \subseteq \mu_{\tilde{B}}, \mu_{\tilde{B}} \subseteq \mu_{\tilde{A}} \Rightarrow \mu_{\tilde{A}} = \mu_{\tilde{B}}$	Yes	Yes
Transitive	$\mu_{\tilde{A}} \subseteq \mu_{\tilde{B}}, \mu_{\tilde{B}} \subseteq \mu_{\tilde{C}} \Rightarrow \mu_{\tilde{A}} \subseteq \mu_{\tilde{C}}$	Yes	Yes
Idempotent	$\mu_{\tilde{A}} \sqcup \mu_{\tilde{A}} = \mu_{\tilde{A}}$	Yes	**NO**
	$\mu_{\tilde{A}} \sqcap \mu_{\tilde{A}} = \mu_{\tilde{A}}$	Yes	**NO**
Commutative	$\mu_{\tilde{A}} \sqcup \mu_{\tilde{B}} = \mu_{\tilde{B}} \sqcup \mu_{\tilde{A}}$	Yes	Yes
	$\mu_{\tilde{A}} \sqcap \mu_{\tilde{B}} = \mu_{\tilde{B}} \sqcap \mu_{\tilde{A}}$	Yes	Yes
Associative	$(\mu_{\tilde{A}} \sqcup \mu_{\tilde{B}}) \sqcup \mu_{\tilde{C}} = \mu_{\tilde{A}} \sqcup (\mu_{\tilde{B}} \sqcup \mu_{\tilde{C}})$	Yes	Yes
	$(\mu_{\tilde{A}} \sqcap \mu_{\tilde{B}}) \sqcap \mu_{\tilde{C}} = \mu_{\tilde{A}} \sqcap (\mu_{\tilde{B}} \sqcap \mu_{\tilde{C}})$	Yes	Yes
Absorption	$\mu_{\tilde{A}} \sqcap (\mu_{\tilde{A}} \sqcup \mu_{\tilde{B}}) = \mu_{\tilde{A}}$	Yes	**NO**
	$\mu_{\tilde{A}} \sqcup (\mu_{\tilde{A}} \sqcap \mu_{\tilde{B}}) = \mu_{\tilde{A}}$	Yes	**NO**
Distributive	$\mu_{\tilde{A}} \sqcap (\mu_{\tilde{B}} \sqcup \mu_{\tilde{C}}) = (\mu_{\tilde{A}} \sqcap \mu_{\tilde{B}}) \sqcup (\mu_{\tilde{A}} \sqcap \mu_{\tilde{C}})$	Yes	**NO**
	$\mu_{\tilde{A}} \sqcup (\mu_{\tilde{B}} \sqcap \mu_{\tilde{C}}) = (\mu_{\tilde{A}} \sqcup \mu_{\tilde{B}}) \sqcap (\mu_{\tilde{A}} \sqcup \mu_{\tilde{C}})$	Yes	**NO**
Involution	$\mu_{\overline{\overline{\tilde{A}}}} = \mu_{\tilde{A}}$	Yes	Yes
De Morgan's Laws	$\overline{\mu_{\tilde{A}} \sqcup \mu_{\tilde{B}}} = \mu_{\overline{\tilde{A}}} \sqcap \mu_{\overline{\tilde{B}}}$	Yes	**NO**
	$\overline{\mu_{\tilde{A}} \sqcap \mu_{\tilde{B}}} = \mu_{\overline{\tilde{A}}} \sqcup \mu_{\overline{\tilde{B}}}$	Yes	**NO**
Identity	$\mu_{\tilde{A}} \sqcup (1/0) = \mu_{\tilde{A}}$	Yes	Yes
	$\mu_{\tilde{A}} \sqcap (1/1) = \mu_{\tilde{A}}$	Yes	Yes
	$\mu_{\tilde{A}} \sqcup (1/1) = 1/1$	Yes	Yes
	$\mu_{\tilde{A}} \sqcap (1/0) = 1/0$	Yes	Yes

*The membership functions in this table are secondary membership functions. Each of the table's laws applies at a specific value of x; but, for notational convenience, we do not show the secondary membership functions as functions of x; i.e. $\mu_{\tilde{A}}$ is short for $\mu_{\tilde{A}}(x)$.

$$\mu_{\tilde{C}}(x) = \int_{w \in J_x^w} h_x(w) / w \quad J_x^w \subseteq [0,1] \tag{B-8}$$

As in [Klir and Yuan (1995)], we define fuzzy set inclusion to mean:

$$\tilde{A} \subseteq \tilde{Q} \Leftrightarrow \mu_{\tilde{A}}(x) \le \mu_{\tilde{B}}(x) \quad \forall x \in X \tag{B-9}$$

The generalized versions of reflexive, anti-symmetric, and transitive laws, as stated in Table B-2, are satisfied because they do not make use of the t-norm or t-conorm. Note that, in these laws, $\mu_{\tilde{A}}(x) = \mu_{\tilde{B}}(x) \Leftrightarrow f_x(u) = g_x(v)$, $\forall u \in J_x^u$ and $\forall v \in J_x^v$.

Commutative laws are satisfied for maximum t-conorm and product t-norm [Mizumoto and Tanaka (1976)]; e.g. using (7-17)

$$\mu_{\tilde{A}}(x) \sqcup \mu_{\tilde{B}}(x) = \left[\int_{u \in J_x^u} f_x(u) / u \right] \sqcup \left[\int_{v \in J_x^v} g_x(v) / v \right]$$

$$= \int_{u \in J_x^u} \int_{v \in J_x^v} f_x(u) \times g_x(v) / (u \vee v) = \int_{u \in J_x^u} \int_{v \in J_x^v} g_x(v) \times f_x(u) / (v \vee u) \tag{B-10}$$

$$= \left[\int_{v \in J_x^v} g_x(v) / v \right] \sqcup \left[\int_{u \in J_x^u} f_x(u) / u \right] = \mu_{\tilde{B}}(x) \sqcup \mu_{\tilde{A}}(x)$$

Associative laws are also satisfied for maximum t-conorm and product t-norm [Mizumoto and Tanaka (1976)]; e.g. using (7-20)

$$\mu_{\tilde{A}}(x) \sqcap (\mu_{\tilde{B}}(x) \sqcap \mu_{\tilde{C}}(x)) = \left[\int_{u \in J_x^u} f_x(u) / u \right] \sqcap \left[\int_{v \in J_x^v} \int_{w \in J_x^w} g_x(v) \times h_x(w) / (v \times w) \right]$$

$$= \int_{u \in J_x^u} \int_{v \in J_x^v} \int_{w \in J_x^w} f_x(u) [g_x(v) h_x(w)] / u \times (v \times w)$$

$$= \int_{u \in J_x^u} \int_{v \in J_x^v} \int_{w \in J_x^w} [f_x(u) g_x(v)] h_x(w) / (u \times v) \times w \tag{B-11}$$

$$= \left[\int_{u \in J_x^u} \int_{v \in J_x^v} f_x(u) g_x(v) / (u \times v) \right] \sqcap \left[\int_{w \in J_x^w} h_x(w) / w \right]$$

$$= (\mu_{\tilde{A}}(x) \sqcap \mu_{\tilde{B}}(x)) \sqcap \mu_{\tilde{C}}(x)$$

Now we proceed to prove the identity laws. They are satisfied for maximum t-conorm and product t-norm if we use normal membership grades, because:

$$\mu_{\tilde{A}}(x) \sqcup (1/0) = \left[\int_{u \in J_x^u} f_x(u)/u \right] \sqcup 1/0$$

$$= \int_{u \in J_x^u} f_x(u) \times 1/(u \vee 0) = \int_{u \in J_x^u} f_x(u)/u = \mu_{\tilde{A}}(x) \tag{B-12}$$

$$\mu_{\tilde{A}}(x) \sqcap (1/1) = \left[\int_{u \in J_x^u} f_x(u)/u \right] \sqcap 1/1$$

$$= \int_{u \in J_x^u} f_x(u) \times 1/(u \times 1) = \int_{u \in J_x^u} f_x(u)/u = \mu_{\tilde{A}}(x) \tag{B-13}$$

$$\mu_{\tilde{A}}(x) \sqcup (1/1) = \left[\int_{u \in J_x^u} f_x(u)/u \right] \sqcup 1/1 = \int_{u \in J_x^u} f_x(u) \times 1/(u \vee 1)$$

$$= \int_{u \in J_x^u} f_x(u)/1 = \left[\sup_u f_x(u) \right]/1 = 1/1 \tag{B-14}$$

$$\mu_{\tilde{A}}(x) \sqcap (1/0) = \left[\int_{u \in J_x^u} f_x(u)/u \right] \sqcap 1/0 = \int_{u \in J_x^u} f_x(u) \times 1/(u \times 0)$$

$$= \int_{u \in J_x^u} f_x(u)/0 = \left[\sup_u f_x(u) \right]/0 = 1/0 \tag{B-15}$$

We have only had to use the fact that the secondary membership functions are normal in (B-14) and (B-15). We did not need to use this fact in the proofs of (B-12) and (B-13); hence, those identity laws hold even in the case of non-normal secondary membership functions.

Next we show, by means of a counter-example, that the first parts of the idempotent and distributive laws, and the second part of the absorption law, which are satisfied in the type-1 case, may not be satisfied for maximum t-conorm and product t-norm in the type-2 case.

Example B-1: Consider the following three normal convex type-1 secondary membership functions:

$$\mu_{\tilde{A}}(x) = 0.5/0.1 + 1/0.7 \tag{B-16}$$

$$\mu_{\tilde{B}}(x) = 0.6/0.3 + 1/0.7 \tag{B-17}$$

$$\mu_{\tilde{C}}(x) = 0.4 / 0.2 + 1 / 0.8 \tag{B-18}$$

Failure of the first part of the idempotent law:

$$\mu_{\tilde{A}}(x) \sqcup \mu_{\tilde{A}}(x) = (0.5 / 0.1 + 1 / 0.7) \sqcup (0.5 / 0.1 + 1 / 0.7)$$
$$= 0.25 / 0.1 + 0.5 / 0.7 + 0.5 / 0.7 + 1 / 0.7 \tag{B-19}$$
$$= 0.25 / 0.1 + 1 / 0.7 \neq \mu_{\tilde{A}}(x)$$

Failure of the first part of the distributive law (details are left to the reader):

$$\mu_{\tilde{A}}(x) \sqcap (\mu_{\tilde{B}}(x) \sqcup \mu_{\tilde{C}}(x)) = 0.12 / 0.03 + 0.2 / 0.07 + 0.5 / 0.08$$
$$+ 0.24 / 0.21 + 0.4 / 0.49 + 1 / 0.56 \tag{B-20}$$

$$(\mu_{\tilde{A}}(x) \sqcap \mu_{\tilde{B}}(x)) \sqcup (\mu_{\tilde{A}}(x) \sqcap \mu_{\tilde{C}}(x)) = 0.06 / 0.03 + 0.1 / 0.07 + 0.25 / 0.08$$
$$+ 0.2 / 0.14 + 0.3 / 0.21 + 0.5 / 0.49 + 1 / 0.56 \tag{B-21}$$

Comparing (B-20) and (B-21), we conclude that

$$(\mu_{\tilde{A}}(x) \sqcap \mu_{\tilde{B}}(x)) \sqcup (\mu_{\tilde{A}}(x) \sqcap \mu_{\tilde{C}}(x)) \neq \mu_{\tilde{A}}(x) \sqcap (\mu_{\tilde{B}}(x) \sqcup \mu_{\tilde{C}}(x))$$

Failure of the second part of the absorption law (details are left to the reader):

$$\mu_{\tilde{A}}(x) \sqcup (\mu_{\tilde{A}}(x) \sqcap \mu_{\tilde{B}}(x)) = 0.25 / 0.1 + 0.3 / 0.21 + 0.5 / 0.49 + 1 / 0.7 \neq \mu_{\tilde{A}}(x) \tag{B-22}$$

■

Observe from Table B-2 that both of the distributive and absorption laws do not hold. So, under maximum t-conorm and product t-norm, meet is totally non-distributive and non-absorptive for the type-2 case.

❀❀❀❀❀❀❀❀❀❀❀

EXERCISES

B-1: Verify (B-4) and (B-5) numerically.

B-2: Show that for type-1 fuzzy sets all the set-theoretic laws are satisfied under maximum t-conorm and minimum t-norm.

B-3: Show that for type-2 fuzzy sets all the set-theoretic laws are satisfied under maximum t-conorm and minimum t-norm.

B-4: Show that, under product t-norm and maximum t-conorm, $\mu_{\tilde{A}}(x) \sqcap \mu_{\tilde{B}}(x) = \mu_{\tilde{B}}(x) \sqcap \mu_{\tilde{A}}(x)$.

B-5: Show that, under product t-norm and maximum t-conorm,

$$\mu_{\tilde{A}}(x) \sqcup (\mu_{\tilde{B}}(x) \sqcup \mu_{\tilde{C}}(x)) = (\mu_{\tilde{A}}(x) \sqcup \mu_{\tilde{B}}(x)) \sqcup \mu_{\tilde{C}}(x).$$

B-6: Show that for type-2 fuzzy sets the involution law is satisfied under maximum t-conorm and product t-norm.

B-7: Complete all the details for Example B-1.

Computation

Although no MATLAB M-files are packaged with this book, more than 30^1 are available as freeware on the Internet at the following URL: http://sipi.usc.edu/~mendel/software. They are being made available so that you will be able to immediately use the results in this book.

Brief descriptions of the M-files appear at the end of each chapter for which the M-file is most applicable. In this appendix we collect all of the M-files together as they are organized on the Internet; i.e. in the three folders: *type-1 fuzzy logic systems*, *general type-2 fuzzy logic systems*, and *interval type-2 fuzzy logic systems*.

C.1 Type-1 FLSs

Singleton Mamdani Type-1 FLS

sfls_type1.m: Compute the output(s) of a singleton type-1 FLS when the antecedent membership functions are Gaussian.

train_sfls_type1.m: Tune the parameters of a singleton type-1 FLS when the antecedent membership functions are Gaussian, using some input–output training data.

svd_qr_sfls_type1.m: Rule-reduction of a singleton type-1 FLS when the antecedent membership functions are Gaussian, using some input–output training data.

---

[1]There are M-files online that are not described here; e.g. some are used within the listed M-files.

Non-Singleton Mamdani Type-1 FLS

nsfls_type1.m: Compute the output(s) of a non-singleton type-1 FLS when the antecedent membership functions are Gaussian and the input sets are Gaussian.

train_nsfls_type1.m: Tune the parameters of a non-singleton type-1 FLS when the antecedent membership functions are Gaussian, and the input sets are Gaussian, using some input–output training data.

svd_qr_nsfls_type1.m: Rule-reduction of a non-singleton type-1 FLS when the antecedent membership functions are Gaussian, and the input sets are Gaussian, using some input–output training data.

TSK FLS

tsk_type1.m: Compute the output(s) of a type-1 TSK FLS (type-1 antecedents and type-0 consequent) when the antecedent membership functions are Gaussian.

train_tsk_type1.m: Tune the parameters of a type-1 TSK FLS (type-1 antecedents and type-0 consequent) when the antecedent membership functions are Gaussian, using some input–output training data.

C.2 General Type-2 FLSs

Operations

join.m: Function to compute the join of n type-1 fuzzy sets under minimum or product t-norms, using Theorem A-1.

meet.m: Function to compute the meet of n type-1 fuzzy sets under minimum t-norm using Theorem A-2.

negation.m: Function to compute the negation of a type-1 fuzzy set using Theorem A-3.

gaussian_meet.m: Function to compute the Gaussian approximation in (A-10) and (A-11) to the meet of n Gaussian type-1 sets under product t-norm.

gaussian_sum.m: Function to compute an affine combination of n Gaussian type-1 sets, as described in Example 7-4.

weighted_avg.m: Function to extend the weighted average of crisp numbers to the case where all the quantities involved are general type-1 sets. It implements the generalized centroid in (9-11).

C.3 INTERVAL TYPE-2 FLSs

Plotting

plot2d1.m: Function to plot two-dimensional representation of the FOU of an interval type-2 fuzzy set. The area between the upper and lower membership functions is shaded uniformly to indicate that all the secondary grades are unity.

Operations

interval_meet.m: Function to compute the meet (or product) of n interval type-1 sets, as described in Theorem 7-2.

interval_sum.m: Function to compute an affine combination of n interval type-1 sets, as described in Theorem 7-4.

interval_wtdavg.m: Function used to implement the iterative procedure described in Theorem 9-1 to compute the maximum and minimum of a weighted average, where both the z_i and the w_i are interval sets.

Interval Singleton Mamdani Type-2 FLS

sfls.m: Compute the output(s) of an interval singleton type-2 FLS when the antecedent membership functions are Gaussian primary membership functions with uncertain means.

train_sfls.m: Tune the parameters of an interval singleton type-2 FLS when the antecedent membership functions are Gaussian primary membership functions with uncertain means, using some input–output training data.

svd_qr_sfls.m: Rule-reduction of an interval singleton type-2 FLS when the antecedent membership functions are Gaussian primary membership functions with uncertain means, using some input–output training data.

Interval Type-1 Non-Singleton Mamdani Type-2 FLS

nsfls1.m: Compute the output(s) of an interval type-1 non-singleton type-2 FLS when the antecedent membership functions are Gaussian primary membership functions with uncertain means and the input sets are type-1 Gaussian.

train_nsfls1.m: Tune the parameters of an interval type-1 non-singleton type-2 FLS when the antecedent membership functions are Gaussian primary membership functions with uncertain means and input sets are type-1 Gaussian, using some input–output training data.

svd_qr_nsfls1.m: Rule-reduction of an interval type-1 non-singleton type-2 FLS when the antecedent membership functions are Gaussian primary membership functions with uncertain means and input sets are type-1 Gaussian, using some input–output training data.

Interval Type-2 Non-Singleton Mamdani Type-2 FLS

nsfls2.m: Compute the output(s) of an interval type-2 non-singleton type-2 FLS when the antecedent membership functions are Gaussian primary membership functions with uncertain means and the input membership functions are Gaussian primary membership functions with uncertain standard deviations.

train_nsfls2.m: Tune the parameters of an interval type-2 non-singleton type-2 FLS when the antecedent membership functions are Gaussian primary membership functions with uncertain means and the input membership functions are Gaussian primary membership functions with uncertain standard deviations, using some input–output training data.

svd_qr_nsfls2.m: Rule-reduction of an interval type-2 non-singleton type-2 FLS when the antecedent membership functions are Gaussian primary membership functions with uncertain means and the input membership functions are Gaussian primary membership functions with uncertain standard deviations, using some input–output training data.

Interval Type-2 TSK FLS

tsk_type2.m: Compute the output(s) of an interval type-2 TSK FLS A2-C1 (type-2 antecedents and type-1 consequent) when the antecedent membership functions are Gaussian primary membership functions with uncertain means.

train_tsk_type2.m: Tune the parameters of an interval type-2 TSK FLS A2-C1 when the antecedent membership functions are Gaussian primary membership functions with uncertain means, using some input–output training data.

References

Adas, A. M., "Using Adaptive Linear Prediction to Support Real-Time VBR Video Under RCBR Network Service Model," *IEEE Trans. on Networking*, vol. 6, pp. 635-644, 1998.

Allendoerfer, C. B. and C. O. Oakley, *Principles of Mathematics*, McGraw-Hill, New York, 1955.

Alspach, D. L. and H. W. Sorenson, "Nonlinear Bayesian Estimation Using Gaussian Sum Approximations," *IEEE Trans. on Automatic Control*, vol. AC-17, pp. 439-448, Aug. 1972.

Autonne, L., "Sur Les Groupes Lineaires, Reels et Orthogonaux," *Bull. Soc. Math. France*, vol. 30, pp. 121-133, 1902.

Baets, B. and E. Kerre, "The Generalized Modus Ponens and the Triangular Fuzzy Data Model," *Fuzzy Sets and Systems*, vol. 59, pp. 305-317, 1993.

Bárdossy, A. and L. Duckstein, *Fuzzy Rule-Based Modeling With Applications to Geophysical, Biological and Engineering Systems*, CRC, Boca Raton, FL, 1995.

Berenji, H. R., "Treatment of Uncertainty in Artificial Intelligence," in *Machine Intelligence and Autonomy Aerospace Systems* (H. Heer and H. Lum, Eds.), pp. 233-247, AIAA, Washington, DC, 1988.

Berenji, H. R. and P. Khedkar, "Learning and Tuning Fuzzy Logic Controllers Through Reinforcements," *IEEE Trans. on Neural Networks*, vol. 3, pp. 724-740, Sept. 1992.

Blum, E. K. and L. K. Li, "Approximation Theory and Feedforward Networks," *Neural Networks*, vol. 4, pp. 511-515, 1991.

Bonissone, P. P. and K. S. Decker, "Selecting Uncertainty Calculi and Granularity: An Experiment in Trading Off Precision and Complexity," in *Uncertainty in Artificial Intelligence* (L. N. Kanal and J. F. Lemmer, Eds.), pp. 217-247, Amsterdam, 1986.

Buckley, J. J., "Fuzzy Hierarchical Analysis," *Fuzzy Sets and Systems*, vol. 17, pp. 233-247, 1985.

Buckley, J. J., "Sugeno-Type-Controllers Are Universal Controllers," *Fuzzy Sets and Systems*, vol. 25, pp. 299-303, 1993.

Bustince, H. and P. Burillo, "Mathematical Analysis of Interval-valued Fuzzy Relations: Application to Approximate Reasoning," *Fuzzy Sets and Systems*, vol. 113, pp. 205-219, 2000.

Casdagli, M., "A Dynamical Systems Approach to Modeling Input–Output Systems," in *Nonlinear Modeling and Forecasting. SFI Studies in the Sciences of Complexity* Process, vol. XII, pp. 265-281, Addison-Wesley, New York, 1992.

Chaneau, J. L., M. Gunaratne and A. G. Altschaeffl, "An Application of Type-2 Sets to Decision Making in Engineering," in *Analysis of Fuzzy Information, vol. II: Artificial Intelligence and Decision Systems* (J. Bezdek, Ed.), CRC, Boca Raton, FL, 1987.

Chang, C.-J., C.-H. Lin, D.-S. Guan and R.-G. Cheng, "A Power-Spectrum Based Neural Fuzzy Connection Admission Mechanism for ATM Networks," *IEEE Proc. of ICC*, Monterey, Canada, pp. 1709-1713, 1997.

Chang, C.-J., C.-H. Lin, D.-S. Guan and R.-G. Cheng, "Design of Power-Spectrum-Based ATM Connection Admission Controller for Multimedia Communications," *IEEE Trans. Industrial Electronics*, vol. 45, pp. 52-59, Feb. 1998.

Chen, C.-L. and F.-Y. Chang, "Design and Analysis of Neural/Fuzzy Variable Structure PID Control Systems," *Proc. Inst. Elect. Eng. Control Theory Applications*, vol. 143, pp. 200-208, 1996.

Chen, C.-L. and Y.-M. Chen, "Self-Organizing Fuzzy Logic Controller Design," *Comput. Indust.*, vol. 22, pp. 240-261, 1993.

Chen, S., S. A. Billings and W. Luo, "Orthogonal Least Squares Methods and Their Application to Nonlinear System Identification," *Int. J. Contr.*, vol 50, pp. 1873-1896, 1989.

Chen, S., C. F. N. Cowan and P. M. Grant, "Orthogonal Least Squares Learning Algorithm for Radial Basis Function Networks," *IEEE Trans. on Neural Networks*, vol. 2, pp. 302-309, 1991.

Chen, S. and B. Mulgrew, "Overcoming Co-Channel Interference Using Adaptive Radial Basis Function Equalizer," *Signal Processing*, vol. 28, pp. 91-107, 1992.

Chen, S., B. Mulgrew and S. McLaughlin, "A Clustering Technique for Digital Communications Channel Equalization Using Radial Basis Function Network," *IEEE Trans. Neural Networks*, vol. 4, pp. 570-579, July 1993a.

Chen, S., B. Mulgrew and S. McLaughlin, "Adaptive Bayesian Equalizer With Decision Feedback," *IEEE Trans. Signal Processing*, vol. 41, pp. 2918-2927, Sept. 1993b.

Chen, S., S. McLaughlin, B. Mulgrew and P. M. Grant, "Adaptive Bayesian Decision Feedback Equalizer for Dispersive Mobile Radio Channels," *IEEE Trans. Communications*, vol. 43, pp. 1937-1956, May 1995.

Chen, S., S. McLaughlin, B. Mulgrew and P. M. Grant, "Bayesian Decision Feedback Equalizer for Overcoming Co-Channel Interference," *IEEE Proc. Communications*, vol. 143, pp. 219-225, August 1996.

Chiang, D. A., L.-R. Chow and N.-C. Hsien, "Fuzzy Information in Extended Fuzzy Relational Databases," *Fuzzy Sets and Systems*, vol. 92, pp. 1-20, Nov. 1997.

Cho, Y., K. Lee, J. Yoo and M. Park, "Autogeneration of Fuzzy Rules and Membership Function for Fuzzy Modeling Using Rough Set Theory," *IEEE Proc. Control Theory and Applications*, vol. 145, pp. 437-442, Sept. 1998.

Chong, S. and S.-Q. Li, "Probabilistic Burstiness-Curve-Based Connection Control Real-Time Multimedia Services in ATM Networks," *IEEE J. of Selected Areas in Communications*, vol. 15, pp. 1072-1086, August 1997.

Chu, P. and J. M. Mendel, "First Break Refraction Event Picking Using Fuzzy Logic Systems," *IEEE Trans. on Fuzzy Systems*, vol. 2, pp. 255-266, Nov. 1994.

Cooper, M. G., "Evolving a Rule-Based Fuzzy Controller," *Simulation*, vol. 65, pp. 67-72, 1995.

Cowan, C. F. N. and S. Semnani, "Time-Variant Equalization Using a Novel Non-Linear Adaptive Structure," *Intl. J. of Adaptive Control and Signal Processing*, vol. 12, pp. 195-206, 1998.

Cox, E. A., "Fuzzy Fundamentals," *IEEE Spectrum*, pp. 58-61, Oct. 1992.

Cox, E. A., *The Fuzzy Systems Handbook*, AP Professional, Cambridge, MA, 1994.

Cox, E. A., *Fuzzy Logic for Business and Industry*, Charles River Media, Rockland, MA, 1995.

Crowder, R. S., "Predicting the Mackey–Glass Time Series With Cascade-Correlation Learning," in *Proc. 1990 Connectionist Models Summer School* (D. Touretsky, G. Hinton and T. Sejnowski, Eds.), Carnegie Mellon Univ., 1990, pp. 117-123.

Cybenko, G., "Approximation by Superpositions of a Sigmoidal Function," *Mathematics of Control, Signals, and Systems*, 1989.

Daley, S. and K. F. Gill, "A Design Study of a Self-Organizing Fuzzy Logic Controller," in *Proc. Inst. Mechan. Eng. Part C, Mechan. Eng. Science*, vol. 200, pp. 59-69, 1986.

Delago, M. and A. Gonzalez, "An Inductive Learning Procedure to Identify Fuzzy Systems," *Fuzzy Sets and Systems*, vol. 55, pp. 121-133, 1993.

Delgado, M., F. Herrera, E. Herrera-Viedma and L. Martinez, "Combining Numerical and Linguistic Information in Group Decision Making," *J. of Information Sciences*, vol. 107, pp. 177-194, 1998.

Dickerson, J. A. and B. Kosko, "Fuzzy Function Learning With Covariance Ellipsoids," in *Proc. IEEE Int'l. Conf. Neural Networks (IEEE ICNN93)*, pp. 1162-1167.

Dickerson, J. A. and B. Kosko, "Ellipsoidal Learning and Fuzzy Throttle Control for Platoons of Smart Cars," in *Fuzzy Sets, Neural Networks, and Soft Computing* (R. Yager and L. A. Zadeh, Eds.), pp. 63-84, Van Nostrand Reinhold, New York, 1994.

Douliger, C. S. and G. Develekos, "Neuro-fuzzy Control in ATM Networks," *IEEE Communication Magazine*, vol. 35, pp. 154-163, May 1997.

Driankov, D., H. Hellendoorn and M. Reinfrank, *An Introduction to Fuzzy Control* (2nd ed.), Springer-Verlag, 1996.

Dubois, D. and H. Prade, "Operations on Fuzzy Numbers," *Int. J. Systems Science*, vol. 9, pp. 613-626, 1978.

Dubois, D. and H. Prade, "Operations in a Fuzzy-Valued Logic," *Information and Control*, vol. 43, pp. 224-240, 1979.

Dubois, D. and H. Prade, *Fuzzy Sets and Systems: Theory and Applications*, Academic Press, NY, 1980.

Dubois, D. and H. Prade, "A Review of Fuzzy Set Aggregation Connectives," *Information Sciences*, vol. 36, pp. 85-121, 1985.

Duda, R. O., "Elements of Pattern Recognition," in *A Prelude to Neural Networks: Adaptive and Learning Systems* (J. M. Mendel, Ed.), Prentice-Hall, Englewood-Cliffs, NJ, pp. 3-33, 1994.

Duda, R. O. and P. E. Hart, *Pattern Classification and Scene Analysis*, John Wiley & Sons, Inc., New York, 1973.

Eckart, C. and G. Young, "A Principal Axis Transformation for Non-Hermitian Matrices," *Bull. Am. Math. Soc.*, vol. 45, pp. 118-121, 1939

Edwards, W. F., *Likelihood*, Cambridge Univ. Press, London, 1972.

Evans, J. S. and D. Everitt," Effective Bandwidth-Based Admission Control for Multiservice CDMA Cellular Networks," *IEEE Trans. Vehicular Tech.*, vol. 48, pp. 36-46, Jan. 1999.

Farmer, J. D., "Chaotic Attractors of Infinite-Dimensional Dynamical Systems," *Physica*, vol. 4-D, pp. 366-393, 1982.

Figueiredo, M. and F. Gomide, "Design of Fuzzy Systems Using Neurofuzzy Networks," *IEEE Trans. on Neural Networks*, vol. 10, pp. 815-827, July 1999.

Filev, D. P., "Toward the Concept of Quasilinear Fuzzy Systems," in *Proc. Int. Conf. Fuzzy Logic Neural Nets*, Iizuka, Japan, pp. 761-765, 1990.

Filev, D. P., "Fuzzy Modeling of Complex Systems," *Int. J. Approx. Reasoning*, vol. 4, pp. 281-290, 1991.

Filev, D. P. and R. R. Yager, "A Generalized Defuzzification Method via BAD Distributions," *International J. of Intelligent Systems*, vol. 6, pp. 687-697, 1991.

Golub, G. H. and C. F. Van Loan, *Matrix Computations*, Johns Hopkins Univ. Press, Baltimore, MD, 1983.

Gonzalez, A. and R. Perez, "Structural Learning Of Fuzzy Rules From Noised Examples," in *Proc. Fourth IEEE Conf. Fuzzy Systems*, vol. 3, pp. 1323-1330, Yokohama, Japan, 1995.

Gorzalczany, M. B., "A Method of Inference in Approximate Reasoning Based on Interval-Valued Fuzzy Sets," *Fuzzy Sets and Systems*, vol. 21, pp. 1-17, 1987.

Habib, I.W., "Applications of Neurocomputing in Traffic Management of ATM Networks," *Proc. of IEEE*, vol. 84, pp. 1430-1441, Oct. 1996.

Habib, I.W., R. Morris, H. Saito and B. Pehrson (Eds.), Special Issue on Computational and Artificial Intelligence in High Speed Networks, *IEEE J. of Selected Areas in Communications*, vol. 15, Feb. 1997.

Hasan, A. R., T. S. Martis and A. H. M. S. Ula, "Design and Implementation of a Fuzzy Controlled Based Automatic Voltage Regulator for a Synchronous Generator," *IEEE Trans. Energy Conv.,* vol. 9, pp. 550-556, 1994.

Haykin, S., *Adaptive Filter Theory* (3rd Ed.), Prentice-Hall, Upper Saddle River, NJ, 1996.

Hellendoorn, H. and C. Thomas, "Defuzzification in Fuzzy Controllers," *J. of Intelligent Systems*, vol. 1, pp. 109-123, 1993.

Hisdal, E., "The IF –THEN ELSE Statement and Interval-Values Fuzzy Sets of Higher Type," *Int'l. J. Man-Machine Studies*, vol. 15, pp. 385-455, 1981.

Hohensohn, J. and J. M. Mendel, "Two-Pass Orthogonal Least-Squares Algorithm to Train and Reduce Fuzzy Logic Systems," in *Proc. Third IEEE Conf. Fuzzy Systems*, vol. 1, pp. 696-700, Orlando, FL, 1994.

Hohensohn, J. and J. M. Mendel, "Two-Pass Orthogonal Least-Squares Algorithm to Train and Reduce the Complexity of Fuzzy Logic Systems," *J. of Intelligent and Fuzzy Systems*, vol. 4, pp. 295-308, 1996.

Horikawa, S., T. Furahashi and Y. Uchikawa, "On Fuzzy Modeling Using Fuzzy Neural Networks with Back-Propagation Algorithm," *IEEE Trans. on Neural Networks*, vol. 3, pp. 801-806, Sept., 1992.

Hornik, K., "Some Results on Neural Network Approximation," *Neural Networks*, vol. 6, pp. 1069-1072, 1993

Hornik, K., M. Stinchcombe and H. White, "Multilayer Feedforward Networks Are Universal Approximators," *Neural Networks*, vol. 2, pp. 359-366, 1989.

Hsu, Y.-Y. and C.-H. Chen, "Design of Power System Stabilizers for Multimachine Power Systems," *Proc. Inst. Elec. Eng. Part C, Generation, Transmission and Distribution*, vol. 137, pp. 233-238, 1990.

Hussain, A., J. J. Soraghan and T. S. Durrani, "A New Adaptive Functional-Link Neural-Network-Based DFE for Overcoming Co-Channel Interference," *IEEE Trans. Communications*, vol. 45, pp. 1358-1362, Nov. 1997.

Izumi, K., H. Tanaka and K. Asai, "Resolution of Composite Fuzzy Relational Equations of Type 2," *Trans. of the Inst. of Electronics and Communication Engineers of Japan (in Japanese), Part D*, vol. J66D, pp. 1107-1113, Oct. 1983.

Jang, J.–S. R., "Self-Learning Fuzzy Controllers Based on Temporal Back-Propagation," *IEEE Trans. on Neural Networks*, vol. 3, pp. 714-723, September, 1992.

Jang, J.-S. R., "ANFIS: Adaptive-Network-Based Fuzzy Inference System," *IEEE Trans. on Systems, Man and Cybernetics*, vol. 23, pp. 665-684, May/June 1993.

Jang, J.-S. R. and C-T. Sun, "Neuro-Fuzzy Modeling and Control,"*IEEE Proc.*, vol. 83, pp. 378-406, March 1995.

Jang, J.-S. R., C-T. Sun and E. Mizutani, *Neuro-Fuzzy and Soft-Computing*, Prentice-Hall, Upper Saddle River, NJ, 1997.

John, R. I., Type-2 Inferencing and Community Transport Scheduling," *Proc. Fourth European Congress on Intelligent Techniques and Soft Computing, EUFIT'96*, pp. 1369-1372, Aachen, Germany, Sept. 1996.

John, R. I., "Type 2 Fuzzy Sets for Knowledge Representation and Inferencing," in *Proc. of IEEE Int'l. Conf. on Fuzzy Systems*, IEEE World Congress on Computational Intelligence, pp. 1003-1008, Anchorage, AK, May 1998.

John, R. I., P. R. Innocent and M. R. Barnes, "Type 2 Fuzzy Sets and Neuro-Fuzzy Clustering or Radiographic Tibia Images," in *Proc. of Sixth Int'l. Conf. on Fuzzy Systems*, pp. 1375-1380, Barcelona, Spain, July 1997; also, in *Proc. of IEEE Int'l. Conf. on Fuzzy Systems*, pp. 1373-1376, Anchorage, AK, May 1998.

Karnik, N. N., *Type-2 Fuzzy Logic Systems*, Ph.D. Dissertation, University of Southern California, Los Angeles, CA 1998.

Karnik, N. N. and J. M. Mendel, "Introduction to Type-2 Fuzzy Logic Systems," in *Proc. 1998 IEEE FUZZ Conf.*, pp. 915-920, Anchorage, AK, May 1998a.

Karnik, N. N. and J. M. Mendel, *An Introduction to Type-2 Fuzzy Logic Systems*, Univ. of Southern Calif., Los Angeles, CA, June 1998b; see http://sipi.usc.edu/~mendel/report.

Karnik, N. N. and J. M. Mendel, "Type-2 Fuzzy Logic Systems: Type-Reduction," in *Proc. IEEE Conference on Systems, Man and Cybernetics*, pp. 2046-2051, San Diego CA, Oct., 1998c.

Karnik, N. N. and J. M. Mendel, Applications of Type-2 Fuzzy Logic Systems to Forecasting of Time-Series," *Information Sciences*, vol. 120, pp. 89-111, 1999a.

Karnik, N. N. and J. M. Mendel, "Applications of Type-2 Fuzzy Logic Systems: Handling the Uncertainty Associated With Surveys," in *Proc. FUZZ-IEEE'99*, Seoul, Korea, August 1999b.

Karnik, N. N. and J. M. Mendel, "Operations on Type-2 Fuzzy Sets," accepted for publication, *Int'l. J. on Fuzzy Sets and Systems*, 2000a.

Karnik, N. N. and J. M. Mendel, "Centroid of a Type-2 Fuzzy Set," submitted for publication, 2000b.

Karnik, N. N., J. M. Mendel and Q. Liang "Type-2 Fuzzy Logic Systems," *IEEE Trans. on Fuzzy Systems*, vol. 7, pp. 643-658, Dec. 1999.

Kaufman, A. and M. M. Gupta, *Introduction to Fuzzy Arithmetic: Theory and Applications*, Van Nostrand Reinhold, NY 1991.

Kim, Y. M. and J. M. Mendel, "Fuzzy Basis Functions: Comparisons With Other Basis Functions," *IEEE Trnas. on Fuzzy Systems*, vol. 3, pp. 158-168, May 1995.

Kiszka, J. B., M. E. Kochanska and D. S. Sliwinska, "The Influence of Some Parameters on the Accuracy of Fuzzy Model," in *Industrial Applications of Fuzzy Control* (M. Sugeno, Ed.), North Holland, Amsterdam, pp. 187-230, 1985a.

Kiszka, J. B., M. E. Kochanska and D. S. Sliwinska, "The Influence of Some Parameters on the Accuracy of a Fuzzy Model—Part I," *Fuzzy Sets and Systems*, vol. 15, pp. 111-128, 1985b.

Kiszka, J. B., M. E. Kochanska and D. S. Sliwinska, "The Influence of Some Parameters on the Accuracy of a Fuzzy Model—Part II," *Fuzzy Sets and Systems*, vol. 15, pp. 223-240, 1985c.

Klema, V. C. and A. J. Laub, "The Singular-Value Decomposition: Its Computation and Some Applications," *IEEE Trans. Automatic Control*, vol. AC-25, pp. 164-176, 1980.

Klir, G. J. and T. A. Folger, *Fuzzy Sets, Uncertainty, and Information*, Prentice Hall, Englewood Cliffs, NJ, 1988.

Klir, G. J. and M. J. Wierman, *Uncertainty-Based Information*, Physica-Verlag, Heidelberg, Germany, 1998.

Klir, G. J. and B. Yuan, *Fuzzy Sets and Fuzzy Logic: Theory and Applications*, Prentice Hall, Upper Saddle River, NJ, 1995.]

Kosko, B., *Neural Network and Fuzzy Systems, A Dynamical Systems Approach to Machine Intelligence*, Prentice Hall, Englewood Cliffs, NJ, 1992.

Kosko, B., "Fuzzy Systems as Universal Approximators," *IEEE Int. Conf. on Fuzzy Systems*, pp. 1153-1162, 1992; also, in *IEEE Trans. on Computers*, 1994.

Kosko, B., *Fuzzy Thinking: The New Science of Fuzzy Logic*, Hyperion, New York, 1993a.

Kosko, B., *Fuzzy Engineering*, Prentice Hall, Upper Saddle River, NJ, 1997.

Kreinovich, V., A. Lakeyev, J. Rohn, and P. Kahl, *Computational Complexity and Feasibility of Data Processing and Interval Computations*, Chapter 10, Kluwer Academic Publishers, The Netherlands, 1998.

Kreinovich, V., G. C. Mouzouris and H. T. Nguyen, "Fuzzy Rule Based Modeling as a Universal Approximation Tool," in *Fuzzy Systems, Modeling and Control* (H. T. Nguyen and M. Sugeno, Eds.), pp. 135-195, Kluwer Ac. Publ., Boston, 1998.

Krunz, M., R. Sass and H. Hughes, "Statistical Characteristics and Multiplexing of MPEG Streams," *Proc. IEEE Int'l. Conf. Computer Communications, INFOCOM'95*, vol. 2, Boston, MA, pp. 455-462, April 1995.

Kuncheva, L. I., *Fuzzy Classifier Design*, Physica-Verlag, Heidelberg, 2000.

Langari, R. and L. Wang, "Fuzzy Models, Modular Control, and Hybrid Learning," in *Proc. Fourth IEEE Conf. Fuzzy Systems*, vol. 3, pp. 1291-1298, Yokohama, Japan, 1995.

Lapedes, A. S. and R. Farber, *Nonlinear Signal Processing Using Neural Networks: Prediction and System Modeling*, Tech. Report LA-UR-87-2662, Los Alamos National Lab., Los Alamos, NM, 1987.

Larkin, L. I., "A Fuzzy Logic Controller for Aircraft Flight Control," in *Industrial Applications of Fuzzy Control* (M. Sugeno, Ed.), Elsevier Science, North-Holland, Amsterdam, The Netherlands, 1985.

Larsen, P. M., "Industrial Applications of Fuzzy Logic Control," *Int. J. Man, Mach. Studies,* vol. 12, pp. 3-10, 1980.

Lea, R. N., V. Kreinovich and R. Trejo, "Optimal Interval Enclosures for Fractionally-Linear Functions and Their Application to Intelligent Control," *Reliable Computing*, vol. 2, pp. 265-285, 1996.

Lee, C.-C., "Fuzzy Logic in Control Systems: Fuzzy Logic Controller, Part II," *IEEE Trans. on Syst., Man, and Cybernetics,* vol. SMC-20, pp. 419-435, 1990.

Lee, K. Y., "Complex Fuzzy Adaptive Filters with LMS Algorithm," *IEEE Trans. Signal Processing*, vol. 44, pp. 424-429, 1996.

Liang, Q. and J. M. Mendel, "An Introduction to Type-2 TSK Fuzzy Logic Systems," in *Proc. FUZZ-IEEE'99*, Seoul, Korea, 1999.

Liang, Q. and J. M. Mendel, "Interval Type-2 Fuzzy Logic Systems," in *Proc. FUZZ-IEEE '00*, San Antonio, TX, May 2000a.

Liang, Q. and J. M. Mendel, "Decision Feedback Equalizer for Nonlinear Time-Varying Channels Using Type-2 Fuzzy Adaptive Filters," in *Proc. FUZZ-IEEE'00*, San Antonio, TX, May 2000b.

Liang, Q. and J. M. Mendel, "Interval Type-2 Fuzzy Logic Systems: Theory and Design," *IEEE Trans. on Fuzzy Systems*, vol. 8, pp. 535–550, 2000c.

Liang, Q. and J. M. Mendel, "Equalization of Nonlinear Time-Varying Channels Using Type-2 Fuzzy Adaptive Filters," *IEEE Trans. on Fuzzy Systems*, vol. 8, pp. 551–563, 2000d.

Liang, Q. and J. M. Mendel, "Designing Interval Type-2 Fuzzy Logic Systems Using an SVD–QR Method: Rule Reduction," *Int'l. J. of Intelligent Systems*, vol. 15, pp. 939–957, 2000e.

Liang, Q. and J. M. Mendel, "Interval Type-2 TSK Fuzzy Logic Systems with Application to MPEG VBR Video Traffic Forecasting," submitted for publication, 2000f.

Liang, Q. and J. M. Mendel, "Overcoming Time-Varying Co-Channel Interference Using Type-2 Fuzzy Adaptive Filter," *IEEE Trans. on Circuits and Systems*, 2000g.

Liang, Q. and J. M. Mendel, "MPEG VBR Video Traffic Modeling and Classification Using Fuzzy Techniques," *IEEE Trans. on Fuzzy Systems*, 2000h.

Liang, Q., N. N. Karnik and J. M. Mendel, "Connection Admission Control in ATM Networks Using Survey-Based Type-2 Fuzzy Logic Systems," *IEEE Trans. on Systems, Man and Cybernetics Part C: Applications and Reviews*, 2000.

Lin, C. J. and C. T. Lin, "Reinforcement Learning for ART-Based Fuzzy Adaptive Learning Control Systems," in *Proc. Fourth IEEE Conf. Fuzzy Systems*, vol. 3, pp. 1299-1306, Yokohama, Japan, 1995.

Lin, C-T. and C. S. G. Lee, *Neural Fuzzy Systems*, Prentice-Hall PTR, Upper Saddle River, NJ, 1996.

Linkens, D. A. and H. O. Nyongesa, "Genetic Algorithms for Fuzzy Control. Part 2: Offline System Development and Application," *Inst. Elect. Eng. Proc. Control Theory Applications*, vol. 142, pp. 161-176, 1995a.

Linkens, D. A. and H. O. Nyongesa, "Genetic Algorithms for Fuzzy Control. Part 2: Online System Development and Application," *Inst. Elect. Eng. Proc. Control Theory Applications*, vol. 142, pp. 177-185, 1995b.

Liu, B. and C. Huang, "Systematic Design Approach for Multivariable Fuzzy Expert System," in *Proc. Third IEEE Conf. Fuzzy Systems*, vol. 3, pp. 2094-2099, Orlando, FL, 1994.

Lo, N. W., D. D. Falconer and A. U. Sheikh, "Adaptive Equalization for Co-Channel Interference in a Multipath Fading Environment," *IEEE Trans. Communications*, vol. 43, pp. 1441-1453, April 1995.

Mabuchi, S., "An Interpretation of Membership Functions and the Properties of General Probabilistic Operators as Fuzzy Set Operators, II: Extension to Three-Valued and Interval-Valued Fuzzy Sets," *Fuzzy Sets and Systems*, vol. 92, pp. 31-50, Nov. 1997.

MacDuffee, C. C., *The Theory of Matrices*, Springer, New York, 1933.

Mackey, M. C. and L. Glass, "Oscillation and Chaos in Physiological Control Systems," *Science*, vol. 197, pp. 287-289, 1977.

Magdon-Ismail, M., A. Nicholson and Y. Abu-Mostafa, "Financial Markets: Very Noisy Information Processing," *Proc. of IEEE*, vol. 86, pp. 2184-2195, 1998.

Mamdani, E. H., "Applications of Fuzzy Algorithms for Simple Dynamic Plant," *Proc. IEEE*, vol. 121, pp. 1585-1588, 1974.

Mancuso, M., P. Moretti and T. Tamagnini, "Fuzzy Algorithms for Machine Vision," *Electron. Eng.*, vol. 67, pp. 51-52, 1995.

Manzoni, P., P. Cremonesi and G. Serazzi, "Workload Models of VBR Video Traffic and Their Use in Resource Allocation Policies," *IEEE Trans. on Networking*, vol. 7, pp. 387-397, 1999.

Marimin, M. Umano, I. Hatono and H. Tamura, "Linguistic Labels for Expressing Fuzzy Preference Relations in Fuzzy Group Decision Making," *IEEE Trans. on Systems, Man and Cybernetics–Part B: Cybernetics*, vol. 28, pp. 205-218, April 1998.

McNeill, D. and P. Freilberger, *Fuzzy Logic: The Discovery of a Revolutionary Computer Technology and How it is Changing Our World*, Simon and Schuster, New York, 1992.

Mehrvar, H. R. and T. Le-Ngoc, "Fuzzy Logic in Estimation of Traffic Burstiness for Admission Control in Broadband Networks," *IEEE Proc. of ICC*, Monterey, Canada, pp. 1090-1094, 1997.

Mendel, J. M., *Optimal Seismic Deconvolution: An Estimation Based Approach*, Academic Press, New York, 1983.

Mendel, J. M., *Maximum-Likelihood Deconvolution: A Journey into Model-Based Signal Processing*, Springer-Verlag, New York, 1990.

Mendel, J. M., "Tutorial on Higher-Order Statistics (Spectra) in Signal Processing and System Theory Theoretical Results and Some Applications," *IEEE Proc.*, vol. 79, pp. 278-305, March 1991.

Mendel, J. M., "Fuzzy Logic Systems for Engineering: A Tutorial," *IEEE Proc.*, Vol. 83, pp. 345-377, March 1995a.

Mendel, J. M., *Lessons in Estimation Theory for Signal Processing, Communications and Control*, Prentice-Hall PTR, Englewood Cliffs, NJ, 1995b.

Mendel, J. M., "Computing With Words, When Words Can Mean Different Things to Different People," in *Proc. of Third International ICSC Symposium on Fuzzy Logic and Applications*, Rochester Univ., Rochester, NY, June 1999.

Mendel, J. M., "Uncertainty, Fuzzy Logic, and Signal Processing," *Signal Proc. J.*, vol. 80, pp. 913-933, 2000.

Mendel, J. M. and Q. Liang, "Pictorial Comparisons of Type-1 and Type-2 Fuzzy Logic Systems," in *Proc. IASTED Int'l Conference on Intelligent Systems & Control*, Santa Barbara, CA, Oct., 1999.

Mendel, J. M. and G. C. Mouzouris, "Designing Fuzzy Logic Systems," *IEEE Trans. on Circuits and Systems–II: Analog and Digital Signal Processing*, vol. 44, pp. 885-895, Nov. 1997.

Mendel, J. M., S. Murphy, L. C. Miller, M. Martin and N. Karnik, "The Fuzzy Logic Advisor for Social Judgments," in *Computing With Words in Information/Intelligent Systems* (L. A. Zadeh and J. Kacprzyk, Ed.), Physica-Verlag, pp. 459-483, 1999.

Mizumoto, M. "Comparison of Various Fuzzy Reasoning Methods," *Proc. 2nd IFSA Congress*, Tokyo, Japan, pp. 2-7, July 1987.

Mizumoto, M. and K. Tanaka, "Some Properties of Fuzzy Sets of Type-2," *Information and Control*, vol. 31, pp. 312-340, 1976.

Mizumoto, M. and K. Tanaka, "Fuzzy Sets of Type-2 Under Algebraic Product and Algebraic Sum," *Fuzzy Sets and Systems*, vol. 5, pp. 277-290, 1981.

Momoh, J. A., X. W. Ma and K. Tomsovic, "Overview and Literature Survey of Fuzzy Set Theory in Power Systems," *IEEE Trans. Power Systems*, vol. 10, pp. 1676-1690, 1995.

Moody, J., "Fast Learning in Multi-Resolution Hierarchies," in *Advances in Neural Information Processing Systems I* (D. S. Touretzky, Ed.), San Mateo, CA: Morgan Kaufman, Chapter 1, pp. 29-39, 1989.

Moody, J. and C. J. Darken, "Fast Learning in Networks of Locally-Tuned Processing Units," *Neural Comp.*, vol. 1, pp. 281-294, 1989.

Moon, J. and T. Jeon, "Sequence Detection for Binary ISI Channels Using Signal Space Partitioning," *IEEE Trans. Communications*, vol. 46, pp. 891-901, July 1998.

Mori, H. and H. Kobayashi, "Optimal Fuzzy Inference for Short-Term Load Forecasting," *IEEE Trans. Power Systems*, vol. 11, pp. 390-396, 1996.

Mouzouris, G. C. and J. M. Mendel, "Non-Singleton Fuzzy Logic Systems: Theory and Applications," *IEEE Trans. on Fuzzy Systems*, vol. 5, pp. 56-71, February 1997.

Mouzouris, G. C. and J. M. Mendel, "Designing Fuzzy Logic Systems for Uncertain Environments Using a Singular-Value–QR Decomposition Method," *Proc. of the Fifth IEEE Int'l. Conf. on Fuzzy Systems*, New Orleans, LA, 1996.

Mouzouris, G. C. and J. M. Mendel, "A Singular-Value–QR Decomposition Based Method for Training Fuzzy Logic Systems in Uncertain Environments," *J. of Intelligent and Fuzzy Systems*, vol. 5, pp. 367-374, 1997.

Nawa, N. E. and T. Furuhashi, "Fuzzy System Parameters Discovery by Bacterial Evolutionary Algorithm," *IEEE Trans. on Fuzzy Systems*, vol. 7, pp. 608-616, Oct. 1999.

Nieminen, J., "On the Algebraic Structure of Fuzzy Sets of Type-2," *Kybernetica*, vol. 13, no. 4, 1977.

Nikias, C. L. and J. M. Mendel, "Signal Processing With Higher-Order Spectra," *IEEE Signal Processing Magazine*, vol. 10, pp. 10-37, July 1993.

Nguyen, H. T., V. Kreinovich and Q. Zuo, "Interval-Valued Degrees of Belief: Applications of Interval Computations to Expert Systems and Intelligent Control," *Int'l. J. of Uncertainty, Fuzziness and Knowledge-Based Systems*, vol. 5, pp. 317-358, 1997.

Patra, S. K. and B. Mulgrew, "Efficient Architecture for Bayesian Equalization Using Fuzzy Filters," *IEEE Trans. Circuits and Systems II: Analog and Digital Signal Processing*, vol. 45, pp. 812-820, 1998a.

Patra, S. K. and B. Mulgrew, "Fuzzy Implementation of Bayesian Equalizer in the Presence of Intersymbol and Co-Channel Interference," *IEE Proc. Communications*, vol. 145, pp. 323-330, 1998b.

Pedrycz, W., "Design of Fuzzy Control Algorithm With the Aid of Fuzzy Models," in *Industrial Applications of Fuzzy Control* (M. Sugeno, Ed.), pp. 139-151, Elsevier Science, North-Holland, Amsterdam, The Netherlands, 1992.

Poggio, T. and F. Girosi, "Networks for Approximation and Learning," *Proc. of IEEE*, vol. 78, pp. 1481-1497, Sept. 1990.

Popoli, R. F. and J. M. Mendel, "Heuristically Constrained Estimation for Intelligent Signal Processing," in *Advances in Geophysical Data Processing*, vol. 3 (M. Simaan and F. Aminzadeh, Eds.), JAI, Greenwich, CT, pp. 107-134, 1989.

Popoli, R. F. and J. M. Mendel, "Estimation Using Subjective Knowledge With Tracking Applications," *IEEE Trans. Aerospace and Electron. Systems*, vol. 29, pp. 610-623, 1993.

Proakis, J. G., *Digital Communications* (2nd Ed.), McGraw-Hill, New York, 1989.

Quinney, D., *An Introduction to the Numerical Solution of Differential Equations*, Research Studies Press, England, 1985.

Rahmoun, A. and M. Benmohamed, "Genetic Algorithm Based Methodology to Generate Automatically Optimal Fuzzy Systems," *IEE Proc. Control Theory and Applications*, vol. 145, pp. 583-586, Nov. 1998.

Rappaport, T. S., *Wireless Communications*, Prentice-Hall, Upper Saddle River, NJ, 1996.

Rasband, S. N., *Chaotic Dynamics of Non-linear Systems*, Wiley, New York, 1990.

Rose, O., *Statistical Properties of MPEG Video Traffic and Their Impact on Traffic Modeling in ATM Systems*, Univ. of Wurzburg, Institute of Computer Science, Research Report 101, 1995.

Rudin, W., *Real and Complex Analysis*, Mc-Graw Hill, New York, 1966.

Sanger, T. D., "A Tree-Structured Adaptive Network for Function Approximation In High-Dimensional Spaces," *IEEE Trans. Neural Networks*, vol. 2, pp. 285-293, March 1991.

Sarwal, P. and M. D. Srinath, "A Fuzzy Logic System for Channel Equalization," *IEEE Trans. Fuzzy Systems*, vol. 3, pp. 246-249, 1995.

Savazzi, P., L. Favalli, E. Costamagna and A. Mecocci, "A Suboptimal Approach to Channel Equalization Based on the Nearest Neighbor Rule," *IEEE J. Selected Areas in Communications*, vol. 16, pp. 1640-1648, Dec. 1998.

Schwartz, D. G., "The Case for an Interval-Based Representation of Linguistic Truth," *Fuzzy Sets and Systems*, vol. 17, pp. 153-165, 1985.

Setnes, M. and H. Hellendoorn, "Orthogonal Transforms for Ordering and Reduction of Fuzzy Rules," in *Proc. FUZZ-IEEE'00*, San Antonio, TX, May 2000, pp. 700-705.

Shi, Y., R. Eberhart and Y. Chen, "Implementation of Evolutionary Fuzzy Systems," *IEEE Trans. on Fuzzy Systems*, vol. 7, pp. 109-119, April 1999.

Specht, D. F., "A General Regression Neural Network," *IEEE Trans. Neural Networks*, vol. 2, pp. 568-576, 1991.

Stachowicz, M. S. and M. E. Kochanska, "Fuzzy Modeling of the Process," *Proc. 2nd IFSA Congress*, Tokyo, Japan, pp. 86-89, July 1987.

Stewart, G. W., *Introduction to Matrix Computations*, Academic Press, New York, 1973.

Sugeno, M., "Fuzzy theory, III," *J. of the Society of Instrument and Control Engineers* (in Japanese), vol. 22, pp. 454-458, May 1983.

Sugeno, M. and G. T. Kang, "Fuzzy Modeling and Control of Multilayer Incinerator," *Fuzzy Sets and Systems*, vol. 18, pp. 329-346, 1986.

Sugeno, M. and G. T. Kang, "Structure Identification of Fuzzy Model," *Fuzzy Sets and Systems*, vol. 28, pp. 15-33, 1988.

Sugeno, M. and K. Tanaka, "Successive Identification of a Fuzzy Model and Its Applications to Prediction of Complex Systems," *Fuzzy Sets and Systems*, vol. 42, pp. 315-334, 1991.

Sugeno, M. and T. Yasukawa, "A Fuzzy-Logic-Based Approach to Qualitative Modeling," *IEEE Trans. on Fuzzy Systems*, vol. 1, pp. 7-31, 1993.

Takagi, T. and M. Sugeno, "Fuzzy Identification of Systems and Its Application to Modeling and Control," *IEEE Trans. on Systems, Man and Cybernetics*, vol. 15, pp. 116-132, 1985.

Tanaka, K., M. Sano and H. Watanabe, "Modeling and Control of Carbon Monoxide Concentration Using a Neuro-Fuzzy Technique," *IEEE Trans. Fuzzy Systems*, vol. 3, pp. 271-279, 1995.

Tanaka, K. and M. Sugeno, "Introduction to Fuzzy Modeling," in *Fuzzy Systems Modeling and Control* (H. T. Nguyen and M. Sugeno, Eds.), pp. 63-89, Kluwer Academic Publ., Boston, MA, 1998.

Tanaka, Y. and S. Hosaka, "Fuzzy Control of Telecommunications Networks Using Learning Technique," *Electr. and Communications in Japan, Part I*, vol. 76, pp. 41-51, Dec. 1993.

Tao, K. M., "A Closer Look at the Radial Basis Function (RBF) Networks," *Proc. 27th Asilomar Conf. on Signals, Systems and Computers*, Pacific Grove, CA, Nov. 1993.

Teodorescu, H.-N., A. Kandel and L. C. Jain et al. (Eds.), *Fuzzy and Neuro-Fuzzy-Systems in Medicine*, CRC, Boca Raton, FL, 1999.

Terano, T., K. Asai and M. Sugeno, *Fuzzy Systems Theory and Its Applications*, Academic Press, New York, 1992.

Terano T., K. Asai and M. Sugeno, *Applied Fuzzy Systems*, Academic Press, Cambridge, MA, 1994.

Tong, R. M., "An Annotated Bibliography of Fuzzy Control," in *Industrial Applications of Fuzzy Control* (M. Sugeno, Ed.), Elsevier Science, North-Holland, Amsterdam, The Netherlands, 1985.

Turksen, I., "Interval Valued Fuzzy Sets Based on Normal Forms," *Fuzzy Sets and Systems*, vol. 20, pp. 191-210, 1986.

Uehara, K. and K. Hirota, "Fuzzy Connection Admission Control for ATM Networks Based on Possibility Distribution of Cell Loss Ratio," *IEEE J. Selected Areas in Communications*, vol. 15, pp. 179-190, Feb. 1997.

Vaccaro, R., Ed., *SVD and Signal Processing Algorithms, II, Algorithms, Analysis and Applications*, Elsevier, New York, 1991.

Vadiee, N. and M. Jamshidi, "A Tutorial on Fuzzy Rule-Based Expert Systems (FRBES) Models. 1: Mathematical Foundations," *J. of Intelligent and Fuzzy Systems*, Vv. 1, pp. 171-188, 1993.

Vidal-Verdu, F. and A. Rodriguez-Vazquez, "Using Building Blocks to Design Analog Neuro-Fuzzy Controllers," *IEEE Micro*, vol. 15, pp. 49-57, 1995.

Wagenknecht, M. and K. Hartmann, "Application of Fuzzy Sets of Type-2 to the Solution of Fuzzy Equation Systems," *Fuzzy Sets and Systems*, vol. 25, pp. 183-190, 1988.

Wang, L.-X., *Analysis and Design of Fuzzy Systems*, Ph.D. Dissertation, University of Southern California, Los Angeles, CA 1992a.

Wang, L.-X., "Fuzzy Systems Are Universal Approximators," *Proc. IEEE Int'l. Conf. on Fuzzy Systems*, San Diego, CA, 1992b.

Wang, L.-X., *Adaptive Fuzzy Systems and Control: Design and Stability Analysis*, PTR Prentice-Hall, Englewood Cliffs, NJ, 1994.

Wang, L.-X., *A Course in Fuzzy Systems and Control*, Prentice-Hall, Upper Saddle River, NJ, 1997.

Wang L.-X., "Analysis and Design of Hierarchical Fuzzy Systems," *IEEE Trans. on Fuzzy Systems*, vol. 7, pp. 617-624, Oct. 1999.

Wang, L.-X. and J. M. Mendel, "Fuzzy Basis Functions, Universal Approximation, and Orthogonal Least Squares Learning," *IEEE Trans. on Neural Networks,* vol. 3, pp. 807-813, Sept. 1992a.

Wang, L.-X. and J. M. Mendel, "Back-Propagation of Fuzzy Systems as Non-Linear Dynamic System Identifiers," *Proc. IEEE Int'l. Conference on Fuzzy Systems,* pp. 1409-1418, San Diego, CA, 1992b.

Wang, L.-X. and J. M. Mendel, "Generating Fuzzy Rules By Learning From Examples," *IEEE Trans. on Systems, Man and Cybernetics*, vol. 22, pp. 1414-1427, Nov./Dec. 1992c.

Wang, L.-X. and J. M. Mendel, "Fuzzy Adaptive Filters, With Application to Nonlinear Channel Equalization," *IEEE Trans. Fuzzy Systems*, vol. 1, no. 3, pp. 161-170, Aug. 1993.

Wu, K. C., "Fuzzy Interval Control of Mobile Robots," *Computers Elect. Eng.*, vol. 22, pp. 211-229, 1996.

Wu, T.-P. and S.-M. Chen, "A New Method For Constructing Membership Functions and Fuzzy Rules From Training Examples," *IEEE Trans. on Systems, Man and Cybernetics, Part B*, pp. 25-40, Feb. 1999.

Xiang, Z., G. Bo and T. Le-Ngoc, "Polynomial Perceptrons and Their Applications to Fading Channel Equalization and Co-Channel Interference Suppression," *IEEE Trans. Signal Processing*, vol. 42, pp. 2470-2480, 1994.

Yager, R. R., "Fuzzy Subsets of Type II in Decisions," *J. of Cybernetics*, vol. 10, pp. 137-159, 1980.

Yager, R. R., "On the Implication Operator in Fuzzy Logic," *Information Sciences*, vol. 31, pp. 141-164, 1983.

Yager, R. R., "A Characterization of the Fuzzy Extension Principle," *J. Fuzzy Sets and Systems*, vol. 18, pp. 205-217, 1986.

Yager, R. R. and D. P. Filev, "Template-Based Fuzzy Systems Modeling," *J. of Intelligent and Fuzzy Systems*, vol. 2, pp. 39-54, 1994a.

Yager, R. R. and D. P. Filev, *Essentials of Fuzzy Modeling and Control*, John Wiley, New York, 1994b.

Yam, Y., P. Baranyi and C.-T. Yang, "Reduction of Fuzzy Rule Base Via Singular Value Decomposition," *IEEE Trans. on Fuzzy Systems*, vol. 7, pp. 120-132, April 1999.

Yasunobu, S. and S. Miyamoto, "Automatic Train Operation System by Predictive Fuzzy Control," in *Industrial Applications of Fuzzy Control* (M. Sugeno, Ed.) Elsevier Science, North-Holland, Amsterdam, The Netherlands, 1985.

Yen, J. and R. Langari, *Fuzzy Logic: Intelligence, Control, and Information*, Prentice-Hall, Upper Saddle River, NJ, 1999.

Yen, J. and L. Wang, "An SVD-Based Fuzzy Model Reduction Strategy," *Proc. of the Fifth Int'l. Conf. on Fuzzy Systems*, New Orleans, LA, pp. 835-841, 1996.

Yen, J. and L. Wang, "Simplifying Fuzzy Rule-Based Models Using Orthogonal Transformations," *IEEE Trans. on Systems, Man and Cybernetics*, vol. 29, Part B, 1999.

Yoshinari, Y., W. Pedrycz and K. Hirota, "Construction of Fuzzy Models Through Clustering Techniques," *Fuzzy Sets and Systems*, vol. 54, pp. 157-165, 1993.

Zadeh, L. A., "Fuzzy sets," *Information and Control,* vol. 8, pp. 338-353, 1965.

Zadeh, L. A., "Outline of a New Approach to the Analysis of Complex Systems and Decision Processes," *IEEE Trans. on Systems, Man, and Cybernetics,* vol. SMC-3, pp. 28-44, 1973.

Zadeh, L. A., "The Concept of a Linguistic Variable and Its Application to Approximate Reasoning-1," *Information Sciences*, vol. 8, pp. 199-249, 1975.

Zadeh, L. A., "Fuzzy Logic = Computing With Words," *IEEE Trans. on Fuzzy Systems*, vol. 4, pp. 103-111, 1996.

Zadeh, L. A., "From Computing With Numbers to Computing With Words—From Manipulation of Measurements to Manipulation of Perceptions," *IEEE Trans. on Circuits and Systems–I: Fundamental Theory and Applications*, vol. 4, pp. 105-119, 1999.

Zeng, X.-J. and M. G. Singh, "Fuzzy Bounded Least-Squares Method the Identification of Linear Systems," *IEEE Trans. on Systems, Man and Cybernetics–Part A; Systems and Humans*, vol. 27, pp. 624-635, Sept. 1997.

Zhang, Y.-Q. and A. Kandel, "Compensatory Neurofuzzy Systems With Fast Learning Algorithms," *IEEE Trans. on Neural Networks*, vol. 9, pp. 83-105, Jan. 1998.

Zhang, J. and A. J. Morris, "Fuzzy Neural Networks Nonlinear Systems Modeling," *Inst. Elect. Eng. Proc., Control Theory Application*, vol. 142, pp. 551-561, 1995.

Zhang, Z.-L., J. Kurose, J. D. Salehi and D. Towsley, "Smoothing, Statistical Multiplexing, and Call Admission Control Stored Video," *IEEE J. of Selected Areas in Communications*, vol. 15, pp. 1148-1166, August 1997.

Zimmermann, H. J., *Fuzzy Set Theory and Its Applications* (2nd Ed.), Kluwer Academic Publ., Boston, MA, 1991.

Index

Prentice Hall: Professional Technical Reference

`http://www.phptr.com/`

P R E N T I C E   H A L L

Professional Technical Reference
Tomorrow's Solutions for Today's Professionals.

Keep Up-to-Date with
PH PTR Online!

We strive to stay on the cutting edge of what's happening in professional computer science and engineering. Here's a bit of what you'll find when you stop by **www.phptr.com**:

Special interest areas offering our latest books, book series, software, features of the month, related links and other useful information to help you get the job done.

Deals, deals, deals! Come to our promotions section for the latest bargains offered to you exclusively from our retailers.

Need to find a bookstore? Chances are, there's a bookseller near you that carries a broad selection of PTR titles. Locate a Magnet bookstore near you at www.phptr.com.

What's new at PH PTR? We don't just publish books for the professional community, we're a part of it. Check out our convention schedule, join an author chat, get the latest reviews and press releases on topics of interest to you.

Subscribe today! Join PH PTR's monthly email newsletter!

Want to be kept up-to-date on your area of interest? Choose a targeted category on our website, and we'll keep you informed of the latest PH PTR products, author events, reviews and conferences in your interest area.

Visit our mailroom to subscribe today! **http://www.phptr.com/mail_lists**

www.phptr.com